Ethical and Professional Issues in Counseling

R. Rocco Cottone
University of Missouri—St. Louis

Vilia M. Tarvydas
The University of Iowa

Merrill
an imprint of Prentice Hall
Upper Saddle River, New Jersey • *Columbus, Ohio*

Library of Congress Cataloging-in-Publication Data

Cottone, R. Rocco.
    Ethical and professional issues in counseling / Robert Rocco Cottone,
Vilia M. Tarvydas.
        p.   cm.
    Includes bibliographical references and index.
    ISBN 0-13-569138-9 (pbk.)
    1. Counselors—Professional ethics.   I. Tarvydas, Vilia M.
II. Title.
BF637.C6C625   1998
174'.915—dc21   97-28262
                                                                 CIP

Cover photo: Hamish MacEwan/Super Stock
Editor: Kevin M. Davis
Production Editor: Sheryl Glicker Langner
Design Coordinator: Julia Zonneveld Van Hook
Text Designer: Rebecca Bobb
Cover Designer: Russ Maselli
Production Manager: Patricia A. Tonneman
Director of Marketing: Kevin Flanagan
Marketing Manager: Suzanne Stanton
Advertising/Marketing Coordinator: Julie Shough

This book was set in Galliard by Carlisle Communications, Ltd. and was printed and bound
by R.R. Donnelley & Sons Company. The cover was printed by Phoenix Color Corp.

 © 1998 by Prentice-Hall, Inc.
Simon & Schuster/A Viacom Company
Upper Saddle River, New Jersey 07458

Printed in the United States of America

10 9 8 7 6 5 4 3 2 1

ISBN: 0-13-569138-9

Prentice-Hall International (UK) Limited, *London*
Prentice-Hall of Australia Pty. Limited, *Sydney*
Prentice-Hall of Canada, Inc., *Toronto*
Prentice-Hall Hispanoamericana, S. A., *Mexico*
Prentice-Hall of India Private Limited, *New Delhi*
Prentice-Hall of Japan, Inc., *Tokyo*
Simon & Schuster Asia Pte. Ltd., *Singapore*
Editora Prentice-Hall do Brasil, Ltda., *Rio de Janeiro*

This book is dedicated to Dr. Francis Tarvydas, who taught many that spirit and principle live beyond the acts themselves, and to Lucia Balčiunas Tarvydas, who demonstrated that it is the heart that gives life and direction to the spirit.

Vilia Tarvydas

This book is dedicated to Molly Jo Cottone, the love of my life.

R. Rocco Cottone

Preface

This book was really initiated years ago when I served on the ethics committee of the National Rehabilitation Counseling Association (NRCA). At the time, Vilia Tarvydas was the chair of the NRCA Professional Development Council, and she was charged with getting the ethics committee together to address concerns about the ethical code for rehabilitation counselors. I watched with amazement as she was able to help a group of strong personalities with disparate interests come to some consensus about the direction and work of the committee. Vilia and I later served on another committee that was charged with rewriting the code of ethics for rehabilitation counselors and to unite the code for all organizations representing rehabilitation counselors, including the NRCA, the American Rehabilitation Counseling Association (a division of the American Counseling Association), and the Commission on Rehabilitation Counselor Certification. It was a difficult task, with countless hearings, drafts, and rewrites. In the end, I was quite proud of the committee, and through the effort, Vilia and I gained a respect for each other as professionals and as friends.

In the years following the work of the rehabilitation counseling ethics committee, Vilia and I worked together on several projects. After several successful efforts, we decided that an ethics text focusing on counseling and counseling psychology was needed. This text, then, was born out of friendship and need. We believed the existing textbooks were not adequately addressing the specialty interests of counseling. We also believed that a different approach was needed. We wanted a format that would serve beginning students well, provide a useful format and structure for professors teaching ethics courses, and inspire some critical thought about ethical issues along the way. This text is designed to be used in courses on ethical or professional issues in counseling or counseling psychology. Also, it is meant to be a useful resource. A special effort was made to provide not only descriptive and narrative information about ethical issues, but to provide case scenarios and reprints of the many codes of ethics that apply to counseling, psychology, and the specialty practices of counseling. In this way, the text serves not only as an introduction to counseling ethics, but also as a compendium of contemporary ethical codes and issues. Practicing professionals may want to keep a copy at hand. Finally, the text was organized to address professional issues. One of the themes of the text is that ethics do not arise out of a vacuum; professions are involved. The text, therefore, provides a summary of professional issues in counseling, psychology, and the specialties of counseling practice. Also, it provides a description of the other mental health professions—their credentials, training, and scopes of practice. In this way, the reader is provided a professional context within which ethical standards can be understood and assessed.

We are grateful to the following reviewers of this text for all of their valuable input and suggestions: Al Carlozzi, Oklahoma State University; Nils S. Carlson, Jr., California State University—Bakersfield; Lane Fischer, Brigham Young University; Margery A. Neely, Kansas State University; and Wayne Lanning, University of Nevada—Las Vegas.

Of course this text could not be completed without the love and patience of our families. Vilia thanks her husband, George Sauerberg, and son, Ted. A special thanks to George for his countless hours editing draft manuscripts. I am thankful to my wife, Molly, and the children (Christopher, Kristina, Maria, and Torre). Most critical to the development of our ideas and the motivation to translate ethical ideas into action is the influence of our many students. They have enlivened our thinking and discussion and helped us to understand how this work is critical to good counseling practice. Most important is the understanding brought to our work by many hours of working with clients and their families as we sought to determine what was the best course of action in sometimes very emotional and difficult circumstances. We would also like to thank the countless professional colleagues who have shaped our ideas or supported our efforts, especially those at the University of Iowa and the University of Missouri–St. Louis. Finally, we are thankful to the staff at Merrill/Prentice Hall for supporting our ideas and helping to shape this project into its final form.

R.R.C.
St. Louis, Missouri

About the Authors

R. Rocco Cottone, Ph.D., is a professor of Behavioral Studies and Coordinator of the Marriage and Family Counseling Sequence at the University of Missouri—St. Louis. He earned a Ph.D. at Saint Louis University and an M.Ed. in counseling from the University of Missouri—Columbia. He holds specialty certifications in rehabilitation counseling and family therapy. He is a member of the American Counseling Association and the American Association for Marriage and Family Therapy. He is licensed as a psychologist and as a professional counselor in Missouri.

Vilia M. Tarvydas, Ph.D., CRC, is an associate professor and Program Coordinator of The Graduate Programs in Rehabilitation at The University of Iowa. She has a Ph.D. in rehabilitation psychology from the University of Wisconsin—Madison, and an M.S. in rehabilitation counseling from the University of Wisconsin—Milwaukee. She is a licensed psychologist in Wisconsin and was a program director for a head injury rehabilitation center in Wisconsin. She is the president of the American Rehabilitation Counseling Association and a vice chair of the Commission on Rehabilitation Counselor Certification. She has practiced as a psychologist in a hospital setting.

Contributors

Fong Chan, Ph.D., CRC, is a professor in the Department of Rehabilitation Psychology and Special Education at the University of Wisconsin—Madison. Dr. Chan received his Ph.D. at the University of Wisconsin—Madison. His research interests are in vocational assessment and evaluation, computer applications in rehabilitation counseling, professional competency studies, and multicultural counseling. He is a certified rehabilitation counselor and a licensed psychologist. He is also a fellow in the Division of Rehabilitation Psychology of the American Psychological Association.

Marijane Fall, Ed.D., LCPC, is an associate professor in the Department of Counseling and Human Development at the University of Southern Maine. Dr. Fall received her Ed.D in counselor education from the University of Southern Maine and her M.S.Ed. in counselor education from the University of Maine. Dr. Fall is a former elementary school counselor. She is a certified play therapist and conducts a limited private practice working with children.

Donna A. Henderson, Ph.D., is an assistant professor in the counselor education program at Wake Forest University. She has a Ph.D. from The University of Tennessee at Knoxville in counselor education, and an M.A. in teaching from James Madison University. She is a licensed professional counselor in Tennessee and a licensed school counselor in North Carolina. Dr. Henderson is also active in the Southern Association of Counselor Education and Supervision. She is a former high school counselor and has taught English and language arts in grades 7–12.

Gerald C. Murray, M.A., CRC, is a doctoral candidate in the rehabilitation counselor education program at The University of Iowa. Mr. Murray has an M.A. in rehabilitation counseling from The University of Iowa, and practices as a vocational rehabilitation counselor for the Iowa Division of Vocational Rehabilitation Services.

Barbara Wolf O'Rourke, Ph.D., R.N., is an adjunct faculty member with The University of Iowa Graduate Programs in Rehabilitation and the Kirkwood Community College. Dr. O'Rourke has a Ph.D. in rehabilitation psychology, an M.A. in counseling and human development, and a B.S.N. in nursing, all from The University of Iowa. She is involved in private practice as a rehabilitation psychologist, and practices as a psychiatric nurse at Mercy Hospital in Iowa City, Iowa.

David B. Peterson, Ph.D., CRC, LHMC, is an assistant professor at The University of Iowa in The Graduate Programs in Rehabilitation. He has a Ph.D. in rehabilitation psychology from the University of Wisconsin—Madison, and a master's degree in deafness rehabilitation from Northern Illinois University. In addition, Dr. Peterson has an applied degree in electronics engineering technology and has worked in the aerospace industry.

Susan Robine, M.Ed., NCC, MAC, is president of Diversified Counseling Services in St. Charles, Missouri. She is a specialist working in the area of addictions, with special emphasis on work with gambling addictions and ex-offenders. She is a doctoral candidate in behavioral/developmental processes at the University of Missouri—St. Louis.

Brief Contents

Contents

PART IV   Ethical Practice Within Counseling Specialties

CHAPTER 12
Mental Health Counseling and Assessment   295

CHAPTER 13
Career and Rehabilitation Counseling   326

CHAPTER 14
Group Counseling   363

Contents

Overview of Ethical and Professional Issues in Counseling

Introduction to Ethical and Professional Issues in Counseling

Aside from counseling theory, there is probably no other area of study that is more related to the everyday practice of counseling than the area of professional ethics. Frequently counselors are confronted with *ethical dilemmas**, conflicts that arise when competing standards of right and wrong apply to a specific situation in counseling practice. Counselors must be alert to professional ethical standards. They must be educated as to what is considered acceptable and competent practice in the field of counseling, in general, and as related to counseling specialty practice, in particular. Counselors must know when serious ethical dilemmas arise so that they may make informed and ethical decisions. In day-to-day practice, this means counselors must, from the very beginning of each case, act in a way that is ethically sensitive.

Professional ethical issues are linked closely to general professional issues. Ethical standards, for example, do not arise in a vacuum. Rather, they derive from the judgments of individuals representing a profession through established and respected professional associations, such as the American Counseling Association or the American Psychological Association. These professional associations act much like the guilds of old, representing individuals of related professional interests. Not only do professional organizations provide a meeting ground for practitioners and researchers, they also play a political role in advocating for the profession. These organizations must communicate to many audiences that the represented professionals are competent, needed, and guided by standards (e.g., ethical codes) that act to minimize or to prevent

---

* Italicized terms are defined in the Glossary for Parts I and II of this text.

harm to served individuals. A profession without enforceable ethical standards is a questionable profession. Therefore, counselors must be alert to political and professional issues in counseling, psychology, and the other mental health professions.

This text focuses on ethical and professional issues in counseling (as a separate profession) and counseling psychology (as a specialty within the profession of psychology). The first part of the text is organized to present definitions and case-related scenarios introducing basic ethical issues and legal issues. Part 2 focuses on ethical theory, values clarification, and ethical decision making, and presents a decision-making model. Part 3 presents emerging issues and current challenges arising in the field, including the ethical climate of the workplace, technology issues, and issues that arise in medical settings. The fourth part provides detailed and targeted summaries of ethical issues and standards in several of the major specialties of counseling, such as school counseling, marriage and family counseling, and mental health counseling. Finally, Part 5 reviews the role of the counselor as an ethical practitioner, including the counselor's duties and responsibilities when confronted with ethically compromising circumstances. The purpose of this text is to provide the professional counselor more than a cursory review of ethical issues; it is meant to instill ethical responsibility through informed practice.

Counseling Versus Counseling Psychology

Counseling and counseling psychology were once considered sister occupations. They developed side by side as advances occurred in measurement/assessment, counseling theory, and mental health services. Counseling emerged from (and is still deeply embedded in) the educational setting, whereas psychology emerged as an academic discipline with applications in mental health settings. The first psychological clinic, for instance, was founded in 1896 at the University of Pennsylvania (Fowler, 1996). Psychology's professional development preceded counseling by approximately 20 or 30 years, especially as related to licensure and independent mental health practice. The psychology speciality of *counseling psychology* was a bridge that spanned the two professions and also acted as a boundary marker between them. If there is any doubt that the professions of counseling and psychology overlap in regard to activities and scope of practice, counseling psychology acts as a symbol of their similarity. On the other hand, if there are any doubts that the former sister occupations have emerged as discrete and competitive mental health professions, licensure standards of the two groups stand as distinguishing criteria. Although counseling psychologists may qualify for licenses in either psychology or counseling, they may find that requisite coursework or other requirements may be different between the two professions, which may require the licensure applicant to seek training beyond courses required for a degree. Master's-level counselors would not meet licensure standards for psychology in states adopting American Psychological Association (APA) standards, which require a doctoral degree in psychology. Even doctoral-level trained counselors would find it difficult to meet psychology licensure standards, as degree requirements for psychology clearly require a degree title in "psychology" (counseling or counselor education doctorates would not qualify). So the provinces of the professions have been defined.

Gelso and Fretz (1992) defined several unifying themes of counseling psychology, which apply to counseling as well: (a) "the focus on intact, as opposed to severely disturbed, personalities"; (b) "the focus on people's assets and strengths and on positive mental health *regardless* of the degree of disturbance"; (c) an emphasis on brief interventions; (d) "an emphasis on person–environment interactions, rather than an exclusive focus on either the person or the environment"; and (e) "an emphasis on educational and career development of individuals and on educational and vocational environments" (pp. 7–9). Further, in comparing counseling to counseling psychology, Gelso and Fretz stated the following:

> The counseling profession, or counselor education, probably adheres to the same unifying themes as counseling psychology. Counselors are found in a wide range of job settings and may function as school counselors, rehabilitation counselors, employment counselors, college counselors, community counselors, and so forth. Many counseling positions require a master's degree rather than a doctorate.
>
> In addition to differences in the level of training, counseling psychology, to a greater extent than the general counseling profession, subscribes to the scientist-practitioner model of training and practice. Because of this, the counseling psychologist receives more training in research and the scientific aspects of psychology.
>
> Also, the counseling psychologist is extensively trained as a psychologist, with required graduate-level coursework in several core areas (e.g., biopsychology, learning) of the discipline of psychology. In contrast, although students who pursue degrees in counseling may take many psychology courses, expectations about what psychology courses they take, as well as how many, vary greatly from training program to training program. (p. 25)

Although the philosophies of the two professions are similar, there are practical differences. As described by Gelso and Fretz (1992), probably the most obvious distinguishing feature at the professional level is the level of required educational attainment. To be licensed as a psychologist (counseling psychologists included) requires a doctoral degree (Doctor of Philosophy, Ph.D., Doctor of Education, Ed.D., or Doctor of Psychology, Psy.D.). To be licensed independently to practice counseling requires most usually a master's degree as the terminal degree. An individual who claims to be a licensed psychologist most likely has doctoral-level training.

In regard to practice, there is little that differentiates the licensed professional counselor from the licensed psychologist. Both provide counseling (or psychotherapy). Both professional licenses allow for assessment of individuals with standardized measurement instruments, such as intelligence tests or personality tests. Both licensed professional counselors and licensed psychologists provide individual or group treatments. The two professions compete in the same market of mental health services, and therefore, have much in common. Accordingly, in this book we will use the term *counselor* to mean both professional counselors and counseling psychologists.

Defining Ethics

In philosophy, the term *ethics* has many meanings, depending on the school of philosophy defining the term (Angeles, 1981). Generally what is common among all definitions is that ethics involves an analysis of what is socially and culturally acceptable, the agreed-on "shoulds" and "oughts" of human action. Ethics, as a philosophy, cannot be separated from morality. *Morality* deals with human conduct where judgments are made as to whether a human act conforms to the accepted rules of righteousness or virtue. In our culture, the term *morality* implies the application of religious standards. What is moral, to many, is determined by one's religious values.

Ethics, on the other hand, involves an attempt to assess and to judge human decisions and behavior against an accepted standard primarily in a nonreligious context.

What is ethical (even legal) practice in medicine may be immoral by certain religious standards (e.g., abortion). What is ethical in counseling practice also may be immoral by certain religious standards (e.g., counseling gay partners about their lifestyle). So in professional practice in the United States, ethics is separated from morality at the level of professional and legal directives. However, individual professionals may choose not to separate the moral from the ethical; for example, some physicians may refuse to perform abortions on moral grounds.

Before proceeding, a distinction must be drawn between what is considered "professional" ethics and "legal" ethics. In the United States, professionals such as counselors or psychologists are directed and bound by the ethical standards of the professional organization or organizations to which they belong. For example, most counselors are members of the American Counseling Association (ACA). Counseling psychologists may have membership in either or both the ACA and the American Psychological Association (APA), professional organizations that provide a forum for counselors to address their educational, personal, and professional needs. The ACA has affiliate organizations, and the APA has divisions devoted to specialty interests. For example, two affiliate organizations of the ACA are the American Rehabilitation Counseling Association (ARCA) and the International Association for Marriage and Family Counseling (IAMFC). Rehabilitation counselors and marriage/family counselors attend the ACA conference and also attend meetings and professional presentations sponsored by their respective affiliate groups and the ACA as a whole. The APA is similar—divisions of the association (e.g., rehabilitation psychology or family psychology) organize activities and presentations for the national APA conference. The ACA and APA also make malpractice and other types of personal insurance available to their members. The ACA and the APA also have established professional standards through committees that oversee ethical standards (including disciplinary procedures) and practice.

The ACA and APA codes of ethics direct members when they are faced with an ethical concern or dilemma, any conflict where competing standards of right and wrong apply to a specific situation in counseling practice. Such a circumstance requires a professional to decide as to the rightness or wrongness of an action (before or at the time of the act) when competing or mutually exclusive ethical or legal standards are involved. Competing rights and responsibilities are involved in ethical dilemmas (Huber, 1994). The ACA and APA ethical codes provide guidance to counselors when they are faced with circumstances that are potentially unethical. The ACA and APA codes of ethics are *professional* ethical standards (see this chapter's appendices).

Counselors who are licensed to practice counseling by one of the licensing states (44 of the 50 states in the United States as of this writing) and psychologists licensed to practice psychology (in any of the 50 states) are also directed by the ethical code referenced in the relevant state's licensure statute. In fact, one of the main reasons for the licensure of professions (such as counseling or psychology) is to protect the public from unqualified or unethical practitioners. Counselors or counseling psychologists who act unethically, as judged by a licensure authority according to the authority's accepted standards, are subject to suspension or revocation of a professional license. Licensure allows a person to practice a profession and prevents the practice of a profession by those who are unlicensed (Dorken, 1976). *Revocation* of a license, therefore, is a loss of the right to practice in the state's jurisdiction. *Suspension* of a license is a temporary loss of the right to practice the profession within the jurisdiction. Licenses are not easy to attain. To be licensed as a professional counselor in most states requires a master's degree with one or more years of supervised professional (postdegree) practice, and licensure candidates must also pass a stringent examination. The standards in psychology are similar, except a doctoral degree is required. Consequently, the prospect of losing a professional license is frightening to most professionals because it means the loss of livelihood. Whereas a breach of the code of ethics of a professional organization (such as the ACA or APA) can result in professional censure or even loss of membership, the breach of an ethical standard required by regulatory law may result in the loss of a license to practice and/or other legal penalty. The distinction, therefore, between professional and legal ethical standards is a critical one.

Fortunately, most professional organizations, such as the ACA or APA, have an ethical standards committee that communicates with the professional counselors that serve on licensure boards in individual states to ensure consistency across both professional and legal standards. In some cases, licensure statutes or regulations simply reference the professional association's code of ethics. Most states incorporate their own standards, but usually ethical standards in licensure statutes are very similar to (or based in large part on) those of the professional association. In psychology, the Association for State and Provincial Psychology Boards (ASPPB), a group made up of state licensing board representatives, has its own code of ethics. (See Sinclair [1996] for a comparison of the ASPPB code of conduct and the APA and Canadian Psychological Association codes of ethics). Regardless, it is imperative that counselors know both the professional and legal ethical standards that direct their practices. Professionals are obligated to know these standards beyond the knowledge gained by a cursory reading of a code. Counselors should commit to memory the general principles that operate in ethical practice, and they should regularly discuss with other counselors or psychologists how such principles apply to professional practice. Chapter 2 provides a summary of ethical issues and the standards involved, and presents case scenarios with practice-relevant contexts for understanding these standards. Chapter 3 contains a summary of legal issues.

But before proceeding, readers are directed to Box 1.1, which is a statement made by a counselor who volunteered to share his own experience related to a serious breach of professional ethics.

Box 1.1   Ethical Errors: Serious and Painful

A Letter from a Counselor Accused of Serious Ethical Misconduct

I remember the day all too well. It was the worst day of my professional life. "My God! What have I done?" Panic surged through my body. My mind raced with worry on the day my boss confronted me with my worst nightmare. He informed me that a former client of mine had accused me of the most serious of ethical violations. Specifically, I was being accused of having a dual relationship with this client—a sexual relationship. My boss had tears in his eyes as if he was saying, "Please tell me it isn't true." But, I could not deny the truth. I had been denying the truth for ten months. It was time to come clean and try to salvage what little integrity I had left.

This is my story. It is serious and extraordinarily painful. I hurt many people. My behavior was completely irresponsible. I have lived through it, and I keep what I did in front of me as a teaching tool. I can never forget what I did, or I may become vulnerable again. It doesn't really matter what is known intellectually about ethical errors. Anyone can read and understand that there are certain things that must not be done, and there are many gray areas as well. But what happens when the human vulnerable side surfaces? What happens when buttons get pushed and countertransference issues arise? I hope what happens is that the truth is faced, that a boss or trusted colleague is consulted, or that personal counseling is undertaken. I didn't face the truth. As a result, I had to talk to a lawyer, to an ethics committee, and to my insurance company. I lost my job, my license, and lots of money. This was certainly an expensive lesson. What I did was wrong. My punishment was deserved.

What I gained from this ordeal was something very important: I gained myself. I'm sure most students of counseling and most practicing professionals have heard the many reasons why people pursue counseling professionally, including meeting one's own personal needs. This was certainly true for me. My need was to be needed. Therefore, I've been vulnerable to needy clients. When clients were hurting, I wanted to rescue and take care of them. I knew this prior to acting out, but I didn't know how strong this need was and how I could lose myself and my professional boundaries.

One of the many ironies is that I could see what was happening. I remember reviewing the ethical guidelines concerning dual relationships. I even informed my spouse that I was attracted to a client prior to acting out. But I was blinded by needs. I needed help, but was ashamed to ask for it. My denial took over and deception began. I held this shameful secret inside. My strong word of caution: Don't keep secrets. Secrets have powerful and destructive energy.

All counselors will be faced with ethical dilemmas throughout their careers. There are no simple answers and no complete guidebook to inform how to respond to the many difficult and ambiguous situations. Experience is a great teacher, but it cannot help with every possible concern. Furthermore, experience often teaches the hard way, by giving the test first, followed by the lesson.

There is little guidance to help those who have been cited for ethical misconduct or legal wrongdoing. A legal specialist for psychologists and counselors informed me that approximately 50 percent of mental health professionals will face some ethical or legal hardship during the course of their careers. How does one prepare for this behaviorally and emotionally? It is all too easy to say, "Just don't make any ethical mistakes." This statement is unrealistic and naive. Like shadows, mistakes lurk in the darkness and catch a person off guard, when one is most vulnerable.

If for some reason you are accused of some wrongdoing, whether you are guilty or not, it will most likely shock your system. Be prepared for an emotional roller coaster. Get help, but be cautious. Get a lawyer if necessary; inform your insurance company if your lawyer recommends that you do so (make sure you carry insurance); and be careful about what you tell friends, family, and colleagues. By all means, talk to a therapist if you are personally struggling.

I experienced a plethora of emotions. That dear old question, "How did it make you feel?" certainly became real for me. I was angry at my client, at first, for turning me in; after all, my client was a willing participant who encouraged my involvement. My denial was still strong for the only person I should have been angry at—myself. A client places a counselor in an authority position whether welcomed or not. I abused my position. I should have been angry at myself for allowing this to happen.

Once I was able to accept complete responsibility for what I did, I could begin to grieve. These were extraordinarily tough days. I had to endure many losses. I experienced many days of depression. For months I was completely ashamed of myself as a human being and could not imagine ever counseling again. Eventually, I realized that although I did a terrible thing, I was not a terrible person. I was a counselor who let personal issues get in the way of my professional responsibilities. Today I am very remorseful for what I did, and I am fortunate that I received a great deal of support when I began to tell the truth.

Not all people forgave me for what I did, and I understand this. I am very sorry for my behavior and I wish I could make amends to all those who suffered. I have developed many resources to help me personally, especially when I'm feeling stressed and overwhelmed, and I use my resources rather than just talk about them. I encourage all counselors to do the same. My resources are personal therapy, a 12-step program, my spouse, and a personal accountability program. It is very easy for counselors to talk and to listen, but more difficult for them to do their own personal work. Frankly, I believe that many counselors are compulsive about their jobs while neglecting themselves personally. Regardless, counselors owe it to their clients, to their profession, to their families, and most of all to themselves to take care of themselves.

Well, that is my story. I wouldn't wish it upon anyone. I have to live with myself everyday knowing what I did. Sometimes it is very difficult and painful for me. But it is important for me to keep my pain and my story in front of me. I need to remind myself of what I did so I can prevent myself from ever doing it again. Mistakes are best prevented by taking an honest accounting of one's life and one's situation. Be alert to "red flags," and consult supervisors, colleagues, friends, or a therapist if personal needs begin to blind you to your professional responsibilities.

I wish you well on your journey

Ethics Governance*

Means to govern ethical practice are necessary to give meaning to professional standards and to enhance the societal stature of the profession. These governance processes guide counselors through education and socialization in their professional role, and subsequently, discipline them if they do not practice within the proscribed standards. Ethical standards of practice can be thought of as being either mandatory or aspirational in the level of direction they provide the practitioner (Corey, Corey, & Callanan, 1993). The most basic level of ethical functioning is guided by *mandatory* ethics. At this level, individuals focus on compliance with the law and the dictates of the professional codes of ethics that apply to their practice. In other words, counselors are concerned at this level with remaining safe from legal action and professional censure. The more ethically sophisticated level is the *aspirational* level.

*This section was adapted from "Standards of Practice: Legal and Ethical" by Vilia M. Tarvydas in T. F. Riggar & D. R. Maki (Eds.), (1997), *Rehabilitation Counseling: Profession and Practice.* Copyright © 1997 by Springer Publishing Company. Used by permission of Springer Publishing Company, Inc., New York 10012.

Here, individuals additionally reflect on the effects of the situation on the welfare of their clients and the effects of their actions on the profession as a whole.

These same concepts of mandatory and aspirational ethics can be applied to the overall structure of governance for counseling's standards of practice. It is important to reiterate that codes of ethics are binding only on persons who hold that particular credential or membership. If a credential holder or a member of a professional group violates an applicable code of ethics, the organization has the responsibility to provide a disciplinary procedure to enforce its standards. In the case of a professional association, the ultimate sanction would typically be loss of membership, with possible referral of the findings of an ethics committee to other professional or legal jurisdictions. For a credentialing entity such as the National Board of Certified Counselors (NBCC), the largest certifying body for professional counselors, or for a counselor licensure board in one of the licensing states, violators could face the more serious option of certificate or license revocation, thus possibly removing their ability to practice. Less serious levels of sanction, such as a reprimand or a period of probation, are also available and utilized. Often when there is reprimand or probation, there is an additional requirement for educational or rehabilitative remedies, such as taking an educational course on ethics, treatment of an addiction, supervised practice, or other remedies to assist counselors in regaining an appropriate level of functioning ethically and/or personally. The assessment of the level of seriousness of the ethical violation will affect the actual choice of sanction once an individual is found to be in violation of the code of ethics. Factors often considered include the intentionality, degree of risk or actual harm to the client, motivation or ability of the violator to change, and recidivism of the violator (Keith-Spiegel & Koocher, 1985).

Responsible practitioners supplement the mandatory level of ethics awareness with advanced knowledge of the scholarly literature on accepted ethical practice. They also consult colleagues who may have experience addressing challenging ethical circumstances and who are respected in the community as ethically wise practitioners. In addition, they may gain guidance from other codes of ethics and specialty guidelines. Sophisticated practitioners will seek these sources to supplement the required mandatory ethical standards with the more aspirational principles. In fact, for certain situations, the course of action suggested by the aspirational guidelines may contradict or exceed those required by mandatory standards. Such situations create stressful ethical dilemmas and place practitioners in need of means to reconcile them responsibly (see Chapter 6 for further guidance on making ethical decisions when involved in ethical dilemmas).

Figure 1–1 presents the contemporary hierarchical structure of ethics governance for counselors. The levels of ethical functioning appear to the side of the pyramid, depicting the professional organizations presented as existing roughly on a continuum from primarily aspirational to primarily mandatory ethical functioning. These organizations are discussed in this order in the following paragraphs.

Colleges and universities are educational institutions that provide professional education and research services. Professional programs at universities or colleges in counseling or psychology usually operate under the review of professional accrediting organizations. *Accreditation* allows for clear recognition of a program (its nature, intent, and quality). The review process is a means to certify that the school program

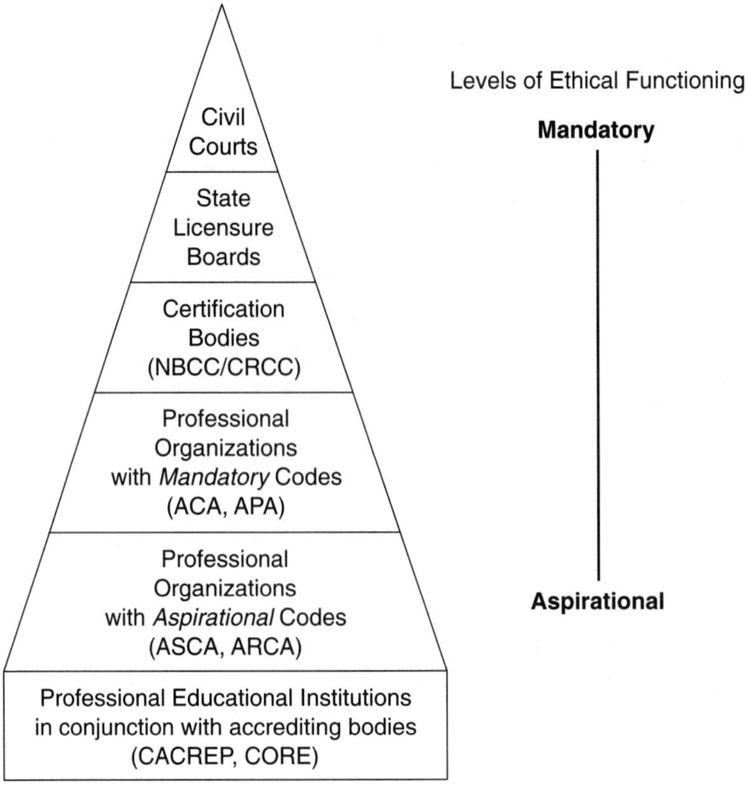
Civil
Courts
State
Licensure
Boards
Certification
Bodies
(NBCC/CRCC)
Professional
Organizations
with Mandatory Codes
(ACA, APA)
Professional
Organizations
with Aspirational Codes
(ASCA, ARCA)
Professional Educational Institutions
in conjunction with accrediting bodies
(CACREP, CORE)
Levels of Ethical Functioning
Mandatory
Aspirational

Figure 1–1
Model of Ethics Governance for Counselors

meets standards set by the accrediting body. *Professional accreditation* is the process whereby a college or university program voluntarily undergoes review by a professional accrediting body, such as the Commission on Rehabilitation Education (CORE) or the Commission on the Accreditation of Counseling and Related Educational Programs (CACREP) or the APA (1995) accreditation body. CORE, CACREP, and the APA are professional accrediting bodies that evaluate graduate education programs in rehabilitation counseling, counseling, and counseling psychology, respectively. *Professional accrediting bodies* essentially qualify educational programs as meeting standards beyond those required of colleges or universities to offer degrees; they certify that the educational institution meets these high professional standards. Professional accrediting bodies have the broadest function to provide aspirational educational guidance in ethics. They help to establish the structural foundation for ethical governance. Additionally, they help to build the theoretical and research base for understanding ethical issues, decision-making processes, and ethical educational methods. These aspects of the aspirational knowledge base are needed to support ethical development of a profession. Colleges and universities also ensure that proper preservice education and professional socialization occurs to inculcate future practitioners and educators with the proper ethics base. Educators play an important part in role modeling and supporting ethical analysis and ethical behavior in teaching, supervision, and actual clinical practice. Educational institutions also serve as a resource to other professional organizations and regulatory bodies to provide teaching, research, and service supporting aspirational and mandatory ethical practice.

At the next level sit the professional organizations with aspirational codes of ethics but with no internal mandatory enforcement mechanisms. For example, the American School Counseling Association (ASCA) and the American Rehabilitation Counseling Association (ARCA), as divisions of the ACA, occupy this position. For such organizations, the primary task is to encourage aspirational ethical practice of their members. Mandatory enforcement is not undertaken by such professional organizations due to factors such as lack of (a) appropriate consumer access and protection in the disciplinary process, (b) appropriate remedies for serious infractions, and (c) substantial financial, staff, and professional resources necessary for responsible enforcement. In some cases the mandatory enforcement function of the organization is referred to a parent organization (e.g., to ACA in the case of ASCA or ARCA), or the complainant is referred to another appropriate jurisdiction (e.g., a state licensure board) to initiate a disciplinary process.

Nonetheless, professional organizations with aspirational codes perform several significant functions within the ethics governance structure. Most usually, they provide for their members supplemental codes of ethics that extend and illuminate other more general codes. Such documents provide guidelines for ethical practice for particular, frequently encountered ethical issues or professional activities. For rehabilitation counselors, as an example, such issues might be (a) assessment of persons with functional limitations due to disability, (b) interdisciplinary team practice issues, (c) managed care practice, and (d) the responsibility of advocacy for persons with disabilities. A supplemental code may take the form of guidelines for practice that address specialty setting or function-specific issues, as is done in the APA (such as the *Guidelines for Computer-based Tests and Their Interpretation* [APA, 1986]). In addition to maintaining supplementary, specialty ethical standards or guidelines, some professional organizations at the aspirational level collect information regarding ethical trends and needs for revision of either the specialty or generalist ethics codes. Their leaders also participate in revision and writing for both types of codes. These organizations identify and supply qualified professionals to serve on the various mandatory enforcement bodies. They provide educational programs to extend the knowledge base and to define better quality ethical practice, performing significant educational and socialization functions. A new and innovative role for these organizations, one that is potentially most meaningful, is identifying or providing remediation or rehabilitation programs for impaired professionals who have been found in violation (or are at risk for violation) of ethical standards.

At the third level of ethical governance are professional organizations that maintain and enforce a mandatory code of ethics (such as the ACA or the APA). These organizations provide an entry-level mandatory code and enforcement process for their members, and, in the case of the ACA, enforce the standards or guidelines of affiliate (specialty) organizations. Organizations at this level consult with certification and licensing bodies and the specialty professional organizations to ensure active participation of all parties in ethics enforcement. They also provide educational programs to increase practitioner knowledge.

At the next two levels of ethics governance are professional regulatory bodies that either certify or license professionals, and that constitute the pre-eminent enforcers of a mandatory code. National certification bodies, such as the NBCC and CRCC, as well as state counselor and psychology licensure boards operate at this level. They perform a pivotal role in the promulgation and enforcement of ethical standards. They do not develop completely novel internal standards; rather, they draw their specific codes of ethical standards from the organizations that constitute the professional body or their constituent counseling communities, and then regulate based on the profession's own internal standards. They also may provide information and consultation to professional organizations in revising and maintaining current codes of ethics. Beyond their ethical regulatory function, these bodies encourage ethical proficiency of their licensees and certificate holders through requiring graduate degree program education and continuing (postgraduate) education in the area of ethics.

At the pinnacle of the ethics governance hierarchy are the courts. One of the primary mechanisms for this type of governance is adjudication of malpractice in the civil courts. In *malpractice* actions, one of the central points is to establish a violation of duty, requiring determining the standard of what constitutes "good professional practice" as applied to the matter at hand. "Good professional practice" is sometimes hard to define and requires many types of considerations. It is not unusual to call various expert witnesses to testify regarding such practices. Additionally, one party to the action might attempt to establish that a blatant violation of the general rules of the profession occurred by reference to the profession's ethical standards (Thompson, 1990).

Another standard of practice applied in court may be consideration of whether the action or service in question was within the *scope of practice* of both the profession and the individual, the extent and limits of activities considered "acceptable" by individuals licensed or certified in a profession or specialty. Licensed counselors or psychologists in many states are governed by the scope of practice described in state statutes, and licensees may be required to declare their personal scopes of practice at the time they are licensed or when renewing a license (e.g., marriage and family counseling or counseling psychology). Practitioners are ethically bound to limit their own scope of practice to areas within that of the profession and in specialites within which they have obtained appropriate training and supervision. They must be able to demonstrate that they are competent to practice by virtue of appropriate education, supervision, and professional experience.

This six-level professional governance structure constitutes a network of mandatory and aspirational ethics. An interactive system of research, education, and enforcement shapes and regulates the ethical practice of counselors. This structure provides a system of knowledge, traditions, rules, and laws, but does not provide practitioners with possibly the most crucial tool for ethical practice—knowledge and experience in applying their ethical decisions. Part 2 of this text, which deals with ethical theory, values, and decision-making, will help the reader make the transition from an informed student or practitioner to an ethical practitioner. But before going further in defining ethical concepts, it is important that counselors and psychologists know the scope of their practice professionally, and the limits of practice in counseling, psychology, and the other mental health professions.

The Mental Health Professions

Beyond a good understanding of the ethical principles that direct the professions of counseling and psychology, it is important for you to be well acquainted with the other mental health professions, especially as related to *limits of practice,* the boundaries that demarcate the acceptable activities associated with a profession.

This section will summarize professional identification and practice-related issues in counseling, psychology, and the other established mental health professions of psychiatry, marital and family therapy, psychiatric nursing, and social work.

Counseling

Counseling is an emerging mental health profession that has developed from the field of professional education. At the time of this writing, 43 states have regulated the independent practice of counseling, which essentially enables the practice outside of the schools or other educational settings. Because of counseling's historical linkage to schools, most professional counselors are educated in college or university departments or schools of education (where they usually have the option of receiving training to become school or nonschool community counselors).

The standard educational credential is the master's degree in counseling. Typically, the specific degree titles are the Master of Education (M.Ed.), the Master of Arts (M.A.) in education or counseling, the Master of Science (M.S.) in education or counseling, or the Master of Counseling (M.C.) degree. Doctoral-level practitioners may hold the Doctor of Philosophy (Ph.D.) in education or counseling. The Ph.D. is considered the highest academic degree in the United States, and traditionally has been viewed as a research degree as well as a practitioner degree in the mental health services. Some practitioners may hold the Doctor of Education (Ed.D.) in counseling, which is considered a professional degree in education, much like the Doctor of Medicine (M.D.) is a professional degree in medicine. Most schools or colleges at research universities offer the Ph.D. or the Ed.D. with an option of the Ph.D.. While there is a trend away from the Ed.D. at large research universities, it is still thriving and appears to be offered by increasing numbers of comprehensive (nonresearch) universities (Osguthorpe & Wong, 1991).

To be a certified school counselor, most states require a master's degree plus documentation of specific coursework in education. Certification is usually granted to individual school counselors and is regulated by the state's department of education. Certification as a school counselor by such a department usually allows counseling practice *only* within elementary, middle, and secondary schools within the state. School certification in no way implies that the counselor has been credentialed to practice counseling *independently* (i.e., in private practice for a fee).

The independent practice of counseling is regulated most usually by state licensure statutes. *Licensure* is a type of regulation that may restrict both the use of a professional title, such as "counselor," and the practice of counseling in fee-for-service independent practice. *Independent practice* is the practice of counseling outside of an exempt institutional or other setting (exempt from oversight by the licensure authority). For example, counselors working for the state government may be exempt from a requirement that they should be licensed. Since the state hires counselors based on some standard and their practice is supervised and monitored by the authority of the state agency, it may be unnecessary to require that employees of the state meet additional state licensure requirements. Exemptions from licensure, if any, vary from state to state, and counselors should know the generally accepted exemptions in order to identify counselors who are practicing legally or illegally. Counselors employed by a state's mental health, vocational rehabilitation, or family services agency may not be required by statute to be licensed by the regulatory board. They may practice counseling consistent with and within the bounds of their employment; however, a person who works in an exempt setting as an employee is still not able to practice independently for a fee outside of that employment. A private practice as a second job, no matter how small a practice, still comes under the jurisdiction of the licensure authority.

Each licensure statute defines the nature and limits of counseling practice controlled by the law *and* defines exceptions (exempt practice). For example, Christian Science practitioners are often exempted, and therefore, so long as they practice within the bounds of religious doctrine, they may counsel Christian Scientists about religious and personal issues. Typical exemptions include pastoral counselors, state and/or federal employees, school counselors so long as they are certified by the state's department of education, hypnotists, and substance abuse treatment personnel. Each state's exemptions may be unique to the politics involved in passing the licensure statute in that state. Exemptions are usually listed in the statute itself.

Counselor licensure for independent practice in most states requires a relevant master's degree from an acceptable educational institution with coursework in identified core areas (such as assessment, group counseling, counseling ethics, and counseling theories). States also often require one or two years of post–master's degree supervised experience. Additionally, subsequent to completion of this experience, the candidate for the license must pass an examination of knowledge in the core areas of counseling by achieving an acceptable passing or "cut" score, which is usually at or near the national mean. The newly licensed professional counselor (often designated "L.P.C." or other letters representing the state's title), is then allowed to charge clients for providing counseling services *independently* of any institutional oversight. Licensed professional counselors are regulated in that, as discussed previously, the licensure board has the right to suspend or to revoke the license for unethical or illegal practice. Additionally, some licensure boards require continuing education of licensed professionals and may impose other requirements to maintain a license. Licensure boards often adopt nationally accepted ethical codes, often the ACA' s code or some derivative, and adopt administrative or disciplinary rules that constitute mandatory standards of practice to protect consumers.

In addition to licensure of independent practice and state regulation or certification of counselors in the schools, there is another type of credential sought by mental health professionals—specialty certification.

Specialty certification (such as in the specialties of rehabilitation, mental health, family, or career counseling) is a voluntary means for professionals to identify themselves as trained and qualified specialists, and is overseen by freestanding, nongovernmental, and national specialty certification boards. Specialty certification is a way of identifying professionals who hold specialized training or experience in a circumscribed practice of counseling, usually assisting a unique subpopulation of clients. For example, certified rehabilitation counselors (CRCs) specialize in assisting individuals with disabilities; marriage or family counseling specialists serve couples or families. Specialists often limit their practices to clients needing their specialized treatment. In effect, specialty certification is a means to identify and to designate counselors who have met specialty standards and who, to some degree, limit their practices to those activities consistent with the specialty.

Many specialty certification boards are given approval or credibility by a large national professional association. For instance, in counseling, the Commission on Rehabilitation Counselor Certification (CRCC) certifies rehabilitation counselors. CRCC was organized with the support of ARCA, a division of what is now the ACA, and in conjunction with the National Rehabilitation Counseling Association (NRCA), a division of the National Rehabilitation Association. Currently, these organizations have seats on the commission that oversees CRCC activity. The CRC credential is the oldest still existing and widely recognized professional counseling specialty designation. The largest recognized specialty board in professional counseling is the National Board of Certified Counselors (NBCC). NBCC currently certifies general counselor practitioners and also certifies in several specialities, such as career counseling or mental health counseling.

Ordinarily, specialty certification requirements are equivalent to or more stringent than licensure standards. But it must be understood, some counselors may be certified by a specialty board and still may not be licensed to practice independently. Specialty certification is simply a practitioner's way of identifying his or her level of training and limits of practice. It is not a legal right to practice for a fee. For example, many counselors employed by a state government's vocational rehabilitation agency (usually a license-exempt setting) attain the CRC credential to demonstrate their commitment and allegiance to their specialty, even though they may be required by law to restrict their practice to their state government job (if they are not licensed).

In the mental health field there has also been a proliferation of questionable certifications. In fact, anyone can set up a specialty certification board by incorporating a "board," getting a post office box, and developing application forms. A number of boards, advertised in professional newspapers and journals, have questionable or nonexistent connections to legitimate professional organizations. These boards may charge exorbitant fees to provide impressive-sounding credentials. However, such certification is considered by most professionals as worthless, except perhaps in deceiving the public. Wise and ethical practitioners seek certification only by specialty boards that are well respected in the professional community. Most generally, well-respected specialty boards have established relationships with recognized organizations representing a profession (such as the ACA). Practitioners who purchase credentials from freestanding and unrecognized certification bodies to imply a level of expertise or training may be considered unethical, if such an action misrepresents their professional qualifications.

The terms most commonly used to describe specialty designation in the counseling and mental health professions are *certification, board certification,* or *diplomate* (such as the diplomate of the American Board of Professional Psychology).

Psychiatry

Psychiatry is the oldest recognized mental health profession. Psychiatry is a medical specialty. All psychiatrists must be physicians, and therefore, must have a medical or equivalent degree. There are two academic-professional degrees in the United States that allow for licensure as a fully qualified physician—the Doctor of Medicine (M.D.) and the Doctor of Osteopathy (D.O.). The Doctor of Chiropractic (D.C.) degree, although sometimes allowing for the title of "Chiropractic Physician," is not consistent with licensure for the full range of treatments typically associated with medical practice (e.g., chiropractors in most states are not allowed to prescribe medication). Graduates of medical schools outside the United States may have the M.D. degree or some variation, but once they pass a state's licensure standards for the Doctor of Medicine, they may legitimately use the "M.D." designation after their names.

The Doctor of Osteopathy (D.O.) degree is awarded by schools of osteopathy. Usually such schools are not associated with universities. Osteopathy is considered an alternative to the traditional training model of the profession of medicine. There is separate licensure for osteopathic physicians. It is a relatively young profession, developed as an offshoot of medicine based on philosophical differences. Osteopaths believe that physical structure is often implicated in the disease process, and physical manipulation is a primary osteopathic treatment. Additionally, osteopaths focus on the individual patient more holistically, and view medication as an adjunct to other treatments. Regardless, osteopaths are licensed to provide the full range of medical treatment, including surgery and the prescription of medication. In a substantial portion of their academic curricula and in actual practice, there may be little that distinguishes a D.O. from an M.D. In fact, some D.O.'s specialize in psychiatry, seeking additional residency training after the education required for licensure as an osteopath.

A licensed physician must have the appropriate degree from an accepted school of medicine or osteopathy. Additionally, a one year general medical "internship" must be completed in a hospital. Upon completion of the internship, if the candidate has passed the required licensure examinations (sometimes called "state board" examinations), then a license to practice as a physician is granted. This license allows the physician to perform all medical procedures and to prescribe medicine. Licensed physicians can practice independently, that is, in private practice on their own.

However, many hospitals will not grant a physician *hospital privileges* (the right to admit patients to and treat patients in the hospital) without postinternship training. Hospital privileges allow the professional to admit patients to the hospital and to treat patients in the hospital. Hospitals usually require a physician to show evidence of three or more years of additional training in a specialty—a residency. A *specialty residency* is a three-year or more hospital-based training program that prepares the physician to practice diagnosis, general treatment, and specialty procedures in a specific area of medical practice, such as orthopedic surgery, internal medicine (diagnostics), pediatrics, dermatology, family practice, or psychiatry. There are many specialties in medicine and osteopathy. Physicians who have completed a specialty residency, can legitimately claim to be specialists and can perform procedures, usually within hospitals where they have been granted hospital privileges. However, many physicians who have completed specialty residencies decide to seek *specialty designation,* certification through a national specialty certifying board. Specialty designation through such a board has become the increasingly acknowledged benchmark for advanced specialty practice.

In psychiatry, the national certifying body is the American Board of Psychiatry and Neurology (ABPN). Physicians who have been licensed and who have completed an approved (by the relevant specialty board) specialty residency may then sit for a specialty examination. The specialty examination is a rigorous test of knowledge within the specialty. Upon passing the test, physicians are granted "diplomate" status—essentially receiving a diploma of completion of specialty training. Diplomates of a specialty board may describe themselves as "board certified" specialists.

It is not necessary to be a board certified specialist to practice a specialty. However, to legitimately and ethically practice a specialty, a physician should have at least completed an approved specialty residency. There are many psychiatrists practicing without the ABPN designation.

Board certification is no guarantee of competence, just as not having board certification is no indication of incompetence. But board certification helps to identify duly trained and knowledgeable specialty practitioners.

Psychiatrists can perform physically intrusive procedures (e.g., surgery, blood tests, etc.), electroconvulsive therapy (ECT), psychotherapy, and medicinal treatment or pharmacotherapy. Additionally, by virtue of their general medical training, they may practice any and all procedures within general medicine. This training allows the psychiatrist to be uniquely qualified to understand and address the biochemical and medical aspects of mental disorders. By nature of their training, they have a knowledge base for treating the co-morbid physical illness with which individuals with mental disorder may be dealing.

Psychology

Unlike psychiatrists, psychologists currently cannot prescribe medications or perform other treatments or diagnostic procedures that are intrusive or insultive of the physical structure of the body. But psychologists, like counselors, can assess individuals with normative tests (such as IQ, aptitude, personality, or interest tests).

Psychiatrists are not typically trained in psychometrics or psychological testing procedures and interpretation, and they should not be involved in such activity unless they have completed appropriate training and supervision. Psychiatrists, psychologists, and counselors, however, are all trained and licensed to perform psychotherapy or counseling.

It is noteworthy, however, that some psychologists, at the direction of some leaders of the APA, are actively seeking the right to prescribe medication before several state legislatures.

To be a psychologist, one must be educated to the level of the academic doctorate (Doctor of Philosophy, Ph.D., Doctor of Education, Ed.D., or Doctor of Psychology, Psy.D.). The Psy.D. is most usually awarded by freestanding, nonuniversity-affiliated schools of psychology; as such, the institutions granting the Psy.D. degree do not usually seek to prepare psychologists for potential research or academic roles. Freestanding schools of psychology primarily train individuals for clinical practice. The Ph.D. is usually awarded in university colleges of arts and science in clinical psychology or counseling psychology. Schools of education at universities or colleges may award the Ph.D. or the Ed.D. in counseling, educational, or school psychology. Any of these psychology degrees, if obtained from a legitimately accredited college or university, may signify doctoral level training in psychology. Increasingly, however, the preferred national standard for academic psychology programs is accreditation through the American Psychological Association's committee on accreditation. In other words, beyond a university's overall accreditation, specific accreditation of its psychology program by the APA is valued.

On completion of the doctorate from an appropriately accredited program, to become licensed as a psychologist usually requires one or two years of postdoctoral experience supervised by a licensed psychologist in a psychology service delivery program accepted or approved by the state licensure authority. Additionally, candidates must pass a stringent licensure examination. Once licensed, psychologists can provide the full range of psychological delivery services for a fee, independently.

Psychologists may become board certified through the American Board of Professional Psychology (ABPP). There are a number of specialties awarding diplomate status, including clinical, counseling, family, rehabilitation, and neuropsychology. Specialty certification requires up to five years of postdoctoral specialized experience under the supervision of a diplomated specialist plus an acceptable score on an examination of knowledge in the specialty.

The largest professional association representing psychologists in the United States is the American Psychological Association (the APA).

Marriage and Family Therapy

Marriage and family therapists as of this writing are licensed in over 30 states. Marital therapy focuses on concerns experienced by couples. The focus is on the relationship itself, with an implied obligation to assist the partners to solve problems so they can maintain their relationship. Family therapy is a treatment approach that treats social concerns or individual problems (including psychopathology) within the context of the family (whether defined by genetics, law, common law, or choice) or recognized household. However, other individuals may be involved in a family's problem and also may be asked to participate in treatment. For example, a dating partner of a household member may be asked to attend a session.

Marital and family therapists are trained to treat relationships from a dyad (a two-person system) to a family system of three (a triad) or more individuals. Unlike other mental health professions, which primarily focus on individual treatment, marital and family therapists are trained primarily in theories of relationships and relationship treatment, which typically are grounded in social systems theory (Cottone, 1992). This unique theoretical and clinical training constitutes a critical difference in how the therapists conceptualize and practice their profession; relationships clearly become the focus.

There is controversy over the existence of marriage and family therapy as a separate or independent mental health profession. Larger, more inclusive professions, such as psychology and counseling, have taken the stance that marital therapy and family therapy are actually treatment approaches that counselors or psychologists may choose with appropriate training and experience. They have argued that marriage and family therapy is not a profession unto itself, but rather reflects a body of specialized techniques. Accordingly, freestanding licenses for marriage and family therapists are criticized, since psychologists and counselors believe that any trained psychiatrist, psychologist, or counselor with specialty training can practice marital and family therapy. Since marital and family therapy is within the scope of practice of the other mental health professions in many states (e.g., counseling or psychology), it is considered a specialty of those professions rather than a separate profession.

Marriage and family therapists represented by the American Association for Marriage and Family Therapy (AAMFT) have taken the position that specialty training and specialty designation is not enough, arguing that in-depth master's-level professional training is needed, primarily with grounding in social systems theory. Further, they convincingly have argued before state legislators that marriage and family therapy should be licensed as a freestanding mental health profession. As a result, in many states the marriage and family therapy license is separate from other mental health professions.

To be licensed as a marriage and family therapist requires a master's degree in marital and family therapy (or a closely related degree), with specialized coursework in systems theory, marital and family treatment approaches, and marital and family therapy ethics, among more general areas. The college or university degrees most often awarded are the Master of Science (M.S.) or Master of Arts (M.A.). Additionally, one or two years of post-master's supervision of practice is required. Upon completion of the supervised experience, applicants must pass an examination covering core knowledge areas.

Currently, there are no formally credentialed suspecialties of marriage and family therapy, and consequently, there are no specialty designations. It can be anticipated that in time there will be specialty boards in marriage counseling, family work, children's issues, and other areas addressed by marriage and family therapists.

The AAMFT has a restricted membership composed of already licensed or highly trained and supervised professionals. The AAMFT offers an advanced membership level (clinical member), which acts much like a specialty credential, since the criteria for "clinical membership" are stringent. Interestingly, no examination is required to become a clinical member of the AAMFT. Rather, it requires two years of close supervision by an AAMFT "approved supervisor" once candidates have completed basic master's-level coursework. The emphasis on the supervisory relationship, rather than on an examination, appears to reflect the overall emphasis of the profession on "relationship."

Psychiatric Nursing

Psychiatric nursing has established itself as a mental health specialty through general certification in psychiatric and mental health nursing and through advanced "clinical specialist" certification as a mental health nurse. Training for the general practice of nursing requires at least two years of college-level preparation leading to state "registration" as a nurse (a registered nurse, RN). This registration is akin to state licensure of other health professions. To become a registered nurse, an individual must have an acceptable degree in nursing, and must pass an examination over nursing theory and practice and meet other registration requirements. There are three educational routes to meet educational requirements: the two-year associate's degree; the three-year diploma from a hospital-based "school" of nursing; and the bachelor's degree in nursing from a college- or university-affiliated nursing school. There is a trend away from the associate's degree and toward the bachelor of nursing degree as an entry-level training requirement.

Registered nurses are allowed to provide the full range of nursing services, primarily treating patients under the direction of a physician. However, in the psychiatric nursing area, certified "clinical specialists" in mental health nursing are master's degree–trained nurses who have specialized coursework in psychotherapeutic approaches. Certified clinical specialists in mental health nursing make the case that they are trained to the level necessary to provide mental health treatments independent of physician oversight. Nurses are not licensed to administer psychological or educational tests or to independently prescribe medications.

The primary certifying body for professional nurses is the American Nurses Credentialing Center (ANCC). The ANCC was established under the auspices of the American Nursing Association. As of 1992, over 90,000 nurses were certified by the ANCC. Effective in 1998, the ANCC will certify only those nurses holding the baccalaureate in nursing, regardless of state registration to practice nursing. Synopses of the two certifications in mental health nursing provided by the ANCC are as follows:

1. *"Psychiatric and mental health nurse" certification.* Generally, this level of certification requires the RN, documented experience in psychiatric nursing, 30 contact hours of continuing education in coursework relevant to mental health practice, and a passing score on an examination over topics including theories/concepts, psychopathology, treatment modalities and nursing interventions, and professional issues and trends.

2. *The "clinical specialist" certification in either adult or child/adolescent psychiatric and mental health nursing.* Generally, this level of certification requires the RN, documented experience in psychiatric nursing, documentation of experience in treatment modalities, a master's degree in psychiatric nursing or a closely related field, post-master's experience in psychiatric nursing, and a passing score on an examination that includes theories, psychopathology, treatment modalities, trends and issues, and other areas.

In addition to the ANA, the National League for Nursing is respected as a professional organization representing nurses.

Social Work

Generally, social workers trained to the level of the master's degree specialize in two areas: public policy or clinical social work. In the mental health field, it is the clinical or psychiatric social worker that is trained to practice as an independent mental health professional.

The degree required for independent practice in clinical social work is the Master of Social Work (M.S.W.) degree, which generally requires 60 to 72 semester hours of graduate coursework. Those individuals seeking to be mental health professionals usually follow a graduate coursework track focusing on psychotherapeutic treatment (rather than on social policy). Social workers often are trained to provide group and family treatments as well as individual psychotherapy, depending on the focus of the degree program. Social workers are not trained or licensed to administer psychological or educational tests or to prescribe psychotropic medications.

Licensure of social workers generally requires the M.S.W. and one to two years of post-master's supervised experience. A passing score on a licensure examination covering social work theory and practice often is required. Psychotherapy, group therapy, and couple or family therapy are all within the scope of practice of most social work licenses.

Master's-level trained social workers wishing to be certified may seek credentialing through the Academy of Certified Social Workers (ACSW) which then allows their acronym to be used after a social worker's name to designate advanced certification. The ACSW is a widely recognized and respected social work credential, and is awarded under the direction of the National Association of Social Workers (NASW). The NASW is the largest national organization representing social workers. To be an ACSW, one must have a master's degree in social work, two years of post-master's paid experience in social work practice under supervision of a social worker, and an acceptable score on an examination over social work knowledge in assessment and service planning, intervention, professional development, ethical standards, and administration. The ACSW is a generic credential and does not necessarily reflect qualifications in "clinical" practice.

Social workers who are specialists in clinical practice may seek listing in the NASW "Register of Clinical Social Workers." There are two levels of certification in the "clinical" category: the "Qualified Clinical Social Worker" and the "Diplomate in

Clinical Social Work." Both clinical credentials require a master's or doctoral degree in social work from a program accredited by the Council on Social Work Education, the social work accrediting body. Additionally the ACSW credential or state licensure in social work and two years of supervised experience in "clinical" social work are needed. No examination is needed for the "Qualified Clinical Social Worker" credential, but candidates must pass an advanced examination to be a "Diplomate." The diplomate credential also requires three additional years of practice.

There is one other social work certification—the "School Social Work Specialist." This specialist must have a master's degree in social work from an accredited program, two years of postgraduate supervised school social work experience, and a passing score on a specialty test for school social workers. The ACSW is not needed.

All in all, social work has established itself as a viable mental health profession. In fact, by level of education, it is the profession most closely competing with master's-level professional counseling. Counselors and social workers may compete for similar jobs in mental health centers, hospitals, educational institutions, and other settings not requiring doctoral-trained professionals.

Summary

This chapter has introduced the professions of counseling and counseling psychology. We have defined the term *ethics,* and linked and discussed ethical and professional issues. We then reviewed the mental health professions as a means to define the limits of ethical practice. The next chapter will review in depth some key ethical issues and concepts.

References

American Psychological Association. (1986). *American Psychological Association guidelines for computer-based tests and interpretations.* Washington, DC: Author.

American Psychological Association, Office of Program Consultation and Accreditation. (1995). *Guidelines and principles for accreditation of programs in professional psychology.* Washington, DC: Author.

Angeles, P. A. (1981). *Dictionary of philosophy.* New York: Barnes & Noble.

Corey, G., Corey, M. S., & Callanan, P. (1993). *Issues and ethics in the helping professions* (4th ed.). Pacific Grove, CA: Brooks/Cole.

Cottone, R. R. (1992). *Theories and paradigms of counseling and psychotherapy.* Needham Heights, MA: Allyn & Bacon.

Dorken, H. (1976). *The professional psychologist.* San Francisco, CA: Jossey-Bass.

Fowler, R. D. (1996, June). Clinical psychology celebrates its 100th. *The APA Monitor, 27* (6), 3.

Gelso, C. J., & Fretz, B. R. (1992). *Counseling psychology.* Fort Worth, TX: Harcourt Brace Jovanovich.

Huber, C. H. (1994). *Ethical, legal, and professional issues in the practice of marriage and family therapy* (2nd ed.). Upper Saddle River, NJ: Merrill/Prentice Hall.

Keith-Spiegel, P., & Koocher, G. P. (1985). *Ethics in psychology.* New York: Random House.

Osguthorpe, R. T., & Wong, M. J. (1991). *The Ph.D. versus the Ed.D.: Time for a decision.* (ERIC document Reproduction Service No. Ed 339 685) Brigham Young University.

Sinclair, C. (1996). A comparison of codes of professional conduct and ethics. In Bass et al. (Eds.), *Professional conduct and discipline in psychology.* Washington, DC: American Psychological Association.

Thompson, A. (1990). *Guide to ethical practice in psychotherapy.* New York: Wiley.

Professional Organizations and Credentialing Bodies

Counseling

The largest professional group representing professional counselors is the American Counseling Association (ACA), 5999 Stevenson Avenue, Alexandria, VA 22304-3300; phone 703-823-9800. The address of the National Board of Certified Counselors (NBCC) is 3-D Terrace Way, Greensboro, NC 27403; phone 910-547-0607. The address of the Commission on Rehabilitation Counselor Certification (CRCC) is 1835 Rohlwing Road, Suite E, Rolling Meadows, IL 60008; phone 847-394-2104.

Psychiatry

The largest professional association representing psychiatrists is the American Medical Association (AMA). Specifically related to psychiatry, however, the American Psychiatric Association (APA) is the largest professional group representing psychiatrists. The American Psychiatric Association is located at 1400 K Street, N.W., Washington, DC 20005, 202-682-6000.

Psychology

The address of the American Psychological Association (APA) is 750 First Street, N.E., Washington, DC 20002-4242; phone 800-374-2721. The address of the American Board of Professional Psychology (ABPP) is 2100 East Broadway (Suite 313), Columbia, MO 65201, phone 573-875-1267.

Marriage and Family Therapy

The address of the American Association for Marriage and Family Therapy (AAMFT) is 1100 17th Street, Washington, DC 20036-4601. The National Academy for Certified Family Therapists (NACFT) is located at 50 South Steele St., Suite 222, Denver, CO 80209-2807; phone 303-377-1970.

Nursing

The address of the National League for Nursing is 350 Hudson Street, New York, NY 10014; phone 212-989-9393. The address of the American Nurse Credentialing Center (ANCC) is 600 Maryland Avenue, S.W., Suite 100 West, Washington, DC 20024-2571, 202-651-7250.

Social Work

The address of the National Association for Social Work (NASW) is 750 First Street N.E., Suite 700, Washington, DC 20002-4241; phone 202-408-8600 or 800-638-8799.

AMERICAN COUNSELING ASSOCIATION
CODE OF ETHICS
AND
STANDARDS OF PRACTICE
(Approved by the Governing Council, April 1995)

PREAMBLE

The American Counseling Association is an educational, scientific and professional organization whose members are dedicated to the enhancement of human development throughout the life span. Association members recognize diversity in our society and embrace a cross-cultural approach in support of the worth, dignity, potential, and uniqueness of each individual.

The specification of a code of ethics enables the association to clarify to current and future members, and to those served by members, the nature of the ethical responsibilities held in common by its members. As the code of ethics of the association, this document establishes principles that define the ethical behavior of association members. All members of the American Counseling Association are required to adhere to the *Code of Ethics* and the *Standards of Practice*. The Code of Ethics will serve as the basis for processing ethical complaints initiated against members of the association.

CODE OF ETHICS

Section A: The Counseling Relationship

A.1. Client Welfare

a. *Primary Responsibility.* The primary responsibility of counselors is to respect the dignity and to promote the welfare of clients.

b. *Positive Growth and Development.* Counselors encourage client growth and development in ways that foster the clients' interest and welfare; counselors avoid fostering dependent counseling relationships.

c. *Counseling Plans.* Counselors and their clients work jointly in devising integrated, individual counseling plans that offer reasonable promise of success and are consistent with abilities and circumstances of clients. Counselors and clients regularly review counseling plans to ensure their continued viability and effectiveness, respecting clients' freedom of choice. (See A.3.b.)

d. *Family Involvement.* Counselors recognize that families are usually important in clients' lives and strive to enlist family understanding and involvement as a positive resource, when appropriate.

e. *Career and Employment Needs.* Counselors work with their clients in considering employment in jobs and circumstances that are consistent with the clients' overall abilities, vocational limitations, physical restrictions, general temperament, interest and aptitude patterns, social skills, education, general qualifications, and other relevant characteristics and needs. Counselors neither place nor participate in placing clients in positions that will result in damaging the interest and the welfare of clients, employers, or the public.

A.2. Respecting Diversity

a. *Nondiscrimination.* Counselors do not condone or engage in discrimination based on age, color, culture, disability, ethnic group, gender, race, religion, sexual orientation, marital status, or socioeconomic status. (See C.5.a., C.5.b., and D.1.i.)

b. *Respecting Differences.* Counselors will actively attempt to understand the diverse cultural backgrounds of the clients with whom they work. This includes, but is not limited to, learning how the counselor's own cultural/ethical/racial identity impacts her/his values and beliefs about the counseling process. (See E.8. and F.2.i.)

A.3. Client Rights

a. *Disclosure to Clients.* When counseling is initiated, and throughout the counseling process as necessary, counselors inform clients of the purposes, goals, techniques, procedures, limitations, potential risks and benefits of services to be performed, and other pertinent information. Counselors take steps to ensure that clients understand the implications of diagnosis, the intended use of tests and reports, fees, and billing arrangements. Clients have the right to expect confidentiality and to be provided with an explanation of its limitations, including supervision and/or treatment team professionals; to obtain clear information about their case records; to participate in the ongoing counseling plans; and to refuse any recommended services and be advised of the consequences of such refusal. (See E.5.a. and G.2.)

b. *Freedom of Choice.* Counselors offer clients the freedom to choose whether to enter into a counseling relationship and to determine which professional(s) will provide counseling. Restrictions that limit choices of clients are fully explained. (See A.1.c.)

c. *Inability to Give Consent.* When counseling minors or persons unable to give voluntary informed consent, counselors act in these clients' best interests. (See B.3.)

A.4. Clients Served by Others

If a client is receiving services from another mental health professional, counselors, with client consent, inform the professional persons already involved and develop clear agreements to avoid confusion and conflict for the client. (See C.6.c.)

A.5. Personal Needs and Values

a. *Personal Needs.* In the counseling relationship, counselors are aware of the intimacy and responsibilities inherent in the counseling relationship, maintain respect for clients, and avoid actions that seek to meet their personal needs at the expense of clients.

b. *Personal Values.* Counselors are aware of their own values, attitudes, beliefs, and behaviors and how these apply in a diverse society, and avoid imposing their values on clients. (See C.5.a.)

A.6. Dual Relationships

a. *Avoid When Possible.* Counselors are aware of their influential positions with respect to clients, and they avoid exploiting the trust and dependency of clients. Counselors make every effort to avoid dual relationships with clients that could impair professional judgment or increase the risk of harm to clients. (Examples of such relationships include, but are not limited to, familial, social, financial, business, or close personal relationships with clients.) When a dual relationship cannot be avoided, counselors take appropriate professional precautions such as informed consent, consultation, supervision, and documentation to ensure that judgment is not impaired and no exploitation occurs. (See F.1.b.)

b. *Superior/Subordinate Relationships.* Counselors do not accept as clients superiors or subordinates with whom they have administrative, supervisory, or evaluative relationships.

A.7. Sexual Intimacies with Clients

a. *Current Clients.* Counselors do not have any type of sexual intimacies with clients and do not counsel persons with whom they have had a sexual relationship.

b. *Former Clients.* Counselors do not engage in sexual intimacies with former clients within a minimum of two years after terminating the counseling relationship. Counselors who engage in such relationship after two years following termination have the responsibility to thoroughly examine and document that such relations did not have an exploitative nature, based on factors such as duration of counseling, amount of time since counseling, termination circumstances, client's personal history and mental status, adverse impact on the client, and actions by the counselor suggesting a plan to initiate a sexual relationship with the client after termination.

A.8. Multiple Clients

When counselors agree to provide counseling services to two or more persons who have a relationship (such as husband and wife, or parents and children), counselors clarify at the outset which person or persons are clients and the nature of the relationships they will have with each involved person.

If it becomes apparent that counselors may be called upon to perform potentially conflicting roles, they clarify, adjust, or withdraw from roles appropriately. (See B.2. and B.4.d.)

A.9. Group Work

a. *Screening.* Counselors screen prospective group counseling/therapy participants. To the extent possible, counselors select members whose needs and goals are compatible with goals of the group, who will not impede the group process, and whose well-being will not be jeopardized by the group experience.

b. *Protecting Clients.* In a group setting, counselors take reasonable precautions to protect clients from physical or psychological trauma.

A.10. Fees and Bartering (See D.3.a. and D.3.b.)

a. *Advance Understanding.* Counselors clearly explain to clients, prior to entering the counseling relationship, all financial arrangements related to professional services including the use of collection agencies or legal measures for non-payment. (A.11.c.)

b. *Establishing Fees.* In establishing fees for professional counseling services, counselors consider the financial status of clients and locality. In the event that the established fee structure is inappropriate for a client, assistance is provided in attempting to find comparable services of acceptable cost. (See A.10.d., D.3.a., and D.3.b.)

c. *Bartering Discouraged.* Counselors ordinarily refrain from accepting goods or services from clients in return for counseling services because such arrangements create inherent potential for conflicts, exploitation, and distortion of the professional relationship. Counselors may participate in bartering only if the relationship is not exploitive, if the client requests it, if a clear written contract is established, and if such arrangements are an accepted practice among professionals in the community. (See A.6.a.)

d. *Pro Bono Service.* Counselors contribute to society by devoting a portion of their professional activity to services for which there is little or no financial return (pro bono).

A.11. Termination and Referral

a. *Abandonment Prohibited.* Counselors do not abandon or neglect clients in counseling. Counselors assist in making appropriate arrangements for the continuation of treatment, when necessary, during interruptions such as vacations, and following termination.

b. *Inability to Assist Clients.* If counselors determine an inability to be of professional assistance to clients, they avoid entering or immediately terminate a counseling relationship. Counselors are knowledgeable about referral resources and suggest appropriate alternatives. If clients decline the suggested referral, counselors should discontinue the relationship.

c. *Appropriate Termination.* Counselors terminate a counseling relationship, securing client agreement when possible, when it is reasonably clear that the client is no longer benefiting, when services are no longer required, when counseling no longer serves the client's needs or interests, when clients do not pay fees charged, or when agency or institution limits do not allow provision of further counseling services. (See A.10.b. and C.2.g.)

A.12. Computer Technology

a. *Use of Computers.* When computer applications are used in counseling services, counselors ensure that: (1) the client is intellectually, emotionally, and physically capable of using the computer application; (2) the computer application is appropriate for the needs of the client; (3) the client understands the purpose and operation of the computer applications; and (4) a follow-up of client use of a computer application is provided to correct possible misconceptions, discover inappropriate use, and assess subsequent needs.

b. *Explanation of Limitations.* Counselors ensure that clients are provided information as a part of the counseling relationship that adequately explains the limitations of computer technology.

c. *Access to Computer Applications.* Counselors provide for equal access to computer applications in counseling services. (See A.2.a.)

Section B: Confidentiality

B.1. Right to Privacy

a. *Respect for Privacy.* Counselors respect their clients' right to privacy and avoid illegal and unwarranted disclosures of confidential information. (See A.3.a. and B.6.a.)

b. *Client Waiver.* The right to privacy may be waived by the client or their legally recognized representative.

c. *Exceptions.* The general requirement that counselors keep information confidential does not apply when disclosure is required to prevent clear and imminent danger to the client or others or when legal requirements demand that confidential information be revealed. Counselors consult with other professionals when in doubt as to the validity of an exception.

d. *Contagious, Fatal Diseases.* A counselor who receives information confirming that a client has a disease commonly known to be both communicable and fatal is justified in disclosing information to an identifiable third party, who by his or her relationship with the client is at a high risk of contracting the disease. Prior to making a disclosure the counselor should ascertain that the client has not already informed the third party about his or her disease and that the client is not intending to inform the third party in the immediate future. (See B.1.c. and B.1.f.)

e. *Court Ordered Disclosure.* When court ordered to release confidential information without a client's permission, counselors request to the court that the disclosure not be required due to potential harm to the client or counseling relationship. (See B.1.c.)

f. *Minimal Disclosure.* When circumstances require the disclosure of confidential information, only essential information is revealed. To the extent possible, clients are informed before confidential information is disclosed.

g. *Explanation of Limitations.* When counseling is initiated and throughout the counseling process as necessary, counselors inform clients of the limitations of confidentiality and identify foreseeable situations in which confidentiality must be breached. (See G.2.a.)

h. *Subordinates.* Counselors make every effort to ensure that privacy and confidentiality of clients are maintained by subordinates including employees, supervisees, clerical assistants, and volunteers. (See B.1.a.)

i. *Treatment Teams.* If client treatment will involve a continued review by a treatment team, the client will be informed of the team's existence and composition.

B.2. Groups and Families

a. *Group Work.* In group work, counselors clearly define confidentiality and the parameters for the specific group being entered, explain its importance, and discuss the difficulties related to confidentiality involved in group work. The fact that confidentiality cannot be guaranteed is clearly communicated to group members.

b. *Family Counseling.* In family counseling, information about one family member cannot be disclosed to another member without permission. Counselors protect the privacy rights of each family member. (See A.8., B.3., and B.4.d.)

B.3. Minor or Incompetent Clients

When counseling clients who are minors or individuals who are unable to give voluntary, informed consent, parents or guardians may be included in the counseling process as appropriate. Counselors act in the best interests of clients and take measures to safeguard confidentiality. (See A.3.c.)

B.4. Records

a. *Requirement of Records.* Counselors maintain records necessary for rendering professional services to their clients and as required by laws, regulations, or agency or institution procedures.

b. *Confidentiality of Records.* Counselors are responsible for securing the safety and confidentiality of any counseling records they create, maintain, transfer, or destroy whether the records are written, taped, computerized, or stored in any other medium. (See B.1.a.)

c. *Permission to Record or Observe.* Counselors obtain permission from clients prior to electronically recording or observing sessions. (See A.3.a.)

d. *Client Access.* Counselors recognize that counseling records are kept for the benefit of clients, and therefore provide access to records and copies of records when requested by competent clients, unless the records contain information that may be misleading and detrimental to the client. In situations involving multiple clients, access to records is limited to those parts of records that do not include confidential information related to another client. (See A.8., B.1.a., and B.2.b.)

e. *Disclosure or Transfer.* Counselors obtain written permission from clients to disclose or transfer records to legitimate third parties unless exceptions to confidentiality exist as listed in Section B.1. Steps are taken to ensure that receivers of counseling records are sensitive to their confidential nature.

B.5. Research and Training

a. *Data Disguise Required.* Use of data derived from counseling relationships for purposes of training, research, or publication is confined to content that is disguised to ensure the anonymity of the individuals involved. (See B.1.g. and G.3.d.)

b. *Agreement for Identification.* Identification of a client in a presentation or publication is permissible only when the client has reviewed the material and has agreed to its presentation or publication. (See G.3.d.)

B.6. Consultation

a. *Respect for Privacy.* Information obtained in a consulting relationship is discussed for professional purposes only with persons clearly concerned with the case. Written and oral reports present data germane to the purposes of the consultation, and every effort is made to protect client identity and avoid undue invasion of privacy.

b. *Cooperating Agencies.* Before sharing information, counselors make efforts to ensure that there are defined policies in other agencies serving the counselor's clients that effectively protect the confidentiality of information.

Section C: Professional Responsibility

C.1. Standards Knowledge

Counselors have a responsibility to read, understand, and follow the *Code of Ethics* and the *Standards of Practice.*

C.2. Professional Competence

a. *Boundaries of Competence.* Counselors practice only within the boundaries of their competence, based on their education, training, supervised experience, state and national professional credentials, and appropriate professional experience. Counselors will demonstrate a commitment to gain knowledge, personal awareness, sensitivity, and skills pertinent to working with a diverse client population.

b. *New Specialty Areas of Practice.* Counselors practice in specialty areas new to them only after appropriate education, training, and supervised experience. While developing skills in new specialty areas, counselors take steps to ensure the competence of their work and to protect others from possible harm.

c. *Qualified for Employment.* Counselors accept employment only for positions for which they are qualified by education, training, supervised experience, state and national professional credentials, and appropriate professional experience. Counselors hire for professional counseling positions only individuals who are qualified and competent.

d. *Monitor Effectiveness.* Counselors continually monitor their effectiveness as professionals and take steps to improve when necessary. Counselors in private practice take reasonable steps to seek out peer supervision to evaluate their efficacy as counselors.

e. *Ethical Issues Consultation.* Counselors take reasonable steps to consult with other counselors or related professionals when they have questions regarding their ethical obligations or professional practice. (See H.1.)

f. *Continuing Education.* Counselors recognize the need for continuing education to maintain a reasonable level of awareness of current scientific and professional information in their fields of activity. They take steps to maintain competence in the skills they use, are open to new procedures, and keep current with the diverse and/or special populations with whom they work.

g. *Impairment.* Counselors refrain from offering or accepting professional services when their physical, mental or emotional problems are likely to harm a client or others. They are alert to the signs of impairment, seek assistance for problems, and, if necessary, limit, suspend, or terminate their professional responsibilities. (See A.11.c.)

C.3. Advertising and Soliciting Clients

a. *Accurate Advertising.* There are no restrictions on advertising by counselors except those that can be specifically justified to protect the public from deceptive practices. Counselors advertise or represent their services to the public by identifying their credentials in an accurate manner that is not false, misleading, deceptive, or fraudulent. Counselors may only advertise the highest degree earned which is in counseling or a closely related field from a college or university that was accredited when the degree was awarded by one of the regional accrediting bodies recognized by the Council on Postsecondary Accreditation.

b. *Testimonials.* Counselors who use testimonials do not solicit them from clients or other persons who, because of their particular circumstances, may be vulnerable to undue influence.

c. *Statements by Others.* Counselors make reasonable efforts to ensure that statements made by others about them or the profession of counseling are accurate.

d. *Recruiting Through Employment.* Counselors do not use their places of employment or institutional affiliation to recruit or gain clients, supervisees, or consultees for their private practices. (See C.5.e.)

e. *Products and Training Advertisements.* Counselors who develop products related to their profession or conduct workshops or training events ensure that the advertisements concerning these products or events are accurate and disclose adequate information for consumers to make informed choices.

f. *Promoting to Those Served.* Counselors do not use counseling, teaching, training, or supervisory relationships to promote their products or training events in a manner that is deceptive or would exert undue influence on individuals who may be vulnerable. Counselors may adopt textbooks they have authored for instruction purposes.

g. *Professional Association Involvement.* Counselors actively participate in local, state, and national associations that foster the development and improvement of counseling.

C.4. Credentials

a. *Credentials Claimed.* Counselors claim or imply only professional credentials possessed and are responsible for correcting any known misrepresentations of their credentials by others. Professional credentials include graduate degrees in counseling or closely related mental health fields, accreditation of graduate programs, national voluntary certifications, government-issued certifications or licenses, ACA professional membership, or any other credential that might indicate to the public specialized knowledge or expertise in counseling.

b. *ACA Professional Membership.* ACA professional members may announce to the public their membership status. Regular members may not announce their ACA membership in a manner that might imply they are credentialed counselors.

c. *Credential Guidelines.* Counselors follow the guidelines for use of credentials that have been established by the entities that issue the credentials.

d. *Misrepresentation of Credentials.* Counselors do not attribute more to their credentials than the credentials represent, and do not imply that other counselors are not qualified because they do not possess certain credentials.

e. *Doctoral Degrees From Other Fields.* Counselors who hold a master's degree in counseling or a closely related mental health field, but hold a doctoral degree from other than counseling or a closely related field do not use the title, "Dr." in their practices and do not announce to the public in relation to their practice or status as a counselor that they hold a doctorate.

C.5. Public Responsibility

a. *Nondiscrimination.* Counselors do not discriminate against clients, students, or supervisees in a manner that has a negative impact based on their age, color, culture, disability, ethnic group, gender, race, religion, sexual orientation, or socioeconomic status, or for any other reason. (See A.2.a.)

b. *Sexual Harassment.* Counselors do not engage in sexual harassment. Sexual harassment is defined as sexual solicitation, physical advances, or verbal or nonverbal conduct that is sexual in nature, that occurs in connection with professional activities or roles, and that either: (1) is unwelcome, is offensive, or creates a hostile workplace environment, and counselors know or are told this; or (2) is sufficiently severe or intense to be perceived as harassment to a reasonable person in the context. Sexual harassment can consist of a single intense or severe act or multiple persistent or pervasive acts.

c. *Reports to Third Parties.* Counselors are accurate, honest, and unbiased in reporting their professional activities and judgments to appropriate third parties including courts, health insurance companies, those who are the recipients of evaluation reports, and others. (See B.1.g.)

d. *Media Presentations.* When counselors provide advice or comment by means of public lectures, demonstrations, radio or television programs, prerecorded tapes, printed articles, mailed material, or other media, they take reasonable precautions to ensure that (1) the statements are based on appropriate professional counseling literature and practice; (2) the statements are otherwise consistent with the *Code of Ethics* and the *Standards of Practice;* and (3) the recipients of the information are not encouraged to infer that a professional counseling relationship has been established. (See C.6.b.)

e. *Unjustified Gains.* Counselors do not use their professional positions to seek or receive unjustified personal gains, sexual favors, unfair advantage, or unearned goods or services. (See C.3.d.)

C.6. Responsibility to Other Professionals

a. *Different Approaches.* Counselors are respectful of approaches to professional counseling that differ from their own. Counselors know and take into account the traditions and practices of other professional groups with which they work.

b. *Personal Public Statements.* When making personal statements in a public context, counselors clarify that they are speaking from their personal perspectives and that they are not speaking on behalf of all counselors or the profession. (See C.5.d.)

c. *Clients Served by Others.* When counselors learn that their clients are in a professional rela-

tionship with another mental health professional, they request release from clients to inform the other professionals and strive to establish positive and collaborative professional relationships. (See A.4.)

Section D: Relationships with Other Professionals

D.1. Relationships with Employers and Employees

a. *Role Definition.* Counselors define and describe for their employers and employees the parameters and levels of their professional roles.

b. *Agreements.* Counselors establish working agreements with supervisors, colleagues, and subordinates regarding counseling or clinical relationships, confidentiality, adherence to professional standards, distinction between public and private material, maintenance and dissemination of recorded information, workload, and accountability. Working agreements in each instance are specified and made known to those concerned.

c. *Negative Conditions.* Counselors alert their employers to conditions that may be potentially disruptive or damaging to the counselor's professional responsibilities or that may limit their effectiveness.

d. *Evaluation.* Counselors submit regularly to professional review and evaluation by their supervisor or the appropriate representative of the employer.

e. *In-Service.* Counselors are responsible for in-service development of self and staff.

f. *Goals.* Counselors inform their staff of goals and programs.

g. *Practices.* Counselors provide personnel and agency practices that respect and enhance the rights and welfare of each employee and recipient of agency services. Counselors strive to maintain the highest levels of professional services.

h. *Personnel Selection and Assignment.* Counselors select competent staff and assign responsibilities compatible with their skills and experiences.

i. *Discriminate.* Counselors, as either employers or employees, do not engage in or condone practices that are inhumane, illegal, or unjustifiable (such as considerations based on age, color, culture, disability, ethnic group, gender, race, religion, sexual orientation, or socioeconomic status) in hiring, promotion, or training. (See A.2.a. and C.5.b.)

j. *Professional Conduct.* Counselors have a responsibility both to clients and to the agency or institution within which services are performed to maintain high standards of professional conduct.

k. *Exploitive Relationships.* Counselors do not engage in exploitive relationships with individuals over whom they have supervisory, evaluative, or instructional control or authority.

l. *Employer Policies.* The acceptance of employment in an agency or institution implies that counselors are in agreement with its general policies and principles. Counselors strive to reach agreement with employers as to acceptable standards of conduct that allow for changes in institutional policy conducive to the growth and development of clients.

D.2. Consultation (See B.6.)

a. *Consultation as an Option.* Counselors may choose to consult with any other professionally competent persons about their clients. In choosing consultants, counselors avoid placing the consultant in a conflict of interest situation that would preclude the consultant being a proper party to the counselor's efforts to help the client. Should counselors be engaged in a work setting that compromises this consultation standard, they consult with other professionals whenever possible to consider justifiable alternatives.

b. *Consultant Competency.* Counselors are reasonably certain that they have or the organization represented has the necessary competencies and resources for giving the kind of consulting services needed and that appropriate referral resources are available.

c. *Understanding with Clients.* When providing consultation, counselors attempt to develop with their clients a clear understanding of problem definition, goals for change, and predicted consequences of interventions selected.

d. *Consultant Goals.* The consulting relationship is one in which client adaptability and growth to-

ward self-direction are consistently encouraged and cultivated. (See A.1.b.)

D.3. Fees for Referral

a. *Accepting Fees from Agency Clients.* Counselors refuse a private fee or other remuneration for rendering services to persons who are entitled to such services through the counselor's employing agency or institution. The policies of a particular agency may make explicit provisions for agency clients to receive counseling services from members of its staff in private practice. In such instances, the clients must be informed of other options open to them should they seek private counseling services. (See A.10.a., A.11.b., and C.3.d.)

b. *Referral Fees.* Counselors do not accept a referral fee from other professionals.

D.4. Subcontractor Arrangements

When counselors work as subcontractors for counseling services for a third party, they have a duty to inform clients of the limitations of confidentiality that the organization may place on counselors in providing counseling services to clients. The limits of such confidentiality ordinarily are discussed as part of the intake session. (See B.1.e. and B.1.f.)

Section E: Evaluation, Assessment, and Interpretation

E.1. General

a. *Appraisal Techniques.* The primary purpose of educational and psychological assessment is to provide measures that are objective and interpretable in either comparative or absolute terms. Counselors recognize the need to interpret the statements in this section as applying to the whole range of appraisal techniques, including test and nontest data.

b. *Client Welfare.* Counselors promote the welfare and best interests of the client in the development, publication, and utilization of educational and psychological assessment techniques. They do not misuse assessment results and interpretations and take reasonable steps to prevent others from misusing the information these techniques provide. They respect the client's right to know the results, the interpretations made, and the bases for their conclusions and recommendations.

E.2. Competence to Use and Interpret Tests

a. *Limits of Competence.* Counselors recognize the limits of their competence and perform only those testing and assessment services for which they have been trained. They are familiar with reliability, validity, related standardization, error of measurement, and proper application of any technique utilized. Counselors using computer-based test interpretations are trained in the construct being measured and the specific instrument being used prior to using this type of computer application. Counselors take reasonable measures to ensure the proper use of psychological assessment techniques by persons under their supervision.

b. *Appropriate Use.* Counselors are responsible for the appropriate application, scoring, interpretation, and use of assessment instruments, whether they score and interpret such tests themselves or use computerized or other services.

c. *Decisions Based on Results.* Counselors responsible for decisions involving individuals or policies that are based on assessment results have a thorough understanding of educational and psychological measurement, including validation criteria, test research, and guidelines for test development and use.

d. *Accurate Information.* Counselors provide accurate information and avoid false claims or misconceptions when making statements about assessment instruments or techniques. Special efforts are made to avoid unwarranted connotations of such terms as IQ and grade equivalent scores. (See C.5.c.)

E.3. Informed Consent

a. *Explanation to Clients.* Prior to assessment, counselors explain the nature and purposes of assessment and the specific use of results in language the client (or other legally authorized person on behalf of the client) can understand, unless an explicit exception to this right has been agreed upon in advance. Regardless of whether scoring and interpretation are completed by counselors, by assistants, or by computer or other outside services, counselors take reasonable steps to ensure that appropriate explanations are given to the client.

b. *Recipients of Results.* The examinee's welfare, explicit understanding, and prior agreement determine the recipients of test results. Counselors include accurate and appropriate interpretations with any release of individual or group test results. (See B.1.a. and C.5.c.)

E.4. Release of Information to Competent Professionals

a. *Misuse of Results.* Counselors do not misuse assessment results, including test results, and interpretations, and take reasonable steps to prevent the misuse of such by others. (See C.5.c.)

b. *Release of Raw Data.* Counselors ordinarily release data (e.g. protocols, counseling or interview notes, or questionnaires) in which the client is identified only with the consent of the client or the client's legal representative. Such data are usually released only to persons recognized by counselors as competent to interpret the data. (See B.1.a.)

E.5. Proper Diagnosis of Mental Disorders

a. *Proper Diagnosis.* Counselors take special care to provide proper diagnosis of mental disorders. Assessment techniques (including personal interview) used to determine client care (e.g., locus of treatment, type of treatment, or recommended follow-up) are carefully selected and appropriately used. (See A.3.a. and C.5.c.)

b. *Cultural Sensitivity.* Counselors recognize that culture affects the manner in which clients' problems are defined. Clients' socioeconomic and cultural experience is considered when diagnosing mental disorders.

E.6. Test Selection

a. *Appropriateness of Instruments.* Counselors carefully consider the validity, reliability, psychometric limitations, and appropriateness of instruments when selecting tests for use in a given situation or with a particular client.

b. *Culturally Diverse Populations.* Counselors are cautious when selecting tests for culturally diverse populations to avoid inappropriateness of testing that may be outside of socialized behavioral or cognitive patterns.

E.7. Conditions of Test Administration

a. *Administration Conditions.* Counselors administer tests under the same conditions that were established in their standardization. When tests are not administered under standard conditions or when unusual behavior or irregularities occur during the testing session, those conditions are noted in interpretation, and the results may be designated as invalid or of questionable validity.

b. *Computer Administration.* Counselors are responsible for ensuring that administration programs function properly to provide clients with accurate results when a computer or other electronic methods are used for test administration. (See A.12.b.)

c. *Unsupervised Test-Taking.* Counselors do not permit unsupervised or inadequately supervised use of tests or assessments unless the tests or assessments are designed, intended, and validated for self-administration and/or scoring.

d. *Disclosure of Favorable Conditions.* Prior to test administration, conditions that produce most favorable test results are made known to the examinee.

E.8. Diversity in Testing

Counselors are cautious in using assessment techniques, making evaluations, and interpreting the performance of populations not represented in the norm group on which an instrument was standardized. They recognize the effects of age, color, culture, disability, ethnic group, gender, race, religion, sexual orientation, and socioeconomic status on test administration and interpretation and place test results in proper perspective with other relevant factors. (See A.2.a.)

E.9. Test Scoring and Interpretation

a. *Reporting Reservations.* In reporting assessment results, counselors indicate any reservations that exist regarding validity or reliability because of the circumstances of the assessment or the inappropriateness of the norms for the person tested.

b. *Research Instruments.* Counselors exercise caution when interpreting the results of research instruments possessing insufficient technical data to support respondent results. The specific purposes for the use of such instruments are stated explicitly to the examinee.

c. *Testing Services.* Counselors who provide test scoring and test interpretation services to support the assessment process confirm the validity of such interpretations. They accurately describe the purpose, norms, validity, reliability, and applications of the procedures and any special qualifications applicable to their use. The public offering of an automated test interpretations service is considered a professional-to-professional consultation. The formal responsibility of the consultant is to the consultee, but the ultimate and overriding responsibility is to the client.

E.10. Test Security

Counselors maintain the integrity and security of tests and other assessment techniques consistent with legal and contractual obligations. Counselors do not appropriate, reproduce, or modify published tests or parts thereof without acknowledgment and permission from the publisher.

E.11. Obsolete Tests and Outdated Test Results

Counselors do not use data or test results that are obsolete or outdated for the current purpose. Counselors make every effort to prevent the misuse of obsolete measures and test data by others.

E.12. Test Construction

Counselors use established scientific procedures, relevant standards, and current professional knowledge for test design in the development, publication, and utilization of educational and psychological assessment techniques.

Section F: Teaching, Training, and Supervision

F.1. Counselor Educators and Trainers

a. *Educators as Teachers and Practitioners.* Counselors who are responsible for developing, implementing, and supervising educational programs are skilled as teachers and practitioners. They are knowledgeable regarding the ethical, legal, and regulatory aspects of the profession, are skilled in applying that knowledge, and make students and supervisees aware of their responsibilities. Counselors conduct counselor education and training programs in an ethical manner and serve as role models for professional behavior. Counselor educators should make an effort to infuse material related to human diversity into all courses and/or workshops that are designed to promote the development of professional counselors.

b. *Relationship Boundaries with Students and Supervisees.* Counselors clearly define and maintain ethical, professional, and social relationship boundaries with their students and supervisees. They are aware of the differential in power that exists and the student's or supervisee's possible incomprehension of that power differential. Counselors explain to students and supervisees the potential for the relationship to become exploitive.

c. *Sexual Relationships.* Counselors do not engage in sexual relationships with students or supervisees and do not subject them to sexual harassment. (See A.6. and C.5.b)

d. *Contributions to Research.* Counselors give credit to students or supervisees for their contributions to research and scholarly projects. Credit is given through coauthorship, acknowledgment, footnote statement, or other appropriate means, in accordance with such contributions. (See G.4.b. and G.4.c.)

e. *Close Relatives.* Counselors do not accept close relatives as students or supervisees.

f. *Supervision Preparation.* Counselors who offer clinical supervision services are adequately prepared in supervision methods and techniques. Counselors who are doctoral students serving as practicum or internship supervisors to master's level students are adequately prepared and supervised by the training program.

g. *Responsibility for Services to Clients.* Counselors who supervise the counseling services of others take reasonable measures to ensure that counseling services provided to clients are professional.

h. *Endorsement.* Counselors do not endorse students or supervisees for certification, licensure, employment, or completion of an academic or training program if they believe students or supervisees are not qualified for the endorsement. Counselors take reasonable steps to assist students or supervisees who are not qualified for endorsement to become qualified.

F.2. Counselor Education and Training Programs

a. *Orientation.* Prior to admission, counselors orient prospective students to the counselor education or training program's expectations, including but not limited to the following: (1) the type and level of skill acquisition required for successful completion of the training, (2) subject matter to be covered, (3) basis for evaluation, (4) training components that encourage self-growth or self-disclosure as part of the training process, (5) the type of supervision settings and requirements of the sites for required clinical field experiences, (6) student and supervisee evaluation and dismissal policies and procedures, and (7) up-to-date employment prospects for graduates.

b. *Integration of Study and Practice.* Counselors establish counselor education and training programs that integrate academic study and supervised practice.

c. *Evaluation.* Counselors clearly state to students and supervisees, in advance of training, the levels of competency expected, appraisal methods, and timing of evaluations for both didactic and experiential components. Counselors provide students and supervisees with periodic performance appraisal and evaluation feedback throughout the training program.

d. *Teaching Ethics.* Counselors make students and supervisees aware of the ethical responsibilities and standards of the profession and the students' and supervisees' ethical responsibilities to the profession. (See C.1. and F.3.e.)

e. *Peer Relationships.* When students or supervisees are assigned to lead counseling groups or provide clinical supervision for their peers, counselors take steps to ensure that students and supervisees placed in these roles do not have personal or adverse relationships with peers and that they understand they have the same ethical obligations as counselor educators, trainers, and supervisors. Counselors make every effort to ensure that the rights of peers are not compromised when students or supervisees are assigned to lead counseling groups or provide clinical supervision.

f. *Varied Theoretical Positions.* Counselors present varied theoretical positions so that students and supervisees may make comparisons and have opportunities to develop their own positions. Counselors provide information concerning the scientific bases of professional practice. (See C.6.a.)

g. *Field Placements.* Counselors develop clear policies within their training program regarding field placement and other clinical experiences. Counselors provide clearly stated roles and responsibilities for the student or supervisee, the site supervisor, and the program supervisor. They confirm that site supervisors are qualified to provide supervision and are informed of their professional and ethical responsibilities in this role.

h. *Dual Relationships as Supervisors.* Counselors avoid dual relationships such as performing the role of site supervisor and training program supervisor in the student's or supervisee's training program. Counselors do not accept any form of professional services, fees, commissions, reimbursement, or remuneration from a site for student or supervisee placement.

i. *Diversity in Programs.* Counselors are responsive to their institution's and program's recruitment and retention needs for training program administrators, faculty, and students with diverse backgrounds and special needs. (See A.2.a.)

F.3. Students and Supervisees

a. *Limitations.* Counselors, through ongoing evaluation and appraisal, are aware of the academic and personal limitations of students and supervisees that might impede performance. Counselors assist students and supervisees in securing remedial assistance when needed, and dismiss from the training program supervisees who are unable to provide competent service due to academic or personal limitations. Counselors seek professional consultation and document their decision to dismiss or refer students or supervisees for assistance. Counselors assure that students and supervisees have recourse to address decisions made, to require them to seek assistance, or to dismiss them.

b. *Self-Growth Experiences.* Counselors use professional judgment when designing training experiences conducted by the counselors themselves that require student and supervisee self-growth or self-disclosure. Safeguards are provided so that students and supervisees are aware of the ramifications their self-disclosure may have, on counselors whose primary role as teacher, trainer, or supervisor requires acting on ethical obligations to the profession. Evaluative components of experiential training experiences explicitly delineate predetermined academic standards that are separate and not dependent on the student's level of self-disclosure. (See A.6.)

c. *Counseling for Students and Supervisees.* If students or supervisees request counseling, supervisors or counselor educators provide them with acceptable referrals. Supervisors or counselor educators do not serve as counselor to students or supervisees over whom they hold administrative, teaching, or evaluative roles unless this is a brief role associated with a training experience. (See A.6.b.)

d. *Clients of Students and Supervisees.* Counselors make every effort to ensure that the clients at field placements are aware of the services rendered and the qualifications of the students and supervisees rendering those services. Clients receive professional disclosure information and are informed of the limits of confidentiality. Client permission is obtained in order for the students and supervisees to use any information concerning the counseling relationship in the training process. (See B.1.e.)

e. *Standards for Students and Supervisees.* Students and supervisees preparing to become counselors adhere to the *Code of Ethics* and the *Standards of Practice.* Students and supervisees have the same obligations to clients as those required of counselors. (See H.1.)

Section G: Research and Publication

G.1. Research Responsibilities

a. *Use of Human Subjects.* Counselors plan, design, conduct, and report research in a manner consistent with pertinent ethical principles, federal and state laws, host institutional regulations, and scientific standards governing research with human subjects. Counselors design and conduct research that reflects cultural sensitivity appropriateness.

b. *Deviation from Standard Practices.* Counselors seek consultation and observe stringent safeguards to protect the rights of research participants when a research problem suggests a deviation from standard acceptable practices. (See B.6.)

c. *Precautions to Avoid Injury.* Counselors who conduct research with human subjects are responsible for the subjects' welfare throughout the experiment and take reasonable precautions to avoid causing injurious psychological, physical, or social effects to their subjects.

d. *Principal Researcher Responsibility.* The ultimate responsibility for ethical research practice lies with the principal researcher. All others involved in the research activities share ethical obligations and full responsibility for their own actions.

e. *Minimal Interference.* Counselors take reasonable precautions to avoid causing disruptions in subjects lives due to participation in research.

f. *Diversity.* Counselors are sensitive to diversity and research issues with special populations. They seek consultation when appropriate. (See A.2.a. and B.6.)

G.2. Informed Consent

a. *Topics Disclosed.* In obtaining informed consent for research, counselors use language that is understandable to research participants and that: (1) accurately explains the purpose and procedures to be followed; (2) identifies any procedures that are experimental or relatively untried; (3) describes the attendant discomforts and risks; (4) describes the benefits or changes in individuals or organizations that might be reasonably expected; (5) discloses appropriate alternative procedures that would be advantageous for subjects; (6) offers to answer any inquiries concerning the procedures; (7) describes any limitations on confidentiality; and (8) instructs that subjects are free to withdraw their consent and to discontinue participation in the project at any time. (See B.1.f.)

b. *Deception.* Counselors do not conduct research involving deception unless alternative procedures are not feasible and the prospective value of the research justifies the deception. When the methodological requirements of a study necessitate concealment or deception, the investigator is required to explain clearly the reasons for this action as soon as possible.

c. *Voluntary Participation.* Participation in research is typically voluntary and without any penalty for refusal to participate. Involuntary participation is appropriate only when it can be demonstrated that participation will have no harmful effects on subjects and is essential to the investigation.

d. *Confidentiality of Information.* Information obtained about research participants during the course of an investigation is confidential. When the possibility exists that others may obtain access to such information, ethical research practice requires that the possibility, together with the plans for protecting confidentiality, be explained to participants as a part of the procedure for obtaining informed consent. (See B.1.e.)

e. *Persons Incapable of Giving Informed Consent.* When a person is incapable of giving informed consent, counselors provide an appropriate explanation, obtain agreement for participation and obtain appropriate consent from a legally authorized person.

f. *Commitments to Participants.* Counselors take reasonable measures to honor all commitments to research participants.

g. *Explanations And Data Collection.* After data are collected, counselors provide participants with full clarification of the nature of the study to remove any misconceptions. Where scientific or human values justify delaying or withholding information, counselors take reasonable measures to avoid causing harm.

h. *Agreements to Cooperate.* Counselors who agree to cooperate with another individual in research or publication incur an obligation to cooperate as promised in terms of punctuality of performance and with regard to the completeness and accuracy of the information required.

i. *Informed Consent for Sponsors.* In the pursuit of research, counselors give sponsors, institutions, and publication channels the same respect and opportunity for giving informed consent that they accord to individual research participants. Counselors are aware of their obligation to future research workers and ensure that host institutions are given feedback information and proper acknowledgment.

G.3. Reporting Results

a. *Information Affecting Outcome.* When reporting research results, counselors explicitly mention all variables and conditions known to the investigator that may have affected the outcome of a study or the interpretation of data.

b. *Accurate Results.* Counselors plan, conduct, and report research accurately and in a manner that minimizes the possibility that results will be misleading. They provide thorough discussions of the limitations of their data and alternative hypotheses. Counselors do not engage in fraudulent research, distort data, misrepresent data, or deliberately bias their results.

c. *Obligation to Report Unfavorable Results.* Counselors communicate to other counselors the results of any research judged to be of professional value. Results that reflect unfavorably on institutions, programs, services, prevailing opinions, or vested interests are not withheld.

d. *Identity of Subjects.* Counselors who supply data, aid in the research of another person, report research results, or make original data available take due care to disguise the identity of respective subjects in the absence of specific authorization from the subjects to do otherwise. (See B.1.g. and B.5.a.)

e. *Replication Studies.* Counselors are obligated to make available sufficient original research data to qualified professionals who may wish to replicate the study.

G.4. Publication

a. *Recognition of Others.* When conducting and reporting research, counselors are familiar with and give recognition to previous work on the topic, observe copyright laws, and give full credit to those to whom credit is due. (See F.1.d. and G.4.c.)

b. *Contributors.* Counselors give credit through joint authorship, acknowledgment, footnote statements, or other appropriate means to those who have contributed significantly to research or concept development in accordance with such contributions. The principal contributor is listed first and minor technical or professional contributions are acknowledged in notes or introductory statements.

c. *Student Research.* For an article that is substantially based on a student's dissertation or thesis, the student is listed as the principal author. (See F.1.d. and G.4.a.)

d. *Duplicate Submission.* Counselors submit manuscripts for consideration to only one journal at a time. Manuscripts that are published in whole or in substantial part in another journal or published work are not submitted for publication without acknowledgment and permission from the previous publication.

e. *Professional Review.* Counselors who review material submitted for publication, research, or other scholarly purposes respect the confidentiality and proprietary rights of those who submitted it.

Section H: Resolving Ethical Issues

H.1. Knowledge of Standards

Counselors are familiar with the *Code of Ethics* and the *Standards of Practice* and other applicable ethics codes from other professional organizations of which they are members, or from certification and licensure bodies. Lack of knowledge or misunderstanding of an ethical responsibility is not a defense against a charge of unethical conduct. (See F.3.e.)

H.2. Suspected Violations

a. *Ethical Behavior Expected.* Counselors expect professional associates to adhere to Code of Ethics. When counselors possess reasonable cause that raises doubts as to whether a counselor is acting in an ethical manner, they take appropriate action. (See H.2.d. and H.2.e.)

b. *Consultation.* When uncertain as to whether a particular situation or course of action may be in violation of Code of Ethics, counselors consult with other counselors who are knowledgeable about ethics, with colleagues, or with appropriate authorities.

c. *Organization Conflicts.* If the demands of an organization with which counselors are affiliated pose a conflict with Code of Ethics, counselors specify the nature of such conflicts and express to their supervisors or other responsible officials their commitment to Code of Ethics. When possible, counselors work toward change within the organization to allow full adherence to Code of Ethics.

d. *Informal Resolution.* When counselors have reasonable cause to believe that another counselor is violating an ethical standard, they attempt to first resolve the issue informally with the other counselor if feasible, providing that such action does not violate confidentiality rights that may be involved.

e. *Reporting Suspected Violations.* When an informal resolution is not appropriate or feasible, counselors, upon reasonable cause, take action such as reporting the suspected ethical violation to state or national ethics committees, unless this action conflicts with confidentiality rights that cannot be resolved.

f. *Unwarranted Complaints.* Counselors do not initiate, participate in, or encourage the filing of ethics complaints that are unwarranted or intend to harm a counselor rather than to protect clients or the public.

H.3. Cooperation with Ethics Committees

Counselors assist in the process of enforcing Code of Ethics. Counselors cooperate with investigations, proceedings, and requirements of the ACA Ethics Committee or ethics committees of other duly constituted associations or boards having jurisdiction over those charged with a violation. Counselors are familiar with the ACA Policies and Procedures and use it as a reference in assisting the enforcement of the Code of Ethics.

STANDARDS OF PRACTICE

All members of the American Counseling Association (ACA) are required to adhere to the *Standards of Practice* and the *Code of Ethics*. The *Standards of Practice* represent minimal behavioral statements of the *Code of Ethics*. Members should refer to the applicable section of the *Code of Ethics* for further interpretation and amplification of the applicable Standard of Practice.

Section A: The Counseling Relationship

Standard of Practice One (SP-1)
Nondiscrimination

Counselors respect diversity and must not discriminate against clients because of age, color, culture, disability, ethnic group, gender, race, religion, sexual orientation, marital status, or socioeconomic status. (See A.2.a.)

Standard of Practice Two (SP-2)
Disclosure to Clients

Counselors must adequately inform clients, preferably in writing, regarding the counseling process and counseling relationship at or before the time it begins and throughout the relationship. (See A.3.a.)

Standard of Practice Three (SP-3)
Dual Relationships

Counselors must make every effort to avoid dual relationships with clients that could impair their professional judgment or increase the risk of harm to clients. When a dual relationship cannot be avoided, counselors must take appropriate steps to ensure that judgment is not impaired and that no exploitation occurs. (See A.6.a. and A.6.b.)

Standard of Practice Four (SP-4)
Sexual Intimacies with Clients

Counselors must not engage in any type of sexual intimacies with current clients and must not engage in sexual intimacies with former clients within a minimum of two years after terminating the counseling relationship. Counselors who engage in such relationship after two years following termination have the responsibility to thoroughly examine and document that such relations did not have an exploitative nature.

Standard of Practice Five (SP-5)
Protecting Clients During Group Work

Counselors must take steps to protect clients from physical or psychological trauma resulting from interactions during group work. (See A.9.b.)

Standard of Practice Six (SP-6)
Advance Understanding of Fees
Counselors must explain to clients, prior to their entering the counseling relationship, financial arrangements related to professional services. (See A.10.a-d. and A.11.c.)

Standard of Practice Seven (SP-7)
Termination
Counselors must assist in making appropriate arrangements for the continuation of treatment of clients, when necessary, following termination of counseling relationships. (See A.11.a.)

Standard of Practice Eight (SP-8)
Inability to Assist Clients
Counselors must avoid entering or immediately terminate a counseling relationship if it is determined that they are unable to be of professional assistance to a client. The counselor may assist in making an appropriate referral for the client. (See A.11.b.)

Section B: Confidentiality

Standard of Practice Nine (SP-9)
Confidentiality Requirement
Counselors must keep information related to counseling services confidential unless disclosure is in the best interest of clients, is required for the welfare of others, or is required by law. When disclosure is required, only information that is essential is revealed and the client is informed of such disclosure. (See B.1.a.-f.)

Standard of Practice Ten (SP-10)
Confidentiality Requirements for Subordinates
Counselors must take measures to ensure that privacy and confidentiality of clients are maintained by subordinates. (See B.1.h.)

Standard of Practice Eleven (SP-11)
Confidentiality in Group Work
Counselors must clearly communicate to group members that confidentiality cannot be guaranteed in group work. (See B.2.a.)

Standard of Practice Twelve (SP-12)
Confidentiality in Family Counseling
Counselors must not disclose information about one family member in counseling to another family member without prior consent. (See B.2.b.)

Standard of Practice Thirteen (SP-13)
Confidentiality of Records
Counselors must maintain appropriate confidentiality in creating, storing, accessing, transferring, and disposing of counseling records. (See B.4.b.)

Standard of Practice Fourteen (SP-14)
Permission to Record or Observe
Counselors must obtain prior consent from clients in order to electronically record or observe sessions. (See B.4.c.)

Standard of Practice Fifteen (SP-15)
Disclosure or Transfer of Records
Counselors must obtain client consent to disclose or transfer records to third parties, unless exceptions listed in SP-9 exist. (See B.4.e.)

Standard of Practice Sixteen (SP-16)
Data Disguise Required
Counselors must disguise the identity of the client when using data for training, research, or publication. (See B.5.a.)

Section C: Professional Responsibility

Standard of Practice Seventeen (SP-17)
Boundaries of Competence
Counselors must practice only within the boundaries of their competence. (See C.2.a.)

Standard of Practice Eighteen (SP-18)
Continuing Education
Counselors must engage in continuing education to maintain their professional competence. (See C.2.f.)

Standard of Practice Nineteen (SP-19)
Impairment of Professionals
Counselors must refrain from offering professional services when their personal problems or conflicts may cause harm to a client or others. (See C.2.g.)

Standard of Practice Twenty (SP-20)
Accurate Advertising
Counselors must accurately represent their credentials and services when advertising. (See C.3.a.)

Standard of Practice Twenty-one (SP-21)
Recruiting Through Employment
Counselors must not use their place of employment or institutional affiliation to recruit clients for their private practices. (See C.3.d.)

Standard of Practice Twenty-two (SP-22)
Credentials Claimed
Counselors must claim or imply only professional credentials possessed and must correct any known misrepresentations of their credentials by others. (See C.4.a.)

Standard of Practice Twenty-three (SP-23)
Sexual Harassment
Counselors must not engage in sexual harassment. (See C.5.b.)

Standard of Practice Twenty-four (SP-24)
Unjustified Gains
Counselors must not use their professional positions to seek or receive unjustified personal gains, sexual favors, unfair advantage, or unearned goods or services. (See C.5.e.)

Standard of Practice Twenty-five (SP-25)
Clients Served by Others
With the consent of the client, counselors must inform other mental health professionals serving the same client that a counseling relationship between the counselor and client exists. (See C.6.c.)

Standard of Practice Twenty-six (SP-26)
Negative Employment Conditions
Counselors must alert their employers to institutional policy or conditions that may be potentially disruptive or damaging to the counselor's professional responsibilities, or that may limit their effectiveness or deny clients' rights. (See D.1.c.)

Standard of Practice Twenty-seven (SP-27)
Personnel Selection and Assignment
Counselors must select competent staff and must assign responsibilities compatible with staff skills and experiences. (See . D.1.h.)

Standard of Practice Twenty-eight (SP-28)
Exploitive Relationships with Subordinates
Counselors must not engage in exploitive relationships with individuals over whom they have supervi-

sory, evaluative, or instructional control or authority. (See D.1.k.)

Section D: Relationship With Other Professionals

Standard of Practice Twenty-nine (SP-29)
Accepting Fees from Agency Clients
Counselors must not accept fees or other remuneration for consultation with persons entitled to such services through the counselor's employing agency or institution. (See D.3.a.)

Standard of Practice Thirty (SP-30)
Referral Fees
Counselors must not accept referral fees. (See D.3.b.)

Section E: Evaluation, Assessment, and Interpretation

Standard of Practice Thirty-one (SP-31)
Limits of Competence
Counselors must perform only testing and assessment services for which they are competent. Counselors must not allow the use of psychological assessment techniques by unqualified persons under their supervision. (See E.2.a.)

Standard of Practice Thirty-two (SP-32)
Appropriate Use of Assessment Instruments
Counselors must use assessment instruments in the manner for which they were intended. (See E.2.b.)

Standard of Practice Thirty-three (SP-33)
Assessment Explanations to Clients
Counselors must provide explanations to clients prior to assessment about the nature and purposes of assessment and the specific uses of results. (See E.3.a.)

Standard of Practice Thirty-four (SP-34)
Recipients of Test Results
Counselors must ensure that accurate and appropriate interpretations accompany any release of testing and assessment information. (See E.3.b.)

Standard of Practice Thirty-five (SP-35)
Obsolete Tests and Outdated Test Results
Counselors must not base their assessment or intervention decisions or recommendations on data or test

results that are obsolete or outdated for the current purpose. (See E.11.)

Section F: Teaching, Training, and Supervision

Standard of Practice Thirty-six (SP-36)
Sexual Relationships with Students or Supervisees
Counselors must not engage in sexual relationships with their students and supervisees. (See F.1.c.)

Standard of Practice Thirty-seven (SP-37)
Credit for Contributions to Research
Counselors must give credit to students or supervisees for their contributions to research and scholarly projects. (See F.1.d.)

Standard of Practice Thirty-eight (SP-38)
Supervision Preparation
Counselors who offer clinical supervision services must be trained and prepared in supervision methods and techniques. (See F.1.f.)

Standard of Practice Thirty-nine (SP-39)
Evaluation Information
Counselors must clearly state to students and supervisees in advance of training, the levels of competency expected, appraisal methods, and timing of evaluations. Counselors must provide students and supervisees with periodic performance appraisal and evaluation feedback throughout the training program. (See F.2.c.)

Standard of Practice Forty (SP-40)
Peer Relationships in Training
Counselors must make every effort to ensure that the rights of peers are not violated when students and supervisees are assigned to lead counseling groups or provide clinical supervision. (See F.2.e.)

Standard of Practice Forty-one (SP-41)
Limitations of Students and Supervisees
Counselors must assist students and supervisees in securing remedial assistance, when needed, and must dismiss from the training program students and supervisees who are unable to provide competent service due to academic or personal limitations. (See F.3.a.)

Standard of Practice Forty-two (SP-42)
Self-Growth Experiences
Counselors who conduct experiences for students or supervisees that include self-growth or self disclosure must inform participants of counselors' ethical obligations to the profession and must not grade participants based on their nonacademic performance. (See F.3.b.)

Standard of Practice Forty-three (SP-43)
Standards for Students and Supervisees
Students and supervisees preparing to become counselors must adhere to the *Code of Ethics* and the *Standards of Practice* of counselors. (See F.3.e.)

Section G: Research and Publication

Standard of Practice Forty-four (SP-44)
Precautions to Avoid Injury in Research
Counselors must avoid causing physical, social, or psychological harm or injury to subjects in research. (See G.1.c.)

Standard of Practice Forty-five (SP-45)
Confidentiality of Research Information
Counselors must keep confidential information obtained about research participants. (See G.2.d.)

Standard of Practice Forty-six (SP-46)
Information Affecting Research Outcome
Counselors must report all variables and conditions known to the investigator that may have affected research data or outcomes. (See G.3.a.)

Standard of Practice Forty-seven (SP-47)
Accurate Research Results
Counselors must not distort or misrepresent research data, nor fabricate or intentionally bias research results. (See G.3.b.)

Standard of Practice Forty-eight (SP-48)
Publication Contributors
Counselors must give appropriate credit to those who have contributed to research. (See G.4.a. and G.4.b.)

Section H: Resolving Ethical Issues

Standard of Practice Forty-nine (SP-49)
Ethical Behavior Expected
Counselors must take appropriate action when they possess reasonable cause that raises doubts as to

whether counselors or other mental health professionals are acting in an ethical manner. (See H.2.a.)

Standard of Practice Fifty (SP-50)
Unwarranted Complaints

Counselors must not initiate, participate in, or encourage the filing of ethics complaints that are unwarranted or intended to harm a mental health professional rather than to protect clients or the public. (See H.2.f.)

Standard of Practice Fifty-one (SP-51)
Cooperation with Ethics Committees

Counselors must cooperate with investigations, proceedings, and requirements of the ACA Ethics Committee or ethics committees of other duly constituted associations or boards having jurisdiction over those charged with a violation. (See H.3.)

References

The following documents are available to counselors as resources to guide them in their practices. These resources are not a part of the *Code of Ethics* and the *Standards of Practice*.

American Association for Counseling and Development/Association for Measurement and Evaluation in Counseling and Development. (1989). *The responsibilities of users of standardized tests (revised).* Washington, DC: Author.

American Counseling Association. (1988). *American Counseling Association Code of Ethics and Standards of Practice.* Alexandria, VA: Author.

American Psychological Association. (1985). *Standards for educational and psychological testing (revised).* Washington, DC: Author.

American Rehabilitation Counseling Association, Commission on Rehabilitation Counselor Certification, and National Rehabilitation Counseling Association. (1995). *Code of professional ethics for rehabilitation counselors.* Chicago, IL: Author.

American School Counselor Association. (1992). *Ethical standards for school counselors.* Alexandria, VA: Author.

Joint Committee on Testing Practices. (1988). *Code of fair testing practices in education.* Washington, DC: Author.

National Board for Certified Counselors. (1989). *National Board for Certified Counselors Code of Ethics.* Alexandria, VA: Author.

Prediger, D.J. (Ed.). (1993, March). *Multicultural assessment standards.* Alexandria, VA: Association for Assessment in Counseling.

AMERICAN PSYCHOLOGICAL ASSOCIATION
ETHICAL PRINCIPLES OF PSYCHOLOGISTS AND
CODE OF CONDUCT

CONTENTS

INTRODUCTION

The American Psychological Association's (APA's) Ethical Principles of Psychologists and Code of Conduct (hereinafter referred to as the Ethics Code) consists of an Introduction, a Preamble, six General Principles (A–F), and specific Ethical Standards. The Introduction discusses the intent, organization, procedural considerations, and scope of application of the Ethics Code. The Preamble and General Principles are *aspirational* goals to guide psychologists toward the highest ideals of psychology. Although the Preamble and General Principles are not themselves enforceable rules, they should be considered by psychologists in arriving at an ethical course of action and may be considered by ethics bodies in interpreting the Ethical Standards. The Ethical Standards set forth *enforceable* rules for conduct as psychologists. Most of the Ethical Standards are written broadly, in order to apply to psychologists in varied roles, although the application of an Ethical Standard may vary depending on the context. The Ethical Standards are not exhaustive. The fact that a given conduct is not specifically addressed by the Ethics Code does not mean that it is necessarily either ethical or unethical.

Membership in the APA commits members to adhere to the APA Ethics Code and to the rules and procedures used to implement it. Psychologists and students, whether or not they are APA members, should be aware that the Ethics Code may be applied to them by state psychology boards, courts, or other public bodies.

This Ethics Code applies only to psychologists' work-related activities, that is, activities that are part of the psychologists' scientific and professional functions or that are psychological in nature. It includes the clinical or counseling practice of psychology, research, teaching, supervision of trainees, development of assessment instruments, conducting assessments, educational counseling, organizational consulting, social intervention, administration, and other activities as well. These work-related activities can be distinguished from the purely private conduct of a psychologist, which ordinarily is not within the purview of the Ethics Code.

The Ethics Code is intended to provide standards of professional conduct that can be applied by the APA and by other bodies that choose to adopt them. Whether or not a psychologist has violated the Ethics Code does not by itself determine whether he or she is legally liable in a court action, whether a contract is enforceable, or whether other legal consequences occur. These results are based on legal rather than ethical rules. However, compliance with or violation of the Ethics Code may be admissible as evidence in some legal proceedings, depending on the circumstances.

In the process of making decisions regarding their professional behavior, psychologists must consider this Ethics Code, in addition to applicable laws and psychology board regulations. If the Ethics Code establishes a higher standard of conduct than is required by law, psychologists must meet the higher ethical standard. If the Ethics Code standard appears to conflict with the requirements of law, then psychologists make known their commitment to the Ethics Code and take steps to resolve the conflict in a responsible manner. If neither law nor the Ethics Code resolves an issue, psychologists should consider other professional materials[1] and the dictates of their own conscience, as well as seek consultation with others within the field when this is practical.

---

[1]Professional materials that are most helpful in this regard are guidelines and standards that have been adopted or endorsed by professional psychological organizations. Such guidelines and standards, whether adopted by the American Psychological Association (APA) or its Divisions, are not enforceable as such by this Ethics Code, but are of educative value to psychologists, courts, and professional bodies. Such materials include, but are not limited to, the APA's *General Guidelines for Providers of Psychological Services* (1987), *Specialty Guidelines for the Delivery of Services by Clinical Psychologists, Counseling Psychologists, Industrial/Organizational Psychologists, and School Psychologists* (1981), *Guidelines for Computer Based Tests and Interpretations* (1987), *Standards for Educational and Psychological Testing* (1985), *Ethical Principles in the Conduct of Research With Human Participants* (1982), *Guidelines for Ethical Conduct in the Care and Use of Animals* (1986), *Guidelines for Providers of Psychological Services to Ethnic, Linguistic, and*

Culturally Diverse Populations (1990), and *Publication Manual of the American Psychological Association* (3rd ed., 1983). Materials not adopted by APA as a whole include the APA Division 41 (Forensic Psychology)/American Psychology—Law Society's *Specialty Guidelines for Forensic Psychologists* (1991).

Note: From 1992, December, *American Psychologist.* Copyright American Psychological Association. Reprinted by permission.

The APA has previously published its Ethical Standards as follows:

American Psychological Association. (1953). *Ethical standards of psychologists.* Washington, DC: Author.

American Psychological Association. (1958). Standards of ethical behavior for psychologists. *American Psychologist, 13,* 268–271.

American Psychological Association. (1963). Ethical standards of psychologists. *American Psychologist, 18,* 56–60.

American Psychological Association. (1968). Ethical standards of psychologists. *American Psychologist, 23,* 357–361.

American Psychological Association. (1977, March). Ethical standards of psychologists. *APA Monitor,* pp. 22–23.

American Psychological Association. (1979). *Ethical standards of psychologists.* Washington, DC: Author.

American Psychological Association. (1981). Ethical principles of psychologists. *American Psychologist, 36,* 633–638.

American Psychological Association. (1990). Ethical principles of psychologists (Amended June 2, 1989). *American Psychologist, 45,* 390–395.

Request copies of the APA's Ethical Principles of Psychologists and Code of Conduct from the APA Order Department, 750 First Street, NE, Washington, DC 20002-4242, or phone (202) 336-5510.

This version of the APA Ethics Code was adopted by the American Psychological Association's Council of Representatives during its meeting, August 13 and 16, 1992, and is effective beginning December 1, 1992. Inquiries concerning the substance or interpretation of the APA Ethics Code should be addressed to the Director, Office of Ethics, American Psychological Association, 750 First Street, NE, Washington, DC 20002-4242.

This Code will be used to adjudicate complaints brought concerning alleged conduct occurring on or after the effective date. Complaints regarding conduct occurring prior to the effective date will be adjudicated on the basis of the version of the Code that was in effect at the time the conduct occurred, except that no provisions repealed in June 1989, will be enforced even if an earlier version contains the provision. The Ethics Code will undergo continuing review and study for future revisions; comments on the Code may be sent to the above address.

The procedures for filing, investigating, and resolving complaints of unethical conduct are described in the current Rules and Procedures of the APA Ethics Committee. The actions that APA may take for violations of the Ethics Code include actions such as reprimand, censure, termination of APA membership, and referral of the matter to other bodies. Complainants who seek remedies such as monetary damages in alleging ethical violations by a psychologist must resort to private negotiation, administrative bodies, or the courts. Actions that violate the Ethics Code may lead to the imposition of sanctions on a psychologist by bodies other than APA, including state psychological associations, other professional groups, psychology boards, other state or federal agencies, and payors for health services. In addition to actions for violation of the Ethics Code, the APA Bylaws provide that APA may take action against a member after his or her conviction of a felony, expulsion or suspension from an affiliated state psychological association, or suspension or loss of licensure.

PREAMBLE

Psychologists work to develop a valid and reliable body of scientific knowledge based on research. They may apply that knowledge to human behavior in a variety of contexts. In doing so, they perform many roles, such as researcher, educator, diagnostician, therapist, supervisor, consultant, administrator, social interventionist, and expert witness. Their goal is to broaden knowledge of behavior and, where appropriate, to apply it pragmatically to improve the condition of both the individual and society. Psychologists respect the central importance of freedom of inquiry and expression in research, teaching, and publication. They also strive to help the public in developing informed judgments and choices concerning human behavior. This Ethics Code provides a common set of values upon which psychologists build their professional and scientific work.

This Code is intended to provide both the general principles and the decision rules to cover most situations encountered by psychologists. It has as its primary goal the welfare and protection of the individuals and groups with whom psychologists work. It is the individual responsibility of each psychologist to aspire to the highest possible standards of conduct. Psychologists respect and protect human and civil rights, and do not knowingly participate in or condone unfair discriminatory practices.

The development of a dynamic set of ethical standards for a psychologist's work-related conduct requires a personal commitment to a lifelong effort to act ethically; to encourage ethical behavior by students, supervisees, employees, and colleagues, as appropriate; and to consult with others, as needed, concerning ethical problems. Each psychologist supplements, but does not violate, the Ethics Code's values and rules on the basis of guidance drawn from personal values, culture, and experience.

GENERAL PRINCIPLES

Principle A: Competence

Psychologists strive to maintain high standards of competence in their work. They recognize the boundaries of their particular competencies and the limitations of their expertise. They provide only those services and use only those techniques for which they are qualified by education, training, or experience. Psychologists are cognizant of the fact that the competencies required in serving, teaching, and/or studying groups of people vary with the distinctive characteristics of those groups. In those areas in which recognized professional standards do not yet exist, psychologists exercise careful judgment and take appropriate precautions to protect the welfare of those with whom they work. They maintain knowledge of relevant scientific and professional information related to the services they render, and they recognize the need for ongoing education. Psychologists make appropriate use of scientific, professional, technical, and administrative resources.

Principle B: Integrity

Psychologists seek to promote integrity in the science, teaching, and practice of psychology. In these activities psychologists are honest, fair, and respectful of others. In describing or reporting their qualifications, services, products, fees, research, or teaching, they do not make statements that are false, misleading, or deceptive. Psychologists strive to be aware of their own belief systems, values, needs, and limitations and the effect of these on their work. To the extent feasible, they attempt to clarify for relevant parties the roles they are performing and to function appropriately in accordance with those roles. Psychologists avoid improper and potentially harmful dual relationships.

Principle C: Professional and Scientific Responsibility

Psychologists uphold professional standards of conduct, clarify their professional roles and obligations, accept appropriate responsibility for their behavior, and adapt their methods to the needs of different populations. Psychologists consult with, refer to, or cooperate with other professionals and institutions to the extent needed to serve the best interests of their patients, clients, or other recipients of their services. Psychologists' moral standards and conduct are personal matters to the same degree as is true for any other person, except as psychologists' conduct may compromise their professional responsibilities or reduce the public's trust in psychology and psychologists. Psychologists are concerned about the ethical compliance of their colleagues' scientific and professional conduct. When appropriate, they consult with colleagues in order to prevent or avoid unethical conduct.

Principle D: Respect for People's Rights and Dignity

Psychologists accord appropriate respect to the fundamental rights, dignity, and worth of all people. They respect the rights of individuals to privacy, confidentiality, self-determination, and autonomy, mindful that legal and other obligations may lead to inconsistency and conflict with the exercise of these rights. Psychologists are aware of cultural, individual, and role differences, including those due to age, gender, race, ethnicity, national origin, religion, sexual orientation, disability, language, and socioeconomic status. Psychologists try to eliminate the effect on their work of biases based on those factors, and they do not knowingly participate in or condone unfair discriminatory practices.

Principle E: Concern for Others' Welfare

Psychologists seek to contribute to the welfare of those with whom they interact professionally. In their professional actions, psychologists weigh the welfare and rights of their patients or clients, students, supervisees, human research participants, and other affected persons, and the welfare of animal subjects of research. When conflicts occur among psychologists' obligations or concerns, they attempt to resolve these conflicts and to perform their roles in a responsible fashion that avoids or minimizes harm. Psychologists are sensitive to real and ascribed differences in power between themselves and others, and they do not exploit or mislead other people during or after professional relationships.

Principle F: Social Responsibility

Psychologists are aware of their professional and scientific responsibilities to the community and the society in which they work and live. They apply and make public their knowledge of psychology in order to contribute to human welfare. Psychologists are concerned about and work to mitigate the causes of human suffering. When undertaking research, they strive to advance human welfare and the science of psychology. Psychologists try to avoid misuse of their work. Psychologists comply with the law and encourage the development of law and social policy that serve the interests of their patients and clients and the public. They are encouraged to contribute a portion of their professional time for little or no personal advantage.

ETHICAL STANDARDS

1. General Standards

These General Standards are potentially applicable to the professional and scientific activities of all psychologists.

1.01 Applicability of the Ethics Code

The activity of a psychologist subject to the Ethics Code may be reviewed under these Ethical

Standards only if the activity is part of his or her work-related functions or the activity is psychological in nature. Personal activities having no connection to or effect on psychological roles are not subject to the Ethics Code.

1.02 Relationship of Ethics and Law

If psychologists' ethical responsibilities conflict with law, psychologists make known their commitment to the Ethics Code and take steps to resolve the conflict in a responsible manner.

1.03 Professional and Scientific Relationship

Psychologists provide diagnostic, therapeutic, teaching, research, supervisory, consultative, or other psychological services only in the context of a defined professional or scientific relationship or role. (See also Standards 2.01, Evaluation, Diagnosis, and Interventions in Professional Context, and 7.02, Forensic Assessments.)

1.04 Boundaries of Competence

a. Psychologists provide services, teach, and conduct research only within the boundaries of their competence, based on their education, training, supervised experience, or appropriate professional experience.

b. Psychologists provide services, teach, or conduct research in new areas or involving new techniques only after first undertaking appropriate study, training, supervision, and/or consultation from persons who are competent in those areas or techniques.

c. In those emerging areas in which generally recognized standards for preparatory training do not yet exist, psychologists nevertheless take reasonable steps to ensure the competence of their work and to protect patients, clients, students, research participants, and others from harm.

1.05 Maintaining Expertise

Psychologists who engage in assessment, therapy, teaching, research, organizational consulting, or other professional activities maintain a reasonable level of awareness of current scientific and professional information in their fields of activity, and undertake ongoing efforts to maintain competence in the skills they use.

1.06 Basis for Scientific and Professional Judgments

Psychologists rely on scientifically and professionally derived knowledge when making scientific or professional judgments or when engaging in scholarly or professional endeavors.

1.07 Describing the Nature and Results of Psychological Services

a. When psychologists provide assessment, evaluation, treatment, counseling, supervision, teaching, consultation, research, or other psychological services to an individual, a group, or an organization, they provide, using language that is reasonably understandable to the recipient of those services, appropriate information beforehand about the nature of such services and appropriate information later about results and conclusions. (See also Standard 2.09, Explaining Assessment Results.)

b. If psychologists will be precluded by law or by organizational roles from providing such information to particular individuals or groups, they so inform those individuals or groups at the outset of the service.

1.08 Human Differences

Where differences of age, gender, race, ethnicity, national origin, religion, sexual orientation, disability, language, or socioeconomic status significantly affect psychologists' work concerning particular individuals or groups, psychologists obtain the training, experience, consultation, or supervision necessary to ensure the competence of their services, or they make appropriate referrals.

1.09 Respecting Others

In their work-related activities, psychologists respect the rights of others to hold values, attitudes, and opinions that differ from their own.

1.10 Nondiscrimination

In their work-related activities, psychologists do not engage in unfair discrimination based on age, gender, race, ethnicity, national origin, religion, sexual orientation, disability, socioeconomic status, or any basis proscribed by law.

1.11 Sexual Harassment

a. Psychologists do not engage in sexual harassment. Sexual harassment is sexual solicitation, physical advances, or verbal or nonverbal conduct that is sexual in nature, that occurs in connection with the psychologist's activities or roles as a psychologist, and that either: (1) is unwelcome, is offensive, or creates a hostile workplace environment, and the psychologist knows or is told this; or (2) is sufficiently severe or intense to be abusive to a reasonable person in the context. Sexual harassment can consist of a single intense or severe act or of multiple persistent or pervasive acts.

b. Psychologists accord sexual-harassment complainants and respondents dignity and respect. Psychologists do not participate in denying a person academic admittance or advancement, employment, tenure, or promotion, based solely upon their having made, or their being the subject of, sexual-harassment charges. This does not preclude taking action based upon the outcome of such proceedings or consideration of other appropriate information.

1.12 Other Harassment

Psychologists do not knowingly engage in behavior that is harassing or demeaning to persons with whom they interact in their work based on factors such as those persons' age, gender, race, ethnicity, national origin, religion, sexual orientation, disability, language, or socioeconomic status.

1.13 Personal Problems and Conflicts

a. Psychologists recognize that their personal problems and conflicts may interfere with their effectiveness. Accordingly, they refrain from undertaking an activity when they know or should know that their personal problems are likely to lead to harm to a patient, client, colleague, student, research participant, or other person to whom they may owe a professional or scientific obligation.

b. In addition, psychologists have an obligation to be alert to signs of, and to obtain assistance for, their personal problems at an early stage, in order to prevent significantly impaired performance.

c. When psychologists become aware of personal problems that may interfere with their performing work-related duties adequately, they take appropriate measures, such as obtaining professional consultation or assistance, and determine whether they should limit, suspend, or terminate their work-related duties.

1.14 Avoiding Harm

Psychologists take reasonable steps to avoid harming their patients or clients, research participants, students, and others with whom they work, and to minimize harm where it is foreseeable and unavoidable.

1.15 Misuse of Psychologists' Influence

Because psychologists' scientific and professional judgments and actions may affect the lives of others, they are alert to and guard against personal, financial, social, organizational, or political factors that might lead to misuse of their influence.

1.16 Misuse of Psychologists' Work

a. Psychologists do not participate in activities in which it appears likely that their skills or data will be misused by others, unless corrective mechanisms are available. (See also Standard 7.04, Truthfulness and Candor.)

b. If psychologists learn of misuse or misrepresentation of their work, they take reasonable steps to correct or minimize the misuse or misrepresentation.

1.17 Multiple Relationships

a. In many communities and situations, it may not be feasible or reasonable for psychologists to avoid social or other nonprofessional contacts with persons such as patients, clients, students, supervisees, or research participants. Psychologists must always be sensitive to the potential harmful effects of other contacts on their work and on those persons with whom they deal. A psychologist refrains from entering into or promising another personal, scientific, professional, financial, or other relationship with such persons if it appears likely that such a relationship reasonably might impair the psychologist's objectivity or otherwise interfere with the psychologist's effectively performing his or her functions as a psychologist, or might harm or exploit the other party.

b. Likewise, whenever feasible, a psychologist refrains from taking on professional or scientific obligations when preexisting relationships would create a risk of such harm.

c. If a psychologist finds that, due to unforeseen factors, a potentially harmful multiple relationship has arisen, the psychologist attempts to resolve it with due regard for the best interests of the affected person and maximal compliance with the Ethics Code.

1.18 Barter (With Patients or Clients)

Psychologists ordinarily refrain from accepting goods, services, or other nonmonetary remuneration from patients or clients in return for psychological services because such arrangements create inherent potential for conflicts, exploitation, and distortion of the professional relationship. A psychologist may participate in bartering *only* if (1) it is not clinically contraindicated, *and* (2) the relationship is not exploitative. (See also Standards 1.17, Multiple Relationships, and 1.25, Fees and Financial Arrangements.)

1.19 Exploitative Relationships

a. Psychologists do not exploit persons over whom they have supervisory, evaluative, or other authority such as students, supervisees, employees, research participants, and clients or patients. (See also Standards 4.05–4.07 regarding sexual involvement with clients or patients..

b. Psychologists do not engage in sexual relationships with students or supervisees in training over whom the psychologist has evaluative or direct authority, because such relationships are so likely to impair judgment or be exploitative.

1.20 Consultations and Referrals

a. Psychologists arrange for appropriate consultations and referrals based principally on the best interests of their patients or clients, with appropriate consent, and subject to other relevant considerations, including applicable law and contractual obligations. (See also Standards 5.01, Discussing the Limits of Confidentiality, and 5.06, Consultations.)

b. When indicated and professionally appropriate, psychologists cooperate with other professionals in order to serve their patients or clients effectively and appropriately.

c. Psychologists' referral practices are consistent with law.

1.21 Third-Party Requests for Services

a. When a psychologist agrees to provide services to a person or entity at the request of a third party, the psychologist clarifies to the extent feasible, at the outset of the service, the nature of the relationship with each party. This clarification includes the role of the psychologist (such as therapist, organizational consultant, diagnostician, or expert witness), the probable uses of the services provided or the information obtained, and the fact that there may be limits to confidentiality.

b. If there is a foreseeable risk of the psychologist's being called upon to perform conflicting roles because of the involvement of a third party, the psychologist clarifies the nature and direction of his or her responsibilities, keeps all parties appropriately informed as matters develop, and resolves the situation in accordance with this Ethics Code.

1.22 Delegation to and Supervision of Subordinates

a. Psychologists delegate to their employees, supervisees, and research assistants only those responsibilities that such persons can reasonably be expected to perform competently, on the basis of their education, training, or experience, either independently or with the level of supervision being provided.

b. Psychologists provide proper training and supervision to their employees or supervisees and take reasonable steps to see that such persons perform services responsibly, competently, and ethically.

c. If institutional policies, procedures, or practices prevent fulfillment of this obligation, psychologists attempt to modify their role or to correct the situation to the extent feasible.

1.23 Documentation of Professional and Scientific Work

a. Psychologists appropriately document their professional and scientific work in order to facilitate provision of services later by them or by other professionals, to ensure accountability, and to meet other requirements of institutions or the law.

b. When psychologists have reason to believe that records of their professional services will be used in legal proceedings involving recipients of or participants in their work, they have a responsibility to create and maintain documentation in the kind of detail and quality that would be consistent with reasonable scrutiny in an adjudicative forum. (See also Standard 7.01, Professionalism, under Forensic Activities.)

1.24 Records and Data

Psychologists create, maintain, disseminate, store, retain, and dispose of records and data relating to their research, practice, and other work in accordance with law and in a manner that permits compliance with the requirements of this Ethics Code. (See also Standard 5.04, Maintenance of Records.)

1.25 Fees and Financial Arrangements

a. As early as is feasible in a professional or scientific relationship, the psychologist and the patient, client, or other appropriate recipient of psychological services reach an agreement specifying the compensation and the billing arrangements.

b. Psychologists do not exploit recipients of services or payors with respect to fees.

c. Psychologists' fee practices are consistent with law.

d. Psychologists do not misrepresent their fees.

e. If limitations to services can be anticipated because of limitations in financing, this is discussed with the patient, client, or other appropriate recipient of services as early as is feasible. (See also Standard 4.08, Interruption of Services.)

f. If the patient, client, or other recipient of services does not pay for services as agreed, and if the psychologist wishes to use collection agencies or legal measures to collect the fees, the psychologist first informs the person that such measures will be taken and provides that person an opportunity to make prompt payment. (See also Standard 5.11, Withholding Records for Nonpayment.)

1.26 Accuracy in Reports to Payors and Funding Sources

In their reports to payors for services or sources of research funding, psychologists accurately state the nature of the research or service provided, the fees or charges, and where applicable, the identity of the provider, the findings, and the diagnosis. (See also Standard 5.05, Disclosures.)

1.27 Referrals and Fees

When a psychologist pays, receives payment from, or divides fees with another professional other than in an employer–employee relationship, the payment to each is based on the services (clinical, consultative, administrative, or other) provided and is not based on the referral itself.

2. Evaluation, Assessment, or Intervention

2.01 Evaluation, Diagnosis, and Interventions in Professional Context

a. Psychologists perform evaluations, diagnostic services, or interventions only within the context of a defined professional relationship. (See also

Standard 1.03, Professional and Scientific Relationship.)

b. Psychologists' assessments, recommendations, reports, and psychological diagnostic or evaluative statements are based on information and techniques (including personal interviews of the individual when appropriate) sufficient to provide appropriate substantiation for their findings. (See also Standard 7.02, Forensic Assessments.)

2.02 Competence and Appropriate Use of Assessments and Interventions

a. Psychologists who develop, administer, score, interpret, or use psychological assessment techniques, interviews, tests, or instruments do so in a manner and for purposes that are appropriate in light of the research on or evidence of the usefulness and proper application of the techniques.

b. Psychologists refrain from misuse of assessment techniques, interventions, results, and interpretations and take reasonable steps to prevent others from misusing the information these techniques provide. This includes refraining from releasing raw test results or raw data to persons, other than to patients or clients as appropriate, who are not qualified to use such information. (See also Standards 1.02, Relationship of Ethics and Law, and 1.04, Boundaries of Competence.)

2.03 Test Construction

Psychologists who develop and conduct research with tests and other assessment techniques use scientific procedures and current professional knowledge for test design, standardization, validation, reduction or elimination of bias, and recommendations for use.

2.04 Use of Assessment in General and With Special Populations

a. Psychologists who perform interventions or administer, score, interpret, or use assessment techniques are familiar with the reliability, validation, and related standardization or outcome studies of, and proper applications and uses of, the techniques they use.

b. Psychologists recognize limits to the certainty with which diagnoses, judgments, or predictions can be made about individuals.

c. Psychologists attempt to identify situations in which particular interventions or assessment techniques or norms may not be applicable or may require adjustment in administration or interpretation because of factors such as individuals' gender, age, race, ethnicity, national origin, religion, sexual orientation, disability, language, or socioeconomic status.

2.05 Interpreting Assessment Results

When interpreting assessment results, including automated interpretations, psychologists take into account the various test factors and characteristics of the person being assessed that might affect psychologists' judgments or reduce the accuracy of their interpretations. They indicate any significant reservations they have about the accuracy or limitations of their interpretations.

2.06 Unqualified Persons

Psychologists do not promote the use of psychological assessment techniques by unqualified persons. (See also Standard 1.22, Delegation to and Supervision of Subordinates.)

2.07 Obsolete Tests and Outdated Test Results

a. Psychologists do not base their assessment or intervention decisions or recommendations on data or test results that are outdated for the current purpose.

b. Similarly, psychologists do not base such decisions or recommendations on tests and measures that are obsolete and not useful for the current purpose.

2.08 Test Scoring and Interpretation Services

a. Psychologists who offer assessment or scoring procedures to other professionals accurately describe the purpose, norms, validity, reliability, and applications of the procedures and any special qualifications applicable to their use.

b. Psychologists select scoring and interpretation services (including automated services) on the basis of evidence of the validity of the program and procedures as well as on other appropriate considerations.

c. Psychologists retain appropriate responsibility for the appropriate application, interpretation, and use of assessment instruments, whether they score and interpret such tests themselves or use automated or other services.

2.09 Explaining Assessment Results

Unless the nature of the relationship is clearly explained to the person being assessed in advance and precludes provision of an explanation of results (such as in some organizational consulting, preemployment or security screenings, and forensic evaluations), psychologists ensure that an explanation of the results is provided using language that is reasonably understandable to the person assessed or to another legally authorized person on behalf of the client. Regardless of whether the scoring and interpretation are done by the psychologist, by assistants, or by automated or other outside services, psychologists take reasonable steps to ensure that appropriate explanations of results are given.

2.10 Maintaining Test Security

Psychologists make reasonable efforts to maintain the integrity and security of tests and other assessment techniques consistent with law, contractual obligations, and in a manner that permits compliance with the requirements of this Ethics Code. (See also Standard 1.02, Relationship of Ethics and Law.)

3. Advertising and Other Public Statements

3.01 Definition of Public Statements

Psychologists comply with this Ethics Code in public statements relating to their professional services, products, or publications or to the field of psychology. Public statements include but are not limited to paid or unpaid advertising, brochures, printed matter, directory listings, personal resumes or curricula vitae, interviews or comments for use in media, statements in legal proceedings, lectures and public oral presentations, and published materials.

3.02 Statements by Others

a. Psychologists who engage others to create or place public statements that promote their professional practice, products, or activities retain professional responsibility for such statements.

b. In addition, psychologists make reasonable efforts to prevent others whom they do not control (such as employers, publishers, sponsors, organizational clients, and representatives of the print or broadcast media) from making deceptive statements concerning psychologists' practice or professional or scientific activities.

c. If psychologists learn of deceptive statements about their work made by others, psychologists make reasonable efforts to correct such statements.

d. Psychologists do not compensate employees of press, radio, television, or other communication media in return for publicity in a news item.

e. A paid advertisement relating to the psychologist's activities must be identified as such, unless it is already apparent from the context.

3.03 Avoidance of False or Deceptive Statements

a. Psychologists do not make public statements that are false, deceptive, misleading, or fraudulent, either because of what they state, convey, or suggest or because of what they omit, concerning their research, practice, or other work activities or those of persons or organizations with which they are affiliated. As examples (and not in limitation) of this standard, psychologists do not make false or deceptive statements concerning (1) their training, experience, or competence; (2) their academic degrees; (3) their credentials; (4) their institutional or association affiliations; (5) their services; (6) the scientific or clinical basis for, or results or degree of success of, their services; (7) their fees; or (8) their publications or research findings. (See also Standards 6.15, Deception in Research, and 6.18, Providing Participants With Information About the Study.)

b. Psychologists claim as credentials for their psychological work, only degrees that (1) were earned from a regionally accredited educational institution or (2) were the basis for psychology licensure by the state in which they practice.

3.04 Media Presentations

When psychologists provide advice or comment by means of public lectures, demonstrations, radio or television programs, prerecorded tapes, printed articles, mailed material, or other media, they take reasonable precautions to ensure that (1) the statements are based on appropriate psychological literature and practice, (2) the statements are otherwise consistent with this Ethics Code, and (3) the recipients of the information are not encouraged to infer that a relationship has been established with them personally.

3.05 Testimonials

Psychologists do not solicit testimonials from current psychotherapy clients or patients or other persons who because of their particular circumstances are vulnerable to undue influence.

3.06 In-Person Solicitation

Psychologists do not engage, directly or through agents, in uninvited in-person solicitation of business from actual or potential psychotherapy patients or clients or other persons who because of their particular circumstances are vulnerable to undue influence. However, this does not preclude attempting to implement appropriate collateral contacts with significant others for the purpose of benefiting an already engaged therapy patient.

4. Therapy

4.01 Structuring the Relationship

a. Psychologists discuss with clients or patients as early as is feasible in the therapeutic relationship appropriate issues, such as the nature and anticipated course of therapy, fees, and confidentiality. (See also Standards 1.25, Fees and Financial Arrangements, and 5.01, Discussing the Limits of Confidentiality.)

b. When the psychologist's work with clients or patients will be supervised, the above discussion includes that fact, and the name of the supervisor, when the supervisor has legal responsibility for the case.

c. When the therapist is a student intern, the client or patient is informed of that fact.

d. Psychologists make reasonable efforts to answer patients' questions and to avoid apparent misunderstandings about therapy. Whenever possible, psychologists provide oral and/or written information, using language that is reasonably understandable to the patient or client.

4.02 Informed Consent to Therapy

a. Psychologists obtain appropriate informed consent to therapy or related procedures, using language that is reasonably understandable to participants. The content of informed consent will vary depending on many circumstances; however, informed consent generally implies that the person (1) has the capacity to consent, (2) has been informed of significant information concerning the procedure, (3) has freely and without undue influence expressed consent, and (4) consent has been appropriately documented.

b. When persons are legally incapable of giving informed consent, psychologists obtain informed permission from a legally authorized person, if such substitute consent is permitted by law.

c. In addition, psychologists (1) inform those persons who are legally incapable of giving informed consent about the proposed interventions in a manner commensurate with the persons' psychological capacities, (2) seek their assent to those interventions, and (3) consider such persons' preferences and best interests.

4.03 Couple and Family Relationships

a. When a psychologist agrees to provide services to several persons who have a relationship (such as husband and wife or parents and children), the psychologist attempts to clarify at the outset (1) which of the individuals are patients or clients and (2) the relationship the psychologist will have with each person. This clarification includes the role of the psychologist and the probable uses of the services provided or the information obtained. (See also Standard 5.01, Discussing the Limits of Confidentiality.)

b. As soon as it becomes apparent that the psychologist may be called on to perform potentially conflicting roles (such as marital counselor to husband and wife, and then witness for one party in a divorce proceeding), the psychologist attempts to clarify and adjust, or withdraw from, roles appropriately. (See also Standard 7.03, Clarification of Role, under Forensic Activities.)

4.04 Providing Mental Health Services to Those Served by Others

In deciding whether to offer or provide services to those already receiving mental health services elsewhere, psychologists carefully consider the treatment issues and the potential patient's or client's welfare. The psychologist discusses these issues with the patient or client, or another legally authorized person on behalf of the client, in order to minimize the risk of confusion and conflict, consults with the other service providers when appropriate, and proceeds with caution and sensitivity to the therapeutic issues.

4.05 Sexual Intimacies With Current Patients or Clients

Psychologists do not engage in sexual intimacies with current patients or clients.

4.06 Therapy With Former Sexual Partners

Psychologists do not accept as therapy patients or clients persons with whom they have engaged in sexual intimacies.

4.07 Sexual Intimacies With Former Therapy Patients

a. Psychologists do not engage in sexual intimacies with a former therapy patient or client for at least two years after cessation or termination of professional services.

b. Because sexual intimacies with a former therapy patient or client are so frequently harmful to the patient or client, and because such intimacies undermine public confidence in the psychology profession and thereby deter the public's use of needed services, psychologists do not engage in sexual intimacies with former therapy patients and clients even after a two-year interval except in the most unusual circumstances. The psychologist who engages in such activity after the two years following cessation or termination of treatment bears the burden of demonstrating that there has been no exploitation, in light of all relevant factors, including (1) the amount of time that has passed since therapy terminated, (2) the nature and duration of the therapy, (3) the circumstances of termination, (4) the patient's or client's personal history, (5) the patient's or client's current mental status, (6) the likelihood of adverse impact on the patient or client and others, and (7) any statements or actions made by the therapist during the course of therapy suggesting or inviting the possibility of a posttermination sexual or romantic relationship with the patient or client. (See also Standard 1.17, Multiple Relationships.)

4.08 Interruption of Services

a. Psychologists make reasonable efforts to plan for facilitating care in the event that psychological services are interrupted by factors such as the psychologist's illness, death, unavailability, or relocation or by the client's relocation or financial limitations. (See also Standard 5.09, Preserving Records and Data.)

b. When entering into employment or contractual relationships, psychologists provide for orderly and appropriate resolution of responsibility for patient or client care in the event that the employment or contractual relationship ends, with paramount consideration given to the welfare of the patient or client.

4.09 Terminating the Professional Relationship

a. Psychologists do not abandon patients or clients. (See also Standard 1.25e, under Fees and Financial Arrangements.)

b. Psychologists terminate a professional relationship when it becomes reasonably clear that the patient or client no longer needs the service, is not benefiting, or is being harmed by continued service.

c. Prior to termination for whatever reason, except where precluded by the patient's or client's conduct, the psychologist discusses the patient's or client's views and needs, provides appropriate pretermination counseling, suggests alternative service providers as appropriate, and takes other reasonable steps to facilitate transfer of responsibility to another provider if the patient or client needs one immediately.

5. Privacy and Confidentiality

These Standards are potentially applicable to the professional and scientific activities of all psychologists.

5.01 Discussing the Limits of Confidentiality

a. Psychologists discuss with persons and organizations with whom they establish a scientific or professional relationship (including, to the extent feasible, minors and their legal representatives) (1) the relevant limitations on confidentiality, including limitations where applicable in group, marital, and family therapy or in organizational consulting, and (2) the foreseeable uses of the information generated through their services.

b. Unless it is not feasible or is contraindicated, the discussion of confidentiality occurs at the outset of the relationship and thereafter as new circumstances may warrant.

c. Permission for electronic recording of interviews is secured from clients and patients.

5.02 Maintaining Confidentiality

Psychologists have a primary obligation and take reasonable precautions to respect the confidentiality rights of those with whom they work or consult, recognizing that confidentiality may be established by law, institutional rules, or professional or scientific relationships. (See also Standard 6.26, Professional Reviewers.)

5.03 Minimizing Intrusions on Privacy

a. In order to minimize intrusions on privacy, psychologists include in written and oral reports,

consultations, and the like, only information germane to the purpose for which the communication is made.

b. Psychologists discuss confidential information obtained in clinical or consulting relationships, or evaluative data concerning patients, individual or organizational clients, students, research participants, supervisees, and employees, only for appropriate scientific or professional purposes and only with persons clearly concerned with such matters.

5.04 Maintenance of Records

Psychologists maintain appropriate confidentiality in creating, storing, accessing, transferring, and disposing of records under their control, whether these are written, automated, or in any other medium. Psychologists maintain and dispose of records in accordance with law and in a manner that permits compliance with the requirements of this Ethics Code.

5.05 Disclosures

a. Psychologists disclose confidential information without the consent of the individual only as mandated by law, or where permitted by law for a valid purpose, such as (1) to provide needed professional services to the patient or the individual or organizational client, (2) to obtain appropriate professional consultations, (3) to protect the patient or client or others from harm, or (4) to obtain payment for services, in which instance disclosure is limited to the minimum that is necessary to achieve the purpose.

b. Psychologists also may disclose confidential information with the appropriate consent of the patient or the individual or organizational client (or of another legally authorized person on behalf of the patient or client), unless prohibited by law.

5.06 Consultations

When consulting with colleagues, (1) psychologists do not share confidential information that reasonably could lead to the identification of a patient, client, research participant, or other person or organization with whom they have a confidential relationship unless they have obtained the prior consent of the person or organization or the disclosure cannot be avoided, and (2) they share information only to the extent necessary to achieve the purposes of the consultation. (See also Standard 5.02, Maintaining Confidentiality.)

5.07 Confidential Information in Databases

a. If confidential information concerning recipients of psychological services is to be entered into databases or systems of records available to persons whose access has not been consented to by the recipient, then psychologists use coding or other techniques to avoid the inclusion of personal identifiers.

b. If a research protocol approved by an institutional review board or similar body requires the inclusion of personal identifiers, such identifiers are deleted before the information is made accessible to persons other than those of whom the subject was advised.

c. If such deletion is not feasible, then before psychologists transfer such data to others or review such data collected by others, they take reasonable steps to determine that appropriate consent of personally identifiable individuals has been obtained.

5.08 Use of Confidential Information for Didactic or Other Purposes

a. Psychologists do not disclose in their writings, lectures, or other public media, confidential, personally identifiable information concerning their patients, individual or organizational clients, students, research participants, or other recipients of their services that they obtained during the course of their work, unless the person or organization has consented in writing or unless there is other ethical or legal authorization for doing so.

b. Ordinarily, in such scientific and professional presentations, psychologists disguise confidential information concerning such persons or organizations so that they are not individually

identifiable to others and so that discussions do not cause harm to subjects who might identify themselves.

5.09 Preserving Records and Data

A psychologist makes plans in advance so that confidentiality of records and data is protected in the event of the psychologist's death, incapacity, or withdrawal from the position or practice.

5.10 Ownership of Records and Data

Recognizing that ownership of records and data is governed by legal principles, psychologists take reasonable and lawful steps so that records and data remain available to the extent needed to serve the best interests of patients, individual or organizational clients, research participants, or appropriate others.

5.11 Withholding Records for Nonpayment

Psychologists may not withhold records under their control that are requested and imminently needed for a patient's or client's treatment solely because payment has not been received, except as otherwise provided by law.

6. Teaching, Training Supervision, Research, and Publishing

6.01 Design of Education and Training Programs

Psychologists who are responsible for education and training programs seek to ensure that the programs are competently designed, provide the proper experiences, and meet the requirements for licensure, certification, or other goals for which claims are made by the program.

6.02 Descriptions of Education and Training Programs

a. Psychologists responsible for education and training programs seek to ensure that there is a current and accurate description of the program content, training goals and objectives, and requirements that must be met for satisfactory completion of the program. This information must be made readily available to all interested parties.

b. Psychologists seek to ensure that statements concerning their course outlines are accurate and not misleading, particularly regarding the subject matter to be covered, bases for evaluating progress, and the nature of course experiences. (See also Standard 3.03, Avoidance of False or Deceptive Statements.)

c. To the degree to which they exercise control, psychologists responsible for announcements, catalogs, brochures, or advertisements describing workshops, seminars, or other non-degree-granting educational programs ensure that they accurately describe the audience for which the program is intended, the educational objectives, the presenters, and the fees involved.

6.03 Accuracy and Objectivity in Teaching

a. When engaged in teaching or training, psychologists present psychological information accurately and with a reasonable degree of objectivity.

b. When engaged in teaching or training, psychologists recognize the power they hold over students or supervisees and therefore make reasonable efforts to avoid engaging in conduct that is personally demeaning to students or supervisees. (See also Standards 1.09, Respecting Others, and 1.12, Other Harassment.)

6.04 Limitation on Teaching

Psychologists do not teach the use of techniques or procedures that require specialized training, licensure, or expertise, including but not limited to hypnosis, biofeedback, and projective techniques, to individuals who lack the prerequisite training, legal scope of practice, or expertise.

6.05 Assessing Student and Supervisee Performance

a. In academic and supervisory relationships, psychologists establish an appropriate process

for providing feedback to students and supervisees.

b. Psychologists evaluate students and supervisees on the basis of their actual performance on relevant and established program requirements.

6.06 Planning Research

a. Psychologists design, conduct, and report research in accordance with recognized standards of scientific competence and ethical research.

b. Psychologists plan their research so as to minimize the possibility that results will be misleading.

c. In planning research, psychologists consider its ethical acceptability under the Ethics Code. If an ethical issue is unclear, psychologists seek to resolve the issue through consultation with institutional review boards, animal care and use committees, peer consultations, or other proper mechanisms.

d. Psychologists take reasonable steps to implement appropriate protections for the rights and welfare of human participants, other persons affected by the research, and the welfare of animal subjects.

6.07 Responsibility

a. Psychologists conduct research competently and with due concern for the dignity and welfare of the participants.

b. Psychologists are responsible for the ethical conduct of research conducted by them or by others under their supervision or control.

c. Researchers and assistants are permitted to perform only those tasks for which they are appropriately trained and prepared.

d. As part of the process of development and implementation of research projects, psychologists consult those with expertise concerning any special population under investigation or most likely to be affected.

6.08 Compliance With Law and Standards

Psychologists plan and conduct research in a manner consistent with federal and state law and regulations, as well as professional standards governing the conduct of research, and particularly those standards governing research with human participants and animal subjects.

6.09 Institutional Approval

Psychologists obtain from host institutions or organizations appropriate approval prior to conducting research, and they provide accurate information about their research proposals. They conduct the research in accordance with the approved research protocol.

6.10 Research Responsibilities

Prior to conducting research (except research involving only anonymous surveys, naturalistic observations, or similar research), psychologists enter into an agreement with participants that clarifies the nature of the research and the responsibilities of each party.

6.11 Informed Consent to Research

a. Psychologists use language that is reasonably understandable to research participants in obtaining their appropriate informed consent (except as provided in Standard 6.12, Dispensing With Informed Consent). Such informed consent is appropriately documented.

b. Using language that is reasonably understandable to participants, psychologists inform participants of the nature of the research; they inform participants that they are free to participate or to decline to participate or to withdraw from the research; they explain the foreseeable consequences of declining or withdrawing; they inform participants of significant factors that may be expected to influence their willingness to participate (such as risks, discomfort, adverse effects, or limitations on confidentiality, except as provided in Standard 6.15, Deception in Research); and they explain other aspects about which the prospective participants inquire.

c. When psychologists conduct research with individuals such as students or subordinates, psychologists take special care to protect the prospective participants from adverse consequences of declining or withdrawing from participation.

d. When research participation is a course requirement or opportunity for extra credit, the prospec-

tive participant is given the choice of equitable alternative activities.

e. For persons who are legally incapable of giving informed consent, psychologists nevertheless (1) provide an appropriate explanation, (2) obtain the participant's assent, and (3) obtain appropriate permission from a legally authorized person, if such substitute consent is permitted by law.

6.12 Dispensing With Informed Consent

Before determining that planned research (such as research involving only anonymous questionnaires, naturalistic observations, or certain kinds of archival research) does not require the informed consent of research participants, psychologists consider applicable regulations and institutional review board requirements, and they consult with colleagues as appropriate.

6.13 Informed Consent in Research Filming or Recording

Psychologists obtain informed consent from research participants prior to filming or recording them in any form, unless the research involves simply naturalistic observations in public places and it is not anticipated that the recording will be used in a manner that could cause personal identification or harm.

6.14 Offering Inducements for Research Participants

a. In offering professional services as an inducement to obtain research participants, psychologists make clear the nature of the services, as well as the risks, obligations, and limitations. (See also Standard 1.18, Barter [With Patients or Clients].)

b. Psychologists do not offer excessive or inappropriate financial or other inducements to obtain research participants, particularly when it might tend to coerce participation.

6.15 Deception in Research

a. Psychologists do not conduct a study involving deception unless they have determined that the use of deceptive techniques is justified by the study's prospective scientific, educational, or applied value and that equally effective alternative procedures that do not use deception are not feasible.

b. Psychologists never deceive research participants about significant aspects that would affect their willingness to participate, such as physical risks, discomfort, or unpleasant emotional experiences.

c. Any other deception that is an integral feature of the design and conduct of an experiment must be explained to participants as early as is feasible, preferably at the conclusion of their participation, but no later than at the conclusion of the research. (See also Standard 6.18, Providing Participants With Information About the Study.)

6.16 Sharing and Utilizing Data

Psychologists inform research participants of their anticipated sharing or further use of personally identifiable research data and of the possibility of unanticipated future uses.

6.17 Minimizing Invasiveness

In conducting research, psychologists interfere with the participants or milieu from which data are collected only in a manner that is warranted by an appropriate research design and that is consistent with psychologists' roles as scientific investigators.

6.18 Providing Participants With Information About the Study

a. Psychologists provide a prompt opportunity for participants to obtain appropriate information about the nature, results, and conclusions of the research, and psychologists attempt to correct any misconceptions that participants may have.

b. If scientific or humane values justify delaying or withholding this information, psychologists take reasonable measures to reduce the risk of harm.

6.19 Honoring Commitments

Psychologists take reasonable measures to honor all commitments they have made to research participants.

6.20 Care and Use of Animals in Research

a. Psychologists who conduct research involving animals treat them humanely.

b. Psychologists acquire, care for, use, and dispose of animals in compliance with current federal, state, and local laws and regulations, and with professional standards.

c. Psychologists trained in research methods and experienced in the care of laboratory animals supervise all procedures involving animals and are responsible for ensuring appropriate consideration of their comfort, health, and humane treatment.

d. Psychologists ensure that all individuals using animals under their supervision have received instruction in research methods and in the care, maintenance, and handling of the species being used, to the extent appropriate to their role.

e. Responsibilities and activities of individuals assisting in a research project are consistent with their respective competencies.

f. Psychologists make reasonable efforts to minimize the discomfort, infection, illness, and pain of animal subjects.

g. A procedure subjecting animals to pain, stress, or privation is used only when an alternative procedure is unavailable and the goal is justified by its prospective scientific, educational, or applied value.

h. Surgical procedures are performed under appropriate anesthesia; techniques to avoid infection and minimize pain are followed during and after surgery.

i. When it is appropriate that the animal's life be terminated, it is done rapidly, with an effort to minimize pain, and in accordance with accepted procedures.

6.21 Reporting of Results

a. Psychologists do not fabricate data or falsify results in their publications.

b. If psychologists discover significant errors in their published data, they take reasonable steps to correct such errors in a correction, retraction, erratum, or other appropriate publication means.

6.22 Plagiarism

Psychologists do not present substantial portions or elements of another's work or data as their own, even if the other work or data source is cited occasionally.

6.23 Publication Credit

a. Psychologists take responsibility and credit, including authorship credit, only for work they have actually performed or to which they have contributed.

b. Principal authorship and other publication credits accurately reflect the relative scientific or professional contributions of the individuals involved, regardless of their relative status. Mere possession of an institutional position, such as Department Chair, does not justify authorship credit. Minor contributions to the research or to the writing for publications are appropriately acknowledged, such as in footnotes or in an introductory statement.

c. A student is usually listed as principal author on any multiple-authored article that is substantially based on the student's dissertation or thesis.

6.24 Duplicate Publication of Data

Psychologists do not publish, as original data, data that have been previously published. This does not preclude republishing data when they are accompanied by proper acknowledgment.

6.25 Sharing Data

After research results are published, psychologists do not withhold the data on which their conclusions are based from other competent professionals who seek to verify the substantive claims through reanalysis and who intend to use such data only for that purpose, provided that the confidentiality of the participants can be protected and unless legal rights concerning proprietary data preclude their release.

6.26 Professional Reviewers

Psychologists who review material submitted for publication, grant, or other research proposal review respect the confidentiality of and the proprietary rights in such information of those who submitted it.

7. Forensic Activities

7.01 Professionalism

Psychologists who perform forensic functions, such as assessments, interviews, consultations, reports, or expert testimony, must comply with all other provisions of this Ethics Code to the extent that they apply to such activities. In addition, psychologists base their forensic work on appropriate knowledge of and competence in the areas underlying such work, including specialized knowledge concerning special populations. (See also Standards 1.06, Basis for Scientific and Professional Judgments; 1.08, Human Differences; 1.15, Misuse of Psychologists' Influence; and 1.23, Documentation of Professional and Scientific Work.)

7.02 Forensic Assessments

a. Psychologists' forensic assessments, recommendations, and reports are based on information and techniques (including personal interviews of the individual, when appropriate) sufficient to provide appropriate substantiation for their findings. (See also Standards 1.03, Professional and Scientific Relationship; 1.23, Documentation of Professional and Scientific Work; 2.01, Evaluation, Diagnosis, and Interventions in Professional Context; and 2.05, Interpreting Assessment Results.)

b. Except as noted in (c), below, psychologists provide written or oral forensic reports or testimony of the psychological characteristics of an individual only after they have conducted an examination of the individual adequate to support their statements or conclusions.

c. When, despite reasonable efforts, such an examination is not feasible, psychologists clarify the impact of their limited information on the reliability and validity of their reports and testimony, and they appropriately limit the nature and extent of their conclusions or recommendations.

7.03 Clarification of Role

In most circumstances, psychologists avoid performing multiple and potentially conflicting roles in forensic matters. When psychologists may be called on to serve in more than one role in a legal proceeding—for example, as consultant or expert for one party or for the court and as a fact witness—they clarify role expectations and the extent of confidentiality in advance to the extent feasible, and thereafter as changes occur, in order to avoid compromising their professional judgment and objectivity and in order to avoid misleading others regarding their role.

7.04 Truthfulness and Candor

a. In forensic testimony and reports, psychologists testify truthfully, honestly, and candidly and, consistent with applicable legal procedures, describe fairly the bases for their testimony and conclusions.

b. Whenever necessary to avoid misleading, psychologists acknowledge the limits of their data or conclusions.

7.05 Prior Relationships

A prior professional relationship with a party does not preclude psychologists from testifying as fact witnesses or from testifying to their services to the extent permitted by applicable law. Psychologists appropriately take into account ways in which the prior relationship might affect their professional objectivity or opinions and disclose the potential conflict to the relevant parties.

7.06 Compliance With Law and Rules

In performing forensic roles, psychologists are reasonably familiar with the rules governing their roles. Psychologists are aware of the occasionally competing demands placed upon them by these principles and the requirements of the court system, and attempt to resolve these conflicts by making known their commitment to this Ethics Code and taking steps to resolve the conflict in a responsible manner. (See also Standard 1.02, Relationship of Ethics and Law.)

8. Resolving Ethical Issues

8.01 Familiarity With Ethics Code

Psychologists have an obligation to be familiar with this Ethics Code, other applicable ethics codes, and their application to psychologists' work. Lack of awareness or misunderstanding of an ethical standard is not itself a defense to a charge of unethical conduct.

8.02 Confronting Ethical Issues

When a psychologist is uncertain whether a particular situation or course of action would violate this Ethics Code, the psychologist ordinarily consults with other psychologists knowledgeable about ethical issues, with state or national psychology ethics committees, or with other appropriate authorities in order to choose a proper response.

8.03 Conflicts Between Ethics and Organizational Demands

If the demands of an organization with which psychologists are affiliated conflict with this Ethics Code, psychologists clarify the nature of the conflict, make known their commitment to the Ethics Code, and to the extent feasible, seek to resolve the conflict in a way that permits the fullest adherence to the Ethics Code.

8.04 Informal Resolution of Ethical Violations

When psychologists believe that there may have been an ethical violation by another psychologist, they attempt to resolve the issue by bringing it to the attention of that individual if an informal resolution appears appropriate and the intervention does not violate any confidentiality rights that may be involved.

8.05 Reporting Ethical Violations

If an apparent ethical violation is not appropriate for informal resolution under Standard 8.04 or is not resolved properly in that fashion, psychologists take further action appropriate to the situation, unless such action conflicts with confidentiality rights in ways that cannot be resolved. Such action might include referral to state or national committees on professional ethics or to state licensing boards.

8.06 Cooperating With Ethics Committees

Psychologists cooperate in ethics investigations, proceedings, and resulting requirements of the APA or any affiliated state psychological association to which they belong. In doing so, they make reasonable ef-

forts to resolve any issues as to confidentiality. Failure to cooperate is itself an ethics violation.

8.07 Improper Complaints

Psychologists do not file or encourage the filing of ethics complaints that are frivolous and are intended to harm the respondent rather than to protect the public.

NOTE: From 1992, December, *American Psychologist.* Copyright American Psychological Association. Reprinted by permission.

Introduction to Ethical Concepts and Practices in Counseling

One of the best ways to get a good understanding of ethical issues and the ethical dilemmas counselors face is to address specific concerns that practicing counselors often encounter. This chapter addresses some basic ethical issues—confidentiality and privacy, privileged communication, avoidance of dual relationships, informed consent, professional responsibility, and competence. First, we define the ethical issue and related concepts, then we present case scenarios to demonstrate how each issue relates to actual practice.

Confidentiality and Privacy

Both the APA and ACA codes of ethics address the issue of privacy as related to confidentiality. The concepts are related, but there are differences. Privacy is a broader issue. Counselors and psychologists, by nature of their work, are privy to the most personal and even intimate information about their clients. The very fact that some individuals have attended counseling is a very private matter to them. It is generally respected in U.S. culture that individuals have a right to maintain certain personal information about themselves as nonpublic, meaning it is not to be shared in an open forum. *Privacy* is the client's right to keep the counseling relationship a secret. Privacy not only deals with communications made by counselors, but also relates to the disposal of records, not being identified in a waiting room, tape recordings, use of credit cards for billing, use of computer services for scoring of tests or billing, and other documentary or business activities of the counselor. For example, if a client uses a credit card to pay for services, and the counselor lists a counseling agency name or profession on the receipt, the credit card company then effectively has information that the individual paid for services to a counselor which is a breach of privacy. As another example, if sessions are scheduled in a way that others may observe clients in a waiting room, privacy may be compromised. Both the ACA and APA codes of ethics state that an individual's privacy should be respected. The ACA (1995) code states, "Counselors respect their client's right to privacy and avoid illegal and unwarranted disclosures of confidential information" (p. 34). The APA (1992) code states that psychologists must "respect the rights of individuals to privacy." Counselors must be mindful of this overriding principle.

Confidentiality more specifically addresses information communicated in the counseling context. Confidentiality was developed as something akin to an antigossip guarantee. "Confidentiality is the obligation of professionals to respect the privacy of clients and the information they provide" (Handelsman, 1987, p. 33). When information is communicated in the privacy of the formal counselor–client relationship, it is to be maintained as a secret within that relationship. Confidentiality is an ethical concept almost universally referenced in both professional association codes of ethics and legal ethical standards. When confidentiality is referenced by law or statute, it is referred to as legal confidentiality. *Legal confidentiality* is a mandate that prevents the discussion of private communications (with a counselor in a professional context) from being revealed to other individuals. Counselors cannot reveal to other individuals what is communicated in counseling without potential penalty of law. Confidentiality guaranteed by a professional association alone (nonlegal confidentiality) does not carry the weight of law; however, it still carries the weight of the professional association, which can censure members or remove them from association membership. Regardless, confidentiality is a guarantee to clients that what they communicate privately in professional counseling will be held "in confidence"—for the ears and eyes of the counselor alone, unless clients specifically release the counselor from the promise.

However, there are limits or exceptions to both professionally mandated and legal confidentiality. For example, in a classic court case, Tarasoff versus the California Board of Regents (VandeCreek & Knapp, 1993), a judgment was made that a psychologist had the "duty to warn" an endangered party when a counseling client made a direct threat on a life. In this case, the psychologist, a counselor at a University of California counseling center, warned the police of the threat. Unfortunately, he failed to warn the threatened individual, whom the client later murdered. The judgment was that in such cases confidentiality is overridden by the *duty to warn* —to protect endangered individuals by informing them of a threat (see the related discussion in Chapter 3). Threats to individuals should not be taken lightly, and the authorities *and* the potential victim must be warned. Most ethical codes in psychology and counseling have now incorporated the practices suggested by the Tarasoff decision, and counselors should be alert to this limit of confidentiality.

Other common limits to confidentiality typically referenced in professional codes or statutes involve the following:

1. Required revelation to authorities of any case of substantiated or suspected child abuse or neglect

2. Required revelation to authorities of intent to do harm to an individual or to society (e.g., through an illegal act)

3. Required revelation of counseling information to a parent or legal guardian of a client who is a minor child, on the request of the parent or legal guardian

4. In-case consultation with other professionals or students of counseling (often however, identifying information must be disguised)

Counselors should inform clients before counseling is initiated of any professional and/or legal limits to the confidential relationship. Otherwise, they may share confidential information with others only with the direct written consent of clients.

It is noteworthy that confidentiality is not only a legal issue at the state level, federal laws also address it. Specifically, there is a federal law that prohibits the disclosure of information of individuals treated for chemical dependency (see Chapter 15). Also, the U.S. Supreme Court on 13 June 1996 ruled that communications between psychotherapists and their clients are confidential and privileged; specifically the decision extended federal privilege, which, according to the ACA (1996), "already applies to psychiatrists and psychologists." The actual Supreme Court case extended privilege to a licensed social worker, which, according to the ACA (1996), "leave[s] the door open for inclusion of other providers of psychotherapy" (p. 10). The Supreme Court decision adds credence to a generally respected concept of confidentiality in counseling and psychology.

Although confidentiality appears to be a straightforward concept, challenging situations may arise that make judgments difficult. One area of contemporary concern is related to individuals with human immunodeficiency virus (HIV) who may transmit the virus to others through intimate relations. Should confidentiality be breached and a partner of an HIV-positive individual be warned? Does Tarasoff apply? What are a counselor's responsibilities? These questions are beginning to receive attention in the literature (e.g., Harding, Gray, & Neal, 1993; Stanard & Hazler, 1995), but there are no clear answers and the codes of the ACA and the APA do not give unquestionable guidance. As with the HIV issue, new problems arise, and, often, acceptable ethical standards are established after a serious concern has been raised in the literature or in the courts. Accordingly, it is important for counselors to be up-to-date on the professional literature to ensure that they are alert to potential ethical dilemmas; in this way they can act to prevent a breach of ethics before it happens.

Case Scenario 1

Confidentiality

A mother of a 21-year-old female client phones concerned about her daughter and wishes to share information with the counselor about the daughter's status. In the course of the conversation between the mother and the counselor, the mother asks about the daughter's progress in counseling. Should the counselor answer?

NO.   The counselor should not answer without specific written consent from the client allowing communications with the mother. In fact, counselors should not even acknowledge that they are seeing any clients to anyone over the phone, especially when they have not placed the phone call with the client's written consent. This would hold true of anyone seeking information about an individual's participation in counseling, even an identified lawyer or judge. Counselors should be leery about communicating about clients over the phone on incoming calls, but may more safely communicate to individuals on calls they place with the permission of their clients.

Case Scenario 2

Confidentiality

A counselor at a party meets a social worker who referred a client to the counselor. The social worker begins to discuss the client with the counselor while other individuals are milling around. Should the counselor discuss the case?

NO.   The counselor should communicate to the social worker that they should not talk about cases at the party. With appropriate permission from the client, they should talk about the case only in a private, professional (not social) context. At that time, they should discuss only such information directly pertinent to the social worker's role in the case and allowed by client consent. It is also prudent in this day of advanced technology (e.g., E-mail and cellular phones) to evaluate the privacy of any professional conversation, however proper, to ensure that confidentiality or privacy is not unintentionally breached.

Case Scenario 3

Confidentiality

The spouse of a counselor meets the counselor at the counselor's office and sees a client walk out of the counseling office. The spouse asks: "What's his problem?" Should the counselor discuss the case with the spouse?

NO.   A counselor's confidentiality does not extend to a spouse. In some cases it does extend to coworkers in agencies or to other professional colleagues, but even in these cases, the coworkers or colleagues must be informed of the confidential nature of the information and must guarantee that they will maintain confidentiality. Regardless, the service-providing counselor is ultimately responsible ethically if confidentiality is breached.

Case Scenario 4

Confidentiality

A counselor has had a rough day and goes to a local cosmetology salon after work. The counselor begins discussing tough cases with the cosmetologist but is careful to disguise names and identifying information about specific clients. Has anything unethical occurred?

YES.   If it is possible that someone can identify a client by context, then confidentiality has been breached. If, for example, a relative or friend of a client overheard such a conversation and could piece together the information, thereby identifying the client, an unethical act has occurred. Only in certain professional situations can a general discussion of disguised cases be ethical, such as a professor's discussion of a case in a relevant college class. Even if the risk of identifying a client is not significant, any practice of public discussion of cases is generally harmful of the trust of confidentiality. It risks decreasing the confidence of the lay public in the profession of counseling and subjects both clients and other counselors to misunderstanding or even ridicule.

Privileged Communication

Privileged communication is a legal right of clients found in state or federal statutes. *Privileged communication* is a client's right that prevents the revelation of confidential information in a legal proceeding (e.g., in a legal hearing or courtroom). A counselor cannot be made to testify on a client's case if the privilege stands. Privileged communication is owned by the client, and only the client can waive the privilege allowing testimony (Hummel, Talbutt, & Alexander, 1985). Privileged communication, being a legal right, is not found in professional codes of ethics. It is statutory.

Like confidentiality, there are limits to privileged communication. For example, in many states, stipulations override any psychotherapist or counselor privileged communication in cases of substantiated or suspected child abuse or neglect. In such cases, a judge can order a counselor to testify on otherwise confidential information. Such disclosure is not illegal, and the counselor is given immunity from prosecution (i.e., cannot be found guilty of breaching privileged communication). Another example where privilege may not stand is when a client sues a counselor.

In many states, by licensure statute, communications are "privileged" in civil but not criminal cases. In other words, if a client is charged with a felony and goes to criminal court, the counseling case files can be requested and the counselor can be made to testify by the judge. Such a request to testify is called a *subpoena*, a court-ordered request to appear in a legal hearing with all requested information. On the other hand, when a counselor is subpoenaed by a civil court (not a criminal court) such as a divorce court, the counselor must refuse to testify about a client's case on the grounds of the client's right by law to privileged communication. Other examples of civil cases in which a counselor cannot testify include workers' compensation disability/injury hearings, social security disability hearings, child custody hearings, termination of parental rights hearings (unless there is an allegation of child abuse or neglect and an exemption to privileged communication), or other legal proceedings where a crime allegedly has not been committed. As with confidentiality, it is important for counselors to know the limits of privileged communication written into licensure laws or other state statutes. Usually the ethics committee of a state counseling association or a licensure board of a state can help a counselor identify those laws that affect professional practice. Most ethical codes require that counselors obey the laws in the jurisdiction within which they practice.

Case Scenario 1

Privileged Communication

A vocational rehabilitation counselor is hired by a workers' compensation insurance company to assess an alleged injured worker. The insurance claims adjuster refers the case and is suspicious that the claimant is malingering (faking an injury or illness) in order to collect workers' compensation injury benefits. The claims adjuster requests that the counselor evaluate the client to plan and recommend rehabilitation services, if necessary. The counselor does not explain any limits of confidentiality and does not have the claimant sign a waiver of privileged communication. Counseling clients in the counselor's state are afforded privileged communication in civil legal proceedings. Later, the counselor is asked to testify on the case by a workers' compensation administrative law judge. Since the counselor was hired by the workers' compensation insurance company the counseling information is owned by the insurance carrier, therefore the counselor must testify. True or false?

FALSE.   The client/claimant owns the privilege, and only the client can waive the privilege in a civil case. If it appears court testimony is going to be part of a case assessment, the counselor should obtain a written waiver of privileged communication before assessing the client. This issue also involves another ethical standard, informed consent, which we address later in this chapter.

Case Scenario 2

Privileged Communication

A marriage counselor sees a husband and wife in counseling conjointly. The counselor then is subpoenaed by a judge regarding divorce proceedings at the request of the husband's attorney. The husband claims that the counselor had evidence of the wife's mental instability from previous medical and hospital records as well as from observation of the wife in marriage counseling. The husband believes the marriage counselor can testify as to the effects of the wife's mental disorder on the marriage. The husband waives privileged communication. The counselor refuses to testify on the basis of the privileged communication of the wife. Did the counselor act legally?

IT DEPENDS.   In some states, privileged communication stands only in cases where there has been one-on-one communication between a client and a therapist. If other persons are present (as in group counseling or marital or family therapy) the privilege may not stand. Whether privilege stands depends on how the statute is written and on past cases with decisions by judges (case law). For example, in some states, relationship theory and family counseling are referenced into the definition of practice in the psychology or counselor licensure statute. Therefore, it can be assumed by the law itself that privilege extends to circumstances involving relational treatment or family counseling. But if there is no case law on this issue in the state, a final conclusion on this issue is not possible. A counselor who is unsure whether privileged communication applies should probably consult or hire an attorney before attending any legal proceeding, thereby seeking representation on that issue before the court.

Case Scenario 3

Privileged Communication

An allegation of child abuse is made against a counselor's client, who is the parent of the child in question. The counselor is subpoenaed by a hearing officer to attend a parental rights termination hearing. The counselor must go to testify. True or false?

TRUE.   In states where privileged communication is overridden by licensure or other statutes in cases of child abuse or neglect, the counselor should appear and be prepared to testify in those cases. However, the counselor should alert the judge or hearing officer of the client's right to privileged communication and should formally request that the privilege should be overridden as a part of the record, based on the relevant statute.

Dual Relationships

Licensure boards often report that mental health professionals have had licenses suspended or revoked on the basis of improper sexual intimacies with patients or supervisees. The sexual contact issue between patients and therapists is very commonly the charge that leads to suspension or revocation of a professional license on ethical grounds.

There is unanimous agreement among ethical codes: *Sexual intimacies with clients are unethical.* In states where psychotherapeutic practice is regulated, it also is illegal. It is considered a breach of the most basic trust between a mental health professional and a client, and is viewed as harmful to clients (Bouhoutsos, Holroyd, Lerman, Forer, & Greenberg, 1983).

Sexual intimacies with clients are the clearest examples of dual relationships in counseling. A *dual relationship* is one that contains both professional (formally established as a treatment or supervisory relationship) and additional personal and nonprofessional components (Swenson, 1993). Examples of dual relationships are (a) friendships and planned social contacts between counselors and clients; (b) bartering for professional services (a client who is a painter trades services with a therapist, or a client babysits for a therapist); (c) planned social or sexual contacts between active therapy students and a professional supervisor; and (d) erotic or nonerotic physical contact with clients (i.e., the client becomes an object of sexual or physical need).

Dual relationships should be avoided always. But, please understand that not all dual relationships are technically illegal or unethical. Certainly a nonplanned, accidental social contact is not unethical; for example, counselors could hardly be blamed for running into a client at a party or at an athletic event. Other cases also may not be unethical:

1. A professor of counseling is impressed by a student. After she graduates, he hires her to work in a counseling service that he owns.

2. A supervisor of counselor licensure candidates gets to know his supervisees over several years of supervision. Friendships develop that last beyond the formal supervision agreement.

3. A counselor encounters a former client whose counseling was terminated several years earlier. The counselor remembers that the client provided a professional service, which she currently needs. She then negotiates to purchase the services from the former client.

These dual relationships are not illegal or technically unethical, but still warrant scrutiny. Counselors generally will know if a dual relationship either currently or in the future holds the potential of impairing professional objectivity or the ability to focus solely on the client's best interests. Counselors should also be mindful that it is important to consider the appearance of impropriety as well as the unintended level of coercion or influence they may have on impressionable clients. The general rule is *avoid dual relationships.* Or, if such a relationship is imminent, clearly examine the ethical or legal ramifications.

Counselors and therapists are human. No licensure board or ethical authority can control feelings. For example, Pope, Keith-Spiegel, and Tabachnick (1986) found that "attraction to clients is a prevalent experience among both male and female psychologists" (p. 155). *Feelings* may develop and may be uncontrollable, but there are controls on *actions* of professionals. The issue really relates to the potential harm of a client or supervisee. The basic question is, "Is the client/supervisee in danger of physical or emotional harm?" But even that question is not easily answered. Thoreson and his associates in a survey of male counselors found that "although relatively few respondents (1.7%) reported having engaged in sexual misconduct with clients during a professional relationship, the prevalence rate increased to 17% when the definition of sexual misconduct was expanded to include (a) students and students under supervision and (b) occurrences of sexual misconduct after the professional relationship" (Thoreson, Shaughnessy, Heppner, & Cook, 1993, p. 429). Further, in a survey of female counselors, "Counselors viewed sexual contact in current professional relationships as less ethical than contact in subsequent relationships, although relationships with former clients were seen as less ethical than relationships with former supervisees or students. Compared with male counselors from a previous study, female counselors were less likely to report sexual contact in their professional roles" (Thoreson, Shaughnessy, & Frazier, 1995, p. 84). As to opinions about the level of unethical practice, there may be differences of opinion depending on the gender of the individual questioned.

As to whether there is danger of physical or emotional harm, a healthy friendship that develops during a formal counseling relationship and lasts beyond the formal contracted services may not be considered harmful. Sexual intimacies, however, are another matter. Research shows that clients most usually are in danger of emotional harm when sexually involved with a counselor or therapist (Bouhoutsos et al., 1983). It is a misuse of power for the therapist to cross the line of sexual intimacy. Remember, clients must be viewed to some degree as emotionally vulnerable, by nature of their status. Seduction by clients is considered a symptom of some emotional disorders, which requires counselors to take extra precautions against any semblance of dual relationships.

In cases where there is question as to whether the therapist is being "set up" by a client, or where there is discomfort regarding a counseling relationship, the counselor should take reasonable precautions. Strategies to consider include leaving the door slightly opened so a secretary or colleague can see in the office, but in a way that the voice is somehow screened to maintain confidentiality; taping all sessions with client consent; and inviting a second therapist to do cotherapy with the client's permission. Care must be taken to protect clients from potential harm from dual relationships; but care must also be taken to protect counselors from some clients' malicious intentions.

There is current controversy over the issue of potential harm. For example, some psychotherapeutic techniques actually encourage touch between therapists and clients. And some therapeutic techniques may involve deep muscle massage or other physical contact. In these cases, it is believed that touch is therapeutic. Some people have even argued that sexual contacts between counselors and their clients are therapeutic. Regardless, the ethical codes are clear—sexual intimacy is banned. Therapists who use touch as part of their therapeutic repertoire should be sure to use it cautiously and appropriately, such as hand holding. Touching a person's knee or thigh can be considered crossing the ethical line. Having a witness available during treatments may also prevent the misinterpretation of touch in therapy or may minimize the legal vulnerability of the therapist.

Counselors who are aware of other counselors or therapists who are involved in potentially harmful dual relationships are obligated to confront the counselor in question. Most ethical codes allow a therapist or counselor *first* to confront the suspected unethical practitioner to attempt to rectify the problem before being obligated to report the concern formally to a legal or ethical authority. Colleagues have great potential influence over a perpetrator of unethical behavior by addressing ethical concerns openly and by re-educating (or educating, in some cases) the unethical party as to his or her ethical obligations. But colleagues should report to authorities serious infractions or persistent concerns subsequent to re-education or even warning. In most cases, the reporting party is given legal or professional protection from retribution (e.g., immunity from any sort of countersuit).

It is a professional counselor's responsibility to confront an unethical colleague. If there is a borderline ethical concern or an ethical dilemma, discussion of the concerns also seems warranted, as well as consultation with an authority on ethical matters (e.g., a member of a professional association's ethical practice committee).

To summarize, counselors need to be cautious about the dual relationship issue. If there are concerns, discussion with another professional knowledgeable about ethical standards is a start. The question must be asked, "Is there potential harm?" Means of rectification other than official report are warranted. Consultation with authorities is warranted if the concerns are persistent or of a serious or sexual nature.

Informed Consent

Informed consent is the client's right to agree to participate in counseling, assessment, or other professional procedures or services after such services are fully described and explained so they are fully comprehensible to that client. Clients have the right to know the potential benefits or detriments of therapy or counseling. They should be fully informed before treatment occurs of significant facts about procedures, what typically occurs during them, and probable outcomes. Also, clients should be informed of treating professionals' credentials or training, especially related to specialized procedures. There should be no counselor coercion involved in a decision to undergo treatment. Alternative treatments, or alternatives to treatment, should also be addressed (see Handelsman & Galvin [1988], for specific issues related to content and format of informed consent procedures).

Counselors generally present this information to clients in writing. The information should be clear and presented at a level that the client can understand (Handelsman, Kemper, Kesson-Craig, McLain, & Johnsrud, 1986). Counselors should ensure that clients are intellectually and emotionally able to understand the information provided so that they may make a true voluntary judgment (Handelsman & Galvin, 1988). Essentially, clients have freedom of choice to participate in counseling services.

Handelsman and Galvin (1988) provided a format for informed consent that lists questions the client can pose to the therapist. This fosters open discussion of therapeutic issues and helps to establish a professional relationship and rapport.

Informed consent is not so serious a concern when clients are of legal (adult) age to consent and when they voluntarily seek treatment. However, it becomes a more serious concern when a client is a minor, when clients may not be fully competent to consent to treatment, or when there is a third party referral. A *third-party referral source* is another individual, an agency, or an organization that directs the client to the provider of services. Sometimes clients referred by a third party go willingly and voluntarily submit to treatment. Other times, therapy is *compulsory,* meaning it is required for some legal reason. Compulsory therapy is initiated by a third-party referral source usually as a form of rehabilitation or ongoing assessment when (a) the client has been involved with, is accused of, or is guilty of an illegal or potentially harmful act, or (b) treatment is viewed as a means to return a person to gainful activity when the person is receiving benefits or services for disability or other conditions. Examples of compulsory counseling are (a) a judge-ordered referral of an ex-offender who, as part of rehabilitation, must undergo counseling; (b) a workers' compensation company–referred injured client at risk of losing benefits who is required to undergo vocational assessment; (c) a chemically dependent parent who is at risk of losing his or her children through parental rights termination unless there is sobriety; and (d) a misbehaving child who is required to undergo assessment or therapy as a condition for return to school or other settings. In all these cases, a third-party requests to correct or to evaluate a client's problem or condition. Remember, it is a client's right to consent to counseling. Even in cases of compulsory counseling, clients have the right to refuse services. Also, if legal issues are involved, clients have the right to know if their counselor will testify on the case. If a counselor may be called to testify, the client must waive privileged communication, if applicable, and must be informed of the possible outcomes *before* accepting counseling services.

In the case of minor children involved in counseling, they technically do not have the right to consent to treatment; their parents or legal guardians have the right to consent for them. This is true in most states, although there are exceptions. For instance, some states allow minor children to seek birth control counseling, counseling related to venereal disease, pregnancy/abortion counseling, or substance abuse/dependence treatment without the consent of a parent or legal guardian. Barring such exceptions, parents or legal guardians not only have the right to consent to their children's counseling, they also in most cases have the right to know what occurs in counseling, and they may request termination of counseling at any time.

Regardless of the legal issues, it is therapeutically and ethically wise for the counselor to consult a minor about treatment issues and to enlist the minor's participation when parental or guardian consent is given, even if there are limits to the confidential relationship. The limits of confidentiality must be addressed with the minor in a way that the minor understands: the minor must know that what is discussed in counseling can be shared with the parent or legal guardian.

Some counselors attempt to get a verbal or written agreement from parents or legal guardians that they will respect the minor's right to confidentiality. This is no guarantee, however. Unless there is clear statutory provision and case law for a parent or legal guardian's ability to waive both informed consent and access to case information, such agreements must be viewed as tenuous, or even potentially misleading. Separate agreements waiving parental rights to informed consent or access to files may not be upheld legally, and certainly a parent or legal guardian would have the right to cancel such an arrangement at any time.

The case of informed consent is even more complicated when persons who are elderly or who have disabilities are involved (Pepper-Smith, Harvey, Silberfeld, Stein & Rutman, 1992). Can an elderly person with serious mental deterioration (e.g., dementia) consent to psychological or counseling assessment or treatment? Can a relative be consulted or informed? Many elderly clients may have diminished capacity to make informed judgments, yet they may legally be considered "competent." These clients may be in vulnerable circumstances if an unscrupulous practitioner is involved. In most cases, it is wise to obtain consent to inform and to consult with involved family members or even to do family intervention in cases were a person's ability to make judgments is diminished. Such a person's "informed consent" to treatment may technically be in order, yet ethically, when there is no legal guardian, the involvement of family members may be necessary to ensure appropriate treatment.

Case Scenario 1

Informed Consent

A physician writes an order for a counselor to assess the IQ of a geriatric patient at a hospital. The patient consents. The IQ test and a thorough mental status assessment produce results of diminished capacity, but overall the IQ is in the low borderline range of measured intelligence. The bill for the assessment is sent to Medicare, with a copayment bill sent to the spouse of the patient, who protests both the rationale for the test and the bill itself. The spouse claims that she should have been informed. Was anything done unethically in this case?

IT DEPENDS.   The question on this case is, "Were the IQ and mental status testing necessary for diagnostic or treatment reasons?" If so, then nothing has been done illegally, although a professional consult with a second opinion would be recommended, and appropriate consultation with family members (with permission) seems justified in such a case.

Case Scenario 2

Informed Consent

A couple attends their first marriage counseling session. They are never informed about the potential length of treatment, the probable results, or alternative treatments. The counselor simply begins doing treatment. Is this ethical?

NO.   Most codes of ethics either explicitly or indirectly require both the counselor to formally present procedure-relevant information and the client to formally consent before treatment is initiated.

Professional Responsibility

Professional responsibility is best defined as the counselor's obligation to clients and to the counseling profession. It relates to the appropriateness of professional actions.

In all cases, a professional counselor's responsibility is to advance the welfare of her or his clients (Margolin, 1982). This means that counselors do not discriminate against those that seek their services, and they do not subjugate their obligations to their clients for the sake of monetary or other rewards. Professional counselors are also obligated to end their services if it becomes clear they are not helping or benefiting their clients.

Generally, professional counselors are obligated to their employers as well as to their clients. They have a responsibility to serve their employers in a way that demonstrates competence and ethical sensitivity.

Sometimes, however, there are conflicts between employing institutions and the best interests of clients. Where such conflicts jeopardize the integrity of professional services rendered to clients, the counselor has an obligation to attempt to remedy conditions that are compromising. When a reconciliation of institutional and professional conflicts is not forthcoming, the counselor has an obligation to terminate the affiliation with the employing institution, rather than to persist or to compound the injustice. Just as physicians should not compromise the health and safety of their patients in a hospital that provides less than minimal standard care, so, too, counselors should refuse to treat clients in settings where clients' best interests are in conflict with institutional interests. In other words, professional counselors should always seek to develop treatment (work) environments where the employing institution's goals and objectives are consistent with a primary responsibility for competent and timely service to clients.

It is also important to recognize that the client is *the person who is served,* not the person or institution paying the bill (Cottone, 1982). It is a common mistake among inexperienced or uninformed counselors, or counselors unduly influenced by their business interests, that their obligation is to the paying party. The counselor's principal obligation is *always* to the person receiving services—the client, or counselee—unless of course there is potential danger to another individual or to society, in which case the counselor has a duty to warn the endangered party and the authorities. The presence of a third party (a person or institution) paying for services does not diminish, redirect, or in any way compromise the counselor's primary obligation to the counselee.

Of course, if there is a third-party payer, there may be limits to confidentiality or privileged communication. In such cases, clients must be fully informed prior to the onset of treatment of any limits to confidentiality or privileged communication to ensure informed consent. The fact that clients have the right to refuse treatment even with the presence of a third-party payer, and that counselors must respect clients' rights to refuse treatment, demonstrates counselors' clear responsibility to persons receiving their counseling services.

Regardless, any person that refuses treatment when there is third-party oversight may suffer consequences directly related to the relationship between the client and the overseeing person or agency (e.g., a third-party referral source or payer). Those consequences should be clearly circumscribed to the client's relationship with the third party and should not impinge on the client's relationship with the counselor. Counselors have a responsibility primarily to assess or to treat fully informed clients competently and to communicate their findings only with the consent of clients.

Case Scenario 1

Responsibility

A counselor receives a referral from a friendly caseworker at the state family services agency. The caseworker communicates with the counselor that he has a case of a woman who is "disturbed" and he wants her evaluated presumably for treatment potential, but notes that the information is really needed for possible parental rights termination. The counselor receives many cases from the referring caseworker at the family services agency, and the counselor agrees to assess the referred individual, saying "I'll see what I can do." The client comes with the full intention of later receiving counseling under the auspices of the family services agency. Instead, the client is evaluated and never later scheduled for treatment, and the counselor's report appears as evidence in a parental rights termination hearing. Was this unethical?

PROBABLY.   Assuming that the counselor informed the client of limits to confidentiality and/or privileged communication, this is still a probable breach of responsibility. This is especially true if the findings were in any way influenced by the prior stated intent of the caseworker to seek parental rights termination. The client should have been fully informed of the intent of the evaluation and its potential uses. Additionally, the evaluation should be as objective as possible in its recommendations, using standard and accepted means of assessment.

Case Scenario 2

Responsibility

A school counselor/evaluator is given a case referred by a teacher who is a close friend. The teacher communicates to the counselor that the student is a "BD" (behavior-disordered) student and the teacher wants this child "out of my class-room" and "placed in special education." The counselor finds that much of the problem may be "embedded in" and "specific to" the teacher–student relationship, meaning there is less support for a diagnosis of BD in other settings. Yet the teacher has documented well the misbehavior of this student. The counselor recommends to the special education panel that a diagnosis/classification of BD is warranted. Was this ethical?

POSSIBLY.   The counselor has an obligation to assess, historically and otherwise, the student's behavior in other settings with other authority figures. If the counselor's recommendation was primarily based on the friend's documentation and without otherwise independent competent assessment of competing outcome/recommendations, there was then a breach of responsibility and probably a case of professional incompetence (we address the competence issue in the next section of this chapter).

Case Scenario 3

Responsibility

A researcher does a followup study on a previously tested hypothesis. The outcome conflicts with the prior conclusion and statistical findings. The researcher writes an article on the initial findings, but fails to acknowledge the followup study. The researcher also fails to acknowledge the work of one of her students who collected the data during the original study. The report is later published. Is this unethical?

YES.   There has been a breach of "responsibility" on two counts. First, the researcher had an obligation to report the findings of the followup study, even if it meant the article might not be published. This omission was a breach of responsibility to the profession. Secondly, there was a breach of responsibility to the student who assisted in the study. The student should have received acknowledgment formally on the manuscript.

Competence

Professional "competence" is an issue that focuses on two aspects of professional practice: (a) the quality of provided services and (b) the boundaries or scope of professional activity. The concept of boundaries of professional activities involve the question of whether the professional is trained, experienced, and licensed appropriately to perform certain procedures or treatments. To say that a professional counselor or therapist is *competent,* in the ethical sense of the word, means that the counselor or therapist is capable of performing a minimum quality of service and that the service provided is clearly within the limits of her or his training, experience, and practice as defined in professional standards or regulatory statutes. For example, a counselor telling a client not to take prescribed medication is unethical and is practicing illegally (literally practicing medicine without a license). But a counselor using hypnotic technique may well be within the ethical and legal bounds of the counseling profession, depending on the counselor's past training and experience with hypnotic technique and regulation of hypnosis by statute. Both the quality issue and the scope of practice issue are implied in any discussion of professional competence.

Relatedly, professional counselors or therapists who may be licensed to practice certain procedures or techniques should not perform those activities unless they have had appropriate specialized training in the area of practice in question. In some cases, they may request a professional consult with a specialist. A *professional consult* is a paid formal arrangement where a consulting counselor obtains a second opinion, professional advice, or even supervision (to the extent of possible cotherapy) on an issue of concern from a knowledgeable, competent colleague. A licensed counselor with a rehabilitation counseling degree who does marriage counseling without ever having had a course or supervision in marriage counseling is practicing unethically (literally crossing the border of professional competence). In such cases, the rehabilitation counselor has an obligation to refer the client to or consult with an appropriately trained and credentialed marriage counselor. Likewise, a marriage counselor should not suddenly begin chemical dependency treatment with a substance-dependent client without specialized training in dealing with chemical dependency; referral to or consultation with an appropriately trained rehabilitation counselor is in order. Just because a professional is licensed to perform a procedure does not mean he or she can ethically perform the procedure. All physicians are *licensed* to do brain surgery, yet only those that have specialized training or experience in the procedure should be actively and independently doing it.

Case Scenario 1

Professional Competence

A school counselor has a client who is showing excess anxiety; the counselor later learns that the client has been diagnosed by a psychiatrist as having "generalized anxiety disorder." The school counselor begins to arrange individual sessions of counseling and performs a technique called systematic desensitization. Systematic desensitization is a behavioral technique used to ameliorate symptoms such as phobic anxiety when the anxiety results from the presentation of a specific object or situation. Is the counselor practicing unethically?

POSSIBLY NOT.   If the anxiety is specifically school related, and the counselor has been trained and supervised successfully in systematic desensitization, this activity is within the realm of competent practice. School anxieties, such as a phobia to testing or speaking in public, are problems treatable ethically by appropriately trained school counselors. On the other hand, if the phobia is not school related, or if the counselor is attempting to treat the generalized anxiety disorder, then this is questionable practice. It is generally understood that generalized anxiety disorder is not best treated by systematic desensitization. Also, the psychiatrist, if he or she was treating the client actively, should have been consulted, even regarding treatment of a circumscribed school phobia.

Case Scenario 2

Professional Competence

A marriage counselor is faced with a couple that is having sexual difficulties. The problem is a complicated one, and the counselor's interventions have not produced a desirable outcome. The counselor has explained to the couple that although he has training to address certain sexual problems, he does not view himself as a sex therapist. Regardless, the husband and wife implore the counselor to continue treatment, because they do not want to start over with another professional. The counselor continues as desired by the couple. Is this unethical?

PROBABLY.   If other trained sex therapists are available, the counselor should either refer the couple to a sex therapist or professionally consult with one. On the other hand, if no other professional is available, then the counselor has an obligation to immediately seek appropriate training or guidance and to serve the couple as best as possible.

Summary

This chapter has introduced basic concepts and terms of ethical practice in counseling. We have identified and discussed issues in the areas of confidentiality and privacy, privileged communication, dual relationships, informed consent, professional responsibility, and competence. Chapter 3 will focus on general legal issues.

References

American Counseling Association. (1995, June). Code of Ethics and Standards of Practice. *Counseling Today, 37*(12), 33–40.

American Counseling Association. (1996, July). Supreme Court extends confidentiality privilege. *Counseling Today, 39*(1), 1, 6, 10.

American Psychological Association. (1992). *Ethical principles of psychologists and code of conduct.* Washington, DC: Author.

Bouhoutsos, J., Holroyd, J., Lerman, H., Forer, B. R., & Greenberg, M. (1983). Sexual intimacy between psychotherapists and patients. *Professional Psychology: Research and Practice, 14,* 185–196.

Cottone, R. R. (1982). Ethical issues in private-for-profit rehabilitation. *Journal of Applied Rehabilitation Counseling, 13*(3), 14–17, 24.

Handelsman, M. M. (1987). Confidentiality: The ethical baby in the legal bathwater. *Journal of Applied Rehabilitation Counseling, 18*(4), 33–34.

Handelsman, M. M., & Galvin, M. D. (1988). Facilitating informed consent for outpatient psychotherapy: A suggested written format. *Professional Psychology: Research and Practice, 19,* 223–225.

Handelsman, M. M., Kemper, M. B., Kesson-Craig, P., McLain, J., & Johnsrud, C. (1986). Use, content, and readability of written informed consent forms for treatment. *Professional Psychology: Research and Practice, 17,* 514–518.

Harding, A. K., Gray, L. A., & Neal, M. (1993). Confidentiality limits with clients who have HIV: A review of ethical and legal guidelines and professional policies. *Journal of Counseling and Development, 71,* 297–305.

Hummel, D. L., Talbutt, L. C., & Alexander, M. D. (1985). *Law and ethics in counseling.* New York: Van Nostrand Reinhold.

Margolin, G. (1982). Ethical and legal considerations in marital and family therapy. *American Psychologist, 37,* 788–801.

Pepper-Smith, R., Harvey, W. R., Silberfeld, M., Stein, E., & Rutman, D. (1992). Consent to a competency assessment. *International Journal of Law and Psychiatry, 15,* 13–23.

Pope, K. S., Keith-Spiegel, P., & Tabachnick, B. G. (1986). Sexual attraction to clients: The human therapist and the (sometimes) inhuman training system. *American Psychologist, 41,* 147–158.

Stanard, R., & Hazler, R. (1995). Legal and ethical implications of HIV and duty to warn for counselors: Does Tarasoff apply? *Journal of Counseling and Development, 73,* 397–400.

Swenson, L. C. (1993). *Psychology and law for the helping professions.* Pacific Grove, CA: Brooks/Cole.

Thoreson, R. W., Shaughnessy, P., & Frazier, P. A. (1995). Sexual contact during and after professional relationships: Practices and attitudes of female counselors. *Journal of Counseling and Development, 74,* 84–89.

Thoreson, R. W., Shaughnessy, P., Heppner, P. P., & Cook, S. W. (1993). Sexual contact during and after the professional relationship: Attitudes and practices of male counselors. *Journal of Counseling and Development, 71,* 429–434.

VandeCreek, L., & Knapp, S. (1993). *Tarasoff and beyond: Legal and clinical considerations in the treatment of life-endangering patients* (2nd ed.). Sarasota, FL: Professional Resource Press.

Ethics and the Law

Many counselors find the relationship between their clinical practices and the dictates of the law unsettling, and this relationship makes them feel vulnerable. In the past it was not uncommon for counselors simply to hope that their basically sound clinical methods would be congruent with appropriate legal practices. Such a reactive posture is no longer adequate for professional counselors, who now need to understand and actively manage the legal aspects of their practices.

Counseling has become a dynamic and well-recognized profession. As a result, counselors have taken on increasingly responsible roles in terms of the independence of their practices and how their work affects their clients. The standing of counselors as independent and responsible professionals has been recognized legally by 43 states through counselor licensure at the time of this writing. It is not unusual for counselors to be involved in such highly charged events as diagnosing their clients as having a serious mental disorder, recommending that custody of a child be terminated, testifying at a hearing regarding the effects of spousal abuse, or counseling an adult with mild mental retardation regarding reproductive rights and options. Counselors also provide forensic services related to their counseling expertise in countless civil, criminal, and administrative hearings. It is only reasonable to assume that with increased visibility and professional status, counselors will be held legally accountable for their actions. More importantly, counselors must understand and protect the legal rights of their clients.

Counselors must approach the relationship between law and ethics with a constructive and clear-headed perspective. Many years ago Ware (1971) considered the relationship between law and professional judgment in reconciling legislated and ethical standards of conduct. She noted that both tend to remain broad and open to situational interpretation, and she provided advice that continues to be meaningful to the profession's contemporary legal environment: Beware the tendency to look to other professions for standards to reconcile these conflicts. Noting counselors' emerging interest in the law, Ware described the phenomenon as a function of two factors: first, a hope that the law would relieve them from the pressure to resolve complex or vague professional dilemmas; second, a fear that they might be sued regarding some legal violation. Ware concluded that although knowledge of legal standards is necessary to address issues in a balanced way, it would be unwise to rest too much hope on legal remedy, or to fear the law too greatly. This goal for ethical decision making of knowledge and respect in balance with all clinically relevant factors is the approach taken in the Integrative Decision-Making Model of Ethical Behavior (Chapter 6).

In this chapter, we introduce you to the basic concepts involved in the relationship between ethics and law, review the basic legal mechanisms you may encounter, then familiarize you with the most common legal issues in counseling practice. Within this discussion we will introduce you to an informed consent process useful for avoiding legal issues, how to respond to subpoenas, and how to use appropriate case documentation techniques.

Relationship Between Law and Ethics

Law and ethics both have an effect on the counselor–client relationship. Generally the law is supportive or neutral in dealing with professional ethical codes and standards. The legal structure is neutral in most instances, allowing the profession to govern its practitioners' conduct and practices. Only in instances in which public health, safety, or welfare is threatened does the legal system tend to intervene and override the ethical codes of the profession. It long has been noted that it is necessary to have a knowledge of both legal and ethical regulatory standards to conduct well-informed practice. Both standards must receive situation-specific interpretation. Codes of ethics are not intended to supersede the law, but rather to clarify existing law and policy. In Chapter 5 this close relationship between societal moral and values and professional values will receive detailed discussion. Instances do occur in which ethical standards appear to conflict with the law and there is difficulty in reconciling legislated and ethical standards of conduct. Both standards are broad and open to situational interpretation, so counseling organizations need to work with bar associations, legislatures, the judiciary, and their own memberships to educate and to achieve better standards.

Counselors must think dynamically about the relationship among the law, the ethical standards of their profession, and their individual professional ethical and moral consciences. On rare occasions, counselors may be required to exercise personal and professional judgment when the legal requirements and the ethical ones appear to be at odds with one another. The codes of ethics for the mental health professions offer limited guidance in this instance. The APA Code of Ethics provides no

Table 3–1
Interactions between Ethics and the Law

		Example
1. Ethical & Legal	Following a just law	Keeping a client's confidences that are also protected by law from disclosure
2. Ethical & Illegal	Disobeying an unjust law	Refusing to breach promised confidentiality even though ordered to by court
3. Ethical & Alegal	Doing good where no law applies	Offering free service to poor clients
4. Unethical & Legal	Following an unjust law	Following the Federal Trade Commission's edict that ethical codes cannot prohibit the use of testimonials in ads for counseling services
5. Unethical & Illegal	Breaking a just law	Disclosing confidential information protected by law from disclosure
6. Unethical & Alegal	Doing harm that no law prohibits	Promoting client dependency to enhance one's own feeling of power

Note: Adapted from *Guide to Ethical Practice in Psychotherapy* by A. Thompson, 1990, New York: John Wiley & Sons. Copyright 1990 by John Wiley & Sons. Adapted by permission.

overall requirement to abide by any legal statute or administrative rule. It does have several more specific standards requiring conformity with legal requirements related to referral practices, fee practices, research and practices with research animals, and being familiar with rules concerning forensic work. APA Ethical Standard 1.02 states only that in cases of conflict that psychologists "make known their commitment to the Ethics Code and take steps to resolve the conflict in a responsible manner" (APA, 1992, p. 1599). Other codes of ethics defer to the law, such as the ACA Code of Ethics and Standards of Practice (Remley, 1996), and the Code of Ethics for Professional Rehabilitation Counselors (CRCC, 1987).

Even in cases where the code of ethics states that the professional should abide by the dictates of the law, the problem of what should be done in a specific instance of conflict is not resolved for two reasons: First, it is the responsibility of the professional to weigh all aspects of a situation, determine which ethical and legal standards apply in general, and how they apply in this instance. Clients vary and each set of circumstances adds situational complexity to the interpretation, so that counselors must exercise their judgment regarding the issues and concerns embedded in the situation. It is through this interpretation that the appropriateness and applicability of the ethical and legal standards can be assessed. It can be argued that the norm of engaging in such a level of independent judgment with the intent of upholding the principles and standards of the profession distinguishes a true profession from a skilled occupation.

Second, there may be instances in which, even after thorough and resourceful efforts to resolve the conflict within the boundaries of the law, the legal option for action is determined to be not in the best ethical interests of the client, who is the counselor's primary ethical obligation. Authorities on moral development and ethical decision-making theory recognize the position that the best solution to an ethical dilemma may violate the law in the interests of a higher moral or conscience level of analysis (Van Hoose & Paradise, 1979; Kohlberg, 1964, 1981). These models are discussed in greater detail in Chapter 5. Generally, then, it is accepted that counselors and other professionals have a strong prima facie obligation to abide by the legal requirements of a situation. *Prima facie* is a Latin phrase meaning that the obligation in question must be considered in every case and set aside only if valid and compelling reasons to do so are present in a specific instance. These reasons would involve ethical or legal reasons of greater importance than the specific legal rule in question.

Thompson (1990) noted that there are six interactions between ethics and the law. Examples of these types of interactions illustrate these distinctions (Table 3–1).

When faced with an apparent conflict between ethics and the law, you must take steps to resolve it. You must recognize that forces other than law and ethics may clash to create conflict. For example, employer policies and procedures, accreditation rules, or funding source rules might be at issue rather than the law. Remley (1996) recommended the following steps to guide the counselor in such conflicts:

1. Identify the force that is at issue regarding the counselor's behavior . . .

2. If a legal question exists, legal advice should be obtained . . .

3. If there is a problem in applying an ethical standard to a particular situation or in understanding the requirements of an ethical standard, the best action a counselor could take is to consult with colleague and with those perceived to be experts in the counseling field . . .

4. If a force other than law or ethics (for example, an employer, an accrediting body, or a funding agency) is suggesting that a counselor take some action he or she perceives to be illegal, the counselor should seek legal advice to determine whether such action is indeed illegal. (p. 288)

Counselors must involve themselves in efforts to change laws they believe are placing their clients at risk or causing them other injury or harm. This determination often is not easy for counselors to make. For example, state law might force counselors to report the physical abuse of a child as soon as they become aware of it. This action might be taken despite the fact that the child must return home at the end of the session pending an investigation and might be in even more danger of serious harm in retaliation for reporting the abuse to the counselor.

At its best, the legal system has stimulated the mental health professions to enhance their ethical standards. The careful ethical practices commonly used by counselors to warn and protect potential victims of their dangerous clients are owed to the lessons learned in the landmark decisions surrounding the Tarasoff v. the Regents of the University of California court case (discussed in Chapter 2). That decision and the related rulings that followed it are now collectively known as the Tarasoff doctrine. They have occasioned intense professional review and, in general, have positively influenced the growth of ethical standards and counseling interventions with dangerous clients for the past two decades.

Legal Mechanisms

Four mechanisms exist through which all mental health professionals are held accountable by society for maintaining proper clinical and ethical standards of practice. These mechanisms are professional ethics committees, state licensure boards, and the criminal and civil courts (Pope & Vasquez, 1991). These bodies, especially those addressing ethical matters, were introduced in Chapter 1. The current chapter deals only with matters as they are addressed in the civil and criminal court systems.

Counselors and other mental health professionals are not expected to have expert knowledge of legal concepts and mechanisms and how they apply to their work at the same level as would an attorney. In fact, they are expected to have no special legal knowledge beyond that of a competent layperson (Shea, 1985), and they must seek legal opinions as needed. Nevertheless, counselors are greatly aided by a knowledge of the basic legal mechanisms that govern their practices. Such knowledge might allow them to avoid important missteps, anticipate possible legal entanglements, and react more appropriately to legal processes should the need arise.

Specific legal information and applications will not be emphasized in this text, because the law is evolving constantly, and counselors are not lawyers or legal experts. The U.S. Constitution and federal, state, and local levels are the essential levels of legal authority (Remley, 1996). In many instances the law pertaining to a particular matter differs from jurisdiction to jurisdiction. Often, the law varies from state to state, either in terms of the laws enacted by the state legislatures or the way the courts within local jurisdictions have interpreted it in specific cases. Thus, the body of court rulings interpreting a law establishes what is known as case law. *Case law* provides precedents that are relevant to the law's interpretation in specific circumstances and jurisdictions, and contributes to the evolution of a legal concept. Therefore, counselors must determine what laws and interpretations are relevant for any legal issues raised in the state and local jurisdictions in which they practice. For instance, all 50 states have some form of law that requires mandatory reporting of child abuse by mental health and other professionals. However, the definition of child abuse, the evidence necessary to report it, and the manner and timing of its reporting varies. For example, some states do not differentiate between neglect and abuse, but others do (Fischer & Sorenson, 1985).

Laws are also classified as civil or criminal. *Civil law* involves the obligation of citizens to one another. The obligation must be asserted by the individual before the obligation is enforced by the government (Remley, 1996). A civil matter involves an offense to an individual, and the remedy is some form of compensation to the victim (Keary, 1985). Malpractice, the most common cause of legal liability for mental health practitioners, is a type of civil action. Malpractice lawsuits against mental health professionals were discussed in Chapter 1.

Criminal law involves conduct required of all citizens or prohibited to all, and is enforced by the government's legal authorities. In criminal matters, the violator is punished by the state, and punishments may involve imprisonment, fines, or death (Remley, 1996). Criminal actions against counselors in matters unrelated to their professional roles likely are just as common as for members of the general public.

However, it would appear that the most frequent type of professionally related criminal offense for psychotherapists is fraud related to third-party billings (Pope & Vasquez, 1991). Engaging in sexual intimacy with a client is also a criminal offense in some states, including Wisconsin, Colorado, and Minnesota (Pope, 1988).

The legal system embodies what society considers a minimum level of acceptable behavior on the part of its citizens. Professional organizations generally wish to strive for higher standards of behavior in professional practice, and enforce these standards upon their members. However, no society will delegate all authority for such enforcement solely to the profession, because it must continue to protect the rights and well-being of its citizenry. Thus, both ethical and legal standards should be complementary in most instances, although requiring differing interpretations to be fully understood.

Common Legal Concerns

Any number of possible legal issues exist that may affect counselors in the course of their service to clients. The legal concerns that are most frequent are fewer and more predictable based on awareness of ethical aspects of the situations that routinely are encountered in the normal course of counseling practice. Practitioners should be able to recognize the more frequent issues and develop a well-informed approach to handling them—a series of "conceptual templates for legal risk situations," if you will. Then, even more inexperienced counselors can anticipate and handle many of the standard issues more capably. They also would be likely to know what initial steps to take when confronted with the more serious and complex ones. Such a proactive mental structure is important for better management of legal risk and liability exposure. One useful template for anticipating important ethical concerns in counseling practice was provided by DePauw (1986). DePauw proposed that counselors adopt a standard, natural timeline perspective for ethical considerations. The timeline approach helps the counselor be alert to specific problems as they arise within the specific stages of client service. This approach allows counselors to anticipate the natural rhythm of issues in their individual relationships with clients. DePauw incorporated many of the key challenges in client services, and noted ethical matters in four phases of the counseling relationship: (a) initiation phase issues, (b) ongoing counseling issues, (c) dangerousness and crisis concerns, and (d) termination phase considerations. Figure 3–1 presents the issues considered within each phase. This general structure will be used to explore several issues within each phase that pose particularly important legal issues that counselors should consider.

Initiation Phase Issues

The initiation phase includes the areas of pre-counseling, anticipating service provision, and informed consent issues. During this phase counselors are reaching out to potential clients and readying them to enter into counseling relationships

I. *Initiation Phase Issues*
   A. Precounseling considerations
      1. advertising
      2. avoiding misuse of institutional affiliations
      3. financial arrangements
      4. donated services
   B. Service provision issues
      1. adequacy of counselor skills, experience, and training (competency)
      2. better service option for client
      3. concurrent counselor involvement
      4. conflicting dual relationships
   C. Informed consent issues
      1. structures to educate regarding purposes, goals, and techniques
      2. explanation of rules of procedure and limitations
      3. supervision and consultation release concerns
      4. experimental methods of treatment

II. *Ongoing Counseling Issues*
   A. Confidentiality
   B. Special issues of confidentiality
      1. children
      2. groups
   C. Consultation
   D. Recordkeeping

III. *Dangerousness and Crisis Concerns*
   A. Threat to self
   B. Threat to others
   C. Child abuse
   D. Gray areas (e.g., HIV/AIDS and dying client issues)

IV. *Termination Phase Issues*

Figure 3–1

Timeline Perspective on Ethical and Legal Considerations

Note: From "Avoiding Ethical Violations: A Timeline Perspective for Individual Counseling" by M.E. DePauw, 1986. *Journal of Counselling & Development, 64(5),* 303–305. Copyright 1986 by American Counseling Association. Reprinted by permission.

appropriately prepared and informed. Discussion follows of several legal areas relevant to this phase.

Counselor competency.   It is critical for the well-being of clients that counselors possess adequate skills, experience, and training to serve them competently. Additionally, it is important that counselors assure themselves and their clients that they have these necessary qualities. By doing so they limit their liability and observe any regulations that require them to practice only within a specific scope of practice.

Counseling and other professional licensure laws commonly include definitions of the profession, as well as the practice and procedures of the profession. Taken together, these statutory definitions, and any regulations that may pertain to them, define the scope of practice for that profession within that jurisdiction. The definitions are usually drawn from those established by the profession's organizations at the national level. For example, the American Counseling Association uses its model counselor licensure bill to encourage a more regularized structure for individual state laws. A *scope of practice* is the extent and limit of practices considered acceptable for an individual who is licensed or certified in a profession. More broadly defined, it is a recognized area of proficiency or competence gained through appropriate education and experience. In most cases, the scope of practice is related closely to the profession's definition of its areas of competency. Professionals licensed under a specific law may operate within the limits of the scope of practice as described within that jurisdiction's law and regulations.

It should be noted that the professional scope of practice is different from the individual counselor's scope of practice, though they will overlap. An individual's scope of practice is based on one's own knowledge and skills that have been gained through education and professional experience. Counselors are bound ethically to limit their practice to the scope of practice for which they are prepared within the profession's larger scope. In addition, the licensure regulations of many states require that professionals must identify their personal scopes of practice and stipulate that they will practice within this area. Sometimes this includes the provision of a written statement of the scope of practice to the licensure board. This statement then constitutes the appropriate legal and ethical limitations to the counselor's practice.

Counselors should not provide or supervise services to clients outside their area of expertise. Their scope of practice should be made clear to prospective clients before they are accepted into one's practice. Referral to another professional is appropriate if the client's problem falls outside the counselor's scope of practice (Anderson, 1996). If counselors work with clients or techniques outside their areas of competency, they could be disciplined if the licensure board becomes aware of it, or the work might become a negative factor in a malpractice lawsuit if it can be demonstrated that the counselor used a technique in which he or she was not trained.

Informed Consent Issues.   Clients have the right to make informed choices about their care. Counselors have the legal duty to provide their clients with sufficient information and to make sure they fully understand it before making their decisions. This practice originated within medical treatment settings and has come to be known as informed consent. *Informed consent* is the client's right to agree to participate in counseling, assessment, or professional procedures or services after such services are fully described and explained in a manner that is comprehensible to the client.

As the counselor and the client enter into the relationship, they enter into a contractual relationship as well. This contract may be formal if it is written, or it may be spoken between the two parties. Either way, it is important that both parties to the relationship understand the basic aspects of the situation into which they may enter. This is important so that it can be documented clearly what the counselor is, and is not, promising to do for the client. If one party thinks that the other party has not provided the items that were agreed on, that person may consider the contract violated, a legal charge called *breach of contract.*

Counselors should begin the informed consent process by engaging in a screening or precounseling consultation—this might be an aspect of the initial intake meeting. If possible, an initial precounseling consultation is an excellent tool to assure that adequate and attentive initial preparation is available to both parties. At that time certain basic information about the client's issues and objectives for counseling and the counselor's competency must be discussed to ascertain if the counselor is the appropriate helper for this individual client (Anderson, 1996).

Although there are many types of information that the counselor would be wise to provide to the client, there are some basic issues that should be part of a thorough precounseling consent process. Bertram and Wheeler (1994) include 20 topics on their checklist for a written informed consent for treatment (Appendix A). This document provides a thorough and useful format. Additionally, the counselor should discuss the same information with the client to reinforce the client's understanding of what is likely to occur in counseling with this particular counselor. Generally a written consent to treatment or related document (i.e., professional disclosure statement or therapeutic contract) should address areas such as (a) the therapeutic process, (b) background of the therapist, (c) costs involved in therapy, (d) length of therapy and termination, (e) consultation with colleagues, (f) interruptions in therapy (e.g., vacations, illness), (g) right of access to files, (h) rights pertaining to diagnostic labeling, (i) nature and purpose of confidentiality, (j) audiotape or videotape recording, (k) dual relationships and informed consent, (l) the benefits and risks of treatment, and (m) alternatives to traditional therapy (Corey, Corey, & Callanan, 1993). Discussing the common limits to confidentiality is important at this stage, as has been noted in Chapter 2. In addition, any written contract or document should be periodically discussed and updated to fit the current nature of the agreed-on work in which the counselor and client are engaged.

Informed consent requires that three legal elements be present: capacity, comprehension of information, and voluntariness. The person must (a) possess the ability to make a rational decision (*capacity*); (b) have sufficient information and be able to understand it (*comprehension*); and (c) give consent by acting freely in the decision making process (*voluntariness*) (Bray, Shepard, & Hayes, 1985). Counselors are encouraged to get informed consent in writing before proceeding with the client, and to make every effort to ensure that this consent is genuine and valid.

Several issues may arise to call this consent into question. Remember that *client competency* is not an all-or-nothing quality. Clients must be competent to make decisions for themselves, a precondition for being able to consent autonomously (Beauchamp & Childress, 1989). The criteria for the ability to make a decision also vary by the context or criteria of the decision to be made (Beauchamp & Childress, 1989). For example, an individual may be able to think rationally enough to decide whether to wear a coat on a given day, but may not be competent to decide whether to sell the family business. Also, limitations in competency may be temporary or more permanent. Factors that might temporarily affect competency might include intoxication or a severe psychological trauma, such as rape. More permanent conditions affecting a person's competency might include dementia (a loss of intelligence due to physical–organic factors) or severe mental retardation. There are other cognitive or emotional states that do not have as consistent or clear an effect on competency, such as major depression or judgment deficits after a traumatic brain injury. If a counselor is in doubt about a client's ability to make rational decisions and evaluation of competency is not within the counselor's scope of practice, consultation should be sought with another professional who can make such a determination. If a person is judged not to be competent, a legal guardian or parent could provide consent. Counselors should always determine if their clients have guardians who must be involved in decision making, and the type of guardianship involved. A guardianship may extend to matters in all areas of a client's life, or may be specific to one area, such as financial or medical matters.

Several informed consent issues beyond client competency are of concern. Counselors have a major responsibility for the client's comprehension or understanding of the matter at hand. Counselors must be sure that information is provided in a manner that maximizes the particular client's ability to understand it and its implications. The counselor must know the client's communication and learning styles and the conditions necessary for the individual to be most likely to understand the information. The counselor must tailor the discussion to meet those needs. Some issues to be considered include the client's (a) verbal (oral and reading) and cognitive abilities, (b) ability to see or hear, (c) emotional state, (d) language of first choice, (e) degree of fatigue or illness, and (f) distractibility or attentional ability. The same information may need to be presented several ways (e.g., discussed, demonstrated, or written), repeated several times or on different occasions, or even provided by different persons.

Special care must be taken with any forms used. They must be free of jargon, written at an appropriate reading grade level, and legible. In addition, the client must be literate in the language used on the form. For example, a recent analysis of mandated consent to psychotherapy forms used in Colorado (Handelsman, Martinez, Geisendorfer, & Jordan, 1995) found that the average readability level of the forms reached upper college grades. Additionally, the majority of the forms contained legally mandated information, but fewer contained ethically desirable information.

Counselors must realize that no specific approach to informed consent works for all clients and that they must use their professional sensitivity and judgment to find the correct method in each case. The client is dependent upon the counselor in this matter. Research has shown some positive results of proper informed consent procedures in counseling and psychotherapy. Results include clients' decreased anxiety, increased compliance with treatment, increased alertness to problems in treatment, and more rapid recovery (Pope & Vasquez, 1991).

Ongoing Counseling Issues

At this point in the process, the counselor and client are engaged in the ongoing work as they have outlined it. Two common issues with legal aspects are especially important in this phase: confidentiality and recordkeeping.

Confidentiality and Privileged Communication.   Confidentiality and privileged communication were defined and given a thorough introduction in Chapter 2; but several more specific points of information will be provided here. There is evidence that these two related client rights are among the most troublesome areas of practice for mental health professionals. In a national study of psychologists, it was found that almost two-thirds of them (61.9%) unintentionally violated client confidentiality (Pope, Tabachnick, & Keith-Spiegel, 1987). Anderson (1996) described the issues of confidentiality as confusing and of concern to counselors.

The ethical obligations of confidentiality and privileged communication stem from the ethical principles of fidelity, or being loyal and keeping promises, autonomy, and the principle of nonmaleficence, or refraining from doing harm to another. These principles support the duty to keep client information private and not to reveal what is said or done within the counseling relationship. This promise of privacy to the client allows for the openness of communication and trust that is considered to be the most basic and essential component of the therapeutic relationship.

The related concept of privileged communication provides clients the legal right that their confidential communications cannot be revealed in a legal proceeding. It stems from English common law in recognizing that clients must have the ability to talk freely to their attorneys if they are to defend themselves effectively in criminal legal proceedings (Anderson, 1996). Additionally, state statutes have established privileged communication similar to that of the attorney-client privilege for some professionals on a state-by-state basis. Over time, privileged communication has been applied through common law or state statute to limited types of relationships, beginning with the priest–penitent, attorney–client, husband–wife relationships and gradually extending to those of physician–patient, psychologist–client, and counselor–client.

This extension of the protection to other types of mental health professionals appears to have continued with the recent Supreme Court decision in *Jaffee v. Redmond* (Remley, Herlihy, & Herlihy, 1997). This decision upheld the ability of licensed psychotherapists to maintain the confidences of their clients in federal court cases. The court case involved the ability of a clinical social worker licensed in Illinois to assert privilege for communications between herself and her client in a lawsuit. The client, Mary Lu Redmond, was a police officer who killed Ricky Allen Sr. after responding to reports of a fight in progress and finding Allen allegedly poised to stab another individual. The lawsuit was brought against Redmond, the City of Hoffman Estates and its police department by Carrie Jaffee, the administrator of the Allen estate, alleging excessive force had been used in the incident. In the course of the legal proceedings, the family petitioned to obtain notes made by the therapist in counseling sessions with Redmond after the incident. Redmond and the therapist refused to provide the notes, the judge instructed the jury to assume the notes were unfavorable to Redmond, and the plaintiff won the case. On appeal in the U.S. Court of Appeals for the 7th Circuit, the jury verdict was thrown out and the case was remanded for new trial with the court opinion stating the trial court had erred by not offering protection to confidential communications. Jaffee appealed this decision to the U.S. Supreme Court, which upheld a strict standard of privileged communication in its June 13, 1996 ruling. The arguments made before the highest court by ACA and APA in friend-of-the-court briefs stem from four longstanding criteria used to support the granting of privilege in the legal system. According to Wigmore (1961),the four criteria are:

1. The communications must originate in confidence that they will not be disclosed.

2. This element of confidentiality must be essential to the full and satisfactory maintenance of the relationship between the parties.

3. The relationship must be one that, in the opinion of the community, ought to be fostered.

4. The injury that would be inflicted to the relationship by the disclosure of the communications must be greater than the benefit gained for the correct disposal of litigation.

The *Jaffee v. Redmond* ruling directly applies only within the federal court system, but it does extend psychotherapist privilege to another group of licensed professionals, clinical social workers. Leadership in the counseling profession has noted the following:

> With this recognition of licensed clinical social workers and the previous recognition of clinical psychologists and psychiatrists, counselors are the largest remaining group of licensed professionals providing psychotherapeutic services that is not explicitly recognized by federal courts. The Supreme Court used the term psychotherapist in its decision and counselors must be considered psychotherapists if they are to be covered by the Jaffee ruling. (National Board for Counselor Certification, 1996, p. 4)

State licensure of clinical social workers was mentioned as a key factor in the decision by the Supreme Court. State licensure, inclusion of the profession in the privilege statutes of each state, and establishment of uniform qualifications for the professionals to be considered psychotherapists appear to be important elements in advancing privileged communication status to counselors in the future (NBCC, 1996).

Special Issues and Exceptions to Confidentiality.   The ethical obligation of counselors to assure clients of confidentiality, and the clients' related legal right of privilege, truly are basic to counseling. So many circumstances vary for counseling in different specialized areas of practice that issues regarding confidentiality and privilege express themselves somewhat differently across these situations as well. For that reason, the ways they are expressed will be discussed further in upcoming chapters. Some areas in which there often are special circumstances related to confidentiality and privilege include counseling with persons who have HIV or AIDS (see Chapter 7), families or couples (see Chapter 10), minors or school settings (see Chapter 11), people with disabilities (see Chapters 12 and 13), groups (see Chapter 14), and clients in drug or alcohol treatment facilities or ex-offenders (see Chapter 15). By using the basic information provided in the earlier chapters of this text, you will more easily be able to appreciate the special requirements of these specific populations and settings.

There are several exceptions to the general requirement that the counselor hold client communications confidential. Arthur and Swanson (1993) have noted the following:

1. Client is dangerous to self or others.
2. Client waives confidentiality and privilege by requesting a release of information.
3. Counselor receives a court order requiring the release of information.
4. Counselor is involved in systematic clinical supervision.
5. Client's information and paper work is processed by clerical workers for routine purposes, and client has been informed of this arrangement prior to counseling.
6. Counselor required legal or clinical consultation, and client is informed of this counselor right before counseling.
7. The issue of the client's mental health is raised by client in a legal proceeding, such as a custody lawsuit.
8. Counseling occurs with a third party in the room, as in group or family counseling.
9. Client is a minor (younger than 18).
10. Client information is made available within the agency or institution as part of the treatment process, with the client receiving precounseling notification of this practice.
11. Information is shared within a penal institution as part of the operation of the institution or the case process.
12. Client discloses the information to advance a criminal or fraudulent activity.
13. Child abuse is suspected by the counselor.

Two additional concerns arise for counselors who are faced with the legal system's demands for information they view as confidential: subpoenas and court appearances.

A legally inexperienced counselor's first impulse upon receiving a subpoena might be to surrender all materials requested in the subpoena. This well-meaning response would not be proper because the ethical and legal duty to protect a client's confidentiality requires that the counselor make appropriate attempts to preserve client privacy.

A *subpoena,* as described in Chapter 2, is a court-ordered request to appear in a legal hearing with all requested information. This legal hearing might be either a court appearance or a deposition. The counselor might be questioned or subpoenaed documents might be examined. Often, subpoenas are drafted broadly to capture any information that might be of assistance to a party to the legal proceeding requesting the information—a "fishing trip" for anything potentially helpful. Counselors should be familiar with state statutes regarding privilege that might apply to them in their jurisdiction before encountering this situation (Anderson, 1996). Arthur and Swanson (1993) and Anderson (1996) provide more specific recommendations to respond to a subpoena (Figure 3–2).

An order to appear in court if the counselor's client is a defendant in a lawsuit presents a similar set of challenges. Similarly, counselors should try to protect their clients' confidences in a manner consistent with the earlier information. Judges may

1. Do not respond to the subpoena automatically. Be sure that all staff members know proper procedures for responding.
2. Determine if the subpoena was requested by a current or former client, or his or her attorney. Legally, this would require you to produce the documents or testify as directed. However, it is ethically important that you review any concerns you might have about detrimental aspects of this information with the these parties so that they may exercise truly informed judgment about proceeding with this request.
3. Consult with your attorney and the client's attorney, after obtaining the client's permission to do so, regarding the situation. If the judgment is that you should respond to the subpoena, obtain written release of information forms specifying what will be released, and to whom, from all clients whose information will be revealed.
4. If it is determined that you should not respond, ask the client's attorney to file a motion to quash the subpoena. In this case, a judge will hear the concerns about the detrimental effects of revealing the materials and privately view them to rule on whether the counselor should be compelled to respond to the subpoena or to further limit the information provided.
5. NEVER ignore a subpoena or defy it without taking some of the measures described here and with legal assistance.
6. Be sure to keep thorough documentation in the client's record of all interactions with the client or the client's attorney in this matter, as well as copies of all subpoenas, releases of information, court rulings, and official communications.

Figure 3–2
Considerations in Responding to a Subpoena

compel counselors to answer questions in legal proceedings even though counselors may argue that it is their ethical responsibility to preserve client confidentiality. If that is the case, Anderson (1996) has several additional suggestions: (a) answer truthfully, but do not volunteer information beyond what is specifically requested, (b) remember the counselor should be protected in the hearing by an attorney (the counselor's or the client's) and should follow the attorney's direction, and (c) use that attorney before the hearing to discuss the concerns regarding confidentiality and prepare for the actual testimony to be provided.

Recordkeeping.   The importance of observing minimum acceptable standards of clinical recordkeeping should be obvious after these discussions about confidentiality and privilege. Case records have been reported to be one of the top five areas of legal liability for counselors (Snider, 1987). Unfortunately, formal training in case-recording methods and procedures is usually limited in the professional education of most counselors. These matters are usually considered to be primarily a part of the clinical experiences of the students. While good methods may certainly be learned in this manner, the resulting training is typically varied in terms of content, depth, and method. Nonetheless, counselors must educate themselves regarding the best practices in recordkeeping in mental health professions while thoroughly acquainting themselves with the methods and requirements of the system and practices used in their own setting. For example, good basic introductions to client case recording methods are provided by Piazza and Baruth (1990), Snider (1987), and Mitchell (1991). Counselors working in schools that receive federal funding should be aware that educational and other records are covered by the Family Educational Rights and Privacy Act (FERPA). FERPA provides rights of access to educational records to students and their parents, and defines *educational record* as any record kept by employees of the educational institution. Anderson (1996) further stated that "records made by and kept in the sole possession of" a professional such as a physician, psychologist of other recognized professional "are excluded from the disclosure requirements, except that notes may be provided to other treating professionals or reviewed by a physician of the student's choice" (p. 38). For further information regarding issues of confidentiality in the schools, refer to Chapter 11.

The issue of adequate recordkeeping is considered so important in the practice of psychology that the American Psychological Association (1993) has adopted *Record Keeping Guidelines*. In addition to considering the principles and purpose underlying clinical records, the guidelines provide specific recommendations in the following areas: content, construction and control, retention of records, procedures with outdated records, and disclosure of recordkeeping procedures. The considerations relevant to electronic recordkeeping are noted in Chapter 9.

It is beyond the scope of this discussion to introduce the technical methods involved in good clinical recordkeeping practices. However, several additional legally relevant points will be made, drawing from the comments of Arthur and Swanson (1993). First, security of files must be maintained and files must not be left anywhere they may be accessed by unauthorized persons. Second, notes should be written in nontechnical, clear, and objective statements with behavioral descriptions. Any subjective or evaluative statements involving professional judgments should be so designated and written in a separate section clearly set aside from factual content. Third, all client records should be written with the understanding that they might be seen by the client, a court, or some other authorized person at some time. Fourth, document only information that is necessary and appropriate to the reason the client is receiving services. Finally, Remley (1990) cautioned that counselors should extensively document critical incidents or interactions with clients. Examples might include emergencies; circumstances in which clients will not follow recommendations, thereby risking a negative outcome or endangering themselves, or when litigation appears possible. In summary, good recording practices should enhance the quality of clinical analysis and service as well as protect client and counselor alike.

Dangerousness and Crisis Concerns

At any point in working with a client, even as early as the first contact with the person, crises and dangerous circumstances may arise. Such situations need to be dealt with effectively to prevent harm to the client and any other parties at risk. As mentioned, the Tarasoff court decision, introduced in Chapter 2, and other related cases have shaped our understanding of how counselors should proceed. The Tarasoff case is arguably the best-known case in mental health and counseling history. Before, the core ethical tendency was preserving client confidentiality, and the results of this case made it clear that therapists had a legal obligation to third parties who are at risk of serious harm from dangerous clients. The California Supreme Court noted in its decision that "the protective privilege ends where the public peril begins" (Tarasoff v. Regents of the University of California, 1976, p. 347). As a result of the original Tarasoff decision (1974), the court held that an affirmative duty existed to warn the identifiable victim despite the right to confidentiality of the client. This ruling established that "liability would attach where the psychotherapist *reasonably believed, or should have believed,* that the client posed a serious danger *to an identifiable potential victim*" (Anderson, 1996, p. 29, italics in original). This doctrine has come to be known as the *duty to warn.* The Tarasoff decision is binding only in California, and other state courts do not have to follow its dictates. However, it has been an influential case, and many other state and federal courts have followed this ruling. Counselors should educate themselves about the legal requirements in their local jurisdictions for the duty to warn and protect others from dangerous clients.

The 1976 Tarasoff ruling (known as Tarasoff II) actually was an appeal of the original 1974 Tarasoff decision (Tarasoff I) by the defendants, alleging that the parents of the client did not have a legal claim in the matter but rather were private third parties and not clients of the therapist. The California Supreme Court reconsidered the case and did find that the parents could sue the defendants. Tarasoff II effectively expanded the original decision from the more limited duty to warn to a more inclusive "duty to protect." In the *duty to protect* standard, warning the intended victim is now only one option available to the therapist to protect others from a dangerous client (VandeCreek, Bennett, & Bricklin, 1994). Other interventions with the potential to be equally effective may be used to control the potential of dangerous behavior. These interventions include (a) voluntary or civil commitment of the client, (b) increase or change in medication to control the condition creating the danger, (c) an increase in the frequency of sessions or supervision, or (d) referral of the client to another provider with better potential to control the violent behavior. Clearly, this does not absolve the therapist from the responsibility to exercise due care and proper professional judgment in assessing and attempting to protect potential victims of dangerous clients. It does expand the range of options to meet the needs of the public for protection and of the client to receive care that does not automatically expose the therapeutic relationship to the same level of potential harm (VandeCreek, Bennett, & Bricklin, 1994). Figure 3–3 presents recommended steps for the counselor to take if the client has been assessed as dangerous.

Several subsequent court decisions have expanded and clarified the duty to protect from dangerous clients. For example, victims who are not specifically identified but are foreseeable, likely targets of client violence, such as family members and others in close proximity to an identifiable victim, should be warned (*Hedlund v. Superior Court,* 1983; *Jablonski v. United States,* 1983). Counselors should continue to educate themselves on additional rulings that influence their duty to protect their clients and people around them from harm. State and federal courts continue to struggle with specific instances of the manner in which this important issue should be resolved in particular circumstances. Costa and Altekruse (1994) provide a set of

- As in all other situations, discuss the issue fully and openly with clients.
- Inform clients of the counselor's legal responsibility to warn others.
- Inform your supervisor of the potentially dangerous situation. If there is no supervisor, consult with another professional.
- Notify the person who might be responsible for the client or contact the police.
- Notify the intended victim.
- Explore other options, which may include commitment to an appropriate psychiatric facility.

Figure 3–3
Steps to Protect Others When Working with a Dangerous Client
Note: From *The ACA Legal Series: Confidentiality and Privileged Communication* (p. 22) by G.L. Arthur & C.D. Swanson, 1993, Alexandria, VA: American Counseling Association. Copyright 1993 by American Counseling Association. Reprinted by permission.

practical guidelines for dealing with duty-to-warn situations, emphasizing practical issues in their application.

Another court case has established that a parallel duty exists to violate confidentiality if a client is judged to be at risk for self-harm. *Eisel v. Board of Education* was a 1991 decision by the Maryland Court of Appeals that established the duty to protect for school counselors. This case involved a child who threatened suicide in the presence of schoolmates, who reported the threats to their parents, who notified the school counselors. The counselors interviewed the child, who denied the threats, and the counselors did not notify the parents or school administration. After the child did commit suicide, the father sued the counselors and the school, alleging breach of duty to intervene to prevent the suicide (Anderson, 1996). This case and others lead Anderson (1996) to caution that counselors do have a duty to protect their clients from harming themselves if it is foreseeable.

Termination Phase Issues

In the final phase of counseling, the focus shifts to ensuring that the client is prepared for the transition out of counseling or into a new relationship if a referral is made. Clearly, termination is a right of either the counselor or the client, and the stage should have been set for the length and nature of the relationship, beginning with the process of informed consent and continuing through the therapy and subsequent reevaluations of the nature of the counseling relationship. If a client requires additional therapy, or counseling beyond the counselor's scope of competence, it is the counselor's ethical responsibility to see that the client is referred properly and her counseling needs are met after the conclusion of the first relationship. The counselor might consider documenting the referral arrangements in a followup letter summarizing the arrangements or names of individuals to whom referral might be made to record the transition precautions.

Particular caution should be taken in two instances at termination. First, clients with serious, unresolved clinical conditions that require further intervention should not be terminated. If their care is beyond the abilities of the counselor, a referral may be made, but counseling must be continued until the referral transition can be made. Second, caution must be exercised in situations where the counselor works for an institution such as a managed care system that mandates termination after a specified number of sessions, whether or not the client's condition is resolved sufficiently to terminate. If a client is improperly prematurely terminated by the counselor, a malpractice suit may be filed for abandonment, or failure to treat or refer. The counselor should seek to continue treatment, at least until appropriate alternate treatment can be arranged (Bennett, Bryant, VandenBos, & Greenwood, 1990).

Pressure on counselors and mental health professionals to terminate services prematurely may become one of the most prominent ethical and legal issues in mental health care. The temptation to terminate a client may be great when a provider's fees run out, the clients cannot afford further care, or the client amasses an increasingly large bill. If the client is in need of further treatment, it continues to be the obligation of the therapists to meet that need until it is resolved or a referral can be arranged. The more appropriate route to dealing with this issue is for the counselor and client to fully understand the financial conditions and limitations involved and determine whether the client's resources likely will be sufficient for the duration of the counseling relationship. Counselors are not obligated to accept a client into counseling if this situation does not seem workable at the outset, and the potential client may be better served by beginning counseling with an agency that has the potential to carry out a reasonable treatment plan for this client.

Summary

This chapter addressed the critical relationship between ethical and legal standards in the practice of counselors. First, we described the dynamic interplay between these standards, particularly when there are conflicts between the guidance of each. A model of possible interactions between law and ethics illustrated this issue. Next, we defined the specific legal mechanisms that govern the practice of all mental health professionals: professional ethics committees, state licensure boards, and the criminal and civil courts. Finally, we provided more detailed consideration of common legal concerns within the specific stages of the individual client service cycle.

References

American Psychological Association. (1993). Record keeping guidelines. *American Psychologist, 48,* 984–986.

American Psychological Association. (1992). Ethical principles of psychologists and code of conduct. *American Psychologist, 47,* 1597–1611.

Anderson, B. S. (1996). *The counselor and the law* (4th ed.). Alexandria, VA: American Counseling Association.

Arthur, G. L., & Swanson, C. D. (1993). *The ACA legal series: Confidentiality and privileged communication.* Alexandria, VA: American Counseling Association.

Beauchamp, T. L., & Childress, J. F. (1989). *Principles of biomedical ethics.* Oxford: Oxford University Press.

Bennett, B. E., Bryant, B. K., VandenBos, G. R., & Greenwood, A. (1990). *Professional liability and risk management.* Washington, DC: American Psychological Association.

Bertram, B., & Wheeler, A. M. (1994). Legal aspects of counseling: Avoiding lawsuits and legal problems. Workshop materials. Alexandria, VA: American Counseling Association.

Bray, J. H., Shepard, J. N., & Hayes, J. R. (1985). Legal and ethical issues in informed consent to psychotherapy. *The American Journal of Family Therapy, 13*(2), 56–60.

Commission on Rehabilitation Counselor Certification. (1987). *Code of professional ethics for rehabilitation counselors.* Rolling Meadows, IL: Author.

Corey, G., Corey, M., & Callanan, P. (1993). *Issues and ethics in the helping professions.* Pacific Grove, CA: Brooks/Cole.

DeCosta, L., & Altekruse, M. (1994). Duty-to-warn guidelines for mental health counselors. *Journal of Counseling & Development, 72,* 346–350.

DePauw, M. E. (1986). Avoiding ethical violations: A timeline perspective for individual counseling. *Journal of Counseling & Development, 69,* 3–36.

Eisel v. Board of Education of Montgomery County, 324 Md. 376, 597 A,2d 447 (Md. Ct. App. 1991).

Fischer, L., & Sorenson, G. P. (1985). *School law for counselors, psychologists, and social workers.* New York: Longman.

Gibson, W. T., & Pope, K. S. (1993). The ethics of counseling: A national survey of certified counselors. *Journal of Counseling & Development, 71,* 330–336.

Handelsman, M. M., Martinez, A., Geisendorfer, S., & Jordan, L. (1995). Does legally mandated consent to psychotherapy ensure ethical appropriateness? *Ethics and Behavior, 5*(2), 119–129.

Hedlund v. Superior Court of Orange County , 669 P.2d41, 191 Cal. Rptr. 805 (1983).

Hinkelday, N. N., & Spokane, A. R. (1985). Effects of pressure and legal guideline clarity on counselor decision making in legal and ethical conflict situations. *Journal of Counseling and Development, 64,* 240–245.

Jablonski v. United States, 712 F.2d 391 (9th Cir., 1983).

Jaffee v. Redmond et al., WL 315841 (U.S. June 13, 1996).

Jagim, R. D., Wittman, W. D., & Noll, J. O. (1978). Mental health professionals' attitudes toward confidentiality, privilege, and third party disclosure. *Professional Psychology: Profession and Practice, 9,* 458–466.

Keary, A. O. (1985). Criminal law and procedure. In N. T. Sidney (Ed.), *Law and ethics: A guide for the health professional* (pp. 63–102). New York: Human Sciences.

Kohlberg, L. (1981). *Philosophy of moral development.* San Francisco: Harper & Row.

Kohlberg, L. (1964). Development of moral character and moral ecology. In M. L. Hoffman & L. W. Hoffman (Eds.), *Review of child development research.* Vol. I. New York: Russell Sage Foundation.

Mitchell, R. W. (1991). *Documentation of counseling records* (AACD Legal Series, Vol. 2). Alexandria, VA: American Association for Counseling and Development.

National Board for Counselor Certification. (1996, Summer). Jaffee v. Redmond: A primer on privilege. *NBCC NewsNotes, 13,* 1–4.

Piazza, N. J., & Baruth, N. E. (1990). Client record guidelines. *Journal of Counseling & Development, 68,* 313–316.

Pope, K. S. (1988). How clients are harmed by sexual conduct with mental health professionals: The syndrome and its prevalence. *Journal of Counseling & Development, 67,* 222–226.

Pope, K., Tabachnick, B., & Keith-Spiegel, P. (1987). Ethics of practice: The beliefs and behavior of psychologists as therapists. *American Psychologist, 42,* 993–1006.

Pope, K., & Vasquez, M. J. T. (1991). *Ethics in psychotherapy and counseling.* San Francisco: Jossey-Bass.

Remley, T. P., Jr. (1996). The relationship between law and ethics. In B. Herlihy & G. Corey (Eds.), *ACA ethical standards casebook* (5th ed.) (pp. 285–292). Alexandria, VA: American Counseling Association.

Remley, T. P., Jr. (1990). Counseling records: Legal and ethical issues. In B. Herlihy & L. Golden (Eds.), *ACA Ethical standards casebook* (4th ed.) (pp. 162–169). Alexandria, VA: American Counseling Association.

Remley, T. P., Jr. & Herlihy, B., Herlihy, S.B. (1997). The U.S. Supreme Court decision in Jaffee v. Redmond: Implications for counselors. *Journal of Counseling and Development, 75,* 213–218.

Shea, T. E. (1985). Finding the law: Legal research and citation. In N. T. Sidney (Ed.), *Law and ethics: A guide for the health professional* (pp. 411–424). New York: Human Sciences.

Snider, P. D. (1987). Client records: Inexpensive liability protection for mental health counselors. *Journal of Mental Health Counseling, 9,* 134–141.

Swoboda, J. S., Elwork, A., Sales, B. D., & Levine, D. (1978). Knowledge of and compliance with privileged communication and child-abuse reporting laws. *Professional Psychology: Profession and Practice, 9,* 448–457.

Tarasoff v. Regents of University of California, 17 Cal. App. 3d 425, 551 P.2d 334 (1976).

Tarasoff v. Regents of University of California, 13 C.3d 177, 529 P.2d 553, 118 Cal. Rptr. 129 (1974).

Thompson, A. (1990). *Guide to ethical practice in psychotherapy.* New York: John Wiley & Sons.

Vandecreek, L., Bennett, B. E., & Bricklin, P. M. (1994). *Risk management with potentially dangerous patients.* Washington, DC: APA Insurance Trust.

Van Hoose, W. H., & Kottler, J. A. (1985). *Ethical and legal issues in counseling and psychotherapy* (2nd ed.). San Francisco: Jossey-Bass.

Van Hoose, W. H., & Paradise, L. V. (1979). *Ethics in counseling and psychotherapy: Perspectives in issues and decision making.* Cranston, RI: Cranston Press.

Ware, M. L. (1971). The law and counselor ethics. *Personnel and Guidance Journal, 50,* 305–310.

Wigmore, J. H. (1961). Evidence in trials at common law. In J. T. McNaughton (Ed.), *Rules of evidence* (Vol. 8, rev. ed.). Boston: Little, Brown.

INFORMED WRITTEN CONSENT FOR TREATMENT CHECKLIST

Requirements vary greatly regarding the necessity or the content of an informed written consent for treatment—sometimes referred to as a Fact Sheet. Agency or institutional policies, state counselor licensing laws and rules, and other binding directives often determine the existence or content of this document. The intent of an informed consent document is to define the basic treatment relationship between counselor and client. Misunderstanding and disappointment, which are often the genesis of a liability claim, can be reduced when clients are made knowledgeable of the ground rules of the counseling relationship. Trust and the therapeutic relationship are enhanced when clients understand what is expected or required of a counselor and of themselves in a successful counseling relationship.

The following topics are recommended for consideration when developing an informed written consent for treatment:

1. *Voluntary Participation.* Clients voluntarily agree to treatment and can terminate at any time without penalty.
2. *Client Involvement.* What level of involvement and what type of involvement will be expected from clients?
3. *Counselor Involvement.* What will the counselor provide? How will this be provided? How can the counselor be reached in the event of an emergency?
4. *No Guarantees.* Counselors cannot guarantee results (e.g., become happier, less tense or depressed, save the marriage, stop drug use, obtain a good job).
5. *Risks Associated with Counseling.* Define what, if any, risks are associated with the counselor's particular approach to counseling.
6. *Confidentiality and Privilege.* Specify how confidentiality will be handled in couple counseling, family counseling, child/adolescent counseling, and group counseling situations. How may confidential and privileged information be released?
7. *Exceptions of Confidentiality and Privilege.* Define specific statutory circumstances where confidentiality and privilege cannot be maintained (e.g., abuse reporting).
8. *Counseling Approach or Theory.* What is the counselor's counseling orientation or theoretical belief system? How will that affect treatment?
9. *Counseling and Financial Records.* What will they include? How long will they be maintained? How will they be destroyed?
10. *Ethical Guidelines.* What standard defines the counselor's practice? How might a client obtain a copy of these guidelines?
11. *Licensing Regulations.* What license does the counselor hold? How may a client check on the status of the license?
12. *Credentials.* What education, training, and experience credentials will the counselor need to provide counseling treatment, including any specialty credentials?
13. *Fees and Charges.* What are the specific fees and charges? How will fees be collected? How are financial records maintained?
14. *Insurance Reimbursement.* What responsibility will the counselor take for filing insurance forms? What fees, if any, are associated with insurance filing? How will co-payments be handled?
15. *Responsibility for Payment.* Who is responsible for payment of counseling charges? How will delinquent accounts be handled, what charges will be assessed for delinquent accounts?
16. *Disputes and Complaints.* How will fee or other disputes be resolved? Provide the address and phone number of the state licensing board for complaints if required by state licensing statute.
17. *Cancellation Policy.* How much notice for cancellation of a scheduled appointment is required? What fees will be charged for late cancellation?
18. *Affiliation Relationship.* Describe independent contractor and/or partnership relationship with any other practitioners in office suite.

19. *Supervisory Relationship.* Describe any required supervisory relationship along with reason for the supervision. Provide supervisor's name and credentials.

20. *Colleague Consultation.* Indicate that, in keeping with generally accepted standards of practice, you frequently consult with other mental health professionals regarding the management of cases. The purpose of the consultation is to ensure quality care. Every effort is made to protect the identity of clients.

NOTE: From "Legal Aspects of Counseling: Avoiding Lawsuits and Legal Problems," by B. Bertram & A.M. Wheeler, 1994, Workshop materials, Alexandria, VA: American Counseling Association.

Values Clarification and Decision-Making

4

Defining Values Philosophically:

Two Extremes and a Middle Ground

This chapter will challenge you to examine two extreme ethical and moral frameworks, and to assess the relevance of these positions to counseling. One position derives from Judeo–Christian thought and the other from a philosophy called "evolutionary naturalism." The intent of this chapter, therefore, is to stimulate critical thought by presenting mutually exclusive extreme positions. A secondary purpose is to facilitate self-examination of your philosophical inclinations. You may find that you tend to agree or disagree with one of the two positions, siding with either Judeo–Christian thinking or the scientific alternative in evolutionary naturalism. A third purpose of this chapter is to introduce new ideas about ethics through published works in the category of post-modernism or social constructivism, an intellectual movement in the mental health field gaining favor among theoreticians and practitioners. *Social constructivism* is a philosophical framework that proposes that reality is a creation of individuals in interaction—a socially, consensually agree-on definition of what is "real." The two established mutually exclusive positions (Judeo–Christian thought and evolutionary naturalism) will be presented in this chapter, and then an alternative "constructivist" framework will be outlined. Accordingly, you should embrace the challenge of foundational theory as a stimulus to facilitate a critical application of the ideas to counseling practice. In chapters 5 and 6, which address values clarification and decision-making, you will be asked to go beyond theory to assess personal values and decision-making processes.

It should be noted that many different philosophical positions can be related to counseling. A whole text could be written on ethical philosophy as related to counseling and psychotherapy. The intent of this chapter is not to review ethical philosophy.

The intent here is to present two mutually exclusive positions and an alternative position to demonstrate how closely linked counseling practice is to personal and disciplinary philosophy.

Foundational Values and the Judeo–Christian Ethic

From a philosophical standpoint, the nature of ethical standards in counseling is clear: The ethical and philosophical foundations of counseling derive from a concern for individuals. Productive activity is viewed as a dignifying and fulfilling aspect of an individual's life in a capitalistic system (Obermann, 1965). As Bozarth (1981) noted, "Clients are to be valued, respected, and considered responsible members of society" (p. 76).

The ethical and philosophical foundations of counseling correspond closely to religious principles that pervade Western culture: Judeo–Christian ideals have significantly influenced counseling. The influence of Eastern religions (e.g., Taoism) has also influenced counseling philosophy, primarily in humanistic philosophy and theory; however, the influence of Judeo–Christian morality is prominent and consistent with a philosophy which purports kindness and compassion for those in need.

As an example, the influence of Judeo–Christian ideals as an ethical standard in counseling is clearly identifiable in the specialty of rehabilitation counseling. In regard to Judeo–Christian ideals and vocational rehabilitation, Obermann (1965) gave the clearest historical linkage: "Perhaps no source of information, inspiration and dogma has had as great an influence on our Western civilization as the Judeo–Christian Bible" (p. 52). Obermann presented excerpts from the Bible that demonstrated both positive and negative responses to individuals with disabilities. However, as the Judeo–Christian ethic developed over the centuries, as Obermann described, the dominant view became one of charity and compassion toward individuals in need. The following quote from Obermann described the development of Judeo–Christian thought through the Middle Ages:

> Thus charity became a device of the Church in the early Christian era, and all through the Middle Ages it was useful in the purchase of salvation. The poor and the unfortunate became necessary for the spiritual well-being of those who could give alms; they were cherished as important in God's scheme of things. Saint John Chrysostom preached, "If there were no poor the greater part of your sins would not be removed; they are the healers of your wounds."
>
> Although this was the dominant view in the medieval Western world, it was not universal. Outside the Roman Church, other views of charity could be found. The Jews saw charity as an essential in the mutual support they so often needed. Among them, charity was of many kinds and levels of laudability, depending on the conditions and attitudes related to practicing it. It might be said that vocational rehabilitation was placed as the highest level by Maimonides (1135–1204); helping an unfortunate person in such a manner that he would not need help again, for example giving him employment or helping him to find employment, was listed as the highest order of charity. (p. 88)

Caring for others in need has become basic to the Judeo–Christian ethical tradition. In rehabilitation counseling, the link is clear.

A more recent example of the influence of Judeo–Christian ideals on rehabilitation counseling is given by Rubin and Roessler (1987); they described the Social Gospel movement of the late 19th century "as compatible with improved attitudes regarding society's responsibility for the rehabilitation of persons with disabilities" (p. 17). Proponents of the Social Gospel movement viewed the role of a Christian as that of "social reformer" (Hofstadter, Miller, & Aaron, 1959, p. 276). Against the backdrop of a Social Darwinism (Hofstadter et al., 1959), the Social Gospel movement was a particularly salient social movement. Social Darwinism, as embodied in the work of Spencer (1893), proposed an ethical philosophy based on "survival of the fittest." Spencer (1893), speaking of the ideal of "survival of the fittest," wrote:

> This law implies that each individual ought to receive the benefits and the evils of his own nature and consequent conduct: neither being prevented from having whatever good his actions normally bring to him, nor allowed to shoulder off on to other persons whatever ill is brought to him by his actions. (p. 17)

By Judeo–Christian ideals, on the other hand, all individuals are valued, as is responsible action for individuals in need. Individual sacrifice for those in less fortunate circumstances is esteemed from a Judeo–Christian perspective, not because human beings have "inherited" sympathy, but because they are directed by a higher moral ideal. There is clear consistency between Judeo–Christian ideals and philosophy in rehabilitation. Many rehabilitation counselors devote their lives to serving those in need for little personal gain. This is also true of counselors in general. Counselors are directed by their vocation to assist others in need, those who have lost jobs, those who are disabled, those who suffer personal loss or serious personal adjustments, or those who suffer with disease. Counseling is a profession that is founded on Judeo–Christian standards.

But how should nonreligious counselors, or those who do not view their work as a religious calling view their ethical obligation? Is there an alternative perspective, a scientific justification for ethical theory in counseling that is both consistent with evolutionary science and more general counseling philosophy? A recent development in theoretical biology offers such a scientific foundation for ethical theory in counseling, thereby providing a competitive viewpoint to a traditional Judeo–Christian perspective.

Religious Thinking and Ethics

In a commentary on MacIntyre's (1981) manuscript titled "Can Medicine Dispense with a Theological Perspective on Human Nature," Ramsey (1981) concluded that "religion is ethics, and ethics is religion" (p. 154). The position that religion and ethics are inextricably intertwined is well supported in the ethics literature, whether one takes a direct religious perspective, citing the Bible, for example, as a source of inspiration and directive, or whether one takes a more philosophical position, for instance, through Kant's (undated/1949) "Categorical Imperative." Several ethical themes predominate on theological or philosophical grounds, the greatest of which is the belief in a divine entity. Even a strictly philosophical analysis of moral philosophy often leads to the conclusion of a divine or greater power. MacIntyre (1981), speaking of Kant's philosophy, concluded:

> Our moral experience presupposes the form of a progress toward a goal never to be achieved in this present world; but this in turn presupposes that the moral agent has a more than earthly identity, and that there is a power in the universe able to sustain our progress toward the goal in and after the earthly life. Morality thus does presuppose our own life after death and the existence of a power that we may call divine. Since the whole point of this power's activity, as belief in it is presupposed by us, is to bring about moral perfection and the *summum bonum,* we cannot, if we see rightly, see our duty as in any way different from precepts of such a power. We must see our duties as divine commands. (pp. 128-129)

Consequently, there is a *summum bonum* (greatest good) because there is something greater than one's living self. Without a sense of "absolute good," ethical theory deteriorates into a relativistic or situational judgmentalism, where "right" or "wrong" depend on the contextual demands. With a sense of absolute good, on the other hand, the existence of an omnipotent god force is the only rational conclusion. Judeo–Christian ethical principles are founded on belief in an absolute good defined as "God." Three other aspects of a moral philosophy founded primarily on Judeo–Christian ideals are noteworthy. Gustafson (1981) summarized them as follows:

1. *The ideal of liberation from oppression.* Gustafson (1981) stated: "Where there is oppression God wills liberation; where there are movements for liberation, there is the presence of God" (p. 182).

2. *The concept of sin.* According to Gustafson (1981), "the consequences of human actions are judged, to be sure, by moral norms" (p. 185). The consequence of a sinful life, of course, is condemnation.

3. *The idea of divine purpose and that there is no need for a rationale other than God.* Gustafson (1981) said: "God makes himself his own end" (p. 186).

Inherent in this philosophy are directives toward helping others in need, including people who are oppressed, ill, disabled, and poor. Those who can help people in need have an obligation to help. Given religious belief along Judeo–Christian lines, there is a good reason for assisting others through counseling. One's religious values are at issue.

Science in Antithesis

Darwin's Natural Selection

From a Judeo–Christian standpoint, Darwin's (1859/1984) *On the Origin of Species by Means of Natural Selection* was revolutionary, even heretical, thinking. Darwin professed that the human species evolved from a lower order, was not created spontaneously by an omnipotent god force, and shared many characteristics of genetic forebearance. From a strict biological perspective of Darwin's work, "good" is what survives. What survives is naturally, not divinely, selected. Even Darwin embraced Herbert Spencer's summarizing phrase, "survival of the fittest" (Korey, 1984), which depicts humankind's procreant role as subordinating the individual to the species. Yet, Darwin like Spencer (1893) who followed his lead, unyieldingly believed that humankind was more than the result of a selfish and survivalistic drive. Darwin (1874) believed that the human being evolved into a sympathetic being which was able to overcome individual and selfish urges for the good of the "tribe" (Pepper, 1960). However, Darwin's position is idealistic and does not account for the human being's selective and socially bounded sympathy. If, in fact, the human being inherited "sympathy" for other human beings, how is it that in some cases humans can war against an enemy closer in genetic makeup than the social group of affiliation? Clearly, humankind's sympathy does not extend to all members of the species.

Regardless, Darwin's "natural selection" when taken to its biological and logical extreme, directly conflicts with the principles of Judeo–Christian morality. Beyond Spencer's (1893) philosophy, the logical extreme of Darwin's ideas is clearly represented in Nietzsche's "Evolutionary Naturalism."

Nietzsche's "Evolutionary Naturalism"

Friedrich Nietzsche, a 19th century German philosopher, rejected the Judeo–Christian ethic and embraced Darwinian ideas. As described by Kaufmann (1968), "Nietzsche is one of the first thinkers with a comprehensive philosophy to complete the break with religion" (p. 17).

Nietzsche believed that the "Judeo–Christian system of moral ideals" constituted "an inversion of natural life-giving instinctive values" (Sahakian, 1968, p. 229). He further believed that Darwin's ideas inevitably led to a natural foundation for ethics, and that sympathy and pity were unacceptable as a moral foundation. To Nietzsche, moral principles were best founded on the basic idea of survival of the fittest. He believed that humankind was driven by a will to power, and that Judeo–Christian based ethics derived from a "slave morality" rather than a "master morality" (Sahakian, 1968). Nietzsche (1888/1968a), in *The Antichrist* stated, "What is good? Everything that heightens the feeling of power in man, the will to power, power itself. What is bad? Everything that is born of weakness" (p. 570). And further he stated, "The weak and the failures shall perish . . . And they shall even be given every possible assistance" (p. 570). In regard to the value of pity, Nietzsche wrote: "Quite in general, pity crosses the law of development, which is the law of *selection*. It preserves what is ripe for destruction; it defends those who have been disinherited and condemned by life; and by the abundance of the failures of all kinds which it keeps alive, it gives life itself a gloomy and questionable aspect" (p. 572).

Nietzsche valued the "overman," or as described by some, the "superman." In *Thus Spake Zarathustra*, Nietzsche (1891/1968b) proclaimed "God is dead!" and, speaking as Zarathustra, he defined the overman as the highest moral being:

> Behold, I teach you the overman. The overman is the meaning of the earth. Let your will say: the overman shall be the meaning of the earth! I beseech you, my brothers, remain faithful to the earth, and do not believe those who speak to you of other-worldly hopes! (p. 125)

It is not hard to understand that Nietzsche's moral philosophy, or some derivative of his philosophy, was embraced by Hitler in his ideal of a master race, with subsequent stigmatization and destruction of Jews and individuals with disabilities. And there is no question that Nietzsche's Evolutionary Naturalism, as an offshoot of Darwin's theoretical biology, is antithetical to ethical principles held dear by human service professionals in Western society. Evolutionary science, therefore, as is demonstrated in its broad application in the moral philosophy of Nietzsche, provides a poor foundation for ethics in counseling, and to the extreme, it can be a foundation for a philosophy that is antithetical to counseling philosophy.

A Reprieve in Maturana and Varela's Autopoiesis: A Constructivist Philosophy

New Biological Theory

In an intriguing work, Maturana and Varela (1973/1980) have attempted to bridge the gap between theoretical biology and philosophy. Maturana and Varela have developed a theoretical framework that accounts for evolutionary theory and provides counseling with a biological foundation that is not antithetical to Judeo–Christian ideals. In so doing, they have provided a scientific theory which can serve as a foundation for ethical theory in counseling.

Maturana and Varela (1973/1980) defined criteria for living systems, which they called "autopoietic machines." *Autopoietic machines* (systems) are essentially made up of autonomous and self-creative relationships. In fact, the word *autopoiesis* means self- (auto-) production (-poiesis). Essentially, the criteria given by Maturana and Varela (1973/1980) for autopoietic machines are as follows:

1. "Autopoietic machines are homeostatic machines" (p. 78), that is, they tend toward a steady operating state (dynamic equilibrium).
2. Autopoietic machines are processes, such as interactions or transformations. These processes continuously regenerate themselves through components which are process generated;
3. Autopoietic machines continually specify their own boundaries by the organization of relationships and through their operations, and not by static organization of components.

To simplify, autopoiesis defines the dynamics of living autonomous systems. Generally, what is viewed as alive can be considered autopoietic. For example, living systems "transform matter into themselves in a manner such that the product of their operation is their own organization" (Maturana & Varela, 1973/1980, p. 82). For example, as living human bodies, human beings eat (they are organized to take things within their boundaries) to maintain an equilibrium, and in the process they regenerate themselves and the organized processes that led to their eating. Essentially, what Maturana and Varela have done is to focus on the organization of relationships in defining "living" things rather than to focus on individual traits or individual processes of such things. To say that one eats and breathes does not define one as living, but to say that one eats and breathes and, in the process, regenerates one's own organization for eating and breathing is to say that one is alive.

But the controversial part of Maturana and Varela's (1973/1980) work from an ethical standpoint is not in defining living systems as autopoietic, but in stating that all autopoietic systems are living systems. This means that any system, if it has autopoietic properties, is essentially alive. They stated:

> If living systems are machines, that they are physical autopoietic machines is trivially obvious. . . . However, we deem the converse to be true: a physical system if autopoietic, is living. In other words, we claim that the notion of autopoiesis is necessary and sufficient to characterize the organization of living systems. (p. 82)

They have taken the position that autopoiesis is the definition of *life*. The question then becomes, does the system have to be "physical" to meet the criteria? Can it be social? Can the mental health service system be alive? If so, what are the ethical implications of "living" social systems?

Beer's Applications to Social Systems

Maturana and Varela (1973/1980), as biologists addressing biological issues, did not address whether social systems are living systems directly. However, Beer (1980), in an introduction to Maturana and Varela's essay, concluded without qualification that "human societies are biological systems," and Beer claimed that Maturana and Varela's work "conclusively proves the point" (p. 70). Maturana (1980) himself, in a separate introduction to his work, acknowledged the social significance of his biological theory. He stated, "To the extent that human beings are autopoietic systems, all their activities as social organisms must satisfy their autopoiesis" (p. xxvi). Likewise, a social system cannot operate if its components cease to be autopoietic. He further stated, "The realization of the autopoiesis of the components of a social system is constitutive to the realization of the social system itself. This cannot be ignored in any consideration about the operation of a social system without negating it" (p. xxv). Therefore, the relationship between living human beings and a living social system (in which they exist) is one of mutuality through interaction, or what Maturana and Varela (1973/l980) called "coupling" (p. 107). Neither of the coupled entities is more important, because each derives from each other. As Maturana and Varela state, "Biological phenomena depend upon the autopoiesis of the individuals involved; thus, there are biological systems that arise from the coupling of autopoietic unities, some of which may even constitute autopoietic systems of a higher order" (p. 118).

Given this conclusion, Maturana and Varela's (1973/1980) work has provided a biological rationale for formation of social systems—the social system is a biological system in itself. It is a biological system of a higher order. Essentially, human beings fulfill roles in a social system that keep the social system alive, and, in so doing, they maintain relationships necessary for their own existence.

Just as living cells are parts of the living body, so are individuals parts of a living social system; they are cells in the larger body of things. At the same time the cells are building blocks of the body, they derive their existence from the relations of which they are a part. Accordingly, individuals in a social system are not dispensable, even after their reproductive role, so long as they continue (or will be able) to fill roles constituting the social system. A soccer team without a goalie is not a soccer team. A baseball team without a pitcher is not a baseball team. And should the soccer goalie or the baseball pitcher become injured, the team must have a means of rehabilitation or replacement, or the team will cease to exist. Being ethical means valuing the individuals that fulfill (or will fulfill) roles in the social system. At the same time, the system must have a means of insuring those who might also be adversely affected in a critical role, which thereby helps to ensure the survival of the system. Being ethical, therefore, means the individual and the social system are on equal terms. Maturana and Varela (1973/1980) stated: "Thus biology cannot be used anymore to justify the dispensability of the individuals for the benefit of the species, society or mankind under the pretense that its role is to perpetuate them. Biologically the individuals are not dispensable" (p. 118).

The indispensability of the individual performing a role in a living social system gives a science-based reason for valuing the individual. Consequently, caring for people in need has new meaning. In caring for the individual in society, one helps guarantee the living properties of the societal system necessary for one's own continued autopoiesis. By being ethical, one helps to ensure one's own survival. By being ethical, an individual is selfish and selfless at the same time. Therefore, belief in a divine entity or god force is not necessitated, except as an organizing principle of relationships.

Challenging the Status Quo

Maturana's work, as previously discussed, is new biological theory. It is controversial, yet it is based on ideas about biology and cognition that have a firm foundation in empirical research. Nevertheless, his ideas are revolutionary not only to biology, but also to social systems theory and the field of cybernetics, two areas that have been influential in the development of counseling theory, especially as related to marriage and family counseling (see Dell, 1985, for a summary of the philosophical implications for marriage and family therapy). For example, as related to social systems theory, a theory of relationships, Maturana and Varela (1973/1980) believed that systems are informationally "closed," which is counter to the traditional systemic–relational idea that biological systems are "open" systems (Bertalanffy, 1952, 1968). According to Maturana and Varela, "cause and effect," from the perspective of a learning, living organism, is the result of what is in the organism (the structure and organization of the nervous system) rather than a direct result of out-side stimulation. You can hit a baseball with a bat and it will fly, but when you hit an uncooked egg with a bat it will splatter; the cause of these two differing responses is not the bat (stimulus) but the differing structures of the baseball and egg in interac-tion with the bat. Simple conceptions of linear, external causality go by the wayside, because the structure of that which is perturbed primarily defines what will result from the perturbation. Efran and Lukens (1985) made the point as follows: "toasters 'toast' and washing machines 'wash' because of how each is built or structured" (p. 25), even though both can be similarly stimulated through an electrical outlet.

Additionally, evolutionary thought as embodied in the phrase "survival of the fittest" has new meaning according to Maturana and Varela's ideas. Fitness, instead of meaning physical, intellectual, or sexual prowess, becomes a matter of social and environmental "fit."

Beyond challenging evolutionary theory and systemic–relational conceptions about the operation of systems, Maturana (1978) has challenged beliefs about the na-ture of reality. Maturana's reality is constructed out of simultaneous relationships among an observer, the social domain (which involves language), and neuronal ac-tivity (which may or may not be related to external perturbation of the perceptual organs). Maturana has placed "objectivity in parentheses" (Simon, 1985), because reality is bounded by the structure of the organism in its operative domain. In other words, Maturana's ideas are consistent with the social constructivist movements in psychology or psychotherapy, because reality is socially constructed. Consequently, an absolute "right" or "wrong," from an ethical standpoint, results from consensus across (coupled autopoietic) systems. Right and wrong are socially agreed on con-structions. For example, it would be highly unlikely that two warring countries would develop relationships to help fulfill each other's continued autopoiesis. And because there would be a lack of autopoietic coupling, a consensus between two warring countries over what is absolutely right or wrong would be difficult to accomplish. On the other hand, it is unlikely that a country would war against another country that is economically and socially linked to its own survival. Countries closely linked would have consensus about "right" or "wrong," which would be absolutely real within iden-tifiable bounds of their interactive domain. The interactive domain of coupled au-topoietic unities, therefore, is the parenthetical boundary of "objectivity." Maturana's ideas certainly offer a different perspective from an ethical standpoint.

The "Living" Mental Health Service Delivery System

To return to a question posed earlier, is the mental health service system alive? An offshoot conclusion of a theory of autopoietic systems is that social systems are liv-ing systems, just as are biological systems. In the one area of counseling where this question has been addressed—rehabilitation counseling—the answer is yes. The state–federal rehabilitation service delivery system, as a social system, clearly meets the criteria for autopoiesis: It is homeostatic (Cottone, 1987; Cottone & Cottone, 1986). It is autonomous within the larger constraints of the societal system in which it operates, and it continually regenerates the components that fulfill roles necessary for its survival. For example, the rehabilitation system continually produces new counselors through rehabilitation education programs. It produces administrators from its own ranks. It essentially produces individuals who fulfill roles that help to maintain its organization and its operative autonomy. At the same time, it is autopoietically coupled to the larger society which it helps to constitute (mutuality through interaction). Accordingly, the way the system behaves will be consistent with the properties of living, autopoietic systems. Consequently, Maturana's work raises additional philosophical questions that are at the heart of the rehabilitation system's existence. It is proposed that the same is true of other areas of mental health service delivery.

Implications

Consistent with a need to analyze the philosophical foundations of ethical theory in counseling, this chapter has provided a scientific viewpoint that is an alternative to the Judeo–Christian ethical perspective or to an evolutionary naturalism. Because individuals in counseling, to some degree, are trained as social scientists–practitioners, the major implication of a scientific foundation for ethical theory in counseling is consistency between counseling approaches, the scientific method, and ethical philosophy in counseling.

Specific to Maturana and Varela's (1973/1980) autopoiesis, clients of professionals in counseling are valued, so long as the individuals can potentially perform as part of the network of social roles in the societal system. Autopoiesis translates to ethical egalitarianism, because no one role is more important than another from the perspective of the larger, complex system of interrelationships. Also, the idea that individuals must be helped out of pity or from fear of condemnation is replaced. Autopoiesis is not a degrading concept as applied to ethical theory because it is developed from the idea of "mutuality through interaction."

To date, an ethical justification for counseling has been scientifically unfounded. What remained was either (a) a philosophy deriving primarily from a religious perspective, (b) dissonance between scientific theories, such as Darwin's "natural selection" and counseling goals, or (c) what can be assumed to be ignorance or denial of the importance of ethical philosophy to counseling practice. The search for a scientific foundation for ethical theory in counseling, therefore, is a step toward critical discourse on such issues.

The arguments provided herein do not necessarily displace the Judeo–Christian ethical tradition, although they challenge it. For example, Jewish or Christian counselors can continue to apply their religious values to professional practice. But individuals who are uncomfortable with the mix of religion and professional practice, especially within a legal system that values division of church and state, may find the scientific alternative a more agreeable option.

Summary

We described counseling philosophy as closely paralleling Judeo–Christian moral principles. From a religious perspective, there is clear justification for assisting individuals in need. But scientific theories of evolution, such as Darwin's "Natural Selection" theory, provide a foundation for ethical theory inconsistent with counseling philosophy and do not clearly account for humankind's socially bounded sympathy. This is demonstrated to the extreme through the works of Nietzsche. We presented a new biological theory incorporating an evolutionary perspective while accounting for humankind's socially bounded sympathy. Maturana and Varela's autopoiesis is described as a constructivist framework for viewing counseling's ethical foundation. Beyond ethical concerns, Maturana's ideas raise additional questions about the operation of mental health service delivery systems.

References

Beer, S. (1980). Preface to "Autopoiesis: The organization of the living." In H. R. Maturana & F. J. Varela, *Autopoiesis and cognition: The realization of the living.* Boston, MA: D. Reidel.

Bertalanffy, L. von. (1952). *Problems of life.* London: C. A. Watts.

Bertalanffy, L. von. (1968). *General systems theory.* New York: George Braziller.

Bozarth, J. D. (1981). Philosophy and ethics in rehabilitation counseling. In R. M. Parker & C. E. Hansen (Eds.), *Rehabilitation counseling: Foundations—consumers—service delivery* (pp. 59–81). Boston: Allyn & Bacon.

Cottone, R. R. (1987). A systemic theory of vocational rehabilitation. *Rehabilitation Counseling Bulletin, 30,* 167–176.

Cottone, R. R., & Cottone, L. P. (1986). A systemic analysis of vocational evaluation in the state–federal rehabilitation system. *Vocational Evaluation and Work Adjustment Bulletin, 19,* 47–54.

Darwin, C. (1874). *The descent of man and selection in relation to sex* (2nd ed.). Chicago: Rand, McNally & Co.

Darwin, C. (1984). On the origin of species by means of natural selection. In R. Jastrow & K. Korey (Ed. & Commentator, respectively), *The essential Darwin,* (pp. 57–228). Boston, MA: Little Brown & Co. (Original work published in 1859)

Dell, P. F. (1985). Understanding Bateson and Maturana: Toward a biological foundation for the social sciences. *Journal of Marital and Family Therapy, 11,* 1–20.

Efran, J., & Lukens, M. D. (1985, May–June). The world according to Humberto Maturana. *The Family Therapy Networker,* pp. 23–28; 72–75.

Gustafson, J. M. (1981). Theology and ethics: An interpretation of the agenda. In D. Callahan & H. T. Engelhardt, Jr. (Eds.), *The roots of ethics: Science, religion, and values* (pp. 175–196). New York: Plenum.

Hofstadter, R., Miller, W., & Aaron, D. (1959). *The American republic since 1865: Volume two.* Upper Saddle River, NJ: Prentice Hall.

Kant, I. (undated/1949). *Critique of practical reason and other writings in moral philosophy,* (L. W. Beck, Trans.). Chicago: University of Chicago Press.

Kaufmann, W. (1968). *The portable Nietzsche.* New York: Penguin.

Korey, K. (1984). *The essential Darwin.* Boston: Little, Brown & Co.

MacIntyre, A. (1981). Can medicine dispense with a theological perspective of human nature? In D. Callahan & H. T. Engelhardt, Jr. (Eds.), *The roots of ethics: Science, religion, and values* (pp. 119–137). New York: Plenum.

Maturana, H. R. (1978). Biology of language: The epistemology of reality. In G. A. Miller & E. Lenneberg (Eds.), *Psychology and biology of language and thought.* New York: Academic Press.

Maturana, H. R. (1980). Introduction. In H. R. Maturana & F. J. Varela, *Autopoiesis and cognition: The realization of the living.* Boston: D. Reidel.

Maturana, H. R., & Varela, F. J. (1980). Autopoiesis: The organization of the living. In H. R. Maturana & F. J. Varela, *Autopoiesis and cognition: The realization of the living.* Boston: D. Reidel. (Original work published in 1973).

Nietzsche, F. (1968a). *The Antichrist.* In W. Kaufmann (Ed. & Trans.), *The portable Nietzsche* (pp. 565–656). New York: Penguin. (Original work written in 1888)

Nietzsche, F. (1968b). Thus spake Zarathustra. In W. Kaufmann (Ed. & Trans.), *The portable Nietzsche* (pp. 103–439). New York: Penguin. (Original work published in 1891).

Obermann, C. E. (1965). *A history of vocational rehabilitation in America.* Minneapolis, MN: T. S. Denison.

Pepper, S. G. (1960). *Ethics.* New York: Appleton-Century-Crofts.

Ramsey, P. (1981). Kant's Moral Theology or a religious ethics? In D. Callahan & H. T. Engelhardt, Jr. (Eds.), *The roots of Ethics: Science, religion, and values* (pp. 139–169). New York: Plenum.

Rubin, S. E., & Roessler, R. T. (1987). *Foundations of the vocational rehabilitation process* (3rd ed.). Austin, TX: Pro-Ed.

Sahakian, W. S. (1968). *History of philosophy.* New York: Barnes & Noble.

Simon, R. (1985, May–June). Structure is destiny: An interview with Humberto Maturana. *The Family Therapy Networker, 9*(3), pp. 32–37; 41–43.

Spencer, H. (1893). *Principles of ethics: Volume II.* New York: D. Appleton.

Values, Valuing, and Principles in Counseling

Counselors and their clients center on issues of value and the meaning of life as they search out solutions for problems, goals, and strategies related to this meaning. They use their unique interpretations of what is good, bad, right, wrong, joyous, and painful in their experiences and realities to guide them. These understandings are called values; and they are abstract, making them difficult to define and communicate. Values must be experienced to be truly grasped. They are powerful and drive our choices about what we wish to do and what we would like to have. They focus our energies and choices. If you doubt this, you need only reflect on the strong emotion and sense of rightness you experience when you hug your child after returning from a long journey; the confusion and disgust you feel as you watch the beating of an individual on television news; or the sense of calm and joy you experience when you see a beautiful sunrise or feel gentle, pine-scented breezes. The beliefs and preferences that underlie these values can be articulated—the love of family, respect for life and personal freedom, and respect for nature and our responsibility to care for these resources. Values are formed over the years through our experience of the beliefs, choices, and actions of significant others and through exposure to cultural institutions such as school and places of worship.

Clients and counselors all hold values, whether they are able to articulate them in the moment or not. When clients come to counselors for assistance in making choices or changing their lives, both parties enact values, either knowingly or unknowingly. The material in this chapter builds on the understanding of how values are defined philosophically provided in Chapter 4. In this chapter, the nature of specific values relevant to counseling and value choices will be discussed in terms of both personal values and the professional principles of ethics. Professional ethical principles are drawn from societal values that professionals have found that guide them best in making difficult choices in their work with clients. We will describe these principles and illustrate how they underpin the codes of ethics used in counseling. Finally, we will discuss the increased importance of value analysis and choice in ethical decision making. We will touch on new developments in ethics, multiculturalism, and feminist streams of thought to illustrate how the value and worldview-based analysis can be reframed to accommodate the diverse lives and perspectives of all people in counseling.

Values: The Basic Concepts

Ethics, Morals, and Values

In a sermon given in Georgia on 4 February 1968 during the height of the Civil Rights movement, the Rev. Martin Luther King Jr. spoke eloquently of a truth about what it takes to truly be a helper:

> Everybody can be great because anybody can serve (the Civil Rights movement). You don't have to have a college degree to serve, you don't have to have to make your subject and verb agree to serve, you don't have to know about Plato and Aristotle to serve, you don't have to know Einstein's "Theory of Relativity" to serve, you don't have to know the Second Theory of Thermodynamics and Physics to serve. . . . You only need a heart full of grace, a soul generated by love. (King, 1968)

The issues surrounding ethical judgment involve a complex interplay of morals, values, and priorities people hold in relationship to themselves, their colleagues, and other professionals. Ethical principles of practice are interrelated with, but distinguishable from, concepts such as morals, values, and codes of ethics. Taken together they form the heart and soul of counseling.

Ethics and Morals.   *Ethics* has been variously defined as "a branch of study in philosophy concerning how people ought to act toward each other, pronouncing judgments of value about those actions" (Kitchener, 1984, p. 18); and "a hierarchy of values that permits choices to be made based on distinguished levels of right or wrong" (Shertzer & Linden, 1979, p. 510). In describing *morals*, the nature of the concepts takes on a clear connotation of the goodness or badness of human behavior or character (Van Hoose & Kottler, 1985) and an element of coercion is implied (Mowrer, 1967). Although ethics also deals with the appropriateness of human action, it connotes more of a basis in reason and objectivity (Van Hoose & Kottler, 1985). In differentiating between ethics and morals, Kitchener (1984) noted that *morals* are more related to the individual's belief structure whereas *ethics* involve the study and evaluation of this belief structure. The importance of this distinction and the evaluative component of ethics becomes clear when one realizes that "it is critical to differentiate between saying 'X' *believes* a certain action is right or good and that action *is* right or good" (Kitchener, 1984, p. 16). It is not difficult to think of examples of people who are steeped in personally or environmentally distorted thinking. Remember the scientists in charge of the Tuskegee experiment that left black men with syphilis intentionally untreated for decades, or the Rev. Jim Jones who led the mass suicide of his cult in Guyana. The individuals involved in these and countless other tragic circumstances that haunt the daily news reports may have acted consistently with their personal moral code, but not ethically, based on a broader analysis of appropriate behavior. The need for evaluation for personal actions against a broader standard of what is right and good is imperative for the well being of all.

Values.   Counselors are required to distinguish their personal moral codes from and reconcile them with the profession's values to behave in an ethical manner. However, some experts in the field maintain that the stated attempt to separate moral outlook and choices from professional skills and practices is both deceptive and deleterious to one of psychotherapy's major sources of legitimacy, direction, and power (Frank, 1961; London, 1986).

Rokeach (1973) defined *value* as "an enduring belief that a specific mode of conduct or end-state of existence is personally or socially preferable to an opposite or converse mode of conduct or end-state of existence" (p. 5). In other words, *values* involve that which is intrinsically worthwhile, or worthy of esteem for its own sake, and reflect the value holder's worldview, culture, or understanding of the world. They arise from individuals' experience and interactions with their culture, the world, and the people around them, such as their parents, friends, religious leaders, and neighbors. Thus, values vary across individuals, but are likely to vary less among persons growing up within similar systems, such as specific cultures or religions. A *value system* is a hierarchical ranking of the degree of preference for the values expressed by a particular person or social entity.

Values usually are thought of as involving a simple expression of personal interest or preference, such as a preference for an automatic rather than a standard transmission in a new car. Actually, values are more complex in that they involve a set of beliefs that include evaluative, emotional, and existential aspects. That is, there are elements of goodness, obligation, or requirement; positive or negative affective orientation; and a sense of the meaningfulness of the situation or choice attached to the object of the valuing process. Values are not directly observable, but are expressed verbally or in how they guide human choice and action through the value preferences expressed in human choices and goals.

There are many systems for describing values including Rokeach's (1973) 18 values reflecting desirable end-states, and Allport, Vernon, and Lindzey (1960) who saw 6 basic values or evaluative attitudes reflected in personality types: theoretical, economic, aesthetic, social, political, and religious. Similarly, Frankena (1963) identified eight distinct realms of value, only one of which is related to ethics: morality, art, science, religion, economics, politics, law, and manner or custom. In all these cases, values can be either *moral* or *nonmoral* in nature; that is, they may or may not involve preferences concerning what is morally right or wrong. For example, a person's choice to become a vegetarian might be based on nonmoral or moral value grounds. It might stem from belief in the importance of social status and a wish to follow lead of a charismatic friend or be "politically correct" (nonmoral values of manner or custom); or the choice might be based on a spiritual belief that all forms of life should be respected and protected from discomfort and violence (moral). Thus, it can be seen that any situation, choice, or action may be valued or prized in a number of disparate and possibly competing ways by different individuals or groups. It also is possible for one individual to hold two or more values that conflict about a particular object or situation, resulting in some level of dissonance if the person becomes aware of the conflicting values. For instance, the vegetarian who believes in the sanctity of all life forms may also value respect for family tradition and a mother's wishes (thus eating Thanksgiving turkey once a year at the family gathering).

The process of socializing neophyte students into a profession can also be construed as introducing them to the profession's specific core values. This process can be seen as a way of assisting these individuals in adopting a specific subculture or worldview that will enhance their professional perspective and judgment, and ability to function responsibly in their new roles. Rokeach and Regan (1980) noted two dimensions of values relevant to counseling: (a) standards of competency and standards of morals, and (b) terminal (desirable end-states) and instrumental (behaviors useful to reach end-state) values. Some examples of terminal values would be wisdom (more desirable than foolishness), truthfulness (more desirable than deceit), and freedom (more desirable than enslavement). Instrumental values concern those idealized or desirable types of behavior useful to attaining the end-state. They are not necessarily good in and of themselves. For example the instrumental value of industriousness may serve either a thief or Mother Theresa, but to very different ends. These dimensions add richness to the considerations of ethics concepts. Thus, unethical practices can be seen as stemming from either ignorance and inadequate training or supervision (violations of the value concerning standards of competency), as well as from personal profit motive, need for self-enhancement or the need to maintain power and status (terminal values). These latter motivations may be related to personal values that are nonmoral values, and are in conflict with the moral values embedded in the profession's values as reflected in its standards regarding particular situations.

Another important differentiation involves acknowledging that some values can be seen as universal, but not necessarily absolute. Historically, anthropologists see such values as the prohibition against killing, a prohibition on marriage or sexual intercourse between members of the immediate family, respect for ownership of property, and truthfulness as values shared by most human cultures (Brandt, 1959; Kluckhorn, 1951). Nevertheless, there are culturally permissible exceptions under specific circumstances that are allowed, such as killing to defend one's own life, or in battle in a war. This acknowledgment is not tantamount to ethical relativism or situational ethics. These exceptions are related to limited circumstances that make the exception permissible. Further, these exceptions are widely understood and supported by the entire cultural group for all people in similar circumstances.

Values in Counseling

Historical Perspective.   The questions of whether we share a common ground of shared values as members of the human race, and the degree to which the values of the counselor should or do influence our clients constitute some of the most troublesome debates in counseling. These issues date to the beginning of psychotherapy's development with Sigmund Freud's psychodynamic approach. In his system of therapy, the therapist was to work assiduously to maintain an absolute neutrality of response to the patient, thus providing a "blank screen" on which the patient can project and play out intrapsychic conflicts. A transference reaction was the desired result of this process. Patients would project the persona of an important figure from their earlier psychic development and engage this persona in reparatory work through playing out conflicts with this figure in the therapist-patient relationship. Therefore, it was seen as essential that characteristics of the therapist, including values and morals, should not be conveyed to the patient; thereby encouraging the projection process.

The substance of orthodox Freudian psychodynamic therapy as well as the enthusiastic adoption of the objective, scientific paradigm, continued to influence the development of all psychotherapy. This legacy resulted in a longterm supposition that counselors and therapists could and should be value-neutral, a belief that persisted into the 1950s (Ginsberg & Herma, 1953; Walters, 1958). Later, authorities began acknowledging the value-based nature of counseling (London, 1964; Bergin, 1985; Pietrofesa, Hoffman, Splete, & Pinto, 1978). Education and research in the profession have continued to value and develop the scientific and technical aspects of professional practice in subsequent decades. However, it is just as critical for counselors to acknowledge and develop ability to address the moral and value dimensions of their expertise (London, 1986; Corey, Corey, & Callanan, 1993). Herr and Niles (1988) noted that it appears that the counselor's values tend to determine the process of counseling; while the values of the client determine the content of counseling. A few philosophical systems that may influence the values expressed in counseling were discussed in Chapter 4. In addition, the content of the problem the client brings to counseling may be value-laden in and of itself for both the counselor and client, such as whether to have premarital sex. Clients also may attempt to camouflage or avoid certain issues affecting them due to struggles with their value systems, such as refusing to discuss the possibility that they may be struggling with issues of gender identity. Some examples of the myriad value-charged issues clients may bring to counseling are provided in Figure 5–1. Counselors should examine their own values and biases in these areas.

The counselor's personal and professional value systems will influence the course of the counseling interaction through a wide range of mechanisms. Examples include (a) if and how the client will be diagnosed, (b) whether certain topics will be focused on or discussed at all through either specific direction or more subtle verbal or nonverbal reinforcement, (c) which goals are considered possible or appropriate for the counseling work they will do, and (d) how they will be evaluated (Strupp, 1980).

abortion	assisted suicide	pre- or extra-marital sex
sexual identity issues	child custody	spousal abuse
substance abuse	illegal means of support	interracial relationships
cross-racial adoption	unsafe sexual activity	child neglect/abuse
controversial religious	racist behavior/attitudes	dishonesty
beliefs	unwed pregnancy	discipline of children
birth control	cosmetic surgery	death and dying
infertility/childlessness	gang membership	suicide
unusual sexual practices		

Figure 5–1
Value-Charged Issues in Counseling

Counselors' Values in the Relationship.   It is recommended strongly that counselors become intensely involved in assessing their own values and how they affect the counseling process (Corey, Corey, & Callanan, 1993; Herr & Niles, 1988). It is increasingly considered unethical for counselors to *impose* their values on a client (Corey, Corey, & Callanan, 1993). However, it may be helpful for the counselor to *disclose* his or her values. Recently, it has been recommended more often that counselors disclose their values and philosophical orientations directly to clients. This discussion might occur either within the context of specific issues that arise within the course of counseling or as part of the process of informed consent and professional disclosure at the outset of counseling (Tjelveit, 1986). As with any advanced counseling technique such as the use of confrontation, it is important for the counselor to disclose values carefully. This disclosure should be intentional, focused on enhancing the client's process, and presented in an open, nonjudgmental manner that carries with it the sense that these values may be accepted or rejected without risking the counseling relationship.

The values the client might experience include the personal values the counselor might hold as well as a more general body of shared values. Traditionally these shared values have been variously described as *mental health values* (Jensen & Bergin, 1988) or *essential therapeutic values* (Strupp, 1980). A national survey by Jensen and Bergin (1988) examined counselors' degree of consensus with key mental health values including autonomy and independence, skill in interpersonal communication, honesty, and self-control. They did find a substantial consensus among surveyed counselors that these are central counseling values.

The essential therapeutic values described by Strupp (1980) are that people (a) have rights and privileges and responsibilities, (b) have the right to personal freedom, (c) have responsibilities to others, (d) should be responsible for conducting their own affairs, as much as they are able, (e) should have their individuality respected, (f) should not be dominated, manipulated, coerced, or indoctrinated, and (g) are entitled to make their own mistakes and learn from them. Values may be observed interpersonally within the counseling relationship through studying the perceived operation of (a) *support,* the receiving of encouragement, understanding, and kindness from others, (b) *conformity,* the following of rules and observation of societal regulations, (c) *recognition,* the attraction of favorable notice and being considered important, (d) *independence,* seeing oneself as being free to make one's own decisions and acting autonomously, (e) *benevolence,* the experience of sharing, helping, and acting generously toward others, and (f) *leadership,* having the sense of responsibility, power, and authority over others (Gordon, 1976). Clearly, the values of counselors are expressed through specific behaviors affecting the client in the counseling relationship.

In addition to these more global value orientations, some theoretical orientations embody and promulgate specific philosophical or value positions as part of the therapeutic system. To the degree that counselors follow these specific systems of therapy, they will directly influence the philosophy and values of their clients, hopefully with the client's direct awareness and consent. Examples of such approaches and associated values include (a) Adlerian Psychotherapy's emphasis on social striving and social interest, (b) Reality Therapy and its focus on personal responsibility and the quality of the individual lifestyle, (c) Existential Therapy and its emphasis on learning this particular philosophical system, including such concepts as self-determination and freedom with responsibility, and (d) Ellis' Rational–Emotive Therapy with its goal of indoctrinating the client with a new set of rational beliefs and values. The theoretical approach and philosophy or value system counselors select for their practices constitute another way in which the counselors' value systems will influence their clients. Therefore, the counselor's theoretical and philosophical system and underlying value structure should be included in the informed consent procedures used at the outset of the relationship. These issues should be thoroughly processed in terms that clients can understand to ensure that the prospective clients truly comprehend these aspects of counseling and how they might influence their treatment, as well as whether they are compatible with their own value system.

Research has demonstrated that the degree to which the values of the counselor and client are congruent influences the outcome of the counseling process. For example, clients who adopted values like their counselors' tend to have more positive outcomes (Beutler, Pollack, & Jobe, 1978; Landfield & Nawas, 1964; Welkowitz, Cohen & Ortmeyer, 1967). This important effect of differing counselor and client value systems is but one reason for the increasing attention to the importance of the counselor being culturally sensitive. Counselors must become aware of the value systems of their clients from different cultures and of their own cultural assumptions and biases. They also must be willing and able to apply the skills necessary to accommodate and work across these diverse cultural perspectives (Sue, 1996; Pederson, 1985).

Values Clarification, Valuing, and Moral Discussion

How can counselors best prepare themselves to recognize their values and the implications of these values in their work? This task can be daunting. However, three general processes have been developed to assist in this task of preparing counselors to work with their value systems and those of their clients: (a) values clarification, (b) the valuing process, and (c) moral discussion.

Values Clarification

The work of Raths, Harmin, and Simon (1966; 1978) sparked a tremendously successful movement among educators, counselors, other helping professionals, and even the public that focused attention on the importance and understanding of values. The work of these scholars addressed the vacuum that many people felt in the 1950s in terms of establishing a sense of meaning and importance of values within their lives and work. This movement appeared to be a reaction to the value-neutral influence of the scientific tradition as well as the increasing popularity of the humanistic philosophical and therapeutic movements of the late 1950s to the 1970s. The contemporary work of Rogers, Perls, Maslow, and others encouraged self-determination, examination of one's own perspectives, and the search for personal meaning and truth through self-examination (Kinnier, 1995). It is within that context that Raths, Harmin, and Simon (1966), noted that many individuals are unaware of the values they hold and suffer from the lack of this focus in their personal and professional relationships and even in the sense of who they are.

Values clarification helps individuals clarify what they believe through a method that focuses on the *process* surrounding assigning value rather than on the *content* of what is valued (Raths, Harmin, & Simon, 1966). There are distinct steps in the values clarification process involving the three main functions of prizing, choosing, and acting on one's values (Figure 5–2). Values chosen through this process are considered *clarified values.*

Figure 5–2
The Values Clarification Process
Source: From *Values Clarification* (p. 19) by S. B. Simon, L.W. Howe, & H. Kirschenbaum, 1978, New York: Dodd, Mead & Co.

Prizing beliefs and behaviors

1. prizing and cherishing
2. publicly affirming, when appropriate

Choosing beliefs and behaviors

3. choosing from alternatives
4. choosing after consideration of consequences
5. choosing freely

Acting on beliefs

6. acting
7. acting with a pattern, consistency and repetition

The box below lists activities you might try that would be consistent with this tradition. Remember that the recommended approach involves a group discussion and processing of your work. In that process you might benefit from the open, thought-provoking discussion of your peers and the opportunity to examine the consequences of your position and to publicly affirm your beliefs.

Countless individuals have taken part and benefited from this type of encounter with their own and others' value systems over the years. The opportunities to examine countless aspects of our personal and professional relationships and lifestyle choices abound in this approach. It is possible to stimulate lively discussion and serious self-examination and tailor the activities to the concerns and needs of quite disparate types of people. It is possible to examine many aspects of being a counselor in this manner as well. For example:

- What is your ideal type of client to work with? Why? Your most dreaded? Why?

- What makes me happiest about my work as a counselor? Over what do I become the most upset or afraid?

- Who is the living person who has most influenced your work? Why and how?

- Who is the historical or prominent celebrity figure who has most influenced your work? Why and how?

What Are Some of My Values?

Activity 1. Imagine that your doctor has told you you have a virulent form of cancer and will be dead soon. This afternoon you have decided you will write your own eulogy. What are the unique traits or meaningful accomplishments that you especially want to include? Why are they particularly important to you? Which one of them is the *most important* of them to you? Why? Which one is most important to your parents? To your spouse, partner, or closest friend? Do these perspectives differ? Why or why not?

Activity 2. Imagine you are in a longstanding relationship with your partner that is very happy, except for one thing—you and your partner are not able to have a biological child despite wanting one badly. You have decided to adopt a child, but are not able to receive a healthy infant of your own race. You are offered the opportunity to choose from among the following babies: a biracial baby, a baby that is moderately mentally retarded, a baby whose biological mother is HIV positive, a 2-year-old who appears to be hyperactive, a child with facial deformities that can only be partially corrected by surgeries, and a toddler who survived the murder–suicide of his biological parents. Would you adopt one of these children or choose not to have a child? If you would adopt, which child would you select and why? For each of the children you did not select, what was your reasoning?

- What is the biggest threat to your effectiveness and why?
- What is the greatest boost to your effectiveness and why?
- What am I proudest of about myself as a counselor? Ashamed?

Values Conflict Resolution and Valuing

Values Conflict Resolution.   Clearly, the ways in which human experience can be explored through values clarification are vast. Nevertheless, values clarification began to lose favor during the 1980s. The most common areas of concern involve the apparently value-neutral position of the group leader or teacher. Many have voiced concern that this experience may create a permissive, self-absorbed atmosphere, and in its extreme, allow abusive or abhorrent values to go unchallenged. Kinnier (1995) suggested that religious conservatism, political conservatism, a therapeutic paradigm shift away from humanistic philosophy, and the inherent flaws within the theory itself are the major forces that have dampened earlier enthusiasm for values clarification. He noted that the core concepts are worth retaining, and recommended several changes to resolve specific problems and extend the usefulness of this approach. Kinnier (1995) forwarded the idea of focusing on one concrete and specific values conflict at a time in a specific area of the person's life because people do not effectively evaluate values in single, abstract form. The emphasis should not be on rank-ordering values, but rather on determining which values are in conflict and the degree of conflict, as well as arriving at an overall statement of how the key values in conflict can be reconciled. This would provide a more specific goal to the process—resolution of a specified values conflict—and thus Kinnier (1995) suggested how more effective interventions could be tailored to assist in this conflict resolution (Table 5–1). The interventions suggested are divided between rational and intuitive-type foci to accommodate differing personal styles of those in conflict, and methods for evaluating these interventions are discussed.

In addition to these concerns about how the process was conceptualized and applied, several authorities reviewed the effectiveness of values clarification in values or moral education. Based on their critical review of the literature in this area, two leading proponents of moral education (Leming, 1993; Lickona, 1991) considered the moral discussion approach of Lawrence Kohlberg (1981) rather than values clarification (Raths, Harmin, & Simon, 1966) to be successful in moral education.

Valuing.   Other issues have arisen as counselors attempt to apply the individualistically oriented concepts of values clarification to group or marriage and family counseling issues. More and more, the role of interdependence in healthy human relationships and the social, political, and cultural context of the individual's experience are becoming an important aspect of the counseling therapeutic and theoretical worldviews beyond the scope of more limited specialty area perspectives. For example Sue (1996) noted that counseling practices that impose monocultural value systems or biases on clients from diverse cultural backgrounds are discriminatory and unethical.

Table 5–1
Strategies for Intrapersonal Values Conflict Resolution

Rational	Intuition-Enhancing
Defining the conflict clearly	Emotional focusing
Gathering information systematically	Brainstorming/Free association
Comparing alternatives & considering consequences logically	Life review
Eliminating alternatives systematically	Psychodrama
	Guided imagery into hypothetical focus
Being vigilant for maladaptive affect regarding the conflict, resolution, or both (e.g., excessive worry, postdecisional regret, irrational beliefs) and using cognitive restructuring, emotional inoculation, or stress-reduction techniques to counter maladaptive affect	Personal rituals
	Incubation (e.g., Vision Quest, meditation)
	Self-confrontational exercises such as the devil's advocate or the two-chair exercise, and confrontation with one's own mortality that involves both rational discourse and a focus on affective reactions

Source: From "A Reconceptualization of Values Clarification: Values Conflict Resolution" by R.T. Kinnier, 1995, *Journal of Counseling & Development, 74*, 18–24. Copyright 1995 by American Counseling Association. Reprinted by permission.

Marriage and family counselors have long struggled with issues of reconciling the conceptualization of the individual's values with those in the relationships of the group or family as a wholistic entity. Doherty and Boss (1991) reviewed the literature on value issues and ethics in the practice of marriage and family and notes that the idea that value neutrality on the part of therapist is no longer viable, and the emphasis in the field should be on accommodating values within the therapeutic process. Thomas (1994) provided a model of value analysis within marriage and family counseling that is an attempt to meld personal and systematically oriented value systems in addressing value dilemmas. He noted that counselors must analyze and reconcile values at (a) the individual level of the counselor microsystem, (b) the family level of the client's microsystem, and (c) the level of the overlapping counseling process itself (mesosystem). These operations are embedded in the context of societal values surrounding the dilemma (macrosystem). While this analysis may be couched in the marriage and family counseling paradigm, it is important for counselors in all settings to consider contextual or hierarchical levels that affect their ethical and values analysis (Tarvydas & Cottone, 1991). Sue (1996) called for a recognition that systems interventions will be necessary for ethical practice as counselors recognize that clients often have experiences embedded in the systems in which they are nested.

Valuing or the *negotiation of values* is a model and practice that has grown out of these concerns for reconciling these disparate and often competing values orientations and better accommodates forces of social change as expressed in various social and cultural value changes (Huber, 1994). Huber (1994) described the valuing process as one in which the counselor:

> Negotiates with a client in emphasizing certain values previously de-emphasized, and at the same time in relegating other values to the background. Within the context of the therapist-client negotiation, values evolve with accompanying behavioral changes that are compatible with values changes. Essentially, the therapist and client come together in negotiating a common world of less pain and conflict...Valuing recognizes that when therapist and client come together, they can negotiate a new, common system containing elements of both subsystems as well as unique properties arising from their interactions. (pp. 235–236)

Counselors must acknowledge several implications in their practice to enact such an approach to reconciling values. Taken together, these assumptions constitute a valuing perspective and worldview that create the conditions for this more interactive alliance around a particular values perspective. Huber (1994) described these key assumptions based on the earlier work of Dell (1983). The practitioner must recognize that:

1. *No such phenomenon as an absolute value* exists that is objectively true or good. Rather, values are a result of the person's processing or reaction of a system's values.

2. Every person must *take responsibility* for selecting, interpreting, and holding their own values, and thus no one can be held ultimately responsible for changing another's values.

3. Therapists must accept responsibility for the tendency to *pathologize their clients,* or to see them in terms of their pathologies or problems, thus de-emphasizing the role of their own values in the process.

4. Counselors must accept that *"what is, is."* They must allow clients to be accepted for who they are, rather than being judged as bad or sick because of behaviors that do not conform to the counselor's values or preferences. In addition to these assumptions, values negotiation or valuing involves several process-related components.

The value assumptions described above are only working assumptions and must be examined critically, Nevertheless, these principles, if they are acknowledged and incorporated within the work of the valuing process, will allow valuing to occur in a constructive and productive manner. The core components of valuing are (a) recognition of mutual obligations and entitlements within the relationships among the parties, or the "give and take" of human interactions, (b) the acknowledgment of those things to which others are entitled, and the valid claims of others, and (c) the balance of fairness (Huber, 1994). If obligations, entitlements, and claims are all taken together and are in balance relatively, then the climate is operating that will facilitate the balance of fairness in terms of values issues in the relationship. While attending to these principles and the valuing process within the counseling relationship may appear to add greatly to its complexity, in reality these considerations recognize and respect the truly shared nature of this important relationship between diverse, autonomous beings. Values issues that arise between counselor and client from the dazzlingly numerous sources of interpersonal diversity are not only accommodated, but have the potential to enrich the counselor, client, and their relationship if they are directly addressed within the valuing process.

Moral Discussion and Levels of Development

As one of the key figures in developmental psychology and the philosophy of morality, Kohlberg (1964; 1971) has led in the understanding of the moral development of children and adults in this century. His work provides a way in which the important process of values education or clarification can be extended and enriched, through providing an understanding of the moral perspectives that underlie these value choices. Kohlberg's work presents a theoretical understanding of how moral reasoning develops and relates values to moral growth. Concerns about the seeming relativity of values in the values clarification are removed in the Kohlberg system, by interpreting moral choice within a particular, developmental moral system that holds justice as the core concept of morality. In other words Kohlberg's theory helps one understand value choices within the context of how people develop higher levels of moral judgment (Reimer, Paolitto, & Hersch, 1983).

The work of Kohlberg (1964; 1971) is drawn from Piaget's developmental psychology, which focused on the reasoning processes underlying the behavior involved in the cognitive developmental stages of children. Similarly, Kohlberg focused specifically on the reasoning processes underlying the behaviors associated with moral development. He also assumed a universal, absolute core of morality that provides structure to this reasoning process. Kohlberg maintained that all human societies believe in certain core moral values, even though there may be moral debates and cultural differences regarding their interpretations: (a) laws and values, (b) conscience, (c) personal roles of affection, (d) authority, (e) civil rights, (f) contract, trust, and justice in exchange, (g) punishment, (h) the value of life, (i) property rights and values, and (j) truth. Kohlberg spent his career studying how moral stages are organized and learned. Kohlberg views children as forming their own moral philosophies and systems as they are exposed to and grapple with moral experiences and dilemmas. This process is creative and is an attempt to make sense out of the information and experiences to which people and the culture surrounding the individual expose the person. It is considered optimal to expose people to these situations and assist them in processing them for themselves within the context of the moral system. Kohlberg and Wasserman (1980) recommended that ethical behavior can best be encouraged by (a) exposing people to the higher stages of moral development, (b) introducing them to irreconcilable ethical dilemmas, thus stimulating awareness and dissatisfaction with the lower, less-sophisticated levels of reasoning, and (c) providing a supportive, therapeutic environment in which the situations and analyses can be freely processed. Van Hoose and Kottler (1985) noted that the counseling session is a likely environment for this process.

This system of moral development stages has been described as Kohlberg's greatest contribution to the study of ethics (Van Hoose & Kottler, 1985), and Van Hoose and Paradise (1979) have adapted them to describe the stages of ethical

Stage I. Punishment Orientation   Counselor decisions, suggestions and courses of action are based on a strict adherence to prevailing rules and standards, i.e., one must be punished for bad behavior and rewarded for good behavior. The primary concern is the strict attention to the physical consequences of the decision.

Stage II. Institutional Orientation   Counselor decisions, suggestions, and courses of action are based on a strict adherence to the rules and policies of the institution or agency. The correct posture is based on the expectations of higher authorities.

Stage III. Societal Orientation   The maintenance of standards, approval of others, and the laws of society and the public characterize this stage of ethical behavior. Concern is for duty and societal welfare.

Stage IV. Individual Orientation   The primary concern of the counselor is for the needs of the individual while avoiding the violation of laws and the rights of others. Concern for law and societal welfare is recognized, but is secondary to the needs of the individual.

Stage V. Principle or Conscience Orientation   Concern for the individual is primary with little regard for the legal, professional, or societal consequences. What is right, in accord with self-chosen principles of conscience and internal ethical formulations, determines counselor behavior.

Figure 5–3

Stages of Ethical Orientation

Source: From *Ethics in Counseling and Psychotherapy: Perspectives in Issues and Decision Making* (p. 117) by W.H. Van Hoose and L.V. Paradise, 1979, Cranston, RI: The Carroll Press.

orientation for counselors. They assumed that counselors, as do all persons, initially mature through stages of development within the context of age and situation-related experiences. Through insight and self-awareness they challenged counselors to identify and explore their individual rationale for particular value or ethical choices to stimulate themselves in reaching more sophisticated levels of ethical reasoning. These stages of ethical orientation presented by Van Hoose and Paradise (1979) are (a) punishment, (b) institutional, (c) societal, (d) individual, and (e) principle or conscience (See Figure 5–3 for descriptions of the stages' characteristics. You may wish to think about the last ethical dilemma you faced, how you responded to it, and at what level your thinking was on this matter). The individual's level of ethical orientation can be thought of as forming that person's intuitive sense of moral judgment. The counselor would use this first general level of orientation or moral thinking to consider ethical dilemmas as described by Kitchener (1984), and discussed within the decision-making arena described in Chapter 6.

In the context of this theoretical framework, a number of assumptions regarding ethical behavior follow: (a) counselor's functioning is not solely at one stage, since this functioning may be affected by situational, educational, and other variables; (b) the orientations are qualitatively discrete stages, and they reflect a continuum of ethical reasoning; (c) the basis for ethical judgment is characterized by the dominant stage of ethical orientation; (d) stages are continuous and overlapping, which suggests development toward higher levels; (e) development in ethical judgment is forward and irreversible, but specific ethical actions need not be so; and (f) internalized ethical conflict may be generated by discrepancies between ethical reasoning and action associated with situational influences (VanHoose & Paradise, 1979). While all stage theories can be criticized for certain structural limitations (e.g., not accommodating individual varia- tions in patterns movement between stages), the stages of ethical orientation for coun- selors presented by VanHoose and Paradise (1979) continue to provide a useful frame- work for counselors to think about their moral development. Counselors may be assisted by realizing that there are hierarchically and developmentally ordered benchmarks against which they measure their current ethical reasoning abilities. Additionally, be- cause their theory is oriented toward continued moral development through ongoing education within a specific moral and principled framework, it provides a positive and structured model for professional education and improvement.

Applying Ethical Principles in Counseling

Ethical principles are the higher order norms or fundamental assumptions that de- velop within society consistent with its moral principles and which constitute higher standards of moral behavior. Counseling and psychology have largely espoused prin- ciple ethics, the model of ethical reasoning traditionally dominant in medicine and bioethics. *Principle ethics* involves objectively applying a system of ethical rules and principles to determine what is the right or moral decision when an ethical dilemma arises. Several ethical principles have risen to prominence over the years as having particular importance for helping with ethical decision making in U.S. culture among helping professions. They can be thought of as "The Golden Five"—autonomy, benef- icence, nonmaleficence, justice (Beauchamp & Childress, 1983), and fidelity (Kitchener, 1984). Simply put, they involve the following obligations:

Autonomy	To honor the right to individual decisions
Beneficence	To do good to others
Nonmaleficence	To do no harm to others
Justice	To be fair, give equally to others
Fidelity	To be loyal, honest, and keep promises

These principles embody lofty concepts as well as practical considered judgments about those qualities that work to the greater good in experiences with others in so- ciety. Principle ethics involves reasoning about the dilemma or choice by *specifying* and *balancing* these principles in an ethical analysis to arrive at an ethical justifica- tion for an ultimate solution to the dilemma. Specifying involves determining and naming the principles that are involved in the situation being considered. The *bal- ancing* of principles involves weighing which principles are more applicable or important in the analysis (Meara, Schmidt, & Day, 1996). Because several principles or moral obligations are usually involved in a dilemma and they are based on well- accepted and generalizable values in society, these principles are said to have *prima facie* merit in the analysis; that is, these principles must be considered in every case and if set aside, valid and compelling reasons must be given. Usually, such reasons are based on the specific facts in the situation and the greater importance of other core principles to the issue. This process allows for maintaining the general structure of moral obligations within a society without thoughtlessly forcing its members into slavish, absolutist compliance with standards that do not fit specific situations well. The Golden Five principles form the substrate on which our most enduring professional ethical obligations are based.

Autonomy

Autonomy is the principle which involves having a right to self-determination of choice and freedom from the control of others. Kitchener (1984) noted that there is a difference between freedom of action and freedom of choice. In other words, while people should have freedom to make choices, their ability to act on these choices is limited by the autonomy of others. If a person's choice abridges the freedom or autonomy of another, as in the case of wishing to murder another, it would be ethical to deny the autonomy in that instance. Counselors create conditions of autonomy for their clients when they do not interfere unnecessarily in the clients' decisions; when they provide all necessary information to their clients in a manner they can understand; and when it is determined that the clients have the ability to use this information to assess their choices, plan them and carry them out (Howie & Gatens-Robinson & Rubin, 1992). In other words, the necessary conditions for autonomy are voluntariness, competence, and full disclosure of information. The specific professional practice responsibilities that are related to this principle are professional disclosure, informed consent, right to privacy and protection of confidentiality, and determination of competency for the types of decisions involved in the situation.

Beneficence and Nonmaleficence

The principles of beneficence and nonmaleficence are closely related, and in some ways represent different aspects of the same concept. *Beneficence* involves a more active concept of contributing to the well-being of others. At its most basic level, it involves the general social obligation to provide mutual aid to members of our society who are in need of assistance. This obligation for mutual aid applies as long as (a) doing so involves a significant need on the part of the other, (b) the person who might assist the other has some particular qualification, such as knowledge or skill to assist the other, (c) the action would have a high probability of succeeding, and (d) the risk or burden to the person rendering aid is not greater than that to the person needing aid (Beauchamp & Childress, 1983).

In addition to the obligation for beneficence all members of society hold, members of a profession such as counseling have additional obligations to assist their clients. The entire existence of a profession is based on the society's recognition of special skills and knowledge, as well as a purpose to help members of the society with certain types of problems and situations. Important professional duties stemming from beneficence would include the obligation to assure that professionals establish, reach, and maintain

1. The client is *actually* limited in his or her ability to act autonomously and to adequately assess his or her own interest. (The client is seriously depressed, mentally ill, uninformed, coerced, drugged, etc.).

2. The authority to act in the interest of another is based in a knowledge of the conditions promoting the clients *real* interests, which is superior to the client's own knowledge.

3. A serious effort has been made to know the particular personal interest of the client and to take those interests as primary.

4. The risk to the client is real and significant and the loss of autonomy is the minimum necessary to promote the good of the client.

Figure 5–4

Justifications for Paternalistic Beneficent Action

Source: From "Applying Ethical Principles in Rehabilitation Counseling" by J. Howie, E. Gatens-Robinson, and S.E. Rubin, 1992, *Rehabilitation Education, 6,* 45. Copyright 1992 by Elliot and Fitzpatrick. Reprinted by permission.

an appropriate level of competency in terms of their knowledge, skills, and ethical practices. Additionally they must balance their decisions to influence the client or actively undertake a course of action that in their professional judgment will result in increased growth or well being for the client against the possibilities that they might at the same time sacrifice some of the client's autonomy or do harm to the client. Counselors must particularly be cautioned against assuming a paternalistic or parentlike stance toward their clients. When working with clients of different backgrounds, classes, races, religions, or abilities, counselors must be ever cautious about assuming that they know better than the clients or their families what is in the clients' best interests. Howie, Gatens-Robinson and Rubin (1992) offer specific guidelines for determining when paternalistic beneficent action might be justified (Figure 5–4).

They make the point that being an expert does not automatically entitle the professional to the moral authority to take paternalistic action on behalf of a client. Counselors who discuss only traditional career choices with female clients because they assume that the clients would benefit more from such a career choice than from the challenges of one the counselor thinks is unusual for women may be taking a morally wrong action.

Nonmaleficence is one of the oldest moral principles in the professions, probably best known as the cornerstone of the Hippocratic Oath taken by ancient Greek physicians to "above all, do no harm." *Nonmaleficence* is the requirement that we refrain from any action that might cause harm, in addition to not intentionally harming others. This principle is often considered the most pressing obligation for professionals, in that their activities have the potential to do either good or harm. Often, as a result of the trust of the client and advanced knowledge of the counselor in the counseling relationship, the counselor has access to special information or opportunities to injure clients either intentionally or unintentionally.

Kitchener (1984) discussed the responsibilities involved in diagnosis of clients as an especially powerful occasion to help or to harm the client. The counselor must determine in conjunction with the client as much as possible, whether the benefits of diagnosis outweigh the possible harm of going through the assessment and diagnostic process. Because diagnosis is related closely to treatment planning, funding, and the effects of labeling, these are important concerns. Kitchener noted that the experience of distress or discomfort is often unavoidable, even necessary, during diagnosis and treatment, and this realization may make it difficult to discern what constitutes sufficient level of harm to justify nonpursuit of a particular course in counseling. It should also be noted that even counselors who do not diagnose clients directly are not absolved from concerns about diagnosis and misdiagnosis. In reality, psychiatrists, psychologists, and counselors who assign diagnoses often must rely on a variety of records, comments, evaluations, and judgments that are (or should be) conveyed to them to assist in making an appropriate diagnosis. Sometimes, it is important for the counselor to take steps to assure that their observations and information are included in this process, or that a diagnosis that appears to be inappropriate is reevaluated. The increased use of the managed health care and the medical model to access psychotherapy have resulted in heavy pressures on mental health professionals to provide diagnoses for funding of care. These pressures are likely to increase the incidence of misdiagnosis and overdiagnosis, while increasing the possibility of harm to our clients.

Justice

The concept of *justice* involves the idea of fairness and equality in terms of access to resources and treatment by others. Counselors are obligated to assure that their process, agencies, and services do not discriminate against others. They also must not operate in such a manner that they advance discrimination at the hands of others. This principle is usually involved in counseling in the sense of *distributive justice*, the issue of who has access to resources and services, which may be considered scarce (Howie, Gatens-Robinson, & Rubin, 1992). The policies and rules of agencies, institutions, eligibility criteria, laws, and social policies that affect the mental-health practice should all be examined regarding whether they meet acceptable criteria for just distribution. If counselors determine after appropriate analysis that serious inequalities exist, they must determine what types of advocacy both within and outside of the given system is needed to address the injustice and seriously consider undertaking advocacy efforts to remediate the situation.

Some criteria for distributive justice that might be considered include (a) equal shares, (b) distribution by need, (c) distribution by motivation or effort, (d) distribution by contribution of person, (e) free market exchange or purchase, (f) fair opportunity, or equalizing unequal opportunity (Howie, Gatens-Robinson, & Rubin, 1992). Therefore it is clear that the process of determining a model of justice for a particular purpose and justifying why a particular approach was taken is a complex and important aspect of enacting the ideal of justice. Counseling practices such as due process considerations, access to grievance processes, and techniques of systems intervention and advocacy are examples of activities related to this principle.

Fidelity

Promise keeping or keeping commitments are characteristics of the principle of *fidelity*. Other obligations include honesty and loyalty. Because the bond of trust in the counseling relationship is considered to be of utmost importance to its effectiveness, this principle holds particular meaning for individuals in counseling and the related professions. Indeed, many theorists, such as Rogers, place particular importance on the healing characteristics engendered by the very qualities nurtured by fidelity. Some interpretations of fidelity emphasize the nature of the promises made to clients, and the social contract between professional and client. However, reducing this concept to a legalistic concern that recognizes only specific, direct promises, and not those implied within the nature of the relationship, is not appropriate to the richness of the counselor–client relationship. Such counseling practices as professional disclosure, informed consent, maintenance of confidentiality, not misrepresenting or withholding the truth or lying, and avoiding or appropriately dealing with dual/multiple relationships are obligations that flow from the important principle of fidelity.

Principles and Codes of Ethics

These generalizable, higher-order justifications for moral action, the five ethical principles discussed in this chapter are drawn from broader sociocultural understandings of what is right and good as addressed in Chapter 4. Therefore, they have great explanatory power regarding how certain rules, such as professional codes of ethics, agree with the common sense and general sense of the moral principles of U.S. society. They are at the heart of any well-written ethical rule when subjected to deeper analysis.

Even though the various professions and professional specialties in counseling have many codes of ethics, they can all be subjected to analysis in terms of which ethical principles their canons and rules uphold. After conducting such an analysis, it is surprising and useful for harmonious cross-disciplinary collaboration that these codes are similar in their basic conceptualizations of ethical practices. Of course, differences exist in specific areas covered and how the details of the core obligations are discharged. Nevertheless, it can be said that the mental-health professions all endorse the core ethical obligations embodied in these five ethical principles.

The practice of selecting a particular rule from a code of ethics to analyze which ethical principles support it is a useful practice. This activity has been used by the Ethical Case Management Practice Training Program developed by Rubin and associates (Wilson, Rubin, & Millard, 1991). This analysis is helpful in strengthening the counselor's levels of familiarity and comfort with the application of these specific ethical principles. It also builds the ability to discern the principles that are behind any number of ethically charged rules, policies, or client situations (see box that follows). Of course, the application of the ethical principles is also a critical stage of the ethical decision-making process as described by many authorities and in Chapter 6.

Ethical Code Rules and Basic Principles

Check your ability to perceive the principles involved in ethical rules by reviewing the analyses in this activity box. To further your understanding, you might wish to select several additional rules from the ACA code of ethics as well as another code of ethics in which you are interested to practice determining which ethical principles underlie specific rules.

Exercise 1

Ethical Rule: ACA Code of Ethics B.1.a. Counselors respect their clients' right to privacy and avoid illegal and unwarranted disclosures of confidential information.

Ethical Principles: Autonomy, Beneficence, and Fidelity

Exercise 2

Ethical Rule: ACA Code of Ethics E.2.b. Counselors are responsible for the appropriate application, scoring, interpretation, and use of assessment instruments, whether they score and interpret such tests themselves or use computerized services.

Ethical Principles: Nonmaleficence, Beneficence, and possibly Justice if information gained will determine access to resources or services

Exercise 3

Ethical Rule: ACA Code of Ethics A.5.a. In the counseling relationship, counselors are aware of the intimacy and responsibilities inherent in the counseling relationship, maintain respect for clients, and avoid actions that seek to meet their personal needs at the expense of clients.

Ethical Principles: Fidelity and Nonmaleficence

Principle ethics and analysis are powerful tools that the counselor must learn to employ in the ethical decision-making process. There have been recent trends to question the exclusive reliance on principle ethics, most notably among feminist scholars and authorities in cross-cultural or multicultural studies. This critique is related to the perception that the cultural assumptions in principle ethics are heavily based on Western, scientific thought, and a generally male-oriented worldview. As a result, the study of ethical discourse is being enriched by the writings on the ethics of care and virtue ethics. These two perspectives offer alternative perspectives for considering ethical reasoning that hold the potential to better accommodate the positions of nonmainstream people, women, and persons from culturally different backgrounds. At this point, it is important to note that the ethics of care and the multicultural perspective can complement the traditional processes of principle ethics that has provided the bulk of ethical tradition within counseling.

Summary

In this chapter we have described values and the concepts related to them in ethical tradition. We discussed the evolving role of values in counseling, as well as three methods that counselors might use to enhance their use of values in their work: values clarification, moral discussion or moral reasoning, and values conflict resolution or negotiation. Finally, we outlined the five basic principles that underlie ethical analysis and decisions in the helping professions. Examples were provided of how they operate to support the rules found within ethical codes. In Chapter 6 on ethical decision-making you will be introduced to the process through which these various concepts become involved in making specific ethical decisions regarding your clients.

References

Allport, G. W., Vernon P. E., & Lindzey, G. (1960). *The study of values*. Boston: Houghton-Mifflin.

Beauchamp, T. L., & Childress, J. F. (1983). *Principles of biomedical ethics*. Oxford: Oxford University Press.

Bergin, A. E. (1985). Proposed values for guiding and evaluating psychotherapy. *Counseling and Values, 29*, 99–116.

Beutler, L. E., Pollack, S., & Jobe, A. (1978). Acceptance, values, and therapeutic change. *Journal of Consulting and Clinical Psychology, 46*, 198–199.

Brandt, R. (1959), *Ethical theory*. Upper Saddle River, NJ: Prentice Hall.

Corey, B., Corey, M. S., & Callanan, P. (1993). *Issues and ethics in the helping professions* (4th ed.). Pacific Grove CA: Brooks/Cole.

Dell, P. (1983). From pathology to ethics. *The Family Therapy Networker, 7*(6), 29–31, 64.

Doherty, W., & Boss, P. (1991). Values and ethics in family therapy. In A. S. Gurman & D. P. Kniskern (Eds.) *Handbook of family therapy:* Vol. 2. New York: Brunner/Mazel.

Frank, J. (1961). *Persuasion and healing*. New York: Schoken.

Frankena, W. K. (1963). *Ethics*. Upper Saddle River, NJ: Prentice Hall.

Ginsberg, S. W., & Herma, J. L. (1953). Values and their relationship to psychiatric principles and practice. *American Journal of Psychotherapy, 7*, 536–573.

Gordon, L. V. (1976). *Survey of interpersonal values: Revised manual*. Chicago: Science Research Associates.

Herr, E. L., & Niles, S. (1988). The values of counseling: Three domains. *Counseling and Values, 33*, 4–17.

Howie, J., Gatens-Robinson, E., & Rubin, S. E. (1992). Applying ethical principles in rehabilitation counseling. *Rehabilitation Education, 6*, 41–55.

Huber, C. H. (1994). Ethical, legal, and professional issues in the practice of marriage and family therapy (2nd ed.). Upper Saddle River, NJ: Merrill/Prentice Hall.

Jensen, J. P., & Bergin, A. E. (1988). Mental health values of professional therapists: A national interdisciplinary study. *Professional psychology: Research and Practice, 19*, 290–297.

King, M. L. Jr. (1968 February 4). Drum Major Instinct sermon. Given at Ebenezer Baptist Church, Atlanta, GA.

Kinnier, R. T. (1995). A reconceptualization of values clarification: Values conflict resolution. *Journal of Counseling & Development, 74*, 18–24.

Kitchener, K. S. (1984). Ethics in counseling psychology: Distinctions and directions. *Counseling Psychologist, 12*(3), 43–55.

Kluckhorn, C. (1951). Values and value-orientations in the theory of action: An exploration in definition and clarification. In T. Parsons & E. A. Shils (Eds.), *Toward a general theory of action* (pp. 338–433). Cambridge, MA: Harvard University Press.

Kohlberg, L. (1964). Development of moral character and moral ecology. In M. L. Hoffman & L. W. Hoffman (Eds.), *Review of child development research.* Vol. I. New York: Russell Sage Foundation.

Kohlberg, L. (1971). Moral development and the education of adolescents. In R. Purnell (Ed.), *Adolescents and the American high school.* New York: Holt, Rinehart & Winston.

Kohlberg, L. (1981). *Philosophy of moral development.* San Francisco, CA: Harper & Row.

Kohlberg, L., & Wasserman, E. R. (1980). The cognitive–developmental approach and the practicing counselor: An opportunity for counselors to rethink their roles. *Personnel and Guidance Journal, 59*, 559–568.

Landfield, A. W., & Nawas, M. M. (1964). Psychotherapeutic improvement as a function of communication and adoption of therapist's values. *Journal of Counseling Psychology, 11*, 336–341.

Leming, J. S. (1993). *Character education: Lessons from the past, models for the future.* Camden, ME: The Institute for Global Ethics.

Lickona, T. (1991). *Educating for character.* New York: Bantam.

London, P. (1986). *Modes and morals of psychotherapy,* 2nd ed. New York: Holt, Rinehart & Winston.

Meara, N. M., Schmidt, L. D., & Day, J. D. (1996). Principles and virtue: A foundation for ethical decisions, policies, and character. *The Counseling Psychologist, 24*(1), 4–77.

Mowrer, O. (1967). *Morality and mental health.* Chicago: Rand McNally.

Pederson, P. (Ed.). (1985). *Handbook of cross-cultural counseling and therapy.* Westport, CT: Greenwood.

Pietrofesa, J. J., Hoffman, A., Splete, H., & Pinto, D. (1978). *Counseling: Theory, research, and practice.* Chicago: Rand McNally.

Raths, L., Harmin, M., & Simon, S. (1966). *Values and teaching: Working with values in the classroom.* Upper Saddle River, NJ: Merrill/Prentice Hall.

Raths, L., Harmin, M., & Simon, S. (1978). *Values and teaching: Working with values in the classroom* (2nd ed.). Upper Saddle River, NJ: Merrill/Prentice Hall.

Reimer, J., Paolitto, D. P., & Hersch, R. H. (1983). *Promoting moral growth: From Piaget to Kohlberg.* New York: Longman.

Rokeach, M. (1973). *The nature of human values.* New York: Free Press.

Rokeach, M., & Regan, J. (1980). The role of values in the counseling situation. *Personnel and Guidance Journal, 58*, 576–583.

Shertzer, B., & Linden, J. (1979). *Fundamentals of individual appraisal: Assessment techniques for counselors.* Boston: Houghton-Mifflin.

Simon, S. B., Howe, L. W., & Kirshenbaun, H. (1978). *Values clarification: A handbook of practical strategies for teachers and students.* New York: Dodd, Mead, & Co.

Strupp, H. H. (1980). Humanism and psychotherapy: A personal statement of the therapist's essential values. *Psychotherapy: Theory, Research and Practice, 17*, 396–400.

Sue, D. W. (1996). Ethical issues in multicultural counseling. In B. Herlihy, & G. Corey, (Eds.), *ACA Ethical standards casebook* (5th ed.). Alexandria, VA: American Counseling Association.

Tarvydas, V. M., & Cottone, R. R. (1991). Ethical responses to legislative, organizational, and economic dynamics: A four-level model of ethical practice. *Journal of Applied Rehabilitation Counseling, 22*(4), 11–18.

Thomas, V. (1994). Value analysis: A model of personal and professional ethics in marriage and family counseling. *Counseling and Values, 38,* 193–202.

Tjelveit, A. C. (1986). The ethics of value conversion in psychotherapy: Appropriate and inappropriate therapist influence on client values. *Clinical Psychology Review, 6,* 515–537.

Van Hoose, W. H., & Kottler, J. A. (1985). *Ethical and legal issues in counseling and psychotherapy* (2nd ed.). San Francisco: Jossey-Bass.

Van Hoose, W. H., & Paradise, L.V. (1979). *Ethics in counseling and psychotherapy: Perspectives in issues and decision making.* Cranston, RI: The Carroll Press.

Walters, O. S. (1958). Metaphysics, religion, and psychotherapy. *Journal of Counseling Psychology, 5,* 243–252.

Welkowitz, J., Cohen, J., & Ortmeyer, D. (1967). Value system similarities: Investigation of patient/therapist dyds. *Journal of Consulting Psychology, 31*(1), 48–55.

Wilson, C. A., Rubin, S. E., & Millard, R. P. (1991). Preparing rehabilitation educators to deal with ethical dilemmas. *Journal of Applied Rehabilitation Counseling, 22*(1), 30–33.

Ethical Decision-Making Processes

Vilia M. Tarvydas

Clients require the services of professional counselors who are grounded in the awareness of their value-laden mission and who are willing and able to assist people through appropriate knowledge and competencies. The value-based nature of counseling and the ethical principles that derive from these values were discussed in Chapter 5. An understanding of these concepts is at the heart of the ethical decision-making skills needed in the day-to-day practice of counseling. This chapter presents an ethical decision-making model that will allow you to apply these concepts and the codes of ethics to your work intentionally and skillfully. Earlier chapters provided the definitions of key concepts in ethics, an introduction to the relevant codes of ethics, a discussion of the role of values and principles in ethics, and two extremes in ethical theory. This information should help you to more fully understand the components of the *Integrative Decision-Making Model of Ethical Behavior* as presented in this chapter. This chapter concludes the sections of this book that introduce basic ethical and professional concepts and issues in counseling. Part 3 will deal with challenges and emerging issues in ethics.

Ethical Judgment

The practice of counseling is an art as well as a science, requiring the practitioner to make both value-laden and rational decisions. Rather than being incompatible stances, both facts and values must be considered together if one is to make good decisions. Within ethical deliberation, the practitioner blends such elements as personal moral sensitivities and philosophies of practice with clinical behavioral objectivity and the quest for efficient care of clients.

The intent of an ethics code is to provide counselors with guidance for specific situations they experience in their practices. However, authorities have long recognized that ethics codes must be general enough that they apply across a wide range of practice settings. They also are reactive in nature; that is, they address situations that have already been part of the profession's experience (Mabe & Rollin, 1986; Kitchener, 1984). As a result, even with the knowledge of the profession's code of ethics, counselors may find that they do not have sufficient guidance to resolve the dilemma in question. They may find that the particular situation they face is not addressed in their code, is addressed by more than one code providing conflicting direction, or that conflicting provisions within one code appear to apply to the situation. It is for that reason that counselors must be prepared to exercise their professional judgment in ethics responsibly. *Ethical dilemmas are not so much a failure of ethical codes as a natural and appropriate juncture recognizing the importance of professional judgment.* In other words, the need to use ethical judgment is affirmation that one is involved in "practice of a profession," rather than "doing a job," however skilled.

To exercise professional judgment, counselors must be prepared to recognize underlying ethical principles and conflicts among competing interests, as well as to apply appropriate decision-making skills to resolve the dilemma and act ethically (Tarvydas, 1987; Kitchener, 1984; Francouer, 1983). Fortunately, professionals are assisted in this task by examination and refinement of their ordinary moral sense, as well as the availability of thoughtful models for the ethical decision-making process. Many components of ethical decision-making involve teachable, learnable skills, to supplement the professional's developing intuitive judgment.

Several models exist which explain and structure the process of ethical decision-making. Some prominent examples view the ethical decision-making process as (a) professional self-exploration (Corey, Corey, & Callanan, 1993), (b) a moral reasoning discourse (Kitchener, 1984), (c) the result of a moral developmental process (Van Hoose & Kottler, 1985), (d) a cognitive, problem-solving process (Forester-Miller & Davis, 1995), (e) a multidimensional, integrative psychological process (Rest, 1984), and (f) involving a hierarchy of four contextual levels that affect the process of decision-making (Tarvydas & Cottone, 1991). Generally, ethical decision-making models can be thought of as having the characteristics of either *principle* or *virtue* ethics (Corey, Corey, & Callanan, 1993). *Principle* ethics focuses on the objective, rational, cognitive aspects of the process. Practitioners who adhere to this perspective tend to view the application of universal, impartial ethical principles, rules, codes, and law as the core elements of ethics. *Virtue* ethics considers the characteristics of the counselors themselves as the critical element for responsible practice. Thus, proponents of virtue ethics approaches would tend to concern themselves more with counselors reflecting on and clarifying their moral and value positions. Additionally, they would examine other personal issues that might influence their ethical practice, such as unresolved emotional needs that might negatively affect their work with their clients. Preferred approaches to ethical decision-making should include both aspects (Meara, Schmidt, & Day, 1996; Corey, Corey, & Callanan, 1993). Among other positive contributions of such a synergistic approach, Meara, Schmidt, and Day (1996) and Vasquez (1996) speculated that the addition of virtue ethical perspectives may improve ethical conduct in multicultural and diverse interactions and settings.

The Integrative Decision-Making Model of Ethical Behavior

The Integrative Decision-Making Model of Ethical Behavior integrates the most prominent principle and virtue aspects of several decision-making approaches and introduces some contextual considerations into the process. It emphasizes the constant process of interaction between the principle and virtue elements, and places a reflective attitude at the heart of the process. The model also focuses on the actual production of ethical behavior within a specified context, rather than prematurely terminating analysis by merely selecting the best ethical course of action. This approach respects the importance of setting and environmental factors that are crucial in counseling. The model is shown in Table 6–1. It's origins and components will be discussed throughout the remainder of this chapter.

Conceptual Origins

The Integrative Model builds on several well-known decision-making models widely used by professionals in the mental health and counseling communities. Rest (1984) provided the Integrative Model with its core understanding of ethical decision-making as a psychological process involving distinct cognitive–affective elements interacting in each component. Cognitions and emotions are seen as unavoidably intertwined at each component of the decision-making process, and in the production of ethical behavior. Rest (1984) conceptualized ethical decision-making as more than a direct expression of moral or value traits, or stage in a moral developmental process. He emphasized considering the completion of ethical behavior as the necessary point for consideration, rather than merely arriving at a cognitive decision or intent to do an ethical act. Therefore Rest's (1984) ethical decision-making components and many of his considerations are the foundation of the Integrative Model as presented here.

The work of Kitchener (1984) provided other core elements to the Integrative Model. She made a useful distinction between the *intuitive* and *critical–evaluative* levels of ethical decision-making, thus providing a forum to incorporate the richness and influence of the everyday personal and professional moral wisdom into the individual professional's process of ethical decision-making. This personal and professional wisdom informs the first level of her process, the intuitive level. At that level, both nonconscious and conscious levels of awareness lead to decisions that call into play the individual's existing morals, beliefs, and experiences. These morals, beliefs,

Table 6–1
The Integrative Decision-Making Model of Ethical Behavior in Counseling

---

Stage I. *Interpreting the Situation through Awareness and Fact Finding*

Component 1   Enhance **sensitivity** and **awareness**

Component 2   Reflect to determine whether a **dilemma** or an **issue** is involved

Component 3   Determine the major **stakeholders** and their ethical claims in the situation

Component 4   Engage in the **fact finding** process

Stage II. *Formulating an Ethical Decision*

Component 1   Review the problem or **dilemma**

Component 2   Determine what ethical **codes, laws, ethical principles,** and **institutional policies and procedures** exist that apply to the dilemma

Component 3   Generate possible and probable **courses of action**

Component 4   Consider potential positive and negative **consequences** for each course of action

Component 5   **Consult** with supervisors and other knowledgeable professionals

Component 6   Select the best **ethical course** of action

Stage III. *Selecting an Action by Weighing Competing, Nonmoral Values*

Component 1   Engage in reflective recognition and analysis of **personal competing values**

Component 2   Consider **contextual influences** on values selection at the collegial, team, institutional, and societal levels

Stage IV. *Planning and Executing the Selected Course of Action*

Component 1   Figure out a reasonable **sequence of concrete actions** to be taken

Component 2   Anticipate and work out personal and contextual **barriers** to effective execution of the plan of action, and effective **counter measures** for them

Component 3   **Carry out, document,** and **evaluate** the course of action as planned

---

Source: Adapted from "Standards of Practice: Legal and Ethical" by Vilia M. Tarvydas, 1997, in T. F. Riggar & D. R. Maki (Eds.), *Rehabilitation Counseling: Profession and Practice,* Copyright 1997 by Springer Publishing Co. Used by permission.

and experiences that constitute our ordinary moral sense will also include professional learning and experiences. She noted that the intuitive level of process often is the professional's main decision-making tool when the situation is not perceived as novel, unusual, or requiring an unusual level of care. The intuitive level of analysis always constitutes the first platform of decision-making, even when the situation requires the more stringent level of analysis involved in the critical–evaluative level of consideration. Thus, a person's ordinary moral sense is relevant to one's ethical decision-making process, reinforcing the concerns raised by proponents of the virtue ethics perspective.

If the ethical issue is not resolved at the intuitive level, the counselor progresses to Kitchener's (1984) critical–evaluative level of ethical analysis. This level involves three hierarchical stages of examination to resolve the dilemma. At the first stage, the counselor seeks to determine if any laws or ethical rules exist that would provide a solution for the dilemma. If they do not exist, or provide conflicting dictates, the counselor progresses to the second stage by considering how the core ethical principles apply to the situation. The seminal work of Beauchamp and Childress (1983) identified autonomy, beneficence, nonmaleficence, and justice as the core ethical principles governing ethical behavior. Kitchener (1984) subsequently added fidelity to these core principles for helping professionals, resulting in five core ethical principles to be considered in ethical decision-making.

If counselors are still uncertain as to the appropriate ethical course of action, counselors proceed to the third stage—assessing the positions suggested by ethical theory. Patterson (1992) recommended that counselors should be concerned with normative ethical theory and may benefit from considering whether they would prefer their action to be decided based on a general or universal law. Kitchener (1984) suggested applying the "good reasons" approach in which counselors attempt to make a decision based on what they would wish for themselves, or someone dear to them. Another standard Kitchener suggested is to take the action that will result in the least amount of harm.

The final conceptual influence on the Integrative Model is the *four level model* of ethical practice introduced by Tarvydas and Cottone (1991). This approach extends consideration of the contextual forces acting on ethical practice beyond the singular focus of the individual practitioner in relationship to the individual client. The four levels are hierarchical, moving to increasingly broader level of social contexts within which ethical practice is influenced. The four levels are (a) the clinical counseling level, (b) the clinical multidisciplinary level, (c) the institutional/agency level, and (d) the societal resource/public policy level. The relationships among the levels are seen as interactive. Peak ethical efficiency and lowest levels of ethical stress are reached when each level holds compatible values and standards, or endorses a mutually acceptable mechanism for ethical dilemma resolution. The first or micro-level in the hierarchy is the traditionally central clinical counseling core, in which the counselor–client relationship is the focus. The second level is the clinical multidisciplinary team interaction. At this point, practitioner-to-practitioner dynamics are considered. Often team relationships and leadership, collaboration skills, and the interplay of the differing ethical codes and traditions becomes important to the process. At the third level, the institutional or agency context and its constraints enter into the process. Dictates of agency policy, practitioner–supervisor style and practices, and staffing patterns are factors that might have an influence. Corporate or administrative operations such as institutional goals, marketing strategies, and corporate oversight processes may also play a role. At the fourth or macro-level, the effects of overall societal resources and public policy have their considerations. Social concern for scarce health-care resources, the movement to managed care and the privatization of mental health care are examples of broad themes and related policies that may affect ethical practices at the practitioner level. Societal values related to such areas as independence and self-sufficiency, work and productivity, physical appearance, and other types of behavior do influence the work of counselors extensively (Gatens-Robinson & Rubin, 1995).

Themes and Attitudes

In addition to the specific elements or steps of the Integrative model, four underlying *themes* or *attitudes* are necessary for the professional counselor to enact. These attitudes involve mindfully attending to the tasks of (a) maintaining a stance of *reflection* concerning one's own awareness of personal issues, values, and decision-making skills, as well as extending effort to understand those of all others concerned with the situation, and their relationship to the decision-maker; (b) addressing the *balance* among various issues, people, and perspectives within the process; (c) maintaining an appropriate level of attention to the *context(s)* of the situation in question, allowing awareness of the counselor–client, treatment team, organizational, and societal implications of the ethical elements; and (d) seeking to use a process of *collaboration* with all rightful parties to the decision, but most especially the client.

By adopting these background attitudes of balance, reflection, context, and collaboration, counselors engage in a more thorough process that will help preserve the integrity and dignity of all parties involved. This will be the case even when outcomes are not considered equally positive for all participants in the process, as is often true in a serious dilemma when such attitudes can be particularly meaningful. Reflection is the overriding attitude of importance throughout the enactment of the specific elements of stages and components that constitute the steps of the Integrative Model. Many complex decision-making processes easily become overwhelming, either in their innate complexity, or in the real-life press of the speed or intensity or events. In the current approach, the counselor is urged always to "stop and think!" at each point in the process. The order of operations is not absolute, nor more important than being reflective and invested in a calm, dignified, respectful, and thorough analysis of the situation. It is not until we recognize that we are involved in the process and appreciate its critical aspects that we can call forth other resources to assist the process and persons within it. Such an attitude of reflection will serve the counselor well at all stages of this process.

Case Scenario 1

Themes & Attitudes

Jimmy W. is in fifth grade and has been sent to see you, his school counselor, by Mrs. James, his teacher. This has been a difficult year for you professionally and personally. You have felt overwhelmed by an increasing number of students assigned to you. You also have had difficulty concentrating since your rather acrimonious divorce that was finalized during the summer. Jimmy has continued to do good work in class since his parents' divorce eight months ago. However, Mrs. James has noticed that Jimmy tears up his worksheets and art projects as soon as they are graded and has not shown his usual enthusiasm for school work. She has talked to him about the situation, but Jimmy denies that anything is wrong. Jimmy finally confides to you that his mother will no longer allow him to send letters and his completed school work to his father who lives in another state. He misses his father and his correspondence with him; he also thinks his work is meaningless and not important enough to be seen by his dad. He asks you if you will send his letters and school work to his father occasionally. Jimmy finally gives you permission to discuss his concerns with his mother. Mother angrily forbids you to communicate with Jimmy's father in any way. She informs you that she is the sole custodial parent and guardian, and that Mr. W. moved away rather than "be bothered with the responsibility of Jimmy." She reluctantly allows you to continue counseling with Jimmy about his "behavior problems" in school, but not to raise his hopes about seeing or communicating with his father. While you will continue to provide supportive counseling to Jimmy, you consider the matter of contact with Mr. W. closed. By the end of the school year, you have not heard from Mr. or Mrs. W. and Jimmy's problems have not worsened. WERE YOU CORRECT?

PROBABLY NOT.   When you stop and reflect on this situation outside of the furor of the meeting with Jimmy and his mom, you realize that two factors probably clouded your thinking. The first factor was your own painful divorce and custody problems. The second factor involved recent situations in which your school principal criticized you before the school staff for refusing to reveal confidential information about a student's family financial matters to him in a controversial case. Your anger at your former spouse and your fear of the principal have blinded you to other questions you must explore. You may discover that either the mother has incorrectly reported the custody arrangements, or the father does have some legal right to the communication his son desires. Even if Mr. W. does not have a legal right to correspondence from his son, Jimmy's rights and desires must be considered primary, and his father may have some moral claim to continue contact with his son apart from the custody decree specifics. Although counseling must occur with parental consent, it might be possible to counsel Jimmy and his mom to preserve some acceptable type and level of contact. A greater ability to communicate might facilitate Jimmy's adjustment and future cooperative communication regarding other aspects of Jimmy's welfare. These deeper considerations would include themes of BALANCING the moral claims of all parties to the situation regardless of the legal aspects of the situation. It also introduces the attitude of COLLABORATION to the decisions involving Jimmy's well-being. None of these issues would have been available for your consideration unless you had first systematically practiced the attitude of REFLECTION about a decision you thought was obvious at first.

Elements

The specific elements that constitute the operations within the Integrative Model have four main *stages* with several *components* including the steps to be taken within each stage. As previously stated, the concepts summarized below are drawn in the main from the work of Rest (1984), Kitchener (1984), and Tarvydas and Cottone (1991).

Stage I: Interpreting the Situation Through Awareness and Fact Finding.   At this stage the primary task of counselors is to be sensitive and aware of the needs and welfare of the people around them, and the ethical implications of these situations. This level of awareness allows counselors to imagine and to investigate the effects of the situation on the parties involved and the possible effects of various actions and conditions. This research and awareness must also include emotional as well as cognitive and fact-based considerations. As with the case scenario, Jimmy may be best served by some contact with his father, assuming that the father is interested and not abusive. Four components constitute the counselors' operations in this stage. *Component 1* involves enhancing one's sensitivity and awareness. *Component 2* requires the counselor to reflect on what is known of the situation to determine whether any dilemma or issue seems to be involved. Rubin, Wilson, Fischer, and Vaughn (1991) set four characteristics that a situation must meet before it is considered an ethical dilemma:

> 1. A choice must be made between two courses of action. 2. There are significant consequences for taking either course of action. 3. Each of the two courses of action can be supported by one or more ethical principles. 4. The ethical principles supporting the unchosen course of action will be compromised. (p. 79)

Not every ethical situation rises to the level of an ethical dilemma. For example, there may be significant emotional turmoil or disatisfaction experienced by the counselor or client, but there may be only one course of action available that is supported by an ethical principle. Therefore, there is no true ethical dilemma in this situation, even though there may be a significant clinical issue to be resolved by the counselor and client.

In *Component 3* the counselor takes an inventory of the people who are major stakeholders in the outcome of the situation. It is important to reflect on any parties who will be affected and what their exact relationship is ethically and legally to the person at the center of the issue, the client. It is useful to imagine dropping a rock into a pond. The point of impact is where the central figure, the client, is situated. However, the client is surrounded by people at varying levels of closeness to them, such as parents, intimate partners, spouse, children, employer, friends, and neighbors. They radiate out from the client in decreasing levels of intimacy and responsibility to the client. The ethical claims on the counselor's level of duty is not uniform. Almost all codes of ethics in counseling make it clear that the client is the person to whom the first duty is owed, but there are others to whom the counselor has lesser, but important levels of duty. It is always important to determine whether any surrogate decision-makers for the client exist, such as a guardian or person with power of attorney, so that they may be brought into the central "circle of duty" early in the process. As with Jimmy in the case scenario, the mother must be counseled and the noncustodial parent does have many rights to contact and even decision-making authority in some jurisdictions. It is useful to be sensitive and proactive in working through situations where the legal relationships involved do not coincide with the social and emotional bonds between the client and other people involved in the dilemma. The final element in Stage I is *Component 4* in which the counselor undertakes an extensive fact-finding investigation of a scope appropriate to the situation. The nature of the fact-finding process should be carefully considered, and is not intended to be a formal investigative or quasilegal process. The intent is that the counselor should carefully review, understand the information at hand, and seek out new information. Only information that is appropriately available to a counselor should be involved. For example, information might be gained from such sources as further discussion with the client, contacts with family (with appropriate permission of the client), case records, expert consultation and reports, legal resources, or agency policy and procedures. As in Jimmy's case scenario, the exact legal nature of the father–son relationship and the mother–father relationship should be explored.

Stage II: Formulating an Ethical Decision.   This aspect of the process is most widely known by professionals, and many may erroneously think it is the end of the process. The central task in this stage is to identify which of the possible ethical courses of action appears to come closest to the moral ideal in the situation under consideration (Rest, 1984). Many decision-making models in other areas of counseling can be applied as a template at this stage, but the following components are drawn from the work of Van Hoose and Kottler (1985).

Component 1 suggests that the counselor review the problem or dilemma to be sure that it is clearly understood in light of any new information. *Component 2* directs the counselor to research the standards of law and practice applicable to the situation. This component includes Kitchener's (1984) attention to ethical codes, laws, and ethical principles; and Tarvydas and Cottone's (1991) concern for the team and organizational context in the examination of institutional policies and procedures to make mention of other useful areas for consideration. If you were the counselor in Jimmy's case scenario, you would need at this point to be sure that you were familiar with the requirements of the Family Educational Rights and Privacy Act of 1974 (see Chapter 11) to be sure what protections are afforded your counseling notes and what records about Jimmy would be released to Jimmy's parents upon their request. *Component 3* initiates the process of formally envisioning and generating possible and probable courses of action. As with all decision-making processes, it is important not to truncate this exploratory process by prematurely censoring the possibilities, or succumbing to a sense of being overwhelmed or limited in options. *Component 4* is the logical outgrowth of considering courses of action, in that positive and negative consequences are identified and assessed in light of the risks, as well as the material and personal resources available. In *Component 5* the counselor is reminded to consult with supervisors and trusted and knowledgeable colleagues for guidance, if this has not been done before this point. Professional standards of practice emphasize the importance of appropriate collegial consultation to resolve difficult clinical and ethical dilemmas. Research has also demonstrated that such consultations can have a significant influence on those seeking such consultation (Cottone, Tarvydas, & House, 1994). At this time, it is valuable to review the reasoning employed so far in working through the ethical dilemma, and the solutions and consequences envisoned to be sure that all potentially useful and appropriate considerations have been taken into account. Finally, the best ethical course of action is determined in *Component 6*.

Stage III: Selecting an Action by Weighing Competing, Nonmoral Values.   Many people would think the ethical decision-making process is concluded at the end of Stage II. This impression is limited in its realization of the many additional forces which may affect the counselor and result in the counselor not actually executing the selected ethical course of action. *Component 1* of Stage III interjects a period of reflection and active processing of what the counselor intends to do in view of competing, nonmoral values (Rest, 1984). For example, the counselor serving Jimmy in the case scenario might have realized upon reflection that the need to avoid controversy with the principal or the identifications with Jimmy's mother's anger with a noncustodial parent and wish to be seen by her as supporting the rights of a single mother may be competing with knowledge of what is legally or ethically right.

It is important that counselors allow themselves to become aware of the strength and attractiveness of other values they hold that may influence whether they will discharge their ethical obligations. If they are self-aware, they may more effectively and honestly compensate for their conflicted impulses at this point. Counselors may have strong needs for acceptance by peers or supervisors, prestige, influence, to avoid controversy, or to be financially successful. These value orientations may come into conflict with the course of action necessary to proceed ethically, and must be reconciled with the ethical requirements if the client is to be ethically served. On the other hand, counselors may place a high value on being moral or ethical, accepted as respected professionals with high ethical standards, or value the esteem of colleagues who place a high value on ethical professional behavior. Those forces should enhance the tendency to select ethical behavioral options. Therefore, *the importance of selecting and maintaining ethically sensitized and positive professional and personal cultures should be recognized as critical to full professional functioning* as the next component would suggest.

In *Component 2* counselors systematically inventory the contextual influences on their choices at the collegial, team, institutional, and societal levels. While this is not a simple process of weighing influences, it should serve as an inventory of influences that may be either dysfunctional or constructive for selecting the ethical course over other types of values present in these other interactions. Counselors may also use this type of information to think strategically about the influences they will need to overcome to provide ethical service in the situation. Beyond the immediate situation, it is important to recognize that counselors should control their exposure to contexts that consistently reinforce values that run counter to the dictates of good ethical practices. Jimmy's counselor in the case scenario might be influenced in one direction if she spends most of her time personally and professionally with staff who are primarily concerned with getting ahead in the school hierarchy and being seen favorably by the administration, in contrast with having a few strong relationships with colleagues who take great pride in their professional identities and reputations. This problem might result in terminating or curtailing certain relationships, changing employment, or selecting another aspect of counseling service to provide.

Stage IV: Planning and Executing the Selected Course of Action.   Rest (1984) described the essential tasks of this stage as planning to implement and executing what one plans to do. This operation includes *Component 1*, in which the counselor figures out a reasonable sequence of concrete actions to be taken. In *Component 2* the task is to anticipate and work out all personal and contextual barriers to effectively executing the plan. It is useful to prepare countermeasures for barriers that may arise. In the case scenario, if indeed Jimmy's father has a legal and ethical right as well as a personal interest in Jimmy, what barriers might arise if Jimmy is given the opportunity to contact his father? It is here that the earlier attention to other stakeholders and their concerns may suggest problems or allies to the process. Additionally, earlier consideration of the contextual influences in Stage III assist the counselor in this type of strategic planning. *Component 3* is the final step of this model in that it provides for the execution, documentation, and evaluation of the course of action as planned. Rest (1984) noted that the actual behavioral execution of ethics is often not a simple task, frequently drawing heavily on the personal, emotional qualities, and professional and interpersonal skills of the counselor. He mentions such qualities as firmness of resolve, ego strength, and social assertiveness. To this list could be added countless skills such as persistence, tact, time management, team collaboration, and conflict-resolution skills. Considerations are limited only by the characteristics and requirements of the counselor and specific situation involved. Clear and thorough documentation of the entire plan and the rationale behind it, and ethical decision-making steps taken in responding to the ethical dilemma as the process unfolds, is critical to protect the interests of both counselor and client. The information gained in this documentation process will prove critical to assisting in evaluating the effectiveness of the entire ethical decision-making process.

Summary

This chapter presented a model of an ethical decision-making process. As such, it provides counselors with a working schema of how theoreticians view ethical decision-making. The next section of this text will describe ethical challenges and emerging issues.

References

Beauchamp, T. L., & Childress, J. F. (1983). *Principles of biomedical ethics.* Oxford: Oxford University Press.

Corey, G., Corey, M. S., & Callanan, P. (1993). *Issues and ethics in the helping professions.* Pacific Grove, CA: Brooks–Cole.

Cottone, R. R., Tarvydas, V., & House, G. 1994). The effect of number and type of consulted relationships on the ethical decision making of graduate students in counseling. *Counseling and Values, 39,* 56–68.

Forester-Miller, H., & Davis, T. E. (1995). *A practitioner's guide to ethical decision-making.* Alexandria, VA: American Counseling Association.

Francouer, R. T. (1983). Teaching decision making in biomedical ethics for the allied health student. *Journal of Allied Health, 12,* 202–209.

Gatens-Robinson, E., & Rubin, S. E. (1995). Societal values and ethical commitments that influence rehabilitation service delivery behavior. In S. E.

Rubin & R. T. Roessler (Eds.), *Foundations of the vocational rehabilitation process* (pp. 157–174). Austin, TX: Pro-Ed.

Kitchener, K. S. (1984). Intuition, critical evaluation and ethical principles: The foundation for ethical decisions in counseling psychology. *The Counseling Psychologist, 12*(3), 43–55.

Mabe, A. R., & Rollin, S. A. (1986). The role of a code of ethical standards in counseling. *Journal of Counseling and Development, 64*, 294–297.

Meara, N. M., Schmidt, L. D., & Day, J. D. (1996). Principles and virtue: A foundation for ethical decisions, policies, and character. *The Counseling Psychologist, 24*(1), 4–77.

Patterson, J. B. (1992). Ethics and ethical decision making in rehabilitation counseling. In R. M. Parker & E. M. Szymanski (Eds.) *Rehabilitation counseling: Basics and beyond* (pp. 165–193). Austin, TX: Pro-Ed.

Rest, J. R. (1984). Research on moral development: Implications for training psychologists. *The Counseling Psychologist, 12*(3), 19–29.

Rubin, S. E., Wilson, C. A., Fischer, J., & Vaughn, B. (1991). *Ethical practices in rehabilitation: A series of instructional modules for rehabilitation education programs.* Carbondale, IL: Southern Illinois University–Carbondale, Rehabilitation Institute.

Tarvydas, V. M. (1987). Decision-making models in ethics: Models for increased clarity and wisdom. *Journal of Applied Rehabilitation Counseling, 18*(4), 50–52.

Tarvydas, V. M., & Cottone, R. R. (1991). Ethical responses to legislative, organizational and economic dynamics: A four level model of ethical practice. *Journal of Applied Rehabilitation Counseling, 22*(4), 11–18.

Van Hoose, W. H., & Kottler, J. A. (1985). *Ethical and legal issues in counseling and psychotherapy.* San Francisco: Jossey-Bass.

Vasquez, M. J. T. (1996). Will virtue ethics improve ethical conduct in multicultural settings and interactions? *The Counseling Psychologist, 24*(1), 98–104.

Ethical Challenges and Emerging Issues

7

Ethics in Health Care Settings

Vilia M. Tarvydas
Barbara O'Rourke

In recent years, we have seen a trend in Westernized medicine toward a more holistic and comprehensive system of health care. This trend includes turning to types of care once considered alternative, as well as including family, community, and other aspects of the individual's life into health care plans. As this trajectory continues counseling is seen as both healing art and science, and is becoming a more integral part of traditional health care. Concurrently, as the field of health care incorporates counseling as an important aspect of healing, counselors are integrating physical aspects of care into their practice. Counseling services now are acknowledged widely as being effective for clients who are experiencing certain types of physical problems. Mental health care is being practiced increasingly within the context of medicine.

Rehabilitation counselors and social workers have been educated to provide counseling service to people with acute and chronic health conditions and have been doing this type of work for years. In the precedent set by these disciplines, it is becoming more common to see counselors as part of a health care team in such a wide range of settings as family health agencies, rehabilitation facilities that assist in recovery from disabilities such as head or spinal injury, chemical dependency treatment centers, and pain clinics. Counselors in these settings provide supportive services such as training in stress management, teaching of coping skills, and coordination of the educational needs of young clients. In fact, major funding sources such as insurance companies and other third-party payer systems are demanding a more comprehensive, interdisciplinary approach to treatment. Thus, the practices of both medicine and counseling are shifting, and the requisite skills and abilities needed by all disciplines for sound practice are also expanding.

The integration of health care services has created a new ethical landscape for all parties, including the counselor who participates within the health care system. Ethical, political, and social norms create a new complexity within this environment for counseling practice. Counselors who work in a health care setting are expected to operate within the prevailing biomedical model. Ethical guidelines that have developed out of the traditions within this model are called *biomedical ethics*. The decision-making climate in which this model is typically embedded was described in Chapter 6.

According to Beauchamp and Childress (1989), *biomedical ethics* is a relatively young field that can best be described as a way of understanding complexity and examining moral life as it pertains to the biological sciences, medicine, and health care. Biomedical ethics applies general ethical theories for specific forms of conduct or moral judgment as they pertain to these areas. Thus this field is a type of practical or applied ethics.

This chapter will examine several issues in counseling relative to practical ethics in contemporary health care. These biomedical issues include managed care systems, euthanasia, and AIDS.

Managed Care

Health care reform is an evolving response to the escalating and devastating costs of health care. DeLeon, VandenBos, and Bulatao (1991) provided a historical overview of the development of managed care as the primary weapon of the health care reform movement. This type of service management typically takes several forms. Some common organizations participating in managed care are (a) health maintenance organizations (HMOs), which provide specified health services using a restricted group of providers at a fixed cost to the consumer; (b) preferred provider organizations (PPOs), which purchase health care from specific providers at a discounted rate; and (c) independent practice associations (IPAs). According to Shore (1996), IPAs allow consumers to choose independent practitioners, but retain a portion of the fees from providers who may be reimbursed either on a fee-for-service or capitated basis. The aim of managed care is twofold: (a) to limit the treatment to that which is required to return a client to a reasonable level of functioning as soon as possible, but not necessarily to deal with the underlying clinical illness; and (b) to address the secondary goal of prevention, on the theory that preventative care will reduce the overall cost of health care.

Reactions to managed care systems in the health care industry have been mixed. Strong emotions have been generated on both sides, particularly in the mental health arena (Haas & Cummings, 1991; Newman & Bricklin, 1991). Benefits for managed care consumers have been identified as (a) lower membership costs than traditional indemnity plans, (b) ease of access to a variety of services, and (c) having no exclusions due to a pre-existing condition. Disadvantages often noted include (a) offering a limited choice in health care providers, (b) creating an inability to consult a specialist directly, and (c) the use of a gatekeeping system. In the gatekeeper procedure, the managed care vendor often assigns the client to the care provider, or dictates treatment options before their approval in an effort to control costs.

Nevertheless, managed care appears to be a reality that is here to stay. The question has become, "what form will it take?" and how this form will affect client care. Hersch (1995) said, "It is time to move beyond our hurt, fear, and anger. It is time to become creative and adaptive by fully using the substantial repertoire of professional skills available" (p. 16) to assure quality client care. In other words, counselors must be informed about managed care and involved in shaping the principles of managed care to provide sound ethical care to clients. According to Richardson and Shaw Austad (1991), whatever their ambivalence or resistance to managed mental health care, mental health professionals may find it difficult to survive financially if they choose not to participate in such systems. This situation is a result of the fact that a majority of the U.S. population likely will obtain its future health care through some form of managed health care organization. In fact, Jensen, Morrisey, Gaffney and Liston (1997) reported that in 1995, 73% of those receiving their health care through private health insurance did so through some type of managed care.

Elements of managed care stand to change the ethical landscape of counseling. Haas and Cummings (1991) cited several ethical issues in managed mental health care that must be addressed. These interrelated issues include: (a) counselor competence, (b) informed consent, (c) confidentiality, and (d) fidelity. Additionally, a relevant issue discussed in the family therapy literature involves the medicalization of mental health and the use of diagnosis (Denton, 1989; Kutchins & Kirk, 1987).

Counselor Competence

The obligation of counselor competence as mandated by the ACA and APA codes of ethics requires that a counselor strive to maintain the highest level of professional services, and neither claim nor imply professional qualifications exceeding those they possess. Counseling practice in a managed care setting may present relevant questions regarding several aspects of a counselor's competence. One implication is that counselors must be trained adequately to appropriately select, diagnose, and treat clients in a managed care situation. The counselor must be able to identify who is appropriate for services, for what kind of treatment, and under what circumstances. Typically, managed care has resulted in more medical services, including mental health services, being rendered on an out-client or non-hospital basis. Moreover, brief, more cost-effective therapy modalities have been the treatment of choice for numerous conditions within managed care situations.

With this context in mind, Haas and Cummings (1991) offered practice guidelines for out-client services. These authors said that practitioners must develop competency in the use of brief therapy and in their ability to screen the needs of prospective clients. As one example, they recommended that practitioners should be able to identify what prospective clients are appropriate for managed care treatment by using both exclusion and inclusion criteria. They offer a summary of criteria and examples from current literature (Figure 7–1).

Exclusion

1. Could not benefit from brief therapy, or requires other treatment modalities.
   Examples: individuals with delirium, dementia, and active psychosis.

2. Unable to attend to the process of verbal interaction.
   Examples: clients with acute panic disorder and schizophreniform disorders.

3. Possesses a characteriological style that precludes enduring the counseling work.
   Examples: a history of repeated suicide attempts, entrenched alcoholism, and chronic obsessional phobic reactions

4. In sum, presents with chronic anger, psychopathy, organicity, or psychosis.

Inclusion

1. Capacity to relate—at least one significant attachment.

2. Psychologically minded.

3. Motivated.

4. Has adaptational strength.

5. Presents with a clear-cut concern that has emerged at identifiable points in time.

Figure 7–1

Criteria for Selection of Managed Care Outpatients

Source: From "Managed Outpatient Mental Health Plans: Clinical, Ethical, and Practical Guidelines for Participation" by L.J. Haas and N.A. Cummings, 1991, *Professional Psychology: Research and Practice, 22* (1). Copyright 1991 by the American Psychological Association. Adapted by permission.

According to Richardson and Shaw Austad (1991), the aim of brief therapy is "to accomplish significant change in a brief period" (p. 56). Hence, brief treatment skills include developing expertise in assessment. These skills aim to identify the core psychological issues quickly and enhance the ability to match each client with the appropriate counselor and treatment. This type of assessment must be based on client's strengths and motivation for change. Regarding counselor competence, Richardson and Shaw Austad (1991) discussed two types of interventions specifically designed for managed care: (a) a developmental model that focuses on the client's developmental stage as the context for conceptualizing the problem and (b) the crisis-intervention model.

Counselor competence for short-term treatments will require that counselors must be prepared and able to focus on achievable, specific treatment goals, and to be active and more directive in conducting treatment. In sum, short-term treatment should not be considered long-term therapy conducted in merely a more abbreviated time frame; it comprises a unique set of skills. Clinicians must be trained for this approach and provide only treatment that falls within their personal scopes of practice as determined by appropriate training and experience. They also must be fully informed and competent in facilitating appropriate client referrals.

Informed Consent and Confidentiality

Although information management is always of critical importance to the counselor, it is even more so within the context of managed care. Data tracking is crucial to both accessing and using the managed care system. Consequently, this necessary exchange of information presents problems and limitations for counselor–client confidentiality, especially given the increasing use of computerized data and facsimile exchanges of information. While accurate and full disclosure by both the client and the counselor is vital to the counseling process, disclosure must now occur in a climate where information can be used to withhold or dictate services. Recordkeeping is a formal process often dictated by managed care systems that threatens a client's autonomous rights by curtailing limits and decreasing an individual's freedom of choice. Counselors must provide their clients with comprehensive informed consent regarding limitations to confidentiality. Further, the potential limitations on a counselor's ability to retain confidentiality must be fully disclosed to the client before establishing a counseling relationship.

Further, due process is significant ethically in that it must include fully informed consent; for example, informed consent should include disclosure of all treatment alternatives that might be most beneficial to the client, regardless of cost or the payer's willingness to provide these services. Institutions must have an ethical grievance process that allows clients to challenge client care decisions in a timely and responsive manner. Patients must also be able in the process to obtain assistance in resolving their problems at an earlier stage—for example, through the use of ombudsman programs and client assistance programs. There must be processes of appeal that address issues of discrimination and protect people who are disadvantaged within a context of client-centered care, wherein the client's preferences and values are important to treatment outcome.

Fidelity

Ethically, counselors must make themselves aware of the potential effects that a managed care situation may have on the counselor-client relationship, and the counselor's ethical obligation to fidelity. They must work to minimize any detrimental effects of this care system on the obligation of fidelity to the best of their abilities. For example, the managed care process could have a significant effect on the client's level of trust in the counselor–client relationship. If the client perceives the counselor as sharing private or negative information with insurers or employers through the managed care system, trust will be compromised. The principle of fidelity requires the counselor to be concerned with issues of loyalty and faithfulness to the bonds created in this trusting relationship. Similarly, they must honor confidentiality and avoid harming their clients. Given the specific needs of each client, it would be useful and ethically sound for the counselors to consider carefully the potential effects of varying forces and intrusions imposed by managed care upon aspects of their relationships with each client. For example, managed care might have an effect on counselors' loyalties, diagnostic, and termination practices.

Conflicted Loyalties The possibility exists that the professional counselor's loyalty could no longer be to the client or even to a professional's peers, but rather to the managers or systems in charge of prior authorization and utilization review of services. The philosophy of managed care demands awareness of limited resources, thereby expanding the moral role of the counselor to include concerns about distribution of resources to groups or populations of individuals, as well as individual clients. Traditionally, counselors have been held to the ethical responsibility of considering their clients' needs above those of others unless direct risk or harm to others can be ascertained. Now mental health professionals are challenged to assume responsibility for population-based practice without losing concern for the individual.

This widening of ethical obligation to include concerns about distributive justice for society more broadly is a revolutionary emphasis for counselors. Managed care has been recognized as involving at least two conflicting interests: the need for counselors (a) to balance their clients' needs with those of other clients in the managed system; and (b) to balance clients' needs with cost containment and financial resources. In managed care, this balance is usually mediated by an individual in a gatekeeping role, often called the case manager. Some authorities maintain that it is important that professionals recognize the overall responsibility for determining such weighty moral questions by challenging the broader community to address these issues through debate and formation of political and social policy. Counselors should participate in this policy debate both individually and through their professional organizations.

Several authors have written about the potential intrusion of the gatekeeper's function into the counselor's ethical analysis and have described the situation as if the managed care representative was present psychologically in the counseling session. Haas and Cummings (1991) offered the opinion that "the symbolic presence of the manager or third party intensifies the issues in vulnerable therapist–client pairs" (p. 49) and stands to erode the trusting relationship in counseling. A decade ago, Pellegrino (1986) warned that "this [gatekeeper] role is morally dubious because it generates a conflict between the responsibility of the [caregiver] as a primary advocate of the client and as guardian of society's resources" (p. 23).

Counseling codes of ethics are clear in their stance that counselors' commitments to their clients come first. Sections in the APA and ACA codes of ethics, for example, protect the welfare of the consumer. However, interpretation of such consumer mandates has become more difficult in the context of managed care. As pressures on counselors mount, the profession will be called on to further clarify ethical standards and practices in managed care settings.

Diagnosis

Managed care has affected the very definition of mental illness. Counselors' moral and ethical responses to these changes are important, not only for the clients who sit in front of them, but also for all potential clients who may need their services in the future. The importance of diagnosis is heightened in the context of managed care, and labeling through diagnosis can be damaging to the clients. The stigma associated with diagnosis or the use of diagnosis to reduce managed care responsibilities to clients are but two examples of possible damaging effects of a diagnosis being assigned to someone. Damage to clients may extend into their futures and include such effects as a decrease in ability to obtain a job, to obtain insurance coverage, or to have the diagnosis used negatively in a custody hearing or other legal matters. Nevertheless, diagnosis generally has come to be accepted as a necessary process, and presents counselors with a significant challenge. Wylie (1995) stated "therapists are increasingly caught in a three-way crunch between diagnostic accuracy (often complicated by ambiguous symptoms), confidentiality, and the power wielded by the insurer, usually around problem diagnoses that are stigmatized" (p. 32). Part of the challenge of appropriate diagnosis to counselors is to clarify the philosophical and moral systems they themselves hold regarding the use of a labeling system in mental health. They must address questions such as whether to use a less severe diagnosis to reduce the effect of labeling on a client; or conversely, they must examine if they have a tendency toward overreporting diagnosing clients' problems to help them qualify for services (Denton, 1989).

In defining *mental illness* as impaired functioning, the proponents of managed care have challenged the traditional definition and subsequently its traditional treatment goals. In some systems this shift may deprive clients with certain diagnoses, such as personality disorder, of longer-term services. The managed care treatment model opts for minimal levels of acceptable function over maximizing the quality of life as its desired outcome. The Diagnostic and Statistical Manual, Fourth Edition (DSM–IV) classification system, is the primary diagnostic schema used by managed care corporations. This requirement has been accused of providing a mechanism for narrowing and constricting treatment and has been adopted as the official justification for denying "medical necessity" (Wylie, 1995). Further, this system of diagnosis is incompatible with some orientations such as systems theory and the psychosocial rehabilitation philosophy, which seeks to demedicalize or depathologize functional limitations and to focus on an asset-based model.

According to Kutchins and Kirk (1987), the original development of a diagnostic system in mental health was done for reasons of enhanced communication and not for economic purposes. However, the current thrust of the DSM system is fiduciary access. This means that payment of services often depends on type of diagnosis according to this nomenclature. Moreover, to use this system of diagnosis accurately requires the evaluation and use of organic/physical information that is typically beyond the expertise of the counselor. If these assumptions are true, diagnosis requires consultation or the collaborative effort of a physician or psychiatrist and a counselor when treating a client.

The DSM–IV classification system's multiaxial approach was developed to facilitate this collaborative effort as a means to include the biological and psychosocial aspects of mental health. However, the reality in practice often results in an imbalance in the importance given to diagnoses placed under certain axes. For example, the use of V codes as "conditions attributable to a mental disorder" (DSM–IV) are often not seen as significant for treatment and therefore not reimbursable by managed care. This barrier to treatment may be applied to other diagnoses as well. Diagnoses that typically may not be reimbursable include adjustment disorders, personality disorders, and disorders that require long-term treatment such as post-traumatic stress disorder.

- All diagnoses should be made with scrupulous regard for correct procedures. Know your boundaries of competence.
- Careful attention should be paid to organic conditions. Work in conjunction with a physician or carefully review all medical reports.
- A physician should be routinely consulted about the medical aspects of a diagnosis.
- Every diagnosis should be accurately reported to the client and to the insurer. Further, the client should be fully informed about the potential ramifications of using the diagnostic label before its use in formal documents.
- Patients should be advised, preferably in writing, that no diagnosis is meant to indicate a definitive judgment about any physical condition.
- Patients should be referred to physicians for the evaluation of any medical condition.

Figure 7–2

Procedures for Using DSM–IV System

Source: From "DSM–III–R and Social Work Malpractice" by H. Kutchins and S. Kirk, 1987, May, *Social Work.* Copyright 1987 by the National Association of Social Work. Adapted by permission.

Even when the diagnosis itself is not in question, the current diagnostic system presents ethical challenges to counselors. For example, problems may arise concerning limitations of confidentiality and the ramifications of new technology with interconnecting computer data banks and Internet networking capabilities. Wylie (1995) asserted that "many diagnoses can still shadow a client's life like hounds from hell and much more efficiently in the cyberspace age than ever before" (p. 32). Clearly, counselors must work at all levels, personally and politically, to address these dilemmas. They also must know and understand their institutions' information management systems and policies so that they can best protect their clients' confidentiality and provide accurate informed consent regarding its limitations.

Kutchins and Kirk (1987) offered counselors a procedural list of suggestions to guide their use of the DSM classification system. A modified version of their list is provided in Figure 7–2.

Termination   Ethical guidelines for terminating a counselor–client relationship state that counselors should not abandon their client unless (a) they no longer need services, (b) are not benefiting from services, or (c) they are being harmed by continued service. Responsible counselors inform their clients of these possibilities before beginning counseling. Nevertheless, a potential conflict may arise when counseling services are no longer sanctioned by the client's managed care system and the financial assistance for the service is terminated. This problem is particularly pressing if a financial burden is potentially harmful to the client. The counselor must choose among several alternatives including to (a) offer pro bono services, (b) provide alternatives that do not involve a financial burden (e.g., community or support groups), (c) negotiate referral, (d) challenge the managed care system, (e) offer continued services on a sliding-scale fee until the client is stabilized, or (f) continue services at present fee schedule but be paid directly by the client.

The counselor's advocacy on behalf of the client and the client's self-advocacy are paramount when such conflicts of interest arise. Proficiency in these advocacy roles will require educating clients to learn to advocate for themselves through skill training interventions, as well as building the professionals' knowledge and skill-base so they might become more proficient in systems advocacy skills. Problems of inappropriate or premature termination may occur more frequently under an increasingly prevalent managed care system, and they will continue to impose moral dilemmas for both counselors and their clients.

Revisions of current ethical codes will need to include guidelines for counseling practice that assist the counselor in allocating resources that would facilitate client advocacy in these situations. The counseling profession and the governmental regulatory bodies must ensure that managed care techniques are implemented in a way that protects clients, the integrity of their relationship with their counselor, and the well-being of the profession itself.

Efforts to preserve the appropriate ethical role of the counselor include the development of appropriate procedures to reduce conflict in at least three ways: (a) developing practice guidelines that have been established at a higher policy-making level, (b) increasing the role of clients in the decision-making process, and (c) establishing a well-structured appeals process for clients who disagree with treatments or termination decisions.

Euthanasia

Euthanasia is one of the most significant and polarizing social issues of our time (Albright & Hazler, 1995). Historically the first references to this practice occurred in the Hippocratic Oath (Emmanuel, 1994) and it has recurred as an issue with varying degrees of intensity since that time. However, both the scholarly literature and codes of ethics in counseling have remained largely silent on this critical issue.

Ethical decisions regarding euthanasia typically center on three key ethical principles. These principles are autonomy, beneficence, and nonmaleficence. Most discussion and writing in this area has been about the role of physicians or the role of a significant other; either, or both, typically serve as the agent who delivers the means to death. However, counselors may be in a special position to understand the wants and needs of both the client and the client's family regarding this decision. Therefore, a counselor's contribution to a debate regarding the relevance of any guiding ethical principle to a client will be significant.

Many dying clients and their families face inadequate counseling, emotional support, and pain control. Counselors must address these inadequacies, along with the ethical issue of euthanasia. First, counselors must identify and reconcile their personal biases and values regarding related issues (e.g., death and quality of life with chronic or terminal illnesses) before working with clients and their families experiencing these issues.

Decisions about euthanasia more often are shaped by the personal values of the parties to this ethical and personal dilemma rather than law. The recognition and reconciliation of issues of diversity—cultural, familial, and individual—are vital to sound ethical practice. This recognition requires an ongoing effort by counselors to better understand cultural and religious views of life and death that may be different from their own. Moreover, they must be intimately familiar with the decision-making context of any individual facing such a decision. Further, counselors must clarify their own roles in providing client and family assistance during the consideration of euthanasia. Counselors must be mindful that their counselor's primary ethical charges are their obligations to respect the integrity and to promote the welfare of the client (ACA, 1995, Section A.1.a). Understanding a working definition of *euthanasia* and the arguments for and against it are important building blocks for a more sound ethical decision-making process.

Definitions

The term *euthanasia* is derived from two Greek words meaning "good death" (Beauchamp & Walters, 1989). Inadequate and often unclear definitions of *euthanasia* have been noted throughout the literature. This definitional problem has affected public perception of the issues surrounding euthanasia, as well as research and professional writing. This problem also has encumbered the resolution of the ethical and legal status of this important issue. The use of terms to describe *euthanasia* typically has been based on three criteria: (1) the basis of intention to die, (2) the nature of the critical action involved in effecting the death, and (3) the consent of the person requesting death. Qualifying terms that have been used to distinguish these elements include *active euthanasia,* and *passive* or *indirect euthanasia.* Further, either of these approaches can be classified as voluntary or involuntary. Emmanuel (1994) has argued that while such definitional distinctions may be useful, the joining of each qualifier with the emotionally charged word *euthanasia,* confuses moral judgment and distorts subsequent public and political debates. However, a clear definition is important to professional counseling research and scope of practice.

Passive euthanasia is the practice of withdrawing or withholding life-sustaining treatments. Legal rulings consistently have supported such practices under certain conditions. According to Emmanuel (1994), the literature in medicine demonstrates a rising consensus supporting the ethical appropriateness of such actions. For example, the ethical principle of double effect has evolved. *Double effect* is the idea that unacceptable consequences such as death are deemed acceptable under certain circumstances. This stance supports the use of medication for pain relief in terminal conditions, even if it shortens a person's life. Such a decision highlights the propensity toward beneficence over nonmaleficence as the guiding ethical principle in these circumstances. Another example of this concept is the common practice of do-not-resuscitate (DNR) orders for certain terminal clients. However, as Beauchamp and Childress (1989) pointed out, the debate is not over. These authors have suggested that the distinctions between treatment and nontreatment are untenable and should be replaced by the distinction between obligatory and optional means of treatment.

Such a conceptual framework would serve to offer a more adequate rationale for any given choice of action.

Beauchamp and Childress (1994) considered further the omission–commission distinctions regarding treatment. They concluded that the decision to stop treatment is often perceived as more momentous and consequential to the caregiver than the withholding of treatment. For example, the initiation of treatment can create expectations and imply responsibility on the part of the caregiver. However, Beauchamp and Childress (1994) argued that "paradoxically, the moral burden of proof often should be heavier when the decision is to withhold than when it is to withdraw treatments. In many cases, only after starting treatments will it be possible to make a proper diagnosis and prognosis" (p. 198). Either approach potentially can lead to the over- or under-treatment of clients. These authors suggested that such decisions should be based on the client's welfare and rights, which include a balanced consideration of the benefits and burdens of the treatment.

Obtaining advanced directives from a person before that person's loss of competence has been urged recently. The initiation of this legal process was based on ethical and legal considerations of individual autonomy. There are two types of advanced directives: "1) *living wills,* which are specific substantive directives regarding medical procedures that should be provided or forgone in specific circumstances, and 2) *durable power of attorney (DPA)* for health care, or proxy directive" (Beauchamp & Childress, 1994, p. 242). The DPA allows individuals to select substitute decision-makers who would be empowered to make health care decisions on their behalf should they be incapacitated.

Active euthanasia is the intentional termination of life, also referred to as mercy killing or assisted suicide. Justifications for such actions are grounded in the principle of beneficence, with regard to the person who delivers the lethal means, and in the principle of autonomy with regard to an individual's right to make the decision to end his or her life. Conversely, it has been argued that such acts are violations of nonmaleficence. Currently such acts are illegal in the United States. At the same time, acts of suicide or attempted suicide have been decriminalized throughout most of the United States, creating a paradoxical situation in the minds of some persons.

The voluntary versus involuntary distinction is a means to further qualify the degree of contribution to the decision made by the individual facing death. Voluntary status assumes that individuals elect and actively seek their own time and manner of death. Involuntary decisions are much more controversial because the individuals facing death have no active part in the decision-making, even if they are not able to express an opinion due to being comatose or otherwise incapacitated. To broaden the context of this discussion, the next sections will discuss contemporary arguments for and against euthanasia.

Arguments for Euthanasia

According to Beauchamp and Childress (1989) and Emmanuel (1994), four basic claims currently support euthanasia as a legitimate health care intervention. These arguments are based on (a) the principle of autonomy as an *a priori* principle,

1. Requests should be made by a competent person on several occasions and in writing.

2. A thorough examination should be made to rule out or treat any prevailing psychological condition.

3. The act of assistance should be restricted to certified physicians who will not receive compensation for their work.

4. Careful documentation with reference to alternative treatments should be offered to the person.

5. All cases should be reported to an official body.

Figure 7–3

Elements of Ethical Procedural Safeguards for Euthanasia

Source: From "Euthanasia: Historical, Ethical, and Empirical Perspectives" by E.J. Emmanuel, 1994, September 12, *Archives of Internal Medicine, 154.* Copyright 1994 by the American Medical Associaton. Reprinted by permission.

(b) the primacy of the principle of beneficence, (c) the assertion that passive euthanasia is an acceptable practice, and that no real distinction between active and passive euthanasia exists, and (d) the argument is based on utility, which supports rules that promote the most favorable consequences for the largest number of people. A presentation of the issues outlined by these authors follows.

The cultural context of the United States is based on individualism and self-determination, and the rights of an individual are viewed as paramount. In this culture, these rights, including the right to die, clearly are supported by the ethical principle of autonomy. The essence of this right is a claim that reflects a belief that all individuals must be given the opportunity to determine what is good and valuable in life for them. This determination would include the right to determine the time and manner of one's own death. Enactment of this right rests on individual consent and assumes that obligations for action naturally follow this right. Put another way, rights form the justified basis of obligations.

Secondly, based on the duty to do good embedded in the principle of beneficence, euthanasia is seen as an acceptable way to end a life that would probably inflict more pain and suffering. In other words, euthanasia could be considered humane. This benevolent act already has been socially sanctioned through the practice of refusing and not providing life-sustaining interventions. In fact, Brock (1992) claimed that such an opportunity may provide individuals with psychological insurance against anxiety over anticipated pain and suffering, and therefore is an integral part of a trusting relationship between the client and care providers. If this claim is accepted, then euthanasia would not be considered separate from other alternatives of care. In fact, there has been discussion of broadening the claim of best interest to include the welfare of an individual's family, a controversial perspective.

The third argument proclaims that there is no distinction between active and passive euthanasia. An act and an omission are viewed as equivalent. Withholding life-sustaining care shares an equal intention of assisting in death. Arguably, there is no moral difference in the final results.

Finally, what is known as the utility argument suggests that rules should promote the greatest good. Proponents of this claim argue that bad consequences of euthanasia are remote and speculative. However, these proponents contend that tight procedures based on careful analysis and review will be necessary to prevent ill effects. Figure 7–3 presents suggestions for such guidelines.

Arguments Against Euthanasia

Currently six primary claims appear in the literature arguing against the use of euthanasia as a sanctioned medical intervention. These arguments include (a) the overextension of the concept of autonomy, (b) the idea that legalization should not be promoted on the basis of beneficence, (c) the ethical distinction between active and passive euthanasia, (d) the potential to extend the practice to the noncompetent or nonconsenting, (e) the intrusion of the courts into the private realm, and (f) the potential for gender bias.

John Stuart Mill warned that not all voluntary acts are justified by the principle of autonomy. Opponents of euthanasia use the analogy of voluntary slavery that is proscribed by our society and argue that not all independent desires are justifiable. Further, they argue that satisfying preferences must not be confused with a legal right to autonomy. In other words, there can and should be boundaries of acceptable behavior. Consequently, not providing life-sustaining measures is clearly distinct from actively facilitating death.

Similarly, remote acts of beneficence that occur in rare cases of assisting the end of suffering do not justify the legalization of these acts in general. Opponents of euthanasia claim that traditional medical practice has not provided adequate treatment of pain and suffering. Therefore, the boundaries between acceptable and unacceptable conditions of pain and suffering have not been defined. In sum, an acceptable practice of euthanasia could undermine the pursuit of a health care goal of well-being.

In fact, some opponents say there is an ethical and true distinction between active and passive euthanasia based on the intentionality of the caregiver. Euthanasia could undermine the trust inherent in the healing relationship as well as the laborious provision of compassionate care. Potential healing might be supplanted by a view of killing as healing.

More specifically, the potential exists for the natural and logical extension of arguments for euthanasia to include vulnerable and unprotected individuals such as incompetent, comatose or mentally deficient clients, children, and other disempowered people. This is known as the *slippery slope* argument. Beauchamp and Childress (1989) describe this effect as the "progressive erosion of moral restraints" (p. 231). They contend that a move in this permissive direction might be used as an argument to decrease the burden on a family or society, to eliminate individuals who have a perceived diminished quality of life based on a disability, and to consequently modify attitudes toward the respect for life.

1. Keep current on the developing legal, social, and ethical information related to euthanasia.
2. Determine what culturally influenced moral theory, personal biases, and personal perspectives guide your practice. Continue to clarify personal belief and values.
3. Become adept at the skill of self-reflection. Assess your ethical decision-making process, understand it, and use it to deal consistently with issues.
4. Examine, understand, and reconcile institutional protocols, legal precedents, and liabilities.
5. Obtain differing professional perspectives.
6. Be knowledgeable about the potential course, prognosis, and all treatment alternatives related to a client's illness.
7. Be familiar with all contextual factors that may be influencing a client—e.g., who constitutes their support system and what are these individuals' perspectives.
8. Seek to understand clients by exploring their world.
9. Act as a resource person and empathic listener. Assist clients with psychic and physical pain. Provide support and maintain substantial autonomy.
10. Help clients understand the importance of various personal and formal documents associated with the end of life.
11. Be available to comfort significant others after a death has occurred.

Figure 7–4
Counselor Implications
Source: From "A Right to Die? Ethical Dilemmas of Euthanasia" by D.E. Albright and R.J. Hazler, 1995, *Counseling and Values, 39*. Copyright 1995 by the American Counseling Association. Reprinted by permission.

The more direct political argument against legalizing practices of euthanasia parallels the abortion debates and warns against the intrusion of the courts into private matters of health and death. Such intrusions are deemed inevitable to ensure sound procedural safeguards for such practices; therefore, they would be unavoidable if the practices of euthanasia were legalized.

Finally, Wolf (1996) cautioned that the debate regarding the use of euthanasia has been incomplete and the actual practice must not precede a more complete analysis. Before deciding to legitimize a euthanasia process, several salient variables must be examined. Gender is prominent among these factors. Wolf (1996) began this analysis and observed that women may request euthanasia at a higher rate than men. Women also seem to seek euthanasia for different reasons than men. These choices more often may be related to the needs of others than relief from personal pain as an aspect of the valorization of women's propensity to self-sacrifice. Finally, Wolf questioned how the image of woman as the candidate for euthanasia may affect the public debate.

Implications for Counselors

Counselors may find themselves in a unique position of helping clients and their families during the decision-making process regarding euthanasia (Figure 7–4). Several authors have been particularly helpful in preparing counselors to engage in this process with clients. These authors include Albright and Hazler (1995) and Humphrey (1991). However, you are advised to review their work for more depth in this area due to the complexity of these issues and the intense need for self-awareness work on the part of the counselor.

AIDS

The AIDS epidemic has presented counselors with new ethical decision-making dilemmas. This uncharted territory has required counselors to carefully examine and consider prudent action on unresolved ethical issues. Legal and professional norms of practice largely have remained undefined. Further, these unresolved dilemmas are now embedded within a managed health care environment, rendering them even more complex. A working knowledge of the basic issues related to working with individuals touched by the AIDS epidemic should serve as a foundation for counselors as they struggle to resolve these emerging ethical issues.

In providing services to people with AIDS, Ryan and Rowe (1988) identified some predictable ethical dilemmas that counselors may encounter. These dilemmas include (a) personal conflicts with clients' values and behaviors, (b) conflicts with colleagues whose personal biases or unresolved issues prevent them from serving clients appropriately, (c) concerns about a caregiver's right to know which clients are HIV infected, (d) concerns about whether to reveal a client's positive status to sexual partners or partners sharing needles when the client refuses to inform others at risk, (e) conflicts with social service agencies that fail to provide appropriate training and supervision for caregivers or services for people with AIDS, and (f) concerns about the increasing accountability of the counseling profession as an organization that should be advocating for people with AIDS more effectively. A summation of the dilemmas provided by Ryan and Rowe (1988) suggested two major areas of ethical concerns in working with people with AIDS. These two areas are confidentiality and informed consent. Both issues will be presented.

In general, counselors must provide the same sound ethical practice to people with AIDS that they provide to any other client. Specifically, they must strive to protect the privacy of their clients while promoting their welfare. Counselors practicing with clients who have AIDS must have an appropriate degree of practitioner competence. In working with these clients, the counselor's competency must include a working knowledge of potential cultural or lifestyle differences; the AIDS disease process (e.g., etiology, prognosis, and treatment); and an explicit degree of self-awareness with regard to the counselor's own values, assumptions, and fears. According to Melton (1988), the injunction to be educated in working with people with AIDS is founded firmly upon the principle of beneficence. Beneficent practice also extends professional responsibilities to include client advocacy. For example, previous attempts at advocacy have extended the Rehabilitation Act of 1973 and the Americans with Disabilities Act to protect people with AIDS as it would any other individuals with disabilities from undue discrimination.

Examining confidentiality as one of the major concerns previously cited, four major issues have been identified that deal with confidentiality and the person with AIDS: (a) the presence of a special relationship between client and counselor and the duty to treat, (b) assessment of the impending degree of dangerousness of the client, (c) the presence of an identifiable victim of client danger, and (d) the articulation of appropriate counselor actions in working with persons with AIDS (Knapp & VandeCreek, 1990; Lamb et al., 1989; Morrison, 1989; Totten et al., 1990). Each of these four issues will be discussed briefly.

Special Relationship and Duty to Protect: Duty to Treat

The Tarasoff outcome (discussed in Chapter 3) and other prevailing evidence has supported the conclusion that entering into a professional relationship is a sufficient condition for counselors to assume some responsibility for their clients. As a result, the counselor assumes some degree of responsibility for any third parties the counselor reasonably knows to be in danger from that client. The conclusions based on the Tarasoff and related decisions suggest that confidentiality is valued highly in the special relationship between the counselor and the client; however it is not bound as an absolute. In other words, under certain circumstances the counselor is bound ethically to act in the face of certain harm to protect a potential victim (Stanard & Hazler, 1995).

According to Melton (1988), most courts have considered the duties to third parties congruent with the Tarasoff logic. In this perspective, often referred to as the duty to warn, the counselor is charged with a duty to exercise reasonable care in warning a specific intended third party who has been threatened by a client. Put another way, Tarasoff has limited the definition of "reasonable foreseeable" harm to include cases that involve a specific identifiable victim. Concurrently this threat must be carefully weighed against the harm that the client may incur by any breach of confidentiality. Given the unique social and emotional threats where fear and anxiety of contagion are common, people with AIDS may be particularly vulnerable to any breach of confidentiality. An intrusion of privacy should be no greater than necessary to exert reasonable care (Melton, 1988).

Figure 7–5 summarizes suggested guidelines for counselors making decisions about limiting the degree of client confidentiality (Cohen, 1990). Ethical practice dictates that boundaries of confidentiality are to be made clear to the counselor and the client before engaging in the counseling process.

Although there always have been implicit risks for health care providers in the course of providing their services, the deadliness of the AIDS epidemic has heightened the debate regarding the counselor's duty to treat. Justification for refusal to treat a client primarily has been based on the risk of contagion or on the presence of values conflicts between counselor and client (Morrison, 1989). Some counselors who elect not to treat people with AIDS may find that the issues they bring to treatment constitute a value conflict they may view as insurmountable; while others may simply

1. Counselors who receive information from clients who may have a communicable disease known to be fatal must disclose information to relevant third parties if, and only if, the counselors have reason to believe that

   a. there is medical evidence.

   b. the clients bear specific relation (e.g., sexual or shared needles) to specified third parties at high risk of contagion.

   c. the clients have not already informed the third parties nor are they likely to make such disclosures in a timely manner.

2. In cases wherein the above conditions are met, counselors' general obligation to third parties is defined by

   a. within the counseling context, before disclosure, counselors must make all reasonable efforts to educate the clients about the disease and to provide the clients with the support, understanding, encouragement, and opportunity to disclose the information to third parties on their own.

   b. the counselor must make third-party disclosure in a timely fashion.

   c. before disclosure, counselors must inform clients of their intention.

   d. counselors must disclose the information only to the parties at risk or to the legal guardian (in the case of minors).

   e. counselors must limit the third-party disclosure to general medical information, in earnest, communicate to the third party a willingness to provide support in the form of counseling or to make an appropriate referral.

Figure 7–5

Limitations of Confidentiality

Source: From "Confidentiality, Counseling, and Clients Who Have AIDS: Ethical Foundations of a Model Rule" by E.D. Cohen, 1990, *Journal of Counseling and Development, 68,* 282–286. Copyright 1990 by the American Counseling Association. Reprinted by permission.

not feel comfortable with people with AIDS, the lifestyle choices related to the types of people, or the life issues related to the decision. While ethical codes of various disciplines suggest that counselors are obligated to respect a client and to protect the welfare of those seeking services, there is no clearly stated duty to treat undesirable or difficult clients. Refusal to treat a client is a moral as well as an ethical and legal decision and must be viewed from this perspective. As discussed earlier in this section, people with AIDS are legally protected from discrimination based on their illness. While it may not be necessary for the counselor to assume an ethical responsibility to treat a person with AIDS, there is an imminent moral responsibility to reflect on the reasons that this decision has been made. Moreover, the ethical obligation remains to assist any individual seeking services in fully and respectfully obtaining appropriate referral services, even if this individual is not accepted as a client.

Assessment of Dangerousness

The prediction of dangerousness has been considered to be significantly unreliable. The reasons for this high degree of unreliability are complex (Morrison, 1989). Certain behaviors, such as a history of violence or assaultive behavior and the availability of weapons, have been shown to be related to future dangerousness; but have not proved to be directly predictive. Moreover, the dynamics of inherent dangerousness involved in the transmission of a fatal disease such as AIDS are substantively different from other assumed types of danger. Therefore, determining the degree of dangerousness of a client who is HIV positive is a significantly difficult task.

Several important factors must be considered before concluding that a client who is HIV positive is an inherent danger to another individual. First, counselors must acknowledge the limit of their own competence in the diagnosis and prognosis of AIDS. The counselor must obtain reliable medical proof that such a condition exists for a client as well as gather current valid and expert medical information regarding the course and transmission of the disease at varying stages and in relationship to this individual client's disease stage. Second, counselors must establish the degree or extent to which this particular client is engaging in high-risk behaviors. Further, the counselor must identify a victim of any dangerous behavior. Lastly, the counselor must assess the degree to which any strategies are being used by the client to reduce the degree of danger to a third party.

Historically, given the prognostic ambiguity in assessing the degree of dangerousness of a client, mental health professionals tend to overpredict the degree of dangerousness. Overprediction has seemed a more prudent error than underprediction. According to most literature, the Tarasoff stance on the assessment of dangerousness has been upheld. However, the counselor first must consider less intrusive means of diffusing any impending risk before violating the confidentiality and trusting relationship with their client. For example, including significant others in the counseling process or encouraging voluntary disclosure by the client to potential victims would protect others while not violating confidentiality.

Another important ethical consideration of dangerousness must not be overlooked. It is known that there is a substantially high risk of suicide among men with AIDS. In a study conducted by Marzuk et al. (1988), men with AIDS were found to be about 36 times more likely to commit suicide than men in the general population. Ethical and legal responsibilities of counselors include preventive measures that range from persuasion to involuntary commitment. As previously discussed regarding euthanasia, the use of rationality in deciding to end one's life is central. For people with AIDS this rational process may become impaired due to the shock of hearing a diagnosis coupled with a lack of accurate information about the disease. It also might be impaired by the progressive cognitive changes that accompany the disease process of AIDS for some people. Ethical issues mirroring those reviewed in the section on euthanasia must be considered.

Identifiable Victim

According to legal rulings, a counselor is required to substantiate the presence of a specific, identified victim before breaching the client's confidentiality to warn the third party. However, courts have extended the counselor's duty to protect

1. Become familiar and continually update medical information regarding AIDS.

2. Be familiar with short- and long-term issues that may arise.

3. Be aware of one's own attitudes, biases, and prejudices as they relate to individuals with AIDS.

4. Seek to inform and encourage all clients in high-risk groups to consider safe methods of having sex and using drugs.

5. Be prepared to refer clients to legal resources if warranted to protect their right to nondiscrimination.

6. Keep current regarding existing state and federal laws concerning the caregiver role in the spread of communicable diseases.

7. Articulate early in the therapeutic relationship the limitations of confidentiality, including the possible use of written formats to facilitate the informed consent process.

8. Determine mutual goals with the client as part of an ongoing assessment.

9. Remember that your principle duty is to your client.

10. Exercise your prerogative to refer or consult with other professionals as needed.

11. Maintain appropriate case notes that document confidentiality issues, understandings with your client, treatment goals and progress, and unusual events. Consider working notes separate from the formal client record.

Figure 7–6
General Counselor Implications for Working with People with AIDS
Source: From "Applying Tarasoff to AIDS-related Psychotherapy Issues" by D.H. Lamb, C. Clark, P. Drumheller, K.Frizzel, and L. Surrey, 1989, *Professional Psychology, 20.* Copyright 1989 by the American Psychological Association. Adapted by permission.

unknown, but readily identifiable, others. For instance, a client may describe a specific person, such as a roommate, with whom the client shares an IV needle and not provide that person's name. It is clear that with limited effort a specific knowable person might be identified. However, it has also been made clear that a counselor is not in the position to interrogate or independently investigate a client to obtain this information. Nevertheless, the identification of a specific victim in impending danger still comes solely from client disclosure.

According to Lamb et al. (1989), the issue of an identifiable victim has several implications for counseling. These issues are included among other useful guidelines for counselors who work with people with AIDS offered in Figure 7–6.

Appropriate Counselor Action

As the likelihood of counselors working with people with AIDS continues to grow, informed, ethical practice must include thoughtful preparation for working with these clients. Such preparation must include considering and learning about the implications of AIDS for all aspects of the counseling process, for example, prudent recordkeeping procedures that protect the client's confidentiality, particularly in the context of managed care (Hughes & Friedman, 1994). Currently, membership in a high-risk group may be considered evidence for cancellation of a client's insurance benefits or may lead to the loss of a client's job. It has been recommended that all contacts with the client, summation of client progress, documents that support informed consent, and all test data should be included in the client's record but that working notes may need to be kept separate from the client's record (Morrison, 1989). While not exhaustive, Figure 7–6 presents implications for ethical counselors' action(s). Clearly, serving people with AIDS involves the full use of all aspects of good ethical and clinical practice throughout the counseling process.

Summary

In this chapter we discussed the ethical challenges for counselors in health care settings, one of today's most complicated and difficult practice settings. We provided information about the basic nature of managed care as a practice environment. Ethical issues in managed care centering on counselor competence, informed consent, confidentiality and fidelity are emerging as key dilemmas for many professionals in medical managed care practices. Several challenges to counselor judgment related to the ethical obligation of fidelity were considered. These issues are conflicts in counselors' loyalties, diagnostic processes and judgment, and termination practices. Euthanasia and working with persons who are HIV positive or have AIDS are two ethically difficult and highly charged issues that increasingly arise for clients in health care environments. Counselors working with these issues must have advanced knowledge of the ethical considerations related to these concerns. This chapter provided a basic overview of essential information relevant to these issues and described the recommendations for addressing these two ethically critical topics.

References

Albright, D. E., & Hazler, R. J. (1995). A right to die?: Ethical dilemmas of euthanasia. *Counseling and Values, 39,* 177–189.

American Counseling Association. (1995). American Counseling Association code of ethics and standards of practice. *Counseling Today, 37,* 33–40.

Beauchamp, T., & Childress, W. (1989). *Principles of biomedical ethics* (4th ed.). Baltimore, MD: Johns Hopkins University Press.

Beauchamp, T., & Walters, L. (Eds.). (1989). *Euthanasia and the prolongation of life. Contemporary issues in bioethics.* (3rd ed.). Belmont, CA: Wadsworth.

Brock, D. W. (1992). Voluntary active euthanasia. *Hastings Center Report, 22,* 10–22.

Cohen, E. D. (1990). Confidentiality, counseling, and clients who have AIDS: Ethical foundations of a model rule. *Journal of Counseling and Development, 68,* 282–286.

DeLeon, P. H., VandenBos, D., & Bulatao, B. (1991). Managed mental health care: A history of the federal policy initiative. *Professional Psychology: Research and Practice, 22,* 15–25.

Denton, W. H. (1989). DSM-III-R and the family therapy: Ethical considerations. *Journal of Marriage and Family Therapy, 15*(4), 367–377.

Emmanuel, E. J. (1994 Sept. 12). Euthanasia: Historical, ethical, and empirical perspectives. *Archives of Internal Medicine, 154,* 1890–1901.

Haas, L. J., & Cummings, N. A. (1991). Managed outpatient mental health plans: Clinical, ethical, and practical guidelines for participation. *Professional Psychology: Research and Practice, 22*(1), 45–51.

Hersch, L. (1995). Adapting to health care reform and managed care: Three strategies for survival and growth. *Professional Psychology: Research and Practice, 26*(1), 16–26.

Humphrey, D. (1991). *Final exit: The practicalities of self-deliverance and assisted suicide for the dying.* New York: Dell Publishing.

Hughes, R. B., & Friedman, A. L. (1994). AIDS-related ethical and legal issues for mental health professionals. *Journal of Mental Health Counseling, 16,* 445–458.

Jensen, G., Morrisey, M. A., Gaffney, S., & Liston, D. K. (1997, January/February). The new dominance of managed care: Insurance trends in the 1990s. *Health Affairs, 16,* 125–136.

Knapp, S., & VandeCreek, L. (1990). Application of the duty to protect to HIV-positive clients. *Professional Psychology: Research and Practice, 21,* 161–166.

Kutchins, H., & Kirk, S. (1987, May). DSM-III-R and social work malpractice. *Social Work,* 205–211.

Lamb, D. H., Clark, C., Drumheller, P., Frizzell, K., & Surrey, L. (1989). Applying Tarasoff to AIDS-related psychotherapy issues. *Professional Psychology: Research and Practice, 20,* 37–43.

Marzuk, P. M., Tierney, H., Tardiff, K., Gross, E. M., Morgan, E. B., Hsu, M., & Mann, J. J. (1988). Increased risk of suicide in persons with AIDS. *Journal of the American Medical Association, 259,* 1333–1337.

Melton, G. B. (1988). Ethical and legal issues in AIDS-related practice. *American Psychologist, 43,* 941–947.

Morrison, C. F. (1989). AIDS: Ethical implications for psychological interventions. *Professional Psychology: Research and Practice, 20,* 166–171.

Newman, R., & Bricklin, P. N. (1991). Parameters of managed mental health care: Legal, ethical and professional guidelines. *Professional Psychology: Research and Practice, 22,* 26–35.

Pellegrino, E. D. (1986). Rationing health care: The ethics of medical gate keeping. *Journal of Contemporary Health, Law Policy, 2,* 23–45.

Richardson, L. M., & Shaw Austad, C. (1991). Realities of mental health practice in managed-care settings. *Professional Psychology: Research and Practice, 22*(1), 52–59.

Ryan, C. C., & Rowe, M. J. (1988). AIDS: Legal and ethical issues. *Social Casework, 69,* 324–333.

Shore, M. (1996, January). Impact of managed care. *New England Journal of Medicine,* 116–118.

Stanard, R., & Hazler, R. (1995). Legal and ethical implications of HIV and duty to warn for counselors: When does Tarasoff apply? *Journal of Counseling and Development, 73,* 397–400.

Totten, G., Lamb, G., & Reeder, G. D. (1990). Tarasoff and confidentiality in AIDS-related psychotherapy. *Professional Psychology: Research and Practice, 21,* 155–160.

Wolf, S. (Ed.). (1996). Feminism and bioethics: *Beyond reproduction.* New York and Oxford: Oxford Press.

Wylie, M. S. (1995, May/June). The power of DSM-IV: Diagnosing for dollars. *Networker,* 22–32.

Ethical Climate

Vilia M. Tarvydas
Barbara J. O'Rourke

Ivey (1994) asserted, "Intentionality is a core goal . . . [of effective counseling]" (p. 11). He stated the following:

> Intentionality is acting with a sense of capability and deciding from among a range of alternative actions. The intentional individual has more than one action, thought, or behavior to choose from in responding to changing life situations. The intentional individual can generate alternatives in a given situation and approach a problem from different vantage points, using a variety of skills and personal qualities, adapting styles to suit different individuals and cultures. (p. 11)

Building on Ivey's concept of intentional theory-based counseling to include ethical decision-making or applied ethics, it is important to understand that an ethical perspective and process must also be skill based and intentional. Further, issues of morality and ethical decision-making are ever-present in the machinations of everyday counseling. Every counseling decision contains an ethical or moral aspect, and each of these decisions is embedded in an influencing context. To achieve a more complete approach to intentional counseling, counselors must be equally aware of and proactive about ethical choices as of the choice of communication techniques.

Research continues to explore significant factors that may influence counselors' degree of effectiveness in ethical decision-making. Factors that have been examined include variables related to the individual counselor such as his or her moral orientation (Liddell, Halpin, & Halpin, 1992), the number and type of consulted relationships (Cottone, Tarvydas, & House, 1994), or level of ethics education (Tarvydas, 1994). Additionally, the effect of context-related factors on ethical decision-making is being examined. Factors such as the effect of working in a certain type of environment, as within a health care team; or with particular people, such as individuals from numerous disciplines, may influence the ethics of practice. The need is great for ongoing research that will continue to identify, clarify, and define factors as they relate to sound ethical decision-making in counseling practice.

This chapter will address several important issues related to applied ethics in counseling as it occurs within an organizational or institutional setting. Examples of typical settings that involve counselors as part of a specific organizational structure include (a) hospital-based counseling, (b) work in community mental health centers, (c) a small mental health private practice group, (d) school counseling, and (e) counseling in rehabilitation settings. Specifically, this discussion will focus on the effect that an ethical climate may have on the *intentional* ethical decision-making process of counselors. The effects of an unethical climate will also be presented. One example of a significant environmental challenge to counselors is the effect of a colleague's unethical behavior on a counselor and their shared working environment.

Organizational Culture

More and more counseling is occurring within the context of an organization or institution. One way to more clearly understand how ethical decision-making can be affected by one's participation in an organizational setting is to think of an organization as a type of culture. The use of a cultural perspective can help counselors realize the organization's complexity and the interactive nature of variables within a setting as they may influence decision-making. This includes a need to understand the unique aspects of group or team experiences. This chapter focuses on issues of ethical decision-making within counseling situations that may occur in an organizational setting. It is important to note that the social, political, and cultural dynamics that occur in a larger organization like a hospital also occur within smaller group settings such as a classroom within a school. Before considering the ethical climate in which counseling occurs, the concept of culture will be explored more fully.

Culture

Conceptual models used to develop an understanding of multicultural and cross-cultural counseling suggest that one must fully examine the potential influence of one's worldview upon one's counseling practice (Ivey, 1994). One's *worldview* is made up of the observable artifacts, values, and underlying assumptions the individual holds. Counselors must strive to understand how a developed worldview may influence (a) the decision-making of members of any culture, (b) any individual who interacts with members of the culture, and (c) the effects of the interaction between the insider (a member of the culture) and an outsider. Typically, multicultural models assume that the counselor is the outsider; however, the converse may also be true. Often when clients are taking an active decision-making role regarding their care within a health care team, or when students and their parents are constructing an education plan, the clients are working to gain acceptance within the team. The team is a cultural group with its own language and style of communicating. The client is the outsider. It also is important to understand how counselors' worldviews that have been shaped partially by their participation in a specific organizational culture may affect their decision-making, including the ethical components of those decisions.

Schein (1990), an organizational psychologist, implied that a specified group of people who have had enough stability over time and a shared history of working together form a culture. The culture is what the group learns over a period of time in regard to problem solving. This type of learning is manifested as observable behaviors, ways of thinking about the world, and ways of feeling. More specifically, Schein stated:

> Culture can [now] be defined as (a) a pattern of basic assumptions, (b) invented, discovered, or developed by a given group, (c) as it learns to cope with its problems of external adaptation and internal integration, (d) that has worked well enough to be considered valid, and therefore (e) is to be taught to new members as the (f) correct way to perceive, think, and feel in relation to those problems. (p. 111)

This description of a working culture clearly reflects experiences reported by counselors who have been part of a working group, whether on a school team with one or two members or on a larger team of health care workers.

Any definable group with a shared history can have a culture within an organization. Therefore an organization can have many subcultures. Using the hospital—which is often described as having an overarching medical culture—as an example, specific units within a given hospital or disciplines within the same organization can have fully functioning subcultures complete with their own language and practices. They may also have their own set of ethical practice ideals and standards. The term *client* will be used to refer to patients in the remainder of this chapter, because counselors strongly prefer the former term to signify their nonpathology-based orientation to those with whom they work.

Ethics and Organizational Culture

Hospital-based practice is a specific type of organizational culture and generally manifests a model of practice reflected by a definable paradigm. The hospital practice model, typically known as the medical model, represents the organic paradigm (Cottone, 1992). This culture is characterized as one in which the physician diagnoses and treats the disease of the client, who is relieved of blame. The role of the physician is often defined as autocratic. Both the role of the client and of ancillary staff (including the counselor) in this model is to trust and cooperate with physician. The historical shaping of this paradigm was developed from the values and procedures of its religious and military roots. Historically, this paradigm contains a deference and deeply rooted respect for chain-of-command orders over and above individual beliefs. Therefore, this approach represents a parentalistic and hierarchically based framework that has potential for creating ethically based tension. For example, the tension inherent in this culture is encountered when the "order" from the physician conflicts with the autonomous needs of the client or other caregivers.

Professional roles are constructed in response to institutional expectations and professional practices. Beauchamp and Childress (1994) stated that such roles also incorporate virtues and obligations. Roles encompass social expectations as well as standards and ideals. The hospital culture is an example of an environment or context with definitive ideas about how the helping process should occur.

Case Scenario 1

A Cultural Setting

A rehabilitation counselor is asked by a client to represent her at a rehabilitation hospital interdisciplinary team meeting. The client's desire is to remain in the hospital until she feels more able to manage her own care. After careful assessment, the counselor concurs with the client that a delayed discharge would be in her best interest. The client's physician orders that the client be prepared for discharge immediately. The implicit rule of the organization is that clients belong to the doctors and that the hospital and its staff are only assisting the physicians in the care of their clients. Dissenting opinions at team meetings are discouraged strongly due to their historically fruitless outcomes and the time they take from the staff. Should the counselor persist in forwarding the desire of the client? How?

YES.   Ethical standards in counseling clearly define counselors' obligation to their clients (ACA Code A.1.a.). Further, collaboration is considered a necessary condition for ethical decision-making.

Political and moral or ethical problems will arise and persist as long as some professionals make the decisions and order their implementation by others who have not participated in the decision-making. Beauchamp and Childress (1994) pointed out that these conflicts are avoidable but must be anticipated and prevented by establishing practices that honor open and collaborative decision-making. For example, obligations of fidelity must be made clear, and open routes to collegial dialogue must be valued. If this is not the case, Beauchamp and Childress (1994) warned, compassion, while cherished as focal virtue, can also cloud judgment and preclude rational and effective decision-making. Based on the levels of organizational practice discussed in Tarvydas and Cottone (1991), a useful ethical decision-making model for use in the larger organizational context is provided in Chapter 6. Given guidelines such as those provided in this model, decision-making that involves complexity and conflict can be dissected into manageable tasks that help facilitate collaborative discussion.

The setting, including the people with whom counselors work, significantly influences ethical decision-making. Doherty (1995) summarized this point well:

Unsupportive and alienating work settings inevitably affect therapists' ability to care, especially for difficult clients at the end of a long workday or workweek. Having our work undermined by other professionals in positions of greater institutional power erodes motivation and investment in clinical care. Seeing too many clients during a workweek does the same, as does having to fit the client's needs to the rigidly enforced restrictions of managed care contracts. Therapists start to go through the motions, it shows, and we know it. We become negative about our clients, we hope for no-shows and cancellations, our natural caring declines, and our ethical caring begins to feel like martyrdom. When such conditions arise, it is time to change the context or get out, in my view, because we cannot sustain the fundamental virtue of caring. (p. 13)

Clearly, the work setting, whether it is an informal group or a more formal organizational structure influences counselors' decision-making processes significantly.

Organizational Climate

Several authors have suggested that an organizational climate is the outward manifestation of its culture (Mohan, 1993; Schein, 1990). *Climate* is a metaphor that suggests an image wherein the environment, as the sum total of energy, presents atmospheric conditions as a type of aura. These conditions hold, support, create, and sustain the type of ethical decision-making that occurs. An awareness of these conditions is particularly important when confronting a decision with an emotional component such as one that presents an ethical dilemma. Like the atmospheric conditions of our weather, the climate may be fair or stormy. Bellah, Madsen, Sullivan, Swidler, and Tipton (1985) described this phenomenon as our moral ecology.

In other words, *organizational climate* is the way people would characterize a system's practices and procedures, such as the sense of safety or fear of retribution that a counselor may feel when faced with big or small decisions within this context. Therefore, the concept of organizational climate, more specifically the ethical climate, is one level of analysis that can help us understand and explain moral behavior as it is observed. An *ethical climate* is one facet of an organizational climate that describes the shared perceptions that colleagues hold concerning ethical procedures and practices within an organization. It upholds or erodes virtues such as compassion, discernment, truthfulness, and integrity.

The dynamic interaction of individual and organizational variables that contribute to the ethicality of the climate are complex and multilayered (Tarvydas & Cottone, 1991). The decision-maker is faced with individual, client, and organizationally contingent factors that must be considered. For example, decisions within an organization are often made by teams or groups rather than individuals, and decisions affect the workings of a team or group within the organization significantly. A growing body of literature is examining the dynamics inherent in team-based ethical decision making (Agich, 1982; Klebe–Trevino, 1986; O'Rourke, 1996). A basic understanding of some of the identified variables, both for the individual and for the team, is essential to intentional ethical counseling within an organizational setting.

Two basic individual skills that have been identified as essential to the collaborative process are (a) the ability to assert one's thoughts and ideas, and (b) the ability to clarify the content of others' contributions to the decision-making process (Weiss & Davis, 1985). These basic skills are useful in any decision-making process involving two or more individuals. These skills have been found to be particularly salient when decision-making occurs in a hierarchically structured context wherein one party has more power than others within the setting.

Given the potential inequities and complexities inherent in making team-based decisions, it is essential that a working team should establish a due process in a particular form for its decision-making practices. The mechanism of such a due process must then be sensitive to multiple perspectives and must be able to facilitate the production of a group decision. Constructing a useful process that is both efficient and equitable is a complex task. For example, the following questions may arise: How to proceed if an individual professional disagrees with a team decision, whether team consensus is necessary to adopt a decision; how to provide client confidentiality when decisions made about the client are nested within the operations of a larger organization, and what an appropriate appeals process is. Similar to the construction of a group culture in group counseling that has established normative behavior, the machinations of a working team are developmental and must be shaped proactively from its inception.

Case Scenario 2

Confidentiality

A school counselor is working with a young woman who has had numerous behavioral problems, including shoplifting. The student has demonstrated significant improvement during the last semester in both her motivation toward school and in her social behavior. Trust was difficult to establish between her and the counselor, but they have developed a working relationship. During the annual IEP meeting, it was suggested by one of her teachers that the student may benefit from having a job. There is an opening in the lost-and-found department of the school office. Should the counselor tell the team, which includes the student's mother, that she has concerns about the student's current ability to handle other people's property? If you do, what could this disclosure do to the trust that has been built with the client?

PROBABLY YES.   The counselor has a responsibility to support the young woman and help her achieve her counseling goal of avoiding behavioral problems such as stealing. Allowing her to be prematurely placed in a setting that exposes her to overwhelming triggers for stealing behavior would present considerable therapeutic risk. Another concern involves the degree to which the team understands the critical importance of confidentiality and their shared responsibility for assisting the student's progress toward dealing with her behavioral problems. The counselor must be an active participant in setting the climate for these team responsibilities. This sets the stage for any appropriate client disclosures. If the team is truly to function as a treatment team, important observations should be shared; but with the shared responsibility to assure that the student's trust and confidentiality is not violated.

Lastly, but most importantly, the integrity of the student must be respected by the counselor's gaining the student's permission (and even direct participation) in bringing this concern to the team and her mother. Her ability to directly evaluate the risk to herself and bring the issue to the team might have significant therapeutic benefits. At the outset of counseling, the student should have been informed that information and counselor judgments integral to her case would be shared with the treatment team, thus setting the stage for this discussion. If the student is reluctant and the counselor still thinks the opinion must be shared, the counselor should at least discuss her reasons for the disclosure and its perceived benefits and risks with the student before the team meeting.

Accountability

The nature of one's counseling environment plays a significant role in one's decision-making process, and ethical standards mandate that counselors are accountable to both their clients and to the organizations in which they work. As a result, it is ethically sound practice for counselors to explore fully and to commit to the mission and standards of practice of any organizations for which they work. Conversely, it is the organization's ethical obligation to disclose fully all relevant information about its mission and practices, including its provision of a due process for resolution of conflict with an employee. Counselors who accept a position with an organization enter into a tacit agreement with that organization to honor its values and standards of practice. At the same time, counselors have an obligation to honor their professional code of ethics. Therefore, intentional practice is served by having a pre-existing plan to resolve any conflicts between organizational and professional obligations. The establishment of working ethics committees and the use of case consultative meetings are ways that institutions have attempted to be more intentional by constructing mechanisms to provide due process. Again, the decisional model described in Chapter 6 is a useful tool for any individual counselor seeking to reconcile professional and institutional aspects of ethical dilemmas.

Consider the effect that a specific overarching philosophy that creates the hospital's climate, such as a religious affiliation, may have on the operations in the hospital organization. Clinical decisions concerning use of client service options such as provision of pregnancy termination and birth control, or withdrawl of nutrition and hydration from a client in a persistant vegetative state, become enmeshed in the ethical value climate of that particular institution. Extend this consideration to a school environment, such as the gender controversy concerning admission of women to previously all-male military schools, such as The Citadel. An institution's values and moral orientation are clearly an overriding aspect of the concerns involved in these situations.

Organizational values and morality subsequently influence the ethical decision-making process of members. This force is particularly evident when moral obligations and religious standards of the institution are in conflict with their espoused ethical practices.

Case Scenario 3

Accountability

A counselor is working with a client who has been hospitalized at a local Catholic hospital for depression. During the course of her hospitalization, the client disclosed that she had been raped several weeks before but is otherwise not sexually active. A pregnancy test reveals that she is pregnant. She is requesting information from the counselor about obtaining a therapeutic abortion. Should the counselor engage in a dialogue about this issue with the client, given that it is strictly forbidden by institutional values?

YES.   As part of informed consent, the counselor must inform the client about the limits of their relationship and offer to help her identify her alternatives (ACA Code A.3.a).

Climate Factors and Ethical Decisions

Factors in the work environment that influence the ethical decision-making climate of service organizations include the organization's socialization practices, interpersonal relationships with significant others in the workplace (peers and superiors), role perceptions, and individual levels of development of the service providers. Research has examined specific elements of an organizational environment that have shown influence on the ethical behavior of employees, including (a) constructs of structure (centralized versus participatory management), (b) ethical climate (reinforceable values, e.g. beneficence), (c) task dimensions, (d) influence of significant others in the environment, (e) role perceptions, and (f) levels of personal development of the individual service provider (Wiles, 1993). These elements include the influence of significant others such as peers and superiors, the opportunity to behave ethically as guided by a code of ethics, and the application of rewards and punishments for both ethical and unethical behavior. Wiles (1993) reviewed the ethical climate literature, and found that organizationally based ethics decision-making models include 11 specific factors as noted in Figure 8–1.

Clearly, an ethical climate is constructed as a product of the interaction among the institution, the individual counselor, and numerous contributing influences from both sources. The ACA recognizes these influences and clearly defines standards of practice regarding personnel administration in Section G of its Code of Ethics. It is the responsibility of the individual counselor to address some of these influences before making a working covenant with the institution. The remainder of this chapter examines factors related to the influence of significant individuals within the counselors' work environment who may have been unethical in their behavior or impaired in their ability to practice.

1. Environmental factors (external forces)

2. Organizational factors (organizational culture; organizational socialization; characteristics of the job/task; significant others in the organization)

3. Opportunity and situational factors

4. Individual factors (personal values; societal and familial socialization experiences; ego strength; locus of control; field dependence; personal knowledge and attitudes; age; education; gender; job tenure)

5. Stage of moral development

6. Characteristics of the moral issue

7. Recognition of the moral issue (moral sensitivity)

8. Moral evaluation (includes moral philosophy, ethical decision ideology; and phased decision process)

9. Intentions

10. Behavior

11. Evaluation of the behavior (ability to self-reflect)

Figure 8–1

Factors in Organizational Climates that Affect Individual Decision Making

Source: From *Socialization and Interpersonal Influence on Ethical Decision-Making Climatein Service Organizations* by J. Wiles, 1993, unpublished dissertation. Memphis, TN: Memphis State University.

Impaired Professionals

The functional impairment of professionals is a growing concern in U.S. society. Impairment is a relative term and is distinct from a disability. A *disability* is an identifiable condition that is more stable and whose functional limitations, when manifested, are recognized and often overcome with appropriate accommodations. In contrast, an *impairment* is a more covert, often insidious condition that suggests a level of diminished function (obtained by documented evidence) that may be manifested on a continuum by varying degrees of loss of optimal function. It may have many causes. A person with a disability may also become impaired, given this perspective. In fact, all counselors are impaired to some degree at some time in their practice. Impairment may be the result of a headache or having the flu. The more dysfunctional and pervasive impairments that may disrupt professional performance typically include unrecognized or treated chronic physical illness, substance abuse, and emotional or psychological factors such as burnout and sexual acting-out behaviors. Lamb, Cochran, and Jackson (1991) defined *impairment* broadly as it is applied to psychology interns in the following way:

> An interference in professional functioning that is reflected in one or more of the following ways: (a) an inability or unwillingness to acquire and integrate professional standards into one's repertoire of professional behavior; (b) an inability to acquire professional skills and reach an accepted level. (p. 293)

In other words, ethically professional impairment is a matter of decreased level of professional competence, and the term can be applied to people in various professional roles, including those of student, counselor, or supervisor.

Counselors who continue to provide professional services while impaired may be in violation of their ethical code. A counselor who is aware that a colleague or student is providing unethical services but fails to intervene may also be behaving unethically due to failure to address this issue.

Awareness that includes a working knowledge of practice standards and a sensitivity to abridgment of these standards is key to ethical behavior. The impaired professional often provides clues over time that a pattern of problem behavior exists. Typically, the unethical behavior of an impaired colleague is not an isolated occurrence. Information will be provided about three common issues related to professional impairment: (a) burnout, (b) violation of professional boundaries, and (c) substance abuse.

Burnout

According to Skorupa and Agresti (1993), *burnout* is an emotional exhaustion in which the professional no longer has any positive feelings, sympathy, or respect for clients. It is often associated with fatigue, frustration, and apathy that seems to result from prolonged stress and overwork. Studies suggest that certain client factors may contribute to therapist burnout. Among these are the number of contact hours with clients and the number of clients in a caseload that present with pervasive stressful behavior such as aggression or limit testing (Hellman, 1986), factors that are of concern in the increasingly dominant environment of managed care. Interestingly, therapists who work in agency settings were more prone to burnout than those working in private settings (Hellman, 1986). These data indicate the importance of climate conditions on an individual. Implications for ethical practice may include (a) setting limits on the size of a caseload, (b) acknowledging a duty to understand the process of burnout and prevention techniques, and (c) conducting research to determine how work settings can affect counselors, and how to mediate untoward effects of workplace stress on the work of counselors.

Case Scenario 4

Burnout

A social worker with many years of experience is working as your colleague and mentor. You have noticed that she has become increasingly judgmental which often is expressed by becoming anxious and rejecting of her clients when they start to place demands on her or when they "don't do what is good for them." However, it is also true that you are now expected to take more and more clients, do more documentation of services, and are no longer offered overtime pay. Is this behavior severe enough to constitute burnout? Impairment? What alternatives can you define to deal with this situation?

YES AND NO.   Yes, certainly this is a sign of counselor fatigue. However, impairment is present only if the judgmental attitudes are influencing actual practice.

Professional Boundaries

Professionals who transgress boundaries with clients, students, or participants in research violate clearly stated ethical standards related to dual relationships. Basic concepts related to dual relationships were overviewed in Chapter 2. Supervisors and educators also have responsibilities to avoid conflicting relationships, which will be discussed in Chapter 16. To further clarify dual relationships, Schoener (1995) has developed a typology of offenders. This typology provides a descriptive educational device to illuminate features associated with professionals who have been reported violators. The six types of counselors Schoener (1995) saw as likely to violate professional boundaries are counselors with (a) psychotic and severe borderline disorders, (b) manic disorders, (c) impulse control disorders, (d) chronic neurosis and isolation, (e) situational offenders, and (f) deficits due to naivete. The features of these types are given in Figure 8–2.

Schoener (1995) called for more sophisticated assessment procedures and asserted that "prior to the last decade, sexual misconduct and other boundary violations by professionals were treated . . . via a combination of reprimand and temporary privilege suspension. [And] only rarely was there a formal evaluation or planned rehabilitation effort" (p. 95). Students and novice practitioners who violate client boundaries typically fall in the naive category. Therefore, adequate educational opportunities to explore these issues and quality supervision are essential to their practice.

Case Scenario 5

Boundary Issues

Last semester, as a graduate assistant, you were supervising a student on a project that reflects your own interests. You met outside of your scheduled supervisory hour on several occasions and began to know more about each other's personal lives. You really liked this student and want to see him succeed. You have just received your class list for the course you are teaching next semester. His name is on the list. Are there any ethical concerns present? What actions can you take to ensure you and the student remain ethical?

YES.   Your friendship with this student has the potential either to make objective judgment difficult or to create the appearance of unfairness in the minds of other students (ACA Code F.1.b. and F.2.e.). You should raise this issue with both the student and the supervising faculty member so that alternate arrangements might be discussed, such as transfer of yourself or the student to another section. It might be possible for the student to continue in your class with the arrangement of more intense faculty review of your grading and cessation of your social relationship.

1. **Psychotic and severe borderline disorders.** These professionals tend to have difficulties with boundaries due to problems with impulse control and thinking.
2. **Manic disorders.** This refers to individuals with manic disorders that are not medically managed and have become impulsive.
3. **Impulse control disorders.** These include a wide range of paraphilias (strong attractions to non-sexual objects) and other impulse disorders.
4. **Chronic neurotic and isolated.** Professionals who tend to be emotionally needy on a chronic basis and meet many needs through relationships with clients.
5. **Situational offenders.** These professionals are generally healthy with good practice history, free of boundary problems, but a situational breakdown in judgment or control has occurred. Occasionally in response to some life crisis or loss.
6. **Naive.** In the absence of pathology, these professionals have difficulty understanding and operating within boundaries due to social deficits or the development of inadequate knowledge base.

Figure 8–2
Predictive Features of Potential Boundary Violators
Source: From "Thinking About Blowing the Whistle?" by A.G. Felie, 1983, *American Journal of Nursing, 83,* 1541–1542. Reprinted by permission of Lippincott-Raven Publishers, Philadelphia, PA.

Substance Abuse

While the etiology of substance dependence and abuse is varied, pre-existing faulty coping mechanisms and certain predictive behaviors seem to precede professional impairment. Knowledge of risk factors related significantly to chemical dependency can aid early recognition and intervention. The following etiologic factors have been consistently cited in the literature: (a) genetic predisposition, (b) poor coping skills, (c) lack of education about impairment, (d) absence of effective prevention strategies, (e) drug and alcohol availability, (f) the context of a permissive environment, and (g) denial.

Ironically, as with any lethal malady, early diagnosis and intervention is critical, but the hallmark of chemical dependency continues to be denial. Waiting for spontaneous insight from an affected colleague has been judged to be unconscionable. While the workplace is traditionally the last area to be affected, professional competence is affected adversely. Barriers to early recognition of chemical dependency include (a) lack of training in recognition of early signs of abuse, (b) the insidious and confusing effect of the progression of the disease on daily function that lends to signs that are easily rationalized away, and (c) the subsequent denial on the part of the impaired professional as well as the individual's colleagues.

The task of differentiating impairment from problematic behaviors is difficult. Acting on the conclusion that impairment is imminent is even more difficult. Few counselors have received training in this area. The literature (Skorina, DeSoto, & Bissell, 1990) suggested that counselors tend to underestimate or fail to recognize impairment in colleagues. Therefore intervention, including the colleague's recovery, may be delayed.

Suggestions for dealing intentionally with potential impairment among one's peers include primary, secondary, and tertiary levels of intervention based on the timing and need of the situation. Primary interventions include involvement in educational programs (e.g., graduate education or in-service programs). These educational programs provide (a) values clarification regarding impairment and the individual conditions that often cause the impairment (e.g., adopting an attitude of assistance and compassion versus one of blame), (b) knowledge of potential signs of impending impairment for each condition, (c) enactment of prevention strategies that address each area of potential impairment (both individually and institutionally). Secondary intervention would include the establishment and knowledge of sound practice standards. These standards include steps to obtain due process for both the individual who may be impaired as well as the individual's colleagues. Tertiary prevention involves understanding and involving the necessary resources to make a direct intervention with a colleague who appears to be impaired.

Case Scenario 6

Substance Abuse

The medical director of the treatment center where you are working as a chemical dependency counselor has started to miss the morning staff meetings fairly regularly. He always has a rational explanation. Two weeks ago, an evening nurse confided in you that she thought she smelled alcohol on the breath of the doctor as he attended to a client one night. Is this enough evidence to initiate an intervention on the physician?

NO. Impairment requires the documentation of significantly impaired function. However, there is enough evidence to discuss your concerns with the physician (ACA Code D.1.b. and C.2.g.).

Whistle Blowing

Counselors are mandated by their codes of ethics and by state licensure guidelines to report questionable or unethical behavior, yet many are hesitant to become whistle blowers. *Whistle blowing* is the term used to characterize the ethical reporting of unethical behavior, and it has often been used in a pejorative sense. It is important to recognize that collegial support may be mixed regarding a colleague who reports the suspected behavior of a peer.

Mixed support may be particularly true in hierarchical organizations such as hospitals when the accused is a physician who also occupies a place on the upper level of the hierarchy, or when whistle blowing disrupts the immediate work team. On the other hand, whistle blowing can be beneficial and override the negative risks by (a) providing a climate that supports the protection of current and future clients as well as co-workers, (b) facilitating communication among colleagues, and (c) encouraging constructive problem-solving. Several laws have been designed to safeguard employees who suspect the unethical behavior of their colleagues. However, court actions suggest that legal protection for whistle blowers is tentative. For example, a 1981 Michigan state law protects employees who expose illegal or dangerous employee activity from wrongful discharge from any government or private-sector organization. However, as stated in Chapter 2, counselors are obligated to their employers as well as to their clients, making the decisions concerning disclosure ethically complex.

Ethical codes for counseling disciplines do provide codified standards of behavior for addressing concerns regarding the ethicality of a colleague. For example, in the Ethical Principle of Psychologists (APA, 1992), Sections 8.04 and 8.05 (Informal Resolution of Ethical Violation and Reporting Ethical Violations) read:

> **8.04** When psychologists believe that there may have been an ethical violation by another psychologist, they attempt to resolve the issue by bringing it to the attention of that individual if an informal resolution appears appropriate and the intervention does not violate any confidentiality rights that may be involved.

> **8.05** If an apparent ethical violation is not appropriate for informal resolution under Standard 8.04 or is not resolved properly in that fashion, psychologists take further action appropriate to the situation, unless such action conflicts with confidentiality rights in ways that cannot be resolved. Such action might include referral to state or national committees on professional ethics or to state licensing boards. (p. 15)

This approach is similar to the guidance provided in the ACA Code of Ethics.

In a more general sense, Felie (1983) suggested several guidelines for whether, when, and how to blow the whistle on a colleague if informal routes prove to be ineffective and if the colleague is not of one's own discipline but works as a peer within an organizational setting. She has outlined five steps for addressing the problem (Figure 8–3).

The act of taking a colleague to task for behavior that is ethically inappropriate is daunting. Nevertheless, counselors have an important obligation to the clients of the profession and society at large to protect them and uphold the trust placed in the profession.

Summary

This chapter has introduced several important influences on the individual counselor's ethical decision-making: general organizational cultural influences, and the ethical climate of the particular organization. We discussed the counselor's accountability to the organizational culture, as well as more specific factors in the organizational culture that affect ethical decision-making. Finally, we discussed the issue of impaired professionals

---

- **Confirm the issue.** Conduct an objective assessment of the situation. Make certain that you are competent to make this determination and that your desire to make this report is not based on personal motives.

- **Check your perceptions with peers.** Examine them against the norms of your institution and your discipline. Compare the activity against your state's practice guidelines and those of your institution. Does the situation truly exceed acceptable standards? Maintain a nonjudgmental attitude throughout the process.

- **Involve others in an action plan.** Develop a plan of action for voicing your concerns. Respect your institution chain of command. Multiple participants are more effective in providing a successful intervention. Have intervention goals established in advance. Anticipate possible reactions.

- **Set deadlines.** They demonstrate that you are serious. Implement your plan after conferring with your immediate supervisor.

- **Document** details of your discussion and include time, date, and the basic content of the conversation. Timing of any intervention is crucial. Soon after a precipitant crisis is optimal.

- **If needed, take the problem upstairs.** If your supervisor dismisses or fails to address the situation, however, be prepared to move up the organizational ladder.

Figure 8–3
Guidelines for Whistle Blowing
(Felie, 1983)

as a key element within the organizational environment affecting ethical practice. Three types of problems that might lead professionals to significant levels of impairment were delineated: burnout, violation of professional boundaries, and substance abuse. Finally, we reviewed the specific obligations of the counselor to act when unethical conduct is identified, including a more detailed consideration of guidelines for whistle blowing.

References

Agich, G. J. (Ed.). (1982). *Responsibility in health care.* Boston: D. Reidel.

American Psychological Association. (1992). Ethical principles of psychologists and code of conduct. *American Psychologist, 47,* 1597–1611.

Beauchamp, T. L., & Childress, J. F. (1994). *Principles of biomedical ethics.* New York & Oxford: Oxford University Press.

Bellah, R. N., Madson, R., Sullivan, W. M., Swidler, A., & Tipton, S. M. (1985). *Habits of the heart:* *Individualism and commitment in American life.* New York: Harper & Row.

Cottone, R. R. (1992). *Theories and paradigms of counseling and psychotherapy.* Needham Heights, MA: Allyn & Bacon.

Cottone, R. R., Tarvydas, V., & House, G. (1994). The effect of number and type of consulted relationships on the ethical decision-making of graduate students in counseling. *Counseling and Values, 39,* 56–68.

Doherty, W. J. (1995). *Soul searching: Why psychotherapy must promote moral responsibility.* New York: Basic Books.

Felie, A. G. (1983). The risks of blowing the whistle. *American Journal of Nursing, 83,* 1387.

Hellman, J. (1986). The stresses of psychotherapeutic work: A replication and extension. *Journal of Clinical Psychology, 42,* 197–204.

Ivey, A. E. (1994). *Intentional interviewing and counseling: Facilitating client development in a multicultural society,* (3rd ed.) Pacific Grove, CA: Brooks/Cole.

Klebe-Trevino, L. (1986). Ethical decision making in organizations: A person-situation interactionist model. *The Academy of Management Review,* 11, 601–617.

Lamb, D. H, Cochran, D. J., & Jackson, V. (1991). Training and organizational issues associated with identifying and responding to intern impairment. *Professional Psychology: Research and Practice, 22,* 291–296.

Liddell, D. L., Halpin. G., & Halpin, W. G. (1992). The measure of moral orientation: Measuring the ethics of care and justice. *Journal of College Student Development, 33,* 325–330.

Mohan, J. (1993). The business of medicine. *Sociology, 22,* 648–649.

O'Rourke, B. (1996). *Individual interdisciplinary team members' perception of ethics decision-making context: A descriptive study.* Unpublished doctoral dissertation, The University of Iowa, Iowa City, IA.

Schein, E. H. (1990). Organizational culture. *American Psychologist, 45,* 109–119.

Schoener, R. (1995). Assessment of professionals who have engaged in boundary violations. *Psychiatric Annals, 25,* 95–98.

Skorina, J. K., DeSoto, C. B., Bissell, L. (1990). Alcoholic psychologists: Routes to recovery. *Professional Psychology: Research and Practice, 21,* 248–251.

Skorupa, J., & Agresti, A. (1993). Ethical beliefs about burnout and continued professional practice. *Professional Psychology: Research and Practice, 24,* 281–285.

Tarvydas, V. M. (1994). Ethical orientations of masters' rehabilitation students. *Rehabilitation Counseling Bulletin, 37,* 202–214.

Tarvydas, V. M., & Cottone, R. R. (1991). Ethical responses to legislative, organizational, and economic dynamics: A four level model of ethical practice. *Journal of Applied Rehabilitation,* 22(4), 11–17.

Weiss, S. J., & Davis, H. P. (1985). Validity and reliability of the collaborative practice scale. *Nursing Research, 34,* 299–305.

Wiles, J. (1993). *Socialization and interpersonal influence on the ethical decision-making climate in service organizations.* Unpublished dissertation. Memphis State University: Memphis, TN.

9

Ethics and Technology

David B. Peterson
Gerald C. Murray
Fong Chan

During the past 30 years, computer capabilities have dramatically increased while costs to implement such technology have decreased significantly (Ford, 1993; Sampson, in press; Simons, 1985). Personal computers (PCs) have increased in sophistication, and PC-based programming languages are powerful and easy to use. These changes have increased the use of such technology in the counseling profession (Colby, 1980; Ford, 1993; Levitan, Willis, & Vogelgesang, 1985; Sampson, in press).

Computer-based applications for clinical situations in counseling-related professions began as early as the 1960s, with computer-based test interpretation (Butcher, 1987; Fowler, 1985). During the 1970s researchers expanded computer-assisted testing capabilities to include administration, scoring, and interpretation of psychological tests (Butcher, 1987). Computer-assisted assessments have increased in number throughout the 1980s and into the 1990s (Butcher, 1987; Ford, 1993; Fowler, 1985), and the use, assets, and limitations of such technology have been well-explored in the counseling literature (Butcher, 1985, 1987; Eyde, 1987; French, 1986; Matarazzo, 1985, 1986; Merrell, 1986; Sampson, 1990; Sampson, in press).

Computer-assisted therapy also began in the 1960s, with much less success than computerized assessment applications (Colby, Watt, & Gilbert, 1966; Colby, Gould, & Aronson, 1989; Ford, 1993). Therapeutic applications received little further attention until the 1980s (Ford, 1993). Since then various types of computer-assisted therapies have been used, including professional consultation programs, client therapeutic learning programs, and on-line therapy. Unlike computer-assisted assessment, little has been written on ethical issues related to the use of computer-assisted therapy until recently (Sampson, Kolodinsky, & Greeno, 1997).

As computer technology has become more affordable, and as desk and laptop computers have grown in number, tasks once dedicated to paper, typewriter, or pen have been transferred to more convenient computerized technologies. The advent of facsimile machines (faxes), computer modems for phone line communication, computer networks (e.g. the Internet) and satellite networks has resulted in new forms of electronic media that the counseling profession uses with increasing frequency. As a result of these technological developments, ethical and professional issues have arisen that the counseling profession has had little time to address (Ford, 1993; Sampson et al., 1997; Sampson, in press).

The ethical codes of practice and the literature associated with counseling and the allied health professions have been hard-pressed to keep pace with the dramatic changes in technology. Some ethical issues related to recent technological developments have been of concern to counselors and psychologists for many years. Other issues are unique to more recent technological developments. Several counseling-related organizations are addressing new standards of practice that will affect the standards and codes used today (APA, 1986; American Educational Research Association, 1985; ACA, 1995; NBCC, 1989). To care for the "welfare and protection of the individuals and groups with whom (they) work" (APA, 1992, preamble), it is essential for counseling professionals to remain current with efforts to develop and establish ethical standards and codes of conduct.

The purpose of this chapter is to consider how recent technological developments affect the practices and ethical decision-making processes of the counseling professional. As managed care continues to place new demands on the allied health professions, it is ethically essential (Erdman & Foster, 1988; Sampson, in press) that counseling-related professions explore using technology to facilitate ethical counseling practice. We begin by exploring ethical issues surrounding the use of electronic media in counseling-related professions. Then we will review computer-assisted counseling, including on-line forums of counseling via the Internet, followed by a review of computer-assisted assessment in counseling (administration, scoring, and interpreting tests with computers and computer software). Next we will address computer-assisted counselor education, including on-line supervision and virtual practica using the Internet or satellite technology. After a brief review of the ethical use of computer software, we will discuss technological counseling interventions for persons with disabilities. Finally, Tarvydas and Cottone's (1991) four-level model of ethical practice will be reviewed as it applies to ethical use of technology in counseling.

Ethical Management of Electronic Media

Ethical codes addressing the maintenance of client records, such as those established by the APA (1992), mandate that psychologists "maintain appropriate confidentiality in creating, storing, accessing, transferring, and disposing of records under their control, whether these are written, automated, or in any other medium" (section 5.04). The American Counseling Association has a similar requirement that the ethical counseling professional protect the client's right to confidentiality regardless of the type of electronic media (ACA, 1995).

All forms of electronic media used in counseling may contain sensitive material protected by client–therapist confidentiality and privileged communication. It is important that ethical practicing counselors are aware of how the use of electronic media influences professional practice. Protocols need to be in place to ensure that electronic media will be accessible only to ethically appropriate parties. Electronic media storage systems may not be immediately visible to the counseling professional, and therefore ethical management of such data may be easily overlooked. In view of this, it is important to discuss the different types of electronic media used in counseling in light of relevant ethics and standards of practice. The following is a review of types of electronic media used in counseling professions, with suggested means of safeguarding against breaches in confidentiality.

Electronic Media on Personal Computers

Personal computer systems commonly used by counseling professionals are composed of hardware and software. Hardware consists of the electrical and mechanical devices of the computer system, including the central processing unit (CPU) of the computer (or the "brains" in the chassis of the computer), the monitor, printer, and various peripheral (outside of the CPU) devices. Hardware that stores electronic media includes (a) a hard disk drive, which is a sealed memory system located either within the chassis of the CPU or in a portable peripheral unit, (b) floppy disk or compact disk–read-only-memory (CD–ROM) drives that are connected to the CPU and store data on portable floppy disks or compact disks (CDs), or (c) a server that has a large data storage drive for a network of computers. Electronic media can be safeguarded at the hardware level with a mechanical lock and key that prevent power from reaching the computer, thus maintaining confidentiality of the information within. Once turned on, such systems should not be left unattended unless protected at the software level.

Software includes the programs written for the CPU to perform various functions, or applications. Common computer applications used by counseling professionals include document production using word processing applications, financial and records management using spreadsheets, and record filing on databases (applications that facilitate therapy and assessment will be reviewed in their respective sections). Word processors generate media formerly produced by typewriters and handwriting, such as case notes, letters, and test reports. Spreadsheets are used for numerical recordkeeping, tasks like client billing and miscellaneous records. Databases are electronic "file cabinets" used to store and control large amounts of information, such as client mailing lists and community referral sources.

In addition to being able to print a paper or "hard" copy of a document created by a word processor, spreadsheet, or database application, documents can be stored as files on the memory systems mentioned earlier. In addition to the need to control access to printed matter generated from computers, the data stored on hard disks, floppy disks, and CDs must be carefully controlled. Personnel with access to such data must be well-trained regarding ethical management of electronic media. For example, a 3 1/2 inch floppy disk containing confidential information may be less obvious than a notebook-size chart containing paper copies of the same information. However, a small computer disk can store information equivalent to many client charts and is much easier to remove from an office than a rack full of confidential records. Storage of paper and electronic information must be locked in tamper-proof surroundings.

The storage of confidential material on a hard drive may be even less obvious than a floppy disk to the counselor. However, all staff members within a counseling organization must be oriented to the appropriate ethical procedures for all client records and the related access protocols. For hard drives on PCs, security software is available that will allow access to certain files only if a person has an access code or password. People issued access codes must protect their codes from misuse. If a PC in a counseling organization does not require a security code to access confidential information, large amounts of data are at risk of being viewed by people who should not have access to such information.

Organizations that use a server for a network of computers, sometimes called a local area network or LAN, need to establish protocols that limit access to ethically relevant parties. Servers can be accessed by personal computers with modems over telephone lines, dramatically increasing the audience potentially having access to the secured data. Computer systems management specialists who set up systems for business organizations must be made aware of the location of sensitive confidential material. They can design the system with the appropriate safeguards and security protocols to maintain confidentiality through security software requiring pass codes and the requisite employee training.

For example, LAN administrators routinely back up or duplicate LAN files as archives in the event of a hardware or software malfunction that results in the loss of data. If a PC user on the network has stored files on the server (e.g. word processor documents, spreadsheet files, database files, e-mail), the archived files may contain confidential material. Even though a given file may be deleted locally by a network user, there may be an archived copy stored somewhere, accessible to potentially inappropriate parties. Protocols must be established with LAN administrators regarding the archiving of potentially confidential information.

Unfortunately, counseling professionals may not be motivated to purchase adequate systems of protection due to ignorance or presumed unlikelihood of unethical file disclosure. Establishing a secure computer system can be time consuming and costly; nevertheless, confidential client information needs to be protected.

Other Electronic Media

Fax machines allow the transmission of information either from paper or directly from a computer file. Generally, faxes are composed of printed matter, which can include any type of client information protected by client–therapist confidentiality. Counselors need to use caution when sending confidential information by fax. Many businesses have centrally located, public fax machines from which it would be inappropriate to send or receive confidential information. It is the counselor's responsibility to assure that confidential fax transmissions arrive in a secured environment. Faxes can be sent directly to a PC by fax/modem. The security precautions mentioned for electronic media storage applies to fax transmissions sent to PCs. A quick phone call to assess the situation before sending a confidential fax is appropriate to assure safe arrival of sensitive information. In the event that a destination PC or fax machine is not secure, phoning ahead before transmitting documents can alert appropriate parties to intercept confidential information.

Other forms of on-line electronic media, such as video conferencing, will be addressed later, as will data exchanged on the Internet. We will explore data encryption as a method of maintaining client confidentiality when using on-line media. Before reviewing on-line counseling technology, the recent use of computer-assisted counseling will be explored, along with its implications for ethical counseling practice.

Computer-Assisted Counseling

Computer-assisted counseling exists in a variety of forms. Some programs function as therapeutic consultants (Goodman, Gingerich, & Shazer, 1989). The advent of the Internet and "chat rooms" has created the opportunity for direct on-line communication between counselor and client, which will be reviewed later in this chapter. The topic of the following section is therapeutic software marketed to operate without therapist assistance (Lawrence, 1986; Sampson, 1986a).

History

Computer-assisted therapy was first developed in the 1960s (Colby et al., 1966), but was relatively unsuccessful. Attempts to computerize psychotherapy were rejuvenated in the 1980s with the popularization of behavioral modes of therapy and the emphasis of bringing about change through education (Ford, 1993; Wagman, 1988). Early versions of counseling software that did not require counselor assistance included MORTON, based on cognitive behavior therapy and designed primarily to treat mild forms of depression (Selmi, Klein, Greist, Johnson, & Harris, 1982). MORTON began with an educational component addressing a cognitive model of depression with subsequent testing of the client's comprehension of the theory, feedback on a test of depression (Beck Depression Inventory), review of homework, and exercises to combat thoughts that perpetuate depression. The program offered response choices to the client, with limited free-responding. One experimental program, GURU, attempted to expand interactive conversation capabilities with the goal of increasing self-awareness (Colby, Colby, & Stoller, 1990).

Most recently, virtual psychotherapy programs have been under development, such as *Avatars* (Duncan, 1997). This software depicts characterizations of the client via a computer image or graphic, with bubbles overhead to indicate ongoing dialogue. Another application, *Palace,* develops an "Intranet" or closed Internet system, allowing for virtual psychotherapy with a controlled audience (Duncan, 1997). These applications are in their nascent stages of development and require further research to be evaluated effectively for counseling practice.

Computerized career counseling was evaluated by Kilvingham, Johnston, Hogan, and Mauer (1994). Clients who were highly motivated and goal directed benefited from the System for Interactive Guidance and Information–Plus (SIGI–PLUS). However, they determined that clients with less-clear goals and less motivation for independence did not benefit as much from the use of this program. Group or individual counseling was proposed as more appropriate in the latter case. In such a case, using computer career counseling software as an adjunct to individual and group counseling would be exemplary of ethical counseling practice.

As early as 1978, video games were used in the later phases of cognitive retraining for persons with head injury. Cognitive retraining falls under the domain of therapy in a rehabilitation hospital setting. Monotonous repetitive exercises to enhance cognitive functioning were made more enjoyable by the novelty of the games (Caplan, 1987). A more sophisticated computerized testing application, the Computer Assisted Cognitive Retraining system (CACR), was developed in 1987 by the Brain Injury Rehabilitation Unit in Palo Alto, California. The CACR used various computer-driven exercises to enhance the individual's alertness, attention, concentration, fine-motor skills, memory, and certain language abilities (e.g., spelling, reading, and word finding). Performance scores were recorded by the computer, and a graph was constructed to indicate progress.

A variety of theoretical orientations have been adapted to computer-assisted counseling, including behavioral, cognitive, educational, and psychodynamic approaches (Ford, 1993). Software has been developed to target AIDS education (Schinke & Orlandi, 1990; Schinke et al., 1989), the treatment of drug and alcohol abuse (Moncher et al., 1985), obesity (Burnett, Magel, Harrington, & Taylor, 1989; Burnett, Taylor, & Agras, 1985; Taylor, Agras, Losch, Plante, & Burnett, 1991), personal distress (Wagman, 1980, 1988; Wagman & Kerber, 1980), sexual dysfunction (Binik, Servan-Schreiber, Freiwald, & Hall, 1988; Servan-Schreiber & Binik, 1989), smoking (Burling et al., 1989; Schneider, 1986; Schneider, Walter, & O'Donnell, 1990), and stress (Smith, 1987). Various clinical populations have benefited from computer-assisted counseling including persons with depression (Selmi, Klein, Greist, Sorell, & Erdman, 1990), persons with phobia (Carr, Ghosh, & Marks, 1988), people who are violent offenders (Ford & Vitelli, 1992), and with patients who have head trauma needing cognitive retraining (Niemann, Ruff, & Baser, 1990).

As computer technology continues to improve, so will the capabilities of computer-assisted therapy. The ethical implications of widespread use of such technology have not been adequately explored (Ford, 1993; Sampson et al., 1997). Research is needed to compare the outcomes of in vivo counseling and newly developed computer-assisted counseling, how they may be used together to effect change, and what factors of such technology contribute to effective therapy.

Computer-Assisted Counseling: Real Therapy?

Counselors with a psychodynamic or humanistic orientation may be most resistant to the use of computer-assisted counseling in lieu of individual face-to-face therapy (Ford, 1993). However, the concepts of counseling and psychotherapy are so inclusive that further clarification of computer-assisted counseling is necessary before the point can be argued successfully. Grencavage and Norcross (1990) suggested their conceptualization of the commonalties among psychotherapies: (a) development of a therapeutic alliance, (b) opportunity for catharsis, (c) acquisition and practice of new behaviors, and (d) clients' positive expectations. The literature supports the contention that computer-assisted counseling can be used to practice new behaviors, test simulated situations, express feelings and emotions, receive feedback, develop insight, and learn how to better interact with others (Ford, 1993). Ford (1993) contended that if sharing a number of commonalties with recognized psychotherapy techniques is the criterion for determining the viability of computer-assisted psychotherapy, then it can be argued strongly that such technology is in fact a form of psychotherapy.

Consumer Acceptance

It is an ethical responsibility of the counselor to use interventions that suit an individual's needs. The acceptance of computer-assisted counseling interventions by the consumers of such services is a critical aspect of the overall ethical viability of such technology. History has shown that, for most consumers, acceptance of the technology is not an issue (Erdman, Klein, & Greist, 1985; French & Beaumont, 1987; Harrell, Honaker, Hetu, & Oberwager, 1987; Rozensky, Honor, Rasinski, Tovian, & Herz, 1986; Wyndowe, 1987). In fact, for some consumers technological alternatives are preferred over face-to-face interventions (Farrell, Camplair, & McCullough, 1987; Ford, & Vitelli, 1992; Lukin, Dowd, Plake, & Kraft, 1985) with clients expressing positive sentiments toward computer-assisted forms of counseling (Binik et al., 1988; Burda, Starkey, & Dominguez, 1991; Clarke & Schoech, 1984; Colby et al., 1989; Ford, 1988; Matthews, De Santi, Callahan, Koblenz-Sulcov, & Werden, 1987; McLemore & Fantuzzo, 1982; Servan-Schreiber & Binik, 1989).

Independent Use

Another ethical quandary of computer-assisted therapy is its use independent from a therapist. Many counselors are opposed to using such technology as a replacement for human therapists (Colby et al., 1989; Davidson, 1985; Ford, 1988, 1993; Ford & Vitelli, 1992; Hartman, 1986a; Selmi et al., 1990). However, many such programs are designed so that at least moderately functioning clients do not need assistance with administration (Ford, 1993; Sampson, 1986a; Sampson & Krumboltz, 1991). One fact is clear: Counselors are necessary for the development and evaluation of effective computer-assisted counseling programs (Ford, 1993).

The ethical question facing counselors is how safe are these technologies for independent users? There are certain benefits associated with making computer-assisted therapy available to independent users: "Cost, convenience, and privacy are just some of the advantages of self-help programs" (Ford, 1993, p. 391). "To the extent that it is possible to offer the public sound, effective programs that do not require professional intervention, it would be socially irresponsible to restrict unduly or to discourage psychologists from making such contributions" (Kieth-Spiegel & Koocher, 1985, p. 217).

The question remains what are the criteria for determining whether a program should be used by someone who requires professional intervention. Due to the cost-effectiveness of computer-assisted therapy, help can be made available to people who otherwise could not afford therapy provided by a counselor (Colby, 1980, 1986; Davidson, 1985; Ford, 1993; Ford & Vitelli, 1992; Sampson & Krumboltz, 1991). However, making such technology available for those who may benefit from it also presents the potential for some to be harmed through its use.

Legal and ethical ramifications exist for improper use of computer-assisted therapy. Three probable malpractice complaints against counselors that may result from improper use of such technology are (a) negligent rendering of services, (b) negligence that leads to suicide, and (c) improper supervision of a disturbed client (Ford, 1993). Perhaps as malpractice suits unfold, the necessary laws, codes, and standards will evolve. With respect to independent use, it seems best that computer-assisted counseling should be an adjunct to the relationship between counselor and client, so that harm to the client will be avoided through careful supervision.

Computer-Assisted Counseling Technology Validation

The ethical codes of the APA and the ACA require that software developers provide empirical evidence of the safety and effectiveness of computer-assisted assessment products before making any claims as to their effectiveness. This is not the case with computer-assisted therapy, and there are no laws or ethical standards in place to require evidence of validity and reliability before developers can make claims in marketing their self-help software (Ford, 1993; Sampson et al., 1997). Given the precedent set by codes associated with computer-assisted assessment, it appears incumbent on software developers to demonstrate treatment effectiveness of their computer-assisted therapy empirically (Ford, 1993). Research can be done through experiments using the software with a sample of the target population, and a peer review process. Standards to require this suggestion should become a priority for the counseling profession.

Another important point to address regarding program effectiveness is the credibility that is so easily extended by lay people toward information conveyed by computers (Hartman, 1986b; Sampson, 1986a). Ford (1993) proposed that it should be deemed unethical to capitalize on consumer naiveté as to the veracity of computer output. Appropriate training standards should be in place to assure the appropriate use of computer-assisted counseling (see Education of Counseling Professionals later in this chapter).

Access to Software

Companies that produce mental health software establish various levels of restricted access to therapeutic and testing software purchasers. However, there are few standards for access to such software, resulting in less-than-rigorous control over distribution (Ford, 1993). If software is designed for a client who should receive some type of therapy that is at least supervised by a clinician, the counseling profession must exercise some control over who has access to such software. Standards should be generated to make counseling-related software available only to qualified professionals, placing the liability for negligent use of the product on the practitioner (Ford, 1993; Schwitzgebel & Schwitzgebel, 1980).

Ethical Dilemmas in Computer-Assisted Counseling

The ACA (1995) established standard A.12 to address the use of computer technology in counseling. In summary, counselors have an obligation to assure that:

(1) the client is intellectually, emotionally, and physically capable of using the computer application; (2) the computer application is appropriate for the needs of the client; (3) the client understands the purpose and operation of the computer applications; and (4) a follow-up of client use of a computer application is provided to correct possible misconceptions, discover inappropriate use, and assess subsequent needs.

These standards do not support the autonomous use of computer-assisted counseling by all clients and acknowledge the potential for misunderstanding and the lack of contact between counselor and client inherent in such cases. The APA has yet to publish standards or codes specifically addressing computer-assisted therapy, but such efforts are under way (see APA Ethics Statement on the World Wide Web at http://www.apa.org/ethics/stmnt01.html). According to Duncan (1997), 20 states have developed some legislation related to on-line counseling services. A comprehensive review of this legislation is outside the scope of this chapter, but suffice to say efforts are under way to regulate the use of "cybercounseling."

The use of computers to assist in the counseling process introduces a logistically related ethical dilemma. If a client is using a computer to assist with the therapeutic process, does this imply that services rendered are of a shorter duration than if the counseling modality used was face-to-face? Counseling service providers will have to decide how to bill when computer applications are used as an adjunct to therapy. The client may ultimately save money because of less direct contact with the therapist. Conversely, if the therapist is maintaining ethical responsibility for the entire therapeutic process and chooses to closely monitor the use of computer technology, the difference in time used for therapy will merely be reappropriated to monitoring the technology introduced into therapy. It will be interesting to see how the ethical codes and standards under development address this financial issue.

The next topic reviewed is the advent of *cybercounseling,* or counseling over the Internet. On-line forums of counseling are increasing, and the ethical ramifications are complex, significant, and deserving of the counseling profession's attention.

On-Line Forums of Counseling

On-line forums of counseling can be found in the counseling research literature under a number of descriptors: psychotherapy in cyberspace (Stricker, 1996); counseling on the information highway (Sampson et al., 1997); cybercounseling (Duncan, 1997); and simply, counseling over the Internet. *On-line forums* of counseling represent one of the most recent technological developments in computer applications to the counseling profession (Duncan, 1997; Sampson et al., 1997).

The Internet

The Internet is a product of computer networks originally used by the military to communicate with academics, government workers, and business people working on military projects (Sampson et al., 1997). The Internet is an international network of computers that allow for the interchange of messages, files, software, and communication between computer systems. Today's Internet has a number of features, including bulletin board systems (BBSs) and list servers, that provide forums for the public exchange of text-based information by computer users.

BBSs are typically organized around a topic of interest; people can read a posting or add their own. An example of a counseling BBS may contain "posted messages on the content and process of counseling from participants who conduct discussions through these postings" (Sampson et al., 1997, pp. 203–204). Discussions can be moderated or unmoderated (Berge, 1994), allowing for controlled quality of discussion groups or potentially inappropriate information exchanges, respectively. Information on BBSs is not protected, and therefore caution must be used to protect confidentiality when posting material.

E-mail uses the Internet to send and receive messages among individuals or groups, simulating the sending and receiving of letters through the "mail." List servers are e-mail type software, providing easy international dissemination of discussion lists and electronic journals (Sampson et al., 1997). Confidential information on e-mail is vulnerable to interception by people other than the designated recipient; therefore, caution must be used when sending counseling-related information. Because of frequent use of e-mail by counselors, it is important to emphasize the ethical vulnerability of such communication.

Internet Relay Chat (IRC) (Duncan, 1997) or chat mode of Internet communication allows two people to correspond in real time, using a split screen, one side for each person (Sampson et al., 1997). Computer conferencing allows groups of individuals to converse simultaneously through text with one person potentially serving as moderator. In addition to the group counseling dynamic of such communication, the same limitations exist on the e-mail level of confidentiality. Chat rooms, a version of IRC with a little more privacy, are in frequent use. Although the audience is more limited in a chat room, the same ethical questions arise (Duncan, 1997). Pow-Wow, located at tribal.com, is a system used to control who is in a chat room at a given time providing some, although not complete, control over the audience (Duncan, 1997).

The World Wide Web (WWW) is composed of computer servers and graphical interfaces that are connected to the Internet. Together they provide an avenue of information exchange, including audio and visual material as well as text-based information. One can establish a home page on the WWW, which is accessed on the Internet. The home page conveys information about a specific person or organization, maintained by the same. A Web site on the WWW comprises a home page with links, which are indicated by various graphical means. When activated (or "clicked" with a mouse) these links open up related home pages, Web sites, and multimedia files. The colloquialism "surfing the Net" has received a lot of attention. Surfing implies searching for information on the WWW, which is connected via the Internet. Various software packages facilitate connection with the WWW, and the associated home pages, Web sites, and links (e.g., Netscape, MOSAIC, or Microsoft Internet Explorer).

Counseling Applications on the Internet

Bulletin Board Systems serve counselors as information resources, allowing access to specialized and current information regarding mental health issues (Marino, 1996). List servers and information databases (e.g. ERIC, PSYCHLIT) assist counselors in accessing diverse information quickly (Walz, 1996). However, the professional accessing this information should treat such information with the same healthy skepticism as any printed material. Career counselors use the WWW, BBSs, and Web sites (Sampson et al., 1997), which provide job vacancy listings and even assistance assembling resumés and submitting them to prospective employers (Allen, 1995; Boles, 1996; Jandt & Nemnich, 1995; Kennedy, 1995; Riley, Roehm, & Oserman, 1996; Woods & Ollis, 1996; Woods, Ollis, & Kaplan, 1996). Career counseling has also benefited from the use of video conferencing. After using the WWW to locate jobs and create and submit resumés, the interview between employer and prospective employee can occur in real time using on-line video interviewing technology (Magnusen & Magnusen, 1995).

E-mail is being used by consumers to access mental health professionals and to ask specific questions about diverse mental health issues (Hannon, 1996). The information exchange is similar to radio, print media, and television forums of advice-giving, in that the exchange is not in real time. A multitude of ethical concerns are associated with this type of counseling: misaddresses, the inability to see non-verbal behavior, increased opportunity for fraud, no guarantee of confidentiality, and limited use for clients without high verbal ability (Duncan, 1997). Direct, on-line counseling services are increasingly prevalent on the Internet (Duncan, 1997; Sampson et al., 1997). A survey of counseling-related home pages conducted between April 1996 and August 1996 revealed a potential annualized increase in such home pages of 55% (Sampson et al., 1997). The same survey revealed charges ranging from a $15 fee for answering a question via e-mail to $65 per hour for a 60-minute chat session. Services ranged from single-treatment interventions to individuals offering 35 specialty services. Credentials of practitioners varied, including Ph.D., M.D., M.A., and L.P.C. Some individuals indicating degree credentials after their names did not indicate what the degrees were in, and many "counselors" did not indicate any credentials or training (Sampson et al., 1997). Section C.3.a. of the ACA Code of Ethics requires that counselors "identify their credentials in an accurate manner that is not false, misleading, deceptive, or fraudulent" (ACA, 1995). As codes and ethical standards are revised, specific guidelines for counseling activities over the Internet are being addressed.

The Information Highway: Future On-Line Counseling

Sampson et al. (1997) predicted that the future information highway will be an integration of the Internet, multimedia-based PCs, cable TV networks, and wired and wireless telephone networks. Application potential of such an information highway is tremendous, enhancing technologies already discussed and creating uses no one has thought of. The future information highway likely will be a reality for many citizens in the United States (Gates, Myhrvold, & Rinearson, 1995). Sampson et al. (1997), after providing a description of the future information highway, forecast potential counseling applications on the information highway. What follows is adapted from their publication.

WWW home pages could be used for advertising on-line counseling services, provided that the methods used comply with standards set in place for advertising, public statements, and soliciting clients (APA, 1992; ACA, 1995). Multimedia presentation of counseling services could be quite creative and allow for much more information dissemination than a typical phone directory. With real-time video conferencing, clients could screen potential therapists before embarking on a therapeutic relationship. The counseling professional would be able to make suitability judgments as well. In the event that a referral is necessary, electronic media (e.g., e-mail) could be used to contact the referral sources and transfer associated records (with appropriate encryption of the transferred data). However, the appropriate encryption software must be used to protect confidential information sent via e-mail. Encryption software uses an algorithm to resequence data codes in an effort to disguise data from parties without the algorithm key. More research is needed to develop ways to prevent computer "hackers" (amateur software developers) from breaking such codes and accessing ethically sensitive material. Therefore, current e-mail communication must be used with caution, controlling for ethically sensitive material.

Ultimately, the actual counseling sessions could occur in real time, using on-line computer technology on the information highway. The information highway will allow "counselors to overcome problems of distance and time to offer opportunities for networking and interacting not otherwise available" (Walz, 1996, p. 417). Orientation to counseling services may occur using computer-assisted instruction reviewed in this chapter (Sampson, 1986a), freeing up on-line and counselor time and subsequently client expense. The protocols necessary to protect such communication over the Internet, such as data encryption and video signal scrambling (as used for premium cable TV channels), need to be in place to guarantee confidential communication. Otherwise such practice could be considered unethical.

Ethical Concerns with On-line Counseling

A literature review of information regarding ethics and counseling-related activity on the Internet is sparse (Duncan, 1997; Sampson et al., 1997). Sampson et al. (1997) survey revealed from a sampling of the 3,764 counseling-related home pages identified in April 1996, that there are at least 275 practitioners offering counseling services over the Internet. Such activity may be increasing at a rate between 55% and 72% per year, based on projections of Sampson et al. (1997). Psychotherapy in cyberspace brings with it a number of ethical concerns: (a) licensing criteria for such practice, (b) confidentiality issues, and (c) client safety issues to name a few (Stricker, 1996). It is not clear whether people offering counseling services over the Internet are using the technological safeguards recommended here to protect confidentiality. Such information should be sought out before using such services, and if the providers are not using appropriate security measures, such practice could be deemed unethical.

As we discussed earlier, a fully functional information highway will need a solid data security system, including means of safely transferring money (Duncan, 1997; Gates et al., 1995). Data encryption will need to become more sophisticated to keep pace with the increasing sophistication of people who illegally break such codes. Biometric technology (e.g., voiceprints or thumbprints), as it becomes more reliable and cost-effective, likely will be used to control users at the receiving end of the information highway (Sampson et al., 1997).

While many users access the Internet free through organizations and educational institutions, enhanced technology for the information highway comes with a price. The counseling profession may be faced with cost-prohibitive factors of using such technology in some institutions. If the counseling profession becomes dependent on the free services currently available, and cannot shift the resources to continue accessing the information highway when costs increase, the people hurt by such a change may be the consumer of on-line counseling services. Counselors are ethically responsible to assess their ability to maintain access to this technology as costs increase, or be prepared to provide reliable referral sources when on-line counseling services become too expensive for consumers to continue.

While on-line technology removes some barriers of distance and time, the question remains whether counselors actually have the time and energy to accommodate the subsequent increase in client contact. The time constraints imposed by distance and circumstance allow counselors to process between client contacts, document interactions, and prepare for the next client. If counselors already have a full docket of clients, the remaining benefit of providing on-line counseling services is that of service availability to remotely located or home-bound individuals. It may be presumptuous to assume that on-line technology will result in more people served per counselor, given the necessary time to process and document counseling interactions.

Another on-line activity affecting counselors is the use of on-line supervision and virtual practica, all of which fall under the umbrella of counselor education, a discussion of which follows. But first, we will examine computer-assisted assessment.

Computer-Assisted Assessment

Computer-Administered Assessment

The application of computers to the area of assessment includes the ability to administer, score, and interpret most of the psychological assessment instruments and procedures that are used by clinicians—such as personality tests, cognitive tests, and structured interviews. Intelligence test scoring and interpretation applications were among the first commercially available programs for PCs and have been the primary focus of software developers (Honaker & Fowler, 1990). Recent development of the application of computerized cognitive and aptitude assessment includes (a) subtests of the Wechsler Adult Intelligence Scale-Revised (French & Beaumont, 1992), (b) Air Force flight performance tests (Park & Lee, 1992), (c) the Wonderlic Personnel Test (Kennedy, Baltzley, Turnage, & Jones, 1989), (d) memory subtests from the Wechsler Memory Scale-Revised and the Benton Tests (Youngjohn, Larrabee, & Crook, 1991), and (e) multidimensional assessment of elderly people (Stones & Kozma, 1989). At the beginning of this decade, computer programs involving personality assessment accounted for the largest single number of assessment software applications available, 45% of all computerized assessment products available (Honaker & Fowler, 1990). Such tests included the Minnesota Multiphasic Personality Inventory–2 (MMPI–2), the California Psychological Inventory (CPI), the Millon Clinical Multiaxial Inventory (MCMI), the 16 Personality Factor Test (16PF), the NEO Personality Inventory–Revised (NEO PI–R), and the Rorschach inkblot test. These tests continue to experience widespread use in their standard and computerized format (Hood & Johnson, 1997).

Benefits of Computer-Assisted Test Administration.   One benefit of computerized test administration is the relief that can be provided in terms of rapid presentation of reliable and repetitive information, which can be taxing on the client as well as the test administrator (Argentero, 1989; Caplan, 1987). The storing and retrieval of test data can be simplified with computer applications, which allow the professional to attend to other important dynamics in the assessment and training process (Honaker & Fowler, 1990). Human error during data collection also can be minimized. Additionally, there is evidence of increased reliability in the scoring of intelligence tests administered in a computer format (Honaker & Fowler, 1990), which further increases the veracity of test results. However, the reliability of computer-assisted assessment relies on the competency of the administrator of the software. The administrator must understand the noncomputerized administration procedures of a given test and how these are influenced by computer technology (Drummond, 1996). A thorough understanding of an assessment tool (i.e., its development, validity, reliability, and theoretical framework) is essential before administration. Unfortunately, the ease of computer-assisted assessment is deceptive: This perception may encourage use by people not trained adequately in measurement and statistics, who are operating outside a given area of competency, and may constitute unethical practice according to the codes established by the APA, ACA, and the NBCC.

Another benefit of the use of computer-administered assessment is the development of adaptive or tailored testing (Weiss, 1985; Wise & Plake, 1990). Computer technology allows the examinee's responses to determine which subsequent items are to be administered. The resultant number of items required generally is reduced by 50%, therefore reducing test time. For higher-ability examinees, boredom is avoided by offering more challenging items. Lower-ability examinees may avoid discouragement that may occur secondary to item difficulty. This provides for more equal and ethical test administration to examinees, regardless of ability level, thus optimizing a given person's performance (Wise & Plake, 1990).

The ethical administration of tests requires precision and consistency. Computerized administration of testing has the potential to improve precision and consistency, thus enhancing the ethical administration of tests. It is important that the counseling field continue to demonstrate the validity and reliability of computerized assessment tools and compare their performance with comparable and better-established paper-and-pencil tests.

Limitations of Computerized Administration.   The benefits of this reported ease of administration and data collection can be misleading. Accurate interpretation of test performance also requires careful observation of the examinee during the administration of any test. Computerized test administration may encourage less vigilance on the administrator's part, possibly resulting in the absence of important clinical data. Specifically, situational factors related to the individual during the testing process may be overlooked. Interpreting a test without taking into account those factors beyond the basic test scores that are generated by a computer program (e.g., environmental stimuli, distracters, arousal level of the client during the assessment process, and fluctuations in performance related to such factors) may result in the unethical use of test data. Thus, the data gathered are essentially incomplete and may not present a holistic view of the person (Maki, 1986).

Some domains of assessment do not transfer well to computerized assessment. One such area is neuropsychological testing. The stimulus-response complexity of most tests of this type make it difficult to duplicate with current computer technology. While computerized assessment has its place in the assessment process, it cannot replace the involvement of the professional. It can, however, serve as a useful adjunct to the assessment process (Binder & Thompson, 1994). Thus, the ethical use of computerized technology must be considered within the context of the discipline using such technology.

A social issue associated with computerized assessment is the socioeconomically limited access to such technology. In a publication addressing the ethical treatment of patients with brain injury, Ackerman and Banks (1990) highlighted the limitations that socioeconomic status of a consumer or providing institution can impose upon the availability of such technology. It is important that technology that improves outcomes in patient treatment is made available to all who need it, regardless of ability to pay.

In summary, the use of computers to administer assessment instruments is not a replacement for the professional counselor. Counseling practice is essentially a human-to-human encounter, the purpose of which is to provide assistance to people in need of counseling interventions. The use of technology in assessment may facilitate such endeavors; however, implementation of technology in the counseling process also requires careful monitoring and supervision by experienced professionals to promote sound ethical practice.

Computer-Generated Assessment Results and Reports

The use of PCs to assist in interpreting psychological test results is increasing and is known as computer-based test interpretation (CBTI). A great deal of controversy surrounds this area of technology. A modular-integrated computerized testing system called ComPsy (Kaplan, Roditty, & Dover, 1991) was developed to meet the demands of the counseling professional. The system scheduled appointments, administered a battery of tests, performed statistical and data management functions, and produced results in the form of computer-generated reports. However, reliability and validity information for integrated systems such as this one is limited or nonexistent. While the sophistication of modular-integrated systems of assessment is increasing, some serious ethical considerations are still involved.

When a counseling professional has access to computer-generated test results from given test data, there is potential for over-reliance on the computer to interpret the protocol. The computer is not able to incorporate qualitative data accessible to the counselor. Qualitative data can take exception to direct interpretation of the quantitative test data. Errors in data entry can also result in inaccurate test scores. Professionals who use such software are obligated ethically to carefully review the data entered. Computer-generated test reports must also be interpreted carefully to avoid unethical assessment practice. Such protocols generally request raw test data, or data collected from a structured interview. The data is then incorporated into a template report that is adjusted, based on the data entered. It is critical that the counseling professional review the entire report for accuracy correspondent to available test data. Individual test results do not always lend themselves to a predictable template interpretation. The professional must critically analyze the report content and edit and supplement the report accordingly. Computer-generated reports can be useful templates for producing reports but should not be provided to referral sources without careful scrutiny by the examiner.

The organizational pressures in today's mental health care settings from managed care and third-party payment sources may force many organizations to do more with less. Such pressure encourages the use of less-qualified technicians who are paid less to perform assessment procedures. Over-reliance on the ease of computer technology is of even greater concern when less-qualified examiners are used in the assessment process. The temptation to take any information that a computer generates, be it data interpretation or a report, and accept it at face value is a reality with potentially serious consequences. Overconfidence in technology can overshadow reasonable interpretation of results. In summary, technology can help make test administration, interpretation, and report generation a more efficient process. However, computerized assessment must be viewed in light of its assets and limitations.

Research Issues in Computerized Assessment

The ethical appropriateness of using PCs to administer tests is being examined in research today. The APA (1986) Committee on Professional Standards, along with the Committee on Psychological Tests and Assessment, developed the *Guidelines for Computer-Based Tests and Interpretations,* which currently is out of print, but is being revised at the time of this writing. Additionally, most codes of ethics address the importance of ethical behavior regarding the application of any technology in the assessment of, and subsequent treatment of, sentient beings (ACA, 1995; APA, 1992).

Equivalence is also a major issue addressed by the APA. The interchange of information between computer-based and conventional (paper-and-pencil) tests has been deemed allowable if (a) the rank order of scores tested in alternative modes closely approximate each other, and (b) the means, dispersions, and shapes of the score distributions are approximately the same, or have been made approximately the same by rescaling the scores from the computer mode. In other words, the computerized version must be psychometrically similar to the paper-and-pencil version. Thus, the term *equivalence.*

Research is also exploring the possibility that the exchange of people, paper, and pencil for computer technology changes how the examinee responds to evaluation. For example, personally sensitive issues appear to be easier to divulge to a computer program than to an actual therapist, which may increase the amount of data available to the counselor (Honaker & Fowler, 1990; Sampson, in press). The psychological constructs tapped by clinical interviews and the traditional methods of testing may be different from those tapped when a computer is used for these same purposes. Because of these potential differences, norms generated by noncomputerized assessment tools may not generalize to the computer format.

To use a computer for ease of administration and then interpret the test by paper-and-pencil norms may not be ethical due to the potential error that may be introduced. More time is needed to establish appropriate norms for computerized test interpretation. This being the case, many computerized assessment instruments must be treated as experimental until further research clarifies the effect that the computer medium has on the overall assessment process. Manuals accompanying any tests that counseling professionals are considering using must be reviewed carefully to determine the appropriateness of the use of the instrument.

Computer-Assisted Counselor Education

On-Line Supervision and Virtual Practica

Cyberspace, or the Internet, is considered an alternative approach to counselor supervision (Myrick & Sabella, 1995). Myrick and Sabella (1995) recommended the use of e-mail to share professional ideas and information with supervisees in remote and distant areas. Such technology also provides opportunity for academic, organizational, or peer supervision. The authors also provided specific scenarios in which elementary school counselors were able to access timely assistance for complex cases, particularly when counselors were practicing in remote locations.

Limitations should be noted for e-mail, or text-based supervision. Removing the one-to-one interaction between supervisor and supervisee limits the data available to which supervisors may respond (e.g., body language, or acceptance of constructive criticism). With the development of satellite and computer technology that allows real-time video and audio interaction, some limitations of text-based supervision are minimized. However, how this technology compares with person-to-person supervision within the same space is unclear. The ethical issues identified in the on-line counseling section of this chapter also apply to on-line supervision and practica. Without sufficient security protocols in place, such activity could be considered unethical. Further research is needed regarding existing systems and protocols.

Distance Learning

Distance learning may be conceptualized as the use of technical equipment to guarantee consistent product quality in mass volumes, and use of technical media (e.g., television, radio, and satellite broadcasting) in place of in vivo teachers in order to broaden accessibility (Stewart, 1992). New technologies are being used to deliver pre-service and in-service training to counselors from various specialty areas (Davis & Yazak, 1995). Since the development of the British Open University in 1969, distance learning programs have expanded worldwide. Within the United States, 1991 estimates of state institutions having access to some form of distance learning (e.g., college-level televised instruction) was as high as 98% (Barron, 1991). Distance learning is useful for persons in remote and rural areas, for learners who are place-bound, and for professionals with busy schedules or economic limitations wishing to further their professional development through licensure and certification (Steele, 1993).

Advancement in technology is a primary factor influencing the increase of the willingness of educators to consider the use of distance learning (Davis & Yazak, 1995). The Internet connects millions of computers worldwide, allowing access to databases and library materials, and facilitating communication between instructors and students. CD–ROM technology and multimedia presentation of written material and high-quality graphics has made learning through computer software a viable alternative or supplement to the traditional classroom experience (Scriven, 1991; Sirkin, 1994).

The U.S. Department of Education has supported efforts to further distance learning initiatives. Three institutions have received grants for delivering rehabilitation counseling education: (a) Utah State University, offering a master's degree program composed of satellite broadcast of videotaped modules, audio teleconferencing, and telephone support; (b) University of Northern Colorado, in cooperation with Mind Extension University (Bitter, Gregg, & Jackson, 1994), offering noncredit seminars, courses, and certificates via live telecasts, videotapes, computer bulletin board, voice mail, phone support, and electronic meeting software; and (c) San Diego

State University, offering credit courses to remote island groups in the Northern Pacific and several U.S. states via state-of-the-art methods designed to keep pace with evolving technologies (Davis & Yazak, 1995).

Ethical Concerns with Distance Learning

Distance learning brings several ethical concerns for counselor educators. Program integrity, continuity, and sophistication affect the quality of education that a given counselor receives. It is critical that the available resources to facilitate a program's capacity to accomplish its objectives through distance learning must be considered case by case. It is ethically irresponsible to assume that an in vivo course of study will readily translate to a distance learning format. An outcome research base is necessary to compare the difference between distance learning programs and exemplary traditional university-based programs, and to examine the effectiveness of distance learning. Program accreditation standards can be developed from such data to ensure quality education of ethical counselors.

In traditional university settings, courses can be evaluated through peer review, where course activity between teacher and student can be observed and evaluated by fellow professionals, to provide developmental suggestions that enhance an instructor's pedagogy, and ultimately the quality of the student's education. In a distance learning setting, the interpersonal dynamic between instructor and student is different from a face-to-face experience. How this difference affects the learning process is not yet known, but it is clear this dynamic cannot be observed for distance learning in the same way it is in the traditional classroom setting. Methods to maintain in vivo professional feedback that contribute to course quality and development within a distance learning context should be explored further.

The dynamic difference between in vivo and remote education may also influence the student learning process. The authors' review of the counseling literature indicates that this dynamic has not been fully explored. Using the taped presentations of a distance learning curriculum, students do not have the ability to ask questions and interact contemporaneously with instructors. How this may affect the learning process is not clear. In a real-time distance learning presentation, if a student is having difficulty grasping a concept, the opportunity for one-to-one interaction for clarification is limited. The logistics of interacting with a classroom or instructor remotely may inherently be more time consuming than a traditional classroom setting (e.g., timing of questions, coordinating multiple inquiries, and keeping the course moving in a timely manner). The difficulty associated with cueing an instructor in a remote setting may discourage active and lively class participation. Student-to-student interaction (e.g., breaking into small groups) is limited, although technologically not impossible. However, these situations introduce a number of factors that affect time, interpersonal interaction, and possibly the willingness to engage others. The effect of these limitations must be clarified before valid comparison of in vivo learning versus distance learning can be made.

In the event that follow-up phone support is available to students, the ability to graphically clarify a concept is limited. People uncomfortable with phone communication are at a distinct disadvantage. The effect of video with phone interaction may alleviate some of this concern. Additionally, the expense of such communication may deter students from taking advantage of such assistance. Person-to-person conferences available to students at a campus setting to assist with clarification of difficult material is not available to remote learners. Some courses may more readily lend themselves to remote presentation than others, again necessitating a case-by-case approach to the development of distance learning curricula.

The limited literature available indicates that students and faculty generally prefer face-to-face interaction over distance learning (Bland, Morrison, & Ross, 1992). Many faculty agree that simply accessing information is inferior to an educational environment that includes two-way communication (Garrison, 1990; Law & Sissons, 1985). Most importantly, in counselor education the personal development of the students is arguably as important as their professional and academic development. It is difficult for faculty to provide mentoring and role modeling of professional behavior without personal contact with students. All things considered, the development of distance learning curricula should be carefully thought out, as discussed in the following section.

Suggestions for Ethical Distance Learning Curricula Development

Davis and Yazak (1995) suggest several areas of focus for the development of accreditation guidelines for distance learning curricula. They modeled their suggestions after the Southern Association of Colleges and Schools' (Staff, 1993) areas of focus for program accreditation standards, which included mission, curriculum delivery, faculty, resources, student support, and evaluation.

Mission.   Faculty should review the mission of their program and institution to consider the long-range strategic effect of distance learning on the fundamental philosophy of the institution and the existing curriculum. Issues such as regional accreditation (proposed catchment area of recruitment), potential student market, admission procedures, and program structure (e.g., time period of course acquisition that maintains program integrity) must be considered. Student skills of self-pacing, goal setting, and self-evaluation may require a greater emphasis in student recruitment. Without the local influence of professors or peers, student motivation becomes critical. It is the ethical responsibility of the institution offering a distance learning curriculum to recruit candidates who will thrive in a distance learning environment.

Curriculum Delivery.   Establishing appropriate modes of information dissemination is crucial to the education process. Distance learning presents a number of factors that influence curriculum delivery. While it may be premature to rule out the viability of certain areas of curricula in distance learning, Eldredge, Gerard, and Smart (1994) suggested that instruction in the areas of counseling skills and testing evaluation "do not lend themselves well to distance education because of the individualized supervision required to assist full skill development" (p. 78). As Davis and Yazak (1995) recommended, "consideration of the characteristics of technical media in relation to the learning requirements of advanced and specialized curriculum is essential" (p. 297).

The presentation of information that is to be organized, generally understood, and memorized, such as historical and theoretical overviews, could perhaps be effectively accomplished through some of the distance learning techniques already discussed (one-way audio-visual transmission, or videotaped curricula). However, course material that requires critical thinking, abstraction, active processing, and synthesis of information, may require active instructor and student discussion that does not lend itself to distance learning formats (Davis & Yazak, 1995). Discussion of counseling scenarios and complex ethical problem-solving skills that emerge from such experience could be jeopardized in such formats, which strongly questions the ethical appropriateness of using such approaches in counselor education. Clearly, to ethically present an entire advanced curriculum exclusively by distance learning technology, more research is required.

Faculty.   Distance learning will present opportunities to instruct more nontraditional students in remote areas. This may present a new audience to many professional counselor educators, which ultimately will have an effect on how existing curricula are presented to suit new audiences. Also, expertise in technology and troubleshooting will be necessary to promote seamless and timely presentation of remote curricula (Davis-Bell, 1991; Fulmer, Hazzard, Jones, & Keene, 1992; Massoumian, 1989; Willis, 1992). "Distance learning faculty must be trained in how to plan lessons that must be precise, well-timed, and supported with high-quality visual aids" (David & Yazak, 1995). Courses in distance learning technology and subsequent curriculum development may be necessary for counselor educators in training, to facilitate proper use of such technology.

Two more issues need to be addressed with respect to faculty who are developing distance learning material. First, faculty may share concerns with others who are creating computer-assisted counseling software: distance learning curriculum development and counseling software development currently are not acknowledged by university administrators in the same spirit as other more quantitative research efforts, although they are equally time consuming. Such efforts must be remunerated effectively if such technology is to move forward. Second, guidelines for the protection of property rights of materials developed for distance learning endeavors must be established. If a professor invests a great deal of time in curriculum development, the same ethical rights and restrictions placed on publications should be extended to distance learning curricula.

Resources.   Some distance learning students, particularly those in remote locations, will not have access to the same resources as students in a campus setting. Therefore, textbooks used in distance learning courses should engage the students in active learning. Educators may choose texts that are accompanied by workbooks that encourage active processing of readings through exercises. Some courses may also require the use of a library or the Internet for in-depth study. If such resources are not available at a distance learning site, and no alternatives exist (e.g., library networking, interlibrary loan services, or facsimile services), courses requiring such resources may not be appropriate for a distance learning curriculum.

Students benefit from speedy instructor feedback on assignments, such as quizzes, papers, and exams. In a distance learning context, rapid turn-around of the student's work is likely to be confounded by proximity. Expedient methods of assignment exchanges are necessary for students to benefit from instructor feedback. In addition to using mail delivery systems and on-line computerized testing, it has been recommended that faculty visit distance classrooms whenever possible (Barker, 1986; Hodgson, 1986). However, travel to some remote areas could be too expensive, so the nature of the course will have to determine the optimal instructor feedback, and therefore dictate what types of courses will be worth offering through distance learning.

Student Support.   As we mentioned earlier, professionals recruiting students to distance learning programs are ethically responsible for assuring that the recruits have the coping skills necessary to thrive in such an environment. Pre-course counseling may help identify students who need remediation before embarking on such an endeavor. Ongoing tutoring services may also be required for students who have taken on more than they are capable of (Davis & Yazak, 1995; Hodgson, 1986).

Students in distance learning programs need advice regarding educational issues such as career counseling, course selection, financial aid, registration, and practica/internship placement. Reasonable accommodations for persons with disabilities may also be an issue. Many program accrediting bodies require a certain advisee-to-faculty ratio for programs to remain accredited. For example, the Council on Rehabilitation Education (CORE) requires a ratio of less than 20:1, (Council on Rehabilitation Education, 1994). The recommended student-to-faculty ratio of the Council for Accreditation of Counseling and Related Education Programs (CACREP) is more rigorous—10:1 (CACREP, 1996). The impact of distance learning upon these requirements, given the temptation to use such technology to educate more students with the same number of faculty members, must be carefully evaluated.

Program Evaluation.   As with the other new technologies we have discussed, evaluation of distance learning effectiveness is an ethical responsibility of program developers. It is a vital component of program accreditation (Davis & Yazak, 1995, Olcott, 1993). Fenwick (1992) described seven common indicators of quality for distance learning curricula: (a) attrition rates, (b) work assignment response rates, (c) student course evaluations, (d) quality of the learning package, (e) the learning process, (f) degree of freedom of pace and method, and (g) the level of student independence. Formal feedback from students is even more critical for distance learning programs because students have comparatively less contact with program faculty (Davis & Yazak, 1995). Audio conferencing, phone communication, and e-mail communication can facilitate frequent feedback to distance learning program developers. Remember that the ethical concerns reviewed in the electronic media section of this chapter are relevant to distance learning as well. (See also Distance Learning Considerations for Rehabilitation Counselor Education Programs at the end of this chapter.)

Computer-Assisted Instruction

Computer-assisted instruction (CAI) uses tutorials to present concepts and examples of instructional tasks to be mastered. Some program applications can measure performance and present feedback to the learner, while other simulations require the learner to use constructs in an applied situation to solve problems (Sampson & Krumboltz, 1991). As with computerized technology used in assessment and counseling, CAI has experienced more widespread use as affordability has improved. The business world has been using CAI extensively (Sampson & Krumboltz, 1991). However, the counseling field has not used it to its fullest potential. As discussed earlier, computerized-assessment and career-counseling software have experienced the widest use by and the greatest financial investment from large software developers. Most CAI software in counseling has been developed by counselors and distributed by vendors marketing software for a number of individuals (Sampson & Krumboltz, 1991). The financial limitations of individual developers has resulted in restricted development and marketing of such software.

One presumably excellent resource for CAI development would be the academic community, particularly those academicians in programs of education. However, as we have pointed out, academic institutions traditionally have failed to recognize software development as viable scholarly activity that applies toward promotion and tenure, much like textbook writing. This situation inherently limits software development efforts by faculty members, who typically have much to do with limited time and resources.

While counseling and CAI may be conceptualized as distinct, separate activities, it is also possible to see similarities between them. The definition of CAI in counseling offered by Sampson and Krumboltz (1991) is similar to Grencavage and Norcross' (1990) description of the commonalties among psychotherapies cited earlier in the computer-assisted counseling section of this chapter. Because of the similarities between computer-assisted counseling and CAI, many of the ethical issues already discussed in that section of this chapter also apply to CAI in counseling. Additionally, the ethical obligations that educators have to use sound theory and peer review processes in curriculum development and instruction are important to consider in the proliferation of CAI in counseling.

"Technocentered" and "Technoanxious"

Counselors' reactions to technology span a continuum from acceptance to anxiety. Brod (1984) dichotomized people's reactions to technology as *technocentered* (comfortable with computer technology) and *technoanxious* (fearful and avoiding computerization of the profession). The resistance to computerization of various counseling tasks by counselors could be explained in part by technoanxiety (Ford, 1993). Although this chapter has focused on ethical problems associated with new technology, it should be noted that the benefits to technological advances are numerous and substantial. The best way to assure the appropriate implementation of progress, both ethically and in addressing the technophobic, is through preservice and inservice training of counseling professionals (Ford, 1993; Hammer & Hile, 1985; Meier & Geiger, 1986).

Not all resistance to the computerization of counseling is related to anxiety. As this chapter suggests, there are many ethical concerns associated with the implementation of new technology, so the use of computers and related technology in the counseling field must be carried out carefully after appropriate research. In addition, standards should be set to assure continued safe use of the same. The very nature of computerization, being objective and related to quantifiable data, also brings limitations to situations requiring complex problem-solving and clinical judgment. Computerization restricts the exchange of questions and answers, emphasizing quantifiable data and perhaps ignoring less-quantifiable phenomena (Murphy & Pardeck, 1988). It is important that counselors-in-training must be aware of these limitations before embarking on their own professional practice.

Distance learning technology provides an opportunity to disseminate information to people in ways that until recently were not possible. Along with this promise are ethical considerations unique to a distance learning program. To provide guidance to programs considering a distance learning curriculum, Appendix A lists questions generated by Davis and Yazak (1995). Rehabilitation counseling programs should review them when considering distance learning activities, but all counseling education programs would benefit from these considerations.

Ethical Use of Software

Software *pirating*, or the illegal copying and use of software, is a blatant breach of ethics. Between professionals, the sharing of software can be considered doing a co-worker a favor. Clearly the motivation is to save several hundred dollars in acquiring a piece of software. However, the unethical reproduction and transfer of computer software results in both increased cost to the consumer and loss of revenue for the author of the product. Because unauthorized reproduction of software is illegal, the ethical integrity of counselors who engage in this behavior may be questionable. Software pirating can easily go undetected, increasing the responsibility of counselors to practice the ethical use of electronic media autonomously.

Having reviewed the use of computer technology in the counseling profession, we now turn to a specific type of technological intervention used with a specific population of clients: assistive technology for persons with disabilities.

Technological Counseling Interventions for People with Disabilities

Assistive Technology and Quality-of-Life Issues

Advances in technology have increased opportunities for people with various limitations of functioning. Physical and sensory limitations can be minimized through the use of assistive devices. The use of technology to integrate people with disabilities more fully into the mainstream of life enhances their quality of life (Rubin & Roessler, 1995). Literature in the area of quality of life, or "personal ecology" (Peterson, 1993, p. 4), generally refers to the individual assessment (both subjective and objective) of life outcomes along personal, social, sociodemographic, and other specific life domains, such as employment (Deiner, 1984; Fabian, 1989, 1995; Livneh, 1987; Maki & Murray, 1995; Roessler, 1990; Schalock, Keith, Hoffman, & Karan, 1989; Spilker, 1990). The assumption generally is made that people (and their unique mix of personal characteristics) individually interact with various factors in their environments, which interaction results in an evaluation process by each individual. Some authors place more emphasis on the person component rather than the environment component (and vice versa), while others view them as equally important. Additionally, this process is more or less ongoing and may be subtle in nature, as measured by the individual, or a more formalized process, as measured by people or groups other than the individual. Because assistive technology has the potential to greatly increase the quality of life of people with disabilities, professionals in the counseling field have an ethical responsibility to be aware of the technology available.

Categories of Assistive Technology

Rubin and Roessler (1995) refer to assistive technology as "the great equalizer" (p. 349) of opportunity for people with disabilities. Equality of opportunity has been discussed in terms of vocational outcomes for people with disabilities (Maki, 1986) and counseling professionals—regardless of their area of expertise—need to be aware of these resources when working with diverse clientele.

The Seventeenth Institute on Rehabilitation Issues (1990) of the Arkansas Research and Training Center in Vocational Rehabilitation published *The Provision of Assistive Technology in Rehabilitation.* A list of categories of assistive technology can be found at the end of this chapter.

Applications of Assistive Technology

The following is a hypothetical example of how knowledge of technology might be useful to a school counselor working with a child with a disability—specifically, a mobility impairment. The student was referred to the counselor because of behavioral problems in an industrial arts course. During an interview, the child complained of being bored during the class. The counselor discovered there were many class activities in which the child could not partake because of the limited use of her arms. The class recently used computers to develop art graphics, and the child was most disappointed that she was not able to participate. It was after this that her behavior deteriorated significantly, and she was referred to the school counselor.

The counselor's knowledge of assistive technology by way of computer applications provided a resource that helped improve the child's experience in the class, and thus her performance. The counselor was aware of computer software that allowed persons with mobility impairments easier access to keyboard functions by way of a mouth stick and a "sticky keys" software function. Upon the school acquiring this technology, the student's behavioral problems diminished, and her class performance improved dramatically. If the counselor had been unaware of the existence of such technology, the child might not have received the assistance she deserved.

Consider another hypothetical situation involving a rehabilitation counselor and a client who was hard of hearing. Some rehabilitation counselors are trained to work with people with hearing impairments and have expertise in assistive technology for persons who are deaf, but in this situation the counselor did not have such training. The issue presented by the client was communication problems with co-workers. To date, the method of communication had been crude hand signals and notes written on scraps of paper and cardboard. Although the rehabilitation counselor did not have specific training in deafness or hearing impairment, he had taken the responsibility of remaining current on assistive technology in general, and was therefore aware of technology that would minimize the communication problem.

A telecommunication device for the deaf (TDD) is a typewriterlike device that has an electronic display and phone hook-up capability. It is typically used for phone communication, but for the current scenario, the TDD could be used as an electronic scratch pad that may facilitate communication between the client who is hearing-impaired and his co-workers. This application of technology provided ready access to an electronic form of communication, minimizing the communication difficulties related to lack of materials, poor penmanship, and the frustration associated with both. Technology provided a means of removing a communication barrier, thus increasing the client's chance of remaining gainfully employed.

Government Provision of Sufficient Funds

The technology available to create new and innovative assistive devices for people with disabilities also presents an ethical dilemma. The benefit of such technology is that it allows persons with disabilities better and more equal access to the environment. However, the technology can be expensive. While technology can result in remarkable gains in quality of life for people with disabilities, the costs of such technology are prohibitive in a market that demands higher efficiency and provides less funding (Tarvydas & Cottone, 1991).

Thus, the issue involves the principle of justice, or the equitable distribution of goods and services given a limitation on those goods and services available for distribution. For example, people with more severe disabilities may require greater financial assistance than someone with a mild or moderate level of impairment. Assistive technology can be very beneficial—and very expensive—and the allocation of large financial expenditures for one person relative to smaller financial expenditures for several people invariably brings with it an ethical dilemma. Research to explore methods of making such technology more affordable is an ethical responsibility of a government that advocates liberty and justice for all.

Educating Counselors: Assistive Technology

Technology has grown so rapidly that it is difficult to remain current with developments. The helping professions have an ethical obligation to be aware of the best services to provide their clients, which may involve being aware of recent innovations in assistive technology. The categories of assistive devices presented earlier are guidelines of the scope of resources available to assist clients. Practitioners benefit from the mind set of being a student for life, meaning that the continuing education process is ongoing and necessary to remain competent in practice. Further information about assistive technology is available at any state vocational rehabilitation facility (e.g., State Department of Rehabilitation Services, Division of Rehabilitation Services; see state government section of your local phone directory) located throughout the United States. Information on assistive devices and job accommodation can also be obtained via computer modem from ABLEDATA and the Job Accommodation Network (JAN) home pages on the World Wide Web. Agencies and other organizations generating technology have an obligation to disseminate this information so that professionals are made aware of and may benefit from technology. Counselors in turn, have a responsibility to educate their clients regarding the availability of this technology.

Technology and the Four-Level Model of Ethical Practice

Tarvydas and Cottone (1991) proposed a hierarchical model of ethical practice. This model is used in Chapter 16 to discuss ethics in education, supervision, and research. Given the ubiquity of technology and its seemingly unlimited applications, a similar approach is used to discuss ethical considerations with technology and its related applications (e.g., assessment, cybercounseling, and distance learning). Thus, each level of the Tarvydas and Cottone's (1991) hierarchical model is presented, followed by a discussion of critical techno-ethical considerations that are related to each level, which organize much of the material presented earlier in this chapter (summarized in Appendix C). *Techno-ethical* implies ethical significance related to the development and use of technology.

Level One

Level One of Tarvydas and Cottone's (1991) model refers to the client–counseling level and is operationalized by the client–counselor relationship. At this level, ethical consideration must be given to clinical assessment. Specifically, counseling professionals must evaluate their use of assessment devices on an individualized basis.

Computer-assisted assessment protocols that are used inappropriately may harm the client. Such misuse is in clear violation of the ethical principle of nonmaleficence. Counselors are ethically obligated to consider each client's needs individually in the assessment process to promote a "best practices" approach to the application of technology in clinical assessment.

Related to assistive technology for people with disabilities, the use of augmentative communication devices opens up new vistas for people unable to communicate through speech. Technology thus expands the service base of the counseling professional to include services for people who cannot speak without these assistive devices. Additionally, people who are deaf may benefit from augmentative communication devices that display text on a screen in hand-held, notebook-size computers. The use of assistive technology allows clients with communication barriers to have greater access to counseling services. This technology may be particularly useful for gerontological counselors, as well as counselors who work with people who have brain injuries that result in expressive or receptive communication difficulties. Privacy of information remains critical, and confidentiality requirements necessarily must be extended to persons using such technology.

Further consideration of the client–counselor level of ethical practice warrants that people engaged in the counseling process must be apprised of the informed consent and confidentiality issues inherent in electronic data gathering and storage, an extension of paper documentation storage and retrieval. While the issues are similar in their respective contexts (e.g., paper versus electronic media), they require different interventions to protect confidential material.

The emergence of cybercounseling (Duncan, 1997) has redefined some logistical aspects of the client–counselor relationship. Therefore the following issues require attention in a level one context: (a) unauthorized persons having access to personal information electronically; (b) professionalism and credentialing of the cybercounselor (Sampson et al., 1997); (c) verification of the continuity of a specific cybercounselor involved with a specific client; and (d) consideration of the emotional bond believed necessary to establish the therapeutic relationship (Gelso & Carter, 1985).

Level Two

Level Two includes the clinical interdisciplinary level and is operationalized by the practitioner–practitioner relationship. All parties involved in the multidisciplinary team must have similar access to electronic communication on relatively equivalent levels of information transfer. However, some practitioners may need remedial training in the use of technology when it comes to data development, storage, and retrieval. One caveat that must be considered is that regardless of the systems used, information should be equally available and accessible to all team members so that client concerns are not compromised. Given the cost of implementing technology in counseling practice, consideration should be given to continuing education to use the technology to its best advantage. Such determination may blur the lines between agency specializations and disciplines, and therefore initially might entail some professional cross-disciplinary political concerns. Also, cost-containment issues potentially jeopardize these same agencies in contemporary practice. The equal use of the resource of staff time for all disciplines to become technically literate is an important factor in increasing an agency's expertise in electronic media and assistive technology. Such approaches to interdisciplinary clinical services must be considered proactively.

Rust (1995) discussed the development of an international counselor network using electronic information resources. While the context of this discussion was professional school counseling and resource sharing (e.g., information dissemination and publication activity), it is conceivable that a client in one geographic location may benefit from an interdisciplinary team member—perhaps a counselor who previously provided a clinical assessment—in another geographic location. These methods may include both e-mail and sites on the WWW. The counselor's information horizons must be expanded to include valuable, yet geographically disparate resources. It is important to remember that ethical concerns such as data collection, storage, and retrieval should be considered when administering consultation and referral communication.

It should be mentioned that consultation with people not usually considered to be ongoing members of an interdisciplinary team (referral sources such as a medical specialist) may also involve the risk of the loss of information control. It is common to transmit information via e-mail or fax relative to a specific client, and the speed of this information transfer is usually considered beneficial. However, nothing is completely error-free, so consideration must be given to (a) securing protection of confidential information transmitted electronically to the greatest extent possible, and (b) notifying the client of the use of this information transfer as a routine aspect of counseling services provision.

Level Three

Level Three is the institutional/agency level and is operationalized by the institution-member relationship. Institutions and agencies—publicly or privately held—are responsible for ensuring adequate protection of confidential information related to the provision of professional counseling services. Thus, it is incumbent on these entities to provide efficient and effective services related to this issue. *Efficient* refers to the use of cost-effective mechanisms that promote cost-containment of services, and *effective* refers to mechanisms that are reliable.

Myrick and Sabella (1995) discussed the opportunities that are offered for both supervision and consultation through the use of e-mail. Additionally, satellite technology creates the opportunity for on-line, real-time communication as described earlier. Counselor supervision and consultation may be offered through these technologies either individually or in groups. If institutions or agencies are to take advantage of these electronic networking opportunities, consideration must be given to security protocols. Security measures may include passwords or codes, signal scrambling, and securing of terminals that receive such information. It would be naive to assume no one would access those systems unethically. In addition, the notion of "respondent superior" (Remley & Hendren, 1989), or the legal responsibility of supervisors for the actions of their supervisees, must be considered. This issue is treated specifically in Chapter 16.

A final consideration at this level is that technology is rapidly changing, and with it the incumbent necessity to stay informed of these changes. Remedial training and continuing education were touched on under the interdisciplinary level, but such training may be managed ultimately at the organizational level. If agencies are responsible for the training of their professional staff, it follows that they must provide up-to-date and functional information and opportunities for suitable continuing education so these professionals may practice effectively.

Clearly related to the above, distance learning may or may not be technical in its instructional content; that is, staying abreast of the most current technological changes. However, this type of learning almost always involves some technical component of instruction. It is necessary to recognize the importance of teacher-student interaction and feedback at this level. In addition, it is important to address instructional integrity. Finally, some aspects of in vivo learning may not be possible with distance learning, such as (a) the process of information exchange that often is more spontaneous with in vivo instruction, and (b) greater dependency on more didactic forms of instruction (vis-à-vis small group interaction) due to lack of spontaneity.

Level Four

Level Four is the societal resources/public policy level and is operationalized by the legislative–constituent relationship. When considering the adequacy of resources, a question relating to the principle of justice is: What is adequate? It is important for professional counselors continually to ask this specific question, both of themselves and of their clients. People cannot engage in client–counselor relationships and completely ignore the context in which clients find themselves. Thus, a "best-practices" approach to counseling interventions includes consideration of client, agency, and societal resources to access technologies available. Periodic review and assessment involves more formalized procedures for review and assessment of resources versus unmet needs. Quality of life issues that were discussed briefly may fall into this category, particularly those on the societal level versus an individual level. Additionally, evaluation of moneys expended compared with outcomes achieved—on a periodic and fair basis—may help to assure that (a) evaluation is inevitable because it is continuing, and (b) efficient and effective use of resources is realized, which satisfies ethical considerations of justice.

As discussed earlier, Sampson et al. (1997) noted that many providers of cybercounseling services do not list their credentials, and of those who do, the information is not specific in nature. In addition, Sampson et al. (1997) noted the dramatic growth of counseling-related home pages, including various fees for services available. It seems reasonable to state that there are at least three entities involved when it comes to credentialing and electronic media: (a) the cybercounselor, (b) the software manufacturer, and (c) professional bodies such as the ACA, the APA, and the NBCC. Responsibility for the ethical provision of electronic counseling services according to a specified set of standards is borne by all of these entities, at some level, and that responsibility must be given consideration by all participants involved.

Ford (1993) discussed the independent use of computer-assisted counseling services. Of importance here are the legal issues that may arise out of both litigation and legislation related to the electronic provision of counseling services. The lack of face-to-face monitoring of clients in computer-assisted counseling and cybercounseling sessions, and issues related to Tarasoff liability (VandeCreek & Knapp, 1993) may result in malpractice lawsuits that shape legislative policy and ethical code development. Due to the nature of a fiduciary relationship established via electronic media, it is critical that counseling professionals using such technology remain apprised of litigious developments that affect practice. Thus, legal issues ultimately may involve federal, state, and local legislation—and litigation. The body of literature that likely will be developed as a result of this new and technological enterprise will be of great importance to counseling professionals.

Finally, at the societal level of Tarvydas and Cottone's (1991) model, reciprocal advocacy ultimately must be considered. *Reciprocal advocacy* means that legislative leadership must be aware continually of constituent needs, and constituents must work to stimulate the proportional financial support that is required to meet those needs. Thus, each advocates for the other in a spirit of reciprocal support. Related to technology, each party must be aware of the demands that come from the competing needs of all members of society, both people and governments (e.g., local, state, and federal). Only in this context can appropriate consideration be given those needs.

Summary

This chapter has addressed the ethical issues that are concomitant to any discussion of technology, specifically as related to the professional practice of counseling. We began with a review of the ethical use of electronic media, computer-assisted counseling, and on-line counseling. Then followed a review of computer-assisted assessment, and computer-assisted counselor education. After a brief recommendation for the ethical use of software, we reviewed technological counseling interventions for people with disabilities. Finally, a four-level model of ethical counseling practice was reviewed to highlight the chapter content. The human element in the counseling endeavor is believed essential to effective practice, with technology facilitating counselors' efforts to provide efficient and effective interventions to the people served by this profession.

References

Ackerman, R. J. & Banks, M. E. (1990). Computers and the ethical treatment of brain-injured patients. *Social Science Computer Review, 8*(1), 83–95.

Allen, C. (1995). job.search@internet. *Journal of Career Planning & Employment, 55*(3), 53–55.

American Counseling Association. (1995). American Counseling Association code of ethics and standards of practice. *Counseling Today, 37,* pp. 33–40.

American Educational Research Association, American Psychological Association, National Council on Measurement in Education. (1985). *Standards for educational and psychological testing.* Washington, DC: American Psychological Association.

American Psychological Association. (1992). *Ethical principles of psychologists and code of conduct.* Washington, DC: Author.

American Psychological Association. (1986). *Guidelines for computer-based tests and interpretations.* Washington DC: Author.

Argentero, P. (1989). Computerized psychological testing: An annotated bibliography. *Bollettino di Psicologia Applicata, 190,* 21–38.

Barker, K. (1986). Dilemmas at a distance. *Assessment and Evaluation in Higher Education, 11,* 219–230.

Barron, D. (1991). Distance education and school library media specialists. *School Library Media Annual, 9,* 20–29.

Berge, Z. L. (1994). Electronic discussion groups. *Communication Education, 43,* 102–111.

Binder, L. M., & Thompson, L. L. (1994). The ethics code and neuropsychological assessment practices. *Archives of Clinical Neuropsychology, 10,* 27–46.

Binik, Y. M., Servan-Schreiber, D., Freiwald, S., & Hall, K. S. (1988). Intelligent computer-based assessment and psychotherapy: An expert system for sexual dysfunction. *The Journal of Nervous and Mental Disease, 176,* 387–400.

Bitter, J., Gregg, J., & Jackson, W. (1994). Leadership training by distance. *Journal of Rehabilitation Administration, 18,* 81–86.

Bland, K., Morrison, G. R., & Ross, S. M. (1992). *Student attitudes toward learning link: A distance education project.* Paper presented at the annual meeting of the Mid-South Educational Research Association, Knoxville, TN.

Boles, R. N. (1996, March). The Internet and the job hunt. *Career Planning and Adult Development Network Newsletter, 18*(3), 1–4.

Brod, C. (1984). *Technostress: The human cost of the computer revolution.* Don Mills, Ontario Canada: Addison-Wesley.

Burda, P. C., Starkey, T. W., & Dominguez, F. (1991). Computer-administered treatment of psychiatric inpatients. *Computers in Human Behavior, 7,* 1–5.

Burling, T. A., Marotta, J., Gonzalez, R., Moltzen, J. O., Eng, A. M., Schmidt, G. A., Welch, R. L., Ziff, D. C., & Reilly, P. M. (1989). Computerized smoking cessation program for the worksite: Treatment outcome and feasibility. *Journal of Consulting and Clinical Psychology, 57,* 619–622.

Burnett, K. F., Magel, P. M., Harrington, S., & Taylor, C. B. (1989). Computer-assisted behavioral health counseling for high school students. *Journal of Counseling Psychology, 36,* 63–67.

Burnett, K. F., Taylor, C. B., & Agras, W. S. (1985). Ambulatory computer-assisted therapy for obesity: A new frontier for behavior therapy. *Journal of Consulting and Clinical Psychology, 53,* 698–703.

Butcher, J. N. (Ed.). (1985). Perspectives on computerized psychological assessment [Special issue]. *Journal of Consulting and Clinical Psychology, 53,* 745–838.

Butcher, J. N. (1987). The use of computers in psychological assessment: An overview of practices and issues. In J. N. Butcher (Ed.), *Computerized psychological assessment: A practitioner's guide* (pp. 3–14). New York: Basic Books.

Caplan, B. (1987). Rehabilitation psychology desk reference. Rockville: Aspen.

Carr, A. C., Ghosh, A., & Marks, I. M. (1988). Computer-supervised exposure treatment for phobias. *Canadian Journal of Psychiatry, 33,* 112–117.

Clarke, B., & Schoech, D. (1984). A computer-assisted game for adolescents: Initial development and comments. In M. D. Schwartz (Ed.),

Using computers in clinical practice: Psychotherapy and mental health applications (pp. 335–353). New York: Hayworth.

Colby, K. M. (1980). Computer psychotherapists. In J. B. Sidorski, J. H. Johnson, & T. A. Williams (Eds.), *Technology in mental health care delivery systems* (pp. 109–117). Norwood, NJ: Ablex.

Colby, K. M. (1986). Ethics of computer-assisted psychotherapy. *Psychiatric Annals, 16,* 414–415.

Colby, K. M., Colby, P. M., & Stoller, R. J. (1990). Dialogues in natural language with GURU, a psychological inference engine. *Philosophical Psychology, 3,* 171–186.

Colby, K. M., Gould, R. L., & Aronson, G. (1989). Some pros and cons of computer-assisted psychotherapy. *The Journal of Nervous and Mental Disease, 177,* 105–108.

Colby, K. M., Watt, J. B., & Gilbert, J. P. (1966). A computer method of psychotherapy: Preliminary communication. *The Journal of Nervous and Mental Disease, 142,* 148–152.

Council for Accreditation of Counseling and Related Education Programs. (1996). *CACREP accreditation standards and procedures manual—rev. ed.* Alexandria, VA: Author.

Council on Rehabilitation Education. (1994). *accreditation manual for rehabilitation counselor education programs.* Rolling Meadows, IL: Author.

Davidson, R. S. (1985). Applications of computer technology to learning therapy. *Journal of Organizational Behavior Management, 6,* 155–168.

Davis, A., & Yazak, D. (1995). Implementation and accreditation issues in the development of distance learning programs. *Rehabilitation Education, 9,* 293–307.

Davis-Bell, J. (1991). Distance learning: New technology and new potential. *Legislative Reports, 16*(6), 1–10.

Deiner, E. (1984). Subjective well-being. *Psychological Bulletin, 95,* 542–575.

Drummond (1996). *Appraisal procedures for counselors and helping professionals.* Upper Saddle River, NJ: Prentice-Hall.

Duncan, D. M. (1997). *Counseling over the Internet: Ethical and legal considerations.* Presentation at the American Counseling Association's 1997 World Conference, Orlando, FL.

Eldredge, G., Gerard, G., & Smart, J. (1994). A distance education model for rehabilitation counseling. *Journal of Rehabilitation Administration, 18,* 75–79.

Erdman, H. P., & Foster, S. W. (1988). Ethical issues in the use of computer-based assessment. In J. W. Murphy & J. T. Pardeck (Eds.), *Technology and human service delivery: Challenges and a critical perspective* (pp. 71–87). New York: Haworth.

Erdman, H. P., Klein, M. H., & Greist, J. H. (1985). Direct patient computer interviewing. *Journal of Consulting and Clinical Psychology, 53,* 760–773.

Eyde, L. D. (Ed.). (1987). Computerized psychological testing [Special issue]. *Applied Psychology: An International Review, 36,* 223–235.

Fabian, E. (1989). Work and the quality of life. *Psychosocial Rehabilitation Journal, 12*(4), 39–49.

Fabian, E. (1995). Quality of life. In A. Dell Orto & R. Marinelli (Eds.), *Encyclopedia of disability and rehabilitation* (pp. 607–609). New York: Simon & Schuster Macmillan.

Farrell, A. D., Camplair, P. S., & McCullough, L. (1987). Identification of target complaints by computer interview: Evaluation of the computerized assessment system for psychotherapy evaluation and research. *Journal of Consulting and Clinical Psychology, 55,* 691–700.

Fenwick, J. (1992). *A question of quality.* Paper presented at the International Council for Distance Education 16th World Conference, Bangkok, Thailand.

Ford, B. D. (1988). *An ongoing computerized adjunct to psychotherapy program: Two years plus in a two years minus correctional center.* Paper presented at Counseling as Education Conference, Lakehead University, Thunder Bay, Ontario, Canada.

Ford, B. D. (1993). Ethical and professional issues in computer-assisted therapy. *Computers in Human Behavior, 9,* 387–400.

Ford, B. D., & Vitelli, R. (1992). Inmate attitudes towards computerized clinical interventions. *Computers in Human Behavior, 8*, 223–230.

Fowler, R. D. (1985). Landmarks in computer-assisted psychological assessment. *Journal of Consulting and Clinical Psychology, 53*, 748–759.

French, C. F. (1986). Microcomputers and psychometric assessment. *British Journal of Guidance and Counseling, 14*, 33–45.

French, C. C., & Beaumont, J. G. (1987). The reaction of psychiatric patients to computerized assessment. *British Journal of Clinical Psychology, 26*, 267–278.

French, C., & Beaumont, J. (1992). Microcomputer version of a digit span test in clinical use. *Interacting with Computers, 4*, 163–178.

Fulmer, J., Hazzard, M., Jones, S., & Keene, K. (1992). Distance learning: An innovative approach to nursing education. *Journal of Professional Nursing, 8*, 289–294.

Garrison, D. R. (1990). An analysis and evaluation of audio teleconferencing to facilitate education at a distance. *The American Journal of Distance Education, 4*(3), 13–24.

Gates, B., Myhrvold, N., & Rinearson, P. (1995). *The road ahead.* New York: Viking.

Gelso, C., & Carter, J. (1985). The relationship in counseling and psychotherapy: Components, consequences and theoretical antecedents. *The Counseling Psychologist, 13*, 155–243.

Goodman, H., Gingerich, W. J., & Shazer, S. (1989). BRIEFER: An expert system for clinical practice. *Computers in Human Services, 5*, 53–68.

Grencavage, L. M., & Norcross, J. C. (1990). Where are the commonalities among the therapeutic common factors? *Professional Psychology: Research and Practice, 21*, 372–378.

Hammer, A. L., & Hile, M. G. (1985). Factors in clinicians' resistance to automation in mental health. *Computers in Human Services, 1*, 1–23.

Hannon, K. (1996, May 13). Upset? Try cybertherapy. *U.S. News & World Report, 81*, 83.

Harrell, T. H., Honaker, L. M., Hetu, M., & Oberwager, J. (1987). Computerized versus traditional administration of the multidimensional aptitude battery-verbal scale: An examination of reliability and validity. *Computers in Human Behavior, 3*, 129–137.

Hartman, D. E. (1986a). Artificial intelligence or artificial psychologist? Conceptual issues in clinical microcomputer use. *Professional Psychology: Research and Practice, 17*, 528–534.

Hartman, D. E. (1986b). On the use of clinical psychology software: Practical, legal, and ethical concerns. *Professional Psychology: Research and Practice, 17*, 462–465.

Hodgson, V. E. (1986). The interrelationship between support and learning materials. *Programmed Learning and Educational Technology, 23*, 56–61.

Honaker, L. M., & Fowler, R. D. (1990). Computer-assisted psychological assessment. In G. Goldstein & M. Hersen (Eds), *Handbook of psychological assessment* (2nd ed.). Elmsford, NY: Pergamon Press.

Hood, A. B., & Johnson, R. W. (1997). *Assessment in counseling: A guide to the use of psychological assessment procedures* (2nd ed.). Alexandria, Virginia: ACA.

Jandt, F. E., & Nemnich, M. B. (1995). *Using the Internet in your job search.* Indianapolis, IN: JIST Works, Inc.

Kaplan, E., Roditty, S., & Dover, S. (1991). A modular-integrated answer to the differential demands of a computerized testing system. *European Review of Applied Psychology, 41*, 303–306.

Kennedy, J. L. (1995). *Hook up, get hired! The Internet job search revolution.* New York: Wiley.

Kennedy, R., Baltzley, D., Turnage, J., & Jones, M. (1989). Factor analysis and predictive validity of microcomputer-based tests. *Perceptual and Motor Skills, 69*, 1059–1074.

Kieth-Spiegel, P., & Koocher, G. P. (1985). *Ethics in psychology.* New York: Random House.

Kilvingham, Jr., F. M., Johnston, J. A., Hogan, R. S., & Mauer, E. (1994). Who benefits from computerized career counseling? *Journal of Counseling and Development, 72*, 289–292.

Law, M., & Sissons, L. (1985). The challenge of distance education. *New Directions for Continuing Education, 26,* 43–54.

Lawrence, G. H. (1986). Using computers for the treatment of psychological problems. *Computers in Human Behavior, 2,* 43–62.

Levitan, K. B., Willis, E. A., & Vogelgesang, J. (1985). Microcomputers and the individual practitioner: A review of the literature in psychology and psychiatry. *Computers in Human Services, 1,* 65–84.

Livneh, H. (1987). Person-environment congruence: A rehabilitation perspective. *International Journal of Rehabilitation Research, 10*(1), 3–19.

Lukin, M. E., Dowd, T., Plake, B. S., & Kraft, R. G. (1985). Comparing computerized versus traditional psychological assessment. *Computers in Human Behavior, 1,* 49–58.

Magnusen, K. O., & Magnusen, O. C. (1995). On the leading edge of video interviewing. *Journal of Career Planning & Employment, 55*(4), 45–47.

Maki, D. (1986). Foundations of applied rehabilitation counseling. In Riggar, T., Maki, D, & Wolf, A. (Eds.), *Applied rehabilitation counseling* (pp. 3–11). New York: Springer.

Maki, D., & Murray, G. (1995). Philosophy of rehabilitation. In A. Dell Orto & R. Marinelli (Eds.), *Encyclopedia of disability and rehabilitation* (pp. 555–561). New York: Simon & Schuster Macmillan.

Marino, T. W. (1996, January). Counselors in cyberspace debate whether client discussions are ethical. *Counseling Today,* 8.

Massoumian, B. (1989). Successful teaching via two-way interactive video. *Tech Trends, 34*(2), 16–19.

Matarazzo, J. D. (1985). Clinical psychological test interpretations by computer: Hardware outpaces software. *Computers in Human Behavior, 1,* 235–253.

Matarazzo, J. D. (1986). Computerized clinical psychological test interpretation: Unvalidated plus all mean and no sigma. *American Psychologist, 41,* 14–25.

Matthews, T. J., De Santi, S. M., Callahan, D., Koblenz-Sulcov, C. J., & Werden, J. L. (1987). The microcomputer as an agent of intervention with psychiatric patients: Preliminary studies. *Computers in Human Behavior, 3,* 37–47.

McLemore, C. W., & Fantuzzo, J. W. (1982). CARE: Bridging the gap between clinicians and computers. *Professional Psychology, 13,* 501–510.

Meier, S. T., & Geiger, S. M. (1986). Implications of computer-assisted testing and assessment for professional practice and training. *Measurement and Evaluation in Counseling and Development, 19,* 29–34.

Merrell, K. W. (1986). Computer use in psychometric assessment: evaluating benefits and potential problems. *Computers in Human Services, 1*(3), 59–67.

Moncher, M. S., Parms, C. A., Orlandi, M. A., Schinke, S. P., Miller, S. O., Palleja, J., & Schinke, M. B. (1985). Microcomputer-based approaches for preventing drug and alcohol abuse among adolescents from ethnic-racial minority backgrounds. *Computers in Human Behavior, 5,* 79–93.

Murphy, J. W., & Pardeck, J. T. (1988). Dehumanization, computers and clinical practice. *Journal of Social Behavior and Personality, 3,* 107–116.

Myrick, R., & Sabella, R. (1995). Cyberspace: A new place for counselor supervision. *Elementary School Guidance and Counseling, 30* (1), 35–44.

National Board of Certified Counselors (1989). *Code of Ethics.* Charlotte, NC: Author.

Niemann, H., Ruff, R. M., & Baser, C. A. (1990). Computer-assisted attention retraining in head-injured individuals: A controlled efficacy study of an outpatient program. *Journal of Consulting and Clinical Psychology, 58,* 811–817.

Olcott, Jr., D. (1993). Access to learning: Integrating telecommunications instruction in university extended degree programs. *The Journal of Higher Education, 41,* 16–24.

Park, K., & Lee, S. (1992). A computer aided aptitude test for predicting flight performance of trainees. *Human Factors, 34,* 189–204.

Peterson, L. (1993). Behavior therapy: The long and winding road. *Behavior Therapy, 24*(1), 1–5.

Remley, Jr., T., & Hendren, G. (1989). Legal liability of supervisors. *Rehabilitation Education, 3,* 177–183.

Riley, M., Roehm, F., & Oserman, S. (1996). *The guide to Internet job searching.* Lincolnwood, IL: VGM Career Books.

Roessler, R. (1990). A quality of life perspective on rehabilitation counseling. *Rehabilitation Counseling Bulletin, 34*(2), 82–90.

Rozensky, R. H., Honor, L. F., Rasinski, K., Tovian, S. M., & Herz, G. I. (1986). Paper-pencil versus computer-administered MMPI's: A comparison of patient's attitudes. *Computers in Human Behavior, 2,* 111–116.

Rubin, S. E., & Roessler, R. T. (1995). *Foundations of the vocational rehabilitation process* (4th ed.). Austin: Pro-Ed.

Rust, E. (1995). Applications of the international counselor network for elementary and middle school counseling. *Elementary School Guidance and Counseling, 30*(1), 16–25.

Sampson, J. P., Jr. (1986a). The use of computer-assisted instruction in support of psychotherapeutic processes. *Computers in Human Behavior, 2,* 1–19.

Sampson, J. P., Jr. (Ed.). (1986b). Computer applications in testing and assessment [Special issue]. *Measurement and Evaluation in Counseling and Development, 19,* 4–61.

Sampson, J. P., Jr. (1990). Computer-assisted testing and the goals of counseling psychology. *The Counseling Psychologist, 18,* 227–239.

Sampson, J. P., Jr. (in press). *Computer applications.* In C. E. Watkins, Jr., & V. L. Campbell (Eds.), Using tests and assessment procedures in counseling (2nd Ed.). Hillsdale, NJ: Lawrence Erlbaum.

Sampson, J. P., Jr., Kolodinsky, R. W., & Greeno, B. P. (1997). Counseling on the information highway: Future possibilities and potential problems. *Journal of Counseling & Development, 75,* 203–212.

Sampson, J. P., Jr., & Krumboltz, J. D. (1991). Computer-assisted instruction: A missing link in counseling. *Journal of Counseling and Development, 69,* 395–397.

Schalock, R., Keith, K., Hoffman, K., & Karan, O. (1989). Quality of life: Its measurement and use. *Mental Retardation, 27,* (1), 25–31.

Schinke, S. P., & Orlandi, M. A. (1990). Skills-based, interactive computer interventions to prevent HIV infection among African-American and Hispanic adolescents. *Computers in Human Behavior, 6,* 235–246.

Schinke, S. P., Orlandi, M. A., Gordon, A. N., Weston, R. E., Moncher, M. S., & Parms, C. A. (1989). AIDS prevention via computer-based intervention. *Computers in Human Services, 5,* 147–156.

Schneider, S. J. (1986). Trial of an on-line behavioral smoking cessation program. *Computers in Human Behavior, 2,* 277–286.

Schneider, S. J., Walter, R., & O'Donnell, R. (1990). Computerized communication as a medium for behavioral smoking cessation treatment: Controlled evaluation. *Computers in Human Behavior, 6,* 141–151.

Schwitzgebel, R. L., & Schwitzgebel, R. K. (1980). *Law and psychological practice.* Toronto: Wiley.

Scriven, B. (1991). Distance education and open learning: Implications for professional development and retraining. *Distance Education, 12,* 297–305.

Selmi, P. M., Klein, M. H., Greist, J. H., Johnson, J. H., & Harris, W. G. (1982). An investigation of computer-assisted cognitive-behavior therapy in the treatment of depression. *Behavior Research Methods and Instrumentation, 14,* 181–185.

Selmi, P. M., Klein, M. H., Greist, J. H., Sorell, S. P., & Erdman, H. P. (1990). Computer-administered cognitive-behavioral therapy for depression. *American Journal of Psychiatry, 147,* 51–56.

Servan-Schreiber, C., & Binik, Y. M. (1989). Extending the intelligent tutoring system paradigm: Sex therapy as intelligent tutoring. *Computers in Human Behavior, 5,* 241–259.

Seventeenth Institute on Rehabilitation Issues. (1990). *The provision of assistive technology in rehabilitation.* Fayetteville, AR: Arkansas

Research and Training Center in Vocational Rehabilitation.

Simons, G. (1985). *Silicon shock*. New York: Basil Blackwell.

Sirkin, J. (1994). Learning at a distance. *On Campus, 14*(3), 7–10.

Smith, J. J. (1987). The effectiveness of computerized self-help stress coping program with adult males. *Computers in Human Services, 2,* 37–49.

Spilker, B. (1990). *Quality of life assessments in clinical trials.* New York: Raven Press.

Staff. (1993). *Evaluation considerations for distance learning activities.* Decatur, GA: Southern Association of Colleges and Schools.

Steele, R. L. (1993). Distance learning delivery systems: Instructional options. *Media and Methods, 29*(4), 14.

Stewart, D. (1992). *Student support systems in distance education.* Paper presented at the world conference of the International Council for Distance Education, Bangkok, Thailand.

Stones, M., & Kozma, A. (1989). Multidimensional assessment of the elderly via a microcomputer: The SENOTS program and battery. *Psychology and Aging, 4,* 113–118.

Stricker, G. (1996). Psychotherapy in cyberspace. *Ethics and behavior, 6*(2), 169, 175–177.

Tarvydas, V. M., & Cottone, R. R. (1991). Ethical responses to legislative, organizational, and economic dynamics: A four level model of ethical practice. *Journal of Applied Rehabilitation Counseling, 22,* 11–18.

Taylor, C. B., Agras, W. S., Losch, M., Plante, T. G., & Burnett, K. (1991). Improving the effectiveness of computer-assisted weight loss. *Behavior Therapy, 22,* 229–236.

VandeCreek, L., & Knapp, S. (1993). *Tarasoff and beyond: Legal and clinical considerations in the treatment of life-endangering patients* (revised edition). Sarasota, FL: Professional Resource Press.

Wagman, M. (1988). *Computer psychotherapy systems.* New York: Gordon and Breach Science Publishers.

Wagman, M. (1980). PLATO DCS: An interactive computer system for personal counseling. *Journal of Counseling Psychology, 27,* 16–30.

Wagman, M., & Kerber, K. W. (1980). PLATO DCS, an interactive computer system for personal counseling: Further development and evaluation. *Journal of Counseling Psychology, 27,* 31–39.

Walz, G. R. (1996). Using the I-Way for career development. In R. Feller, & G. Walz (Eds.), *Optimizing life transitions in turbulent times: Exploring work, learning and careers* (pp. 415–427). Greensboro: University of North Carolina, ERIC Clearinghouse on Counseling and Student Services.

Weiss, D. J. (1985). Adaptive testing by computer. *Journal of Consulting and Clinical Psychology, 53,* 774–789.

Willis, B. (1992). From a distance. *Educational Technology, 32*(6), 35–37.

Wise, S., & Plake, B. S. (1990). Computerized testing in higher education. *Measurement and Evaluation in Counseling and Development, 23,* 3–10.

Woods, J. F., & Ollis, H. (1996). Labor market, job information proliferates on-line. *Workforce Journal, 5*(1), 32–44.

Woods, J. F., Ollis, H., & Kaplan, R. (1996). *To spin a web: Job, career, and labor market on the Internet* (Occasional Paper No. 8). Washington, DC: National Occupational Information Coordinating Committee.

Wyndowe, J. (1987). The Microcomputerized Diagnostic Interview Schedule: Clinical use in an out-patient setting. *Canadian Journal of Psychiatry, 32,* 93–99.

Youngjohn, J., Larrabee, G., & Crook, T. (1991). First-Last Names and the Grocery List Selective Reminding Test: Two computerized measures of everyday verbal learning. *Archives of Clinical Neuropsychology, 6,* 287–300.

DISTANCE-LEARNING CONSIDERATIONS FOR REHABILITATION COUNSELOR EDUCATION PROGRAMS

MISSION:

Will distance learning component operate within the mission parameters of the program and the institution?

Will program policies regarding admissions standards, curriculum content, degree completion, and instructional procedures be similar to those used in the campus-based program? If not, are the differences within the role and scope of the program and the institution?

CURRICULUM DELIVERY:

What distance learning modes will be used for the delivery of the program?

Will the modes of delivery be appropriate for the course offered?

FACULTY:

Will academic qualifications of faculty involved in distance learning activities be similar to those of faculty teaching in the campus-based program?

How will the program prepare and train faculty to teach in distance learning component?

Will the amount and quality of interaction between faculty and students of distance learning activities be adequate in relation to the nature of course work?

In what ways will the department head, dean, administration and other faculty not directly involved, support faculty involved in distance learning activities?

RESOURCES:

How will the program provide students with access to learning resources?

Do sufficient learning resources exist to carry out a distance learning program?

How will students be encouraged to make adequate use of learning resources?

How will the program ensure timely delivery of textbooks to distance learning students?

STUDENT SUPPORT:

How will the program ensure that academic advising, counseling, financial aid, and registration assistance are adequately provided to distance learning students?

Will the distance learning component significantly change the program's student to advisor ratio?

PROGRAM EVALUATION:

Has the program developed a systematic plan for evaluating effectiveness of distance learning?

Will evaluation methods be appropriate for the distance learning mode used? How will evaluation results be used?

Source: From A. Davis and D. Yazak, Implementation and accreditation issues in the development of distance learning programs, 1995, *Rehabilitation Education, 9,* 293—307.

CATEGORIES OF ASSISTIVE TECHNOLOGY

1. **Aids for daily living:** Self-help aids for use in activities such as eating, bathing, cooking, dressing, toileting, and home maintenance.

2. **Augmentative communication:** Electronic and nonelectronic devices that provide a means for expressive and receptive communication for persons without speech.

3. **Computer applications:** Input and output devices (e.g., voice and Braille), alternate access aids (e.g., headsticks and light pointers), modified or alternate keyboards, switches, special software, and other devices that enable people with disabilities to use a computer.

4. **Environmental control systems:** Primarily electronic systems that enable people without mobility to control various appliances, electronic aids, security systems, and other devices in their room, home, or other surroundings.

5. **Home/worksite modifications:** Structural adaptations or fabrications in the home, worksite, or other areas (e.g., ramps, lifts, and bathroom accommodations) that remove or reduce physical barriers for an individual with a disability.

6. **Prosthetics and orthotics:** Replacement, substitution, or augmentation of missing or malfunctioning body parts with artificial limbs or other orthotic aids (e.g., splints and braces).

7. **Seating and positioning:** Accommodations to a wheelchair or other seating system to provide greater body stability, trunk/head support and an upright posture, and reduction of pressure on the skin surface (e.g., cushions, contour seats, and lumbar supports).

8. **Aids for vision/hearing impairment:** Magnifiers, Braille or speech-output devices, large-print screens, hearing aids, TDDs, visual altering systems, and other related devices.

9. **Wheelchairs/mobility aids:** Manual and electric wheelchairs, mobile bases for custom chairs, walkers, three-wheel scooters, and other utility vehicles for increasing personal mobility.

10. **Vehicle modifications:** Adaptive driving aids, hand controls, wheelchair and other lifts, modified vans, or other motor vehicles used for personal transportation.

Note: Adapted from *The Provision of Assistive Technology in Rehabilitation* (p. 109) by Seventeenth Institute on Rehabilitation Issues, 1990, Fayetteville: Arkansas Research and Training Center in Vocational Rehabilitation.

TECHNO-ETHICAL CONSIDERATIONS WITHIN THE FOUR LEVEL MODEL

Ethical Levels	Techno-Ethical Considerations
Level 1: Clinical Counseling *Operational Context:* Counselor–Client	• Use of clinical assessment materials • Augmentative communication devices • Confidentiality of information/informed consent • Cybercounseling
Level 2: Clinical Multidisciplinary *Operational Context:* Practitioner–Practitioner	• Information dissemination • Resource allocation • Electronic information sources • Consultation
Level 3: Institutional/Agency *Operational Context:* Institution–Member	• Data management and storage • Supervision • Continuing education • Distance learning
Level 4: Social Resources/ Public Policy *Operational Context:* Legislative–Constituent	• Adequacy of resources • Periodic review and assessment • Legal issues • Reciprocal advocacy

Ethical Practice Within Counseling Specialties

10

Marriage and Family Counseling

Marriage and family counseling is developing and growing as a counseling specialty. It is also recognized by some individuals as a profession separate from the larger profession of "counseling." Marital and family "therapy," represented by the professional organization known as the American Association for Marriage and Family Therapy (AAMFT), has its own training standards, accreditation of graduate programs, and licensure. However, many counselor licensure statutes allow for the practice of marriage and family counseling within the purview of the general counseling license. Therefore, marriage and family counseling is unique in that it is viewed by some as a separate profession *and* by others as a counseling specialty. This dual professional standard has its pros and cons. On the negative side, competing professional associations are seeking members from an overlapping pool of mental health professionals. Credentials sponsored by the associations also compete. And rivalry and even debate exist over the legitimacy of the two professions. On the positive side, two groups are seeking to legitimize the practice of marriage and family counseling, or therapy, and two groups are lobbying for such services to be included in health care and other service provider programs. Regardless, the dual professional identity is confusing, and beginning students in counseling are asked to suspend judgment on who is right or wrong in the debate over professional identity until a thorough study of the matter is undertaken. This chapter, in addition to defining ethical dilemmas in marriage and family counseling, will address the professional issues surrounding professional identification and credentialing in the field.

Defining the Specialty, Setting, and Clients

The specialty of marital and family counseling has found a home in the International Association for Marriage and Family Counseling (IAMFC), an affiliate of the American Counseling Association (ACA). The IAMFC became a recognized affiliate of the ACA in 1989, and since that time, it has been one of the fastest growing affiliates in the ACA. In conjuction with several other family therapy organizations, the IAMFC was successful in helping to sponsor the National Academy for Certified Family Therapists (NACFT), a free-standing certification body that identifies qualified marriage and family counselors. Currently, then, counselors who wish to affiliate with other counselors in the area of marriage and family counseling can congregate through a professional organization and seek certification as recognized and qualified marriage and family counselors.

But, as mentioned earlier, there are other organizations seeking to represent marriage and family therapists. The AAMFT is the largest and most visible. Its membership is composed of individuals who may have educational backgrounds in counseling, social work, medicine, or specifically in marriage and family therapy. In the past, the AAMFT has been an interdisciplinary interest and certifying group. More recently, the AAMFT has sought to carve a niche for a separate profession in the name of "marriage and family therapy." The AAMFT is a recognized leader in advocating for the practice of marriage and family therapy, and it is a visible reminder of the interdisciplinary roots of the professional specialty of marriage and family counseling.

Generally, marriage and family counselors work in settings that provide services to couples or families, such as family service agencies, clinics, counseling centers, private practices, hospitals, and other general mental health service settings. Unless marriage and family counselors are trained in the more general counseling field as a mental health practitioner, they limit their practices to work with couples or families. It is unusual for marriage and family counselors to choose to provide individual counseling as a service of preference. The reason they choose to work with couples or families is primarily theoretical. Marriage and family counselors are directed, to a large degree, by social systems theory, or what has been also identified as systemic–relational theory (Cottone, 1992). Systemic–relational theory is a set of assumptions about the nature of mental health problems. Problems are defined as deriving from relationships, which are viewed as real and assessable processes *between* people. It is what happens *between* people that is of interest to the marriage and family counselor trained in systemic–relational theory.

The clients of marriage and family counselors are couples or families with identified problems of a relational nature. But even if the problem is not identified as relational, the marriage and family counselor will probably conceptualize the problem as such. Even in cases of identified patients, individuals viewed as "problems" needing to be fixed, the marriage and family counselor will probably redefine the concern as the interpersonal pattern of interaction in which problematic behavior manifests itself. Even when marriage and family counselors see individuals in treatment, they most usually focus the counseling on relationship concerns.

Issues of Significance to the Specialty

Professional Differentiation

The ACA is composed of affiliate organizations representing groups such as rehabilitation counselors, school counselors, mental health counselors, group counselors, and others. The IAMFC is the only ACA affiliate that specifically addresses concerns of a marital or family nature. Marriage and family counseling is unique among the counseling specialties represented by the ACA. It is the only specialty with theorists and counselors subscribing to a form of treatment that does not focus attention on the individual. Instead, couples and families are the targets of marriage and family counseling.

Ethical Issues

Confidentiality and Privileged Communication.   Confidentiality, as an anti-gossip guarantee, is designed to prevent revelation of privately communicated information to other individuals. In the classic one-client/one-counselor relationship, confidentiality is a simple issue of counselor responsibility. Counselors are bound by their ethical codes or legal ethical standards (e.g., ethical standards in licensure statutes) to maintain the information communicated in counseling sessions in confidence, that is, in a way that does not share information with others, unless there are extenuating circumstances in which confidentiality would not stand (recognized exemptions). Marriage or family counseling, however, presents complications. First, such counseling almost always involves more than one person as a client. In other words, marriage and family counselors, by philosophy, often treat relationship "systems" as the unit or target of intervention. Often, therefore, two or more people overhear what other individuals communicate in a session. In this sense, there is no one-to-one confidential relationship.

Most ethical codes and licensure statutes were designed primarily for one-to-one counseling relationships. However, the AAMFT Code of Ethics does address the issue of more than one person being the unit of treatment. The AAMFT Code of Ethics (1991) states:

> Marriage and family therapists have unique confidentiality concerns because the client in a therapeutic relationship may be more than one person. Therapists respect and guard confidences of each individual client. (p. 2)

Further, the code states, "In circumstances where more than one person in a family receives therapy, each such family member who is legally competent to execute a waiver must agree to the waiver" (p. 2). Essentially *all* legally responsible parties in marriage or family therapy are required to release the information before it can be communicated to other individuals. But not all ethical codes or licensure standards are as clear as the AAFMT Code of Ethics on this issue. It is especially important for licensed professionals to examine their licensure statutes and any ethical standards referenced in those statutes. First, the statutes must be examined to ensure that provision of services to couples or families is clearly within the purview of the practice of the profession, meaning that the definition of professional practice must clearly reference couples, relationships, systems or family work. Second, if couples or family counseling is referenced in the legal definition of professional practice, ethical standards should then be examined in light of the definition of professional practice. Is a confidential relationship described in the statute's ethical guidelines? Does confidentiality extend to relationships beyond the one-on-one counseling relationship? These questions must be addressed in an examination of relevant ethical standards.

Regardless, unique circumstances in marriage and family counseling still exist that are worth noting in any discussion of confidentiality and privileged communication. For example, even in a situation where legal confidentiality exists by statute for communications made within the context of relationship treatment, certain information may be allowed to be communicated to a therapist in private by one member of a family or couple in treatment. In fact Margolin (1982) stated: "Some therapists, in fact, arrange for sessions with individual family members to actively encourage the sharing of 'secrets' to better understand what is occurring in the family" (p. 791). When secrets are privately revealed to the counselor by one member of a couple or family in treatment, the counselor is faced with the decision as to whether that privately communicated information is confidential in a one-to-one sense. Can that information be communicated subsequently in the context of relationship treatment? For example, what if one member of a couple communicates that he or she is involved in a secret extramarital sexual relationship? Obviously this information is crucial to marital counseling, but if it is communicated in a formal counseling setting with no other parties present, it is considered confidential. But for a counselor to continue relationship counseling with such information (essentially counseling in a way that does not acknowledge the infidelity) is ethically compromising. Margolin (1982) believed that therapists have several options in such a situation: The therapist can choose (a) to keep the secret, (b) to reveal the secret, or (c) to reveal the secret in certain circumstances. But, importantly, it is crucial that counselors should communicate their policy on such matters before counseling is initiated. Margolin (1982) stated, "The most difficult predicament for the therapist would be if she or he failed to convey a policy on confidentiality" (p. 792). The same is true for any communication made by one individual in private to a counselor when that party is involved in relationship treatment with the counselor. Secrets, such as physical or sexual abuse, child molestation, sexual preference, or drug involvement, often are revealed to counselors, and counselors must be prepared to reiterate their policy on confidentiality (with legal exceptions noted) and to follow whatever policy has been communicated and agreed to by the involved parties.

However, there is the additional problem that some secrets may involve illegal activity. For example, adultery is considered a punishable crime in some states, and should the counselor keep a secret of adultery from a spouse, it is possible (although highly unlikely) that the counselor could be charged by the spouse with criminal conspiracy or "alienation of affection" (Cottone, Mannis, & Lewis, 1996; Margolin, 1982). Some argue (Cottone et al., 1996) that counselors must not condone illegal activity by keeping secrets; counselors are most ethically and legally safe when they maintain a policy that such secrets will be openly discussed in counseling sessions with all involved parties present.

Privileged communication, like confidentiality, is more complicated in the context of marriage and family counseling. Privileged communication is referenced in statutes most typically as related to one-to-one communication. In other words, communications made by one person in private to a counselor are considered safe from revelation in a legal proceeding, unless there are legal exceptions or the client waives the privilege. But what about cases in which more than one person is involved in counseling? As with confidentiality, the way the statute is written is critical to interpreting this legal standard. If the statute provides for privileged communication, it must be examined as to whether the privilege extends to all people in a session, or whether it is limited to one-on-one communications made to a counselor. Also, state case law (judgments in past relevant legal cases) will be crucial to determining the extent of coverage of privileged communication. Unfortunately, legal standards are often unclear. Further, many states lack definitive case law. Consequently, counselors must act conservatively. Margolin (1982) stated: "Lacking definitive legislation on these issues . . . family therapists cannot comfortably assume that existing privilege statutes protect the communications that occur during family therapy" (p. 794). Clients should know the risks of communicating secrets in circumstances in which there is no clear privacy.

Informed Consent.   Vesper and Brock (1991) stated: "The doctrine of *informed consent* was originally designed to require physicians and surgeons to explain medical procedures to patients and to warn them of any risks or dangers that could result from treatment. The intent of the doctrine was to permit the patient to make an intelligent, informed choice as to whether to undergo the proposed treatment or procedure" (p. 50). As with medical patients, clients of counselors have the right to consent to treatment or to refuse treatment. Discussions of informed consent are often juxtaposed with discussions of the issue of client competency, which usually refers to clients' abilities to understand and to make judgments or decisions in their best interests. Clients judged to be competent to make decisions in their best interests have a right to be fully informed about the nature of treatments, the professional's qualifications and experience performing procedures or treatments, the risks and benefits of treatment, and alternative treatments. Generally speaking, children are considered not competent to make such decisions; parents or guardians must be consulted when a child is involved. Also, when people who have disabilities or are elderly are legally defined as not competent to make such decisions, a guardian must be consulted and must provide approval before treatment is initiated. In marriage and family counseling it is accepted procedure to have adult participants (or otherwise competent individuals) sign a statement of "consent to treatment" once treatment issues have been addressed. However, compromising situations exist. One or more competent parties in the family may refuse to sign the consent form; in such a case, family treatment with all family members present cannot proceed. In effect, the legal and ethical autonomy of the individual overrides the consensus of the family. One person's hesitance can lead to a decision to abandon certain types of relationship counseling. Counselors, therefore, should encourage and seek the informed consent of all competent participants in marriage and family counseling.

Dual Relationships.   The issue of dual relationships (e.g., a counselor and client establishing a relationship outside the office, whether sexual or nonsexual) in marriage and family counseling has aroused some debate in the field (e.g., Ryder & Hepworth, 1990). The reason for the debate probably centers on marriage and family counseling's underlying philosophical position that relationships have great potential in the process of aiding others. In effect, social systems theory posits that relationships are the primary cause of disturbance in individuals and can affect a positive change in observed behavior, as defined within a specified cultural context. In effect, establishing healthy relationships with clients is basic to the systemic–relational framework. The question of dual relationships, then, is an important one. Certain dual relationships may be viewed as very helpful to clients.

Obviously, certain types of relationships can be harmful. But should all dual relationships be considered harmful or potentially harmful? It has been argued (Ryder & Hepworth, 1990) that a closer examination of the issue is warranted, because a blanket ban on dual relationships may prevent the development of some healthy interactions between a counselor and client. For example, Ryder and Hepworth (1990) suggested that the AAMFT dual relationship ethical rule (that dual relationships should be avoided), which was expanded to nonsexual and apparently nonromantic relationships in 1988, was undesirable. They argued that such a rule masked a complex issue that should be addressed by students in marriage and family therapy. They took the position that it is more important that dual relationship issues should be viewed as complex, and they believed the issues of exploitation and power were the crucial concerns. In effect, they argued against a blanket ban on all dual relationships while arguing in favor of a "serious emphasis" in training and supervision programs on the assessment of complex relationship issues. They stated:

> Our argument is, thus, really very simple. We think the blanket admonition to avoid nonsexual dual relationships with supervisees is a bad idea. We think it is a bad idea because we should stand for dealing effectively with inevitable complexity in relationships, and we should not stand for trying, quixotically, to legislate simplicity into relationships. (p. 131)

So the issue of dual relationships, which may be viewed as straightforward by many, actually presents a dilemma for those who value relationships as elements in facilitating the emotional health of clients or the professional development of supervisees.

Regardless, as the ethical codes in marriage and family counseling now read, dual relationships are considered unethical (the IAMFC code) or are to be avoided (the AAMFT code). The issues, as discussed earlier in this text, are really the issues of potential harm, exploitation, and power. The intent of the person in the power position is also a concern. As described in Chapter 2, sexual relations with clients have been found to be potentially harmful. The ban on sexual relationships with current or former clients has support in the research literature regarding the negative consequences of such acts. Unfortunately, not all dual relationship issues are so clear-cut. Is it harmful to counsel a couple in which one partner is the counselor's car dealer or insurance agent? Is it harmful for a professor to counsel a student about the student's relationship problems while teaching a lecture class in which the student is a member? These circumstances are technically unethical, but may in fact be beneficial to the parties involved.

From a practical standpoint, marriage and family counselors are bound to avoid dual relationships. But the issue needs further clarification, and continued dialogue is bound to occur in the professional literature and at professional conferences.

Responsibility.   The issue of responsibility to clients, which seems uncomplicated when only one client is being seen in individual treatment, becomes a concern when more than one person is in the counselor's office. Margolin (1982) stated:

> The dilemma with multiple clients is that in some situations an intervention that serves one person's best interests may be countertherapeutic to another. Indeed, the very reason that families tend to seek therapy is because they have conflicting goals and interests. (p. 789)

Marriage and family counselors are in the unique counseling circumstance in which competing interests may enter into therapeutic decision-making, if, in fact, the individuals in treatment are viewed as clients to be served. Fortunately, systemic–relational theory provides guidance in supporting a contention that the system of relationships is the focus of treatment. This theoretical focus allows the therapist the flexibility to define the system itself, or the relationship of significance, to be the target of treatment. Allegiance, therefore, can be given to the system or relationships. Margolin described this as relationship advocacy. She stated, "The family therapist then becomes an advocate of the family system and avoids becoming an agent of any one family member" (p. 789). Of course, there are circumstances in which advocating for the system or relationships must be abandoned, such as cases of child abuse or neglect, or situations in which one party is endangered by the threats or actions of another member in the family. In such situations, relationship advocacy must be abandoned to protect the endangered party (Margolin, 1982). But for the vast majority of cases, relationship advocacy is a legitimate position. Counselors simply define the *marriage* or the *family* as the unit to which they are responsible, and activities of the counselor are then focused on doing what is right for the relationship or family as a whole. Relationship advocacy is one option of the marriage and family counselor that is not available to counselors doing individual treatment. It is a difference of ethical significance that is theoretically and practically unique to systemic-relational practice.

Values.   Huber (1994) stated: "Values are a core component of any professional endeavor and are particularly critical to the professional practice of marriage and family therapy" (p. 225). *Values* are beliefs about what is desirable. Values may be highly individual, or they may be shared within a social context. Marriage and family counseling poses value dilemmas that are not usually encountered in other types of counseling. For example, a counselor's view of divorce is significant to the tone of marital therapy. Some counselors do all that is possible to guide clients away from consideration of divorce. Other counselors may openly discuss divorce as an option, even early in counseling. Of course, it is implicit in marriage counseling that the marriage is valued. Both the IAMFC and AAMFT ethical codes place value on the well-being or welfare of the family. But to what degree is the individual practitioner bound to a strict value-driven practice? On the issue of divorce, for example, the AAMFT code specifically states that decisions on marital status are the responsibility of the client. This appears to give the practitioner latitude in recommending trial separation as an option, but it appears also to prevent a practitioner from stating, unconditionally, that a person should seek divorce or separation. Value issues are involved, and beyond the directives of the code, a counselor's values may be highly relevant to what actually occurs in counseling. For example, according to some religions, such as the Roman Catholic religion, divorce is not accepted, because marriage is viewed as a sacrament. A Roman Catholic practitioner counseling a Roman Catholic couple may undertake therapy with this overriding religious value directing the options for the couple. So certain values, religious and otherwise, enter into marriage and family counseling practice that may only be tangentially or incompletely addressed by a code of ethics. Also, certain value issues relevant to marriage and family counseling may not be relevant in other specialties of counseling, and ethical codes covering general practice (e.g., the ACA code) may not adequately address the value issues at the heart of marriage and family counseling.

Other value issues typically encountered by marriage and family counselors include judgments about extramarital affairs (sexual or otherwise), sex roles, parenting roles, division of labor in the marital relationship, multicultural or mixed cultural relations, marital sexuality, birth control, involvement with the extended family, decision-making and control of resources, and others.

Most textbooks on professional ethics in the human services (e.g., Corey, Corey & Callanan, 1993; Huber, 1994) direct practitioners to assess their values through a process of value clarification and to be alert to circumstances in practice that may activate a value judgment. In situations where it is apparent that the values of the counselor may be in conflict with the couple or family in treatment, the counselor must decide whether counseling can be undertaken in a way that is consistent with the family values or whether referral to another counselor is appropriate.

Counselor Competence.   Given that marriage and family counseling is founded on a theoretical framework that is philosophically quite distinct from the foundations of individual psychotherapy (Cottone, 1992), it is imperative that marriage and family counselors have special training and supervision in systemic–relational treatment. Both the AAMFT and the National Academy of Certified Family Therapists have set standards for professional marriage and family counselors. The standards are specific in defining the need for a thorough understanding of relationship theory. The standards are also quite demanding regarding adequate supervision: those who aspire to be specialists in marriage and family counseling must obtain supervision under the direction of qualified supervisors. In fact, the AAMFT certifies individuals as "approved supervisors" for the oversight of clinicians in training. It is not enough for a counselor to receive a general counseling degree and then begin seeing couples or families in practice without adequate coursework or supervision specifically in marriage or family counseling.

Code Comparisons

Two ethical codes apply to counselors in the specialty of marriage and family counseling. The first is the American Association for Marriage and Family Therapy Code of Ethics (AAMFT, 1991). The second is the Ethical Code for the International Association of Marriage and Family Counselors (IAMFC, 1993). The IAMFC is an affiliate organization of the larger ACA; therefore, members of the IAMFC are bound by both the IAMFC code and also the more general ACA code. Both the IAMFC and AAMFT codes are reprinted at the end of this chapter. The ACA code is reprinted in Chapter 1. For the purposes of this analysis, only the IAMFC and AAMFT codes will be compared.

Generally both codes promote the welfare of both families and individuals. This is different from more general codes of ethics, which often focus on the individual in a one-on-one or group counseling context. Both codes, for example, provide for confidentiality of communications made in counseling/therapy. But they also require that all competent parties involved in counseling sign a waiver of confidentiality before any information can be released to a third party. Both codes address issues of competence, recognizing that practitioners should not diagnose or treat problems outside the scope of their professional training and supervision, which, in this case directly relates to relationship treatment. Both recognize ethical concerns related to supervision of students, employees, or supervisees.

There are differences in the codes. The IAMFC code has a section specifically dealing with assessment, which reflects the counseling profession's scope of practice, including use of educational and psychological testing devices. AAMFT members may not have training in psychological or counseling assessment. The AAMFT code has a section on advertising and specifically addresses the use of the AAMFT "Clinical Member" designation, which is recognized nationally as a professional credential. Whereas the AAMFT code addresses "financial arrangements" specifically, the IAMFC code addresses "private practice" in general.

The codes have other similarities and differences, and readers are directed to the codes themselves to analyze their contents. Regardless, it is noteworthy that this professional specialty of marriage and family counseling requires knowledge of how treating relationships compounds ethical issues in clinical practice.

Issues of Diversity

Given that marriage and family counseling is founded on systemic–relational theory, both positive and negative implications exist from a multicultural perspective. Systemic–relational theory offers a perspective of cause and effect that relieves the individual of individual blame. Accordingly, it is the system of relationships that is considered causative of what can be observed to be a problem. For example, if there is a misbehaving child in a family, the family dynamics and patterns of interactions would be analyzed and the child's behavior would be interpreted within the context of the family system. The "cause" of the child's problem would not be identified as within the individual psychology or learning of the child; rather the family system's patterns of interactions would be implicated. When a relationship is considered problematic, neither individual in the relationship would be culpable. Blame would be placed on the larger relationship pattern, and further, the relationship problem would be interpreted within an encompassing system of relationships within which the problem is imbedded. For example, a marital concern might be interpreted as a lack of fit between two family systems interacting through the marital relationship. The influences of family relationships currently and historically would be analyzed in assessing the nature of the problem and a means to solution.

Feminist theorists have attacked this cause-and-effect perspective (Bograd, 1984). For example, in the case of physical abuse of a spouse (95% of victims being females) to blame the relationship and relational dynamics is to implicate the victim in the abuse. The position that a perpetrator is not culpable is viewed by feminist theorists as indefensible. The concerns raised by feminist theorists are even more salient when child abuse is the issue. Can a 3-year-old child be viewed in any way as dynamically "causative" of his or her sexual abuse? To somehow relieve the blame of a child abuser is essentially a double victimization of the child. Several theorists (Cottone, 1992; Dell, 1989) have attempted to accommodate this critique of systemic–relational theory by modifying the theory to account for linear causal processes, that is, processes whereby one individual, in a power position, has straightforward causal influence. Thereby the person in power can be blamed in abusive circumstances.

On the positive side, revision of systemic–relational theory has led to a position that within certain contexts, cause can be viewed as either circular and relational or linear and individual. Systemic–relational theorists are embracing theoretical developments in psychology and biology, which have adopted a position that *realities* are defined and constructed socially. Such theoretical developments have come forward under the rubric of "social constructivism," "social constructionism," "contextualism," and "post-modernism" (Cottone, 1992; Gergen, 1985; Hoffman, 1988). Accordingly, a social consensus can be developed around a circumstance, such as abuse, that an individual is culpable. In such circumstances, individual treatment along with relational treatments would be indicated. In this sense, a relational definition of a problem can lead to treatment of an individual.

Additionally, advances in systemic–relational theory allow for an understanding of cultural difference as arising from socially constructed "realities." When reality is viewed as socially constructed, that is, arising from a consensus in a group, it is then possible to conceive of competing, but equally legitimate realities (Maturana, 1978). No cultural group or cultural norm can be viewed as better or more valid than any other. Each cultural norm derives from a reality established within the context of social relations within cultural boundaries. Before such advances, systemic–relational theorists depended on theories that defined what was considered right or acceptable in families; for example, Minuchin (1974), a preeminent family therapist, theoretically defined hierarchy in families as important to what is viewed as healthy family organization. Likewise, other theorists defined what they believed to be healthy family organizations or interactional patterns. Currently, counselors are not bound by absolute conceptions of mental health within a family relational framework; rather, they can accommodate cultural diversity in their techniques and approaches to family systems because no one family norm exists.

Summary

This chapter has summarized ethical issues deriving from the specialty practice of marriage and family counseling. Professional issues were addressed and relevant ethical codes were reviewed. The practice of marriage and family counseling is unique among the counseling specialties, primarily based on a philosophical position that values relationships as crucial to mental health and observable behavioral difficulties. This unique philosophical position allows for unique ethical considerations, including concerns over multicultural issues; it also allows for unique solutions to ethical concerns, which would otherwise not be forthcoming from other counseling specialties.

References

American Association for Marriage and Family Therapy. (1991). *AAMFT Code of Ethics.* Washington, DC: Author.

Bograd, M. (1984). Family systems approaches to wife battering: A feminist critique. *American Journal of Orthopsychiatry, 54,* 558–568.

Corey, G., Corey, M. S., & Callanan, P. (1993). *Issues and ethics in the helping professions.* Pacific Grove, CA: Brooks/Cole.

Cottone, R. R. (1992). *Theories and paradigms of counseling and psychotherapy.* Needham Heights, MA: Allyn & Bacon.

Cottone, R. R., Mannis, J., & Lewis, T. (1996). Uncovering secret extramarital affairs in marriage counseling. *The Family Journal, 4,* 109–115.

Dell, P. F. (1989). Violence and the systemic view: The problem of power. *Family Process, 28,* 1–14.

Gergen, K. J. (1985). The social constructionist movement in modern psychology. *American Psychologist, 40,* 266–275.

Hoffman, L. (1988). A constructivist position for family therapy. *The Irish Journal of Psychology, 9,* 110–129.

Huber, C. H. (1994). *Ethical, legal, and professional issues in the practice of marriage and family therapy.* Upper Saddle River, NJ: Merrill/Prentice Hall.

International Association of Marriage and Family Counseling. (1993). Ethical code for the International Association of Marriage and Family Counselors. *The Family Journal: Counseling and Therapy for Couples and Families, 1,* 73–77.

Margolin, G. (1982). Ethical and legal considerations in marital and family therapy. *American Psychologist, 37,* 788–801.

Maturana, H. R. (1978). Biology of language: The epistemology of reality. In G. A. Miller & E. Lenneberg (Eds.), *Psychology and biology of language and thought.* New York: Academic Press.

Minuchin, S. (1974). *Families and family therapy.* Cambridge, MA: Harvard University Press.

Ryder, R., & Hepworth, J. (1990). AAMFT ethical code: "Dual relationships." *Journal of Marital and Family Therapy, 16,* 127–132.

Vesper, J. H., & Brock, G. (1991). *Ethics, legalities, and professional practice issues in marriage and family therapy.* Needham Heights, MA: Allyn & Bacon.

AAMFT
CODE OF ETHICS

The Board of Directors of the American Association for Marriage and Family Therapy (AAMFT) hereby promulgates, pursuant to Article 2, Section 2.013 of the Association's Bylaws, the Revised AAMFT Code of Ethics, effective August 1, 1991.

The AAMFT Code of Ethics is binding on Members of AAMFT in all membership categories, AAMFT Approved Supervisors, and applicants for membership and the Approved Supervisor designation (hereafter, AAMFT Member).

If an AAMFT Member resigns in anticipation of, or during the course of an ethics investigation, the Ethics Committee will complete its investigation. Any publication of action taken by the Association will include the fact that the Member attempted to resign during the investigation.

Marriage and family therapists are strongly encouraged to report alleged unethical behavior of colleagues to appropriate professional associations and state regulatory bodies.

1. RESPONSIBILITY TO CLIENTS

Marriage and family therapists advance the welfare of families and individuals. They respect the rights of those persons seeking their assistance, and make reasonable efforts to ensure that their services are used appropriately.

1.1 Marriage and family therapists do not discriminate against or refuse professional service to anyone on the basis of race, gender, religion, national origin, or sexual orientation.

1.2 Marriage and family therapists are aware of their influential position with respect to clients, and they avoid exploiting the trust and dependency of such persons. Therapists, therefore, make every effort to avoid dual relationships with clients that could impair professional judgment or increase the risk of exploitation. When a dual relationship cannot be avoided, therapists take appropriate professional precautions to ensure judgment is not impaired and no exploitation occurs. Examples of such dual relationships include, but are not limited to, business or close personal relationships with clients. Sexual intimacy with clients is prohibited. Sexual intimacy with former clients for two years following the termination of therapy is prohibited.

1.3 Marriage and family therapists do not use their professional relationships with clients to further their own interests.

1.4 Marriage and family therapists respect the right of clients to make decisions and help them to understand the consequences of these decisions. Therapists clearly advise a client that a decision on marital status is the responsibility of the client.

1.5 Marriage and family therapists continue therapeutic relationships only so long as it is reasonably clear that clients are benefiting from the relationship.

1.6 Marriage and family therapists assist persons in obtaining other therapeutic services if the therapist is unable or unwilling, for appropriate reasons, to provide professional help.

1.7 Marriage and family therapists do not abandon or neglect clients in treatment without making reasonable arrangements for the continuation of such treatment.

1.8 Marriage and family therapists obtain written informed consent from clients before videotaping, audiorecording, or permitting third party observation.

2. CONFIDENTIALITY

Marriage and family therapists have unique confidentiality concerns because the client in a therapeutic relationship may be more than one person. Therapists respect and guard confidences of each individual client.

2.1 Marriage and family therapists may not disclose client confidences except: (a) as mandated by law; (b) to prevent a clear and immediate danger to a person or persons; (c) where the therapist is a defendant in a civil, criminal, or disciplinary action arising from the therapy (in which case client confidences may be disclosed only in the course of that action); or (d) if there is a waiver previously obtained in writing, and then such information may be revealed only in accordance with the terms of the waiver. In circumstances where more than one person in a family receives therapy, each such family member who is legally competent to execute a waiver must agree to the waiver required by subparagraph (d). Without such a waiver from each family member legally competent to execute a waiver, a therapist cannot disclose information received from any family member.

2.2 Marriage and family therapists use client and/or clinical materials in teaching, writing, and public presentations only if a written waiver has been obtained in accordance with Subprinciple 2.1(d), or when appropriate steps have been taken to protect client identity and confidentiality.

2.3 Marriage and family therapists store or dispose of client records in ways that maintain confidentiality.

3. PROFESSIONAL COMPETENCE AND INTEGRITY

Marriage and family therapists maintain high standards of professional competence and integrity.

3.1 Marriage and family therapists are in violation of this Code and subject to termination of membership or other appropriate action if they: (a) are convicted of any felony; (b) are convicted of a misdemeanor related to their qualifications or functions; (c) engage in conduct which could lead to conviction of a felony, or a misdemeanor related to their qualifications or functions; (d) are expelled from or disciplined by other professional organizations; (e) have their licenses or certificates suspended or revoked or are otherwise disciplined by regulatory bodies; (f) are no longer competent to practice marriage and family therapy because they are impaired due to physical or mental causes or the abuse of alcohol or other substances; or (g) fail to cooperate with the Association at any point from the inception of an ethical complaint through the completion of all proceedings regarding that complaint.

3.2 Marriage and family therapists seek appropriate professional assistance for their personal problems or conflicts that may impair work performance or clinical judgment.

3.3 Marriage and family therapists, as teachers, supervisors, and researchers, are dedicated to high standards of scholarship and present accurate information.

3.4 Marriage and family therapists remain abreast of new developments in family therapy knowledge and practice through educational activities.

3.5 Marriage and family therapists do not engage in sexual or other harassment or exploitation of clients, students, trainees, supervisees, employees, colleagues, research subjects, or actual or potential witnesses or complainants in investigations and ethical proceedings.

3.6 Marriage and family therapists do not diagnose, treat, or advise on problems outside the recognized boundaries of their competence.

3.7 Marriage and family therapists make efforts to prevent the distortion or misuse of their clinical and research findings.

3.8 Marriage and family therapists, because of their ability to influence and alter the lives of others, exercise special care when making public their professional recommendations and opinions through testimony or other public statements.

4. RESPONSIBILITY TO STUDENTS, EMPLOYEES, AND SUPERVISEES

Marriage and family therapists do not exploit the trust and dependency of students, employees, and supervisees.

4.1 Marriage and family therapists are aware of their influential position with respect to students, employees, and supervisees, and they avoid exploiting the trust and dependency of such persons. Therapists, therefore, make every effort to avoid dual relationships that could impair professional judgment or increase the risk of exploitation. When a dual relationship cannot be avoided, therapists take appropriate professional precautions to ensure judgment is not impaired and no exploitation occurs. Examples of such dual relationships include, but are not limited to, business or close personal relationships with students, employees, or supervisees. Provision of therapy to students, employees, or supervisees is prohibited. Sexual intimacy with students or supervisees is prohibited.

4.2 Marriage and family therapists do not permit students, employees, or supervisees to perform or to hold themselves out as competent to perform professional services beyond their training, level of experience, and competence.

4.3 Marriage and family therapists do not disclose supervisee confidences except: (a) as mandated by law; (b) to prevent a clear and immediate danger to a person or persons; (c) where the therapist is a defendant in a civil, criminal, or disciplinary action arising from the supervision (in which case supervisee confidences may be disclosed only in the course of that action); (d) in educational or training settings where there are multiple supervisors, and then only to other professional colleagues who share responsibility for the training of the supervisee; or (e) if there is a waiver previously obtained in writing, and then such information may be revealed only in accordance with the terms of the waiver.

5. RESPONSIBILITY TO RESEARCH PARTICIPANTS

Investigators respect the dignity and protect the welfare of participants in research and are aware of federal and state laws and regulations and professional standards governing the conduct of research.

5.1 Investigators are responsible for making careful examinations of ethical acceptability in planning studies. To the extent that services to research participants may be compromised by participation in research, investigators seek the ethical advice of qualified professionals not directly involved in the investigation and observe safeguards to protect the rights of research participants.

5.2 Investigators requesting participants' involvement in research inform them of all aspects of the research that might reasonably be expected to influence willingness to participate. Investigators are especially sensitive to the possibility of diminished consent when participants are also receiving clinical services, have impairments which limit understanding and/or communication, or when participants are children.

5.3 Investigators respect participants' freedom to decline participation in or to withdraw from a research study at any time. This obligation requires special thought and consideration when investigators or other members of the research team are in positions of authority or influence over participants. Marriage and family therapists, therefore, make every effort to avoid dual relationships with research participants that could impair professional judgment or increase the risk of exploitation.

5.4 Information obtained about a research participant during the course of an investigation is confidential unless there is a waiver previously obtained in writing. When the possibility exists that others, including family members, may obtain access to such information, this possibility, together with the plan for protecting confidentiality, is explained as part of the procedure for obtaining informed consent.

6. RESPONSIBILITY TO THE PROFESSION

Marriage and family therapists respect the rights and responsibilities of professional colleagues and participate in activities which advance the goals of the profession.

6.1 Marriage and family therapists remain accountable to the standards of the profession when acting as members or employees of organizations.

6.2 Marriage and family therapists assign publication credit to those who have contributed to a publication in proportion to their contributions and in accordance with customary professional publication practices.

6.3 Marriage and family therapists who are the authors of books or other materials that are published or distributed cite persons to whom credit for original ideas is due.

6.4 Marriage and family therapists who are the authors of books or other materials published or distributed by an organization take reasonable precautions to ensure that the organization promotes and advertises the materials accurately and factually.

6.5 Marriage and family therapists participate in activities that contribute to a better community and society, including devoting a portion of their professional activity to services for which there is little or no financial return.

6.6 Marriage and family therapists are concerned with developing laws and regulations pertaining to marriage and family therapy that serve the public interest, and with altering such laws and regulations that are not in the public interest.

6.7 Marriage and family therapists encourage public participation in the design and delivery of professional services and in the regulation of practitioners.

7. FINANCIAL ARRANGEMENTS

Marriage and family therapists make financial arrangements with clients, third party payors, and supervisees that are reasonably under-standable and conform to accepted professional practices.

7.1 Marriage and family therapists do not offer or accept payment for referrals.

7.2 Marriage and family therapists do not charge excessive fees for services.

7.3 Marriage and family therapists disclose their fees to clients and supervisees at the beginning of services.

7.4 Marriage and family therapists represent facts truthfully to clients, third party payors, and supervisees regarding services rendered.

8. ADVERTISING

Marriage and family therapists engage in appropriate informational activities, including those that enable laypersons to choose professional services on an informed basis.

General Advertising

8.1 Marriage and family therapists accurately represent their competence, education, training, and experience relevant to their practice of marriage and family therapy.

8.2 Marriage and family therapists assure that advertisements and publications in any media (such as directories, announcements, business cards, newspapers, radio, television, and facsimiles) convey information that is necessary for the public to make an appropriate selection of professional services. Information could include: (a) office information, such as name, address, telephone number, credit card acceptability, fees, languages spoken, and office hours; (b) appropriate degrees, state licensure and/or certification, and AAMFT Clinical Member status; and (c) description of practice. (For requirements for advertising under the AAMFT name, logo, and/or the abbreviated initials AAMFT, see Subprinciple 8.15, below).

8.3 Marriage and family therapists do not use a name which could mislead the public concerning the identity, responsibility, source, and status of those practicing under that name and do not hold themselves out as being partners or associates of a firm if they are not.

8.4   Marriage and family therapists do not use any professional identification (such as a business card, office sign, letterhead, or telephone or association directory listing) if it includes a statement or claim that is false, fraudulent, misleading, or deceptive. A statement is false, fraudulent, misleading, or deceptive if it (a) contains a material misrepresentation of fact; (b) fails to state any material fact necessary to make the statement, in light of all circumstances, not misleading; or (c) is intended to or is likely to create an unjustified expectation.

8.5   Marriage and family therapists correct, wherever possible, false, misleading, or inaccurate information and representations made by others concerning the therapist's qualifications, services, or products.

8.6   Marriage and family therapists make certain that the qualifications of persons in their employ are represented in a manner that is not false, misleading, or deceptive.

8.7   Marriage and family therapists may represent themselves as specializing within a limited area of marriage and family therapy, but only if they have the education and supervised experience in settings which meet recognized professional standards to practice in that specialty area.

Advertising Using AAMFT Designations

8.8 The AAMFT designations of Clinical Member, Approved Supervisor, and Fellow may be used in public information or advertising materials only by persons holding such designations. Persons holding such designations may, for example, advertise in the following manner:

- *Jane Doe, Ph.D., a Clinical Member of the American Association for Marriage and Family Therapy.*

Alternately, the advertisement could read:

- *Jane Doe, Ph.D., AAMFT Clinical Member.*
- *John Doe, Ph.D., an Approved Supervisor of the American Association for Marriage and Family Therapy.*

Alternately, the advertisement could read:

> *John Doe, Ph.D., AAMFT Approved Supervisor.*

- *Jane Doe, Ph.D., a Fellow of the American Association for Marriage and Family Therapy.*

Alternately, the advertisement could read:

> *Jane Doe, Ph.D., AAMFT Fellow.*

More than one designation may be used if held by the AAMFT Member.

8.9   Marriage and family therapists who hold the AAMFT Approved Supervisor or the Fellow designation may not represent the designation as an advanced clinical status.

8.10 Student, Associate, and Affiliate Members may not use their AAMFT membership status in public information or advertising materials. Such listings on professional resumes are not considered advertisements.

8.11 Persons applying for AAMFT membership may not list their application status on any resume or advertisement.

8.12 In conjunction with their AAMFT membership, marriage and family therapists claim as evidence of educational qualifications only those degrees (a) from regionally accredited institutions or (b) from institutions recognized by states which license or certify marriage and family therapists, but only if such state regulation is recognized by AAMFT.

8.13 Marriage and family therapists may not use the initials AAMFT following their name in the manner of an academic degree.

8.14 Marriage and family therapists may not use the AAMFT name, logo, and/or the abbreviated initials AAMFT or make any other such representation which would imply that they speak for or represent the Association. The Association is the sole owner of its name, logo, and the abbreviated initials AAMFT. Its committees and divisions, operating as such, may use the name, logo, and/or the abbreviated initials AAMFT in accordance with AAMFT policies.

8.15 Authorized advertisements of Clinical Members under the AAMFT name, logo, and/or the abbreviated initials AAMFT may include the following: the Clinical Member's name, degree, license or certificate held when required by state law, name of business, address, and telephone number. If a business is listed, it must follow, not precede the Clinical Member's name. Such listings may not include AAMFT offices held by the Clinical Member, nor any specializations, since such a listing under the AAMFT name, logo, and/or the abbreviated initials, AAMFT, would imply that this specialization has been credentialed by AAMFT.

8.16 Marriage and family therapists use their membership in AAMFT only in connection with their clinical and professional activities.

8.17 Only AAMFT divisions and programs accredited by the AAMFT Commission on Accreditation for Marriage and Family Therapy Education, not businesses nor organizations, may use any AAMFT-related designation or affiliation in public information or advertising materials, and then only in accordance with AAMFT policies.

8.18 Programs accredited by the AAMFT Commission on Accreditation for Marriage and Family Therapy Education may not use the AAMFT name, logo, and/or the abbreviated initials AAMFT. Instead, they may have printed on their stationery and other appropriate materials a statement such as:
The (name of program) *of the* (name of institution) *is accredited by the AAMFT Commission on Accreditation for Marriage and Family Therapy Education.*

8.19 Programs not accredited by the AAMFT Commission on Accreditation for Marriage and Family Therapy Education may not use the AAMFT name, logo, and/or the abbreviated initials AAMFT. They may not state in printed program materials, program advertisements, and student advisement that their courses and training opportunities are accepted by AAMFT to meet AAMFT membership requirements.

Violations of this Code should be brought in writing to the attention of the AAMFT Ethics Committee, 1100 17th Street, NW, The Tenth Floor, Washington, DC 20036-4601, (telephone 202/452-0109).
Effective August 1, 1991.

ETHICAL CODE FOR THE INTERNATIONAL ASSOCIATION OF MARRIAGE AND FAMILY COUNSELORS

PREAMBLE

The IAMFC (The International Association of Marriage and Family Counselors) is an organization dedicated to advancing the practice, training, and research of marriage and family counselors. Members may specialize in areas such as: premarital counseling, intergenerational counseling, separation and divorce counseling, relocation counseling, custody assessment and implementation, single parenting, stepfamilies, nontraditional family and marriage lifestyles, healthy and dysfunctional family systems, multicultural marriage and family concerns, displaced and homeless families, interfaith and interracial families, and dual career couples. In conducting their professional activities, members commit themselves to protect and advocate for the healthy growth and development of the family as a whole, even as they conscientiously recognize the integrity and diversity of each family and family member's unique needs, situations, status, and member's unique needs, situations, status, and member's unique needs, situations, status, and condition. The IAMFC member recognizes that the relationship between the provider and consumer of services is characterized as an egalitarian process emphasizing co-participation, co-equality, co-authority, co-responsibility, and client empowerment.

This code of ethics promulgates a framework for ethical practice by IAMFC members and is divided into eight sections: client well-being, confidentiality, competence, assessment, private practice, research and publications, supervision, and media and public statements. The ideas presented within these eight areas are meant to supplement the ethical standards of the American Counseling Association (ACA), formerly the American Association for Counseling and Development (AACD), and all members should know and keep to the standards of our parent organization.

Although an ethical code cannot anticipate every possible situation or dilemma, the IAMFC ethical guidelines can aid members in ensuring the welfare and dignity of the couples and families they have contact with, as well as assisting in the implementation of the Hippocratic mandate for healers: Do no harm.

SECTION I: CLIENT WELL-BEING

A. Members demonstrate a caring, empathic, respectful, fair, and active concern for family well-being. They promote client safety, security, and place-of-belonging in family, community, and society. Due to the risk involved, members should not use intrusive interventions without a sound theoretical rationale and having thoroughly thought through the potential ramifications to the family and its members.

B. Members recognize that each family is unique. They respect the diversity of personal attributes and do not stereotype or force families into prescribed attitudes, roles, or behaviors.

C. Members respect the autonomy of the families that they work with. They do not make decisions that rightfully belong to family members.

D. Members respect cultural diversity. They do not discriminate on the basis of race, sex, disability, religion, age, sexual orientation, cultural background, national origin, marital status, or political affiliation.

E. Members strive for an egalitarian relationship with clients by openly and conscientiously sharing information, opinions, perceptions, processes of decision making, strategies of problem solving, and understanding of human behavior.

F. Members pursue a just relationship that acknowledges, respects, and informs clients of their

SOURCE: Reprinted from *The Family Journal: Counseling and Therapy for Couples and Families,* Vol. 1, January 1993 (pp. 73–77). Reprinted by permission.

rights, obligations, and expectations as a consumer of services, as well as the rights, obligations, and expectations of the provider(s) of service. Members inform clients (in writing if feasible) about the goals and purpose of the counseling, the qualifications of the counselor(s), the scope and limits of confidentiality, potential risks and benefits associated with the counseling process and with specific counseling techniques, reasonable expectations for the outcomes and duration of counseling, costs of services, and appropriate alternatives to counseling.

G. Members strive for a humanistic relationship that assists clients to develop a philosophy of meaning, purpose, and direction of life and living that promotes a positive regard of self, of family, of different and diverse others, and of the importance of humane concern for the community, nation, and the world at large.

H. Members promote primary prevention. They pursue the development of clients' cognitive, moral, social, emotional, spiritual, physical, educational, and career needs, as well as parenting, marriage, and family living skills, in order to prevent future problems.

I. Members have an obligation to determine and inform all persons involved who their primary client is—i.e., is the counselor's primary obligation to the individual, the family, a third party, or an institution? When there is a conflict of interest between the needs of the client and counselor's employing institution, the member works to clarify his or her commitment to all parties. Members recognize that the acceptance of employment implies that they are in agreement with the agency's policies and practices, and so monitor their place of employment to make sure that the environment is conducive to the positive growth and development of clients. If, after utilizing appropriate institutional channels for change, the member finds that the agency is not working toward the well-being of clients, the member has an obligation to terminate his or her institutional affiliation.

J. Members do not harass, exploit, coerce, engage in dual relationships, or have sexual contact with any current or former client or family member to whom they have provided professional services.

K. Members have an obligation to withdraw from a counseling relationship if the continuation of services is not in the best interest of the client or would result in a violation of ethical standards. If a client feels that the counseling relationship is no longer productive, the member has an obligation to assist in finding alternative services.

L. Members maintain accurate and up-to-date records. They make all file information available to clients unless the sharing of such information would be damaging to the status, goals, growth, or development of the client.

M. Members have the responsibility to confront unethical behavior conducted by other counselors. The first step should be to discuss the violation directly with the counselor. If the problem continues, the member should first use procedures established by the employing institution and then those of the IAMFC. Members may wish to also contact any appropriate licensure or certification board. Members may contact the IAMFC executive director, president, executive board members, or chair of the ethics committee at any time for consultation on remedying ethical violations.

SECTION II: CONFIDENTIALITY

A. Clients have the right to expect that information shared with the counselor will not be disclosed to others and, in the absence of any law to the contrary, the communications between clients and marriage and family counselors should be viewed as privileged. The fact that a contact was made with a counselor is to be considered just as confidential as the information shared during that contact. Information obtained from a client can only be disclosed to a third party under the following conditions.

1. The client consents to disclosure by a signed waiver. The client must fully understand the nature of the disclosure (i.e., give informed consent), and only information described in the waiver may be disclosed. If more than one person is receiving counseling, each individual who is legally competent to execute a waiver must sign.

2. The client has placed him- or herself or someone else in clear and imminent danger.

3. The law mandates disclosure.

4. The counselor is a defendant in a civil, criminal, or disciplinary action arising from professional activity.

5. The counselor needs to discuss a case for consultation or education purposes. These discussions should not reveal the identity of the client or any other unnecessary aspects of the case and should only be done with fellow counseling professionals who subscribe to the IAMFC ethical code. The consulting professional counselor has an obligation to keep all shared information confidential.

B. All clients must be informed of the nature and limitations of confidentiality. They must also be informed of who may have access to their counseling records, as well as any information that may be released to other agencies or professionals for insurance reimbursement. These disclosures should be made both orally and in writing, whenever feasible.

C. All client records should be stored in a way that ensures confidentiality. Written records should be kept in a locked drawer or cabinet and computerized record systems should use appropriate passwords and safeguards to prevent unauthorized entry.

D. Clients must be informed if sessions are to be recorded on audio- or videotape and sign a consent form for doing so. When more than one person is receiving counseling, all persons who are legally competent must give informed consent in writing for the recording.

E. Unless alternate arrangements have been agreed upon by all participants, statements made by a family member to the counselor during an individual counseling or consultation contact are to be treated as confidential and are not disclosed to other family members without the individual's permission. If a client's refusal to share information from individual contacts interferes with the agreed upon goals of counseling, the counselor may have to terminate treatment and refer the clients to another counselor.

SECTION III: COMPETENCE

A. Members have the responsibility to develop and maintain basic skills in marriage and family counseling through graduate work, supervision, and peer review. An outline of these skills is provided by the Council for Accreditation of Counseling and Related Educational Programs (CACREP) *Environmental and Specialty Standards for Marriage and Family Counseling/Therapy.* The minimal level of training shall be considered a master's degree in a helping profession.

B. Members recognize the need for keeping current with new developments in the field of marriage and family counseling. They pursue continuing education in forms such as books, journals, classes, workshops, conferences, and conventions.

C. Members accurately represent their education, areas of expertise, training, and experience.

D. Members do not attempt to diagnose or treat problems beyond the scope of their abilities and training.

E. Members do not undertake any professional activity in which their personal problems might adversely affect their performance. Instead, they focus their energies on obtaining appropriate professional assistance to help them resolve the problem.

F. Members do not engage in actions that violate the moral or legal standards of their community.

SECTION IV: ASSESSMENT

A. Members utilize assessment procedures to promote the best interests and well-being of the client in clarifying concerns, establishing treatment goals, evaluating therapeutic progress, and promoting objective decision making.

B. Clients have the right to know the results, interpretation, and conclusions drawn from assessment interviews and instruments, as well as how this information will be used.

C. Members utilize assessment methods that are reliable, valid, and germane to the goals of the client. When using computer-assisted scoring, members obtain empirical evidence for the reliability and validity of the methods and procedures used.

D. Members do not use inventories and tests that have outdated test items or normative data.

E. Members do not use assessment methods that are outside the scope of their qualifications, training, or statutory limitations. Members using tests or inventories have a thorough understanding of measurement concepts.

F. Members read the manual before using a published instrument. They become knowledgeable about the purpose of the instrument and relevant psychometric and normative data.

G. Members conducting custody evaluations recognize the potential impact that their reports can have on family members. As such, they are committed to a thorough assessment of both parents. Therefore, custody recommendations should not be made on the basis of information from only one parent. Members only use instruments that have demonstrated validity in custody evaluations and do not make recommendations based solely on test and inventory scores.

H. Members strive to maintain the guidelines in the *Standards for Educational and Psychological Testing,* written in collaboration by the American Educational Research Association, American Psychological Association, and National Council on Measurement in Evaluation, as well as the *Code of Fair Testing Practices,* published by the Joint Committee on Testing Practices.

SECTION V: PRIVATE PRACTICE

A. Members assist the profession and community by facilitating, whenever feasible, the availability of counseling services in private settings.

B. Due to the independent nature of their work, members in private practice recognize that they have a special obligation to act ethically and responsibly, keep up to date through continuing education, arrange consultation and supervision,

and practice within the scope of their training and applicable laws.

C. Members in private practice provide a portion of their services at little or no cost as a service to the community. They also provide referral services for clients who will not be seen pro bono and who are unable to afford private services.

D. Members only enter into partnerships in which each member adheres to the ethical standards of their profession.

E. Members should not charge a fee for offering or accepting referrals.

SECTION VI: RESEARCH AND PUBLICATIONS

A. Members shall be fully responsible for their choice of research topics and the methods used for investigation, analysis, and reporting. They must be particularly careful that findings do not appear misleading, that the research is planned to allow for the inclusion of alternative hypotheses, and that provision is made for discussion of the limitations of the study.

B. Members safeguard the privacy of their research participants. Data about an individual participant are not released unless the individual is informed about the exact nature of the information to be released and gives written permission for doing so.

C. Members safeguard the safety of their research participants. Members receive approval from, and follow guidelines of, any institutional research committee. Prospective participants are informed, in writing, about any potential danger associated with a study and are notified that they can withdraw at any time.

D. Members make their original data available to other researchers.

E. Members only take credit for research in which they made a substantial contribution, and give credit to all such contributors. Authors are listed from greatest to least amount of contribution.

F. Members do not plagiarize. Ideas or data that did not originate with the author(s) and are not common knowledge are clearly credited to the original source.

G. Members are aware of their obligation to be a role model for graduate students and other future researchers and so act in accordance with the highest standards possible while engaged in research.

SECTION VII: SUPERVISION

A. Members who provide supervision acquire and maintain skills pertaining to the supervision process. They are able to demonstrate for supervisees the application of counseling theory and process to client issues. Supervisors are knowledgeable about different methods and conceptual approaches to supervision.

B. Members who provide supervision respect the inherent imbalance of power in the supervisory relationship. They do not use their potentially influential positions to exploit students, supervisees, or employees. Supervisors do not ask supervisees to engage in behaviors not directly related to the supervision process, and they clearly separate supervision and evaluation. Supervisors also avoid dual relationships that might impair their professional judgment or increase the possibility of exploitation. Sexual intimacy with students or supervisees is prohibited.

C. Members who provide supervision are responsible for both the promotion of supervisee learning and development and the advancement of marriage and family counseling. Supervisors recruit students into professional organizations, educate students about professional ethics and standards, provide service to professional organizations, strive to educate new professionals, and work to improve professional practices.

D. Members who provide supervision have the responsibility to inform students of the specific expectations surrounding skill building, knowledge acquisition, and the development of competencies. Members also provide ongoing and timely feedback to their supervisees.

E. Members who provide supervision are responsible for protecting the rights and well-being of their supervisees' clients. They monitor their supervisees' counseling on an ongoing basis, and create procedures to protect the confidentiality of clients whose sessions have been electronically recorded.

F. Members who provide supervision strive to reach and maintain the guidelines provided in the *Standards for Counseling Supervisors* published by the ACA Governing Council (cf. *Journal of Counseling & Development,* 1990, Vol. 69, pp. 30–32).

G. Members who are counselor educators encourage their programs to reach and maintain the guidelines provided in the CACREP *Environmental and Specialty Standards for Marriage and Family Counseling/Therapy.*

SECTION VIII: MEDIA AND PUBLIC STATEMENTS

A. Members accurately and objectively represent their professional qualifications, skills, and functions to the public. Membership in a professional organization is not to be used to suggest competency.

B. Members have the responsibility to provide information to the public that enhances marriage and family life. Such statements should be based on sound, scientifically acceptable theories, techniques, and approaches. Due to the inability to complete a comprehensive assessment and provide follow-up, members should not give specific advice to an individual through the media.

C. The announcement or advertisement of professional services should focus on objective information that allows the client to make an informed decision. Providing information such as highest relevant academic degree earned, licenses or certifications, office hours, types of services offered, fee structure, and languages spoken can help clients decide whether the advertised services are appropriate for their needs. Members advertising a specialty within marriage and family counseling should provide evidence of training, education, and/or supervision in the area of specialization. Advertisements about workshops or seminars should contain a description of the audience for which the program is intended. Due to their subjective nature, statements either from clients or from the counselor about the uniqueness, effectiveness, or efficiency of services should be avoided. Announcements and advertisements should never contain false, misleading, or fraudulent statements.

D. Members promoting psychology tapes, books, or other products for commercial sale make every

effort to ensure that announcements and advertisements are presented in a professional and factual manner.

Reader's Note: Mary Allison, R. P. Ascano, Edward Beck, Stuart Bonnington, Joseph Hannon, David Kaplan (chair), Patrick McGrath, Judith Palais, Martin Ritchie, and Judy Ritterman are members of the IAMFC ethics committee who formulated the IAMFC code of ethics.

11

School Counseling

Donna A. Henderson
Marijane Fall

Children in the United States attend schools that are microcosms reflecting the diversity of demographic, economic, and social variables in our nation. That combination provides school counselors, as much as any other counseling specialty, with the opportunity to serve a wide variety of clients. The varied roles of school counselors, the range of services they provide to students and adults in the educational setting, the dynamic and diverse population with whom they work, and the transformative setting that schools create, constitute the complexity of school counseling. This complexity breeds challenging situations requiring immediate action. Those often demanding circumstances necessitate school counselors' knowledge of both the ethical implications as well as the legal consequences of any action chosen. This chapter focuses on the ethical responsibilities of school counselors.

Defining the Specialty, Setting, and Clients

School counseling evolved as a profession within the past 100 years. In the early 1900s Jesse Davis established a program in the public schools of Grand Rapids, Michigan. The program was a forerunner of school counseling—a preventive education program to teach character development to students. About the same time Frank Parsons was building another program in Boston. The focus of that effort was vocational guidance aimed at growth and prevention. These were the foundations of the steadily growing profession of school counseling. Later, the National Defense

Education Act of 1958 provided federal funds for upgrading school counseling programs and for training school counselors (Gladding, 1996). This impetus expanded the numbers and increased the quality of school counselors who have continued to advance the profession and its significance in the schools of the United States.

A school counseling program is designed to complement the educational enterprise. The American School Counselor Association (ASCA) endorses a developmental guidance approach to school counseling and states that "developmental guidance should be an integral part of every school counseling program and be incorporated into the role and function of every school counselor" (ASCA, 1984, p. 4). The ASCA position statement defines developmental guidance as a combination of efforts that are planned systematically for the purpose of facilitating the total personal development of all students. The content of this approach varies according to the ages, developmental levels, and needs of the students who are being served.

Currently, school counselors work within elementary, middle, junior high school, and secondary school settings. They practice some combination of the three helping processes of counseling, consulting, and coordinating. Within those processes the principle interventions recognized by the American School Counselor Association (1990) are the following:

- individual counseling
- small group counseling
- large group guidance
- consultation with teachers, administrators, and parents
- coordination of the school counseling program

The school counselor's functions vary across communities as a result of the views of parents, the school board or policy-setting body, the school administration, the teachers, and the students. Therefore, school counselors may not always be able to define the job as they wish. For example, some counselors are hired only to do career counseling, or individual counseling, or handle scheduling and administrative duties. Further, some school districts restrict personal counseling to helping students make career decisions, and other districts choose to do without developmental programs in classrooms.

The clients of school counselors will vary according to individual job descriptions, as well. Counselors who work with parents, teachers, and administrators in a consultant role, as well as counseling children, have the school children as their principle clients. Counselors who facilitate parenting groups will have parents of school children as clients. Some counselors serve as a referral source for teachers and other adults; those adults will be the clients of that referral interview. Thus, the variation in school counseling reflects the various clients that the counselor serves. National standards for school counseling programs currently are being developed to define more clearly a programmatic approach to counseling in schools.

Each of the fifty states requires that school counselors be licensed, certified, endorsed, or credentialed in some manner. The requirements for those designations vary significantly from state to state. Most often these standards are defined by the state departments of education and are related to the process followed by teachers in being certified or licensed. In 1995 ASCA resolved that the designation "Professional School Counselor" be used as the title for individuals who engage in the practice of school counseling, provide the services listed previously, have specialized training in school counseling at a minimum master's degree level, meet the state certification standards, and abide by the laws in the states where they are employed. A national credential, National Certified School Counselor, can be attained by school counselors who meet requirements for the National Certified Counselor (NCC) credential and, who additionally complete specialized courses and experiences that are specific to school counseling (Paisley & Borders, 1995).

As is evident in the outline of the Ethical Standards for School Counselors (ASCA, 1992), school counselors have responsibilities to each group they serve as well as to themselves. The following section of this chapter will include an expanded discussion of those guidelines with some information specific to ethical concerns that may challenge school counselors. These standards are reprinted at the end of this chapter. Huey (1986) noted that ethical standards are only guidelines and seldom provide concrete answers; each situation must be judged in context. The standards of the ASCA, professional association of school counselors, are most specific to that profession and deserve diligent studying by practicing counselors. These standards constitute the basis of the following discussion.

Issues of Significance to the Specialty

Ethical Issues

Responsibilities to Students

Full Vision.   The primary ethical obligation of the school counselor is to be loyal and respectful to students (ASCA, 1992). The ethical standards provide guidelines for discharging this responsibility. A comprehensive counseling program addresses the total needs of the students to enhance the students' growth and development. As counselors design and implement such a program, they recognize the educational, vocational, personal, and social goals for all children and center their services and the program of the school on those goals.

Information.   Ethical standards stipulate that school counselors inform students about the purposes, goals, techniques, and rules of procedure at the beginning of a counseling relationship. The student should also be informed about the meaning and limits of confidentiality, privileged communication, and the possibility that the counselor may want to consult with other professionals. This explanation should occur at the onset of a counseling relationship. This requirement, called informed consent, is also discussed in Chapters 2 and 3. Muro and Kottman (1995) suggested that a written disclosure statement to clients, which includes all the information listed earlier, makes the process of informed consent more concrete for students.

Confidentiality.   A counselor actively protects information received in a counseling relationship according to both legal and ethical standards. Counselors reveal such information to others only with the consent of the parents and student and in accordance with professional obligations. When the condition of the student indicates the presence of a clear and imminent danger to the student or to others, the counselor is responsible for informing authorities and parents or guardians. The student should be informed of the actions the counselor takes when information is revealed. ASCA ethical standards state that such information is disclosed only after careful deliberation and, if possible, consultation with other professionals. More detailed discussions on this issue can be found in the section of this chapter on confidentiality.

Testing.   The standards state that a counselor is obligated to explain clearly the nature, purposes, and results of assessment instruments to students. Counselors are required to apply relevant psychometric standards in selecting, administering, and interpreting assessment techniques. Talbutt (1983b) presented practical recommendations for school counselors and testing in schools. She suggested reviewing school policy in order to become knowledgeable about the counselor's responsibilities related to testing. Counselors should follow all regulations and guidelines from the state and local boards of education, abide by professional guidelines, keep abreast of current testing information, and be diligent in selection and interpretation of testing instruments.

According to ASCA ethical standards, the special situation of computer-based testing requires training specifically for that application in counseling services. When using computers in testing, counselors must ensure the confidentiality of the student data which is generated. Counselors should monitor for the possibility of scoring errors that may be difficult to determine in computer-based testing applications. Overcoming the inadequacies of the generalized test interpretations that accompany the test results is an important counselor obligation, as is the need for follow-up with the computer user. Sampson and Pyle (1988) suggested ensuring the accuracy and proper functioning of computer programs as safeguards to the concerns identified by them and outlined above. The principles for data storage and follow-up are discussed in a later section in responsibilities to students which is titled *computers*. Lengthier discussions about the ethical use of computers and technology in counseling disciplines can be found in Chapter 9.

Personal Influence.   Huey (1986) cautioned that "counselors who work with children need to be particularly careful not to promote acceptance of the counselor's values as the 'right' ones" (p. 321). ASCA ethical standards state that counselors should refrain from imposing their own personal orientations about values, plans, decisions, or beliefs on students and must be careful never to direct a student's decision based on the counselor's ideas of right and wrong. Varhely and Cowles (1991) discussed the counselor's responsibility to engage in self-examination continually. These authors outlined a process for this self scrutiny. The first step is recognizing that personal beliefs, values, and needs may bias behavior in ways that are beyond consciousness. A thoughtful, ongoing exploration of one self is the next step. These two processes lead to the counselor becoming more aware of cues that may imply a conflict between personal issues and professional responsibilities. Constantly examining their own values will allow counselors to be sensitive to whether they are influencing students unconsciously. Situations in which a counselor may choose to express personal values may arise. In such situations the counselor may explain that these beliefs were established after thought and exploration and may not be right for all people (Huey, 1986). If personal values are so strong that a counselor cannot be effective in a relationship, the counselor should refer the student to another person for help. The role of values in counseling is complex and the reader is encouraged to study the information provided on the role of values in ethics in chapters 5 and 6.

Dual Relationships.   Whenever a counselor interacts with a client in more than one capacity, dual relationships can occur (Fisher & Hennessy, 1994). The ethical standards (ASCA, 1992) state that counselors must avoid dual relationships if possible. Corey, Corey, and Callanan (1993) stated that in these situations, incompatible roles have the potential for drastically decreasing the effectiveness of the professional relationship. The ethical standards include the examples of counseling relatives, counseling close friends or children of close friends, and counseling children of associates as dual relationships to be avoided. If it is not at all possible to avoid conflicting relationships, the counselor must be active in eliminating or reducing the potential for harm in those relationships. Dual relationships vary from those that are potentially very harmful to those with little potential for harm. Counselors are always obligated to reduce the potential for harm if the situations cannot be avoided. Counselors need to monitor the relationship closely, gauging the benefits of counseling with the risks of impaired judgment or exploitation of the student client. Counselors also should evaluate the effectiveness of their counseling constantly, and refer the student to another counselor if possible (Fisher & Hennessy, 1994). Seeking consultation or supervision, using informed consent, and documenting carefully are precautions counselors may want to take (Muro & Kottman, 1995) to reduce the potential for harm inherent in dual relationships. Sexual relationships with students who are clients is prohibited in the ethical standards of all mental health organizations and is illegal in many states (Kitchner & Harding 1990).

In determining action to take in ethical dilemmas presented by dual relationships, school counselors may follow these steps:

- Identify the primary client (in most cases, the students in school).
- Identify the ethical issues or dilemma involved.
- Consult the necessary codes and experts.
- Think carefully before acting.

Using the ethical decision-making model presented in Chapter 6 may also help school counselors make responsible and ethical choices. Herlihy and Corey (1992) noted that the harm to clients is derived from the practitioner who exploits the relationship rather than from the duality itself.

Competency.   Counselors should be aware of their own limitations and competencies, and should also be informed about appropriate and available resources for referrals. School counselors should refer students to other professionals when adequate services cannot be provided. Counselors should refer clients to avoid acting unethically, but they may also want to do so to ensure that students receive the level of attention they need. While the ASCA proposes a counselor/student ratio of 1:100 minimum and 1:300 maximum (ASCA, 1988b), in reality, a single counselor can be individually responsible for 1,200 or more students. When a counselor cannot see all students requesting appointments, the counselor should prioritize student needs and take steps to ensure that all those seeking help receive it. School counselors constantly must evaluate situations quickly with very little information, and remain aware that teenagers can think and act on impulses (such as suicidal ideation) very abruptly (Capuzzi & Gross, 1993).

Monitoring one's own psychological health, participating in continuing education and staying current with literature in the profession can help counseling professionals maintain competence in a school counseling setting. Formal education, professional training, and supervised experience are the criteria used to define competence (Carroll, Schneider, & Wesley, 1985).

Computers.   Two examples of expanded counseling services to students include computer applications and peer helper programs. The ethical standards specify that the counselor is responsible for explaining the benefits and limitations of computer applications. The use of computers in counseling should be determined by an assessment of the appropriateness of the use of the computer for the student's needs, the student's understanding of the application, and follow-up counseling assistance. All groups should have equal access to computer applications that are unbiased by discriminatory information and values. The ethical standards related to using computers in counseling services are enhanced by guidelines that Sampson and Pyle (1988), Childers (1988) and Sampson, Kolodinsky, and Greeno (1997) present. These authors discuss ways of safeguarding data stored on the computer by maintaining security procedures, restricting content and access, preserving anonymity when possible, and limiting the time period of storage. If a counselor is using computer applications with a client, the counselor should provide guidelines that include informed consent and release forms specific to the computer use. These authors identify potential problems and provide safeguards as solutions. Additional discussions of ethical issues involved in computer use can be found in Chapter 9.

Responsibility to Groups

Working with Groups and Peer Groups.   Unique ethical considerations exist for school counselors who work with students in counseling groups. The Ethical Guidelines for Group Counselors (Association for Specialists in Group Work, 1989), as well as the ASCA standards outlined previously, provide direction for school counselors working with groups. The importance of screening potential group members, of attending to group members' safety and growth, and of establishing a norm of confidentiality are three stipulations of the ASCA ethical standards. Chapter 14 discusses ethical issues in group counseling in greater detail, but some discussion of group counseling in school environments merits attention here.

Terres and Larrabee (1985) and Corey, Corey, Callanan, and Russell (1988) have emphasized the possibility for ethical dilemmas in the planning and implementation of groups in schools. At the planning stage, school counselors must determine their competence as group leaders of the specific type of group they will be facilitating. Counselors need to determine the appropriateness of the group experience for the specific children and the appropriateness of the specific child to the group and to the group experience. Student and parent rights, as well as internal and external constraints of the school setting, also must be considered in planning group counseling in schools. To implement groups, counselors should provide information about the purpose of the group, the leader's qualifications, and other facts about the group process both to the participating students and to their parents. Experts suggest discussing the importance of confidentiality initially and at each meeting. School counselors recognize they can only guarantee that they personally will abide by the standard of confidentiality in group counseling but should stress to the group members the importance of keeping private the information shared in the group. Group implementation occurs after provisions for space, privacy, participant factors, and session length and duration are determined with all decisions informed by the developmental stages of the students who are involved. The guidelines provided by Terres and Larrabee (1985) will be helpful to school counselors who conduct group counseling.

The ethical standards also clarify the responsibilities of school counselors who coordinate peer helping groups. The pertinent standard states that counselors are responsible for the welfare of students in peer programs under their direction.

Responsibility to Parents.   The difficulties of ethical practice often emerge when school counselors try to balance the responsibilities to students with those to parents. Counselors must determine how to maintain confidentiality for a student and provide information to parents. The ASCA (1992) ethical standards stipulate the counselor has the following obligations to parents:

1. To respect the rights and responsibilities of all parents, custodial and noncustodial, for their children

2. To establish a cooperative relationship with parents, maintaining the confidentiality of their communications with the counselor

3. To inform parents about the role of the school counselor, emphasizing the importance of confidentiality in that role

4. To give parents "accurate, comprehensive, and relevant information in an objective and caring manner, as appropriate and consistent with ethical responsibilities to the counselee" (p. 3)

5. To share information about the student only with people who are authorized to receive it with the permission of the parents and student

6. To recognize legal and local guidelines when helping parents with family difficulties which are interfering with the students' welfare and to provide appropriate assistance and/or referrals

Balancing the responsibilities to students and to parents presents counselors with ethical dilemmas that often have to be decided case by case. Consultation with another counselor and supervision may be helpful in making those decisions.

Responsibility to Colleagues and Professional Associations.   Establishing and maintaining a professional, cooperative relationship with the faculty, staff, and administration is the counselor's obligation. Counselors should inform colleagues about guidelines regarding confidentiality, public and private information, and consultation. Counselors should also be active in cooperating and collaborating with community agencies, organizations, and individuals in the best interests of students and, therefore, establish a network to be used in referring students and their families. Muro and Kottman (1995) suggested providing at least three referral sources.

Counselors who work with parents and with teachers or other school personnel may function as consultants. The ethical issues that may arise from these consultative relationships are outlined and discussed by Dougherty (1992). The competency of the school counselor in the role of consultant centers on the requirements of consultation and whether the counselor has those abilities. The consultant–consultee–client relationship creates issues around the work-related focus, dual relationships, and freedom of choice. Dougherty noted that rights of consultees in the areas of confidentiality and informed consent are issues to be resolved in consultative relationships. The potential for imposing one's own values or for having a conflict of values is a concern. Being knowledgeable and having consultation skills, being aware of personal values, being clear about consultation services, and building collaborative relationships are guidelines he provided for counselors in the role of consultant.

Responsibility to School and Community.   School counselors have obligations to the school program and to the community as well as to the groups of people mentioned above. The ethical standards (ASCA, 1992) stipulate those obligations as follows:

1. Counselors protect the educational program from anything that is not in the best interests of the students.

2. Potentially disruptive or damaging conditions that may threaten the school's mission, personnel, and property are reported to appropriate authorities.

3. The counselor's role and function are defined clearly and conditions that may impede the effectiveness of the program and services are reported to school officials by the counselor.

4. The school counselor is to help in developing a positive school environment, an educational program to meet student needs, and an evaluation process for the counseling program, service, and personnel. The information from the evaluation process is used for planning programs and services.

Huey (1986) stated, "counselors should adhere to local school policies, whether determined by the principal or the board of education, to the extent possible without compromising their primary responsibility to the client" (p. 321). When conflicts exist between loyalty to the student client and to the employee, Huey (1986) suggested a resolution that protects the rights of the student. Counselors may actively pursue changing existing policies that cause the conflicts.

The dilemma of parents' rights in educational control is an ongoing controversy. Counselors may be targeted by parents who challenge the content and activities of school counseling programs. Kaplan (1997) reviewed the current status of parents' rights and lists ways for counselors to prevent and to respond to parental concerns.

Responsibility to Self.   School counselors also have obligations to themselves and to their ability to accomplish their duties. These include operating within the boundaries of their individual professional competence, as well as being aware of personal strengths and limitations. School counselors are to monitor their personal performance and effectiveness, always avoiding any inadequacy in professional services or any harm to students. As previously stated, counselors are to be aware of their own biases and personal characteristics and the potential effects of those on students. School counselors recognize that they may need specific training to ensure they provide appropriate and effective services to people who have differences related to age, gender, race, religion, sexual orientation, and socioeconomic and ethnic backgrounds. Hobson and Kanitz (1996) considered multicultural counseling an ethical issue for school counselors and challenge school counselors to assess their level of multicultural competence and seek training opportunities to overcome any deficiencies.

Continuing education and personal growth are professional obligations of school counselors. Throughout this chapter counselors are urged to stay abreast of changes in school counseling. The Internet is a valuable resource for helping counselors accomplish this. Some web sites which may be useful can be found at the end of this chapter.

Responsibility to the Profession.   Maintaining professionally appropriate conduct, participating in advancing knowledge in the field of counseling, and belonging to professional organizations are parts of the obligation a school counselor has to the profession. School counselors abide by ethical standards of the profession as well as other official policy statements and relevant legal mandates.

Legal Issues

A consideration of the ethical standards for school counselors would be incomplete without discussing the legal standards that affect school counselors' responsibilities. A review of all the legalities related to school counseling is beyond the scope of this chapter; the reader is referred to various sources in law and in education, as well as the recommended reading at the end of the chapter and the general discussion of legal aspects of counseling in Chapter 3 for additional information. Issues that will be discussed here are confidentiality; exceptions to confidentiality, including the duty to warn and reporting child abuse; the Family Educational Rights and Privacy Act; and the Education for All Handicapped Children Act.

Confidentiality.   Confidentiality, the assurance to the client that what is said in a counseling relationship will not be revealed, is an ethical responsibility of counselors in all settings, as we have mentioned earlier in this text. School counselors have unique challenges in trying to honor that obligation because they work with minors. Three subjects related to confidentiality will be discussed—privileged communication, the ASCA position statement, and employer policy and expectations.

Privileged Communication.   Remley (1985) noted that in the legal structure of the United States, children have some of the protection granted adults; however, in many ways the protection of children's rights depends on interpretations made by their parents, guardians, or the courts. The legal status pertinent to the discussion of confidentiality is privileged communication, which means that a client is protected from confidential communications being disclosed in court.

Knapp and Vandecreek (1983) offered a review of privileged communication and judicial hearing in general, and Herlihy and Sheeley (1987) and Sheeley and Herlihy (1987) summarized their survey of the provision of privileged communication to the clients of school counselors.

In approximately 20 states, students in schools are granted the legal right of privileged communication when talking with a school counselor (Taylor & Adelman, 1989). Those statutes vary among states as to the restrictions that are placed on the privileged communication. School counselors should study carefully whether privilege is granted as well as examine the limits that exist in the statute.

The level of privilege to which a minor is entitled is a complicated legal determination (Waldo & Malley, 1992) that must be investigated by school counselors in the state in which they are employed. Additionally, a recent decision by the U.S. Supreme Court decision in *Jaffee v. Redmond* has possible implications about privileged communication for all counselors according to Remley, Herlihy, and Herlihy (1997). In that decision the court ruled that the communications between a master's level social worker and her client were privileged communication under the Federal Rules of Evidence. The social worker was referred to as therapist or psychotherapist in the decision and the activities were referred to as counseling sessions, counseling, or psychotherapy. The decision is important for establishing a precedent in an official federal court that provides protection to communications between therapists and their patients (Remley, Herlihy, & Herlihy, 1997). School counselors need to remain informed about how the implications from that decision may extend to minors and to the school setting.

ASCA Position Statement on Confidentiality.   Regardless of whether privilege has been mandated to protect student communications with counselors, confidentiality within that relationship is imperative. The position statement on the school counselor and confidentiality of the American School Counselor Association (1986) details the obligations of a school counselor for establishing and maintaining confidentiality in schools and places no age limitation on who is entitled to a confidential relationship. The position paper contains definitions and limitations pertinent to school counselors' practice and should be reviewed carefully. One significant point in the statement is that counselors have a responsibility to protect the privacy of information received from students, from parents, and from teachers.

Employer Policy and Expectations.   Tompkins and Mehring (1993) stated that the third consideration of student–counselor privacy is the policy and expectation of the employer. Counselors are specialized members of the school community who receive requests from teachers, the school administration or staff, and others concerned with the educational enterprise. They must respect, and presumably follow, dictates from the school principal and superintendent (Remley, 1993). Because teachers and administrators are able to reveal all that a child says to them, it is often difficult for these individuals to understand why school counselors should not do so as well.

Case Scenario 1

Responding to the Policies of the School and Maintaining Confidentiality

An elementary school counselor was attending a school team meeting with administrators, teachers, and a school psychologist about a student, Joey, who was increasingly disruptive in the classroom. Joey's behavior was interfering with his own as well as his classmates' learning. The counselor had been working with the child, who had been severely physically abused in the last six months, and with the Department of Human Services. During the school team meeting the principal of the school asked the counselor to explain what had been happening to Joey. Should the counselor provide this information to the principal and team?

NO.   The counselor should maintain the confidentiality of Joey's communication and respond that Joey had been encountering some stressful situations and the effects were obviously being expressed in the classroom. The counselor should continue by saying that perhaps together the school team would be able to determine strategies to help him control his classroom behavior.

The competing demands of maintaining confidentiality for the student and some employer policies further complicate the counselor's responsibilities. Before accepting employment, counselors may want to clarify the policy and expectations of the school.

Options for Counselors in Matters Related to Confidentiality.   This portion of the chapter is a review of options that have been proposed to help school counselors in matters related to confidentiality. The following is a summary of some of the suggestions from Tompkins and Mehring (1993) and Davis and Ritchie (1993).

1.   Stay informed about the law and written policy in the area of the practice.

2.   Operate within the ethical code of the professional organization.

3. Review expectations and policy before employment is accepted.

4. Operate within one's personal limits of expertise.

5. Keep the best interest of the children the predominant concern.

Providing informed consent for the child and for the parent when dealing with sensitive issues or before engaging in long-term counseling is a way to establish a climate of confidentiality. Remley (1985) stated that by informing the child before consulting with anyone about the child's problem, involving the child in the decision-making process, and keeping the child informed will allow counselors to fulfill their confidentiality responsibilities. The guidelines provided by Zingaro (1983) included some specifics helpful to the practice of school counseling. He suggested that when it is in the best interest of the child for a significant adult to have information, the counselor may respond by telling the adults ways in which they may help the child rather than revealing specific information that the child has disclosed. Finally Strein and Hershenson (1991) offered suggestions for using a "need-to-know" basis as an alternative guideline to confidentiality when counselors work in situations that are not one-to-one relationships, a common occurrence in schools.

Case Scenario 2

Sharing Information on a "Need-to-Know" Basis

If you were a counselor approached by one of your client's teachers in the teacher's lounge, how would you respond to this request?

Teacher: *What is going on with James? He has asked to go to your office twice in the last two days. I hate to stop him, but of course I cannot let him come to see you unless I know he has a legitimate reason.*

Should you provide the teacher with the specific circumstances creating James' difficulty?

NO. You should phrase your response in such a way that protects James' confidentiality yet tells the teacher what specific actions they may take to assist him. An example of such a response follows.

Counselor: *I'm glad you dropped by. I know how interested you are in your students. James does need time with me right now and I appreciate your letting him come to talk with me. You may notice that he is preoccupied and appears not to pay attention as he did in the past. This is because of other concerns and should get better in time. In the meantime you might talk with him and arrange a signal to help him pull his attention back to the class as you did with Eloise a few months ago. I remember how well that worked for you both.*

Varhely and Cowles (1991) suggested that an overlooked dilemma in the conflicts over confidentiality involve the counselor's personal beliefs, experiences, and values. They stated that counselors must strive to determine their personal beliefs about the rights and responsibilities of children, their needs for belonging and a sense of adequacy, and their personal value system. Without a continual process to develop self-awareness in these areas, counselors may further complicate the difficulties inherent in maintaining confidentiality in school settings. The following example illustrates a situation in which a counselor's values might shape the way in which the situation is treated.

Case Scenario 3

The Influence of Personal Values and Beliefs on Professional Decisions

You are a school counselor on your way home after a long day. A teacher walks you to your car in the school parking lot and starts a discussion about one of the students you both know. Imagine how you would respond.

Teacher of eighth grade to school counselor: *Thank goodness I got a chance to see you. You need to do something about that Duvoe child. Danny is in my class and I can't do anything with him! He's so unkempt; his hair is falling over his shoulders! I told him the second day of class that he needed a haircut, but it's as if he is defying me. Now he doesn't even tie it back. It falls all over his face. I can't even see his eyes when I look at him!*

Danny's teacher is asking the school counselor to "do something" because his hair is long. Is that a problem in which a counselor should be involved?

NO.   While Danny does not appear to be behaving in a manner that indicates he has a personal problem, it is the counselor's responsibility to provide support and assistance to the teachers who may be struggling to meet the needs of diverse students. You probably should attempt to better understand the situation and demonstrate your support to this teacher in a manner that will not encourage undue imposition of either the teacher or the counselor's values upon Danny. One response might be the following:

"I'm not sure I understand how Danny's long hair is a problem." Counselors need to be responsive to teachers in order to be considered a part of the learning team, however, acting on the above teacher's request may not be in line with the values of a counselor who believes in allowing students to be individuals.

Exceptions to Confidentiality.   Some exceptions to confidentiality are the duty to warn and reporting child abuse. These exceptions and their legal and ethical implications will be considered next. School counselors should be aware that, as with privileged communication, the statutes that determine a counselor's liability in situations of duty to warn and of reporting child abuse are mandated by the state in which the counselor is practicing. Only a careful review of the legislative updates and judicial opinion in that state will be sufficient for decisions in a particular setting (Hopkins & Anderson, 1990). Regardless, some generalizations can be made.

Duty to Warn and Protect.   Counselors must determine actions to take in the delicate balance between confidentiality and the duty to warn others on a case-by-case basis (Sheeley & Herlihy, 1989). They may be vulnerable to a lawsuit if they breach confidentiality; however, if counselors could have prevented the incident, they may be sued if a student client is injured, injures someone else, or commits suicide. The decision between breaching confidentiality and warning others should be done with diligence and careful judgment. Being fully informed about state laws and court decisions are first steps counselors can take. Legal mandates and statutes are continually interpreted and revised; keeping abreast of the laws and decisions is an ongoing process. If the school district does not have a policy on confidentiality and its limitations, school counselors should work actively to develop one. That local policy should be adequately disclosed to all students and all parents.

Sheeley and Herlihy (1989) and Remley and Sparkman (1993) have additional suggestions for school counselors working with students who may be suicidal. Their suggestions are useful in establishing policy and procedures for this difficult situation:

1. Be able to recognize the warning signs of students with suicidal potential.
2. Have an established plan for dealing with the crisis.
3. Have referral sources for crisis situations.
4. Develop the skills to help students and families if a student threatens suicide.
5. Take action if it is determined that a student is at risk of harming himself or herself.
6. Consider actions that are the least intrusive steps, but which will nevertheless ensure the safety of the person who is suicidal.
7. Consult with colleagues in determining risk as well as the appropriate action to take.
8. Inform school administrators and parents when counselors have determined that a student client is at risk of attempting suicide.
9. If these adults are reluctant to become involved, school counselors have an ethical responsibility to do all they can do to prevent the suicide.

Counselors should be aware of a court decision in a case involving a student suicide. Friends of a middle school student, Nicole, reported to school counselors that she intended to kill herself. The counselors questioned Nicole and she denied making suicidal statements. The counselors did not inform school officials or Nicole's parents. Nicole died in a suicide pact with another student, and her parents sued. On appeal of the original verdict which favored the school personnel, the question of the counselor's duty to warn the parents was considered. The court found "a special relationship sufficient to create a duty of care when an adolescent in a school setting expresses an intention to commit suicide and the counselor becomes aware of such intention" (Fisher & Sorenson, 1996). This decision has strong implications that school counselors should warn parents of the suicidal intentions of students.

Eating disorders, substance abuse, reckless sexual behavior, cult membership, criminal activity, and other dangerous activities may also be viewed as instances of harm to self. School counselors should question the degree to which such behaviors constitute a potential for harm to self that might necessitate breaching confidentiality. The guidelines listed earlier and throughout this chapter may be helpful in reaching the decision.

Coll (1995) discussed the legal and ethical concerns about confidentiality in substance abuse prevention programs and in reports of criminal activity. His guidelines may provide additional insights. Federal guidelines (42 U.S.C. 290 dd-3 and ee-3; 42 CFR Part 2) govern the circumstances of disclosure of the records of people who are receiving treatment for substance abuse or who are participating in prevention or referral activities. Generally the confidentiality of the records is protected. Exceptions are made for medical emergencies, child abuse or neglect, or the endangering of a third party. These are considered situations in which the benefits produced or the harm prevented justifies overriding confidentiality. Even in those cases only information pertinent to the current problem should be revealed. The federal regulations about minors in substance abuse treatment, prevention, or referral programs permit notification of parents of the involvement of the child unless state laws are more restrictive in requiring or prohibiting notice (Stadler, 1990).

Another situation that probably calls for breaching confidentiality is when a student client indicates harm to others. The Tarasoff decision was a call for reasonable action by a therapist to protect third parties. In a discussion of this legal duty Gehring (1982) reviewed and analyzed the court interpretations of the decision. More recently Waldo and Malley (1992) concluded that this duty to protect requires several actions on the part of a therapist, not only the duty to warn an intended victim. They explain the four criteria used to assess what might be expected of school counselors in a decision involving the duty to protect:

- special relationship to the dangerous person or to the potential victim
- the presence of a clear threat and the imminence of danger
- the ability to identify potential victim(s)
- reasonable care when making decisions

According to these authors, courts have defined the obligations of school counselors in such cases. These obligations are (a) to assemble necessary background information, (b) to confer with a psychiatrist when consultation is needed, and (c) to keep careful records. Seeking professional legal advice is a suggestion but not an obligation. The actions school counselors may take to protect a person at risk are (a) making referrals by notifying the parents of the student client, (b) notifying a probation officer, (c) notifying the police, (d) designating someone to inform the intended victim, (e) warning the potential victim, (f) detaining the client, and (g) seeking voluntary or involuntary commitment. Counselors may choose one or more of these possibilities (Waldo & Malley, 1992).

Assessing the dangerousness of the situation is difficult. Gross and Robinson (1987) and Thompson and Rudolph (1994) discussed case studies with guidelines and procedures for each situation. Counselors may find these useful practice scenarios.

Case Scenario 4

Assessing Dangerousness

As a school counselor you have been conducting a small group for children whose parents are recently divorced. A 13-year-old from that group, Eleanor, has told a friend that she cannot stand her life with her mother and the live-in boyfriend at home any more. Her mother's boyfriend is "impossible," no one is paying any attention to her, and her father refuses to intervene. Eleanor has said that she isn't sure how she is going to do it but she's going to end the lives of the people who are making her feel so miserable so that she can go live with her father. Eleanor's friend has told you about these threats. Should you intervene?

YES.   The counselor should assess the dangerousness of the situation before determining how to work with Eleanor to resolve the situation. Involved in that determination would be whether Eleanor has a specific plan and the plausibility of the plan, whether she has the means to carry out the plan and how accessible those means are, and how pervasive these thoughts are to her. If the counselor considered the possibility of Eleanor carrying out her threat was remote, some of the options below would be the subsequent action. If the counselor considered the threat a distinct possibility, the counselor would then inform Eleanor that the seriousness of her threats necessitate reporting them at least to her parents and possibly to the police. The counselor would make the reports and document the actions. Consultation with another professional would be advisable. Other actions which are directed at supporting Eleanor in resolving her difficult situation may proceed simultaneously. Some possibilities which may be chosen are to arrange an agreement with Eleanor to come to the counselor individually in order to consider alternative actions, with Eleanor's permission to arrange a meeting with all the parties to work on acceptable solutions to the home situation, or to refer Eleanor to another professional for more intensive counseling.

Two sensitive dilemmas with which counselors deal revolve around youth sexuality, counseling minors about birth control or abortion, and counseling students with AIDS. McWhirter, McWhirter, McWhirter, and McWhirter (1993) and Gustafson and McNamara (1987) discussed the difficulties in determining whether to tell parents about the sexual activity of a minor, especially in relation to seeking birth control or abortion information. State laws that mandate reporting, or protecting counselors from such reports, are as varied as other laws. In some states minors may discuss sexually transmitted diseases or pregnancy prevention or cessation with counselors without the legal requirement of parents' notification (Stadler, 1989). In other states notification is mandated. Counselors should remain informed about the legal issues, consult with colleagues, and be deliberate about the decisions they make. Talbutt (1983a) reviewed court cases related to abortions. She noted legal and ethical issues in schools or school employees providing abortion information and concluded that counselors should be familiar with the school district's policy as well as with laws and current court rulings that have implications for abortion counseling. Urging minors to discuss plans with parents may be a legal mandate as well as a counseling goal. She noted that procedures for the situation need to be established before a crisis approach is taken and that the steps within the procedure should involve including family members and local referral agencies.

Likewise, Lynch (1993) provided a thoughtful discussion of the process of counseling someone with AIDS in which counselors balance confidentiality concerns with the duty to protect. Her overview is for those who work in college counseling centers, but the dilemmas she recognizes are applicable to other school settings. Both her article and the position statement *The School Counselor and AIDS* (ASCA, 1988a) promote positive health education, familiarity with current resources, and prudent adherence to the primary role of counselors. Melton (1988) discussed the multiple duties of a counselor related to the danger of a person's disease status and the behaviors related to transmitting the disease. McWhirter et al. (1993) suggested that counselors notify state public health agencies of possible communicable or reportable diseases after the counselor has determined the measures which are taken to protect confidentiality. Those authors proposed that such disclosure protects the third person and the client's confidentiality, and demonstrates the counselor's measures to prevent harm. Lynch (1993) provided alternative decisions involving counselors and students who have AIDS.

Reporting Child Abuse.   All states require some type of reporting of suspected cases of child abuse. As with other state mandates, the specifics of the law vary from state to state (Sandberg, Crabbs, & Crabbs, 1988). Counselors should understand the requirements of the laws in their states and the procedures in their districts. Just as with other legal matters, laws in states are being revised constantly and must be monitored by school counselors. Sandberg, Crabbs, and Crabbs (1988) provided responses to frequently asked questions about legal issues in child abuse.

The School Counselor and Child Abuse/Neglect Prevention is an ASCA (1993) position statement, which outlines various responsibilities counselors have beyond the reporting of child abuse. Included in this statement is a useful set of definitions as well as examples of the signs of abuse and neglect, summarized here. According to the ASCA position statement (1993), *abuse* is the infliction by other than accidental means of physical harm upon the body of a child, continual psychological damage, or denial of emotional needs. Some signs and examples of child abuse cited in this statement are the following:

- Extensive bruises or patterns of bruises
- Burns or burn patterns
- Lacerations, welts or abrasions
- Injuries inconsistent with information offered
- Sexual abuse
- Emotional disturbances caused by continuous friction in the home, marital discord, or mentally ill parents
- Cruel treatment

Neglect is defined in the ASCA position statement (1993) as the failure to provide necessary food, care, clothing, shelter, supervision, or medical attention for a child. According to this statement, children who suffer from neglect include those who are:

- Malnourished, ill-clad, dirty, without proper sleeping arrangements, lacking in appropriate health care
- Unattended, lacking adequate supervision
- Ill and lacking essential medical attention
- Irregularly and illegally absent from school
- Exploited and overworked
- Lacking essential psychological/emotional nurturance
- Abandoned

Counselors are encouraged to implement activities to educate and to support other school personnel involved in protecting children from abuse and neglect. They are also charged with providing ongoing services to the children and/or the family in the crisis or to refer them to an appropriate agency. Providing child abuse/neglect prevention programs also are among counselors' duties (Minard, 1993). Remley and Fry (1993) identified the multiple roles of the counselor in reporting child abuse: informant, counselor to the victim or perpetrator, employee, liaison, court witness, and counselor to the family. Clearly, the potential for role conflict, as well as the burden of being a resource for so many people, makes this area a difficult one for school counselors. Awareness, knowledge, commitment, and effective communication skills are the qualities that counselors must use in facing the process of reporting and preventing child abuse and neglect (Howell-Nigrelli, 1988).

Case Scenario 5

Reporting Suspected Cases of Child Abuse

You are a school counselor who has just met with a student referred to you by her classroom teacher. Based on that session, you arranged an appointment that same morning with your school principal. The meeting leaves you conflicted:

School Counselor: *Mr. B., I need to report this case of suspected abuse to the state reporting agency. Angela Adams has a series of bruises on her arm that look like the prints of large fingers. In addition, she has a large bruise, just darkening, on her shoulder. Her teacher brought her to see me due to these marks, and Angela said she and her dad got into a fight last weekend. She said that her brother looks worse than she does because, "Dad really beat him up."*

Principal: *Angela Adams? This is surprising. I met her mom at open house this year, and she and her husband have helped out on several school and community projects. I really doubt that this could be the right story. Angela can be very obstinate, you know. I had her in my office twice last year for not following teacher directives. I think we should wait on this, and see if anything further happens. I know the Adams' neighbors. I'll ask if they ever hear anything.*

Do you think you have discharged your responsibility to report this suspected child abuse by leaving matters in the principal's hands?

NO.   The counselor has both a legal mandate to report suspected abuse and a personal belief that the incident should be reported. Others in the school system do not agree. The counselor should carefully consider the dilemma and be prepared to convince others of his or her position.

An issue of abuse that is not addressed clearly in the ethical standards is psychological maltreatment in the schools, either by educators or the students' peers. Although currently ASCA provides no position statement and no ethical standards are available, counselors need to monitor the emerging literature about bullying and psychologically abusive teachers (Neese, 1989).

Family Educational Rights and Privacy Act (FERPA).   In November 1974 the Family Educational Rights and Privacy Act (FERPA), or the Buckley Amendment, became law. The intent of this federal mandate was to provide parents and eligible students (older than 18) the right to inspect school records and to protect the dissemination of educational records. The act is reprinted at the end of this chapter. School districts that do not adhere to the policy of allowing parents access to records and denying access without parental permission may have federal funds withheld. A records policy statement and established procedures of access and protection are developed by each school district to explain how the regulations are implemented in that district. The U.S. Department of Education at 600 Independence, SW, Washington, DC 20202-4605 has available a model policy *Student Records Policies and Procedures for the Alpha School District.* However, specific guidelines for counselors may be lacking. Walker and Larrabee (1985) and Fisher and Sorenson (1996) presented useful information on the application of FERPA guidelines:

1.   Parents or eligible students should be informed of their rights under this act. This right is extended to custodial and noncustodial parents, unless a court order restrains the access of the noncustodial parent.

2.   Information about types of educational records that exist and the procedures for accessing those records is disseminated. The content of educational records may include academic progress, test scores, identification data, home background, health information, educational history, anecdotal remarks, case summaries, and recommendations.

3.   Parents or eligible students may review educational records, request changes, pursue a hearing if the change is disallowed, and add personal statements as explanations, if necessary.

4. Personally identifiable information is not released without prior written consent of a parent or an eligible student.

5. Parents and eligible students are allowed to see the school's record of disclosure.

6. Records made by educators that remain in the sole possession of the maker and therefore are not accessible or revealed to any other individual are not subject to disclosure under this act (Fisher & Sorenson, 1996; Hummel, Talbutt, & Alexander, 1985). This indicates that private notes do not have to be revealed.

School counselors who have administrative responsibility for the educational records of children should comply with local policy, state law, and the Buckley amendment. Remley (1990) discussed whether counselors have a legal or ethical obligation to keep counseling records and the content of the records. He described circumstances in which personnel may be obligated to disclose counseling records, and outlined procedures for maintaining, transferring, and discarding counseling records.

The Education for all Handicapped Children Act (PL 94-142).   The Education for all Handicapped Children Act is Public Law 94-142. In 1990 that act was amended by PL 101-476 and renamed the Individuals with Disabilities Education Act. This law guarantees a free and appropriate education in the least restrictive environment possible to all students regardless of the nature and degree of their handicapping conditions. While the law does not refer to school counselors specifically, they are involved in offering many services to students with handicapping conditions and may be included in the Individual Education Plan (IEP) for the students with exceptionalities. School counselors need to be aware of federal guidelines that apply.

Comparisons of Codes of Ethics

School counselors should abide by the codes of ethics of the American Counseling Association, the National Board of Certified Counselors, the National Peer Helpers Association, the Association for Specialists in Group Work, as well as the more specific Ethical Standards for School Counselors discussed earlier. The mechanisms for aspirational and mandatory enforcements of ethical standards are described in Chapter 1. Counselors are subject only to the enforcement of the ethical codes of those organizations of which they are members or of those credentials which they hold, even though they should aspire to the ethical standards endorsed by these organizations. The latter standards differ from the others in that specific responsibilities of school counselors to students, parents, colleagues and professional associations, schools and communities, self, and the profession are more clearly delineated. These responsibilities derive from four basic tenets of the counseling process:

1. Each person has the right to receive respect and dignity as a unique human being and to counseling services without prejudice as to person, character, belief, or practice.

2. Each person has the right to self-direction and self-development.

3. Each person has the right of choice and the responsibility for decisions reached.

4. Each person has the right to privacy and thereby the right to expect the counselor–client relationship to comply with all laws, policies, and ethical standards pertaining to confidentiality (ASCA, 1992).

The specificity of the standards can assist counselors in two important ways. First, school counselors can prepare themselves to be ethical practitioners. For instance, school counselors who inform parents of the counselor role and emphasize the nature of the confidential relationship between the counselor and the students guard the confidentiality of the student at the same time they accord parents the same privilege. The second way standards can assist school counselors is by providing a reference document to educate individuals who have no knowledge about the guidelines. Members of a school board, principals, parent organizations, and others directly involved with schools will benefit by reading the guidelines provided by a national professional organization.

Summary

A synthesis of research indicates that school counselors make significant contributions to the educational and personal development of students (Borders & Drury, 1992). However, while delivering a school counseling program, school counselors may encounter multiple dilemmas in providing services to students, parents, and teachers. The ethical standards of the American School Counselor Association outline the responsibilities counselors have to the groups with whom they work. Knowing the guidelines, the local, state, and federal laws and procedures, seeking consultation, and keeping informed of changes are important activities that help school counselors make decisions ethically. Informed counselors who have a decision-making process such as the one proposed in this volume will be prepared in situations which demand careful judgment to protect the best interest of the child.

References

American School Counselor Association (ASCA). (1984). *ASCA position statement: The school counselor and developmental guidance* (rev. ed.). Alexandria, VA: Author.

American School Counselor Association (ASCA). (1986). *ASCA position statement: The school counselor and confidentiality* (rev. ed.). Alexandria, VA: Author.

American School Counselor Association (ASCA). (1988a). *ASCA position statement: The school counselor and AIDS.* Alexandria, VA: Author.

American School Counselor Association (ASCA). (1988b). *ASCA position statement: The school counselor and counselor/student ratio.* Alexandria, VA: Author.

American School Counselor Association (ASCA). (1990). *Role statement: The school counselor.* Alexandria, VA: Author.

American School Counselor Association (ASCA). (1992). *Ethical standards for school counselors.* Alexandria, VA: Author.

American School Counselor Association (ASCA). (1993). *ASCA position statement: The school counselor and child abuse/neglect prevention* (rev. ed.). Alexandria, VA: Author.

Association for Specialists in Group Work. (1989). *Ethical guidelines for group counselors.* Alexandria, VA: Author.

Borders, L., & Drury, S. (1992). Comprehensive school counseling programs: A review for policy makers and practitioners. *Journal of Counseling and Development, 70,* 487–498.

Capuzzi, D., & Gross, D. R. (1993) *Youth at risk: A resource for counselors, teachers and parents.* Alexandria, VA: American Counseling Association.

Carroll, M. A., Schneider, H. G., & Wesley, G. R. (1985). *Ethics in the practice of psychology.* Upper Saddle River, NJ: Prentice-Hall.

Childers, J. H., Jr. (1988). The counselor's use of microcomputers: Problems and ethical issues. In W. C. Huey & T. P. Remley, Jr. (Eds.), *Ethical and legal issues in school counseling* (pp. 262–270). Alexandria, VA: American School Counselor Association.

Coll, K. M. (1995). Legal challenges in secondary prevention programming for students with substance abuse problems. *The School Counselor, 43,* 35–41.

Corey, G., Corey, M. S., & Callanan, P. (1993). *Issues and ethics in the helping professions* (4th ed.). Pacific Grove, CA: Brooks/Cole.

Corey, G., Corey, M. S., Callanan, P., & Russell, J. M. (1988). Ethical considerations in using group techniques. In W. C. Huey & T. P. Remley, Jr. (Eds.), *Ethical and legal issues in school counseling* (pp. 211–222). Alexandria, VA: American School Counselor Association.

Davis, T., & Ritchie, M. (1993). Confidentiality and the school counselor: A challenge for the 1990s. *The School Counselor, 41,* 23–30.

Dougherty, A. M. (1992). Ethical issues in consultation. *Elementary School Guidance and Counseling, 26,* 214–220.

Fischer, L., & Sorenson, G. P. (1996). *School law for counselors, psychologists, and social workers* (3rd ed.). White Plains, NY: Longman.

Fisher, C. B., & Hennessy, J. (1994). Ethical Issues. In Ronch, J. L., Van Ornum, W., & N. C. Stilwel (Eds.), *The counseling sourcebook: A practical reference on contemporary issues* (pp. 175–185). New York: Crossroad.

Gehring, D. D. (1982). The counselor's "duty to warn." *The Personnel and Guidance Journal, 61,* 208–210.

Gladding, S. T. (1996). *Counseling: A comprehensive profession* (3rd ed.). Upper Saddle River, NJ: Prentice-Hall.

Gross, D. R., & Robinson, S. E. (1987). Ethics, violence, and counseling: Hear no evil, see no evil, speak no evil? *Journal of Counseling and Development, 65,* 340–344.

Gustafson, K. E., & McNamara, J. R. (1987). Confidentiality with minor clients: Issues and guidelines for therapists. *Professional Psychology: Research and Practice, 18,* 503–508.

Herlihy, B., & Corey, G. (1992). *Dual relationships in counseling.* Alexandria, VA: American Association for Counseling and Development.

Herlihy, B., & Sheeley, V. L. (1987). Privileged communication in selected helping professions: A comparison among statutes. *Journal of Counseling and Development, 65,* 479–483.

Hobson, S. M., & Kanitz, H. M. (1996). Multicultural counseling: An ethical issue for school counselors. *The School Counselor, 43,* 245–255.

Hopkins, B. R., & Anderson, B. S. (1990). *The counselor and the law.* Alexandria, VA: American Association for Counseling and Development.

Howell-Nigrelli, J. (1988). Shared responsibility for reporting child abuse cases: A reaction to Spiegel. *Elementary School Guidance and Counseling, 22,* 289–290.

Huey, W. C. (1986). Ethical concerns in school counseling. *Journal of Counseling and Development, 64,* 321–322.

Hummel, D. L., Talbutt, L. C., & Alexander, M. D. (1985). *Law and ethics in counseling.* New York: Van Nostrand Reinhold.

Kaplan, L. S. (1997). Parents' rights: Are school counselors at risk? *The School Counselor, 44,* 334–343.

Knapp, S., & Vandecreek, L. (1983). Privileged communication and the counselor. *The Personnel and Guidance Journal, 62,* 83–85.

Lynch, S. K. (1993). AIDS: Balancing confidentiality and the duty to protect. *Journal of College Student Development, 34,* 148–153.

McWhirter, J. J., McWhirter, B. T., McWhirter, A. M., & McWhirter, E. H. (1993). *At-risk youth: A comprehensive response.* Pacific Grove, CA: Brooks/Cole.

Melton, G. B. (1988). Ethical and legal issues in AIDS-related practice. *American Psychologist, 43,* 941–947.

Minard, S. M. (1993). The school counselor's role in confronting child sexual abuse. *The School Counselor, 41,* 9–15.

Muro, J. J., & Kottman, T. (1995). *Guidance and counseling in the elementary and middle schools: A practical approach.* Madison, WI: Brown & Benchmark.

Neese, L. A. (1989). Psychological maltreatment in schools: Emerging issues for counselors. *Elementary School Guidance and Counseling, 23,* 194–200.

Paisley, P. O., & Borders, L. D. (1995). School counseling: An evolving specialty. *Journal of Counseling and Development, 74,* 150–153.

Remley, T. P., Jr. (1985). The law and ethical practices in elementary and middle schools. *Elementary School Guidance and Counseling, 19,* 181–189.

Remley, T. P., Jr. (1990). Counseling records: Legal and ethical issues. In B. Herlihy & L. Golden (Eds.), *AACD Ethical Standards Casebook* (4th ed.)

(pp. 162–169). Alexandria, VA: American Association for Counseling and Development.

Remley, T. P., Jr. (1993). What responsibilities do I have for student counseling records? *The American Counselor, 2*(4), 32–33.

Remley, T. P., Jr., & Fry, L. J. (1993). Reporting suspected child abuse: Conflicting roles for the counselor. *The School Counselor, 40,* 253–259.

Remley, T. P., Jr., Herlihy, B., & Herlihy, S. B. (1997). The U.S. Supreme Court decision in Jaffee v. Redmond: Implications for counselors. *Journal of Counseling and Development, 75,* 213–218.

Remley, T. P., Jr., & Sparkman, L. B. (1993). Student suicides: The counselor's limited legal liability. *The School Counselor, 40,* 164–169.

Sampson, J. P., Jr., & Pyle, K. R. (1988). Ethical issues involved with the use of computer-assisted counseling, testing, and guidance systems. In W. C. Huey and T. P. Remley, Jr. (Eds.), *Ethical and legal issues in school counseling* (pp. 249–261). Alexandria, VA: American School Counselor Association.

Sandberg, D. N., Crabbs, S. K., & Crabbs, M. A. (1988). Legal issues in child abuse: questions and answers for counselors. *Elementary School Guidance and Counseling, 22,* 268–274.

Sheeley, V. L., & Herlihy, B. (1987). Privileged communication in school counseling: Status update. *The School Counselor, 34,* 268–272.

Sheeley, V. L., & Herlihy, B. (1989). Counseling suicidal teens: A duty to warn and protect. *The School Counselor, 37,* 89–97.

Stadler, H. A. (1989). Balancing ethical responsibilities: Reporting child abuse and neglect. *The Counseling Psychologist, 17,* 102–110.

Strein, W., & Hershenson, D. B. (1991). Confidentiality in nondyadic counseling situations. *Journal of Counseling and Development, 69,* 312–316.

Talbutt, L. C. (1983a). Current legal trends regarding abortions for minors: A dilemma for counselors. *The School Counselor, 31,* 120–124.

Talbutt, L. C. (1983b). The counselor and testing: Some legal concerns. *The School Counselor, 30,* 245–250.

Taylor, L., & Adelman, H. (1989). Reframing the confidentiality dilemma to work in children's best interests. *Professional Psychology Research and Practice, 20,* 79–83.

Terres, C. K., & Larrabee, M. J. (1985). Ethical issues and group work with children. *Elementary School Guidance and Counseling, 19,* 190–197.

Thompson, C. L., & Rudolph, L. B. (1996). *Counseling children* (4th ed.). Pacific Grove, CA: Brooks/Cole.

Tompkins, L., & Mehring, T. (1993). Client privacy and the school counselor: Privilege, ethics, and employer policies. *The School Counselor, 40,* 335–342.

Varhely, S. C., & Cowles, J. (1991). Counselor self-awareness and client confidentiality: A relationship revisited. *Elementary School Guidance and Counseling, 25,* 269–276.

Waldo, S. L., & Malley, P. (1992). *Tarasoff* and its progeny: Implications for the school counselor. *The School Counselor, 40,* 46–54.

Walker, M. M., & Larrabee, M. J. (1985). Ethics and school records. *Elementary School Guidance and Counseling, 19,* 210–216.

Zingaro, J. C. (1983). Confidentiality: To tell or not to tell. *Elementary School Guidance and Counseling, 17,* 261–267.

Internet Resources for Ongoing Professional Development in School Counseling

American Counseling Association
http://www.counseling.org

American School Counselor Association
http://www.edge.net/asca

American Psychological Association
http://www.apa.org

THOMAS: Legislative Information
http://thomas.loc.gov

U.S. Department of Education
http://www.ed.gov

AASA Legislative Alerts
http://www.aasa.org/legis/legis.htm

ASCA Legislative Update
http://www.edge.net/asca/legis1096.html

NACA On the Hill
http://www.nacac.com/hill.html

NAESP Federal Relations Update
http://www.naesp.org/updt.htm

Institute of Government
http://ncinfo.iog.unc.edu

International Counselor Network
listerv@utkvm1.utk.edu (subscribe ICN)

Counselor Educators
listserv@univscvm.csd.scarolina.edu

Counselor Net
http://plaid.hawk.plattsburgh.edu/cnet/

AMERICAN SCHOOL COUNSELOR ASSOCIATION
Ethical Standards for School Counselors

PREAMBLE

The American School Counselor Association (ASCA) is a professional organization whose members have a unique and distinctive preparation, grounded in the behavioral sciences, with training in counseling skills adapted to the school setting. The school counselor assists in the growth and development of each individual and uses his/her specialized skills to ensure that the rights of the counselee are properly protected within the structure of the school program. School counselors subscribe to the following basic tenets of the counseling process from which professional responsibilities are derived:

1. Each person has the right to respect and dignity as a unique human being and to counseling services without prejudice as to person, character, belief or practice.

2. Each person has the right to self-direction and self development.

3. Each person has the right of choice and the responsibility for decisions reached.

4. Each person has the right to privacy and thereby the right to expect the counselor-client relationship to comply with all laws, policies, and ethical standards pertaining to confidentiality.

In this document, the American School Counselor Association has specified the principles of ethical behavior necessary to maintain and regulate the high standards of integrity and leadership among its members. The Association recognizes the basic commitment of its members to the *Ethical Standards* of its parent organization, the American Association for Counseling and Development (AACD), and nothing in this document shall be construed to supplant that code. *The Ethical Standards for School Counselors* was developed to complement the AACD standards by clarifying the nature of ethical responsibilities for present and future counselors in the school setting. The purposes of this document are to:

1. Serve as a guide for the ethical practice of all professional school counselors regardless of level, area, population served, or membership in this Association.

2. Provide benchmarks for both self-appraisal and peer evaluations regarding counselor responsibilities to students, parents, colleagues and professional associates, school and community, self, and the counseling profession.

3. Inform those served by the school counselor of acceptable counselor practices and expected professional deportment.

A. RESPONSIBILITIES TO STUDENTS

The School Counselor:

1. Has a primary obligation and loyalty to the student, who is to be treated with respect as a unique individual, whether assisted individually or in a group setting.

2. Is concerned with the total needs of the student (educational, vocational, personal and social) and encourages the maximum growth and development of each counselee.

3. Informs the counselee of the purposes, goals, techniques and rules of procedure under which she/he may receive counseling assistance at or before the time when the counseling relationship is entered. Prior notice includes confidentiality issues such as the possible necessity for consulting with other professionals, privileged communication, and legal

SOURCE: Reprinted from American School Counselor Association *Ethical Standards for School Counselors.* Reprinted with permission

or authoritative restraints. The meaning and limits of confidentiality are clearly defined to counselees.

4. Refrains from consciously encouraging the counselee's acceptance of values, lifestyles, plans, decisions, and beliefs that represent only the counselor's personal orientation.

5. Is responsible for keeping abreast of laws relating to students and strives to ensure that the rights of students are adequately provided for and protected.

6. Avoids dual relationships which might impair his/her objectivity and/or increase the risk of harm to the client (e.g., counseling one's family members, close friends or associates). If a dual relationship is unavoidable, the counselor is responsible for taking action to eliminate or reduce the potential for harm. Such safeguards might include informed consent, consultation, supervision and documentation.

7. Makes appropriate referrals when professional assistance can no longer be adequately provided to the counselee. Appropriate referral requires knowledge of available resources.

8. Protects the confidentiality of students records and releases personal data only according to prescribed laws and school policies. Student information maintained through electronic data storage methods is treated with the same care as traditional student records.

9. Protects the confidentiality of information received in the counseling relationship as specified by law and ethical standards. Such information is only to be revealed to others with the informed consent of the counselee and consistent with the obligations of the counselor as a professional person.

    In a group setting, the counselor sets a norm of confidentiality and stresses its importance, yet clearly states that confidentiality in group counseling cannot be guaranteed.

10. Informs the appropriate authorities when the counselee's condition indicates a clear and imminent danger to the counselee or others. This is to be done after careful deliberation and, where possible, after consultation with other professionals. The counselor informs the counselee of actions to be taken so as to minimize confusion and clarify expectations.

11. Screens prospective group members and maintains an awareness of participants' compatibility throughout the life of the group, especially when the group emphasis is on self disclosure and self-understating. The counselor takes reasonable precautions to protect members from physical and/or psychological harm resulting from interaction within the group.

12. Provides explanations of the nature, purposes, and results of tests in language that is understandable to the client(s).

13. Adheres to relevant standards regarding selection, administration, and interpretation of assessment techniques. The counselor recognizes that computer-based testing programs require specific training in administration, scoring and interpretation which may differ from that required in more traditional assessments.

14. Promotes the benefits of appropriate computer applications and clarifies the limitations of computer technology. The counselor ensures that (1) computer applications are appropriate for the individual needs of the counselee, (2) the counselee understands how to use the applications, and (3) follow-up counseling assistance is provided. Members of underrepresented groups are assured of equal access to computer technologies and the absence of discriminatory information and values within computer applications.

15. Has unique ethical responsibilities in working with peer programs. In general, the school counselor is responsible for the welfare of students participating in peer programs under her/his direction. School counselors who function in training and supervisory capacities are referred to the preparation and supervision standards of professional counselor associations.

B. RESPONSIBILITIES TO PARENTS

The School Counselor:

1. Respects the inherent rights and responsibilities of parents for their children and endeavors to establish a cooperative relationship with par-

ents to facilitate the maximum development of the counselee.

2. Informs parents of the counselor's role, with emphasis on the confidential nature of the counseling relationship between the counselor and counselee.

3. Provides parents with accurate, comprehensive and relevant information in an objective and caring manner, as appropriate and consistent with ethical responsibilities to the counselee.

4. Treats information received from parents in a confidential and appropriate manner.

5. Shares information about a counselee only with those persons properly authorized to receive such information.

6. Adheres to laws and local guidelines when assisting parents experiencing family difficulties which interfere with the counselee's effectiveness and welfare.

7. Is sensitive to changes in the family and recognizes that all parents, custodial and noncustodial, are vested with certain rights and responsibilities for the welfare of their children by virtue of their position and according to law.

C. RESPONSIBILITIES TO COLLEAGUES AND PROFESSIONAL ASSOCIATES

The School Counselor:

1. Establishes and maintains a cooperative relationship with faculty, staff and administration to facilitate the provision of optimal guidance and counseling programs and services.

2. Promotes awareness and adherence to appropriate guidelines regarding confidentiality, the distinction between public and private information and staff consultation.

3. Treats colleagues with respect, courtesy, fairness and good faith. The qualifications, views and findings of colleagues are represented accurately and fairly to enhance the image of competent professionals.

4. Provides professional personnel with accurate, objective, concise and meaningful data necessary to adequately evaluate counsel and assist the counselee.

5. Is aware of and fully utilizes related professions and organizations to whom the counselee may be referred.

D. RESPONSIBILITIES TO THE SCHOOL AND COMMUNITY

The School Counselor:

1. Supports and protects the educational program against any infringement not in the best interest of students.

2. Informs appropriate officials of conditions that may be potentially disruptive or damaging to the school's mission, personnel and property.

3. Delineates and promotes the counselor's role and function in meeting the needs of those served. The counselor will notify appropriate school officials of conditions which may limit or curtail their effectiveness in providing programs and services.

4. Assists in the development of: (1) curricular and environmental conditions appropriate for the school and community, (2) educational procedures and programs to meet student needs, and (3) a systematic evaluation process for guidance and counseling programs, services and personnel. The counselor is guided by findings of the evaluation data in planning programs and services.

5. Actively cooperates and collaborates with agencies, organizations, and individuals in the school and community in the best interest of counselees and without regard to personal regard or remuneration.

E. RESPONSIBILITIES TO SELF

The School Counselor:

1. Functions within the boundaries of individual professional competence and accepts responsibility for the consequences of his/her actions.

2. Is aware of the potential effects of her/his own personal characteristics on services to clients.

3. Monitors personal functioning and effectiveness and refrains from any activity likely to lead to inadequate professional services or harm to a client.

4. Recognizes that differences in clients relating to age, gender, race, religion, sexual orientation, socioeconomic and ethnic backgrounds may require specific training to ensure competent services.

5. Strives through personal initiative to maintain professional competence and keeps abreast of innovations and trends in the profession. Professional and personal growth is continuous and ongoing throughout the counselor's career.

F. RESPONSIBILITIES TO THE PROFESSION

The School Counselor:

1. Conducts herself/himself in such a manner as to bring credit to self and the profession.

2. Conducts appropriate research and reports findings in a manner consistent with acceptable educational and psychological research practices. When using client data for research, statistical or program planning purposes, the counselor ensures protections of the identity of the individual client(s).

3. Actively participates in local, state and national associations which foster the development and improvement of school counseling.

4. Adheres to ethical standards of the profession, other official policy statements pertaining to counseling, and relevant statutes established by federal, state and local governments.

5. Clearly distinguishes between statements and actions made as a private individual and as a representative of the school counseling profession.

6. Contributes to the development of the profession through the sharing of skills, ideas and expertise with colleagues.

G. MAINTENANCE OF STANDARDS

Ethical behavior among professional school counselors, association members and nonmembers, is expected at all times. When there exists serious doubt as to the ethical behavior of colleagues, or if counselors are forced to work in situations or abide by policies which do not reflect the standards as outlined in these *Ethical Standards for School Counselors* or the *AACD Ethical Standards,* the counselor is obligated to take appropriate action to rectify the condition. The following procedure may serve as a guide.

1. If feasible, the counselor should consult with a professional colleague to confidentially discuss the nature of the complaint to see if she/he views the situation as an ethical violation.

2. Whenever possible, the counselor should directly approach the colleague whose behavior is in question to discuss the complaint and seek resolution.

3. If resolution is not forthcoming at the personal level, the counselor shall utilize the channels established within the school and/or school district. This may include both informal and formal procedures.

4. If the matter still remains unresolved, referral for review and appropriate action should be made to the Ethics Committees in the following sequence:

   - local counselor association
   - state counselor association
   - national counselor association

5. The ASCA Ethics Committee functions in an educative and consultative capacity and does not adjudicate complaints of ethical misconduct. Therefore, at the national level, complaints should be submitted in writing to the AACD Ethics Committee for review and appropriate action. The procedure for submitting complaints may be obtained by writing the AACD Ethics Committee, c/o The Executive Director, American Association for Counseling and Development, 5999 Stevenson Avenue, Alexandria, VA 22304.

H. RESOURCES

School counselors are responsible for being aware of, and acting in accord with, the standards and positions of the counseling profession as represented in official documents such as those listed below.

Code of Ethics (1989). National Board for Certified Counselors. Alexandria, VA

Code of Ethics for Peer Helping Professionals (1989). National Peer Helpers Association. Glendale, CA

Ethical Guidelines for Group Counselors (1989). Association for Specialists in Group Work. Alexandria, VA

Ethical Standards (1988), American Association for Counseling and Development, Alexandria, VA

Position Statement: The School Counselor and Confidentiality (1986). American School Counselor Association. Alexandria, VA

Position Statement: The School Counselor and Peer Facilitation (1984). American School Counselor Association. Alexandria, VA

Position Statement: The School Counselor and Student Rights (1982). American School Counselor Association. Alexandria, VA

Ethical Standards for School Counselors was adopted by the ASCA Delegate Assembly, March 19, 1984. This revision was approved by the ASCA Delegate Assembly, March 27, 1992.

FAMILY EDUCATIONAL RIGHTS AND PRIVACY ACT OF 1974 (FERPA)
Public Law 93-380

Sec. 513.(a) Part C of the General Education Provisions Act is further amended by adding at the end thereof the following new section:

PROTECTION OF THE RIGHTS AND PRIVACY OF PARENTS AND STUDENTS

Sec. 438.(a)(1) No funds shall be made available under any applicable program to any State or local educational agency, any institution of higher education, any community college, any school, any agency offering a preschool program, or any other educational institution which has a policy of denying, or which effectively prevents, the parents of students attending any school of such agency, or attending such institution of higher education, community college, school, preschool, or other educational institution, the right to inspect and review any and all official records, files, and data directly related to their children, including all material that is incorporated into each student's cumulative record folder, and intended for school use or to be available to parties outside the school or school system, and specifically including, but not necessarily limited to identifying data, academic work completed, level of achievement (grades, standardized achievement test scores), attendance data, scores on standardized intelligence, aptitude, and psychological tests, interest inventory results, health data, family background information, teacher or counselor ratings of serious or recurrent behavior patterns. Where such records or data include information on more than one student, the parents of any student shall be entitled to receive, or be informed of, that part of such record or data as pertains to their child. Each recipient shall establish appropriate procedures for the granting of a request by parents for access to their child's school records within a reasonable period of time, but in no case more than forty-five days after the request has been made.

(2) Parents shall have an opportunity for a hearing to challenge the content of their child's school records, to insure that the records are not inaccurate, misleading, or otherwise in violation of the privacy or other rights of students, and to provide an opportunity for the correction or deletion of any such inaccurate, misleading, or otherwise inappropriate data contained therein.

(b)(1) No funds shall be made available under any applicable program to any State or local educational agency, any institution of higher education, any community college, any school, any agency offering a preschool program, or any other educational institution which has a policy of permitting the release of personally identifiable records or files (or personal information contained therein) of students without the written consent of their parents to any individual, agency, or organization, other than to the following—

(A) other school officials, including teachers within the educational institution or local educational agency who have legitimate educational interests;

(B) officials of other schools or school systems in which the student intends to enroll, upon condition that the student's parents be notified of the transfer, receive a copy of the record if desired, and have an opportunity for a hearing to challenge the content of the record;

(C) authorized representatives of (i) the Comptroller General of the United States, (ii) the Secretary, (iii) an administrative head of an educational agency (as defined in section 409 of this Act), or (iv) State educational authorities, under the conditions set forth in paragraph (3) of this subsection; and

(D) in connection with a student's application for, or receipt of, financial aid.

(2) No funds shall be made available under any applicable program to any State or local educational agency, any institution of higher education, any community college, any school, agency offering a preschool program, or any other educational institution which has a policy of practice of furnishing, in any form, any personally identifiable information contained in personal school records, to any persons other than those listed in subsection (b)(1) unless—

(A) there is written consent from the student's parents specifying records to be released, the reasons for such release, and to whom, and with a copy of the records to be released to the student's parents and the student if desired by the parents, or

(B) such information is furnished in compliance with judicial order, or pursuant to any lawfully issued subpoena, upon condition that parents and the student are notified of all such orders or subpoenas in advance of the compliance therewith by the educational institution or agency:

(3)Nothing contained in this section shall preclude authorized representatives of (A) the Comptroller General of the United States, (B) the Secretary, (C) an administrative head of an educational agency or (D) State educational authorities from having access to student or other records which may be necessary in connection with the audit and evaluation of Federally-supported education programs, or in connection with the enforcement of the Federal legal requirements which relate to such programs: *Provided* that, except when collection of personally identifiable data is specifically authorized by Federal law, any data collected by such officials with respect to individual students shall not include information (including social security numbers) which would permit the personal identification of such students or their parents after the data so obtained has been collected.

(4)(A) With respect to subsections (c)(1) and (c)(2) and (c)(3), all persons, agencies, or organizations desiring access to the records of a student shall be required to sign a written form which shall be kept permanently with the file of the student, but only for inspection by the parents or student, indicating specifically the legitimate educational or other interest that each person, agency, or organization has in seeking this information. Such form shall be available to parents and to the school official responsible for record maintenance as a means of auditing the operation of the system.

(B) With respect to this subsection, personal information shall only be transferred to a third party on the condition that such party will not permit any other party to have access to such information without the written consent of the parents of the student.

(c) The Secretary shall adopt appropriate regulations to protect the rights of privacy of students and their families in connection with any surveys or data-gathering activities conducted, assisted, or authorized by the Secretary or an administrative head of an

education agency. Regulations established under this subsection shall include provisions controlling the use, dissemination, and protection of such data. No survey or data-gathering activities shall be conducted by the Secretary, or an administrative head of an education agency under an applicable program, unless such activities are authorized by law.

(d) For the purpose of this section, whenever a student has attained eighteen years of age, or is attending an institution of postsecondary education the permission or consent required of and the rights accorded to the parents of the student shall thereafter be required of and accorded to the student.

(e) No funds shall be made available under any applicable program unless the recipient of such funds informs the parents of students, or the students, if they are eighteen years of age or older, or are attending an institution of postsecondary education, of the rights accorded them by this section.

(f) The Secretary, or an administrative head of an education agency, shall take appropriate actions to enforce provisions of this section and to deal with violations of this section, according to the provisions of this Act, except that action to terminate assistance may be taken only if the Secretary finds that there has been a failure to comply with the provisions of this section, and he has determined that compliance cannot be secured by voluntary means.

(g) The secretary shall establish or designate an office and review board within the Department of Health, Education, and Welfare for the purpose of investigating, processing, reviewing, and adjusting violations of the provisions of this section and complaints which may be filed concerning alleged violations of this section, according to the procedures contained in sections 434 and 437 of this Act.

(b)(1)(i) The provisions of this section shall become effective ninety days after the date of enactment of section 438 of the General Education Provisions Act.

(2)(i) This section may be cited as the "Family Educational Rights and Privacy Act of 1974."

PROTECTION OF PUPIL RIGHTS

Sec. 514. (a) Part C of the General Education Provisions Act is further amended by adding after section 438 the following new section:

Protection of Pupil Rights

Sec. 439. All instructional material, including teacher's manuals, films, tapes, or other supplementary instructional material which will be used in connection with any research or experimentation program or project shall be available for inspection by the parents or guardians of the children engaged in such program or project. For the purpose of this section "research or experimentation program or project" means any program or project in any applicable program designed to explore or develop new or unproven teaching methods or techniques.

(b) The amendment made by subsection (a) shall be effective upon enactment of this Act.

12

Mental Health Counseling and Assessment

Mental health counseling, once a fledgling specialty struggling to develop an identity, has become a dominating force in defining how the overall profession of counseling presents itself in the mental health arena. It is to counseling what clinical psychology has become to psychology. Of course, the development of a specialty that begins to politically flex its muscles has its good and bad points. For example, it can be argued that mental health counseling is the "tail" that is wagging the larger profession of counseling "dog," meaning the larger profession has begun to follow the specialty's lead, perhaps reluctantly. Mental health counselors, as represented by the American Mental Health Counseling Association (AMHCA), have organized to the extent they are making demands on the organization representing counseling as a whole, the ACA. As of 1996, there was even a concerted effort by a constituency of AMHCA to disaffiliate from the ACA. As of this writing, no decisions have been made, but the ACA Governing Council has voted to revoke the AMHCA charter (affiliation), if AMHCA fails to comply with ACA Bylaws (Governing Council, 1996). However, with such demands as the AMHCA is making, there is some influence about how the profession develops.

Beyond influencing the larger profession of counseling, mental health counselors are also influencing mental health services nationally though efforts to ensure that mental health counselors and their services are available to individuals served by government and private health service providers. Mental health counselors, both through AMHCA and the ACA, have become outspoken advocates for the benefits of counseling; and both groups have lobbied for the inclusion of counseling in laws overseeing health service provision.

It seems that just as mental health counseling has taken flight, it has encountered the "wind shear" of managed care. With the growth of managed care, mental health counselors, like other (competing) mental health professionals, are being challenged to provide services under the scrutiny of a managing agency. This is a significant and recent change from the days when mental health professionals just billed their standard fee to an insurance program for reimbursement that was almost guaranteed. Today, mental health professionals must be on a managed care company's provider list (meeting the company's standards) before payment is allowed, and referrals are often made through a "case manager." The case manager defines the number of sessions of psychotherapy to be provided within the financial constraints of the managed care contract. A *managed care contract* is an agreement between the managed care company and the provider of counseling services (usually a counselor in independent practice or an agency providing counseling services). The contract usually defines the type of services that can be provided, the amount of money to be paid for provided services, and other limitations of services. Counselors must agree to abide by the managed care company's contract or they risk being left off the panel and not receiving referrals. If a client should self-refer and the counselor is not on the managed care panel overseeing the client's benefits, no services would be reimbursed by the insurer. Because it has become competitive to be accepted by a managed care company as a provider, the fees for services under managed care are often less than those traditionally billed for services to insurance companies or to individuals paying on their own. In effect, managed care has changed the rules of reimbursement for health services. Regardless, mental health counseling may be well positioned to take a leading role in the mental health enterprise of the future, even with managed care.

This chapter will define the specialty of mental health counseling. Additionally, because assessment of clients for mental health treatment is a major aspect of mental health counselors' work, assessment will be addressed in this chapter. *Assessment* is the process whereby a client is evaluated against a normative standard, or a set of criteria for classification, in diagnosis, planning, or treatment. Assessment in counseling usually involves objective testing. Ethical issues specific to assessment and mental health practice will be addressed. Emergent professional issues will also be explored.

Defining the Specialty, Setting, and Clients

Mental health counselors usually work in clinical settings (state, private, or nonprofit clinics, hospitals, and other health service agencies) and in private practice. In fact, in the early years of AMHCA, the membership was employed primarily in community mental health centers; however, by the mid-1980s there was a shift to private practice as the predominant employment setting (Hershenson & Power, 1987). Mental health counselorsand rehabilitation counselors specialized in phychiatric rehabilitation also are being hired by managed care companies to be case managers, overseeing services provided by their colleagues in the field.

Mental health counselors primarily assess and treat individuals with mental disorders, with an emphasis on promoting healthy development and coping rather than "cure" (Hershenson & Power, 1987). Most services are provided to individuals who meet criteria for a diagnosis or diagnoses according to the *Diagnostic and Statistical Manual of Mental Disorders, Fourth Edition (DSM–IV),* published by the American Psychiatric Association (1994). The *DSM–IV* provides a detailed listing of mental disorders classified by larger groupings of disorders, such as mood disorders, anxiety disorders, and schizophrenia and other psychotic disorders. In addition, each disorder is described by its characteristic behaviors, and behavior-specific criteria are listed for a diagnosis to be met. Statistical data are provided on the prevalence of disorders, and a complete description of associated features, cultural and age related factors, the course of the disorder, and predisposing factors are given. Guidance also is provided for *differential diagnosis,* the process whereby one disorder is considered over another disorder with similar diagnostic signs, symptoms, or course. Mental health counseling is considered the specialty of counseling most suited, by educational and supervised training standards, to serve individuals with mental disorders. However, there is a subtle distinction related to the definition of mental health counseling compared with other "clinical" mental health professions (e.g., clinical psychology; clinical social work). Hershenson and Power (1987) stated:

> As its name implies, mental health counseling does not seek to cure illness (implicit in the terms *psychiatric* and *clinical* in the names of . . . most of the other mental health fields), but rather seeks to promote healthy development and coping. It works with both the client and the environment, building on existing strengths wherever possible and using scientifically evaluated methods. (p. 5)

The focus of treatment in the mental health specialty is the individual with the mental disorder. According to Hershenson and Power (1987), the role of the mental health counselor includes (a) prevention of problems, (b) facilitation of healthy growth, (c) remediation of maladaption, (d) rehabilitation, and (e) enhancing and improving the quality of life.

To a large degree, the types of clients that will be encountered by the mental health counselor will vary by setting. For example, a counselor working in a state acute care facility will probably be faced with seriously disturbed individuals who lack resources to obtain medical benefits coverage through private insurers. On the other hand, a counselor working in a private clinic in a rich community primarily may treat clients with adjustment concerns to everyday living situations. However, mental health counselors must be prepared to serve the full range of mental disorders and to deal with situations involving serious psychopathology. Clients may suffer from mild symptoms of anxiety or depression, or they may be severely disabled by a mental condition such as chronic schizophrenia.

Assessment or diagnostic procedures may be undertaken to provide a clear evaluation of the individual's concerns and the effect of the mental disorder on the individual's daily activities. Along this line, mental health counselors may assess clients through a diagnostic interview, which typically involves a detailed history of the individual's symptoms, stressors, and family background. Additionally, a mental status examination may be performed. A *mental status examination* is a structured interview designed to provide a controlled, interpersonal setting for the emergence and observation of symptoms and signs of mental disorders (Cottone, 1992). Treatment usually involves individual psychotherapy, but mental health counselors may also be involved in group treatment. They may choose to specialize further, by focusing on children, adolescents, or adults. They may specialize in working with clients having one mental disorder (e.g., panic disorder) or one type of mental disorder (e.g., anxiety disorders). Treatment may vary according to the disorder. Regardless, in contrast to psychiatry or clinical psychology, the mental health counselor's emphasis should be on building strengths, facilitating healthy growth, preventing future problems, and rehabilitating the client.

Mental health counselors often work side-by-side with other mental health professionals in their settings. For example, in a hospital setting, a psychiatrist and social worker may often be assigned to a client, and treatment may follow the dictates of a team decision. Most typically, mental health counselors work with psychiatric nurses, social workers, rehabilitation counselors, psychologists, and psychiatrists. The professional who will lead in team decision-making is often defined by the rules of the employing organization. Regardless, the mental health counselor works primarily from an "asset-oriented" model rather than an "illness-oriented" model (Hershenson & Power, 1987), focusing on building the strengths of the individual rather than simply ameliorating symptoms or deficiencies.

At present, AMHCA is the organization that best represents the interests of the mental health counselor. Since its inception, it has been an advocate for the specialty and has facilitated the development of specialty designation through the National Board of Certified Counselors (NBCC). Currently, NBCC offers a specialty designation in mental health counseling. To be certified, NBCC requires that the candidate must meet the general requirements for certification as a National Certified Counselor (NCC), which is a generic credential. In addition, candidates for the Clinical Mental Health Counselor certificate must complete 60 semester hours of graduate training (the NCC requires only an acceptable master's degree, but does not specify semester hours). Graduate courses are required in areas such as theories of counseling, psychopathology or abnormal psychology, ethics, social and cultural foundations, and group counseling. Three thousand hours of post-master's supervised experience is required under a supervisor acceptable to the board. In effect, the standards for the Clinical Mental Health Counselor certificate are among the highest in the counseling profession.

As with all members of the ACA, mental health counselors are directed by the ACA's Responsibilities of Users of Standardized Tests (RUST), originally drafted in 1978 but revised in 1989 in cooperation with the Association for Assessment in Counseling, an affiliate of the ACA. The RUST spells out specific guidelines of test use decisions, the qualification requirements for those who administer tests, test selection, test administration, scoring, and interpretation. Guidance is also given for communicating test results.

Issues of Significance to the Specialty

Professional Differentiation

Mental health counseling has identified itself as the "health" specialty of counseling specialties. Where other specialties in counseling also are involved with medical concerns (e.g., rehabilitation counseling), mental health counseling focuses on the provision of services to prevent and to facilitate healthy development and growth in individuals diagnosed with mental disorders. Mental health counselors focus on building the strengths of people with problems; the focus is on the development of the individual beyond deficiency (Hershenson & Power, 1987). Unique ethical concerns arise due to the medical nature of the settings within which mental health counselors work and due to the nature of the work itself. Like rehabilitation counselors, mental health counselors must be prepared to work with severely disabled individuals in need of urgent care.

Ethical Issues

Privacy. Privacy issues in mental health counseling are complicated by the presence of a third paying party, usually an insurance company, sometimes through a managed care overseer, or through government or other agencies funding services. Occasionally clients will pay for counseling out of their own pockets, but not as often as some specialties of counseling in which clients are sometimes willing to pay for services separate from medical insurance (e.g., marriage counseling). As was addressed earlier in this textbook, privacy relates to the "freedom of individuals to choose for themselves the time and the circumstances under which and the extent to which their beliefs, behavior, and opinions are to be shared or withheld from others" (Spiegel, 1979, p. 251). It is an ethical principle that both (a) the information that a person has sought counseling, and (b) what is communicated in counseling, is private; the client has control over how the information will be used. Privacy and confidentiality, although different concepts, are related; they both involve the right of the client regarding information or behaviors that are shared with a counselor. Whereas privacy issues relate to a constitutional right (Huber, 1994), confidentiality issues address the specific counseling context. Privacy issues extend to such areas as (a) discrete scheduling of sessions to prevent clients from encountering other clients in waiting rooms, (b) billing, administration of case records, (c) use of client information over computer or phone lines or through testing services, and (d) other activities that do not necessarily relate to information provided in counseling sessions. Confidentiality is generally understood to deal with the content of counseling sessions. Huber (1994) stated: "These [privacy] questions are particularly important when insurance companies and other third-party payers attempt to gain access to therapy information about clients or when therapists are bound by law and/or professional codes of ethics to break confidentiality" (p. 23). Ethically sensitive counselors do their best to ensure that information about clients is considered private.

Confidentiality and Privileged Communication.   Mental health counselors, more so than any other type of counselor (except rehabilitation counselors) are faced with clients who are not competent to make judgments about such issues as money management, treatment compliance, or privacy issues. It may be too easy for the unethical practitioner to get the permission of a mentally disturbed individual to share information with other individuals, or even to share the information in legal proceedings. One of the most prevalent traits of individuals with mental disorders listed in the *DSM–IV* is the presence of poor judgment. Clients who have limitations of judgment or ability must be given special treatment as related to the confidentiality issue, because they may release information inadvertently to serve a counselor's agenda rather than their own needs. Ethical counselors ensure that every effort is made to explain fully the relevant issues and that clients makes fully informed decisions.

Confidentiality was defined earlier in this text as akin to an anti-gossip guarantee. Counselors must be alert to the need to keep information learned in counseling as private as is legally possible. Because mentally disordered individuals often manifest behaviors that are odd or unusual, their behaviors make for interesting general conversation. At more than one social gathering, counselors have been overheard entertaining others by talking about the strange behaviors of their clients. Such behavior shows poor respect for individuals in serious personal situations, and it shows poor regard for the profession, which allows counselors the privilege of serving people in need. No matter how seriously disturbed a client's behavior may be, it is incumbent on the counselor to respect the individual and to maintain the privacy of client information.

Costa and Altekruse (1994) provided a detailed guideline of actions for mental health counselors when duty to warn is an issue. Their duty-to-warn guidelines included (a) get informed consent, (b) plan ahead through consultation, (c) develop contingency plans, (d) obtain professional liability insurance, (e) be selective about clients, (f) involve the client, (g) obtain a detailed history, (h) document in writing, and (i) implement procedure to warn. Further, they provided vignettes of potential dilemmas working with families and analyses of the circumstances according to three conditions related to duty to warn: a special relationship, a prediction of harmful conduct, and a forseeable victim. Duty-to-warn situations may arise in mental health counseling, because many of the served clients experience acute symptoms of a serious nature which may affect their judgment. In cases of imminent danger, a breach of confidentiality is acceptable.

As was described in Chapter 2, privileged communication relates to revelation of confidential information in legal proceedings. As with many specialties of counseling, counselors may be called upon to testify at legal proceedings, and it is important that mental health counselors know the laws that apply related to privileged communication in their states.

Informed Consent.   In a recent actual case, a young woman (diagnosed with a reading disorder, depression, and borderline intelligence), unwittingly had her children taken away when she signed a form presented to her by a family services agency caseworker. The caseworker had full knowledge of the person's limitations and inability to read and did not inform the woman of the contents of the form fully, even when the woman asked for an explanation. The children later were returned after much legal maneuvering, when it was learned that the client signed a paper she could not read and which was not thoroughly explained to her.

Mental health counselors must be sure that their clients have the capability to consent to treatment. Handelsman, Kemper, Kesson-Craig, McLain, and Johnsrud (1986) found that the readability of consent forms for therapy was considered difficult, equivalent to an academically oriented periodical. At this level, few clients of even average intelligence can understand a consent document fully. Clients who are emotionally disabled may not be in a state of mind to fully comprehend their rights related to accepting or refusing treatment.

The APA code of ethics gives detailed guidance on this issue of informed consent. Standard 4.02 reads as follows:

> (a) Psychologists obtain appropriate informed consent to therapy or related procedures, using language that is reasonably understandable to participants. The content of informed consent will vary depending on many circumstances; however, informed consent generally implies that the person (1) has the capacity to consent, (2) has been informed of significant information concerning the procedure, (3) has freely and without undue influence expressed consent, and (4) consent has been appropriately documented.

Further, the APA code states that consent from a legally authorized person is sought for those that are "legally incapable of giving informed consent"; yet the incapable person is still consulted and informed of the actions to be taken by the therapist, and that person's "assent" is still sought (where *assent* implies agreement). The APA guidelines are exemplary, and would relate to individuals diagnosed as mentally retarded, organically impaired, or seriously emotionally disturbed. It also would apply to individuals under adult age as defined in the legal jurisdiction of practice.

Dual Relationsh ips.   The AMHCA Code of Ethics (1987) specifically states under a section titled Welfare of the Consumer: "Mental health counselors make every effort to avoid dual relationships with clients and/or relationships which might impair their professional judgment or increase the risk of client exploitation. Examples of such dual relationships include treating an employee or supervisor, treating a close friend or family relative and sexual relationships with clients" (pp. 9–10). In a section titled, Moral and Legal Standards the code also states, "Sexual conduct, not limited to sexual intercourse, between mental health counselors and clients is specifically in violation of this code of ethics. This does not, however, prohibit the use of explicit instructional aids including films and video tapes. Such use is within accepted practices of trained and competent sex therapists" (pp. 5–6).

According to the AMHCA Code of Ethics (AMHCA, 1987), as with the ACA code, dual relationships should be avoided. The APA code states that the psychologist refrains from "multiple relationships" if they might impair the psychologist's judgment or "harm or exploit the other party." Sex between a counselor and a client is prohibited. It is interesting to note the exception in the AMHCA code to sex therapy, which allows for the use of films or videotapes (purportedly on sexuality issues). As with marriage counseling, sexuality issues are addressed by mental health counselors, but it must be understood that being a mental health counselor does not, in and of itself, mean that a person is trained and competent to act as a sex therapist. Certainly, specialized training is necessary.

Responsibility.   The AMHCA Code of Ethics is vague on the issue of responsibility to clients; yet a section dealing with professional competence contains a statement that the mental health counselor has "a responsibility both to the individual who is served and to the institution with which the service is performed to maintain high standards of professional conduct." The ACA code, on the other hand, has a clear-cut statement of responsibility: "The principle responsibility of counselors is to respect the dignity and to promote the welfare of clients" (p. 33). Professional obligation should always start with the client. This is especially true of the mental health counselor, who may be working with individuals vulnerable to the whims of other involved individuals or to agencies involved in the client's treatment. For example, what should a mental health counselor do if a request for additional services is denied by a managed care provider, when such a denial is to the detriment of the patient or even endangers the patient or other parties. Obviously, the mental health counselor's primary obligation should be to the patient, and an effort should be made to inform the managed care provider that actions to deny services may, in fact, endanger individuals or be to the detriment of a patient. The counselor should inform the provider in an appropriate and professional manner, and, if necessary, provide and seek written documentation of correspondence with the managed care provider. It is imperative that counselors not accede to the insurance company's decisions when serious issues of client survival or welfare are imminent. If not successful in appealing what may appear to be an unwise decision to discontinue treatment by an insurer (managed or not) then the counselor must consider treating the client *pro bono publico*, for the public good (without a fee). Regardless, the counselor must be prepared to take the appeal to higher authorities if it is believed that a client has been treated unjustly. Mental health counselors must never confuse their primary responsibility to patients with secondary obligations to paying parties or employers.

Values.   Value issues enter into mental health counseling when counselors must make a judgment or take an action that may conflict with their personal values. What should a counselor do when confronted with a patient who confesses to repeatedly and seriously sexually abusing children? Treating such an individual may be abhorrent to the counselor, who might prefer to assist and to counsel the victims of abuse. Treating abusers or perpetrators may clash with the counselor's most basic values related to children; how can one view perpetrators in a way that they can be treated fairly and competently if their actions are seriously objectionable? Counselors continually must assess their personal values and make appropriate judgments about their own limitations. If counselors find that working with a particular patient or a type of patient is objectionable, they must assess whether they can serve the client competently and objectively. Obviously, referring to another counselor or therapist who specializes in counseling such problems is recommended. But, in some cases, for example, in sparsely populated areas without available mental health alternatives, counselors may have to make judgments to serve clients that they otherwise would refuse to treat. In such cases, counselors are obliged to inform the patient of their concerns or feelings, and counseling should proceed only under the full and informed consent of the patient. Many issues may arise in counseling that produce a circumstance where value conflicts arise (see Chapter Five). In such cases, counselors must be prepared to address the concerns professionally and ethically. Some of the more common value issues arising in mental health counseling involve (a) abuse of children or defenseless/dependent individuals, (b) pregnancy issues (e.g., abortion), (c) current, recent, or past illegal actions by a patient, (d) sexuality concerns or deviant sexual practices, or (e) alcohol or drug abuse.

Counselor Competence.   As was discussed in Chapter 2, counselor competence involves (a) the quality of the provided service, and (b) the boundaries or scope of professional activity. The AMHCA Code of Ethics (AMHCA, 1987) provides a detailed section outlining the principle of "competence." High standards are to be maintained, according to the code. Mental health counselors must (a) know their boundaries of practice, (b) be "up-to-date and scholarly" as a teacher, (c) seek appropriate continuing education, (d) represent accurately their background, (e) seek help for personal problems or cease treatment of clients if personal problems impair their practice, and (f) rectify ethical dilemmas where possible.

Regarding the boundaries of professional practice, there are continual "turf battles" over the extent of services to be provided by counselors and other mental health providers. At this writing, such a battle is brewing in Ohio, where the attorney general offered a legal opinion allowing licensed professional or clinical counselors to use the term *psychological* to "describe their work of testing and evaluating people for mental and emotional disorders" ("Ohio," 1996, p. 9). The opinion is being opposed by the Ohio Board of Psychology and the Ohio Psychological and School Psychologist Associations, according to the report. In essence, counselors, by the opinion of the leading law enforcement agency of the state, have been told they can use a term that has been associated historically only with the practice of psychology. Some view this opinion as a major challenge to psychology in Ohio. Typically, battles over scope of practice of mental health counselors involve the issues of testing, diagnosis, and the use of the term *psychotherapy.* Counselors are required by licensure laws to practice within the limits of their defined competence and training and consistent with definitions of practice within licensure statutes.

Assessment.   To a large degree, issues of assessment pervade many of the ethical issues addressed in the previous sections. But the RUST standards (ACA, 1989) should be consulted for detailed guidelines on assessment matters. (The RUST standards can be found at the end of this chapter). For example, individuals who administer tests should be competently trained to do so. The RUST standards (section III, Qualifications of Test Users) state:

> While all professional counselors and personnel workers should have formal training in psychological and educational measurement and testing, this training does not necessarily make one an expert and even an expert does not have all the knowledge and skills

appropriate to some particular situations or instruments. Questions of user qualifications should always be addressed when testing is being considered. . . . Lack of proper qualifications can lead to errors and subsequent harm to clients. Each professional is responsible for making judgments on this in each situation and cannot leave that responsibility either to clients or to others in authority. It is incumbent upon the individual test user to obtain appropriate training or arrange for proper supervision and assistance when engaging in testing. Qualifications for test users depend on four factors.

The four factors identified in the RUST document are (a) the purposes of testing, (b) characteristics of tests, (c) settings and conditions of test use, and (d) roles of test selectors. The test should be selected on the purpose of testing, the validity of instruments (how well a test measures what it purports to measure), and other technical standards related to test quality (e.g., reliability—how consistently a test measures what it purports to measure). The test should be administered in a way that will produce a valid and accurate assessment of the individual. Test scoring should be done in a standardized way against proper norms, if applicable. Interpretation should be according to guidelines in test manuals and as objective as possible. Safeguards should be taken to ensure a client's privacy and to prevent misuse of the test data.

Code Comparisons

The AMHCA Code of Ethics (found at the end of this chapter) is not as thorough as the ACA or APA codes of ethics, but it need not be. It is more aspirational in nature, because most members of AMHCA are also members of ACA, which provides a code that is a mandatory professional standard. It can also be argued that the AMHCA code, developed in 1987, is outdated. The ACA and APA codes are more contemporary, being implemented in 1995 and 1992 respectively. Should the AMHCA disaffiliate with the ACA, or should the ACA revoke the AMHCA charter, then the AMHCA code will need to be updated and a mechanism for enforcement will need to be established. Regardless, the RUST standards provide specialized guidance on issues of tests and measurement that are not addressed adequately in the ACA, AMHCA, or APA codes. Additional standards related to testing are also published by the APA, including the "Standards for Educational and Psychological Tests," and the "Code for Fair Testing Practices in Education."

Issues of Diversity

Probably one of the most predominant issues in mental health counseling related to multiculturalism is the issue of deviance or maladjustment. For example, Axelson (1993) described the "cultural model" of *maladjustment* as defining:

A normal person as one who is in harmony with self and environment. The definition emphasizes conformity with the cultural requirements, mores, and injunctions of the community. Thus, normality tends to be equated with what is conventional and abnormality with what is viewed as antisocial conduct and/or different behavior. (p. 275)

This view of maladjustment is in contrast to the American Psychiatric Association's (1994) definition in the *Diagnostic and Statistical Manual of Mental Disorders, Fourth Edition (DSM–IV)*. The *DSM–IV* defines a mental disorder as:

A clinically significant behavioral or psychological syndrome or pattern that occurs in an individual and that is associated with present distress (e.g., a painful symptom) or disability (e.g., impairment in one or more important areas of functioning) or with a significantly increased risk of suffering death, pain, disability, or an important loss of freedom. In addition, this syndrome or pattern must not be merely an expectable and culturally sanctioned response to a particular event, for example, the death of a loved one. Whatever its original cause, it must currently be considered a manifestation of a behavioral, psychological, or biological dysfunction in the individual. Neither deviant behavior (e.g., political, religious, or sexual) nor conflicts that are primarily between the individual and society are mental disorders unless the deviance or conflict is a symptom of a dysfunction in the individual, as described above. (pp. xxi–xxii)

As can be seen, the cultural definition of maladjustment takes into consideration cultural variation, whereas the *DSM–IV* definition plays down, minimizes, or subsumes cultural factors by focusing on disorders "in the individual."

For the mental health counselor working in a context that requires diagnosis of mental disorders according to *DSM–IV* criteria, cultural sensitivity may produce discomfort with standardized procedures. This is so because the culturally sensitive counselor recognizes that mental disorders may not be equally prevalent across cultural contexts. Should inner-city inhabitants be diagnosed as "antisocial personality disorders" because they act out of the norm to survive in a difficult environment? Should bulimia or anorexia be interpreted outside of a cultural context which promotes unnaturally thin standards of body weight and attractiveness?

Issues of diversity also are predominant when objective tests are being used. Because minorities are usually outnumbered in norm bases, it can be argued that tests, no matter how broadly normed, cannot reflect cultural differences accurately in the development of abilities, interests, aptitudes, or achievement. Although some tests are more culturally sensitive than others, it is imperative that test data are not interpreted out of social or cultural context.

The greatest challenge to culturally sensitive mental health counselors is to view clients in context, and to dispute labels that require an internalistic or broadly normative view of mental disorder. As Sue (1996) stated:

If we believe that many problems reside outside the person (prejudice and discrimination) and not within (person-blame), ethical practice dictates that professionals develop alternative helping roles that are aimed at *system intervention*. The traditional counseling role has been primarily confined to a one-to-one, remediation-oriented, in-the-office form of help, but recognition that problems may reside in the social system dictates use of nontraditional roles. These roles may include adviser, advocate, consultant, change agent, facilitator of indigenous support systems, and facilitator of indigenous healing systems. Most counselor education programs do not train us in these roles, yet they are some of the most effective in multicultural helping. (p. 196).

As to whether problems should be viewed as internal or external to individuals is a challenge that may best be met by the profession as a whole. But certainly, counselors should be alert to the pressure to view disorders or measured characteristics according to "clinical" standards at the expense of clients acting to survive in difficult or unusual cultural contexts. The emphasis on client assets and the development of potential that rests at the base of the mental "health" counselor's philosophy may be an asset when addressing issues of diversity.

Summary

Mental health counseling has taken a lead in the mental health field and represents a health specialty in counseling. Through specialty certification by means of the NBCC and through development of a specialized code of ethics, mental health counselors have established themselves as a viable and identifiable specialty. Although the pressures of managed care may affect the practice of mental health counseling, the specialty may also be positioned well to interface with the managed care system. Mental health counselors may find jobs opening in managed care companies as case managers and service providers. Because mental health counselors, like social workers, are primarily master's-level trained mental health professionals, they may suit the needs of managed care's cost containment efforts by undercutting the rates and salaries of doctoral-level trained professionals (such as psychology and psychiatry). Mental health counseling may be situated ideally to survive the managed care movement in the mental health field. Yet the field, which has defined itself a "health" specialty must also deal with the issue that mental health may be a culturally relative issue, and not just a matter of diagnosing and treating individual deviance.

References

American Counseling Association (in cooperation with the Association for Assessment in Counseling). (1989). *Responsibilities of users of standardized tests*. Alexandria, VA: Author.

American Mental Health Counseling Association. (1987). *AMHCA code of ethics*. Alexandria, VA: Author.

American Psychiatric Association. (1994). *Diagnostic and statistical manual of mental disorders*, (4th ed.). Washington, DC: Author.

Axelson, J. A. (1993). *Counseling and development in a multicultural society*. Pacific Grove, CA: Brooks/Cole.

Costa, L., & Altekruse, M. (1994). Duty-to-warn guidelines for mental health counselors. *Journal of Counseling and Development, 72,* 346–350.

Cottone, R. R. (1992). *Theories and paradigms of counseling and psychotherapy*. Needham Heights, MA: Allyn & Bacon.

Governing Council (1996, August). *Counseling Today*, p. 1.

Handelsman, M. M., Kemper, M. B., Kesson-Craig, P., McLain, J., & Johnsrud, C. (1986). Use, content, and readability of written informed consent forms for treatment. *Professional Psychology: Research and Practice, 17,* 514–518.

Hershenson, D. B., & Power, P. W. (1987). *Mental health counseling: Theory and practice.* New York: Pergamon.

Huber, C. H. (1994). *Ethical, legal, and professional issues in the practice of marriage and family therapy* (2nd ed.). Upper Saddle River, NJ: Merrill/Prentice Hall.

Ohio A-G legal opinion allows counselors to call testing and evaluations 'psychological.' (1996, July/August). *The National Psychologist,* p. 9.

Spiegel, S. B. (1979). Separate principles for counselors of women: A new form of sexism. *The Counseling Psychologist, 8*(1), 49–50.

Sue, D. W. (1996). Ethical issues in multicultural counseling. In B. Herlihy & G. Corey (Eds.), *Ethical standards casebook,* (5th ed.). Alexandria, VA: American Counseling Association.

AMHCA CODE OF ETHICS

PREAMBLE

Mental health counselors believe in the dignity and worth of the individual. They are committed to increasing knowledge of human behavior and understanding of themselves and others. While pursuing these endeavors, they make every reasonable effort to protect the welfare of those who seek their services or of any subject that may be the object of study. They use their skills only for purposes consistent with these values and do not knowingly permit their misuse by others. While demanding for themselves freedom of inquiry and community, mental health counselors accept the responsibility this freedom confers: competence, objectivity in the application of skills and concern for the best interests of clients, colleagues, and society in general. In the pursuit of these ideals, mental health counselors subscribe to the following principles:

PRINCIPLE 1.   RESPONSIBILITY

In their commitment to the understanding of human behavior, mental health counselors value objectivity and integrity, and in providing services they maintain the highest standards. They accept responsibility for the consequences of their work and make every effort to insure that their services are used appropriately.

a. Mental health counselors accept ultimate responsibility for selecting appropriate areas for investigation and the methods relevant to minimize the possibility that their finding will be misleading. They provide thorough discussion of the limitations of their data and alternative hypotheses, especially where their work touches on social policy or might be misconstrued to the detriment of specific age, sex, ethnic, socio-economic, or other social categories. In publishing reports of their work, they never discard observations that may modify the interpretation of results. Mental health counselors take credit only for the work they have actually done. In pursuing research, mental health counselors ascertain that their efforts will not lead to changes in individuals or organizations unless such changes are part of the agreement at the time of obtaining informal consent. Mental health counselors clarify in advance the expectations for sharing and utilizing research data. They avoid dual relationships which may limit objectivity, whether theoretical, political, or monetary, so that interference with data, subjects, and milieu is kept to a minimum.

b. As employees of an institution or agency, mental health counselors have the responsibility of remaining alert to institutional pressures which may distort reports of counseling findings or use them in ways counter to the promotion of human welfare.

c. When serving as members of governmental or other organizational bodies, mental health counselors remain accountable as individuals to the Code of Ethics of the American Mental Health Counselors Association (AMHCA).

d. As teachers, mental health counselors recognize their primary obligation to help others acquire knowledge and skill. They maintain high standards of scholarship and objectivity by presenting counseling information fully and accurately, and by giving appropriate recognition to alternative viewpoints. As practitioners, mental health counselors know that they bear a heavy social responsibility because their recommendations and professional actions may alter the lives of others. They, therefore, remain fully cognizant of their impact and alert to personal, social, organizational, financial or political situations or pressures which might lead to misuse of their influence.

e. As practitioners, mental health counselors know that they bear a heavy social responsibility because their recommendations and professional actions may alter the lives of others. They, therefore, remain fully cognizant of their impact and alert to personal, social, organizational, financial or political situations or pressures which might lead to misuse of their influence.

f. Mental health counselors provide reasonable and timely feedback to employees, trainees, supervisors, students, clients, and others whose work they may evaluate.

PRINCIPLE 2.   COMPETENCE

The maintenance of high standards of professional competence is a responsibility shared by all mental health counselors in the interest of the public and the profession as a whole. Mental health counselors recognize the boundaries of their competence and the limitations of their techniques and only provide services, use techniques, or offer opinions as professionals that meet recognized standards. Throughout their careers, mental health counselors maintain knowledge of professional information related to the services they render.

a. Mental health counselors accurately represent their competence, education, training and experience.

b. As teachers, mental health counselors perform their duties based on careful preparation so that their instruction is accurate, up-to-date and scholarly.

c. Mental health counselors recognize the need for continuing training to prepare themselves to serve persons of all ages and cultural backgrounds. They are open to new procedures and sensitive to differences between groups of people and changes in expectations and values over time.

d. Mental health counselors with the responsibility for decisions involving individuals or policies based on test results should know and understand literature relevant to the tests used and testing problems with which they deal.

e. Mental health counselors and practitioners recognize that their effectiveness depends in part upon their ability to maintain sound interpersonal relations, that temporary or more enduring aberrations on their part may interfere with their abilities or distort their appraisals of others. Therefore, they refrain from undertaking any activity in which their personal problems are likely to lead to inadequate professional services or harm to a client, or, if they are already engaged in such activity when they become aware of their personal problems, they would seek competent professional assistance to determine whether they should suspend or terminate services to one or all of their clients.

f. The mental health counselor has a responsibility both to the individual who is served and to the institution with which the service is performed to maintain high standards of professional conduct. The mental health counselor strives to maintain the highest levels of professional services offered to the individuals to be served. The mental health counselor also strives to assist the agency, organization or institution in providing the highest caliber of professional services. The acceptance of employment in an institution implies that the mental health counselors is in substantial agreement with the general policies and principles of the institution. If, despite concerted efforts, the member cannot reach agreement with the employer as to acceptable standards of conduct that allow for changes in institutional policy conducive to the positive growth and development of counselors, then terminating the affiliation should be seriously considered.

g. Ethical behavior among professional associates, mental health counselors and non-mental health counselors, is expected at all times. When information is possessed which raises serious doubt as to the ethical behavior of professional colleagues, whether association members or not, the mental health counselor is obligated to take action to attempt to rectify such a condition. Such action shall utilize the institution's channels first and then utilize procedures established by the state, division, or association.

h. The mental health counselor is aware of the intimacy of the counseling relationship and maintains a healthy respect for the personhood of the client and avoids engaging in activities that seek to meet the mental health counselor's personal needs at the expense of the client. Through awareness of the negative impact of both racial and sexual stereotyping and discrimination, the member strives to ensure the individual rights and personal dignity of the client in the counseling relationship.

PRINCIPLE 3.   MORAL AND LEGAL STANDARDS

Mental health counselors moral, ethical and legal standards of behavior are a personal matter to the same degree as they are for any other citizen, except as these may compromise the fulfillment of their professional responsibilities, or reduce the trust in counseling or counselors held by the general public. Regarding their own behavior, mental health counselors should be aware of the prevailing community standards and of the possible impact upon the quality of professional services provided by their conformance to or deviation from these standards. Mental health counselors should also be aware of the possible impact of their public behavior upon the ability of colleagues to perform their professional duties.

a. To protect public confidence in the profession of counseling, mental health counselors will avoid public behavior that is clearly in violation of accepted moral and legal standards.

b. To protect students, mental health counselors/ teachers will be aware of the diverse backgrounds of students and, when dealing with topics that may give offense, will see that the material is treated objectively, that it is clearly relevant to the course, and that is treated in a manner for which the student is prepared.

c. Providers of counseling services conform to the statutes relating to such services as established by their state and its regulating professional board(s).

d. As employees, mental health counselors refuse to participate in employer's practices which are inconsistent with the moral and legal standards established by federal or state legislation regarding the treatment of employees or of the public. In particular and for example, mental health counselors will not condone practices which result in illegal or otherwise unjustifiable discrimination on the basis of race, sex, religion or national origin in hiring, promotion or training.

e. In providing counseling services to clients mental health counselors avoid any action that will violate or diminish the legal and civil rights of clients or of others who may be affected by the action.

f. Sexual conduct, not limited to sexual intercourse, between mental health counselors and clients is specifically in violation of this code of ethics. This does not, however, prohibit the use of explicit instructional aids including films and video tapes. Such use is within accepted practices of trained and competent sex therapists.

PRINCIPLE 4.   PUBLIC STATEMENTS

Mental health counselors in their professional roles may be expected or required to make public statements providing counseling information, professional opinions, or supply information about the availability of counseling products and services. In making such statement, mental health counselors take full account of the limits and uncertainties of present counseling knowledge and techniques. They represent, as objectively as possible, their professional qualification, affiliations, and functions, as well as those of the institutions or organizations with which the statements may be associated. All public statements, announcements of services, and promotional activities should serve the purpose of providing sufficient information to aid the consumer public in making informed judgments and choices on matters that concern it.

a. When announcing professional counseling services, mental health counselors limit the information to: name, highest relevant degree conferred, certification or licensure, address, telephone number, office hours, cost of services, and a brief explanation of the other types of services offered but not evaluative as to their quality or uniqueness. They will not contain testimonials by implication. They will not claim uniqueness of skill or methods beyond those acceptable and public scientific evidence.

b. In announcing the availability of counseling services or products, mental health counselors will not display their affiliations with organizations or agencies in a manner that implies the sponsorship or certification of the organization or agency. They will not name their employer or professional associations unless the services are in fact to be provided by or under the responsible, direct supervision and continuing control of such organizations or agencies.

c. Mental health counselors associated with the development of promotion of counseling device, books, or other products offered for commercial sale will make every effort to insure that announcements and advertisements are presented in a professional and factually informative manner without unsupported claims of superiority and must be supported by scientifically acceptable evidence or by willingness to aid and encourage independent professional scrutiny or scientific test.

d. Mental health counselors engaged in radio, television or other public media activities will not participate in commercial announcements recommending to the general public the purchase or use of any proprietary or single-source product or service.

e. Mental health counselors who describe counseling or the services of professional counselors to the general public accept the obligation to present the material fairly and accurately, avoiding misrepresentation through sensationalism, exaggeration or superficiality. Mental health counselors will be guided by the primary obligation to aid the public in forming their own informed judgments, opinions and choices.

f. As teachers, mental health counselors ensure their statements in catalogs and course outlines are accurate, particularly in terms of subject matter to be covered, bases for grading, and nature of classroom experiences.

g. Mental health counselors accept the obligation to correct others who may represent their professional qualifications or associations with products or services in a manner incompatible with these guidelines.

h. Mental health counselors providing consultation, workshops, training, and other technical services may refer to previous satisfied clients in their advertising, provided there is no implication that such advertising refers to counseling services.

PRINCIPLE 5.   CONFIDENTIALITY

Mental health counselors have a primary obligation to safeguard information about individuals obtained in the course of teaching, practice, or research. Personal information if communicated to others only with the person's written consent or in those circumstances where there is clear and imminent danger to the client, to others or to society. Disclosures of counseling information are restricted to what is necessary, relevant and verifiable.

a. All materials in the official record shall be shared with the client who shall have the right to decide what information may be shared with anyone beyond the immediate provider of service and to be informed of the implications of the materials to be shared.

b. The anonymity of clients served in public and other agencies is preserved, if at all possible, by withholding names and personal identifying data. If external conditions require reporting such information, the client shall be so informed.

c. Information received in confidence by one agency or person shall not be forwarded to another person or agency without the client's written permission.

d. Service providers have a responsibility to insure the accuracy and to indicate the validity of data shared with their parties.

e. Case reports presented in classes, professional meetings, or in publications shall be so disguised that no identification is possible unless the client or responsible authority has read the report and agreed in writing to its presentation or publication.

f. Counseling reports and records are maintained under conditions of security and provisions are made for their destruction when they have outlived their usefulness. Mental health counselors insure that privacy and confidentiality are maintained by all persons in the employ or volunteers, and community aides.

g. Mental health counselors who ask that an individual reveal personal information in the course of interviewing, testing or evaluation, or who allow such information to be divulged, do so only after making certain that the person or authorized representative is fully aware of the purposes of the interview, testing or evaluation and of the ways in which the information will be used.

h. Sessions with clients are taped or otherwise recorded only with their written permission or the written permission of a responsible guardian. Even with guardian written consent one should not record a session against the expressed wishes of a client.

i. Where a child or adolescent is the primary client, the interests of the minor shall be paramount.

j. In work with families, the rights of each family member should be safeguarded. The provider of service also has the responsibility to discuss the contents of the record with the parent and/or child, as appropriate, and to keep separate those parts which should remain the property of each family member.

PRINCIPLE 6.   WELFARE OF THE CONSUMER

Mental health counselors respect the integrity and protect the welfare of the people and groups with whom they work. When there is a conflict of interest between the client and the mental health counselor employing institution, the mental health counselors clarify the nature and direction of their loyalties and responsibilities and keep all parties informed of their commitments. Mental health counselors fully inform consumers as to the purpose and nature of any evaluative, treatment, educational or training procedure, and they freely acknowledge that clients, students, or subjects have freedom of choice with regard to participation.

a. Mental health counselors are continually cognizant both of their own needs and of their inherently powerful position *vis-a'-vis* clients, in order to avoid exploiting the client's trust and dependency. Mental health counselors make every effort to avoid dual relationships with clients and/or relationships which might impair their professional judgment or increase the risk of client exploitation. Examples of such dual relationships include treating an employee or supervisor, treating a close friend or family relative and sexual relationships with clients.

b. Where mental health counselors work with members of an organization goes beyond reasonable conditions of employment, mental health counselors recognize possible conflicts of interest that may arise. When such conflicts occur, mental health counselors clarify the nature of the conflict and inform all parties of the nature and directions of the loyalties and responsibilities involved.

c. When acting as supervisors, trainers, or employers, mental health counselors accord recipients informed choice, confidentiality, and protection from physical and mental harm.

d. Financial arrangements in professional practice are in accord with professional standards that safeguard the best interests of the client and that are clearly understood by the client in advance of billing. This may best be done by the use of a contract. Mental health counselors are responsible for assisting clients in finding needed services in those instances where payment of the usual fee would be a hardship. No commission or rebate or other form of remuneration may be given or received for referral of clients for professional services, whether by an individual or by an agency.

e. Mental health counselors are responsible for making their services readily accessible to clients in a manner that facilitates the client's ability to make an informed choice when selecting a service provider. This responsibility includes a clear description of what the client may expect in the way of tests, reports, billing, therapeutic regime and schedules and the use of mental health counselor's statement of professional disclosure.

f. Mental health counselors who find that their services are not beneficial to the client have the responsibility to make this know to the responsible persons.

g. Mental health counselors are accountable to the parties who refer and support counseling services and to the general public and are cognizant of the indirect or long-range effects of their intervention.

h. The mental health counselor attempts to terminate a private service or consulting relationship when it is reasonably clear to the mental health counselor that the consumer is not benefiting from it. If a consumer is receiving services from another mental health professional, mental health counselors do not offer their services directly to the consumer without informing the professional persons already involved in order to avoid confusion and conflict for the consumer.

i. The mental health counselor has the responsibility to screen prospective group participants, especially when the emphasis is on self-understanding and growth through self-disclosure. The member should maintain an awareness of the group participants compatibility throughout the life of the group.

j. The mental health counselor may choose to consult with any other professionally competent person about a client. In choosing a consultant, the mental health counselor should avoid placing the consultant in a conflict of interest situation that would preclude the consultant's being a proper party to the mental health counselors efforts to help the clients.

k. If the mental health counselor is unable to be of professional assistance to the client, the mental health counselor should avoid initiating the counseling relationship or the mental health counselor terminates the relationship. In either event, the member is obligated to suggest appropriate alternatives. (It is incumbent upon the mental health counselors to be knowledgeable about referral resources so that a satisfactory referral can be initiated.) In the event the client declines the suggested referral, the mental health counselor is not obligated to continue the relationship.

l. When the mental health counselor has other relationships, particularly of an administrative, supervisory, and/or evaluative nature, with an individual seeking counseling services, the mental health counselor should not serve as the counselor but should refer the individual to another professional. Only in instances where such an alternative is unavailable and where the individual's situation definitely warrants counseling intervention should the mental health counselor enter into and/or maintain a counseling relationship. Dual relationships with clients which might impair the member's objectivity and professional judgment (such as with close friends or relatives, sexual intimacies with any client, etc.) must be avoided and/or the counseling relationship terminated through referral to another competent professional.

m. All experimental methods of treatment must be clearly indicated to prospective recipients, and safety precautions are to be adhered to by the mental health counselor instituting treatment.

n. When the member is engaged in short-term group treatment/training programs e.g., marathons and other encounter-type or growth groups, the member ensures that there is professional assistance available during and following the group experience.

PRINCIPLE 7.   PROFESSIONAL RELATIONSHIPS

Mental health counselors act with due regard to the needs and feelings of their colleagues in counseling and other professions. Mental health counselors respect the prerogatives and obligations of the institutions or organizations with which they are associated.

a. Mental health counselors understand the areas of competence of related professions and make full use of other professional, technical, and administrative resources which best serve the interests of consumers. The absence of formal relationships with other professional workers does not relieve mental health counselors from the responsibility of securing for their clients the best possible professional service; indeed, this circumstance presents a challenge to the professional competence of mental health counselors, requiring special sensitivity to problems outside their areas of training, and foresight, diligence, and tact in obtaining the professional assistance needed by clients.

b. Mental health counselors know and take into account the traditions and practices of other professional groups with which they work and cooperate fully with members of such groups when research, services, and other functions are shared or in working for the benefit of public welfare.

c. Mental health counselors strive to provide positive conditions for those they employ and they spell out clearly the conditions of such employment. They encourage their employees to engage in activities that facilitate their further professional development.

d. Mental health counselors respect the viability, reputation, and the proprietary right of organizations which they serve. Mental health counselors show due regard for the interest of their present or prospective employers. In those instances where they are critical of policies, they attempt to effect change by constructive action within the organization.

e. In the pursuit of research, mental health counselors give sponsoring agencies, host institutions, and publication channels the same respect and opportunity for giving informed consent that they accord to individual research participants. They are aware of their obligation to future research workers and insure that host institutions are given feedback information and proper acknowledgment.

f. Credit is assigned to those who have contributed to a publication, in proportion to their contribution.

g. When a mental health counselor violates ethical standards, mental health counselors who know firsthand of such activities should, if possible, attempt to rectify the situation. Failing an informal solution, mental health counselors should bring such unethical activities to the attention of the appropriate state, and/or national committee on ethics and professional conduct. Only after all professional alternatives have been utilized will a mental health counselor begin legal action for resolution.

PRINCIPLE 8.   UTILIZATION OF ASSESSMENT TECHNIQUES

In the development, publication, and utilization of counseling assessment techniques, mental health counselors follow relevant standards. Individuals examined, or their legal guardians, have the right to know the results, the interpretations made, and where appropriate, the particulars on which final judgment was based. Test users should take precautions to protect test security but not at the expense of an individual's right to understand the basis for decisions that adversely affect that individual or that individual's dependents.

a. The client has the right to have and the provider has the responsibility to give explanations of test results in language the client can understand.

b. When a test is published or otherwise made available for operational use, it should be accompanied by a manual (or other published or readily available information) that makes every reasonable effort to describe fully the development of the test, the rationale, specifications followed in writing items analysis or other research. The test, the manual, the record forms and other accompanying material should help users make correct interpretations of the test results and should warn against common misuses. The test manual should state explicitly the purposes and applications for which the test is recommended and identify any special qualifications required to administer the test and to interpret it properly. Evidence of validity and reliability, along with other relevant research data, should be presented in support of any claims made.

c. Norms presented in test manuals should refer to defined and clearly described populations. These populations should be the groups with whom users of the test will ordinarily wish to compare the persons tested. Test users should consider the possibility of bias in tests or in test items. When indicated, there should be an investigation of possible differences in validity for ethnic, sex, or other subsamples that can be identified when the test is given.

d. Mental health counselors who have the responsibility for decisions about individuals or policies that are based on test results should have a thorough understanding of counseling or educational measurement and of validation and other test research.

e. Mental health counselors should develop procedures for systematically eliminating from data files test score information that has, because of the lapse of time, become obsolete.

f. Any individual or organization offering test scoring and interpretation services must be able to demonstrate that their programs are based on appropriate research to establish the validity of the programs and procedures used in arriving at interpretations. The public offering of an automated test interpretation service will be considered as a professional-to-professional consultation. In this the formal responsibility of the consultant is to the consultee but his/her ultimate and overriding responsibility is to the client.

g. Counseling services for the purpose of diagnosis, treatment, or personalized advice are provided only in the context of a professional relationship, and are not given by means of public lectures or demonstrations, newspapers or magazine articles, radio or television programs, mail, or similar media. The preparation of personnel reports and recommendations based on test data secured solely by mail is unethical unless such appraisals are an integral part of a continuing client relationship with a company, as a result of which the consulting clinical mental health counselor has intimate knowledge of the client's personal situation and can be assured thereby that his written appraisals will be adequate to the purpose and will be properly interpreted by the client. These reports must not be embellished with such detailed analyses of the subject's personality traits as would be appropriate only for intensive interviews with the subjects.

PRINCIPLE 9.   PURSUIT OF RESEARCH ACTIVITIES

The decision to undertake research should rest upon a considered judgment by the individual mental health counselor about how best to contribute to counseling and to human welfare. Mental health counselors carry out their investigations with respect for the people who participate and with concern for their dignity and welfare.

a. In planning a study the investigator has the personal responsibility to make a careful evaluation of its ethical acceptability, taking into account the following principles for research with human beings. To the extent that this appraisal, weighing scientific and humane values, suggests a deviation from any principle, the investigator incurs an increasingly serious obligation to seek ethical advice and to observe more stringent safeguards to protect the rights of the human research participants.

b. Mental health counselors know and take into account the traditions and practices of other professional groups with members of such groups when research, services, and other functions are shared or in working for the benefit of public welfare.

c. Ethical practice requires the investigator to inform the participant of all features of the research that reasonably might be expected to influence willingness to participate, and to explain all other aspects of the research about which the participant inquires. Failure to make full disclosure gives added emphasis to the investigators abiding responsibility to protect the welfare and dignity of the research participant.

d. Openness and honesty are essential characteristics of the relationship between investigator and research participant. When the methodological requirements of a study necessitate concealment or deception, the investigator is required to insure as soon as possible the participant's understanding of the reasons for this action and to restore the quality of the relationship with the investigator.

e. In the pursuit of research, mental health counselors give sponsoring agencies, host institutions, and publication channels the same respect and opportunity for giving informed consent that they accord to individual research participants. They are aware of their obligation to future research workers and insure that host institutions are given feedback information and proper acknowledgment.

f. Credit is assigned to those who have contributed to a publication, in proportion to their contribution.

g. The ethical investigator protects participants from physical and mental discomfort, harm and danger. If the risk of such consequences exists, the investigator is required to inform the participant of that fact, secure consent before proceeding, and take all possible measures to minimize distress. A research procedure may not be used if it is likely to cause serious and lasting harm to participants.

h. After the data are collected, ethical practice requires the investigator to provide the participant with a full clarification of the nature of the study and to remove any misconceptions that may have arisen. Where scientific or humane values justify delaying or withholding information the investigator acquires a special responsibility to assure that there are no damaging consequences for the participants.

i. Where research procedure may result in undesirable consequences for the participant, the investigator has the responsibility to detect and remove or correct these consequences, including, where relevant, long-term after effects.

j. Information obtained about the research participants during the course of an investigation is confidential. When the possibility exists that others may obtain access to such information, ethical research practice requires that the possibility, together with the plans for protecting confidentiality be explained to the participants as a part of the procedure for obtaining informed consent.

PRINCIPLE 10.   PRIVATE PRACTICE

a. A mental health counselor should assist where permitted by legislation or judicial decision the profession in fulfilling its duty to make counseling services available in private settings.

b. In advertising services as a private practitioner the mental health counselor should advertise the services in such a manner so as to accurately inform the public as to services, expertise, profession, techniques of counseling in a professional manner. A mental health counselor who assumes an executive leadership role in the organization shall not permit his/her name to be used in professional notices during periods when not actively engaged in the private practice of counseling. The mental health counselor may list the following: highest relevant degree, type and level of certification or license, type and/or description of services and other relevant information. Such information should not contain false, inaccurate, misleading, partial, out-of-context or deceptive material or statements.

c. The mental health counselors may join in partnership/corporation with other mental health counselors and/or other professionals provided that each mental health counselor of the partnership or corporation makes clear the separate

specialties by name in compliance with the regulations of the locality.

d. A mental health counselor has an obligation to withdraw from a counseling relationship if it is believed that employment will result in violation of the code of ethics, if their mental capacity or physical condition renders it difficult to carry out an effective professional relationship, or if the mental health counselor is discharged by the client because the counseling relationship is no longer productive for the client.

e. A mental health counselor should adhere to and support the regulations for private practice of the locality where the services are offered.

f. Mental health counselors are discouraged from deliberate attempts to utilize one's institutional affiliation to recruit clients for one's private practice. Mental health counselors are to refrain from offering their services in the private sector, when they are employed by an institution in which this is prohibited by stated policies reflecting conditions for employment.

PRINCIPLE 11.   CONSULTING

a. The mental health counselor acting as consultant must have a high degree of self-awareness of his/her own values, knowledge, skills and needs in entering a helping relationship which involves human and/or organizational change and that the focus of the relationship be on the issues to be resolved and not on the person(s) presenting the problem.

b. There should be understanding and agreement between the mental health counselor and client for the problem definition, change goals and predicted consequences of interventions selected.

c. The mental health counselor must be reasonably certain that she/he or the organization represented have the necessary competencies and resources for giving the kind of help which is needed now or may develop later and that appropriate referral resources are available to the consultant, if needed later.

d. The mental health counselor relationship must be one in which client adaptability and growth

toward self-direction are encouraged and cultivated. The mental health counselor must maintain this role consistently and not become a decision maker or substitute for the client.

e. When announcing consultant availability for services, the mental health counselor conscientiously adheres to professional standards.

f. The mental health counselor is expected to
refuse a private fee or other remuneration for
consultation with persons who are entitled to
these services through the member's employing
institution or agency. The policies of a particular
agency may make explicit provisions for private
practice with agency counselees by members of
its staff. In such instances, the counselees must
be apprised of other options open to them should
they seek private counseling services.

PRINCIPLE 12.   CLIENTS' RIGHTS

The following apply to all consumers of mental health
services, including both in- and out-patients in all
state, county, local, and private care mental health facilities, as well as clients of mental health practitioners in private practice.

The client has the right:

a. to be treated with consideration and respect;

b. to expect quality service provided by concerned,
competent staff;

c. to a clear statement of the purposes, goals, techniques, rules of procedure, and limitations as well
as potential dangers of the services to be performed and all other information related to or likely
to affect the on-going counseling relationship;

d. to obtain information about their case record and
to have this information explained clearly and directly;

e. to full, knowledgeable, and responsible participation in the on-going treatment plan, to the maximum feasible extent;

f. to expect complete confidentiality and that no
information will be released without written
consent.

g. to see and discuss their charges and payment
records; and

h. to refuse any recommended services and be advised of the consequences of this action.

SOURCE: Adopted by AMHCA Board of Directors
Revised 1987. Reprinted eith permission of the American
Counseling Association.

RESPONSIBILITIES OF USERS OF STANDARDIZED TESTS

I. INTRODUCTION

Background:

At the 1976 AACD (then APGA) Convention, the Board of Directors requested the development of a statement on the responsible use of standardized tests to promote proper test use, reflecting the advantages of assessment along with concerns about negative effects, and to help its members employ safeguards against misuse of tests. A committee representing all AACD Divisions and Regions spent two years studying the issues and developed a statement, published in the October, 1978, issue of *Guidepost,* titled "Responsibilities of Users of Standardized Tests." The Association for Measurement and Evaluation in Counseling and Development was charged with maintaining ongoing review of the so-called RUST Statement. The present statement has grown out of that review.

Target Audience:

The statement is intended to address the needs of the members of AACD and its Divisions, Branches, and Regions, including counselors and other human service workers. Although it may interest test developers, teachers, administrators, parents, the press, or the general public, it is not specifically designed for these audiences.

Organization and Focus:

The statement is organized into eight sections: Introduction, Test Decisions, Qualifications of Test Users, Test Selection, Test Administration, Test Scoring, Test Interpretation, and Communicating Test Results. Basic to the statement is the assumption that test data are merely numbers and that guidelines can help to promote their constructive use. The statement specifies general principles and activities which constitute responsible practice. These are grouped around similar issues and are indexed for ease of reference.

II. TEST DECISIONS:

Decisions should be based on data. In general, test data improve the quality of decisions. However, deciding whether or not to test creates the possibility of three kinds of errors. First, a decision not to test can result in misjudgments that stem from inadequate or subjective data. Second, tests may produce data which could improve accuracy in decisions affecting the client, but which are not used in counseling. Third, tests may be misused. The responsible practitioner will determine, in advance, the purpose for administering a given test, considering protections and benefits for the client, practitioner, and agency.

A. Define purposes for testing by developing specific objectives and limits for the use of test data in relation to the particular assessment purpose:

1. Placement: If the purpose is selection or placement, the test user should understand the programs or institutions into which the client may be placed and be able to judge the consequences of inclusion or exclusion decisions for the client.

2. Prediction: If the purpose is prediction, the test user should understand the need for predictive data as well as possible negative consequences (e.g., stereotyping).

3. Description: If the purpose is diagnosis or description, the test user should understand the general domain being measured and be able to identify those aspects which are adequately measured and those which are not.

4. Growth: If the purpose is to examine growth or change, the test user should understand the practical and theoretical difficulties associated with such measurement.

5. Program Evaluation: If the purpose of assessment is the evaluation of an agency's programs, the test user should be aware of the various information needs for the evaluation and of the limitations of each instrument used to assess those needs, as well as how the evaluation will be used.

B. Determine Information Needs and Assessment Needs:

1. Determine whether testing is intended to assess individuals, groups, or both.
2. Identify the particular individual and/or group to be tested with regard to the agency's purposes and capabilities.
3. Determine the limitations to testing created by an individual's age; racial, sexual, ethnic, and cultural background; or other characteristics.
4. Avoid unnecessary testing by identifying decisions which can be made with existing information.
5. Assess the consequences for clients of deciding either to test or not to test.
6. Limit data gathering to the variables that are needed for the particular purpose.
7. Cross-validate test data using other available information whenever possible.

III. QUALIFICATIONS OF TEST USERS:

While all professional counselors and personnel workers should have formal training in psychological and educational measurement and testing, this training does not necessarily make one an expert and even an expert does not have all the knowledge and skills appropriate to some particular situations or instruments. Questions of user qualifications should always be addressed when testing is being considered.

Lack of proper qualifications can lead to errors and subsequent harm to clients. Each professional is responsible for making judgments on this in each situation and cannot leave that responsibility either to clients or to others in authority. It is incumbent upon the individual test user to obtain appropriate training or arrange for proper supervision and assistance when engaged in testing. Qualifications for test users depend on four factors:

A. Purposes of Testing: Technically proper testing for ill-understood purposes may constitute misuse. Because the purposes of testing dictate how the results are used, qualifications of test users are needed beyond general testing competencies to interpret and apply data.
B. Characteristics of Tests: Understanding the nature and limitations of each instrument used is needed by test users.

C. Settings and Conditions of Test Use: Assessment of the quality and relevance of test user knowledge and skill to the situation is needed before deciding to test or to participate in a testing program.
D. Roles of Test Selectors, Administrators, Scorers and Interpreters: Test users must be engaged in only those testing activities for which their training and experience qualify them.

IV. TEST SELECTION:

The selection of tests should be guided by information obtained from a careful analysis of the characteristics of the population to be tested; the knowledge, skills, abilities or attitudes to be assessed; the purposes for testing; and the eventual use and interpretation of the test scores. Use of tests should also be guided by criteria for technical quality recommended by measurement professionals (i.e., the APA/AERA/NCME "Standards for Educational and Psychological Tests" and the APA/AERA/NCME/ AACD/ASHA "Code of Fair Testing Practices in Education").

A. Relate Validity to Usage:

1. Determine the validity of a test (whether the test measures what is meant to be measured) through evidence of the constructs used in developing the test, the correlation of the test performance with other appraisals of the characteristics being measured, and/or the predictions of specified behaviors from the test performance.
2. Determine whether a test is congruent with the users' definition of the characteristics of human performance to be appraised.
3. Use tests for selection purposes only when they show predictive validity for the specific tasks or competencies needed in an educational or employment experience and when they maintain legal and ethical prescriptions for non-discriminatory practices in program selection, employment, or placement.

B. Use Appropriate Tests:

1. Document tests as appropriate for the characteristics of the population to be tested.

2. Only use tests within the level of skills of administration and interpretation possessed by the practitioner.

3. Use tests consistent with local needs:
   a. Give attention to how the test is designed to handle variation of motivation, working speed, language facility, and experiential background among persons taking it; bias in response to its content; and effects of guessing in response to its questions.
   b. Determine whether a common test or different tests are required for accurate measurement of groups with special characteristics.
      i. Recognize that the use of different tests for cultural, ethnic and racial groups may constitute ineffective means for making corrections for differences.
      ii. Determine whether persons or groups that use different languages should be tested in either or both languages and in some instances, tested first for bilingualism or language dominance.

C. Consider Technical Characteristics:
   1. Select only tests that have documented evidence of reliability or consistency.
   2. Select only tests that have adequate documented evidence of the effectiveness of the measure for the purpose to be served and justification of the inferences based on the results.
   3. Scrutinize standardization and norming procedures for relevance to the local population and use of the data.
   4. Use separate norms for men and women or other subgroups when empirical evidence indicates they are appropriate.
   5. Determine the degree of technical quality demanded of a test on the basis of the nature of the decisions to be made.
   6. Include ease and accuracy of the procedures for scoring, summarizing, and communicating test performance among the criteria for selecting a test.
   7. Consider practical constraints of cost, conditions, and time for testing as secondary test selection criteria.

D. Employ User Participation in Test Selection: Actively involve everyone who will be using the assessments (administering, scoring, summarizing, interpreting, making decisions) as appropriate in the selection of tests so that they are congruent with local purposes, conditions, and uses.

V. TEST ADMINISTRATION:

Test administration includes procedures to ensure that the test is used in the manner specified by the test developers and that the individuals being tested are working within conditions which maximize opportunity for optimum, comparable performance.

A. Provide Proper Orientation:
   1. Inform testing candidates, parents, and institutions or agencies in the community as appropriate about the testing procedures. The orientation should make the test meaningful for the individual or group being tested, and should include the purposes of the test, the kinds of tasks it involves, how it is administered and how the scores will be reported and used.
   2. Provide persons being tested sufficient practice experiences prior to the test.
   3. Prior to testing, check all test takers' ability to record their responses adequately (e.g., in the use of machine-scorable answer sheets).
   4. Provide periodic training by qualified personnel for test administrators within agencies or institutions using tests.
   5. Review test materials and administration sites and procedures prior to the time for testing to ensure standardized conditions and appropriate response to any irregularities which may occur.

B. Use Qualified Test Administrators:
   1. Acquire any training required to administer the test.
   2. Ensure that individuals taking self-administered or self-scored instruments have the necessary understanding and competencies.

C. Provide Appropriate Testing Conditions:
   1. Ensure that the testing environment (seating, work surfaces, lighting, heating, freedom

from distractions, etc.) and psychological climate is conducive to the best possible performance of the test-takers.

2. Carefully observe, record, and attach to the test record any deviation from prescribed test administration procedure.

3. Use a systematic and objective procedure for observing and recording environmental, health, or emotional factors, or other elements which may invalidate test performance. This record should be attached to the test scores of the persons tested.

4. Use sufficiently trained personnel to provide uniform conditions and to observe the conduct of the examinees when large groups of individuals are tested.

D. Give Proper Directions:

1. Present each test in the manner prescribed in the test manual to ensure that it is fair to each test taker.

2. Administer standardized tests with the verbatim instructions, exact sequence and timing, and identical materials that were used in the test standardization.

3. Demonstrate verbal clarity, calmness, empathy for the examinees, and impartiality toward all being tested. Because taking a test may be a new and frightening experience or stimulate anxiety or frustration for some individuals, the examinees should attempt each task with positive application of their skills and knowledge and the expectation that they will do their best.

E. Coordinate Professional Collaboration: In settings where skill and knowledge is pooled and responsibility shared, consider the qualifications of the testing team as a whole as more important than those of individuals. However, coordination and consistency of responsibilities with expertise must be maintained.

VI. TEST SCORING:

Accurate measurement of human performance necessitates adequate procedures for scoring the responses of examinees. These procedures must be audited as necessary to ensure consistency and accuracy of application.

A. Consider Accuracy and Interpretability: Select a test scoring process that maximizes accuracy and interpretability.

B. Rescore Samples: Routinely rescore samples of examinee responses to monitor the accuracy of the scoring process.

C. Screen Test Results: Screen reports of test results using personnel competent to recognize unreasonable or impossible scores.

D. Verify Scores and Norms: Verify the accuracy of computation of raw scores and conversion to normative scales prior to release of such information to examinees or users of test results.

E. Communicate Deviations: Report as part of the official record any deviation from normal conditions and examinee behaviors.

F. Label Results: Clearly label the date of test administration along with the scores.

VII. TEST INTERPRETATION:

Test interpretation encompasses all the ways that meaning is assigned to the scores. Proper interpretation requires knowledge about the test which can be obtained by studying its manual and other materials along with current research literature with respect to its use; no one should undertake the interpretation of scores on any test without such study.

A. Consider Reliability: Reliability is important because it is a prerequisite to validity and because the degree to which a score may vary due to measurement error is an important factor in its interpretation.

1. Estimate test stability using a reliability (or other appropriate) coefficient.

2. Use the standard error of measurement to estimate the amount of variation due to random error in individual scores and to evaluate the precision of cut-scores in selection decisions.

3. Consider, in relationship to the uses being made of the scores, variance components attributed to error in the reliability index.

4. Evaluate reliability estimates with regard to factors that may have artificially raised or lowered them (e.g., test speededness, biases in population sampling).

5. Distinguish indices of objectivity (i.e., scorer reliability) from test reliability.

B. Consider Validity: Proper test interpretation requires knowledge of the validity evidence available for the intended use of the test. Its validity for other uses is not relevant. Indeed, use of a measure for a purpose for which it was not designed may constitute misuse. The nature of the validity evidence required for a test depends upon its use.

1. Use for Placement: Predictive validity is the usual basis for valid placement.

  a. Obtain adequate information about the programs or institutions in which the client may be placed to judge the consequences of such placement.

  b. Use all available evidence to infer the validity of an individual's score. A single test score should not be the sole basis for a placement or selection recommendation. Other items of information about an individual (e.g., teacher report, counselor opinion) frequently improve the likelihood that proper judgments and decisions will be made.

  c. Consider validity for each alternative (i.e., each placement option) when interpreting test scores and other evidence.

  d. Examine the possibility that a client's group membership (socioeconomic status, gender, subculture, etc.) may affect test performance and, consequently, validity.

  e. Estimate the probability of favorable outcomes for each possible placement before making recommendations.

  f. Consider the possibility that outcomes favorable from an institutional point of view may differ from those that are favorable from the individual's point of view.

2. Use for Prediction: The relationship of the test scores to an independently developed criterion measure is the basis for predictive validity.

  a. Consider the reliability and validity of the criterion measure(s) used.

  b. Consider the validity of a measure in the context of other predictors available (i.e., does the test make a valid contribution to prediction beyond that provided by other measures).

  c. Use cross validation to judge the validity of prediction processes.

  d. Consider the effects of labeling, stereotyping, and prejudging people (e.g., self-fulfilling prophecies that may result from labeling are usually undesirable).

  e. If a statistically valid predictor lacks both construct and content validity, analyze the mechanism by which it operates to determine whether or not its predictive validity is spurious.

3. Use for Description: Comprehensiveness of information is fundamental to effective description, since no set of test scores completely describes an individual.

  a. Clearly identify the domain assessed by any measure and the adequacy of the content sampling procedures used in developing items.

  b. Clarify the dimensions being measured when multiple scores from a battery or inventory are used for description.

    i. Examine the content and/or construct validity of each score separately.

    ii. Consider the relative importance of each of the separate elements for interpretation.

    iii. Give appropriate weights to reflect the variabilities (e.g., standard deviations) and relationships (e.g., correlations) of scores which are to be combined.

  c. Distinguish characteristics that can be validated only empirically and those for which content specifications exist.

4. Use for Assessment of Growth: Assessment of growth or change requires valid tests as well as a valid procedure for combining them.

  a. Specifically evaluate the reliability of differences between scores as measures of change.

  b. Establish the validities of the measures used to establish change in relation to one another as well as individually.

  c. Consider comparability of intervals in scales used to assess change.

i. Evaluate derived or extrapolated scores (e.g., grade equivalents) for possible different meanings at different score levels.

ii. Consider problems in interpretation and comparability of tests (e.g. floor or ceiling effects, content changes from level to level, poor articulation in multilevel tests, lack of comparability of alternate forms, inadequacy of score-equating across forms, and differences in administration and timing of tests from that of their norming).

d. Assess potential for undesirable correlations of difference scores with the measures entering into their calculations (e.g., regression toward the mean).

e. Recognize the potential lack of comparability between norms for differences derived from norms and norms for differences derived from differences (i.e. mathematically derived norms for differences are not necessarily equivalent to norms based on distributions of actual differences).

5. Use for Program Evaluation: Assessments of group differences (between groups or within groups over time) are based on research designs which to varying degrees admit competing interpretations of the results.

a. Use procedures in the evaluation which ensure that no factors other than those being studied have major influence on the results (i.e., internal validity).

b. Use statistical procedures which are appropriate and have all assumptions met by the data being analyzed.

c. Evaluate the generalizability (external validity) of the results for different individuals, settings, tests, and variables.

C. Scores, Norms, and Related Technical Features: The result of scoring a test or subtest is usually a number called a raw score which by itself is not interpretable. Additional steps are needed to translate the number directly into either a verbal description (e.g., pass or fail) or into a derived score (e.g., a standard score). Less than full understanding of these procedures is likely to produce errors in interpretation and ultimately in counseling or other uses.

1. Examine appropriate test materials (e.g., manuals, handbooks, users' guides, and technical reports) to identify the descriptions or derived scores produced and their unique characteristics.

a. Know the operational procedures for translating raw scores into descriptions or derived scores.

b. Know specific psychological or educational concepts or theories before interpreting the scores of tests based on them.

c. Consider differential validity along with equating error when different tests, different test forms, or scores on the same test administered at different times are compared.

2. Clarify arbitrary standards used in interpretation (e.g., mastery or nonmastery for criterion-referenced tests).

a. Recognize that when a score is interpreted based on a proportion score (e.g., percent correct), its elements are being given arbitrary weights.

b. Recognize that the difficulty of a fixed standard (e.g., 80 percent right) varies widely and thus does not have the same meaning for different content areas and for different assessment methods.

c. Report the number (or percentage) of items right in addition to the interpretation when it will help others understand the quality of the examinee's performance.

3. Employ derived scores based on norms which fit the needs of the current use of the test.

a. Evaluate whether available norm groups are appropriate as part of the process of interpreting the scores of clients.

i. Use norms for the group to which the client belongs.

ii. Recognize that derived scores based on different norm groups may not be comparable.

iii. Use local norms and derived scores based on them whenever possible.

b. Choose a score based on its intended use.

       i. Consider relative standing scores (e.g., percentile ranks) for comparison of individuals to the norm or reference group.

      ii. Consider standard or scaled scores whenever means and variances or other arithmetic operations are appropriate.

     iii. When using a statistical technique, use the test's derived score which best meets the assumptions of the analysis.

D. Administration and Scoring Variation: Stated criteria for score interpretations assume standard procedures for administering and scoring the test. Departures from standard conditions and procedures modify and often invalidate these criteria.

1. Evaluate unusual circumstances peculiar to the administration and scoring of the test.

   a. Examine reports from administrators, proctors, and scorers concerning irregularities or unusual conditions (e.g., excessive anxiety) for possible effects on test performance.

   b. Consider potential effects of examiner-examinee differences in ethnic and cultural background, attitudes, and values based on available relevant research.

   c. Consider any reports of examinee behavior indicating the responses were made on some basis other than that intended.

   d. Consider differences among clients in their reaction to instructions about guessing and scoring.

2. Evaluate scoring irregularities (e.g., machine scoring errors) and bias and judgment effects when subjective elements enter into scoring.

VIII. COMMUNICATING TEST RESULTS:

The responsible counselor or other practitioner reports test data with a concern for the individual's need for information and the purposes of the information. There must also be protection of the right of the person tested to be informed about how the results will be used and what safeguards exist to prevent misuse (right to information) and about who will have access to the results (right to privacy).

A. Decisions About Individuals: Where test data are used to enhance decisions about an individual, the practitioner's responsibilities include:

1. Limitations on Communication:

   a. Inform the examinee of possible actions that may be taken by any person or agency who will be using the results.

   b. Limit access to users specifically authorized by the law or by the client.

   c. Obtain the consent of the examinee before using test results for any purpose other than those advanced prior to testing.

2. Practitioner Communication Skills:

   a. Develop the ability to interpret test results accurately before attempting to communicate them.

   b. Develop appropriate communication skills, particularly with respect to concepts that are commonly misunderstood by the intended audience, before attempting to explain test results to clients, the public, or other recipients of the information.

3. Communication of Limitations of the Assessment:

   a. Inform persons receiving test information that scores are not perfectly accurate and indicate the degree of inaccuracy in some way, such as by reporting score intervals.

   b. Inform persons receiving test information of any circumstances that could have affected the validity or reliability of the results.

   c. Inform persons receiving test information of any factors necessary to understand potential sources of bias for a given test result.

   d. Communicate clearly that test data represent just one source of information and should rarely, if ever, be used alone for decision making.

4. Communication of Client Rights:

   a. Provide test takers or their parents or guardians with information about any rights they may have to obtain test copies and/or their completed answer sheets, to retake tests, to have tests rescored, or to cancel test scores.

b. Inform test takers or their parents or guardians about how long the test scores will remain on file along with the persons to whom, and circumstances under which, they may be released.

c. Describe the procedures test takers or their parents or guardians may use to register complaints or have problems resolved.

B. Decisions About Groups: Where standardized test data are being used to describe groups for the purpose of evaluation, the practitioner's responsibilities include:

1. Background Information:
   a. Identify the purposes for which the reported data are appropriate.
   b. Include additional information (e.g., population characteristics) if it can improve accuracy of understanding.

2. Averages and Norms:
   a. Clarify the amount of meaning that can be attached to differences between groups (e.g., statistical significance should not be taken as a judgment of importance).
   b. Qualify norms based on their appropriateness for the group being tested.

3. Use obsolescence schedules so that stored data are systematically relocated to historical files or destroyed.

4. Process data used for research or program evaluation to assure individual anonymity (e.g., released only in aggregated form).

5. Political Usage:
   a. Emphasize that test data should be used only for the test's stated purposes.
   b. Public release of test information provides data for many purposes. Take steps to minimize those which may be adverse to the interests of those tested.

6. Agency Policies:
   a. Advocate agency test-reporting policies designed to benefit the groups being measured.
   b. Advocate the establishment of procedures for periodic review of test use.

IX. EXTENSIONS OF THESE PRINCIPLES:

This statement is intended to address current and emerging problems and concerns that are generic to all AACD divisions, branches, and regions by formulating principles that are specific enough to serve as a template for more closely focused statements addressed to specific situations. Individual divisions, branches, and regions are encouraged to elaborate upon this statement to reflect principles, procedures, and examples appropriate to their members.

SOURCE: Reprinted by permission of the American Counseling Association, 1987.

This revision of the 1978 RUST Statement was prepared by a standing committee of AMECD chaired by William D. Schafer. Participating in the revision were Esther E. Diamond, Charles G. Eberly, Patricia B. Elmore, Jo-Ida C. Hansen, William A. Mehrens, Jane E. Myers, Larry Rawlins, and Alan G. Robertson.

Additional copies of the RUST Statement may be obtained from the American Association for Counseling and Development, 5999 Stevenson Avenue, Alexandria, VA 22304. Single copies are free.

Career and Rehabilitation Counseling

The specialties of career counseling and rehabilitation counseling have a common origin in the tremendous interest in vocational guidance and counseling that began in the early decades of the 20th century. Both fields evolved out of powerful events in the history of the United States: societal changes surrounding the Industrial Revolution and immigration patterns in the late 1800s and early 1900s, the Great Depression, and World Wars I and II. The resulting needs to understand the world of work, how to best prepare individuals to enter it, and how to find a suitable match between the demands of the workplace and the skills and needs of individuals within it, became leading concerns during these critical times. Whether those requiring guidance and counseling were students, adults with industrial injuries, or veterans, the need to understand the individual and how that person's individual needs and skills could be used to find a satisfying and satisfactory match with vocational opportunities became a powerful impetus to both these fields.

There was significant social and political support for studying the world of work and training professionals to help people make vocational choices and adjust to problems of vocational placement. Both career and rehabilitation counseling received significant legislative support for the emergence and continued growth of information and methods in their fields. The evolution of both career and rehabilitation counseling has been influenced greatly by social and cultural forces affecting Americans' work lives and the legislation and programs created as a result of these forces.

Although closely related since their inception, rehabilitation counseling and career counseling have taken on individualized identities. Their services and professional development have been tailored to the needs of the populations they have specialized in serving. Historically, rehabilitation counselors have adapted their vocational approaches to meet the needs of people with disabilities across various settings, while career counselors have focused on vocational counseling of nondisabled people facing career planning and choice issues. This parallel evolution has resulted in complementary development of knowledge and skills that can be drawn on by both fields.

Vocational counseling underlies both career and rehabilitation counseling. Parsons (1909) is credited with defining practice in the field of career or vocational guidance through the development of the theoretical model underlying the trait and factor approaches that have permeated the development of career and rehabilitation counseling (Salomone, 1996; Zunker, 1994). This model of career counseling identifies three core factors in vocational choice: (a) a clear self-understanding; (b) a knowledge of occupations; and (c) the ability to understand relationships between the self and information about occupations. The traditional focus of both specializations has been on counseling with individuals to help them successfully enter the world of work. This theoretical underpinning is shared with counseling psychology, a specialty within psychology, that is represented in the American Psychological Association by Division 17 (Counseling Psychology). Counseling psychology had an early and significant influence on the evolution of vocational counseling and psychology. Historically, these professionals have done extensive vocational counseling, and their most frequent employment settings are in educational settings such as colleges and universities. In the evolution of counseling psychology's research base and the training model that has guided its curriculum, many scholarly and practice interventions have been added that enhance the skills and knowledge available to all career counselors.

Over time, these specializations have elaborated on the importance of placing work within the context of other life pursuits. It has long been recognized that many clients of career counselors cannot make vocational decisions as a result of personal or psychological problems, for which they may need counseling before they can successfully deal with the vocational issues facing them. More recently, career counseling has increasingly taken a total life-role perspective to understand the place of work within the total context of people's lives (Brown & Brooks, 1991). This holistic focus primarily has been pursued through the development of various career–life planning approaches. Career–life perspectives emphasize a wide range of factors that influence career choice including needs related to work, family, home, and leisure. Rehabilitation counselors have had a long-standing tradition incorporating the philosophical and practical importance of addressing clients holistically, even while addressing vocational concerns. This phenomenon likely is due to the pervasive psychosocial effects of disability on all life areas and has resulted in a dual focus on vocational and psychosocial adjustment counseling in rehabilitation counseling. Since the 1970s, the independent living movement has stimulated use of rehabilitation counseling skills to provide community rehabilitation services for people with disabilities, and thus has underscored the emphasis on addressing problems across all areas of individual and functioning environmental demands.

There is an ongoing tension in both fields concerning the relationship between personal and career counseling. Of course, the degree of focus for all practitioners will depend on the needs of the clients, the institutional mission within which they practice, and their professional scopes of competency. Salomone (1996) provided a description of the areas of personal, career, and rehabilitation counseling that clarifies the relationships among these areas of professional practice. *Personal* or *generic counseling* involves professional helpers who help clients "understand, accept, and resolve their problems" by using "basic counseling techniques so that their clients can lead more satisfying, well-adjusted lives." In contrast, *"career counseling* focuses on a certain realm of the counselee's life—the world of work" (Salomone, 1996, p. 368). It is not correct to say that career counseling is distinct from personal counseling, because a counselor may assist the client personally as part of the vocational counseling process. It could be said that "it is impossible to do career counseling without simultaneously doing personal counseling" (Salomone, 1996, p. 369). Lastly, rehabilitation counseling builds on personal and career counseling by centering on unique issues related to people with disabilities. These areas include the medical, psychological, and social effects of disability; the vocational effect of disability; and how the effects of the disability influence the ability of the client to transfer skills from one type of job to another (Salomone, 1996).

Clearly a close relationship exists between career and rehabilitation counseling. The remainder of this chapter will focus on professional identification and credentialing issues affecting the standards of practice for these specialties. In addition, common ethical dilemmas in both career and rehabilitation counseling will be discussed.

Defining the Specialties, Setting, and Clients

As counseling specialties, career and rehabilitation counseling share two structural characteristics important to understanding their organization and professional positioning. First, both were key groups in establishing the earliest professional organizational structures for the counseling movement. The National Career Development Association (NCDA), the primary organization representing career counseling and development professionals, is the oldest counseling organization. The group's ethical standards are reprinted at the end of this chapter. It was established in 1913 as the National Vocational Guidance Association (NVGA), and was a founding division of ACA (Engels, 1994). The National Certified Career Counselor (NCCC) was a national certification credential originally developed by NVGA that became the first specialty credential offered by the National Board for Counselor Certification (NBCC). To hold an NBCC specialty certification, the professional counselor must first attain certification as a National Certified Counselor (NCC), the more general level of counseling certification. About 800 people hold the NCCC specialty credential through NBCC (Engels, Minor, Sampson, & Splete, 1995).

Rehabilitation counseling also has enjoyed prominence within the history of the counseling profession. The American Rehabilitation Counseling Association (ARCA) was founded as a division of ACA in 1958, and rehabilitation counseling established both the first accreditation of professional educational programs and national certification of individual counseling practitioners in the profession of counseling. The Council on Rehabilitation Education (CORE) was incorporated in 1972 by a group that included ARCA, and the National Rehabilitation Counseling Association (NRCA). CORE is based on an innovative multiple-stakeholder, field-tested approach to accreditation. There are 79 accredited rehabilitation counseling master's degree programs (Leahy & Szymanski, 1995). Similarly, the Commission on Rehabilitation Counselor Certification (CRCC), established in 1973, is the oldest and most well-established professional counselor certification. Both the CORE and CRCC processes continue to be at the forefront of credentialing in counseling. The ongoing CORE/CRCC Knowledge Validation Study provides continuous empirical validation of the professional standards of this professional group. CORE and CRCC are recognized by ACA as parallel to credentialing by the Council on Accreditation of Counseling and Related Education Programs (CACREP) and NBCC, respectively. More than 23,000 professionals have participated in the CRCC certification process, and it is estimated that more than 13,000 CRCs practice in the United States and several foreign countries (Leahy & Holt, 1993).

The final structural characteristic shared by the two specialties is that each has several types of constituencies. These constituencies both enrich their practices and also affect each group's ability to define its organizational base easily. It sometimes has been unclear whether career counseling constitutes a specialty unto itself, or whether it is a specialized or advanced practice area within a number of other professional counseling groups. Even the NCDA has noted in its career counseling competencies document (Engels, 1994) that its standards provide guidelines for people interested in a variety of career development occupations. These standards state that career counselors should be trained at the master's level or higher with a specialty in career counseling. They further define 10 competency areas that constitute minimum training for career counseling specialists. Counseling professional groups that might consider themselves to have a specialized background in career counseling, depending on their individual programs of preparation and practice, might include school counselors, counseling psychologists, college counselors, private practice counselors, employment counselors, and rehabilitation counselors.

As the level of professionalization in career counseling has increased, the NCDA has strongly endorsed the NBCC standards for career counseling, and cautions that it must be differentiated from other career services such as job placement specialists, outplacement consultants, and employment agents. Members of the latter occupational groups often provide limited or specific career services, rather than working more broadly to place career concerns within a comprehensive approach to increase client career- and self-awareness and development (Engels, 1994). Often the clients for these groups are employers rather than employees or prospective employees. However, NCDA has acknowledged the following career development specialties and set minimum training and competence standards for each:

(a) career counseling (private and public settings);

(b) human resource, career development, and employee assistance specialists (in-house organizational setting, external HR/DC/EAP firms);

(c) career and employment search consultants (private setting);

(d) cooperative education instructors (educational setting);

(e) employment agents (private setting);

(f) outplacement consultants;

(g) job placement specialists (public setting);

(h) school counselors, community college and college counselors and counselors in postsecondary technical institutes (Engels, 1994).

Clearly, career counselors may practice in a variety of settings that demand proficiency in the core career counseling knowledge and skill areas. The 10 minimum competency areas required by NCDA are

1. career development theory

2. individual and group counseling skills

3. individual/group assessment

4. information/resources

5. program management and implementation

6. consultation

7. special populations

8. supervision

9. ethical/legal issues

10. research/evaluation.

While many organizations may relate to the specialized practice of career counseling, the core organizations that most clearly represent this area are NCDA and NCCC, a specialty certification of the NBCC.

The same issue of multiple professional constituencies is expressed differently in rehabilitation counseling. Rehabilitation counseling has arrived at unified professional credentials and standards through collaborative work among its major professional organizations—primarily ARCA and NRCA and the related rehabilitation organizations. This collaboration has resulted in unified accreditation (CORE), certification processes (CRCC), and a code of ethics (reprinted at the end of this chapter). However, this historical duality of the major organizations has created problems of definition regarding which core identity underlies the profession of rehabilitation counseling—counseling or rehabilitation (Tarvydas & Leahy, 1993).

The first perspective historically casts rehabilitation counselors as counselors who work in a variety of rehabilitation and community counseling agencies with people who have disabilities. This perspective appears to be more aligned with an emphasis on counseling through ARCA and its parent organization, ACA (Salomone, 1996). The counseling point of view is grounded firmly in the developmental and psychoeducational counseling approaches that are so important to the profession. The alternate position adds emphasis on case management or coordination with rehabilitation counselors practicing within more of a medical model. This perspective emphasizes rehabilitation as the profession's core function and is seen as more closely related to NRCA and its parent group, the National Rehabilitation Association (Salomone, 1996). It allows for the incorporation of the clinical treatment perspective; and it allows the use of medical information and collaboration with medical treatment systems that are important to serve clients with certain types of rehabilitation needs. The discussion in Chapter 7 has described many of the specialized issues that exist for rehabilitation counselors and others working within a medical model of treatment. In some cases, rehabilitation counselors practicing within this latter point of view deal with many of the same issues discussed in Chapter 12 on mental health counseling and in Chapter 15 on addictions counseling.

It is important to realize that rehabilitation counseling practitioners most often are trained as generalist rehabilitation counselors and thus are conversant with both perspectives and possess basic skills useful in both areas. The profession's scope of practice statement (see *Scope of Practice for Rehabilitation Counseling* at the end of this chapter) involves a blending of the two points of view. Often, it is only in increasingly specialized practice over the course of their careers that rehabilitation counselors may become more fully involved in one of the most differentiated modes of practice. Leahy (1997) summarized this blending of elements into a unique practice by stating the following:

> It is the specialized knowledge of disabilities and of environmental factors that interact with disabilities, as well as the range of knowledge and skills required in addition to counseling that serves to differentiate the rehabilitation counselor from social workers, other types of counselors (e.g., mental health counselors, school counselors, career counselors) and other rehabilitation practitioners (e.g., vocational evaluators, job placement specialists) in today's service delivery environments. (p. 97)

The discussion of individual scope of practice in Chapter 3 is important to all counselors in discerning how they develop an appropriate and ethical specialty practice for themselves.

In terms of the organizational issues in rehabilitation counseling, Leahy and Szymanski (1995) have provided a reality-based analysis by noting that the two organizations have often found methods to collaborate on important projects. In 1993 they formed the Alliance for Rehabilitation Counseling (ARC) as a stable, formal structure to continue this process of melding the two perspectives into an effective working structure for professional policy and strategic planning while still preserving historic ties to their parent groups.

The practice of both career and rehabilitation counseling involves a diverse group of settings and clients. When reflecting on the need for career counseling, Crites (1981) remarked that the need for it is even greater than the need for psychotherapy. This observation is borne out by a recent Gallup poll that was sponsored by NCDA and the National Occupational Information Coordinating Committee (NOICC). This survey documented a tremendous need for career counseling and development services throughout all segments of our society (Brown & Minor, 1989). Economic and political changes nationally and globally are creating monumental and rapid changes in business and industry that complicate career choice and career–life development. These elements challenge career counselors to provide career services to an extremely diverse population.

Traditionally, the clients with whom career counselors have worked most often were students preparing themselves for career choice and adults seeking to make career choices and to enter or re-enter the work force and were found in a variety of organizational settings. Career counseling is most often provided in primary and secondary schools, postsecondary institutions (e.g., college counseling or career placement centers), employment service settings (both public and private), VR settings (both public and private), other organizations serving their own employees (e.g., employee assistance or outplacement programs), and private practice career counseling (Engels, 1994). Thus, for many career counselors, the material on ethical issues in school counseling covered in Chapter 11 or in this chapter about rehabilitation counseling may be of particular interest. Within all of these contexts, an increasingly diverse clientele wish to address their career decisions and career-life planning issues. In addition to the more traditional clients, groups such as middle school and elementary school students, retirees, people whose career development has suffered because of bias or stereotyping, or people who wish to advance in their careers are also seeking career counseling services (Engels, 1994).

It is important to note that in some instances the career counseling service is not being rendered to an individual, but to a corporation or some other organization, often through a consulting relationship. These and other innovative aspects of career counseling make the professional and ethical demands on this group ever more challenging.

At first glance, rehabilitation counselors may seem to practice within a more restricted or specialized range of clients and settings. Nothing could be further from the truth. Rehabilitation counselors work with people who have physical, mental, developmental, cognitive, emotional, and addiction disabilities and help them achieve their personal, career, and independent living goals in the most integrated settings possible (CRCC, 1994). It has been estimated that more than 43 million Americans have disabilities that restrict some of their life activities and prevent them from attaining or maintaining jobs. The diversity of types, degrees, and combinations of disabilities that individuals bring to rehabilitation counselors is immense. Examples of clients served include people who have orthopedic work injuries, brain injuries sustained in an automobile crash, hearing or visual impairments, "invisible" disabilities such as epilepsy, AIDS, or pulmonary disease, developmental disabilities such as mental retardation or cerebral palsy, drug or alcohol addictions, or a psychiatric disorder such as schizophrenia or depression. In recent years, services to individuals with severe disabilities have been emphasized in many settings, and often individuals being served have combinations of several of these disabilities, thus providing more complex issues to the rehabilitation counselors with whom they work.

The primary employment settings for rehabilitation counselors are similarly diverse and include state rehabilitation agencies, alcohol and drug programs, hospitals, independent living centers, educational settings, private rehabilitation companies and practice settings, halfway houses, supported living and employment agencies, rehabilitation facilities, and mental health centers. These facilities may be public, private nonprofit, or private-for-profit.

Due to the traditional emphasis on holistic practice, rehabilitation practice is typically conducted within a rehabilitation team context. The composition of the team is dictated by the nature of the treatment setting and disability-related needs of the clients. Whether the team is in-house or is physically dispersed, rehabilitation counselors have been trained to work within a collaborative team framework. They generally provide the coordination necessary to help the team function for the client's benefit. Often they also provide the broader case management functions for this process to occur unless another team member has been formally designated to do so. *Case management* is "focused on interviewing, counseling, planning rehabilitation programs, coordinating services, interacting with significant others, placing clients on jobs and following up with them, monitoring a client's progress, and solving problems" (CRCC, 1994, p. 2).

In recent years, a number of employment settings have begun to emerge as important areas for rehabilitation counseling practice. These areas include employee assistance programs, employer-based disability management programs, school-based transition programs, disabled student services offices in post-secondary educational settings, and agencies that serve people with HIV and AIDS (Leahy & Szymanski, 1995). Thus, it is apparent that both career and rehabilitation counselors are involved in wide-ranging spheres of professional counseling practice and might affect the lives of more members of our society than better-known mental health professions such as clinical psychology and social work.

Issues of Significance to the Specialties

Professional Differentiation

Both of these counseling specialties have broad areas of practice and diverse practitioner bases, yet each has clearly identified standards for what constitutes appropriate professional practice. NCDA is the organization most closely aligned with career counseling and is an affiliate of ACA. NCDA has strongly endorsed the training standards of NBCC for NCCCs. These standards include (a) a graduate degree in counseling or in a related professional field from a regionally accredited higher education institution, (b) graduate level coursework pertinent to the practice of career counseling and related specialties, (c) supervised counseling experience that includes career counseling, and (d) successful completion of a knowledge-based certification examination (Engels, 1994).

The standards for a qualified rehabilitation counselor have been established by the professional organizations in RC including ARCA, NRCA, and the ARC. These standards require that rehabilitation counselors have (a) completed a master's degree in rehabilitation counseling or a closely related program (e.g., counseling), (b) achieved national certification as a CRC, and (c) attained the appropriate state licensure (e.g., Licensed Professional Counselor) in states that require this level of credential for counseling practice and that allow for the licensing of counselors with a rehabilitation counseling background. Both certification and licensure have requirements for supervised professional practice in rehabilitation counseling and passing a knowledge-based national examination in counseling.

Ethical Issues

Confidentiality and Privileged Communication.   Any number of complications can arise for career and rehabilitation counselors with regard to confidentiality and privilege. As with all professional counselors, the trust engendered by the assurance of confidentiality is the most critical element of the counseling relationship. Confidentiality, as discussed earlier, is the ethical obligation that counselors should not disclose to others material that clients reveal during the counseling relationship. Privilege is the client's legal or statutory right to protect confidences shared within the counseling relationship from being revealed in a legal proceeding. More detailed information about both of these important concepts is provided in Chapter 3.

Rehabilitation counselors may have particularly pressing issues regarding confidentiality in their work. Issues regarding confidentiality that emerged in a survey of CRCs (Patterson & Settles, 1992) were (a) maintaining confidentiality in institutional settings, (b) knowing that a client is driving with poorly controlled seizures, (c) recommending a client who is suspected of abusing substances to an employer, (d) sharing information with family members about a client with chronic mental illness, (e) conflicts between workers' compensation and state laws related to confidentiality, (f) the requirement to report client information to an agency that results in disciplinary action against the client, (g) learning that a client who has AIDS is not practicing safe sex, and (h) discussing clients with others without signed written consent.

Many rehabilitation counselors and some career counselors are involved in legal and third party consultant roles as vocational experts in civil court matters, administrative hearings, or Social Security or Workers' Compensation work (Blackwell, Martin, & Scalia, 1994). Several newer areas of practice—such as vocational or forensic expert practices—require that counselors take particular care in observing requirements to guard client confidentiality. They must clearly address confidentiality limitations with all the individuals involved. The ARCA/NRCA/CRCC code of ethics provides a rule that embodies well-accepted advice in such situations:

> Rehabilitation counselors who provide services at the request of a third party will clarify the nature of their relationships to all involved parties. They will inform all parties of their ethical responsibilities and take appropriate action. Rehabilitation counselors employed by third parties as case consultants or expert witnesses, where there is no pretense or intent to provide rehabilitation counseling services directly to clients, beyond file review, initial interview and/or assessment, will clearly define, through written or oral means, the limits of their relationship, particularly in the areas of informed consent and privileged communications, to involved individuals. (ARCA, CRCC, & NRCA, 1995, p. 2)

There are too many instances of clients having misunderstood the nature of the services being provided by a career or rehabilitation counselor. Clients may think that information they provided to the professional would be held in confidence, only to be shocked and angered later to discover that it is included in a report or deposition that resulted in a negative outcome for them, such as a loss of benefits. Such anecdotal reports are unfortunate illustrations of a need for greater care in observing the informed consent procedures regarding confidentiality limitations. The client must be informed clearly when the counselor is being employed by a third party. Clients must be helped to understand fully how that relationship will influence the way any information is given to the client, or how services provided to the client will be limited or changed.

Another potentially devastating and costly misunderstanding on the part of career and rehabilitation counselors alike is the uncritical assumption that privileged communication extends to their practices. Since privileged communication is granted only through statute and legal precedent, the types of professionals covered by this privilege varies by jurisdiction (Cottone, Pullen, & Wilson, 1983). In other words, possessing a national certification, such as CRC or NCCC, does not entitle one to legal privilege for therapeutic communications in and of itself. Counselors in these two specialties especially must research the nature of the laws governing the granting of privilege in their own areas. Generally privileged communication is extended only to licensed professionals. The recent *Jaffee v. Redmond* ruling by the U.S. Supreme Court has underscored this position (see Chapter 3 for more specific information about privileged communication). Unfortunately, rehabilitation counselors' involvement in the state-by-state counselor licensure movement has been inconsistent and unintegrated compared with some counseling specialties, such as mental health counseling. It is unclear how many rehabilitation and career counselors hold licensure in their states of residence. However, it is almost certain that a great number of them must be in practice without state licensure and the benefit of privileged communication protections for their clients. It is imperative that both the counselors and clients in these relationships are aware of this.

Rehabilitation counselors and many career counselors in educational institutions perform their work within a multi- or interdisciplinary team context. Such a clinical arrangement is often considered the intervention of choice, but it does present additional factors for the counselor to be mindful of in terms of confidentiality. Different team members have varying levels of training and understanding of this ethical obligation and may have a legitimate desire and need to know information the counselor may have about the client. While generally it is acknowledged that professionals may have an appropriate need to communicate information to other people involved in the client's care, the client must be informed clearly and fully of this common limitation to confidentiality at the outset of counseling. Indeed, it is a common and sensible practice to obtain suitable written release of information regarding this and other limitations to confidentiality in a written consent to treatment document (see Chapter 3), as well as discussing this practice with the client. The client should be informed of when, how, to whom, to what extent, and what type of information will be shared with others. This process must be done in such a way as to avoid coercion of clients or the implication that they will not be served if they do not grant blanket permission.

Even when consent is obtained, the counselor still must be circumspect about revealing information to others. Just being a member of the treatment team does not entitle one automatically to know whether a young man with a spinal cord injury is capable of erection and penile penetration while having sex, or that a student involved in a work-study placement through the high school was a victim of incest. The counselor must determine the appropriateness of the disclosure before providing information by asking "is it likely that the information that I am about to share with my team member(s) will *substantially* enhance that person's work with the client" (Strein & Hershenson, 1991, p. 313). The same analysis should be applied to decisions about including material in case records that will be viewed by these individuals. Strein and Hershenson (1991) provided additional benchmark concepts to be considered when fostering confidentiality within a team context. Their recommendations include taking steps to (a) articulate the specific rules the treatment team will follow regarding confidentiality, (b) reinforce the obligation of confidentiality with the team in any circumstance in which it appears that a team member may not realize the confidentiality of the information, and (c) inform the client before material will be shared with members of the team.

Rehabilitation counselors especially also should be aware of other important limitations to confidentiality, because it would not be unusual to a have higher number of clients with issues that could limit confidentiality. Examples might include people with psychiatric or addictions disabilities, HIV/AIDS, and clients with correctional histories who might become dangerous to themselves or others. Clients of rehabilitation and career counselors may be involved in group treatment or counseling for purposes ranging from job-seeking skills and support groups to more traditional psychotherapeutic adjustment counseling groups. Counselors must be certain that they inform the clients involved in these experiences of confidentiality limitations (although the norm of confidentiality is set, confidentiality cannot be guaranteed in a group context) and that the courts generally have not upheld privilege for therapeutic communication in a group setting. It is imperative that the counselor become skilled and comfortable providing informed consent opportunities to clients, for it is never possible to anticipate when these issues might arise with any client. Rehabilitation or career counselors working in certain specialized settings also must become knowledgeable about specific additional state or federal laws that apply to confidentiality and privilege in those settings. Examples include the access to records of minors by their parents as required by the federal Family and Educational Rights and Privacy Act (FERPA), and the laws extending stricter confidentiality to those in treatment in any addictions treatment facility receiving federal funding (see Chapters 3 and 11; and Chapter 15 respectively).

Informed Consent.   As described in Chapter 3, informed consent involves the counselor in ensuring that clients are given sufficient information in a manner the clients can understand regarding the treatment or services in which they will be involved. The intent is to be sure that clients have a sufficient understanding of the circumstances so they can exercise their autonomy and make informed choices. The three required elements of informed consent are (a) capacity, (b) comprehension, and (c) voluntariness.

Rehabilitation counseling has a long-standing philosophical and political tradition endorsing the ideal of the client participating as an equal partner with the counselor in the counseling process. In terms of the normalization principle, the right of persons with disabilities to have access to informed choices is a keystone right in this movement. *Normalization* is a rehabilitation principle that dictates that people with disabilities "should be treated in a manner that allows them to participate both symbolically and actually in roles and lifestyles that are 'normal' for a person of their age and culture" (Greenspan & Love, 1995, p. 75). This tradition of client participation has become institutionalized in rehabilitation treatment settings in diverse ways, including the powerful accreditation standards for rehabilitation programs such as the Commission on Accreditation of Rehabilitation Facilities (CARF) and the Joint Commission on Accreditation of Healthcare Organizations (JCAHO).

Historically, this point of view is one of the values that differentiates the rehabilitation service from the medical treatment model. It received resounding affirmation through the passage of the Rehabilitation Act of 1973 that emphasized consumer involvement of the client in the state–federal VR process in a number of its provisions. The most striking example of this focus was the mandated involvement in the rehabilitation services planning process through the completion of an Individual Written Rehabilitation Program (IWRP) (Rubin & Roessler, 1995). In this plan and its contemporary version, the IWRP is co-developed by counselor and client, written, and reviewed periodically by both as part of the ongoing evaluation of the services plan. The required elements of the IWRP are (a) a statement of the long-term goals for the client and intermediate steps related to it, (b) a statement of the particular rehabilitation services to be provided, (c) the methods to be used in determining whether the intermediate objectives or the long-term goals are being attained, and (d) information from the client regarding how the client was involved in choosing from among alternative goals (Rubin & Roessler, 1995). Career counselors working in school settings may participate in the Individual Educational Plan (IEP), an analogous requirement of providing educational services to students with disabilities.

It is important that the rehabilitation counselor consider it an aspect of the rehabilitation counseling process *to prepare* clients to participate in this collaborative rehabilitation process on a meaningful basis, rather than just offering an opportunity to decide. This process may involve some preparatory counseling, skill teaching, or motivation-enhancing techniques. Due to their disabilities, some clients may not have had a chance to develop decision-making skills; or they may have a limited base of life experiences or other cognitive or psychological limitations.

While rehabilitation philosophy clearly is in support of full informed consent and inclusion, it is a significant ethical challenge to rehabilitation counselors to fulfill the actual intent, rather than just the letter, of these guidelines. The determination of when a client is legally or ethically competent to provide informed consent is a critical consideration for career and rehabilitation counselors. If your client is a minor, but psychosocially and cognitively mature; has a traumatic brain injury; or appears to be under the influence of a drug, you must think carefully about whether informed consent is possible, or whether other measures are needed. The counselor might need to involve a parent or guardian, or wait until the person is in a better position to decide regarding to consent. Haffey (1989) has provided guidance on the assessment of clinical competency for rehabilitation interventions, including differentiating the legal from the clinicoethical issues involved.

It is important to note that some clients may have a legal guardian who may need to be involved in the informed consent process. A *legal guardian* is a person who is appointed by the court to make decisions regarding an individual's person or property. This concept presumes that individual is incompetent to make these decisions (Anderson & Fearey, 1989). While the legal guardian always must consent to services for the client with a guardian, there are a number of ways in which the legal requirements of achieving this consent can be reconciled with the ethical responsibility of respectfully allowing the client to participate in the decision as fully as his or her abilities allow. Often the client can be educated about this process over time. Minors and clients with limited experience or capacity can benefit from the process over time and responsibly assume their own power of consent when it is legally possible.

Dual Relationships.   Dual relationships are an important and common issue for counselors working in all areas of the profession. Career and rehabilitation counselors are no exceptions, and the codes of both specialties prohibit engaging in overlapping or dual relationships (see Chapter 2). The core issues that make dual relationships so potentially dangerous to client and counselor are the power differential between the two parties and a potential loss of objectivity on the part of the counselor. The effects of dual relationships may range from harmful to positive or no appreciable effect. However, due to the potential for harm, the principle is to avoid these overlapping roles wherever possible. Of course, sexual intimacy is strictly prohibited with current clients by both NCDA and ARCA/NRCA/CRCC, because the potential for serious harm to the client in such relationships has been documented as very high.

In rehabilitation and career counseling, several involvements routinely may be incorporated into career and independent living skill or behavioral interventions that may result in additional tensions around the issue of dual relationships. By necessity, many of these interventions take place in natural social, recreational, residential, or vocational settings. For example, social skills training intentionally may simulate some behavioral elements of, but not the emotional content of, relationships such as friend or co-worker. For a naive client or an emotionally needy counselor, the climate can create confusion about relationship boundaries. On the other hand, innovative and constructive intervention styles such as mentoring, coaching, and providing a personalized climate for successful achievement, such as that found in a job club, may be beneficial for many of the nontraditional, diverse clients needing vocational and life skills seen by these specialty counselors.

Herlihy and Corey (1992) provided five specific safeguards to assist counselors in managing dual relationships if they appear to be necessary or desirable after careful consideration. They recommended:

- *Informed consent:* The counselor should fully inform the client of all possible risks involved, the limitations of the relationships, and the safeguards in place.
- *Ongoing discussions:* The counselor should have periodic discussions with all the parties involved in the relationships to identify and work through any conflicts or concerns that develop.
- *Consultation:* If the counselor does proceed with the dual relationship, an ongoing consultation with a colleague should be in place so that all aspects of the situation will be evaluated to guard against overlooking a problem.

- *Supervision:* If the situation involves a high risk for harm, more continuous supervision may be warranted.
- *Documentation:* Counselors should document all aspects of the dual relationship and issues that arise within the process, including the techniques used to manage the situation.

The last major issue in rehabilitation and career counseling concerns the emergence of issues that could be described loosely as multiple relationships, involving conflicts of interest for the counselor. In these situations, counselors provide services that involve a group or team of professionals affiliated with the same client. If one team member has a monetary or business interest in a certain outcome for the client's case, such as an attorney in litigation or a managed care case manager paid through capitation, there may be potential for danger to the client if the counselor begins a noncollegial type of relationship with the first team member. An example would be a counselor entering into a sexually intimate relationship with the plaintiff's attorney in a client's workers' compensation case, or becoming a business partner of this person. If there is only a professional relationship between the counselor and the other professional, there is no unusual conflict for the counselor in protecting the client's interests. However, if the counselor is the other professional's lover or business partner, there could be considerable negative pressure exerted on the counselor. Even the appearance of such undue influence is ethically troublesome. Because various private practice options are being pursued by rehabilitation and career counselors, the possibilities for business and personal concerns creating multiple and conflicting loyalties will be an increasing danger in the future. Often, consultants and vocational experts are hired from among people who are well-known to the organization or hiring professional. Thus the potential for conflicts of interest increases and must be carefully evaluated before entering into, or continuing a professional service relationship (Newman, 1993), even if direct counseling services are not to be provided.

Responsibility. The codes of ethics for both NCDA and ARCA/CRCC/NRCA clearly assert that the primary responsibility of the counselor is to the client. Interestingly, the code for rehabilitation counselors realistically found it necessary to define clients as "people with disabilities receiving services from rehabilitation counselors" (ARCA/NRCA/CRCC, 1995, p. 1) due to the sometimes uncritical use of the term client in contemporary counseling. In the areas of these two specialties, it is clear that there are secondary responsibilities to other parties in counseling. For example, rehabilitation counselors are told in R2.7 that they will recognize that families are usually important to the client's rehabilitation and that counselors should seek to enlist their families' understanding and positive involvement in rehabilitation, with client permission. Another relationship that is acknowledged is the rehabilitation counselor's need to "neither place nor participate in placing clients in positions that will result in damaging the interest and welfare of either clients or employers" (ARCA/NRCA/CRCC, 1995, p. 2). It would seem that the imperative need in contemporary counseling is to acknowledge the important moral theme of interdependence as the true human condition rather than the traditional and excessive U.S.

emphasis on the myth of possessive individualism and independence (Gatens-Robinson & Tarvydas, 1992).

Both rehabilitation and career counseling have had a long history of practicing primarily within agency or institutional settings. This fact is embodied by standards that enjoin them to respect the rights and responsibilities that they owe to their employing agencies and the need to try to resolve disputes with them through constructive internal processes. The NCDA elaborates about the nature of that obligation by stating:

> The acceptance of employment in an institution implies that the career counselor is in agreement with the general policies and principles of the institution. . . . If, despite concerted efforts, the career counselor cannot reach agreement with the employer as to acceptable standards of conduct that allow for changes in institutional policy that are conducive to the positive growth and development of clients, then terminating the affiliation should be seriously considered. (Engels, 1994, p. 28)

There has been substantial documentation in the sociological, political science, and anthropological literatures on disability in society that the basic human rights of people with disabilities are often denied to them. Additionally, even well-meaning individuals and institutions inadvertently have denied these individuals equal opportunities for participation and inclusion. For that well-recognized reason, the rehabilitation counseling code of ethics contains a canon on the obligation to advocate on behalf of their clients and other people with disabilities. This provision is unique among professional codes of ethics and has become an important aspect of the self-definition for this profession. It requires the rehabilitation counselor to "promote access for people with disabilities in programs, facilities, transportation, and communication, so that clients will not be excluded from opportunities to participate fully in rehabilitation, education and society" (ARCA/CRCC/NRCA, 1995, p. 3). The canon goes on to detail the many facets of this advocacy role. The concept is laudatory, but must be updated at revision of the code. The more appropriate construction should acknowledge the leadership and primary role of people with disabilities in advocating for their own interests, and the responsibilities of RCs to assist and teach self-advocacy skills as needed (Vash, 1987).

While the need to work for the best interests of the rehabilitation client is clear, the exact nature of the balance to be struck between the ethical principles of autonomy and beneficence in actual rehabilitation practice situations is not determined so easily. This tension centers on the temptation of paternalism, which originated within the tradition of medical practice in acute rehabilitation. This tendency toward paternalism is difficult to resolve. It originated in the observations of caregivers that clients at some early points in their adjustment to disability might not be able to discern what they might want or need at some later point in their recovery when they were better equipped emotionally to make stable judgments regarding their needs and wishes. Unfortunately, the beneficence of the caregiver wishing to influence the process for the good of the client through controlling information and decision making clashes with the client's right to autonomous ability to exercise his or her discretion in one's own matters (Gatens-Robinson & Tarvydas, 1992). Greenspan and Love (1995) provided a perspective on this issue:

> In disability services, the perception has been that a majority of persons with disabilities (particularly those with cognitive limitations) have sufficiently limited access to autonomy as to justify the substituted decision making of weak paternalism. The reality, however, is that the vast majority of people with disabilities (including cognitive limitations) do have access to autonomy (sometimes with assistance, but more often not). This fact suggests that much of the weak paternalism that is perceived as ethically permissible is, in reality, a form of strong paternalism that should be considered much less acceptable than it is. (p. 80)

It can be expected that all areas of counseling will need to address issues of counselor stereotyping and treatment system bias and how it affects clients' rights as counseling attempts to better serve an increasingly multicultural and diverse population of clients in the future (Sue, 1996). The future of counseling technical innovations to accommodate the needs of multicultural populations may well lie in this traditional area of RC skill. Sue (1996) has stated:

> If we believe that many problems reside outside the person (prejudice and discrimination) and not within (person-blame), ethical practice dictates that professionals develop alternative helping roles that are aimed at *system intervention.* (p. 196, italics in original)

Values.   Clearly, there might be any number of value issues that could be addressed in the areas of career and rehabilitation counseling. The richness and complexity of values and the valuing process and how it influences counseling was explored in chapters 4 and 5. At this point, one overriding value of concern might be overlooked for its obviousness—work! The central importance that U.S. society places on work is so pervasive and strong that it is assumed that not only must we all value work but we also must share similar preferences and interpretations regarding what constitutes meaningful and valuable work. Both rehabilitation and career counseling originated as counseling specialties in answer to the powerful societal approbation of this valued role in our culture and the need to give others more effective access to this all-defining status. It is at the very core of the entire vocational counseling process for both rehabilitation and career counselors to examine the work-related meanings, needs, and interests of their clients and to help them find their niche in this world of work.

Counselors must understand that societal attitudes toward work can affect them in both positive and negative ways as they serve their clients (Gatens-Robinson & Rubin, 1995). Counselors, their agencies, and clients receive support for their vocational counseling activities as long as the outcomes of the process result in productive or visible economic contributions through work. If a career counselor's client achieved great financial success through dealing drugs or illegally trading stocks, the work of that counselor will not be considered professionally appropriate. Also, if the work obtained by clients is not considered by society (or even counselors themselves) to be valuable, those who find alternative or nonremunerative activities or those who cannot be competitive in the employment market may be devalued. A variety of counseling ethical dilemmas may ensue from our uncritical assumption of values regarding work. Counselors may choose not to work with more difficult vocational clients if the agency only rewards particular types of placements or closures. Counselors may not react positively to clients who choose to work in the home as caregivers to children or elders, or who will work only part time to pursue avocational interests. They may pressure clients to take jobs that are not suited for, or are even harmful to them, to appear successful. What reactions do vocational counselors have to clients who choose to work in the hidden job market, not reporting income or bartering for payment? These forms of activity may be the only ones preferred or realistically available to the client due to disincentives to employment, but counselors may be tremendously conflicted by working with such issues in vocational counseling. These tensions are likely only to increase as tremendous changes in the nature of employment and business and industrial structures continue into the 21st century. In addition to the other value issues that confront all counselors, they will be required to lead the professions in interpreting and supporting work-related values in collaboration with their clients.

Counselor Competence.   Competence issues occur in the work of all counselors on an ongoing basis. It becomes imperative that counselors are able to develop and practice an approach to quality control in their work that assures quality and the safety of services they provide to their clients and that counselors work within the legal and ethical boundaries of their scopes of practice. Career and rehabilitation counselors monitor competence in at least two specific areas of contemporary practice: (a) the integration of a mental health counseling or diagnostic focus with their usual practices, and (b) competence around assessment services.

The managed care treatment paradigm has grown tremendously through health care reform efforts as well as the forceful advocacy of AMCHA for mental health specialization as the core clinical counseling specialization. Both of these forces have required all counselors to reevaluate the role of diagnosis and clinical models of practice in their work. For some rehabilitation counselors, the issue of adopting a medically based diagnostic paradigm has profoundly troubling implications for the long-valued asset-focused, nonstigmatizing rehabilitation model that centered on functional assessment and not diagnosis of medical problems or pathologies as a basis for treatment. Other rehabilitation counselors do not find the task of reconciling a medical diagnostic framework as a background to functionally based treatment strategies to be problematic. The psychiatric rehabilitation model developed by Anthony, Cohen, and Farkas (1990) is an example of such a model. The model builds from a medical rehabilitation model used with physical disabilities, and allows for medical diagnosis; yet it emphasizes rehabilitation intervention using a behaviorally oriented, highly supportive, client directed, and positive model.

The career counseling tradition is significant to both fields in this regard in that it is a counseling model that is highly focused on developmental counseling traditions and interventions and thus is at odds with any model based on psychopathological interpretations. Niles and Pate (1989) described the distinction between career counseling and mental health counseling as artificial. They saw the fields as needing to be integrated in that mental health and work concerns are inextricably linked in the human experiences brought to counseling. As result of this reasoning, they make a case for examining how the competence and training standards of both groups would have to be enhanced. They view the lack of NVGA competence stan-

dards (knowledge and skill) in standards related to treatment of mental and emotional disorders as distressing. If adding diagnostic and treatment planning competencies will be required of rehabilitation and career counselors in the future, this
will occasion a re-design of training standards in the field to ensure that practitioners meet minimum levels of knowledge and skill in this complex area. Of
course, individual practitioners may reach these levels of capability through their
individualized programs of specialized professional experience and preparation.
The reader is urged to review the discussion of the ethical considerations in diagnosis as given in Chapter 8, because both rehabilitation and career counselors are
likely to be required to know more about this process in the future.

The second area of specialized emphasis on counselor competence is assessment
and testing. Both career and rehabilitation counselors spend substantial portions of
their time in performing these functions. The use of various vocational assessment
devices has been integral to the development of the trait and factor model of career
counseling that has been discussed as being at the core of this specialized area. It is
a primary tool to gain information to be used by client and counselor alike in the career and vocational rehabilitation processes (Hood & Johnson, 1991; Rubin &
Roessler, 1995). As such there is tremendous potential for assistance or harm to the
clients served by these counselors. Blackwell, Martin and Scalia (1994) distinguished
between testing and assessment. *Testing* is the use of a specific tool to gather information or measure some individual quality or characteristic, such as vocational interests or aptitudes or educational achievement. *Assessment* refers to the process
that involves the coordinated planning of information collection and evaluation to involve addressing a client's counseling or rehabilitation concern or problem. The assessment function requires a higher level of professional training for proper service
(Blackwell, Martin & Scalia, 1995).

The issue of who has sufficient knowledge and training to administer the different types and levels of tests properly is critical in counselor competence. Tests vary
greatly in the complexity of administration and interpretation required for appropriate usage. At one extreme are tests such as the individually administered intelligence
tests, the Weschler Intelligence Tests, and at the other are simple tests of vocational
skills, including typing or language skills like spelling. Copious work has been done
to develop competence standards for the qualifications required of test users as well
as other standards for educational and psychological tests. These standards primarily have exerted an influence in controlling the qualifications of test users through a
statement of qualifications required by the purchasers of tests through many of the
major test distributors. This statement embodies qualifications developed by the
Test User Qualifications Group in consultation with test developers (Hood &
Johnson, 1991). The Test User Qualifications Group was composed of a number of
the professional associations whose members perform assessment and testing services, including ACA and APA. Counselors should review and seek to conform to
these qualification requirements for any and all tests that they utilize in their practices. Both the NCDA and ARCA/NRCA/CRCC codes of ethics have specific and detailed requirements concerning the ethical obligations of their members in observing
the competence standards set for use of these instruments and techniques.

Recent controversies are raging around the attempts of psychology to restrict the ability of nonpsychologists to administer various testing instruments, and they demonstrate the tremendously important role of user competence standards. In recent years, several psychology boards have taken a variety of legal actions to restrict other helping professionals from using various tests. States where actions have been taken include California, Georgia, Indiana, Louisiana, and Ohio (Marino, 1996). While this effort is not yet national, there is a disturbing increase in these actions. As a result, various concerned professional groups formed a coalition to develop strategies to deal with this threat to professional autonomy in scope of practice. The group is the Fair Access Coalition on Testing (FACT), and is said to represent more than 500,000 professionals (Marino, 1996). The concerns of rehabilitation and career counselors have been represented by the leaders of NCDA, ARCA, and CRCC in the activities of FACT. While the issues may be resolved in the future, the importance of preserving this essential function of the counselor's role in practice is clear. Career and rehabilitation counselors always have worked closely with vocational testing and other types of assessment. It is obvious that the ethical obligations of these groups should be affirmed by these professionals as they work to preserve this aspect of their services to clients.

Code Comparisons

In terms of ethical standards, NCDA indicates that career counselors are expected to follow the ethical guidelines of the organizations pertinent to them, including NCDA, NBCC, ACA, and APA. The NCDA ethical standards were developed by NBCC and adopted with only minor revision. Because NCDA is a division of ACA, its members also are subject to discipline through that body. The NCDA standards were the focus of the earlier discussions.

The ethical practices of rehabilitation counselors are governed by the codes of the organizations to which they belong. However, in rehabilitation counseling, the professional organizations have provided a unified code of ethics through the endorsement by ARCA, NRCA, and CRCC of one code of ethics for the entire profession. Of course, rehabilitation counselors who are ARCA members are subject to enforcement of ethics through ACA, its parent organization. NRCA and ARCA do not provide disciplinary processes to enforce the rehabilitation counseling code within their organizations. The CRCC does provide active enforcement of the unified code for all rehabilitation counselors who hold the CRC certification.

Summary

The counseling specialties of career counseling and rehabilitation counseling are united by their historical embeddedness in the vocational guidance and counseling movements. While they have evolved differently since these origins in response to the specialized needs of their clients and settings of choice, they continue to experience dynamic issues in their current ethical and professional issues that share common characteristics. This chapter introduced the major characteristics of the specialties, their clients, settings, and standards. Common ethical issues that are experienced in their practices were discussed. Topics in the areas of confidentiality and privileged communication, informed consent, dual relationships, responsibility, values, and counselor competence were considered from the perspectives of career and rehabilitation counselors.

References

American Rehabilitation Counseling Association, Commission on Rehabilitation Counselor Certification, & the National Rehabilitation Counseling Association. (1995). *Code of professional ethics for rehabilitation counselors.* Chicago: Author.

Anderson, T. P., & Fearey, M. S. (1989). Legal guardianship in traumatic brain injury rehabilitation: Ethical implications. *Journal of Head Trauma Rehabilitation, 4,* 57–64.

Anthony, W., Cohen, M., & Farkas, M. (1990). *Psychiatric rehabilitation.* Boston: Center for Psychiatric Rehabilitation.

Blackwell, T. L., Martin, W. E., & Scalia, V. A. (1994). *Ethics in rehabilitation.* Athens, GA: Elliott & Fitzpatrick.

Brown, D., & Brooks, L. (1991). *Career counseling techniques.* Boston: Allyn & Bacon.

Brown, D., & Minor, C. W. (1989). *Working in America: A status report on planning and problems.* Alexandria, VA: National Career Development Association.

Commission on Rehabilitation Counselor Certification (CRCC). (1994). *CRCC Certification Guide.* Rolling Meadows, IL: Author.

Cottone, R. R., Pullen, J. R., & Wilson, W. C. (1983). Counselor licensure, confidentiality, and privileged communication: Implications for private practice in rehabilitation. *Journal of Applied Rehabilitation, 14,* 6–8.

Crites, J. O. (1981). *Career counseling: Models, methods, and materials.* New York: McGraw-Hill.

Engels, D. W. (1994). *The professional practice of career counseling and consultation: A resource document* (2nd ed.). Alexandria, VA: National Career Development Association.

Engels, D. W., Minor, C. W., Sampson, J. P. Jr., & Splete, H. H. (1995). Career counseling specialty: History, development, and prospect. *Journal of Counseling & Development, 37,* 134–138.

Gatens-Robinson, E., & Rubin, S. E. (1995). Societal values and ethical commitments that influence rehabilitation service delivery behavior. In S. E. Rubin & R. T. Roessler (Eds.), *Foundations of the vocational rehabilitation process* (pp. 157–174). Austin, TX: Pro-Ed.

Gatens-Robinson, E., & Tarvydas, V. (1992). Ethics of care, women's perspectives and the status of the mainstream rehabilitation analysis. *Journal of Applied Rehabilitation Counseling, 23,* 26–33.

Greenspan, S., & Love, P. (1995). Ethical challenges in supporting persons with disabilities. In O. C. Karan & S. Greenspan (Eds.), *Community rehabilitation services for people with disabilities* (pp. 71–89). Boston: Butterworth-Heinemann.

Haffey, W. J. (1989). The assessment of clinical competency to consent to medical rehabilitation interventions. *Journal of Head Trauma Rehabilitation, 4,* 43–56.

Herlihy, B., & Corey, G. (1992). *Dual relationships in counseling.* Alexandria, VA: American Counseling Association.

Hood, A. B., & Johnson, R. W. (1991). *Assessment in counseling: A guide to the use of psychological assessment procedures.* Alexandria, VA: American Counseling Association.

Leahy, M. J. (1997). Qualified providers of rehabilitation counseling services. In D. R. Maki, & T. F. Riggar (Eds.), *Rehabilitation counseling: Profession and practice.* New York: Springer.

Leahy, M. J., & Holt, E. (1993). Certification in rehabilitation counseling: History and process. *Rehabilitation Counseling Bulletin, 37,* 71–80.

Leahy, M. J., & Szymanski, E. M. (1995). Rehabilitation counseling: Evolution and current status. *Journal of Counseling & Development, 74,* 163–166.

Marino, T. W. (1996, November). Fair Access Coalition on Testing holds meeting in Washington D.C. *Counseling Today, 13,* 19.

Newman, J. L. (1993). Ethical issues in consultation. *Journal of Counseling & Development, 72,* 148–156.

Niles, S. G., & Pate, R. H. Jr. (1989). Competency and training issues related to the integration of career counseling and mental health counseling. *Journal of Career Development, 16,* 63–71.

Parsons, F. (1909). *Choosing an occupation.* Boston: Houghton Mifflin.

Patterson, J. B., & Settles, R. (1992). The ethics education of certified rehabilitation counselors. *Rehabilitation Education, 6,* 179–184.

Rubin, S. E., & Roessler, R. T. (1995). *Foundations of the vocational rehabilitation process.* Austin, TX: Pro-Ed.

Salomone, P. R. (1996). Career counseling and job placement: Theory and practice. In E. M. Szymanski & R. M. Parker (Eds.), *Work and disability: Issues and strategies in career development and job placement* (pp. 365–420). Austin, TX: Pro-Ed.

Strein, W., & Hershenson, D. (1991). Confidentiality in nondyadic counseling situations. *Journal of Counseling & Development, 69,* 312–316.

Sue, D. W. (1996). Ethical issues in multicultural counseling. In B. Herlihy, & G. Corey (Eds.), *ACA Ethical standards casebook* (pp. 193–204). Alexandria, VA: American Counseling Association.

Tarvydas, V. M., & Leahy, M. J. (1993). Licensure in rehabilitation counseling: A critical incident in professionalization. *Rehabilitation Counseling Bulletin, 37,* 92–108.

Vash, C. (1987). Canon 3—Client advocacy: Fighting another's battles: Is it helpful? Professional? Ethical? *Journal of Applied Rehabilitation Counseling, 18,* 15–17.

Zunker, V. G. (1994). *Career counseling: Applied concepts of life planning.* Pacific Grove, CA: Brooks/Cole.

NATIONAL CAREER DEVELOPMENT ASSOCIATION ETHICAL STANDARDS
(Revised 1991)

These Ethical Standards were developed by the National Board for Certified Counselors (NBCC), an independent, voluntary, not-for-profit organization incorporated in 1982. Titled "Code of Ethics" by NBCC and last amended in February 1987, the Ethical Standards were adopted by the National Career Development Association (NCDA) Board of Directors in 1987 and revised in 1991, with minor changes in wording (e.g., the addition of specific references to NCDA members).

Preamble:

NCDA is an educational, scientific, and professional organization dedicated to the enhancement of the worth, dignity, potential, and uniqueness of each individual and, thus, to the service of society. This code of ethics enables the NCDA to clarify the nature of ethical responsibilities for present and future professional career counselors.

SECTION A: GENERAL

1. NCDA members influence the development of the profession by continuous efforts to improve professional practices, services, and research. Professional growth is continuous through the career counselor's career and is exemplified by the development of a philosophy that explains why and how a career counselor functions in the helping relationship. Career counselors must gather data on their effectiveness and be guided by their findings.

2. NCDA members have a responsibility to the clients they are serving and to the institutions within which the services are being performed. Career counselors also strive to assist the respective agency, organization, or institution in providing the highest caliber of professional services. The acceptance of employment in an institution implies that the career counselor is in agreement with the general policies and princi-

ples of the institution. Therefore, the professional activities of the career counselor are in accord with the objectives of the institution. If, despite concerted efforts, the career counselor cannot reach agreement with the employer as to acceptable standards of conduct that allow for changes in institutional policy that are conducive to the positive growth and development of clients, then terminating the affiliation should be seriously considered.

3. Ethical behavior among professional associates (e.g., career counselors) must be expected at all times. When accessible information raises doubt as to the ethical behavior of professional colleagues, the NCDA member must take action to attempt to rectify this condition. Such action uses the respective institution's channels first and then uses procedures established by the American Counseling Association, of which NCDA is a division.

4. NCDA members neither claim nor imply professional qualifications which exceed those possessed, and are responsible for correcting any misrepresentation of these qualifications by others.

5. NCDA members must refuse a private fee or other remuneration for consultation or counseling with persons who are entitled to their services through the career counselor's employing institution or agency. The policies of some agencies may make explicit provisions for staff members to engage in private practice with agency clients. However, should agency clients desire private counseling or consulting services, they must be apprised of other options available to them. Career counselors must not divert to their private practices, legitimate clients in their primary agencies or of the institutions with which they are affiliated.

6. In establishing fees for professional counseling services, NCDA members must consider the financial status of clients and the respective locality.

In the event that the established fee status is inappropriate for the client, assistance must be provided in finding comparable services of acceptable cost.

7. NCDA members seek only those positions in the delivery of professional services for which they are professionally qualified.

8. NCDA members recognize their limitations and provide services or only use techniques for which they are qualified by training and/or experience. Career counselors recognize the need, and seek continuing education, to assure competent services.

9. NCDA members are aware of the intimacy in the counseling relationship, maintain respect for the client, and avoid engaging in activities that seek to meet their personal needs at the expense of the client.

10. NCDA members do not condone or engage in sexual harassment which is defined as deliberate or repeated comments, gestures, or physical contacts of a sexual nature.

11. NCDA members avoid bringing their personal or professional issues into the counseling relationship. Through an awareness of the impact of stereotyping and discrimination (e.g., biases based on age, disability, ethnicity, gender, race, religion, or sexual preference), career counselors guard the individual rights and personal dignity of the client in the counseling relationship.

12. NCDA members are accountable at all times for their behavior. They must be aware that all actions and behaviors of a counselor reflect on professional integrity and, when inappropriate, can damage the public trust in the counseling profession. To protect public confidence in the counseling profession, career counselors avoid public behavior that is clearly in violation of accepted moral and legal standards.

13. NCDA members have a social responsibility because their recommendations and professional actions may alter the lives of others. Career counselors remain fully cognizant of their impact and are alert to personal, social, organizational, financial, or political situations or pressures which might lead to misuse of their influence.

14. Products or services provided by NCDA members by means of classroom instruction, public lectures, demonstrations, written articles, radio or television programs, or other types of media must meet the criteria cited in Sections A through F of these Ethical Standards.

SECTION B: COUNSELING RELATIONSHIP

1. The primary obligation of NCDA members is to respect the integrity and promote the welfare of the client, regardless of whether the client is assisted individually or in a group relationship. In a group setting, the career counselor is also responsible for taking reasonable precautions to protect individuals from physical and/or psychological trauma resulting from interaction within the group.

2. The counseling relationship and information resulting from it remains confidential, consistent with the legal obligations of the NCDA member. In a group counseling setting, the career counselor sets a norm of confidentiality regarding all group participants' disclosures.

3. NCDA members know and take into account the traditions and practices of other professional groups with whom they work, and they cooperate fully with such groups. If a person is receiving similar services from another professional, career counselors do not offer their own services directly to such a person. If a career counselor is contacted by a person who is already receiving similar services from another professional, the career counselor carefully considers that professional relationship and proceeds with caution and sensitivity to the therapeutic issues as well as the client's welfare. Career counselors discuss these issues with clients so as to minimize the risk of confusion and conflict.

4. When a client's condition indicates that there is a clear and imminent danger to the client or others, the NCDA member must take reasonable personal action or inform responsible authorities. Consultation with other professionals must be used where possible. The assumption of re-

sponsibility for the client's behavior must be taken only after careful deliberation, and the client must be involved in the resumption of responsibility as quickly as possible.

5. Records of the counseling relationship, including interview notes, test data, correspondence, audio or visual tape recordings, electronic data storage, and other documents are to be considered professional information for use in counseling. They should not be considered a part of the records of the institution or agency in which the NCDA member is employed unless specified by state statute or regulation. Revelation to others of counseling material must occur only upon the expressed consent of the client; career counselors must make provisions for maintaining confidentiality in the storage and disposal of records. Career counselors providing information to the public or to subordinates, peers, or supervisors have a responsibility to ensure that the content is general; unidentified client information should be accurate and unbiased, and should consist of objective, factual data.

6. NCDA members must ensure that data maintained in electronic storage are secure. The data must be limited to information that is appropriate and necessary for the services being provided and accessible only to appropriate staff members involved in the provision of services by using the best computer security methods available. Career counselors must also ensure that electronically stored data are destroyed when the information is no longer of value in providing services.

7. Data derived from a counseling relationship for use in counselor training or research shall be confined to content that can be disguised to ensure full protection of the identity of the subject/client and shall be obtained with informed consent.

8. NCDA members must inform clients, before or at the time the counseling relationship commences, of the purposes, goals, techniques, rules and procedures, and limitations that may affect the relationship.

9. All methods of treatment by NCDA members must be clearly indicated to prospective recipients and safety precautions must be taken in their use.

10. NCDA members who have an administrative, supervisory, and/or evaluative relationship with individuals seeking counseling services must not serve as the counselor and should refer the individuals to other professionals. Exceptions are made only in instances where an individual's situation warrants counseling intervention and another alternative is unavailable. Dual relationships with clients that might impair the career counselor's objectivity and professional judgment must be avoided and/or the counseling relationship terminated through referral to another competent professional.

11. When NCDA members determine an inability to be of professional assistance to a potential or existing client, they must, respectively, not initiate the counseling relationship or immediately terminate the relationship. In either event, the career counselor must suggest appropriate alternatives. Career counselors must be knowledgeable about referral resources so that a satisfactory referral can be initiated. In the event that the client declines a suggested referral, the career counselor is not obligated to continue the relationship.

12.. NCDA members may choose to consult with any other professionally competent person about a client and must notify clients of this right. Career counselors must avoid placing a consultant in a conflict-of-interest situation that would preclude the consultant's being a proper party to the career counselor's efforts to help the client.

13. NCDA members who counsel clients from cultures different from their own must gain knowledge, personal awareness, and sensitivity pertinent to the client populations served and must incorporate culturally relevant techniques into their practice.

14. When NCDA members engage in intensive counseling with a client, the client's counseling needs should be assessed. When needs exist outside the counselor's expertise, appropriate referrals should be made.

15. NCDA members must screen prospective group counseling participants, especially when the emphasis is on self-understanding and growth through self-disclosure. Career counselors must maintain an awareness of each group participant's welfare throughout the group process.

16. When electronic data and systems are used as a component of counseling services, NCDA members must ensure that the computer application, and any information it contains, are appropriate for the respective needs of clients and is nondiscriminatory. Career counselors must ensure that they themselves have acquired a facilitation level of knowledge with any system they use including hands-on application, search experience, and understanding of the uses of all aspects of the computer-based system. In selecting and/or maintaining computer-based systems that contain career information, career counselors must ensure that the systems provide current, accurate, and locally relevant information. Career counselors must also ensure that clients are intellectually, emotionally, and physically compatible with the use of the computer application and understand its purpose and operation. Client use of a computer application must be evaluated to correct possible problems and assess subsequent needs.

17. NCDA members who develop self-help, stand-alone computer software for use by the general public must first ensure that it is initially designed to function in a stand-alone manner, as opposed to modifying software that was originally designed to require support from a counselor. Secondly, the software must include program statements that provide the user with intended outcomes, suggestions for using the software, descriptions of inappropriately used applications, and descriptions of when and how counseling services might be beneficial. Finally, the manual must include the qualifications of the developer, the development process, validation data, and operating procedures.

SECTION C: MEASUREMENT AND EVALUATION

1. NCDA members must provide specific orientation or information to an examinee prior to and following the administration of assessment instruments or techniques so that the results may be placed in proper perspective with other relevant factors. The purpose of testing and the explicit use of the results must be made known to an examinee prior to testing.

2. In selecting assessment instruments or techniques for use in a given situation or with a particular client, NCDA members must evaluate carefully the instrument's specific theoretical bases and characteristics, validity, reliability, and appropriateness. Career counselors are professionally responsible for using unvalidated information with special care.

3. When making statements to the public about assessment instruments or techniques, NCDA members must provide accurate information and avoid false claims or misconceptions concerning the meaning of psychometric terms. Special efforts are often required to avoid unwarranted connotations of terms such as IQ and grade-equivalent scores.

4. Because many types of assessment techniques exist, NCDA members must recognize the limits of their competence and perform only those functions for which they have received appropriate training.

5. NCDA members must note when tests are not administered under standard conditions or when unusual behavior or irregularities occur during a testing session and the results must be designated as invalid or of questionable validity. Unsupervised or inadequately supervised assessments, such as mail-in tests, are considered unethical. However, the use of standardized instruments that are designed to be self-administered and self-scored, such as interest inventories, is appropriate.

6. Because prior coaching or dissemination of test materials can invalidate test results, NCDA members are professionally obligated to maintain test security. In addition, conditions that produce most favorable test results must be made known to an examinee (e.g., penalty for guessing).

7. NCDA members must consider psychometric limitations when selecting and using an instrument, and must be cognizant of the limitations when interpreting the results. When tests are used to classify clients, career counselors must ensure that periodic review and/or retesting are conducted to prevent client stereotyping.

8. An examinee's welfare, explicit prior understanding, and agreement are the factors used

when determining who receives the test results. NCDA members must see that appropriate interpretation accompanies any release of individual or group test data (e.g., limitations of instrument and norms).

9. NCDA members must ensure that computer-generated assessment administration and scoring programs function properly, thereby providing clients with accurate assessment results.

10. NCDA members who are responsible for making decisions based on assessment results, must have appropriate training and skills in educational and psychological measurement including validation criteria, test research, and guidelines for test development and use.

11. NCDA members must be cautious when interpreting the results of instruments that possess insufficient technical data, and must explicitly state to examinees the specific purposes for the use of such instruments.

12. NCDA members must proceed with caution when attempting to evaluate and interpret performances of minority group members or other persons who are not represented in the norm group on which the instrument was standardized.

13. NCDA members who develop computer-based interpretations to support the assessment process must ensure that the validity of the interpretations is established prior to the commercial distribution of the computer application.

14. NCDA members recognize that test results may become obsolete, and avoid the misuse of obsolete data.

15. NCDA members must avoid the appropriation, reproduction, or modification of published tests or parts thereof without acknowledgment and permission from the publisher.

SECTION D: RESEARCH AND PUBLICATION

1. NCDA members will adhere to relevant guidelines on research with human subjects. These include:

   a. *Code of Federal Regulations,* Title 45, Subtitle A, Part 46, as currently issued.

   b. American Psychological Association. (1982). *Ethical principles in the conduct of research with human participants.* Washington, DC: Author.

   c. American Psychological Association. (1981). Research with human participants. *American Psychologist, 36,* 633–638.

   d. Family Educational Rights and Privacy Act. (Buckley Amendment to P. L. 93-380 of the Laws of 1974).

   e. Current federal regulations and various state privacy acts.

2. In planning research activities involving human subjects, NCDA members must be aware of and responsive to all pertinent ethical principles and ensure that the research problem, design, and execution are in full compliance with the principles.

3. The ultimate responsibility for ethical research lies with the principal researcher, although others involved in research activities are ethically obligated and responsible for their own actions.

4. NCDA members who conduct research with human subjects are responsible for the subjects' welfare throughout the experiment and must take all reasonable precautions to avoid causing injurious psychological, physical, or social effects on their subjects.

5. NCDA members who conduct research must abide by the following basic elements of informed consent:

   a. a fair explanation of the procedures to be followed, including an identification of those which are experimental.

   b. a description of the attendant discomforts and risks.

   c. a description of the benefits to be expected.

   d. a disclosure of appropriate alternative procedures that would be advantageous for subjects.

   e. an offer to answer any inquiries concerning the procedures.

   f. an instruction that subjects are free to withdraw their consent and to discontinue participation in the project or activity at any time.

6. When reporting research results, explicit mention must be made of all the variables and conditions

known to the NCDA member that may have affected the outcome of the study or the interpretation of the data.

7. NCDA members who conduct and report research investigations must do so in a manner that minimizes the possibility that the results will be misleading.

8. NCDA members are obligated to make available sufficient original research data to qualified others who may wish to replicate the study.

9. NCDA members who supply data, aid in the research of another person, report research results, or make original data available, must take due care to disguise the identity of respective subjects in the absence of specific authorization from the subject to do otherwise.

10. When conducting and reporting research, NCDA members must be familiar with, and give recognition to, previous work on the topic, must observe all copyright laws, and must follow the principles of giving full credit to those to whom credit is due.

11. NCDA members must give due credit through joint authorship, acknowledgment, footnote statements, or other appropriate means to those who have contributed significantly to the research and/or publication, in accordance with such contributions.

12. NCDA members should communicate to others the results of any research judged to be of professional value. Results that reflect unfavorably on institutions, programs, services, or vested interests must not be withheld.

13. NCDA members who agree to cooperate with another individual in research and/or publication incur an obligation to cooperate as promised in terms of punctuality of performance and with full regard to the completeness and accuracy of the information required.

14. NCDA members must not submit the same manuscript, or one essentially similar in content, for simultaneous publication consideration by two or more journals. In addition, manuscripts that are published in whole or substantial part in another journal or published work should not be submitted for publication without acknowledgment and permission from the previous publication.

SECTION E: CONSULTING

Consultation refers to a voluntary relationship between a professional helper and help-needing individual, group, or social unit in which the consultant is providing help to the client(s) in defining and solving a work-related problem or potential work-related problem with a client or client system.

1. NCDA members acting as consultants must have a high degree of self-awareness of their own values, knowledge, skills, limitations, and needs in entering a helping relationship that involves human and/or organizational change. The focus of the consulting relationship must be on the issues to be resolved and not on the person(s) presenting the problem.

2. In the consulting relationship, the NCDA member and client must understand and agree upon the problem definition, subsequent goals, and predicted consequences of interventions selected.

3. NCDA members must be reasonably certain that they, or the organization represented, have the necessary competencies and resources for giving the kind of help that is needed or that may develop later, and that appropriate referral resources are available to the consultant.

4. NCDA members in a consulting relationship must encourage and cultivate client adaptability and growth toward self-direction. NCDA members must maintain this role consistently and not become decision makers for clients or create a future dependency.

5. NCDA members conscientiously adhere to the NCDA Ethical Standards when announcing consultant availability for services.

SECTION F: PRIVATE PRACTICE

1. NCDA members should assist the profession by facilitating the availability of counseling services in private as well as public settings.

2. In advertising services as private practitioners, NCDA members must advertise in a manner that accurately informs the public of the professional services, expertise, and counseling techniques available.

3. NCDA members who assume an executive leadership role in a private practice organization do not permit their names to be used in professional notices during periods of time when they are not actively engaged in the private practice of counseling.

4. NCDA members may list their highest relevant degree, type, and level of certification and/or license, address, telephone number, office hours, type and/or description of services, and other relevant information. Listed information must not contain false, inaccurate, misleading, partial, out-of-context, or otherwise deceptive material or statements.

5. NCDA members who are involved in partnership or corporation with other professionals must, in compliance with the regulations of the locality, clearly specify the separate specialties of each member of the partnership or corporation.

6. NCDA members have an obligation to withdraw from a private-practice counseling relationship if it violates the NCDA Ethical Standards, if the mental or physical condition of the NCDA member renders it difficult to carry out an effective professional relationship, or if the counseling relationship is no longer productive for the client.

PROCEDURES FOR PROCESSING ETHICAL COMPLAINTS

As a division of the American Counseling Association (ACA) the National Career Development Association (NCDA) adheres to the guidelines and procedures for processing ethical complaints and the disciplinary sanctions adopted by ACA. A complaint against an NCDA member may be filed by any individual or group of individuals ("complainant"), whether or not the complainant is a member of NCDA. Action will not be taken on anonymous complaints.

For specifics on how to file ethical complaints and a description of the guidelines and procedures for processing complaints, contact:

ACA Ethics Committee
c/o Executive Director
American Counseling Association
5999 Stevenson Avenue
Alexandria, VA 22304
(800) 347-6647

SOURCE: From the American Counseling Association. Reprinted with permission.

CODE OF PROFESSIONAL ETHICS FOR REHABILITATION COUNSELORS

The Commission on Rehabilitation Counselor Certification has adopted a Code of Professional Ethics for its Certified Rehabilitation Counselors. The following organizations have adopted the same Code for their memberships: the American Rehabilitation Counseling Association, the National Rehabilitation Counseling Association, and the National Council on Rehabilitation Education. Portions of the Code are derived from the American Psychological Association's Ethical Principles of Psychologists.

PREAMBLE

Rehabilitation counselors are committed to facilitating the personal, social, and economic independence of individuals with disabilities. In fulfilling this commitment, rehabilitation counselors work with various people, programs, institutions, and service delivery systems. Rehabilitation counselors recognize that their actions (or inaction) can either aid or hinder clients in achieving their rehabilitation objectives, and they accept this responsibility as part of their professional obligations. Rehabilitation counselors may be called upon to provide various kinds of assistance including: counseling; vocational explorations; psychological and vocational assessments; evaluations of social, medical, vocational, and psychiatric information; job placement and job development activities; and other types of rehabilitation services. They are required to do so in a manner that is consistent with their education and experience. Moreover, rehabilitation counselors must demonstrate their adherence to ethical standards and ensure that these standards are vigorously enforced. The Code of Professional Ethics (henceforth referred to as the Code) is designed to facilitate the achievement of these goals.

The primary obligation of rehabilitation counselors is to their clients (defined in the Code as individuals with disabilities who are receiving services from rehabilitation counselors). The objective of the Code is to promote public welfare by specifying and enforcing ethical standards of behavior expected of rehabilitation counselors. Accordingly, the Code contains two kinds of standards: Canons and Rules of Professional Conduct.

The Canons are general standards of an aspirational and inspirational nature that reflect the fundamental spirit of caring and respect which professionals share. They are maxims designed to serve as models of exemplary professional conduct. The Canons also express general concepts and principles from which the more specific Rules are derived. Unlike the Canons, the Rules are exacting standards intended to provide guidance in specific circumstances.

Rehabilitation counselors who violate the Code are subject to disciplinary action. A violation of a Rule is interpreted as a violation of the applicable Canon and the general principles it embodies. Since the use of the Certified Rehabilitation Counselor (CRC) designation is a privilege granted by the Commission on Rehabilitation Counselor Certification (CRCC), the Commission reserves unto itself the power to suspend or revoke this privilege or to impose other penalties for a Rule violation. Disciplinary penalties are imposed as warranted by the severity of the offense and its attendant circumstances. All disciplinary actions are undertaken in accordance with published procedures and penalties that are designed to ensure proper enforcement of the Code within a framework of due process and equal protection under the law.

When there is reason to question the ethical propriety of specific behavior, individuals are encouraged to refrain from such behavior until the matter has been clarified. CRCs who need assistance in interpreting the Code should write to the Commission to request an advisory opinion. Counselors who are not certified should request such opinions from their own professional organizations.

Canon 1: Moral and Legal Standards

Rehabilitation counselors shall behave in a legal, ethical, and moral manner in the conduct of their profession, maintaining the integrity of the Code and avoiding any behavior that would cause harm to others.

Rules of Professional Conduct
R1.1 Rehabilitation counselors will obey the laws and statutes of the legal jurisdiction in which

they practice, and are subject to disciplinary action for any violation, to the extent that such violation suggests the likelihood of professional misconduct.

R1.2   Rehabilitation counselors will be thoroughly familiar with and observe the legal limitations of the services they offer to clients. They will discuss these limitations as well as all benefits available to the clients they serve in order to facilitate open, honest communications and avoid unrealistic expectations.

R1.3   Rehabilitation counselors will be alert to the legal parameters relevant to their practices as well as to any disparities that may exist between legally mandated ethical and professional standards and the Code. Where disparities exist, rehabilitation counselors will follow the legal mandates and formally communicate such disparities to the appropriate committee on professional ethics. In the absence of any legal guidelines, the Code is ethically binding.

R1.4   Rehabilitation counselors will not engage in any act or omission of a dishonest, deceitful or fraudulent nature in the conduct of their professional activities. They will not allow the pursuit of financial gain or other personal benefits to interfere with the exercise of sound professional judgment and skills, nor will they abuse the relationship with a client to promote their personal or financial gain or the financial gain of an employer.

R1.5   Rehabilitation counselors will understand and abide by the Canons and Rules of Professional Conduct prescribed in the Code.

R1.6   Rehabilitation counselors will not advocate, sanction, participate in, cause to be accomplished, carry out through another or condone any act which they themselves are prohibited from performing by the Code.

R1.7   Moral and ethical standards of behavior are a personal matter for rehabilitation counselors to the same degree as they are for any other citizen, except as such standards may compromise the fulfillment of the individual's professional responsibilities or reduce public trust in rehabilitation counselors.

R1.8   Rehabilitation counselors will respect the rights and reputation of any institution, organization or firm with which they are associated when making oral or written statements. In those instances where they are critical of policies, they will attempt to effect changes through constructive action within the organization.

R1.9   Rehabilitation counselors will refuse to participate in employment practices that are inconsistent with the moral or legal standards regarding the treatment of employees or the public. Rehabilitation counselors will not condone practices that result in illegal or otherwise unjustifiable discrimination on any basis in hiring, promotion or training.

Canon 2: Counselor-Client Relationship

Rehabilitation counselors shall respect the integrity and protect the welfare of the people and groups with whom they work. The primary obligation of rehabilitation counselors is to their clients (defined as individuals with disabilities who are receiving services from rehabilitation counselors). At all times, rehabilitation counselors shall endeavor to place their clients' interests above their own.

Rules of Professional Conduct

R2.1   Rehabilitation counselors will make clear to clients the purposes, goals, and limitations that may affect the counseling relationship.

R2.2   Rehabilitation counselors will not misrepresent their role or competence to clients. If requested, they will provide information about their credentials, and will refer clients to other specialists as the needs of the clients dictate.

R2.3   Rehabilitation counselors will be continually cognizant of their own needs and values as well as of their potential influence over clients, students, and subordinates. They will avoid exploiting the trust or dependency of such persons. Rehabilitation counselors will make every effort to avoid dual relationships that could impair their professional judgment or increase the risk of exploitation. Examples of dual relationships include, but are not limited to, research with and treatment of employees, students, supervisors, close friends or relatives. Sexual intimacy with clients is unethical.

R2.4 Rehabilitation counselors who provide services at the request of a third party will clarify the nature of their relationships to all involved. They will inform all parties of their ethical responsibilities and take other action as appropriate. Rehabilitation counselors who are employed by third parties as case consultants or expert witnesses, where there is no pretense or intent to provide rehabilitation counseling services directly to clients (beyond file review, initial interview and/or assessment) will clearly define, through written or oral means, the limits of their relationship (particularly in the areas of informed consent and legally privileged communications) to all involved. When serving as case consultants or expert witnesses, rehabilitation counselors have an obligation to provide unbiased, objective opinions.

R2.5 Rehabilitation counselors will honor the rights of clients to consent to participate in rehabilitation services. They will inform the clients or their legal guardians of factors that may affect the clients' decision to take part in rehabilitation services, and they will obtain written consent once the clients or their guardians are fully informed of these factors. Rehabilitation counselors who work with minors or other persons who are unable to give informed, voluntary consent will take special care to protect the best interests of their clients.

R2.6 Rehabilitation counselors will avoid initiating or continuing consulting or counseling relationships if it appears there can be no benefit to the client; in these cases, the rehabilitation counselor will suggest appropriate alternatives to the client.

R2.7 Rehabilitation counselors will recognize that families are usually an important factor in the client's rehabilitation and will strive to enlist their understanding and involvement as a positive resource in achieving rehabilitation goals. The client's permission will be secured prior to any family involvement.

R2.8 Rehabilitation counselors and their clients will work together to devise an integrated, individualized rehabilitation plan that promises reasonable success and is consistent with each client's circumstances and abilities.

Rehabilitation counselors will continually monitor such plans to ensure their ongoing viability and effectiveness, remembering that clients have the right to make their own choices.

R2.9 Rehabilitation counselors will work with their clients in evaluating potential employment opportunities, considering only those jobs and circumstances that are consistent with the client's overall abilities, vocational limitations, physical restrictions, general temperament, interests and aptitude patterns, social skills, education, general qualifications, and other relevant characteristics and needs. Rehabilitation counselors will neither place or participate in the placing of clients in positions that could damage the interests and welfare of either the client or the employer.

Canon 3: Client Advocacy

Rehabilitation counselors shall serve as advocates for individuals with disabilities.

Rules of Professional Conduct

R3.1 Rehabilitation counselors will be obligated at all times to promote better access for individuals with disabilities to facilities, programs, transportation, and communication so that clients will not be excluded from opportunities to participate fully in rehabilitation, education and society.

R3.2 Rehabilitation counselors will ensure that programs, facilities and employment settings are appropriately accessible before referring clients to them.

R3.3 Rehabilitation counselors will strive to understand the accessibility problems of individuals with cognitive, hearing, mobility, visual and/or other disabilities, and to demonstrate this understanding in the practice of their profession.

R3.4 Rehabilitation counselors will strive to eliminate attitudinal barriers, including stereotyping and discrimination, toward individuals with disabilities and to increase their own awareness and sensitivity to such individuals.

R3.5 Rehabilitation counselors will remain aware of the actions taken by cooperating agencies on behalf of their clients and will act as the advocates of such clients to ensure effective service delivery.

Canon 4: Professional Relationships

Rehabilitation counselors shall act with integrity in their relationships with colleagues, organizations, agencies, institutions, referral sources, and other professions in order to provide clients with optimum benefits.

Rules of Professional Conduct

R4.1 Rehabilitation counselors will ensure that there is a mutual understanding of the rehabilitation plan by all agencies involved in the rehabilitation of clients and that all rehabilitation plans are developed with such mutual understanding.

R4.2 Rehabilitation counselors will abide by and help to implement "team" decisions when formulating rehabilitation plans and procedures, even if not in personal agreement with such decisions, unless they constitute a breach of ethical conduct.

R4.3 Rehabilitation counselors will not commit receiving counselors to any prescribed course of action in relation to clients they may transfer to other colleagues or agencies.

R4.4 Rehabilitation counselors, when acting as referring counselors, will promptly supply all information needed for a cooperating agency or counselor to begin serving a transferred client.

R4.5 Rehabilitation counselors will not offer ongoing professional counseling or case management services to clients who are receiving such services from another counselor without first notifying that individual. File reviews and second-opinion services are not included in the concept of professional counseling and case management services.

R4.6 Rehabilitation counselors will secure appropriate reports and evaluations from other specialists when such reports are essential for rehabilitation planning and/or service delivery.

R4.7 Rehabilitation counselors will not discuss the competency of other counselors or agencies (including the judgments made, methods used or quality of rehabilitation plans) in a disparaging way with their clients.

R4.8 Rehabilitation counselors will not use their professional relationships with supervisors, colleagues, students or employees to exploit them sexually or otherwise. Neither will they engage in or condone sexual harassment (defined as deliberate or repeated comments, gestures, or physical contacts of a sexual nature that are unwanted by the recipients).

R4.9 Rehabilitation counselors who know of an ethics violation by another counselor will attempt to resolve the issue informally with that person provided the misconduct is minor in nature and/or appears to be due to a lack of sensitivity, knowledge or experience. If the violation is more serious or not amendable to an informal resolution, the counselor will bring it to the attention of the appropriate committee on professional ethics.

R4.10 Rehabilitation counselors possessing information of an alleged violation of this Code will reveal such information to the Commission or another authority empowered to investigate or act upon the alleged violation, if requested to do so. This does not apply to information that is protected by law.

R4.11 Rehabilitation counselors who employ or supervise students or other professionals will provide appropriate working conditions, timely evaluations, constructive consultations, and suitable experience opportunities to facilitate the professional development of these individuals.

Canon 5: Public Statements/Fees

Rehabilitation counselors shall adhere to professional standards in establishing fees and promoting their services.

Rules of Professional Conduct
R5.1 Rehabilitation counselors will consider carefully the value of their services and the financial resources of their clients in order to establish reasonable fees for their professional services.

R5.2 Rehabilitation counselors will not accept a fee or any other form of remuneration for their work from clients who are entitled to their services through an institution, agency or other benefit structure, unless the client has been fully informed of the availability of such services from those sources.

R5.3 Rehabilitation counselors will neither give nor receive commissions, rebates or any other form of remuneration when referring clients for professional services.

R5.4 Rehabilitation counselors who describe the counseling and other services offered to the public will present such information fairly and accurately, avoiding misrepresentation through sensationalism, exaggeration or superficiality. Rehabilitation counselors will be guided by their primary obligation to aid the public forming valid opinions and making informed choices and judgments.

Canon 6: Confidentiality

Rehabilitation counselors shall respect the confidentiality of information obtained from clients in the course of their work.

Rules of Professional Conduct

R6.1 Rehabilitation counselors will inform clients of the limits of confidentiality at the onset of the counseling relationship.

R6.2 Rehabilitation counselors will take reasonable personal action, inform responsible authorities or inform those persons at risk if the condition or actions of a client indicate there is clear and imminent danger to the client or others; counselors will take such actions only after advising the client of what must be done. Consultations with other professionals may be used where appropriate. Such assumptions of responsibility for a client must be taken only after careful deliberation, and clients must be permitted to resume responsibility as quickly as possible.

R6.3 Rehabilitation counselors will not forward any confidential information to another person, agency or potential employers without the written permission of the client or the client's legal guardian.

R6.4 Rehabilitation counselors will ensure that the agencies which cooperate in serving their clients have specific policies and practices in place to protect client confidentiality.

R6.5 Rehabilitation counselors will safeguard the maintenance, storage, and disposal of client records so unauthorized persons cannot gain access to them. Any non-professional who must be given access to a client's records will be thoroughly instructed about the confidentiality standards to be observed by the rehabilitation counselor.

R6.6 Rehabilitation counselors will present only germane data in preparing oral and written reports, and will make every effort to avoid undue invasions of privacy.

R6.7 Rehabilitation counselors will obtain written permission from clients or their legal guardians prior to taping or otherwise recording counseling sessions. Even if a guardian's consent is obtained, counselors will not record sessions against the expressed wishes of their client.

R6.8 Rehabilitation counselors will persist in claiming the privileged status of confidential information obtained from their clients where communications between counselors and clients have been accorded privileged status under the law.

R6.9 Rehabilitation counselors will provide only relevant information about clients seeking jobs to prospective employers. Before releasing any information that might be considered confidential, the counselor will secure the permission of the client or legal guardian.

Canon 7: Assessment

Rehabilitation counselors shall promote the welfare of clients in the selection, use and interpretation of assessment measures.

Rules of Professional Conduct
R7.1 Rehabilitation counselors will recognize that different tests require different levels of competence to administer, score and interpret; they will also recognize the limits of their competence and will perform only those functions for which they are trained.

R7.2 Rehabilitation counselors will carefully consider the specific validity, reliability, and appropriateness of tests when selecting them for use in a given situation or for particular clients. They will proceed with caution in attempting to evaluate and interpret the performance of individuals with disabilities, members of minority groups or persons who are not represented in standardized norms. Rehabilitation counselors will take into consideration the effects of socio-economic, ethnic, disability, and cultural factors on test scores.

R7.3 Rehabilitation counselors will administer tests under the conditions established when the tests were standardized. When non-standard conditions are required to accommodate clients with disabilities, or when unusual behaviors or irregularities occur during the testing session, those circumstances will be noted and taken into account when interpreting the test results.

R7.4 Rehabilitation counselors will ensure that instrument limitations are not exceeded, and that periodic assessments are made to prevent client stereotyping.

R7.5 Rehabilitation counselors will inform clients of the purpose of any testing and the explicit use of the results before administration. Recognizing the right of clients to their test results, counselors will explain such results in language the clients can understand.

R7.6 Rehabilitation counselors will ensure that specific interpretations accompany any release of individual data. The client's welfare and explicit prior permission from the client will determine who is to receive test results. Assessment data will be interpreted on the basis of the particular goals of the evaluation.

R7.7 Rehabilitation counselors will attempt to ensure that the interpretations produced by computerized assessment programs or procedures have been validated through appropriate research. Public offerings of automated test interpretation services will be considered as professional-to-professional consultations. In these instances, the formal responsibility of the consultant is to the consultee, but the ultimate and overriding responsibility is to the client.

R7.8 Rehabilitation counselors will recognize that assessment results may become outdated and will make every effort to avoid the use of obsolete measures.

Canon 8: Research Activities

Rehabilitation counselors shall assist in efforts to expand the knowledge needed to serve individuals with disabilities more effectively.

Rules of Professional Conduct

R8.1 Rehabilitation counselors will ensure that research data meet rigid standards of validity, accuracy, and protection of confidentiality.

R8.2 Rehabilitation counselors will be aware of and responsive to all pertinent guidelines on research with human subjects. When planning such research, counselors will ensure that the project, design, and execution are in full compliance with such guidelines.

R8.3 Rehabilitation counselors who present case studies in classes, professional meetings or publications will confine the content to information that can be sufficiently disguised to ensure full protection of client identity.

R8.4 Rehabilitation counselors will credit those who contribute to publications in proportion to the size of their contribution.

R8.5 Rehabilitation counselors recognize that openness and honesty are essential to relationships between counselors and research participants. When a study's methodology requires concealment or deception, the counselor will ensure that participants understand the reasons for such action.

Canon 9: Competence

Rehabilitation counselors shall establish and maintain their professional competence at a level which ensures their clients will receive the benefit of the highest quality of service the profession is capable of offering.

Rules of Professional Conduct

R9.1 Rehabilitation counselors will function within the limits of their defined role, training and technical competency, accepting only those positions for which they are professionally qualified.

R9.2 Rehabilitation counselors will continuously strive, through reading, attending professional meetings, and taking courses of instruction, to remain aware of developments, concepts and practices that are essential in providing the highest quality of services to their clients.

R9.3 Rehabilitation counselors, recognizing that personal problems may interfere with their professional effectiveness, will refrain from undertaking any activity in which such problems could lead to inadequate performance. If they are already engaged in such a situation when they become aware of a problem, they will seek competent professional assistance to determine if they should limit, suspend or terminate their professional activities.

R9.4 Rehabilitation counselors who are educators will perform their duties based on careful preparation so that their instruction is accurate, up-to-date, and scholarly.

R9.5 Rehabilitation counselors who are educators will ensure that statements made in catalogs and course outlines are accurate, particularly in terms of subject matter, basis for grading, and nature of classroom experiences.

R9.6 Rehabilitation counselors who are educators will maintain high standards of knowledge and skill by presenting information in their field fully and accurately, and by giving appropriate recognition to alternative viewpoints.

Canon 10: CRC Credential

Rehabilitation counselors holding the designation of Certified Rehabilitation Counselor (CRC) shall honor its integrity and respect the limitations placed on its use.

Rules of Professional Conduct

R10.1 Certified Rehabilitation Counselors will use the CRC designation only in accordance with

the relevant Guidelines promulgated by the Commission on Rehabilitation Counselor Certification (CRCC).

R10.2 Certified Rehabilitation Counselors will not claim a depth or scope of knowledge, skills or professional capabilities that are greater than warranted simply because they have achieved the CRC designation.

R10.3 Certified Rehabilitation Counselors will not make unfair comparisons between persons who hold the designation and those who do not.

R10.4 Certified Rehabilitation Counselors will not write, speak or act in such a way as to lead another to reasonably believe the counselor is an official Commission representative unless authorized to do so in writing by the Commission.

R10.5 Certified Rehabilitation Counselors will not claim possession of unique skills or devices not available to others in the profession unless the existence and efficacy of such skills or devices has been scientifically demonstrated.

R10.6 Certified Rehabilitation Counselors will not initiate or support the candidacy of an individual for certification if that individual is known to engage in professional practices that violate this Code.

Referenced documents, statements, and sources for the development of this revised Code are as follows: National Rehabilitation Counseling Association Code of Ethics, National Academy of Certified Clinical Mental Health Counselors, and the Ethical Standards of the American Association for Counseling and Development. Portions of the Code are also derived from the "Ethical Principles of Psychologists" of the American Psychological Association.

SCOPE OF PRACTICE FOR REHABILITATION COUNSELING

I. ASSUMPTIONS

- The Scope of Practice Statement identifies knowledge and skills required for the provision of effective rehabilitation counseling services to persons with physical, mental, developmental, cognitive, and emotional disabilities as embodied in the standards of the profession's credentialing organizations.

- The several rehabilitation disciplines and related processes (e.g., vocational evaluation, job development and job placement, work adjustment, case management) are tied to the central field of rehabilitation counseling. The field of rehabilitation counseling is a specialty within the rehabilitation profession with counseling at its core, and is differentiated from other related counseling fields.

- The professional scope of rehabilitation counseling practice is also differentiated from an individual scope of practice, which may overlap, but is more specialized than the professional scope. An individual scope of practice is based on one's own knowledge of the abilities and skills that have been gained through a program of education and professional experience. A person is ethically bound to limit his/her practice to that individual scope of practice.

II. UNDERLYING VALUES

- Facilitation of independence, integration, and inclusion of people with disabilities in employment and the community.

- Belief in the dignity and worth of all people.

- Commitment to a sense of equal justice based on a model of accommodation to provide and equalize the opportunities to participate in all rights and privileges available to all people; and a commitment to supporting persons with disabilities in advocacy activities to enable them to achieve this status and empower themselves.

- Emphasis on the holistic nature of human function which is procedurally facilitated by the utilization of such techniques as:
  1. interdisciplinary teamwork.
  2. counseling to assist in maintaining a holistic perspective.
  3. a commitment to considering individuals within the context of their family systems and communities.
- Recognition of the importance of focusing on the assets of the person.
- Commitment to models of service delivery that emphasize integrated, comprehensive services which are mutually planned by the consumer and the rehabilitation counselor.

III. SCOPE OF PRACTICE STATEMENT

Rehabilitation counseling is a systematic process which assists persons with physical, mental, developmental, cognitive, and emotional disabilities to achieve their personal, career, and independent living goals in the most integrated setting possible through the application of the counseling process. The counseling process involves communication, goal setting, and beneficial growth or change through self-advocacy, psychological, vocational, social, and behavioral interventions. The specific techniques and modalities utilized within this rehabilitation counseling process may include, but are not limited to:

- assessment and appraisal;
- diagnosis and treatment planning;
- career (vocational) counseling;
- individual and group counseling treatment interventions focused on facilitating adjustments to the medical and psychosocial impact of disability;
- case management, referral, and service coordination;
- program evaluation and research;
- interventions to remove environmental, employment, and attitudinal barriers;

- consultation services among multiple parties and regulatory systems;

- job analysis, job development, and placement services, including assistance with employment and job accommodations; and

- the provision of consultation about, and access to, rehabilitation technology.

IV. SELECTED DEFINITIONS

The following definitions are provided to increase the understanding of certain key terms and concepts used in the Scope of Practice Statement for Rehabilitation Counseling.

Appraisal: Selecting, administering, scoring, and interpreting instruments designed to assess an individual's attitudes, abilities, achievements, interests, personal characteristics, disabilities, and mental, emotional, or behavioral disorders as well as the use of methods and techniques for understanding human behavior in relation to coping with, adapting to, or changing life situations.

Diagnosis and Treatment Planning: Assessing, analyzing, and providing diagnostic descriptions of mental, emotional, or behavioral conditions or disabilities; exploring possible solutions; and developing and implementing a treatment plan for mental, emotional, and psychosocial adjustment or development. Diagnosis and treatment planning shall not be construed to permit the performance of any act which rehabilitation counselors are not educated and trained to perform.

Counseling Treatment Intervention: The application of cognitive, affective, behavioral, and systemic counseling strategies which include developmental, wellness, pathologic, and multicultural principles of human behavior. Such interventions are specifically implemented in the context of a professional counseling relationship and may include, but are not limited to: appraisal; individual, group, marriage, and family counseling and psychotherapy; the diagnostic description and treatment of persons with mental, emotional, and behavioral disorders or disabilities; guidance and consulting to facilitate normal growth and development, including educational and career development; the utilization of functional assessments and career counseling for persons requesting assistance in adjusting to a disability or handicapping condition; referrals; consulting; and research.

Referral: Evaluating and identifying the needs of a counselee to determine the advisability of referrals to other specialists, advising the counselee of such judgments, and communicating as requested or deemed appropriate to such referral sources.

Case Management: A systematic process merging counseling and managerial concepts and skills through the application of techniques derived from intuitive and researched methods, thereby advancing efficient and effective decision-making for functional control of self, client, setting, and other relevant factors for anchoring a proactive practice. In case management, the counselor's role is focused on interviewing, counseling, planning rehabilitation programs, coordinating services, interacting with significant others, placing clients and following up with them, monitoring a client's progress, and solving problems.

Program Evaluation: The effort to determine what changes occur as a result of a planned program by comparing actual changes (results) with desired changes (stated goals), and by identifying the degree to which the activity (planned program) is responsible for those changes.

Research: A systematic effort to collect, analyze, and interpret quantitative or qualitative data that describe how social characteristics, behavior, emotions, cognition, disabilities, mental disorders, and interpersonal transactions among individuals and organizations interact.

Consultation: The application of scientific principles and procedures in counseling and human development to provide assistance in understanding and solving current or potential problems that the consultee may have in relation to a third party, be it an individual, group, or organization.

14

Group Counseling

Group counseling, like no other type of counseling, raises some interesting ethical dilemmas, because treatment is undertaken with more than one client present. In addition, the clients are usually unrelated (nonfamily members). So certain ethical issues (such as confidentiality, privileged communication, and privacy) come to the forefront.

Group counseling is a popular style of counseling. Corey and Corey (1997) stated:

> Group therapy originated in response to a shortage during World War II of personnel trained to provide individual therapy. At first, the group therapist assumed a traditional therapeutic role, frequently working with a small number of clients with a common problem. Gradually, leaders began to experiment with different roles and various approaches. Over time, practitioners discovered that the group setting offered unique therapeutic possibilities. Exchanges among the members of a therapy group are viewed as instrumental in bringing about change. This interaction provides support, caring, confrontation, and other qualities not found in individual therapy. Within the group context, members are able to practice new social skills and apply some of their new knowledge. (p. 11)

Beyond therapeutic benefits, group counseling is economical for clients. The economic benefits are both financial and time-related. Group counseling is usually much less expensive than individual counseling; fees for one hour of treatment may be one-fourth or one-fifth the standard fee for individual therapy. In addition counselors can treat 8 to 10 people at one time. With constraints of limited government resources, and under the veil of managed care, group therapy may have an expanded role in the mental health service enterprise.

This chapter introduces some of the ethical nuances of group counseling. You will become acquainted with some of the crucial issues addressed by counselors who provide group therapy services. Additionally, specialty concerns will be addressed. Although some people view group counseling as a mode of treatment, others view group counseling as a separate specialty, requiring specialized training and supervision.

Defining the Specialty, Settings, and Clients

Group counseling occurs in a variety of settings: private counseling practices, clinics, college counseling centers, chemical dependency treatment programs, hospitals, schools, and just about any counseling context where there is enough physical space (for three or more individuals) and where there is a pool of available clients. Group counseling usually occurs in a room with chairs arranged in a circular fashion. But the variety of group types, and the variety of configurations of groupings is unlimited. Some counselors allow clients to sit on the floor, or they may recline. Group decision-making about how counseling is to be accomplished is common, usually with a defined theme or topic as central to the group task. However, some groups are highly structured and may imitate a classroom-like atmosphere. The directiveness of groups varies widely, along with the purpose of the group. For example, a group addressing issues of teen drug use may involve open facilitated discussion, may be educational, or may involve some combination of discussion and didactic activities. A group addressing recovery from trauma may involve open-discussion, so individuals can vent their feelings in a supportive environment. There are also differences around the makeup of the group. Groups may be organized by such factors such as gender, age, common experiences, conditions of individuals (e.g., physical or mental disorders), or interests. They may be composed of individuals, couples, families, or other groups. The nature of groups vary widely, and the subsequent dynamics of a group vary according to its nature, makeup, and purpose.

At the current time, there is no recognized certifying body for group specialists established under the auspices or direction of the American Psychological Association (APA) or the American Counseling Association (ACA). There is, however, an affiliate organization in the ACA, the Association for Specialists in Group Work (ASGW) which has a code of ethics specifically written for group counseling practice. Also, the APA has a division (Division 49, Group Psychology and Group Psychotherapy) that serves as a formal organization for psychologists interested in the study and practice of group counseling. Accordingly, group counseling is a specialty that does not meet formal specialty criteria, where such criteria would involve the credentialing of individuals through a formal specialty board and through specialty designation at the level of training. In essence, group counseling represents a mode of treatment that is distinct in its involvement of more than one person as a client at the same time. This distinct treatment modality leads to interesting ethical dilemmas, some of which are not adequately addressed by codes of ethics that focus primarily on individual treatment. The ASGW code of ethics, therefore, is a useful document and gives clear guidance for counselors using group methods.

Issues of Significance to the Specialty

Professional Differentiation

As addressed in the previous section, group counseling does not meet the typical criteria for a formal specialty of counseling, even though the ASGW uses the term *specialists* in its title. Group counseling should be considered a specialized mode of treatment. Where specialties such as school counseling or rehabilitation counseling imply a type of setting (schools or rehabilitation agencies, respectively) and a type of client (students or individuals with disabilities, respectively), group counseling has no such boundaries. It can be used with many types of clients in many types of settings. Regardless, it is imperative that counselors who use this mode of treatment seek supervision and training in group procedures and processes. Even specialized training for certain types of groups is warranted because there are so many variations among groups themselves. Group types range from the "encounter groups" of the 1960s and 1970s, which emphasized personal growth (Rogers, 1970), to a plethora of applications developed since World War II, such as psychodrama groups, behavior therapy groups, Gestalt therapy groups (see Gazda's, 1975, classic text). Generally, group supervision can be obtained from individuals who have credentials in a type of therapy (e.g., Gestalt, Rational–Emotive) or who hold credentials in addressing a type of concern (e.g., chemical dependency, sexual dysfunction) and who additionally are trained and experienced in group procedures.

Ethical Issues

Confidentiality and Privileged Communication.   Complex ethical circumstances arise in groups that do not arise in other counseling situations. In a recently publicized case in a Midwestern state, a member of an Alcoholics Anonymous group revealed to the group that he had committed murder. The revelation was revealed to the press and reported in the newspapers. The individual was subsequently investigated by the authorities. Questions of group counseling confidentiality were raised, and the consensus of the mental health community was that there was no confidentiality except as was voluntarily agreed on by the members of the group. In the absence of a licensed professional, no protection can be given legally to the information provided in a group. But even in the presence of a licensed professional who is afforded legal confidentiality, the presence of other individuals in a group (nonprofessionals) compromises confidentiality; other group members are not required by law to keep information private or secret. In an article addressing confidentiality in a support group for individuals with Acquired Immune Deficiency Syndrome (AIDS), Posey (1988) described some circumstances unique to group treatment:

> In our group, discussions of confidentiality have been triggered by people dropping in, one member identifying another at a bar, issues of how or whether to leave telephone messages, and how to respond to a member's family and friends at the hospital. Initially, a member distributed names and telephone numbers of the group members but recalled them when members expressed discomfort. Once, a news reporter appeared at a meeting

and wanted to sit in, and he guaranteed that identities would be protected. The group agreed to discuss his interest but would not allow him to attend the meeting. (p 226)

Unusual, and sometimes unpredictable issues of confidentiality arise in group settings. This is partly because nonprofessional group members may reveal information communicated in a group at their discretion, judgment, or in some cases, misjudgment. The ASGW *Ethical Guidelines for Group Counselors* make a clear statement about this special circumstance:

> Group counselors stress the importance of confidentiality and set a norm of confidentiality regarding all group participants' disclosures. The importance of maintaining confidentiality is emphasized before the group begins and at various times in the group. The fact that confidentiality cannot be guaranteed is clearly stated. (Section 2b)

It is important for clients to know that although counselors will act to protect the clients' right to confidentiality, counselors cannot enforce a ban on gossip among other members of the group or between members of the group and outsiders. The ASGW code reads: "Group counselors can only ensure confidentiality on their part and not on the part of the members" (Section 2d). The *Ethical Guidelines for Group Counselors* is reprinted at the end of this chapter.

Confidentiality is also complicated in groups when other individuals have access to records. For example, if a group of minors is being counseled, then technically the parents of the minors have the right to have information about the nature and content of counseling (unless there is a legal exemption to parental consent or oversight). Parents even have legal access to case file information. Revelation of group counseling case file information to parents of one or more members of a group (such as group counseling case notes) who reference other individuals in the group, essentially breaches the confidentiality of the other group members, unless those other group members' parents allow for such revelation.

Group counselors have a special responsibility to ensure that case notes for group counseling are written for each individual in the group. Further, information about other group members should be deleted or omitted from the case files of the group member on which the case notes are being written. This situation is complicated further by federal law. The federal Family Education Rights and Privacy Act of 1974 (FERPA), which covers all educational institutions receiving federal funding from preschool through university graduate training clearly states:

> The parents of students [have] the right to inspect and review any and all official records, files, and data directly related to their children, including all material that is incorporated into each student's cumulative record folder. . . . Where such records or data include information on more than one student, the parents of any student shall be entitled to receive or be informed of, that part of such record or data as pertains to their child. (Section 438.[a][1])

In effect, counselors in educational settings must document group counseling case files carefully in light of a legal standard that allows parents full access to such information, even if a parent's child is referenced in someone else's case notes.

Regardless of the specific situation in which an issue of confidentiality arises, the counselor must inform each group participant of the limits of confidentiality before that individual's consent to initiate treatment. The APA (1992), ACA (1995), and ASGW (1989) codes of ethics all agree that the limits of confidentiality must be discussed with clients. Initiation of groups should not occur until all members of the group are privy to and informed of the limits of confidentiality, and clients should be made to acknowledge such awareness (e.g., by signing a statement of understanding).

Standards exemptions to confidentiality apply in group as in individual counseling (see Chapter 2). Depending on the state law that applies, counselors must breach confidentiality in situations where there is (a) suspected or substantiated child abuse or neglect, (b) evidence or suspicion that a client intends to do harm to an individual or society (e.g., through an illegal act), (c) a request by a parent or legal guardian, (d) client permission to reveal, (e) the need to confer with other involved professionals, and (f) in other cases covered by law or specific ethical standard.

The issue of privileged communication, too, is complicated in group treatment circumstances. As was discussed in Chapter 2, privileged communication prevents the revelation of confidential information in a legal proceeding. A counselor cannot be made to testify on a client's case if the privilege stands. The client owns the privilege. But privileged communication, historically, has been accorded most usually in one-to-one communication circumstances. It may not apply to circumstances where there are other individuals present in counseling. Unless group counseling is specifically addressed in laws that provide for privileged communication, it is probably wise to assume that group communications will not be considered privileged, and counselors may be required to testify. On the other hand, if group counseling is referenced in the law that provides for privileged communication, then counselors may proceed with the intent to hold information as privileged that is communicated in group contexts. However, even in those cases where group counseling is referenced in laws providing the privilege, unless there is clear case law in the legal jurisdiction within which the counselor practices, there may be no definitive standard as to whether clients will be protected from revelation of private information in a legal proceeding. In such cases, clients should know that there is a possibility that information may be vulnerable to revelation in a legal context, though the counselor will make every effort to prevent such revelation. State statutes should be studied carefully on this matter.

Finally, some statutes provide for privilege under certain circumstances. Many state licensure statutes allow for privileged communication on civil, not criminal, cases only. Most states allow for revelation of suspected or substantiated child abuse or neglect, and state statutes that cover such matters may override any privileged communication provided to clients of counselors. In group settings where such matters are commonly discussed, clients should have prior knowledge of the limits on their privilege.

Finally, often when individuals seek group therapy they may be involved in individual therapy as well. This occurs in private practice as well as in institutional settings. In institutional settings, there should be clear guidelines for the sharing of group information among agency employees. The ACA (1995) code requires that when there is a relationship between professionals there should be an agreement regarding issues of confidentiality. When a group counselor consults with a client's individual counselor (with the client's permission) the group counselor should be assured that the information communicated will be held in confidence and protected from revelation to outsiders.

Informed Consent.   In establishing groups, counselors must play a special role that extends beyond the informed consent of clients agreeing to group treatment. Of course, as with any type of counseling, clients have the right to consent to treatment as well as to refuse treatment. But it is also true that an individual can be misplaced in a group, being a member of a group that is not consistent with the client's interests or concerns. Obviously, it is the ethical obligation of the counselor to screen clients in or out of groups to ensure that there is appropriate placement. The ASGW (1989) code reads as follows: "Insofar as possible, the counselor selects group members whose needs and goals are compatible with the goals of the group, who will not impede the group process, and whose well-being will not be jeopardized by the group experience" (Section 2). The ASGW recommends several methods of screening, including an individual interview, a group interview with prospective group members, an interview done by a team of leaders, or screening through written questionnaires. Care must be given to prevent a serious misplacement, such as putting a victim of sexual abuse in a group of sexual perpetrators, or placing an abstinent drug abuser in a group where others are actively abusing substances. Even more subtle misplacement may occur, and the counselor must be alert to the possible consequences of misplacement and must act to prevent problems by careful group assignment. When it is obvious that a misplacement has occurred, then procedures should be in place to provide a formal means for an individual "to terminate" services "in an effective way" (ASGW, 1989). Termination procedures should be discussed with members of a group before a group begins, so that they are aware that they may leave the group at any time, but that there may be repercussions for premature withdrawal from the group (especially in cases of mandatory treatment) (ASGW, 1989). And the ASGW recommends a trial period after which members can formally exit the group of their own volition. Certainly, clients should be informed of their obligation to alert the group leader and other group members of their concerns or intentions regarding group attendance.

Coercion is not acceptable; if group pressure comes to bear on a client's decision to remain in or participate in group activities in a way that may be interpreted as "undue pressure," then a client's rights have been breached. Counselors must protect clients from coercion, physical threats, undue pressure, and intimidation (ASGW, 1989).

Conversely, individual clients should be able to screen the group before committing to attend sessions. Counselors have an obligation to provide prospective members with enough information about the group so that they can make fully informed decisions about group attendance. This includes: information about the counselor's credentials and background, procedures or rules of the group, the purpose of the group, counselor expectations regarding client behavior, and the rights, responsibilities, and risks of group membership (ASGW, 1989).

Dual Relationships.   As with any type of counseling, dual relationships are to be avoided. Group counseling does present some different ethical configurations, however. Although it would be unethical for a counselor to establish a romantic relationship with a group member, can group members establish romantic or other dual relationships among themselves? The counselor must discourage such activity. The ASGW (1989) code reads that "Group counselors discuss with group members the potential detrimental effects of group members engaging in intimate inter-member relationships outside of the group" (section 9f). The reason dual relationships among group members are discouraged relates to a possible negative effect on group process and possible detrimental personal outcomes. Obviously, if a member of a group is privy to outside information about another member or is intimately involved with another member, revelations of information that otherwise would be considered private may be made. Also there is the potential for covert coalitions among members of a group, which could result in scapegoating another member. *Scapegoating* is a process whereby one member of a group is placed in an "odd person out" position or is treated by others as a deviant, thereby receiving negative messages from some other members of the group. Scapegoating has been implicated in producing an unhealthy social context, or a two (or more) against one scenario (Hoffman, 1981).

Also, some authors (e.g., Brittain & Merriam, 1988) have recommended that with certain types of groups it is unwise to lead other groups in which other family members (or significant others) may be counseled. For example, a counselor should not lead a group of survivors of child sexual abuse and also lead a group of significant others to survivors of child sexual abuse. In such cases, the objectivity of the counselor may be jeopardized (Brittain & Merriam, 1988).

Responsibility.   Group leaders have a dual responsibility. They have a responsibility to individual members of the group, and they have a responsibility to the group itself. But it must be recognized that the responsibility to the group does not supersede responsibility to individual members of the group. For example, if a counselor began to recognize that one member of a group was being scapegoated and the counselor believed that continued participation in the group could be detrimental to the individual's mental health, then the counselor would be obligated to take actions to protect the individual participant, even if it meant that the group membership and process might be negatively affected. Counselors are directed by the ASGW code to be "equitable" in their treatment to all members, and they are directed by the ACA code to "protect clients from physical or psychological trauma" (ACA, 1995, p. 33). Implicit in such directives is recognition that when there are conflicts between the needs of the group and the needs of an individual member who is potentially traumatized by the group, the counselor must protect the individual. This is not to say that the group counselor should abdicate his or her responsibility to the group, but it is to say that the group leader must clearly take action to protect the individual. Corey, Corey, and Callanan (1993) stated:

> One way of minimizing psychological risks in groups is to use a contract, in which leaders specify what their responsibilities are and members specify their commitment to the group by declaring what they're willing to do. If members and leaders operate under a contract that clarifies expectations, there is less chance for members to be exploited or damaged by a group experience. (p. 338)

Where one person needs to end affiliation with a group, the formal "termination" procedures should be followed (which were established and communicated before the client consented to group treatment), and appropriate referral should be made so the client can receive appropriate treatment, if necessary. The ASGW code reads: "If the needs of a particular member cannot be met within the type of group being offered, the group counselor suggests other appropriate professional referrals." (Section 15).

There will be cases, however, where the needs of the individual and the needs of the group are not in serious conflict. For example, if a group member in a cancer support group raises concerns over disciplining a misbehaving child, the group leader must weigh the needs of the individual against the needs of the group. To focus on the issue of a misbehaving child, which may be tangential to the group purpose, would be a disservice to other group members. In such a case, the counselor would be wise to refer the member to an appropriate treatment source for the child-rearing concern. In this case, neither the individual client nor the group as a whole was placed in a position of lesser priority. Of course, the counselor must ensure that the focus of the group was clearly stated initially, so that referral for such a concern does not seem out of the ordinary.

But ethical codes alone are not enough to ensure responsible group counselors. Kotter (1982) suggested self monitoring related to personal responsibility as important to group leadership. Gregory and McConnell (1986) stated:

> The notion of equal treatment of all group members is often more myth than reality. Therapists like mere human beings are more attracted to some persons than others. Despite efforts to equalize interactions, therapists are prone to give more time, attention, and to be more responsive to group members whom they find personally reinforcing. (p. 60)

Counselors must recognize their own limits and ensure that they do not inadvertently scapegoat members of the group. Counselors, therefore, have a responsibility to self-monitor throughout the group process and to take appropriate corrective action if serious biases reveal themselves.

Values.   Biases and values may affect the group leader and the group process. Corey, Corey, and Callanan (1993) stated:

> Group counselors are sometimes timid about making their values known, lest they influence the direction that the members are likely to take. Practitioners are not value-neutral, however, for the interventions they use are based on values. What is critical is an awareness of how values operate and influence strategies. (p. 346).

Obviously, a group counselor should not be put in a position of leading a group that involves the behavior of clients that is abhorrent or unacceptable to the counselor. A counselor who is a right-to-life (anti-abortion) advocate who works in a hospital setting or mental health center should not be required by agency or other directives to counsel a group of individuals who have had abortions. A counselor who feels uncomfortable addressing issues of sexuality should not be made to direct a group where sexual concerns may be frequently and appropriately raised. However, there are circumstances where a counselor may have a value conflict with one or more members of a group unrelated to the group purpose. In such cases, the counselor is obligated to address such value differences. The ASGW code states:

> Although group counselors take care to avoid imposing their values on members, it is appropriate that they expose their own beliefs, decisions, needs, and values, when concealing them would create problems for the members. (Section 7a)

Importantly, when value conflicts arise that may affect the group process, the counselor is obligated to discuss these conflicts openly and in a way that is not imposing upon the members of the group.

Counselor Competence.   As described in Chapter 2, counselor competence relates to two issues: (a) the quality of provided services, and (b) the boundaries or scope of professional activity. The position taken in this text is that individual counselors must be trained and appropriately credentialed (e.g., licensed) professionals; yet this position is somewhat controversial in the specialty of group counseling. A number of self-help groups are led by peers, nonprofessionals, or paraprofessionals (individuals trained usually to the level of a bachelor's degree). Some of the best examples of these are 12-step groups such as Alcoholics Anonymous, Narcotics Anonymous, Overeaters Anonymous, and others. Some facilities also will have paraprofessionals leading groups; this is common in the field of rehabilitation where individuals with bachelor's degrees serve as group educators/counselors for individuals needing guidance on job procurement, social skills, money management, or grooming. It can be argued that there is no need to have a highly trained counselor directing such groups when nonprofessionals and paraprofessionals are able to provide quality services. But such a response does not take into account issues of ethics other than the obligation to provide quality services. When a professional counselor or psychologist is involved, the client is guaranteed some protection legally (depending on the laws and statutes in the legal jurisdiction). In states where there are licensure statutes with ethical standards, an unlicensed provider or paraprofessional does not accord the group member legal or professional confidentiality (or in some cases privileged communication). Also clients have no recourse should they think that there has been a breach of privacy or malpractice, unless the client sues the agency directing the nonlicensed provider. In other words, having a professional lead a group is some protection to group members. Attending a group with a nonprofessional group leader puts clients at added risk, should there be dissatisfaction with the group or the group leader. When seeking any service for a fee, it is always wise to learn the credentials of the provider and to address protection or limits under the law.

Assuming that a counselor does possess appropriate licensure as a counselor or psychologist, is this an acceptable standard for group counseling practice? Licensure in and of itself is no guarantee that a counselor has been adequately trained and experienced in leading groups. Even though group counseling has been defined as a "mode of treatment" in this text (not meeting other criteria for a specialty designation), group counseling still qualifies as requiring special training, meaning that general credentials are not enough to provide the group leader adequate background in group processes and ethical standards. It is strongly recommended that otherwise qualified counselors who plan to lead groups have a formal graduate course in group procedures/processes and supervision in providing group services through practica, internships, and post-graduate training. This helps to ensure that the counselor has adequate knowledge and experience directing groups. This position is consistent with the position of the Council for Accreditation of Counseling and Related Educational Programs (1994), which requires accredited graduate programs in counseling to include training in "group work." CACREP (1994) requires study of group topics such as (a) group dynamics, (b) group leadership, (c) theories of group counseling, (d) methods of group counseling, (e) variations of group work, and (f) ethical considerations. Additionally, the CACREP standards related to practicum and internship training (as part of the degree program) require development of "individual counseling and group work skills under supervision" (p. 54). Subsequent to receipt of the degree, it is incumbent on the ethical counselor planning to provide group services to seek supervision that provides for training in group counseling.

Code Comparisons

The ASGW is an affiliate organization of the ACA. The ASGW *ethical guidelines* is an aspirational code, that is, without a mechanism for adherence, and is in addition to the ACA code of ethics, a mandatory code of ethics for all ACA members (including ASGW members). In fact, the preamble of the ASGW code states that the ASGW standards are meant "to complement" the ACA code; further it states that "nothing in this document shall be construed to supplant that code" (p. 119). See a reprint of the ASGW ethical guidelines at the end of this chapter.

The ASGW standards, obviously, focus on activities of counselors involved in counseling individuals in group contexts. Topics such as orienting prospective group members through providing them with information about entrance procedures, role expectations, group goals, group policies, and fees are addressed in the code. Guidelines for screening potential members of a group are provided. Issues related to confidentiality and enforcement of privacy rules are presented. Some other practice-relevant topics include involuntary group participation, guidelines for leaving a group, coercion, counselor values, fair and equitable treatment of members, and dual relationships. As can be gleaned from the above discussion, the ASGW "Guidelines" are required reading for counselors involved in group treatment. Not only do the "Guidelines" address issues only addressed in a cursory fashion in more general codes, but very specific guidance is given to the practitioner.

The more general code of ethics of the APA (1992) does not specifically, by heading or subheading, address group counseling. The ACA (1995) code does have a section titled "Group Work," which is composed of two subsections dealing with screening and protecting clients. In effect, the ASGW code is far superior in addressing group-relevant issues, and should be a well-studied reference of counselors involved in group counseling.

Issues of Diversity

In what many consider a milestone publication on the topic of multicultural counseling, Sue, Arrendondo, and McDavis (1992) outlined the need for counselors to have a multicultural perspective and presented cross-cultural competencies and standards. Building on the work of Sue and Sue (1990), Sue, Arrendondo, and McDavis (1992) described the culturally competent counselor as:

> First . . . one who is actively in the process of becoming aware of his or her own assumptions about human behavior, values, biases, preconceived notions, personal limitations, and so forth . . . . Second . . . one who actively attempts to understand the worldview of his or her culturally different client without negative judgments. . . . Third . . . one who is in the process of actively developing and practicing appropriate, relevant, and sensitive intervention strategies and skills in working with his or her culturally different clients. (p. 481)

In group counseling it is crucial for the counselor to be culturally sensitive, not only to direct the counselor's own actions, but to observe any cross-cultural differences among group members that may affect or potentially affect the group process. Differences on issues of value arise; "difference" is a given in a multicultural and diverse society. Accordingly, counselors must be alert to how differences manifest themselves in interactions, and they must ensure that actions are neither discriminatory nor disenfranchising of individuals or groups of individuals. Especially in screening group members for participation in groups, counselors must not simply "screen out" individuals due to differences of culture, race, religion, or sexual preference, unless there would be serious detriment to a group member or members. In fact, it may be wise for the counselor to ensure that there is variation among group members along factors of diversity; in this way the counselor may facilitate an acquaintance or acceptance of difference. As biases reveal themselves, they may be addressed by means of the trained and culturally sensitive counselor. Sue et al. (1992) stated, as related to counselor interventions: "When they [counselors] sense that their helping style is limited and potentially inappropriate, they can anticipate and ameliorate its negative impact" (p. 483).

Also, there may be differences across nations or by national origin. Yamaguchi (1986), for example, described some differences between Western culture groups and those in Japan: Group leaders appear to have a more influential role and privacy issues are prominent (consistent with Japanese tradition related to "intimate" information). Counselors who work with individuals who are culturally different without knowledge of those cultural differences and without making an effort to understand them are counseling in a disadvantaged way. Such a disadvantage may, ultimately, be a disservice or even a detriment to clients.

The ACA code of ethics is clear on this issue: Counselors do not condone or engage in discrimination. And further, on respecting differences:

> Counselors will actively attempt to understand the diverse cultural backgrounds of the clients with whom they work. This includes, but is not limited to, learning how the

counselor's own cultural/ethnic/racial identity impacts her/his values and beliefs about the counseling process. (Section A.2.b.)

In a culture that values equality in a context rich in human diversity, counseling must acknowledge difference nonjudgmentally. Group counselors should facilitate a nonjudgmental discourse on cross-cultural issues.

Summary

This chapter has summarized ethical issues specific to group counseling. Because of the presence of individuals other than a counselor and one client, group counseling poses some interesting ethical dilemmas. The general codes of the APA and the ACA give limited guidance related to group work. However, the ASGW provides detailed and specific guidance in addressing issues typically faced in the practice of group counseling. Although group counseling does not clearly meet the criteria of a formal designated specialty of counseling, it does have unique theory at its base and it has a set of methods or techniques that is not shared with individual, couples, or family therapies. Special training, therefore, is required of the counselor who plans to provide group counseling services ethically and in the context of a multicultural society.

References

American Counseling Association. (1995, June). Code of ethics and standards of practice. *Counseling Today, 37* (12), 33–40.

American Psychological Association. (1992). *Ethical principles of psychologists and code of conduct.* Washington, DC: Author.

Association for Specialists in Group Work. (1990). Ethical guidelines for group counselors—ASGW 1989 Revision. *The Journal for Specialists in Group Work, 15,* 119–126.

Brittain, D. E., & Merriam, K. (1988). Groups for significant others of survivors of child sexual abuse. *Journal of Interpersonal Violence, 3*(1), 90–101.

Corey, G., Corey, M. S., & Callanan, P. (1993). *Issues and ethics in the helping professions.* Pacific Grove, CA: Brooks/Cole.

Corey, M. S., & Corey, G. (1997). *Groups: Process and practice.* Pacific Grove, CA: Brooks/Cole.

Council for Accreditation of Counseling and Related Educational Programs. (1994). *CACREP accreditation standards and procedures manual.* Alexandria, VA: Author.

Gazda, G. M. (1975). *Basic approaches to group psychotherapy and group counseling.* Springfield, IL: Charles C. Thomas.

Gregory, J. C., & McConnell, S. C. (1986). Ethical issues with psychotherapy in group contexts. *Psychotherapy in Private Practice, 4*(1), 51–62.

Hoffman, L. (1981). *Foundations of family therapy.* New York: Basic.

Kotter, J. A. (1982). Ethics comes of age: Introduction to the special issue. *Journal for Specialists in Group Work, 7*(3), 138–139.

Posey, E. C. (1988). Confidentiality in an AIDS support group. *Journal of Counseling and Development, 66,* 226–227.

Rogers, C. (1970). *On encounter groups.* New York: Harper & Row.

Sue, D. W., Arrendondo, P., & McDavis, R. J. (1992). Multicultural counseling competencies and standards: A call to the profession. *Journal of Counseling and Development, 70,* 477–486.

Sue, D. W., & Sue, D. (1990). *Counseling the culturally different: Theory and practice.* New York: Wiley.

Yamaguchi, T. (1986). Group psychotherapy in Japan today. *International Journal of Group Psychotherapy, 36*(4), 567–578.

ETHICAL GUIDELINES FOR GROUP COUNSELORS
Association for Specialists in Group Work 1989 Revision

PREAMBLE

One characteristic of any professional group is the possession of a body of knowledge, skills, and voluntarily, self-professed standards for ethical practice. A Code of Ethics consists of those standards that have been formally and publicly acknowledged by the members of a profession to serve as the guidelines for professional conduct, discharge of duties, and the resolution of moral dilemmas. By this document, the Association for Specialists in Group Work (ASGW) has identified the standards of conduct appropriate for ethical behavior among its members.

The Association for Specialists in Group Work recognizes the basic commitment of its members to the Ethical Standards of its parent organization, the American Association for Counseling and Development (AACD) and nothing in this document shall be construed to supplant that code. These standards are intended to complement the AACD standards in the area of group work by clarifying the nature of ethical responsibility of the counselor in the group setting and by stimulating a greater concern for competent group leadership.

The group counselor is expected to be a professional agent and to take the processes of ethical responsibility seriously. ASGW views "ethical process" as being integral to group work and views group counselors as "ethical agents." Group counselors, by their very nature in being responsible and responsive to their group members, necessarily embrace a certain potential for ethical vulnerability. It is incumbent upon group counselors to give considerable attention to the intent and context of their actions because the attempts of counselors to influence human behavior through group work always have ethical implications.

The following ethical guidelines have been developed to encourage ethical behavior of group counselors. These guidelines are written for students and practitioners, and are meant to stimulate reflection, self-examination, and discussion of issues and practices. They address the group counselor's responsibility for providing information about group work to clients and the group counselor's responsibility for providing group counseling services to clients. A final section discusses the group counselor's responsibility for safeguarding ethical practice and procedures for reporting unethical behavior. Group counselors are expected to make known these standards to group members.

ETHICAL GUIDELINES

1. *Orientation and Providing Information:*
   Group counselors adequately prepare prospective or new group members by providing as much information about the existing or proposed group as necessary.

Minimally, information related to each of the following areas should be provided.

   (a) Entrance procedures, time parameters of the group experience, group participation expectations, methods of payment (where appropriate), and termination procedures are explained by the group counselor as appropriate to the level of maturity of group members and the nature and purpose(s) of the group.

   (b) Group counselors have available for distribution, a professional disclosure statement that includes information on the group counselor's qualifications and group services that can be provided, particularly as related to the nature and purpose(s) of the specific group.

   (c) Group counselors communicate the role expectations, rights, and responsibilities of group members and group counselor(s).

   (d) The group goals are stated as concisely as possible by the group counselor including "whose" goal it is (the group counselor's,

These guidelines were approved by the Association for Specialists in Group Work (ASGW) Executive Board, June 1, 1989.

the institution's, the parent's, the law's, society's, etc.) and the role of group members in influencing or determining the group's goal(s).

(e) Group counselors explore with group members the risks of potential life changes that may occur because of the group experience and help members explore their readiness to face these possibilities.

(f) Group members are informed by the group counselor of unusual or experimental procedures that might be expected in their group experience.

(g) Group counselors explain, as realistically as possible, what services can and cannot be provided within the particular group structure offered.

(h) Group counselors emphasize the need to promote full psychological functioning and presence among group members. They inquire from prospective group members whether they are using any kind of drug or medication that may affect functioning in the group. They do not permit any use of alcohol and/or illegal drugs during group sessions and they discourage the use of alcohol and/or drugs (legal or illegal) prior to group meetings which may affect the physical or emotional presence of the member or other group members.

(i) Group counselors inquire from prospective group members whether they have ever been a client in counseling or psychotherapy. If a prospective group member is already in a counseling relationship with another professional person, the group counselor advises the prospective group member to notify the other professional of their participation in the group.

(j) Group counselors clearly inform group members about the policies pertaining to the group counselor's willingness to consult with them between group sessions.

(k) In establishing fees for group counseling services, group counselors consider the financial status and the locality of prospective group members. Group members are not charged fees for group sessions where the group counselor is not present and the policy of charging for sessions missed by a group member is clearly communicated. Fees for participating as a group member are contracted between group counselor and group member for a specified period of time. Group counselors do not increase fees for group counseling services until the existing contracted fee structure has expired. In the event that the established fee structure is inappropriate for a prospective member, group counselors assist in finding comparable services of acceptable cost.

2. *Screening of Members:* The group counselor screens prospective group members (when appropriate to their theoretical orientation). Insofar as possible, the counselor selects group members whose needs and goals are compatible with the goals of the group, who will not impede the group process, and whose well-being will not be jeopardized by the group experience. An orientation to the group (i.e., ASGW Ethical Guideline #1), is included during the screening process.

• Screening may be accomplished in one or more ways, such as the following:

(a) Individual interview,

(b) Group interview of prospective group members,

(c) Interview as part of a team staffing, and,

(d) Completion of a written questionnaire by prospective group members.

3. *Confidentiality:* Group counselors protect members by defining clearly what confidentiality means, why it is important, and the difficulties involved in enforcement.

(a) Group counselors take steps to protect members by defining confidentiality and the limits of confidentiality (i.e., when a group member's condition indicates that there is clear and imminent danger to the member, others, or physical property, the group counselor takes reasonable personal action and/or informs responsible authorities).

(b) Group counselors stress the importance of confidentiality and set a norm of confidentiality regarding all group participants' disclosures. The importance of maintaining confidentiality is emphasized before the group begins and at various times in the group. The fact that confidentiality cannot be guaranteed is clearly stated.

(c) Members are made aware of the difficulties involved in enforcing and ensuring confidentiality in a group setting. The counselor provides examples of how confidentiality can non-maliciously be broken to increase members' awareness, and help to lessen the likelihood that this breach of confidence will occur. Group counselors inform group members about the potential consequences of intentionally breaching confidentiality.

(d) Group counselors can only ensure confidentiality on their part and not on the part of the members.

(e) Group counselors video or audio tape a group session only with the prior consent, and the members' knowledge of how the tape will be used.

(f) When working with minors, the group counselor specifies the limits of confidentiality.

(g) Participants in a mandatory group are made aware of any reporting procedures required of the group counselor.

(h) Group counselors store or dispose of group member records (written, audio, video, etc.) in ways that maintain confidentiality.

(i) Instructors of group counseling courses maintain the anonymity of group members whenever discussing group counseling cases.

4. *Voluntary/Involuntary Participation:* Group counselors inform members whether participation is voluntary or involuntary.

(a) Group counselors take steps to ensure informed consent procedures in both voluntary and involuntary groups.

(b) When working with minors in a group, counselors are expected to follow the procedures specified by the institution in which they are practicing.

(c) With involuntary groups, every attempt is made to enlist the cooperation of the members and their continuance in the group on a voluntary basis.

(d) Group counselors do not certify that group treatment has been received by members who merely attend sessions, but did not meet the defined group expectations. Group members are informed about the consequences for failing to participate in a group.

5. *Leaving a Group:* Provisions are made to assist a group member to terminate in an effective way.

(a) Procedures to be followed for a group member who chooses to exit a group prematurely are discussed by the counselor with all group members either before the group begins, during a pre-screening interview, or during the initial group session.

(b) In the case of legally mandated group counseling, group counselors inform members of the possible consequences for premature self-termination.

(c) Ideally, both the group counselor and the member can work cooperatively to determine the degree to which a group experience is productive or counterproductive for that individual.

(d) Members ultimately have a right to discontinue membership in the group, at a designated time, if the predetermined trial period proves to be unsatisfactory.

(e) Members have the right to exit a group, but it is important that they be made aware of the importance of informing the counselor and the group members prior to deciding to leave. The counselor discusses the possible risks of leaving the group prematurely with a member who is considering this option.

(f) Before leaving a group, the group counselor encourages members (if appropriate) to discuss their reasons for wanting to discontinue membership in the group. Counselors intervene if other members use undue pressure to force a member to remain in the group.

6. *Coercion and Pressure:* Group counselors protect member rights against physical

threats, intimidation, coercion, and undue peer pressure insofar as is reasonably possible.

(a) It is essential to differentiate between "therapeutic pressure" that is part of any group and "undue pressure," which is not therapeutic.

(b) The purpose of a group is to help participants find their own answer, not to pressure them into doing what the group thinks is appropriate.

(c) Counselors exert care not to coerce participants to change in directions which they clearly state they do not choose.

(d) Counselors have a responsibility to intervene when others use undue pressure or attempt to persuade members against their will.

(e) Counselors intervene when any member attempts to act out aggression in a physical way that might harm another member or themselves.

(f) Counselors intervene when a member is verbally abusive or inappropriately confrontive to another member.

7. *Imposing Counselor Values:* Group counselors develop an awareness of their own values and needs and the potential impact they have on the interventions likely to be made.

(a) Although group counselors take care to avoid imposing their values on members, it is appropriate that they expose their own beliefs, decisions, needs, and values, when concealing them would create problems for the members.

(b) There are values implicit in any group, and these are made clear to potential members before they join the group. (Examples of certain values include: expressing feelings, being direct and honest, sharing personal material with others, learning how to trust, improving interpersonal communication, and deciding for oneself.)

(c) Personal and professional needs of group counselors are not met at the members' expense.

(d) Group counselors avoid using the group for their own therapy.

(e) Group counselors are aware of their own values and assumptions and how these apply in a multicultural context.

(f) Group counselors take steps to increase their awareness of ways that their personal reactions to members might inhibit the group process and they monitor their countertransference. Through an awareness of the impact of stereotyping and discrimination (i.e., biases based on age, disability, ethnicity, gender, race, religion, or sexual preference), group counselors guard the individual rights and personal dignity of all group members.

8. *Equitable Treatment:* Group counselors make every reasonable effort to treat each member individually and equally.

(a) Group counselors recognize and respect differences (e.g., cultural, racial, religious, lifestyle, age, disability, gender) among group members.

(b) Group counselors maintain an awareness of their behavior toward individual group members and are alert to the potential detrimental effects of favoritism or partiality toward any particular group member to the exclusion or detriment of any other member(s). It is likely that group counselors will favor some members over others, yet all group members deserve to be treated equally.

(c) Group counselors ensure equitable use of group time for each member by inviting silent members to become involved, acknowledging nonverbal attempts to communicate, and discouraging rambling and monopolizing of time by members.

(d) If a large group is planned, counselors consider enlisting another qualified professional to serve as a co-leader for the group sessions.

9. *Dual Relationships:* Group counselors avoid dual relationships with group members that might impair their objectivity and professional judgment, as well as those which are likely to compromise a group member's ability to participate fully in the group.

(a) Group counselors do not misuse their professional role and power as group leader to advance personal or social contacts with members throughout the duration of the group.

(b) Group counselors do not use their professional relationship with group members to further their own interest either during the group or after the termination of the group.

(c) Sexual intimacies between group counselors and members are unethical.

(d) Group counselors do not barter (exchange) professional services with group members for services.

(e) Group counselors do not admit their own family members, relatives, employees, or personal friends as members to their groups.

(f) Group counselors discuss with group members the potential detrimental effects of group members engaging in intimate inter-member relationships outside of the group.

(g) Students who participate in a group as a partial course requirement for a group course are not evaluated for an academic grade based upon their degree of participation as a member in a group. Instructors of group counseling courses take steps to minimize the possible negative impact on students when they participate in a group course by separating course grades from participation in the group and by allowing students to decide what issues to explore and when to stop.

(h) It is inappropriate to solicit members from a class (or institutional affiliation) for one's private counseling or therapeutic groups.

10. *Use of Techniques:* Group counselors do not attempt any technique unless trained in its use or under supervision by a counselor familiar with the intervention.

(a) Group counselors are able to articulate a theoretical orientation that guides their practice, and they are able to provide a rationale for their interventions.

(b) Depending upon the type of an intervention, group counselors have training commensurate with the potential impact of a technique.

(c) Group counselors are aware of the necessity to modify their techniques to fit the unique needs of various cultural and ethnic groups.

(d) Group counselors assist members in translating in-group learnings to daily life.

11. *Goal Development:* Group counselors make every effort to assist members in developing their personal goals.

(a) Group counselors use their skills to assist members in making their goals specific so that others present in the group will understand the nature of the goals.

(b) Throughout the course of a group, group counselors assist members in assessing the degree to which personal goals are being met, and assist in revising any goals when it is appropriate.

(c) Group counselors help members clarify the degree to which the goals can be met within the context of a particular group.

12. *Consultation:* Group counselors develop and explain policies about between-session consultation to group members.

(a) Group counselors take care to make certain that members do not use between-session consultations to avoid dealing with issues pertaining to the group that would be dealt with best in the group.

(b) Group counselors urge members to bring the issues discussed during between-session consultations into the group if they pertain to the group.

(c) Group counselors seek out consultation and/or supervision regarding ethical concerns or when encountering difficulties which interfere with their effective functioning as group leaders.

(d) Group counselors seek appropriate professional assistance for their own personal problems or conflicts that are likely to impair their professional judgment and work performance.

(e) Group counselors discuss their group cases only for professional consultation and educational purposes.

(f) Group counselors inform members about policies regarding whether consultation will be held confidential

13. *Termination from the Group:* Depending upon the purpose of participation in the group, counselors promote termination of

members from the group in the most efficient period of time.

   (a) Group counselors maintain a constant awareness of the progress made by each group member and periodically invite the group members to explore and reevaluate their experiences in the group. It is the responsibility of group counselors to help promote the independence of members from the group in a timely manner.

14. *Evaluation and Follow-up:* Group counselors make every attempt to engage in ongoing assessment and to design follow-up procedures for their groups.

   (a) Group counselors recognize the importance of ongoing assessment of a group, and they assist members in evaluating their own progress.

   (b) Group counselors conduct evaluation of the total group experience at the final meeting (or before termination), as well as ongoing evaluation.

   (c) Group counselors monitor their own behavior and become aware of what they are modeling in the group.

   (d) Follow-up procedures might take the form of personal contact, telephone contact, or written contact.

   (e) Follow-up meetings might be with individuals, or groups, or both to determine the degree to which: (i) members have reached their goals, (ii) the group had a positive or negative effect on the participants, (iii) members could profit from some type of referral, and (iv) as information for possible modification of future groups. If there is no follow-up meeting, provisions are made available for individual follow-up meetings to any member who needs or requests such a contact.

15. *Referrals:* If the needs of a particular member cannot be met within the type of group being offered, the group counselor suggests other appropriate professional referrals.

   (a) Group counselors are knowledgeable of local community resources for assisting group members regarding professional referrals.

   (b) Group counselors help members seek further professional assistance, if needed.

16. *Professional Development:* Group counselors recognize that professional growth is a continuous, ongoing, developmental process throughout their career.

   (a) Group counselors maintain and upgrade their knowledge and skill competencies through educational activities, clinical experiences, and participation in professional development activities.

   (b) Group counselors keep abreast of research findings and new developments as applied to groups.

SAFEGUARDING ETHICAL PRACTICE AND PROCEDURES FOR REPORTING UNETHICAL BEHAVIOR

The preceding remarks have been advanced as guidelines which are generally representative of ethical and professional group practice. They have not been proposed as rigidly defined prescriptions. However, practitioners who are thought to be grossly unresponsive to the ethical concerns addressed in this document may be subject to a review of their practices by the AACD Ethics Committee and ASGW peers.

• For consultation and/or questions regarding these ASGW Ethical Guidelines or group ethical dilemmas, you may contact the Chairperson of the ASGW Ethics Committee. The name, address, and telephone number of the current ASGW Ethics Committee Chairperson may be acquired by telephoning the AACD office in Alexandria, Virginia at (703) 823-9800.

• If a group counselor's behavior is suspected as being unethical, the following procedures are to be followed:

   (a) Collect more information and investigate further to confirm the unethical practice as determined by the ASGW Ethical Guidelines.

   (b) Confront the individual with the apparent violation of ethical guidelines for the purposes of protecting the safety of any clients and to help the group counselor correct any inappropriate behaviors. If satisfactory resolution is not reached through this contact then:

(c) A complaint should be made in writing, including the specific facts and dates of the alleged violation and all relevant supporting data. The complaint should be included in an envelope marked "CONFIDENTIAL" to ensure confidentiality for both the accuser(s) and the alleged violator(s) and forwarded to all of the following sources:

1. The name and address of the Chairperson of the state Counselor Licensure Board for the respective state, if in existence.
2. The Ethics Committee
   c/o The President
   American Association for Counseling and Development
   5999 Stevenson Avenue
   Alexandria, Virginia 22304
3. The name and address of all private credentialing agencies that the alleged violator maintains credentials or holds professional membership. Some of these include the following:

National Board for Certified Counselors, Inc.
c/o NBCC
3-D Terrace Way
Greensboro, NC 27403

National Council for Credentialing of Career Counselors
c/o NBCC
3-D Terrace Way
Greensboro, NC 27403

National Academy for Certified Clinical Mental Health Counselors
c/o NBCC
3-D Terrace Way
Greensboro, NC 27403

Commission on Rehabilitation Counselor Certification
1835 Rohlwing Rd.
Suite E
Rolling Meadows, IL 60008

American Association for Marriage and Family Therapy
1100 17th St., N.W., 10th Floor
Washington, D.C. 20036

American Psychological Association
750 First St., N.E.
Washington, D.C. 20002-4242

American Group Psychotherapy Association, Inc.
25 East 21st Street, 6th Floor
New York, New York 10010

Source: From the American Counseling Association. Reprinted with permission.

Addictions and Ex-Offender Counseling

R. Rocco Cottone
Susan Robine

This chapter describes the counseling specialty that serves ex-offenders and individuals with addictions. The unique ethical issues relevant to assessment and treatment of ex-offender or addicted individuals will be addressed. This chapter is organized around the interests of individuals who are serving clients who have behaviors or sets of behaviors that seriously disrupt the functioning of society. In most cases, ex-offenders or addicted individuals are seeking services because an addiction or pattern of behaviors has caused significant difficulty in a social context, most usually requiring third-party intervention. In recognition of this counseling specialization, the ACA has an affiliate group, the International Association of Addictions and Offender Counselors (IAAOC), which operates under the ACA (1995) *Code of Ethics and Standards of Practice,* which can be found at the end of Chapter 1.

At first glance, one may question what counseling issues associated with ex-offenders have in common with those of individuals with addictions. According to Peele and Brodsky (1991), addictions are habits the individual believes cannot be changed or controlled, that are detrimental to the individual's lifestyle, self esteem, and employment. Whether the addictive object is alcohol, drugs, tobacco, food, shopping, gambling, excessive exercise, relationships, sex, criminal activities or aggression, the behavioral patterns are similar. Simply stated, an addiction is an addiction, regardless of how it is acted out. Researchers are only now learning the full extent of the physiological aspects of chemical addictions; it is now postulated that addictive behaviors in addition to chemical dependency, may be attributed to defects in an individual's physiology (see Maraizzilli et al., 1993). However the question still remains, does brain chemistry alter behavior, or does behavior bring about a change in brain chemistry?

The four-step addiction cycle as presented by Carnes (1992) clearly illustrates the repetitive nature of self-destructive behaviors. In developing an addiction the first step is preoccupation, during which individuals experience obsessional thoughts centering on obtaining gratification through the object of their addiction. The second step is ritualization, which is a series of behaviors designed to obtain the addictive object. In observing ex-offender or addicted individuals one will quickly notice a unique language, nonverbal communications, and behavioral patterns that communicate membership in this special group. The gambler "gaslights," the pedophile "grooms," the burglar "cases," the drug addict "scores," the alcoholic "gets trashed," and the list goes on. The third step is acting out the compulsive behavior. At this stage the individual is unable to refrain from obtaining gratification. The addicted individual describes this as a "craving," the ex-offender uses descriptions of poor impulse control or an "urge." Regardless of semantics, a compulsion to act out in a possibly self-destructive manner occurs. The fourth and final step in an addiction is despair and the feeling of powerlessness, which is characterized by condemning self-talk and internalized guilt. In an effort to regain a sense of personal control and inner harmony (Balint, 1979; Kohut, 1971), the cycle begins again.

A high correlation exists between addictive behaviors and criminal activity. Yochelson and Samenow (1986) explained this correlation by postulating that it is not the addictive object, but the individual's view of life as dull or constrained without such activities that affects recovery. Thus personal choice, more than physical addiction, is emphasized in recovery.

Another issue unique to addictions and ex-offender treatment is the role of group counseling, or specifically, programs such as Alcoholics Anonymous (AA), Narcotics Anonymous (NA), Gambler's Anonymous (GA), and Sexaholic's Anonymous (SA). Related to group treatment in general, many treatment programs may rely (or overrely) on group treatment at the expense of individual or family treatment models. Additionally, group treatment through self-help organizations is not supervised by licensed professionals and thus may not afford group members the protection of the professional license, especially related to confidentiality or privileged communications. These issues will be addressed in the following sections of this chapter. (See Chapter 14 for a related discussion on group counseling.)

Additionally, addictions and ex-offender counseling is known for its high "burn out" rate, meaning that many counselors suffer dissatisfaction in their jobs or change jobs frequently. George (1990) stated the following related to work with chemically dependent individuals:

> One of the disturbing aspects of chemical-dependency counseling is the high turnover of treatment staff. This results from counselors choosing to find other work, as well as from a great deal of switching from one treatment program to another. Such a turnover is generally the result of individuals becoming frustrated and unhappy in their current job. Frustration is most likely the response of *burnout* that occurs with many helping professionals, but is particularly found among chemical-dependency counselors. (p. 224)

There is a high relapse, or recidivism, rate among individuals completing structured treatment programs for addictions, generally understood to be as high as 70% over the long-term (George, 1990). Within the ex-offender population, continued criminal activities are also likely (Yochelson & Samenow, 1977). Counselors working with such treatment-resistant groups may show the signs of stress or even exasperation related to treatment success, dealing primarily with "revolving door" phenomena—treating people who have already been unsuccessfully treated, or seeing first-time treatment clients soon returning as relapsed cases. Counselors entering the field of addictions and ex-offender counseling should be alert to the personal and emotional risks involved in such work.

There is some noteworthy controversy in the field of chemical dependency treatment related to the qualifications necessary to adequately provide chemical dependency treatment. As George (1990) stated:

> The ongoing question of whether one is adequately trained to be a chemical-dependency counselor is a source of difficulty in the field. Unfortunately, those who currently work as chemical-dependency counselors have tended to adopt one of two extreme positions: that chemical dependency counselors must be recovering addicts (or, at the very least, have a recovery program as codependents), or that chemical dependency counselors must have a minimum of a master's degree in such related fields as counseling, social work, or psychology. Unfortunately, this polarization often results in unnecessary conflict among counselors and a lack of respect and appreciation for what each group offers to the treatment process. (p. 216)

Although George (1990) recommended an emphasis on skills, the position taken here is a strictly professional counselor position; that is, professionals providing front-line chemical dependency treatment first should be master's-level educated practitioners who, in addition, have adequate coursework and experience related to serving individuals with chemical dependency issues. Regardless, counselors must understand that many individuals who do not hold professional academic credentials perform chemical dependency counseling. In fact, some states exempt chemical dependency treatment personnel from licensure or other standards, and some states have developed separate standards for individuals counseling clients with chemical dependency concerns. So long as other professionals can legally perform chemical dependency treatment services, it is the counselor's ethical obligation to work with these professionals in a way that does not strain professional relations, so long as the services provided by the other professional are provided competently and within applicable ethical standards.

Defining the Specialty, Setting, and Clients

Once trained in the general field of counseling, individuals may seek credentials to further identify themselves as specialists in the field of addictions or chemical dependency. The term *addictions counselor* has gained some prominence recently; however, the term *addictions counselor* implies a treatment professional who is competently trained and experienced in working with addictions in general. Addictions are not limited to substances. Some individuals are addicted to gambling, overeating, sex, or other activities. Some individuals are recurrent perpetrators of sexual abuse of children (pedophiles) who show classic signs of addictive behavior. Addictions counselors should be able to treat individuals demonstrating an addictive behavior, regardless of the nature of the addiction. However, individuals who are chemical dependent do show symptoms or signs unique to chemical dependency, and, beyond any credential, a duly trained and experienced chemical dependency counselor should be able to demonstrate some competence in the diagnosis and treatment of individuals with substance abuse problems across a broad spectrum of substances. In-depth knowledge of chemical effects (short- and long-term) and signs of intoxication or recent use is critical. Specialized knowledge of treatment approaches related to chemical dependency treatment is necessary (Hester & Miller, 1989). In other words, although treatment is similar across many addictions, differences also exist, and chemical dependency does represent a subcategory of addictions requiring special knowledge and training.

Most chemical dependency treatment begins with a hospitalization of the identified patient. In-patient treatment initially attempts to detoxify the individual who is physically addicted and may suffer withdrawal symptoms. At the detoxification stage, physicians and nurses are involved to oversee the individual's physical response to drug use cessation. Medications may ease the discomfort associated with the withdrawal syndrome. Initial detoxification may take from two to four (or in some cases more) days under close medical oversight. Once detoxification is complete, psychologists or psychiatrists may become involved to assess the mental status of the individual and to make a diagnosis. Additional mental disorders are often associated with chemical dependency, such as organic brain disorders or other emotional or personality disorders. When a person is diagnosed with chemical dependency and additionally meets the diagnostic criteria for a second or even third mental disorder, he or she is considered a dual diagnosis case. It is common for individuals to be dually diagnosed. Chemical dependency may facilitate the development of a mental disorder. Data suggest that individuals with mental disabilities are also more prone to substance abuse and dependence (Evans & Sullivan, 1990). Chemical dependency counselors must be alert to the signs and symptoms of compounding mental disturbance so that other professionals may be involved. The diagnostic process, undertaken usually by a psychiatrist or psychologist, helps to identify initial signs of other difficulties.

Once diagnoses are made, the counselor and the social worker begin to provide treatments. Usually, counselors are involved in individual counseling related to the chemical dependency or other problems that may arise. Social workers may provide group treatment and arrange for services once hospitalization is ended (e.g., referral for vocational rehabilitation services or housing assistance). Marriage or family treatment may be provided by a professional trained to deal with family and relationship problems. However, the chemical dependency counselor is often viewed as the frontline professional in providing counseling and psychotherapy for individuals in in-patient treatment programs. Out-patient treatment programs (those provided without hospitalization of the individual) are often staffed by counselors who perform a wide range of diagnostic and treatment services, except for diagnostic or treatment services of a medical nature. Chemical dependency does not appear to be gender specific, associated with one race and not another, or localized to one geographic lo-cale. Some studies, however, have shown different prevalence rates among national-ities or ethnicities (Ray, 1983), although no sweeping generalizations appear war-ranted. Overall, rich and poor, young and old, north or south, chemical dependency appears to be a prevalent problem.

In addressing the unique needs of the ex-offender, it is essential for the compe-tent counselor of this population to obtain proper training. In addition to the basic skills necessary for a professional counselor, special knowledge of the legal system, community safety, and criminology would be advised. Distorted cognitive processes, a pattern of deceitful behaviors, hostility and general suspiciousness within the ex-offender population (Samenow, 1984) makes this an extremely difficult and resistant population to counsel. In addition, treatment outcomes are closely monitored by the legal system (e.g., judicial reviews, probation officers, parole boards), with treatment models at times even dictated by these agencies. Public accountability is also high when working with ex-offenders. For example, in a midwestern state, should a pe-dophile relapse, it is possible for him or her to be sentenced to 30 years incarceration without parole, thus leaving little margin for error within the counseling process. The high client profile and close scrutiny of the progress of clients places additional stress on the ex-offender counselor.

Issues of Significance to the Specialty

Professional Differentiation

As mentioned earlier in this chapter, controversy exists over the professional cre-dential necessary to be involved in chemical dependency treatment. The position taken in this text is that "counselors" providing chemical dependency treatment should be duly trained to the master's degree level, and where required or avail-able, they should meet licensure standards as professional counselors. In regard to further specialty designation, several professional credentials can be sought by counselors wishing to specialize in chemical dependency or addictions treatment. Two that are closely linked to the professional organizations representing coun-seling professionals are (a) the National Board of Certified Counselors (NBCC) specialty designation of Master Addictions Counselor (MAC); and (b) the Commission on Rehabilitation Counselor Certification (CRCC) specialty designa-tion credential titled "Substance Abuse Credential" (SAC). Both of these creden-tials require the broader certification of the sponsoring certifying board (the NCC or the CRC respectively) and, in addition, they require specialty coursework or continuing education related to addictions or chemical dependency treatment, experience under supervision in a setting where addictions are treated, and/or passing a specialty examination developed by the board. Both the NBCC and CRCC specialty designations would serve a professional counselor well, identify-ing that individual as a highly trained counseling professional who has additionally sought specialty certification (beyond general counseling criteria) in a field often staffed with individuals who are less professionally trained.

Ethical Issues

Confidentiality and Privileged Communication.   Confidential communications in the area of addictions and ex-offender counseling is complicated by several factors. First, in addition to state law requiring confidential relations between individuals treated by licensed professionals, there is a federal law that limits release of information related to chemical dependency treatments. For example, federal laws regulate service providers who receive federal funds directly, by way of state distribution, or by way of tax-exempt status. Any provider receiving such funding is bound by federal confidentiality laws. The federal confidentiality laws protect information about any client applying for or receiving services, including assessment, diagnosis, counseling, group counseling, or referral for other treatment. Information about a client protected by federal confidentiality laws may be disseminated only with client consent. In several situations client consent is not needed, such as in cases of medical emergencies, child abuse, or when program staff are involved. Federal law prohibits the use of information in criminal investigation or prosecution of a patient unless a court order has been issued according to federal guidelines, *even if client consent is obtained.* In other words, federal law protects the chemically dependent client beyond what is offered by licensure statute confidentiality or privileged communication provisions. Even when consent is granted, federal guidelines require consent forms to meet federal standards. Consent forms must include (a) the name of the disclosing program, (b) the name and titles of the party receiving the information, (c) the client's name, (d) the purpose of the information disclosure, (e) a statement allowing the client to revoke the consent at any time, (f) a date at which the consent will expire if not revoked, (g) the signature of the client, and (h) the date the consent was signed. The rules were developed to prevent the disclosure of information about a client's past chemical dependency treatment and to protect the client's privacy rights. The intent of these laws is to engage people in treatment for chemical dependency problems who otherwise might be cautious about the legal implications of seeking such treatment. In effect, treatment of a chemically dependent client in a program directly or indirectly receiving federal funds requires additional ethical precautions.

An additional concern related to confidentiality and privileged communication in treatment of ex-offenders or individuals with addictions is confidentiality in group treatment. Depending on state statute or federal regulation, communications made in a group setting, even if a licensed professional is involved, may not be considered confidential or privileged in the classic sense of these terms. Most usually, if group treatment is referenced in a licensure statute, the licensed professional is in most cases bound to keep what is communicated confidential. But other group members, being peers to each other and nonprofessionals (in their roles as group members) are not bound by law to keep information secret. Group members may gossip about other group members without repercussion.

They may also report to others, even authorities, about information communicated at group meetings. Therefore, if a group member confesses a crime in a group meeting, other group members can take this information to authorities, even testify as to what was said, without legal repercussion. If a counselor is present, the counselor may be bound to confidentiality if, in fact, group counseling is within the purview of the license that is held, and if the crime reported does not come under an exception to the statute's confidentiality provision (such as child abuse). However, even if there is a confidential relationship in a group context for the counselor, privileged communication may not stand, since in many state laws there is privileged communication for civil court cases, but not criminal court cases. Counselors should study their state statutes closely in this regard. Counselors may be compelled to testify on criminal allegations, even if a revelation of such was made in a confidential counseling context. In most cases, counselors have group members sign an agreement about keeping group-disclosed information confidential; but such agreements may not be legally binding and may serve only as a promise to not discuss group information in other settings. Accordingly, group members should know, before they enter a group, that there are limits to the confidentiality of what is disclosed in counseling sessions. Likewise, chemically dependent clients should know that there are extra protections from federal law provided to them if they seek treatment in a program that is obligated to honor federal confidentiality law.

With ex-offenders, the counselor must be especially sensitive to any threats they may make to other parties, mindful of Tarasoff and the duty to warn (see chapters 2 and 3).

Informed Consent.   As was discussed in Chapter 2, clients have the right to consent to counseling services, and they must be fully informed of the nature of the service, alternative treatments, the qualifications of the professionals involved, or other information that would help them make an educated decision. Informed consent with ex-offenders and addicted clients is complicated, however, by the fact that treatment services are often initiated when a person is not in a condition or state to make an informed decision. Treatment services are most needed when individuals are under the direct or recent effects of drugs or alcohol or in the throes of an addictive episode. Under the influence of substances or blinded by an addiction it is questionable whether a person can make an educated decision of his or her own accord. Often, other family members must be consulted, and it may be necessary to involve their cooperation in directing an individual to in-patient or out-patient treatment. Regardless, once a client has been initially treated (especially detoxified in cases of chemical dependency), it is incumbent upon the counselor to respect the client's right to further consent to treatment or to withdraw from treatment on his or her own accord.

It is no secret that ex-offenders and addicted clients are highly resistant to treatment. There is a denial process related to recognition of the individual's dependency on drugs or alcohol (George, 1990) as with other addictions. Initial treatment must address the denial process in resistant clients. Initial treatment should also encourage continued treatment.

Unfortunately, some chemical dependency treatment programs have been implicated for unusual tactics in seeking patients. One such program in Kansas City in the 1980s was the focus of a television expose—counselors were visiting potential patients' homes and "arm twisting" family members to admit the identified patient without a reasonable screening of the person for chemical dependency. Tactics that result in hasty admissions without adequate screening and without the educated permission of the client may be considered breaches of professional responsibility as well as informed consent.

Of course, there are numerous referrals for addictions or ex-offender treatment that can be considered compulsory. In many states, treatment may be mandated for traffic offenders identified as substance abusers. Judges may also order treatment for other offenders before a judgment is made about such decisions as child custody or sentencing. In many cases treatment may be mandated as part of a judicial sentence or condition of parole. In these cases, it must be understood that the client, no matter how the client is referred, still has the right to refuse treatment. It is not the counselor's responsibility to persuade clients sent for compulsory treatment that they must remain in treatment. It would however, be appropriate to explore the alternatives and possible consequences with ex-offenders should they choose to terminate counseling prematurely. The counselor should then simply report to the referral source, with client consent, that clients have or have not initiated treatment or have ceased treatment. In such cases, it is important for the counselor to obtain consent (from the beginning of treatment) to report (release information) at least on the client's compliance with mandated treatment.

In the case of minors, some states make provisions for minors to receive chemical dependency treatment without the consent of parents or guardians. In most cases, however, states require the consent of parents or guardians before treatment can be initiated. Also, parents or guardians have the right to review assessment or treatment files. In cases in which minors do not have the right to consent to their own treatment or are not provided confidentiality protection by law, they should be informed from the outset of treatment that the information they provide is subject to review by parents or legal guardians.

Informed consent, then, in ex-offender and addictions treatment has some special circumstances that require ethical sensitivity on the part of the counselor.

Dual Relationships.   The dual relationship issue is complicated in addictions treatment when a counselor is also recovering. When a counselor is in the role of a therapist, but is also a peer in groups such as Alcoholics Anonymous, obviously anonymity is compromised, and a complex web of potential dual relationships is formed. Obviously, recovering treatment professionals should make efforts to avoid dual relationships and to seek treatment in contexts that will decrease the likelihood of nontreatment contacts with clients. Regardless, in some areas, the community of addicted individuals or ex-offenders is a limited one, and inadvertent contacts outside of treatment may be unavoidable. In such cases, the intention of such contacts is the critical issue, and the counselor is obligated to make efforts to avoid such contacts or to ensure that future contacts are prevented.

The issue of sexual relations with current or recent clients is the same for addictions and ex-offender treatment as with any area of counseling: It is unethical. Most ethical codes and ethical standards in licensure statutes prohibit such contacts during active treatment and for up to two years after treatment has been ceased.

Responsibility.   The responsibility of addictions and ex-offender counselors is first and foremost to their clients. Clients hold the highest priority in terms of the actions of the counselor. Additionally, counselors are obligated to their employers and profession. However, as stated earlier in this text, if there is a conflict between a counselor's responsibility to a client and to a third party (such as an employer) the counselor must act to rectify the conflict. But in the end, the counselor should take actions in accordance with a client's welfare.

A client's welfare is a responsibility of the treating counselor. Counselors must do their best to serve their clients, recognizing that services may not be providing the intended purpose. If it is recognized that the client is not benefiting from services, it is the counselor's responsibility to cease treatment, and where necessary, to refer the client to appropriate services provided by other professionals or in other treatment contexts.

Even in cases of family treatment of an individual with an addiction, if the individual with the addiction is the identified patient and has sought treatment primarily for the addiction, then the counselor must advocate for the individual with the addiction, and the counselor should not compromise the client's treatment progress even with the intent of serving the larger system of relationships in the family. In other words, if treatment is undertaken primarily as a means of assisting in the recovery of the addicted or offending individual, then that individual's welfare is the focus of counselor responsibility.

Values.   Individuals treating clients with chemical dependency should clearly define their values related to use of alcohol or drugs in society. There is controversy in the field about the issue of abstinence. Some programs require that clients maintain total abstinence. Other programs attempt to produce a pattern of controlled drinking (Hester & Miller, 1989). The traditional wisdom, especially following the 12-step programs of AA or NA, holds that abstinence is an absolute necessity. Twelve-step programs value abstinence and also have a spiritual foundation (Alcoholics Anonymous, 1976; 1953). When referring clients to AA, counselors should be aware of the 12 traditions of AA (Alcoholics Anonymous, 1976, p. 564), which are:

> One—Our common welfare should come first; personal recovery depends upon A. A. unity.
>
> Two—For our group purpose there is but one ultimate authority—a loving God as He may express Himself in our group conscience. Our leaders are but trusted servants; they do not govern.
>
> Three—The only requirement for A.A. membership is a desire to stop drinking.
>
> Four—Each group should be autonomous except in matters affecting other groups or A. A. as a whole.

Five—Each group has but one primary purpose—to carry its message to the alcoholic who still suffers.

Six—An A. A. group ought never endorse, finance or lend the A.A. name to any related facility or outside enterprise, lest problems of money, property and prestige divert us from our primary purpose.

Seven—Every A. A. group ought to be fully self-supportive, declining outside contributions.

Eight—Alcoholics Anonymous should remain forever nonprofessional, but our service centers may employ special workers.

Nine—A. A., as such, ought never be organized; but we may create service boards or committees directly responsible to those they serve.

Ten—Alcoholics Anonymous has no opinion on outside issues; hence the A. A. name ought never be drawn into public controversy.

Eleven—Our public relations policy is based on attraction rather than promotion; we need always maintain personal anonymity at the level of press, radio and films.

Twelve—Anonymity is the spiritual foundation of all our Traditions, ever reminding us to place principles before personalities. (p. 564)

These twelve traditions of AA clearly reflect the values of the alliance. It is spiritual, anonymous, voluntary, nonfinancially focused, and primarily intended to help people who wish to remain sober.

The 12 "steps" of AA are different from the 12 traditions but follow from them philosophically; the 12 steps are the individual's self-commitments in accordance with AA philosophy.

Not all addiction treatment programs follow the traditions of AA or even encourage involvement in a 12-step program. Some programs having a professional orientation may even discourage involvement in a 12-step program.

Another issue that is unique to addictions or ex-offender treatment involves philosophy related to the use of specialized techniques that may cause the client some pain or discomfort. These include antidipsotropic medications, which deter the alcoholic from drinking by producing an unpleasant physical reaction if alcohol is ingested (Fuller, 1989) and aversion therapies (Rimmele, Miller & Dougher, 1989). Typically these types of therapies produce nausea, apnea, electric shock or unpleasant imagery. Counselors involved in such programs may experience discomfort themselves over the type of treatment being administered.

The values and philosophy of the program within which the professional counselor works should be thoroughly analyzed and studied, to ensure that the counselor can assess program philosophy against his or her personal philosophy.

Value issues come to the fore when dealing with ex-offenders who have committed crimes that are objectionable, heinous, or that seriously challenge the counselor's personal values. For example, working with pedophiles (individuals charged or convicted of sexually molesting or abusing children) may be abhorrent to a counselor. The counselor has an obligation to refer such individuals to specialists who are trained and experienced with such issues. In circumstances in which no alternative mental health treatment is available, counselors must fully inform the client of their concerns, respecting the right of the client to consent to treatment. Further, counselors must act as objectively as possible to prevent punitive or condemning responses. The ACA (1995) code includes the following:

> Counselors offer clients the freedom to choose whether to enter into a counseling relationship and to determine which professional(s) will provide counseling. Restrictions that limit choices of clients are fully explained. (Section A.3.b.)

Any value restrictions on the part of the counselor need to be addressed before beginning counseling.

Counselor Competence.   It is not enough for a counselor to receive a general or community counseling degree and then to practice primarily as an addictions or ex-offender counselor without additional training and specialized supervision. The intricacies of addictions and ex-offender treatment, especially related to chemical effects, the denial process, specialized treatment approaches, and adjunctive involvement of 12-step or other self-help groups, requires in-depth knowledge (best gained in academic settings or accredited continuing education) and supervision under the direction of a counselor well versed in treating addictions.

However, the competence issue is more complex than the adequacy of preparation of the treating counselor. It also relates to professional relations with other professionals who are almost always involved in cases receiving treatment for addictions or legal offenses (including physicians, social workers, lawyers, judges, probation officers, and vocational rehabilitation counselors). And it relates to the boundaries of professional practice. Counselors must be cautious not to overstep their professional bounds, because other professionals have valid and important roles in the treatment of the complex addictive disorders.

Finally, due to the high burnout of professionals serving clients with addictions or legal offenses, counselors must be alert to their own limitations. If counselors recognize they are becoming impatient or uncompromising, they should consider methods for professional rejuvenation, including linkage to a professional organization, continuing education, or even a sabbatical from addictions or ex-offender treatment. This is especially true of counselors who are recovering themselves. The counseling role should not be so stressful as to produce undue distress in the treating professional.

Summary

Working with individuals who manifest addictive behavior patterns presents ethical challenges to the counselor that are unique and require special knowledge and ethical awareness. The competent professional counselor will ensure that a client's rights are respected, no matter how uncomfortable the counselor may be with the individual's past behaviors. It is incumbent upon the counselor to maintain current knowledge, ongoing training, skill assessment, and ethical sensitivity. Because burnout is common among counselors working with ex-offenders and individuals with addictive behaviors, counselors must also be aware of their own limitations and stress levels; in circumstances where the counselor experiences serious burnout, the counselor should seek professional guidance, continuing education, or counseling.

References

Alcoholics Anonymous. (1953). *Twelve steps and twelve traditions.* New York: Author.

Alcoholics Anonymous. (1976). *Alcoholics Anonymous.* New York: Author.

American Counseling Association. (1995, June). Code of ethics and standards of practice. *Counseling Today, 37*(12), 33–40.

Balint, M. (1979). *The basic fault: Therapeutic aspects of regression.* New York: Brunner & Mazel.

Carnes, P. (1992). *Out of the shadows.* Minneapolis, MN: CompCare.

Evans, K., & Sullivan, M. J. (1990). *Dual diagnosis: counseling the mentally ill substance abuser.* New York: Guilford.

Fuller, R. K. (1989). Antidipsotropic medications. In R. K. Hester & W. R. Miller (Eds.), *Handbook of alcoholism treatment approaches* (pp. 117–127). Boston: Allyn & Bacon.

George, R. L. (1990). *Counseling the chemically dependent: Theory and practice.* Boston: Allyn & Bacon.

Hester, R. K., & Miller, W. R. (1989). *Handbook of alcoholism treatment approaches: Effective alternatives.* Boston: Allyn & Bacon.

Kohut, H. (1971). *The analysis of the self: A systematic approach to the psychoanalytic treatment of narcissistic personality disorder.* New York: University International Press.

Maraizzilli, D., Rotondo, A., Presta, S., Pnacioli-Guadagnucci, M., Pagleo, L., & Conti, L. (1993). Role of serotonin in human aggression behavior. *Aggressive Behavior, 19,* 347–353.

Peele, S., & Brodsky, A. (1991). *The truth about addiction and recovery.* New York: Simon & Schuster.

Ray, O. (1983). *Drugs, society, and human behavior.* St. Louis, MO: Mosby.

Rimmele, C. T., Miller, W. R., & Dougher, M. J. (1989). Aversive therapies. In R. K. Hester & W. R. Miller (Eds.), *Handbook of alcoholism treatment approaches* (pp. 128–140). Boston: Allyn & Bacon.

Samenow, S. (1984). *Inside the criminal mind.* USA: Random House.

Yochelson, S., & Samenow, S. (1977). *The criminal personality: Volume II: The change process.* New York: Jason Aronson.

Yochelson, S., & Samenow, S. (1986). *The criminal personality: Volume III: The drug user.* New York: Jason Aronson.

16

Education, Supervision, and Research

Gerald C. Murray
Vilia M. Tarvydas

This chapter discusses three specific areas in which professional counselors, or counselors-in-training, need to be aware: (a) education, whether it be professional preparation or professional maintenance (e.g., continuing education), (b) supervision, whether it is being performed as part of professional preparation or professional practice; and (c) research, which considers both research subjects and methodology, as well as dissemination and future application of research results.

Obviously, these three areas are not only cross-disciplinary in nature, but also tend to pervade both professional preparation and professional practice. Thus, the notion that these areas are independent of each other must be avoided. Additionally, the notion of levels of application is instructive. Supervision is part of education (and practice), while research contributes to both. Each of these areas is inextricably interrelated, although an effort is made to provide specific information relative to each, along with a corresponding sense of integration.

Given the inherent tendency for the interrelationship of one or more of these areas in any given context, it is useful to employ the hierarchical model of ethical practice advanced by Tarvydas and Cottone (1991), and discussed in Chapter 6. Although this model is complex and goes beyond simply describing four specific levels of ethical practice, it is helpful in guiding this discussion of ethical behavior in education, supervision, and research.

In its most basic form, this model postulates that there are four distinct, yet interactive, levels of ethical practice involved in helping people through the human services delivery system. Each level is a separate context that affects the ethical decision-making process.

Level 1 is the most basic level and involves the counselor–client relationship and the importance of clients' ethical rights, such as informed consent and confidentiality. Level 2 is referred to as a team, or practitioner-to-practitioner, level. This level reflects the fact that many human service and counseling professionals do not provide isolated services to clients. Often, professionals from various disciplines, or levels within those disciplines, work together to present a "package" of services for a client. Thus, the importance of practitioner-to-practitioner information and decision-making comes into play; and with it, clients' rights to ethical treatment in this multidisciplinary context.

Level 3 reflects the importance of the institution or agency role—clearly important given the fact that most professional counselors work for an institution or an agency. Level 4 reflects, for lack of a better term, the "big picture," and addresses primarily the principle of justice, or fairness. The question at this level is, Given the resources available to provide "x" amount of services to "y" number of people, which public policy (and subsequent professional preparation and program development) will best meet clients' needs?

In addition, Tarvydas and Cottone (1991) further stated that each level "represents a social domain of practice" (p. 16). As such, there is not only overlap or interaction across levels, but this interaction is multidimensional as well, so that fair and viable ethical practices derive from (and between) each level.

The Tarvydas and Cottone (1991) hierarchical model can be extended to a larger arena. That is, the content areas of education, supervision, and research have inherently analogous (similar) levels, and application of this hierarchical model as an overarching framework for discussion of those content areas for purposes of information clarity seems warranted. Table 16.1 provides a general description of the operational context at each level of this original hierarchy. It is important to emphasize that all levels are viewed as equally important, and distinct, contextual levels of ethical behavior. An associated analogue level for each of the content areas of education, supervision, and research also is presented in Table 16–1.

Education

As mentioned in Chapter 1, colleges and universities provide the broadest function in ethics education and subsequent ethical practice by counseling professionals. These institutions work to ensure that quality professional preparation leads to quality professional practice. Thus, the analog to this institutional level from the original model most closely associated with the educational operational context is the college-program level. Educational institutions are governed by accrediting bodies, such as the Council on Rehabilitation Education (CORE), the Commission on the Accreditation of Counseling and Related Educational Programs (CACREP), and the American Psychological Association (APA), which further provide standards, or authoritative guidelines, by which to disseminate information.

Table 16–1
Four-Level Model and Content Analog Model.

Original Four-Level Model

Level	Operational Context
1. Clinical–Counseling	Counselor–Client
2. Clinical Multidisciplinary	Practitioner–Practitioner
3. Institutional/Agency	Institution–Member
4. Social Resources/Public Policy	Legislative–Constituent

EDUCATION

Level	Operational Context
1. Clinical–Counseling	Instructor–Student
2. Clinical Multidisciplinary	Instructor–Instructor
3. Institutional/Agency	College Program
4. Social Resources/Public Policy	Funding Bodies–College

SUPERVISION

Level	Operational Context
1. Clinical–Counseling	Supervisor–Supervisee
2. Clinical Multidisciplinary	Supervisor–Supervisor
3. Institutional/Agency	Program–Supervisor
4. Social Resources/Public Policy	Standards–Professional

RESEARCH

Level	Operational Context
1. Clinical–Counseling	Researcher–Subject
2. Clinical Multidisciplinary	Researcher–Researcher
3. Institutional/Agency	Department–Researcher
4. Social Resources/Public Policy	Funding Bodies–College

(Tarvydas & Cottone, 1991).

Responsibilities and Expectations

A number of issues come to mind that relate specifically to the educational enterprise. Chief among these are the responsibilities and expectations of both the educator and the student.

Educator.   Governed by the accrediting bodies mentioned earlier, educational institutions have a responsibility to provide unbiased and timely instruction in relevant information areas to their respective students. One goal of all counselor education programs is to ensure competence of professional performance. Standards for various programs (e.g., rehabilitation counselor education) reflect this goal and these responsibilities in great detail. For example, Part V of the CORE Accreditation Manual (1994) sets forth standards for rehabilitation counselor education programs. Additionally, Section VI of the CACREP accreditation manual (1994) provides comparative standards for counseling and related educational programs. Examination of these standards, which must be made available to students, reveals the multiple responsibilities of these educational programs. These include a statement of mission and objectives, periodic program evaluation, curriculum, clinical experience expectations, specificity of educational outcomes, faculty and administration issues (including issues related to instructor–student communication), and program support and resources. A thorough review of these standards should apprise the student of the level of detail that is involved in (one specific) counselor program development and review.

Another issue related to the college-program level is the established policies and procedures for the ethical recruitment and selection of appropriate candidates (students) for training. Corey, Corey, and Callanan (1993) noted the importance of establishing clear and unbiased selection criteria, which must be made available to students upon application. Often, selection committees provide an initial screening of prospective students, with additional procedures specified for students with extenuating circumstances. This latter issue may involve, for example, students being admitted "on probation" to the respective program. Additionally, personal interviews of candidates may be used to clarify applicant information or to address issues or concerns brought about by the application process.

Most, if not all, qualified counselor education programs specify policies and procedures for admission, retention, and appropriate action to be taken in the event that students encounter academic or personal difficulty during the academic process. Included in all of these issues is the fair and ethical treatment of students and the right of appeal of students in the event of an adverse action that affects academic status, which may occur at either Level 1 or Level 3 in the education analog (see Table 16–1).

Another issue relevant to educators is the determination of counselor competence. Clearly, no counselor-in-training will ever be prepared to work with *all* clients or *all* client issues. At a minimum, students need to recognize their limitations and to know both when to refer a client elsewhere for services or assistance, and the process to follow in doing so (Corey et al., 1993); all within the context of ethical treatment of the client (Level 1, original model in Table 16.1). Thus, quality instruction, assessment, and evaluation by the program faculty is necessary to ensure, to the greatest extent possible, competent program graduates.

The CORE standards previously referenced clearly detail competence (for rehabilitation counselors) through their educational outcomes section. This involves two levels in the education content area (see Table 16–1); that is, the instructor–student level (Level 1) and the instructor–instructor level (Level 2). It is important that students receive a fair and unbiased assessment of their skills and abilities. In the event of student difficulty, a plan of remediation to correct those difficulties should be identified. Students in any counseling program benefit from the instruction of several faculty members, or instructors, each with their own specialty areas.

Thus, information sharing between instructors (Level 2) is not uncommon and will certainly occur, at a minimum, at the time of comprehensive examinations. Students have a right to expect fair and ethical evaluation in a climate of respect; and confidentiality is especially important to protect that information from causing harm to the student.

Additionally, instructor–student relationships always include the importance of dual relationship issues, or those factors that may blur the line between teacher responsibilities and student responsibilities. Thus, personal or intimate relationships between teachers and students is a violation of ethical behavior. This is a Level 1 issue in the education analog, and such unethical behavior may cause harm, both personally and academically, to both parties. Students are more vulnerable in these situations due to issues related to lack of autonomy and power associated with the student role (Kitchener, 1988).

Students should be provided both scope and depth of information related to specific coursework rather than just what represents the instructor's bias. Students have the right, and instructors the responsibility, to survey all the domains of information available. This is an instructor–student and college-program responsibility (Levels 1 and 3). Additionally, this scope is enhanced when students are not subjected to the same information, or needless redundancy, from different instructors. As much as possible, faculty have an obligation to present information relevant to their own area of expertise and avoid this redundancy, unless the subject matter is additive to conceptual or practical understanding. This is reflective of the instructor-instructor level (Level 2).

Finally, instructors have a responsibility to accommodate students with disabilities who request it, given a fair and unbiased assessment of the request. For example, a student with a learning disability may need additional time to complete examinations; or a student with a physical disability may require assistance taking notes during class time. Instructors must know the general procedure for fulfilling accommodation requests and the student's associated responsibilities, such as documenting the request in writing. Students may be apprised of their right to accommodation via college-program manuals, registration catalogues, or specific course syllabi. Because it is the course syllabus that generally outlines the expectations of both the instructor and the student, with attendant evaluation procedures, this vehicle is appropriate to address these accommodation needs. Thus, accommodations protocol may be dealt with primarily at Levels 1 and 3.

Student.   Responsibilities of students have been noted somewhat implicitly throughout the foregoing discussion. When various materials are presented to students, be they application materials or course syllabi, it is the responsibility of the student not only to read the material, but also to ask questions if they do not fully understand it.

For example, how can counselors know when to refer a client if they are unable to ask for assistance themselves? These requests are identical in nature, except for the fact that one occurs in an educational setting and one occurs in a practice setting; both involve Levels 1, 2, and 3.

The role of the student is active rather than passive; students should respect both instructors and the educational enterprise. It is inconsistent for students to expect fair and ethical treatment from instructors and then deceive or derogate instructors without their knowledge. This latter behavior is a violation of the principle of maleficence and is unacceptable. Students must ask themselves what effect this may have, not only on the instructor(s) themselves, but also on the instructor's subsequent performance and the receipt of that information by other students—the instructor's audience. Clearly, the place for academic, not personal, disagreement is in the classroom; students have a right to this format, but so do instructors. Such derogation violates sound ethical practice at both the instructor–student level (Level 1), and potentially at the college-program level (Level 3) in terms of the public reputation of the institution.

Another issue regarding student responsibility can best be described as integrity of performance, or performance based on sound moral principles. When coursework demands include the preparation of works, such as student papers, those works should be prepared within the instructor's specifications and must be original work (not plagiarized). *Plagiarism* is the act of stealing or passing off the ideas or words of another author or person as one's own work. Acknowledging others' work is not only tantamount to professional conduct, it represents the ethical treatment and respect of others. Plagiarism is unacceptable in any form, and the issue obviously pervades all levels in the education analog.

Finally, students in any counselor education program must avoid cheating in *any* capacity, whether it be on a quiz (Level 1) or comprehensive examinations (Levels 2 and 3). Cheating is a form of deception that masks the integrity of students and their subsequent performance in any capacity. This latter component—in any capacity—is potentially dangerous, because this deceptive behavior may carry over into professional practice settings (see Table 16.1, original model), where individuals place themselves and their clients at great risk. That risk may also be litigious in nature. Colleges and universities have rules of conduct that address these issues and under which students can be disciplined. Is there a formal student code of ethics that goes beyond college/program expectations? No. Should there be one? Yes, particularly at the graduate level of education, given the continuum of professional preparation to professional practice.

Supervision

Counselor supervision is the second of the three content areas discussed in this chapter, and this area interacts with that of education. Counselor education programs always include supervision of students at various levels of practica, and this requirement involves at least three people: the client (or analog client, in the case of a pre-practicum course), the counselor, and the university supervisor. For community-based practica, a fourth person gets involved: the practicum–internship agency supervisor. In programs that offer post-graduate opportunities, a fifth person may become involved: an advanced doctoral student who is learning applied supervision as part of his or her own education.

It should be apparent, then, that multiple levels of supervision will occur for the student in this "learning alliance" (Flemming & Benedek, 1966). Supervision is relatively important, in its own right, at Levels 1 through 3 (see Table 16.1). At Level 4, standards specify the number of practica hours and the amount of supervision required to meet those standards.

The Association for Counselor Education and Supervision (ACES) (1990) published standards for counseling supervisors that subsequently were adopted by the American Association for Counseling and Development (AACD), now known as the American Counseling Association (ACA), in July 1989. These standards addressed 11 core areas believed necessary for effective counselor supervision (see the end of this chapter for a reprint of the standards).

Responsibilities and Expectations

Certain issues are relevant with respect to the content area of supervision in mind. These are addressed with the responsibilities and expectations of both the educator and the student.

Educator.   Supervision is regarded by Bernard and Goodyear (1992) as:

> An intervention that is provided by a senior member of a profession to a junior member or members of that same profession. This relationship is evaluative, extends over time, and has the simultaneous purposes of enhancing the professional functioning of the junior member(s), monitoring the quality of the professional services offered to the clients she, he, or they see(s), and serving as a gatekeeper for those who are to enter the particular profession. (p. 4)

At the same time, Bernard and Goodyear (1992) distinguished between education and supervision based on the individuality of the teaching endeavor. That is, clinical supervision is "tailored to meet the needs of individual trainees and their clients" (p. 5). Thus, both content areas involve teaching but, in the case of supervision, the teaching component is much more individualized and specifically related to the clientele served. As with counseling theory, there are a number of models on which supervisors may base their intervention (see Bernard & Goodyear, 1992, for a more thorough review of the available models).

One such model is the Structured Developmental Model (SDM) (Figure 16–1). This model of supervision was advanced by Maki and Delworth (1995) specifically for rehabilitation counselors, but is equally applicable to the many other counseling specialties discussed within this text. Educators are required to present a variety of models so that students are apprised of the scope and depth of supervision knowledge and are thus free to choose their own model with which to identify. The Maki and Delworth model is selected for review here due to the (a) similarity to the core areas addressed by ACES (1990), and (b) the overriding importance of professional ethics inherent in this model.

Levels of Counselor Development

Level One

Level Two

Level Three

Level Three–Integrated

Indices of Clinical Behavior

Self-Awareness vs. Awareness of Others

Motivation

Dependency vs. Autonomy

Primary or Meta Domains

Sensitivity to Individual Differences   Theoretical Orientation   Professional Ethics

Counseling Process Domains

Interpersonal Assessment

Individual Client Assessment

Case Conceptualization

Treatment Goals and Plans

Intervention Strategies

Figure 16-1

Structured Developmental Model (SDM) of Counselor Supervision

Source: Based on an idea from "Clinical Supervision: A Definition and Model for the Rehabilitation Counseling Profession" by D. Maki and U. Delworth, 1995, *Rehabilitation Counseling Bulletin, 38*(4).

Building on the work of Stoltenberg and Delworth (1987), Maki and Delworth (1995) postulated that counselors-in-training develop from the lowest level, Level One (not to be confused with the levels described in Table 16.1), to an experienced professional counselor, or Level Three-Integrated, along three structures or indices of clinical behavior. These clinical indices include whether counselors are more aware of themselves (Level One) or more aware of their clients (Level Three). A second index, counselor motivation, waxes and wanes throughout this process, eventually stabilizing at higher levels of development. Thus, new counselors-in-training are highly motivated to "help" clients, but over time that stabilizes on a more realistic level. Finally, newer counselors are more dependent on supervisors (and subsequently more vulnerable), but over time become more autonomous. This autonomy generally stabilizes at a collegial level, where experienced counselors rely on each other's expertise. It should be apparent that ethical issues—specifically informed consent and confidentiality of information—are both related to client protection, and are of paramount importance.

Maki and Delworth (1995) gave particular importance to professional ethics, and refer to this area as one of three primary (or meta) domains. Additionally, sensitivity to individual differences may be viewed within an ethical framework and is related to consideration of factors such as culture and gender. Thus, sensitivity to individual differences promotes beneficent treatment of clients. A third primary domain, theoretical orientation, relates to the basis of intervention provided by the counselor.

These three domains are regarded as primary because they virtually permeate the remaining five process domains, or those domains involved in the counseling process. These five process domains are summarized briefly as follows (see Maki & Delworth, 1995, for a thorough discussion of this model): (a) interpersonal assessment, which refers to the importance of the counseling relationship in evaluating the social skills, personality characteristics, and interactional style of the client; (b) individual client assessment, which refers to the focus on the person and related psychometric and/or situational assessment; (c) case conceptualization, or an integration of interpersonal assessment and individual client assessment to form a holistic view of clients and their situations; (d) treatment goals or plans, or what the client and the counselor hope to accomplish together; and (e) intervention strategies, or a plan of action.

It should be clear that the three primary domains individually and collectively influence each of the five process domains. In terms of professional ethics, for example, ethical treatment of clients is required in each process domain; so too with the remaining two primary domains, sensitivity to individual differences and theoretical orientation.

Thus, educators have a responsibility to provide a format or model for supervision, and apprise the student of the application of this model. This protocol is related to informed consent, such that students know what is expected of them and the criteria by which they will be evaluated. Additionally, supervision models specify the role of the supervisor in relation to the supervisee, and this specificity assists to avoid dual relationship issues (Tarvydas, 1995).

A final issue related to educators is one that Remley and Hendren (1989) discussed within the context of legal liability of supervisors. Remley and Hendren discussed the "legal maxim of respondeat superior" (p. 179), whereby supervisors are responsible for the wrongful acts of their supervisees. These authors go on to note that "there is no way to avoid or escape this responsibility" (p. 179). Thus, supervisors are obligated to supervise counselors-in-training in order for due process (e.g., fairness, honesty, and informed consent) of these trainees to occur (Tarvydas, 1995).

In summary, counselors-in-training are supervised, as a distinct intervention, by clinically trained supervisors within a specific model of supervision that ensures the ethical treatment of all parties concerned, not the least of which is the client. Additionally, multiple levels of supervision are involved (see Table 16.1), such that counselors-in-training are supervised by, potentially, agency supervisors (as part of their community-based practica), university supervisors (which may include doctoral students in training), and ultimately program faculty. From an ethical point of view, and specifically a due process consideration (Tarvydas, 1995), students must be made aware of this programmatic supervisory obligation.

Student.   From a practical standpoint, students should know the situation in which they are getting involved when they enter a counselor education program. Students should understand clearly what supervision involves and what specific responsibilities they have in this endeavor. It has been pointed out that students, following a developmental model of counselor-in-training process (Maki & Delworth, 1995), may at first become dependent on their supervisors. Additionally, they may be motivated to help clients out of their own basic need to get involved, not necessarily what the clients may need.

Given these potential risks, it is important that students, to some degree, monitor their own behavior and have a sound understanding of basic ethical principles. It has been mentioned that the potential for dual relationships between supervisors and supervisees is of concern, so it is equally important that students be ethically equipped to deal with this potential issue. Besides, a fully trained, Level Three–Integrated counselor (Maki & Delworth, 1995; Stoltenberg & Delworth, 1987) certainly is not immune to dual relationship issues in a supervisory context. Thus, students must learn to monitor their own behavior early in the training process. Students must be accorded a safe learning climate, but they must also take advantage of that climate to ensure the quality of their own professional development. At a minimum, educators must provide regular and timely supervision for their students, but students must work cooperatively within that system.

Information sharing is an additional concern, specifically in community-based practica. Students must be apprised of agency regulations regarding releases of information so that supervisors can monitor both client treatment and counselor development adequately (Tarvydas, 1995). Thus, students are required to learn and to know their responsibilities within their own context of learning. If a student shares information about a client with a supervisor that the student does not have a right to share for the purposes of any evaluation, that student has violated the client's right to confidentiality. Thus, educators impart information about ethical requirements, but the student is obligated to know and apply this information. If that is not the case, it is incumbent upon the student to ask for clarification.

Finally, students should understand their own value systems. Corey et al. (1993) offered a 50-item, self-assessment inventory that attempts to assess the attitudes and beliefs that the counselor-in-training may hold about ethical and professional issues. Additionally, informal self-assessment on the part of the student is reflective in nature and may be beneficial (see chapters 4 and 5 for a detailed consideration of values). Such an assessment may reveal one's personal feelings about sensitive issues, such as gender or race or sexual orientation, that may affect their interactions with clients if these issues are not at least identified.

Whatever the area of counseling specialty, clients come in all shapes and colors, with all types and degrees of problems. A proactive approach to ensuring counselor versatility is to examine one's own feelings and beliefs about these, and other, sensitive areas. The importance of sensitivity to individual differences is underscored by the fact that Maki and Delworth (1995) viewed this domain of practice as a primary one that pervades all process domains.

One last note—the importance of duty to warn, immortalized in the counseling process by the Tarasoff case (VandeCreek & Knapp, 1993), pervades both education and supervision. Given the special relationship between psychotherapist and patient, professional counselors also have an affirmative obligation, in some cases, to control the behavior of another in order to protect a third party. Clearly, this is an area of information that must be presented to students in an educational format and monitored throughout counselor–client contact, both during and following professional preparation. VandeCreek and Knapp provided an excellent overview of this obligation, and the student should review and understand this information thoroughly. The issues involved in addressing dangerousness are addressed in Chapters 3 and 7.

Research

The last content area of discussion is research, specifically research in counseling and psychology. This is an area that is not of great interest to many counselors-in-training. At the same time, it is important in professional preparation (and practice) for at least three good reasons: (a) counseling research involves human beings that are sentient in nature; (b) counseling research provides a structured inquiry into counseling effectiveness, as free from all types of bias (systematic error) as possible; and (c) all research, counseling or otherwise, must include ethical considerations of subjects, procedures, and results. However, all research is not quality research. Thus, good counseling practitioners must know how to distinguish quality research from flawed research.

Responsibilities and Expectations

Educators, researchers, supervisors and students are all consumers of research. As before, a quick review of Table 16.1 delineates the analog of the four-level model (Tarvydas & Cottone, 1991) when specifically applied to research. It should be clear that there are multiple levels involved in the research enterprise. Additionally, the student is (or may be) typically involved with faculty that are conducting research at the first three levels of the analog model; gathering data (Level 1), involvement in a research team (Level 2), and working within department or program guidelines (Level 3), including sponsorship and publication of research results.

Educators.   It is clearly the responsibility of educators to teach basic research knowledge to students. This includes, at a minimum, basic terminology, ethical considerations, and the ability to critique and thus apply (or not), research results. Research generally is divided along two lines of inquiry: (a) quantitative research, which includes statistical measurement of objective information; and (b) qualitative research, which involves written and verbal description of subjective information (Heppner, Kivlighan, & Wampold, 1992). A basic review of these methods follows.

Quantitative research usually is conducted within a specific design, or structured plan, that helps to remove (or better account for) error in the results. Without controlling error, mistakes certainly will result in the application and effectiveness of the

Table 16–2
Four Types of Validity

Type of Validity	Relevant Question
1. Internal Validity	Does the study adequately state that a "cause-and-effect" relationship has taken place, or does it discuss "associations" only between factors under study?
2. External Validity	To what group(s) of persons can these results be applied?
3. Construct Validity	Are the factors or concepts under study operationalized properly (e.g., defined clearly and measured accurately)?
4. Statistical Conclusion Validity	Are the appropriate statistical tests employed in the analysis of the data?

results. Researchers measure error to determine the effect on the factors, or variables, under study. Additionally, because quantitative researchers usually study random samples of people (e.g., subjects), or smaller groups of specific populations, some error is inevitable. Thus, researchers attempt to make inferences, or conclusions, from these smaller samples to those larger populations that they represent.

Thus, quantitative research studies generally try to reflect reliable and valid results. *Reliable results* are those that, following the same procedures in different situations with different subjects, generally will result in the same outcome(s). Thus, the notion of stability comes to mind. *Valid results* are those that are well grounded on principle or evidence. Heppner, Kivlighan, and Wampold (1992) referred to validity as "the degree to which inferences reflect the actual state of affairs" (p. 45). Four types of research validity that should be considered in the evaluation of any research study are found in Table 16–2 (see Heppner et al., 1992, pp. 44–67) for a thorough review of this topic.

Qualitative research, quite basically, involves the study of selected samples of subjects (typically smaller in number than quantitative studies) and attempts to provide a more holistic (integrated) view of the topic under study. This generally includes the subjective viewpoint of the members of the sample, or the natural setting in which the qualitative research takes place (Heppner et al., 1992). Miles and Huberman (1984) described qualitative data as those that are in the form of words rather than numbers. A much greater focus is placed on subjectivity, because qualitative researchers believe it is important to study factors (or variables) of interest in more of a natural setting, and that persons respond in unique ways to diverse settings. Thus, settings are viewed as just as important as the subjects of qualitative research.

Because terminology is an issue previously mentioned as important to the content area of research, a comparative analysis of the terminology (Borland, 1990; Lincoln & Guba, 1985) discussed thus far across these two methods of research is found in Table 16–3.

One final caveat is in order. Students must know that it is not the intention of one type of research to replace the other. Quantitative and qualitative research each make different assumptions about the nature of reality, the type of data that is necessary, the way in which subjects should be selected, and so forth. For example, the fact that a student (or a researcher) does not like statistics is not a good reason to

Table 16–3
Comparative Terminology

Quantitative Research	Qualitative Research
Internal Validity: The degree to which objective causality can be determined.	*Credibility:* The degree to which the multiple subjective realities of the respondents (subjects) is credible to them as individuals.
External Validity: The degree to which sample results may be generalized to larger populations.	*Transferability:* Results are interpreted in terms of the particulars of a given setting; generalization to other settings is not possible.
Reliability: Stability or consistency is the key to controlling error that will otherwise adversely effect results.	*Dependability:* The accurate depiction of the inevitable change that occurs over time.

use qualitative research methods. Each type of research offers potentially reliable and valid results within its own methods of inquiry.

Regarding ethical considerations most, if not all, codes of ethics address the importance of ethical considerations regarding the use of subjects in research. The Directory of the American Psychological Association (1993) specified the code of ethical conduct expected of psychologists, and research issues are discussed throughout the Code. Additionally, Heppner et al. (1992) have provided a thorough discussion of ethical issues in counseling research. Of particular importance is the fact that educators must, at a minimum, impart knowledge of the five basic ethical principles used to guide most ethical decisions (Kitchener, 1984). Subjects selected as respondents in a research study that is conducted in a university setting (Level 3) may only be selected following approval by the department or program responsible for assuring the safety of the subjects involved. These usually are referred to as Human Subjects Review Committees.

Because students likely will be conducting literature reviews and collecting data (Table 16.1, Level 1), they must be apprised of the respective pitfalls of plagiarism and lack of integrity with regard to data gathering. They must also understand that (a) potential benefits and risks exist with any research study (and the subjects involved); and (b) *any* study has limitations, regardless of how well it is designed or analyzed. Thus, students need both instruction and guidance on research conduct.

Finally, educators must apprise students of ethical publication responsibility and credit (e.g., authorship). Generally speaking, credit is based on commensurate contribution, a term that is difficult to define (Heppner et al., 1992). Thus, students should be informed explicitly by faculty researchers what various options for publication credit apply, and faculty should not take advantage of student's abilities for their own professional gain (Level 1). Heppner et al. suggested that one way to resolve the authorship dilemma is to negotiate explicitly the order of authorship before beginning the study.

Students may also become part of a research team with their involvement in data-collection, analysis, and writing, so Level 2 also applies. It should also be clear that the potential for dual relationships is also inherent in faculty-conducted research (Level 1). At the same time, without faculty to guide research, learning opportunities are lost for the student.

Student.   Counseling students who become exposed to research, either by participation in the conduct of research or the critique of published studies, must understand the purposes of specific research, the specific research questions addressed, the procedures followed to answer those questions, and the potential for application of the specific results. This applies to counseling practitioners as well. Thus, students assisting with research studies have an ethical responsibility to understand instructions and methodology clearly, apply learned principles, and conduct relevant literature reviews with integrity.

At the same time, data collection is not a guessing game, so students must understand procedures that are proposed and any potential difficulties involved in the data gathering process. In the context of research, having no data is better than arbitrary data. Although neither will answer research questions, the latter may result in falsity that will obscure applicable results. In fact, it may bring harm to those to whom application is intended. In qualitative terms, it would clearly affect both credibility and transferability (see Table 16–3).

Students must also judiciously guard the right to privacy of subjects, or respondents, and the confidentiality of data (Heppner et al., 1992). Subjects must be protected from potential harm as a result of information exposure, or from exposure of themselves as a participant. Thus, information related to research that is being conducted must stay within the confines of the levels depicted in Table 16–1. The only acceptable departure from this is when research results are reported to sources that provide funding (Level 4), or in the case of publication; however the former may be entitled to results as a contingency of funds provided. Even then, confidentiality promised in the form of subject (or respondent) anonymity must be adhered to. Violation of these (and other) ethical considerations may be grounds for legal action, and would certainly be grounds for professional discredit.

Diversity

Issues of diversity are important to any discussion of ethics. In the manner of the Maki and Delworth (1995) supervision model, they are treated as a primary or meta domain due to their overriding importance. This importance also extends to the other two content areas of discussion in this chapter, education and research. Of course, diversity is not relegated solely to race and culture. Other factors, such as age, sexual orientation, intellectual function, disability, and socioeconomic status may also come into play—perhaps simultaneously—in any discussion of diversity.

Responsibilities and Expectations

In a departure from the previous format, the respective responsibilities and expectations with regard to diversity are discussed generally in relation to the three content areas of education, supervision, and research. It should also be noted that issues of diversity pervade all levels of the original and the analog models presented in Table 16–1.

Education.   Corey et al. (1993) discussed multicultural awareness as a "developmental perspective" (p. 260), clearly consistent with the Maki and Delworth (1995) supervision model. The range of this developmental perspective may span total lack of awareness of cultural issues to a sophisticated sensitivity of these issues. Sue and Sue (1990), in their discussion of the characteristics of culturally skilled counselors, summarized this perspective as follows. Culturally skilled counselors:

1) actively examine their own assumptions and biases about human behavior.
2) actively attempt to understand their clients' worldviews.
3) actively seek culturally sensitive interventions.
4) do not view cultural differences as problematic.

For educators, three issues are clearly important. First, it should be noted that culture historically has not been a factor in the development of counseling theories in general. Second, counseling researchers need to know if differential treatment practices are warranted with culturally diverse groups, and such practices are "considered psychology's goal to promote human welfare" (Sue, Zane, & Young, 1994, p. 783). Third, other issues of diversity, such as socioeconomic status, may come into play during counseling sessions.

Counselors must be prepared, via their respective professional preparation programs, to address these issues of diversity. Recall that Maki and Delworth (1995) referred to diversity as a primary domain, describing it as sensitivity to individual differences (see Figure 16.1). Ethical education demands that diversity issues be addressed.

Speight, Myers, Cox, and Highlen (1991) discussed a redefinition of multicultural counseling. These authors proposed an approach that balanced both cultural similarities (or etic) and cultural differences (or emic); they believed that "the new decade of multiculturalism calls for balance" (p. 31).

Supervision.   Bernard and Goodyear (1992) noted that "there is only modest attention given in the literature to the dynamics and experiences of multicultural supervision" (p. 205). They further noted that this may be a result of few minorities in the helping professions. Bernard and Goodyear finally noted that there is much more information related to the cross-cultural training of nonminority, "(presumably) white, middle-class students" (p. 205), to work with racial and ethnic minorities. These authors also make reference to a continuum of awareness of differences much like that previously addressed by Corey et al. (1993). From this discussion, it would appear that there is much to be learned, and much more to be gained, from a renewed focus on diversity in supervision, particularly given the levels of supervision that are implicit for counselors-in-training.

Another issue involves the importance of bias. Bias is an issue that cannot be overestimated, and numerous potential differences (or issues of diversity) come to mind that may emerge in various situations: (a) the sexual orientation of the supervisor or the clients that are served vis-a-vis the sexual orientation of the counselor-in-training; (b) the supervisor's attitude toward working with the "poorest of the poor" in society; or (c) attitudes and biases that may emerge in working with clients that are physically or cognitively challenged. The list goes on. It takes all kinds of people to make a world; thus the use of the term *diversity.*

The chapter authors agree with the Maki and Delworth's (1995) supervision model. Bernard and Goodyear (1992) and Sue et al. (1994) agree that building an awareness of diversity issues is an essential starting place to begin developing the levels of sensitivity to individual differences that are needed for ethical counseling practice.

Research.   Research results that are going to be applicable to multicultural populations must come from multiculturally appropriate samples. Additionally, assessments conducted on multicultural populations should be compared with multiculturally representative norm (standard) groups to properly interpret assessment results. Otherwise, comparisons may be suspect.

Sue et al. (1994) noted different rates of service use (e.g., general and psychiatric hospital admissions) as a function of ethnic minority groups. Additionally, these authors made reference to several other studies that addressed differential drop-out rates (from counseling) and length of treatment, also as a function of ethnic minority status. Thus, the importance of issues of diversity has empirical support.

One method used in counseling research is to analyze comparative results through the use of factorial research designs (Heppner et al. 1992) to better understand the influences of these factors. A more complicated treatment of these issues would include a discussion of such factors as assignability versus nonassignability (i.e., whether certain factors may be "assigned" to subjects). Clearly, multicultural factors and diversity characteristics are becoming more prominent in counseling research as time goes on, and issues related to bias in measurement also are being addressed. The result of these efforts, of course, will improve the integrity of research results and the application of these results for the benefit of all persons.

Summary

This chapter has addressed the ethical issues that pervade the content areas of education, supervision, and research. Information has been presented in a systematic format, given the fact that these content areas are mutually interactive and inherently have multiple levels. An analog model for each content area was developed by the authors, based on the work of Tarvydas and Cottone (1991), where human services provision was viewed in a hierarchical, multiple-context format.

References

Association for Counselor Education (ACES) (1990). Standards for counseling supervisors. *Journal of Counseling and Development, 69,* 30–32.

American Psychological Association. (1993). *Directory of the American Psychological Association.* Washington, DC: Author.

Bernard, J., & Goodyear, R. (1992). *Fundamentals of clinical supervision.* Boston: Allyn & Bacon.

Borland, J. (1990). Postpositivist inquiry: Implications of the "new philosophy of science" for the field of the education of the gifted. *Gifted Child Quarterly, 34*(4), 161–167.

Corey, G., Corey, M., & Callanan, P. (1993). *Issues and ethics in the helping professions* (4th ed.). Pacific Grove: Brooks/Cole.

Council for Accreditation of Counseling and Related Educational Programs (CACREP). (1994). *Accreditation manual for counselor education programs.* Alexandria, VA: Author.

Council on Rehabilitation Education (CORE). (1994). *Accreditation manual for rehabilitation counselor education programs.* Chicago, IL: Author.

Flemming, J., & Benedek, T. (1966). *Psychoanalytical Supervision.* New York: Grune and Stratton.

Heppner, P., Kivlighan, Jr., D., & Wampold, B. (1992). *Research design in counseling.* Pacific Grove: Brooks/Cole.

Kitchener, K. (1984). Intuition, critical evaluation, and ethical principles: The foundation for ethical decisions in counseling psychology. *The Counseling Psychologist, 12*(3), 43–55.

Kitchener, K. (1988). Dual role relationships: What makes them so problematic? *Journal of Counseling and Development, 67,* 217–221.

Lincoln, Y., & Guba, E. (1985). *Naturalistic inquiry.* Beverly Hills, CA: Sage.

Maki, D., & Delworth, U, (1995). Clinical supervision: A definition and model for the rehabilitation counseling profession. *Rehabilitation Counseling Bulletin, 38*(4), 282–293.

Miles, M. & Huberman, A. (1984). *Qualitative data analysis.* Beverly Hills, CA: Sage.

Remley, Jr., T., & Hendren, G. (1989). Legal liability of supervisors. *Rehabilitation Education, 3,* 177–183.

Speight, S., Myers, L., Cox, C., & Highlen, P. (1991). A redefinition of multicultural counseling. *Journal of Counseling and Development, 70,* 29–36.

Stoltenberg, C., & Delworth, U. (1987). *Supervising counselors and therapists: A developmental approach.* San Francisco: Jossey-Bass.

Sue, D. W., & Sue, D. (1990). *Counseling the culturally different: Theory and practice* (2nd ed.). New York: Wiley.

Sue, S., Zane, N., & Young, K. (1994). Research on psychotherapy with culturally diverse populations. In A. Bergin & S. Garfield (Eds.), *Handbook of psychotherapy and behavior change* (4th ed.) (pp. 783–817). New York: Wiley.

Tarvydas, V. (1995). Ethics and the practice of rehabilitation counselor supervision. *Rehabilitation Counseling Bulletin, 38*(4), 294–306.

Tarvydas, V., & Cottone, R.R. (1991). Ethical responses to legislative, organizational, and economic dynamics: A four level model of ethical practice. *Journal of Applied Rehabilitation Counseling, 22*(4), 11–18.

VandeCreek, L., & Knapp, S. (1993). *Tarasoff and beyond: Legal and clinical considerations in the treatment of life-endangering patients* (rev. ed.). Sarasota: Professional Resource Press.

STANDARDS FOR COUNSELING SUPERVISORS
Supervision Interest Network, Association for Counselor Education and Supervision

The Standards for Counseling Supervisors consist of 11 core areas of knowledge, competencies, and personal traits that characterize effective supervisors.

STANDARDS FOR COUNSELING SUPERVISORS

(As Adopted by the AACD Governing Council, July 13–16, 1989)
The Standards include a description of eleven core areas of personal traits, knowledge and competencies that are characteristic of effective supervisors. The level of preparation and experience of the counselor, the particular work setting of the supervisor and counselor and client variables will influence the relative emphasis of each competency in practice.

These core areas and their related competencies have been consistently identified in supervision research and, in addition, have been judged to have face validity as determined by supervisor practitioners, based on both select and widespread peer review.

1. Professional counseling supervisors are *effective counselors* whose knowledge and competencies have been acquired through training, education, and supervised employment experience.
   The counseling supervisor:
   1.1 demonstrates knowledge of various counseling theories, systems, and their related methods;
   1.2 demonstrates knowledge of his/her personal philosophical, theoretical and methodological approach to counseling;
   1.3 demonstrates knowledge of his/her assumptions about human behavior; and
   1.4 demonstrates skill in the application of counseling theory and methods (individual, group, or marital and family and specialized areas such as substance abuse, career-life rehabilitation) that are appropriate for the supervisory setting.

2. Professional counseling supervisors demonstrate *personal traits and characteristics* that are consistent with the role.
   The counseling supervisor:
   2.1 is committed to updating his/her own counseling and supervisory skills;
   2.2 is sensitive to individual differences;
   2.3 recognizes his/her own limits through self-evaluation and feedback from others;
   2.4 is encouraging, optimistic and motivational;
   2.5 possesses a sense of humor;
   2.6 is comfortable with the authority inherent in the role of supervisor;
   2.7 demonstrates a commitment to the role of supervisor;
   2.8 can identify his/her own strengths and weaknesses as a supervisor; and
   2.9 can describe his/her own pattern in interpersonal relationships.

3. Professional counseling supervisors are knowledgeable regarding *ethical, legal and regulatory aspects* of the profession, and are skilled in applying this knowledge.
   The counseling supervisor:
   3.1 communicates to the counselor a knowledge of professional codes of ethics (e.g., AACD, APA);
   3.2 demonstrates and enforces ethical and professional standards;
   3.3 communicates to the counselor an understanding of legal and regulatory documents and their impact on the profession (e.g., certification, licensure, duty to warn, parents' rights to children's records, third party payments, etc.);
   3.4 provides current information regarding professional standards (NCC, CCMHC, CRC, CCC, licensure, certification, etc.);
   3.5 can communicate a knowledge of counselor rights and appeal procedures specific to the work setting; and

3.6 communicates to the counselor a knowledge of ethical considerations that pertain to the supervisory process, including dual relationships, due process, evaluation, informed consent, confidentiality, and vicarious liability.

4. Professional counseling supervisors demonstrate conceptual knowledge of the *personal and professional nature of the supervisory relationship* and are skilled in applying this knowledge.
The counseling supervisor:

4.1 demonstrates knowledge of individual differences with respect to gender, race, ethnicity, culture and age and understands the importance of these characteristics in supervisory relationships;

4.2 is sensitive to the counselor's personal and professional needs;

4.3 expects counselors to own the consequences of their actions;

4.4 is sensitive to the evaluative nature of supervision and effectively responds to the counselor's anxiety relative to performance evaluation;

4.5 conducts self-evaluations, as appropriate, as a means of modeling professional growth;

4.6 provides facilitative conditions (empathy, concreteness, respect, congruence, genuineness, and immediacy);

4.7 establishes a mutually trusting relationship with the counselor;

4.8 provides an appropriate balance of challenge and support; and

4.9 elicits counselor thoughts and feelings during counseling or consultation sessions, and responds in a manner that enhances the supervision process.

5. Professional counseling supervisors demonstrate conceptual knowledge of *supervision methods and techniques,* and are skilled in using this knowledge to promote counselor development.
The counseling supervisor:

5.1 states the purposes of supervision and explains the procedures to be used;

5.2 negotiates mutual decisions regarding the needed direction of learning experiences for the counselor;

5.3 engages in appropriate supervisory interventions, including role-play, role-reversal, live supervision, modeling, interpersonal process recall, micro-training, suggestions and advice, reviewing audio and video tapes, etc.;

5.4 can perform the supervisor's functions in the role of teacher, counselor, or consultant as appropriate;

5.5 elicits new alternatives from counselors for identifying solutions, techniques, responses to clients;

5.6 integrates knowledge of supervision with his/her style of interpersonal relations;

5.7 clarifies his/her role in supervision;

5.8 uses media aids (print material, electronic recording) to enhance learning; and

5.9 interacts with the counselor in a manner that facilitates the counselor's self-exploration and problem solving.

6. Professional counseling supervisors demonstrate conceptual knowledge of the *counselor developmental process* and are skilled in applying this knowledge.
The counseling supervisor:

6.1 understands the developmental nature of supervision;

6.2 demonstrates knowledge of various theoretical models of supervision;

6.3 understands the counselor's roles and functions in particular work settings;

6.4 understands the supervisor's roles and functions in particular work settings;

6.5 can identify the learning needs of the counselor;

6.6 adjusts conference content based on the counselor's personal traits, conceptual development, training, and experience; and

6.7 uses supervisory methods appropriate to the counselor's level of conceptual development, training and experience.

7. Professional counseling supervisors demonstrate knowledge and competency in *case conceptualization and management.*
The counseling supervisor:

7.1 recognizes that a primary goal of supervision is helping the client of the counselor;

7.2 understands the roles of other professionals (e.g., psychologists, physicians, social workers) and assists with the referral process, when appropriate;

7.3 elicits counselor perceptions of counseling dynamics;

7.4 assists the counselor in selecting and executing data collection procedures;

7.5 assists the counselor in analyzing and interpreting data objectively;

7.6 assists the counselor in planning effective client goals and objectives;

7.7 assists the counselor in using observation and assessment in preparation of client goals and objectives;

7.8 assists the counselor in synthesizing client psychological and behavioral characteristics into an integrated conceptualization;

7.9 assists the counselor in assigning priorities to counseling goals and objectives;

7.10 assists the counselor in providing rationale for counseling procedures; and

7.11 assists the counselor in adjusting steps in the progression toward a goal based on ongoing assessment and evaluation.

8. Professional counseling supervisors demonstrate knowledge and competency in client *assessment and evaluation.*
The counseling supervisor:

8.1 monitors the use of tests and test interpretations;

8.2 assists the counselor in providing rationale for assessment procedures;

8.3 assists the counselor in communicating assessment procedures and rationales;

8.4 assists the counselor in the description, measurement, and documentation of client and counselor change; and

8.5 assists the counselor in integrating findings and observations to make appropriate recommendations.

9. Professional counseling supervisors demonstrate knowledge and competency in *oral and written reporting and recording.*
The counseling supervisor:

9.1 understands the meaning of accountability and the supervisor's responsibility in promoting it;

9.2 assists the counselor in effectively documenting supervisory and counseling-related interactions;

9.3 assists the counselor in establishing and following policies and procedures to protect the confidentiality of client and supervisory records;

9.4 assists the counselor in identifying appropriate information to be included in a verbal or written report;

9.5 assists the counselor in presenting information in a logical, concise, and sequential manner; and

9.6 assists the counselor in adapting verbal and written reports to the work environment and communication situation.

10. Professional counseling supervisors demonstrate knowledge and competency in the *evaluation of counseling performance.*
The counseling supervisor:

10.1 can interact with the counselor from the perspective of evaluator;

10.2 can identify the counselor's professional and personal strengths, as well as weaknesses;

10.3 provides specific feedback about such performance as conceptualization, use of methods and techniques, relationship skills, and assessment;

10.4 determines the extent to which the counselor has developed and applied his/her own personal theory of counseling;

10.5 develops evaluation procedures and instruments to determine program and counselor goal attainment;

10.6 assists the counselor in the description and measurement of his/her progress and achievement; and

10.7 can evaluate counseling skills for purposes of grade assignment, completion of internship requirements, professional advancement, and so on.

11. Professional counseling supervisors are knowledgeable regarding *research in counseling and counselor supervision* and consistently incorporate this knowledge into the supervision process.
The counseling supervisor:

11.1 facilitates and monitors research to determine the effectiveness of programs, services and techniques;

11.2 reads, interprets, and applies counseling and supervisory research;

11.3 can formulate counseling or supervisory research questions;

11.4 reports results of counseling or supervisory research and disseminates as appropriate (e.g., inservice, conferences, publications); and

11.5 facilitates an integration of research findings in individual case management.

The Education and Training of Supervisors

Counseling supervision is a distinct field of preparation and practice. Knowledge and competencies necessary for effective performance are acquired through a sequence of training and experience which ordinarily includes the following:

1. Graduate training in counseling;

2. Successful supervised employment as a professional counselor;

3. Credentialing in one or more of the following areas: certification by a state department of education, licensure by a state as a professional counselor, and certification as a National Certified Counselor, Certified Clinical Mental Health Counselor, Certified Rehabilitation Counselor, or Certified Career Counselor;

4. Graduate training in counseling supervision including didactic courses, seminars, laboratory courses, and supervision practica;

5. Continuing educational experiences specific to supervision theory and practice (e.g., conferences, workshops, self-study); and

6. Research activities related to supervision theory and practice.

The supervisor's primary functions are to teach the inexperienced and to foster their professional development, to serve as consultants to experienced counselors, and to assist at all levels in the provision of effective counseling services. These responsibilities require personal and professional maturity accompanied by a broad perspective on counseling that is gained by extensive, supervised counseling experience. Therefore, training for supervision generally occurs during advanced graduate study or continuing professional development. This is not to say, however, that supervisor training in the preservice stage is without merit. The presentation of basic methods and procedures may enhance students' performance as counselors, enrich their participation in the supervision process, and provide a framework for later study.

Note: From Standards for Counseling Supervisors, September/October, 1990, *Journal of Couseling and Development, 69,* 30–32. Reprinted with permission of Association for Counselor Education and Supervision.

Conclusion

17

The Ethical Professional Counselor

The study of ethics is a like a journey. After a first reading of a code of ethics, one may feel confident about one's knowledge and have a sense that nothing can create a serious ethical crisis in one's professional life. But as the journey progresses, it becomes clearer that the practice of counseling or psychology is complex. Often, no easy answers emerge. At the end of the journey there is the realization that ethical dilemmas do arise, and they challenge even the most sophisticated and ethically sensitive practitioner.

No professional is immune to ethical dilemmas. No matter how ethically sensitive one is, circumstances will always arise that place individuals in a quandary. It is important, however, to recognize when you are facing a serious ethical challenge. With such recognition, wise counselors protect themselves from a naive decision and a possible breach of ethical standards.

No professional is immune from being accused of ethical misconduct. Complaints against mental health professionals have increased dramatically in recent years. Bass et al. (1996) reported a 500% increase in disciplinary actions by state and provincial licensing boards in psychology over a 10-year period. They stated the following:

> A wide range of behaviors and practices may lead to disciplinary or legal action before a regulatory board, professional association, or court of law. . . . Common problem areas include (a) competence, (b) informed consent and confidentiality, (c) dual relationships, and (d) financial arrangements. (p. 71)

Even counselor educators are concerned about the ethics of educating counselors (Schwab & Neukrug, 1994). Clients and students of counseling are becoming more sophisticated about their rights. Licensure and regulatory boards are more experienced at addressing complaints. The U.S. society is also a litigious culture. It can be expected that a good percentage of counselors will be accused formally of unethical or illegal practice during their careers. Innocent or not, the consequences can be serious. Professional careers can be ruined by poor decisions made in the moments of an ethical dilemma or in the face of an ethical complaint.

Consequences of a Breach of Ethics for the Counselor

Of course, the professional consequences of a breach of an ethical standard can range from no formal repercussions to serious repercussions, such as professional and personal censure and the loss of a license to practice. Chauvin and Remley (1996) recommended that once confronted with an allegation of unethical conduct, it is wise for the counselor not to discuss the complaint openly with family or friends, to contact the malpractice insurance carrier, and to retain the services of an attorney. Chauvin and Remley stated:

> The immediate reaction of most counselors would be shock and disbelief accompanied by deep sorrow, embarrassment, or extreme anger, or very likely a combination of all three. A first inclination of most counselors would be to call a best friend or family member and describe the details of the accusation and lament the injustice of what has been alleged. A lawyer most likely would advise against such a response. (p. 565)

To consult other individuals with details of a client's allegation of impropriety is, in effect, a breach of client's confidentiality and/or privacy; such action essentially compounds an already tenuous professional situation. Personal needs must be dealt with in a way that will not complicate the situation. Chauvin and Remley (1996) recommend that counselors suffering serious emotional pain over an allegation of unethical behavior should seek confidential treatment for themselves by mental health professionals. Even then, what is said should be said carefully, because the mental health professional may not be able to guarantee privileged communications in certain cases (especially of a criminal nature).

Revelation of serious unethical practice can be devastating to the professional. One's guilt may prevent an unfettered return to practice. Remorseful counselors will be faced with guilt over possible damage done to any victims involved in the ethical breach. They may feel anxiety over the professional consequences related to licensure or other certifying board actions. Legal problems may arise, such as malpractice. Malpractice insurance companies, valued by counselors as a shield against financial ruin, may be untrusting and unwilling participants in defense of charges of unethical conduct.

There are always the cases of professional counselors who are accused falsely of serious ethical misconduct. In addition to the issues addressed earlier in this chapter, the added issue of anger exists. If cleared of all allegations of misconduct, the exonerated counselors may have done themselves serious professional damage by having communicated to others about the complaint. Trusted colleagues from the past may view them with suspicion or disdain. For their own benefit, counselors are well advised to maintain the secrecy of an ethical complaint against them or be willing to suffer the consequence of professional stigmatization, even in cases of total innocence. In many cases, licensure or certifying bodies will keep the complaint confidential, unless legal standards exist that require public knowledge or public hearing of such complaints (Chauvin & Remley, 1996). It is possible that the complaint will be dismissed by the licensure board as unfounded, without merit, or poorly supported. In cases where a certifying or licensing authority dismisses a case, the dismissal may signify the end of the charge, unless the client brings legal action (e.g., malpractice charges). In a report of the ACA ethics committee (Garcia, Glosoff, & Smith, 1994), 32 complaints were processed, but only 11 decisions were made on those complaints. Of the 11 decisions, eight were decisions of "no violation." In effect, counselors should not panic; they should address complaints as a professional faced with a matter of professional business. If personal stress somehow affects the practitioner's judgment, then professional counsel should be sought from an attorney and a mental health professional.

Consequences of a Breach of Ethical Standards on the Client

Unethical situations are even more difficult for a client who suffers an injustice. Victimized clients have to deal with the unacceptable actions of the counselor, but they must also deal with a professional system which may be reluctant to discipline one of its own. The legal system may also become involved, and once the legal wheels begin to roll, it is difficult to steer into a new direction. Financial and personal commitments may place a strain on the victim of unethical practice. In some cases, there may be degrees of embarrassment or public humiliation. Just the revelation of treatment by a mental health professional may be embarrassing to some individuals. Also, the conduct of the professional may be embarrassing to the client or may inadvertently or inappropriately reflect on the morals or judgment of the client. Friendships may be strained or destroyed. In the end, the brave victims of serious unethical practice who file formal complaints may place themselves in positions of double or multiple victimization.

Filing a Complaint to a Licensure Authority

Procedures for filing complaints about unethical practitioners in the mental health field are fairly standard. The licensed professionals practicing in a particular state are bound legally to the ethical and administrative standards of practice as adopted by statute and regulation in that state. These standards and disciplinary procedures are usually available to the public through the state's department of regulation or licensure. Related to psychology licensure, Reaves (1996) stated:

Virtually all jurisdictions require that complaints concerning psychologists' behavior be in writing. Unless a complaint is determined to be frivolous or made in bad faith, an investigation ensues. In some jurisdictions, trained investigators are employed to perform this task. In smaller jurisdictions, a board member may be assigned as an investigating officer. The method used to investigate a complaint varies with the type or substance of the complaint. For example, an allegation that a licensee has been convicted of a felony would involve obtaining documentation from the court where the conviction occurred, whereas an allegation of sexual intimacies with a client would likely involve interviews and possible collection of other evidence. (p. 102)

Reaves further noted that a license to practice a profession is considered a "property," and, therefore, a license cannot be taken away without due process of law.

If a professional is accused of unethical conduct and simply admits to the conduct, then the case is uncontested. Settlement on such cases may be a matter of the regulatory board's disposition—in such cases the board may make a decision as to the consequences of the unethical conduct. Contested cases, where the professional essentially pleads innocent to some or all of the charges, typically leads to a civil court style (versus criminal court) hearing or legal proceeding. In such cases a hearing officer is present, and attorneys may be involved. In some jurisdictions, hearings may be open to the public (Chauvin & Remley, 1996). Chauvin and Remley (1996) stated, "If a hearing is held, the complainant, the witnesses, and the accused counselor would be given an opportunity to present their positions and would be questioned by the board members" (p. 565). After a hearing, the board most typically would make a decision, which could include the following consequences: reprimand, probation, suspension of a certificate or license, or revocation of a certificate or a license. The counselor or psychologist is allowed to appeal. According to Chauvin and Remley, "After an appeal, if the counselor still disagreed with the board's findings, he or she could sue the board in court in an effort to have the board's decision overturned" (p. 565).

Clients or involved laypersons who desire to file complaints should be provided adequate information to file such complaints. Responsible counselors who are knowledgeable about the questionable or unethical practices of colleagues, are obligated by law in most cases and by ethical codes adopted by professional organizations to file complaints. Filing of a complaint is required if direct, informal attempts to resolve the issue with the offending professional fail or if the conduct either is serious or repetitive.

It is standard procedure for a complaint to be filed in writing. Any member of the public or of the profession may file a complaint, regardless of residence (in or outside of the state of the alleged ethical violation). Complaints may be based on personal knowledge, public record, or information received from third-party sources. The complainant and the individual filing the complaint (often the same person) must be identified fully in the complaint by name and address and in writing. Complaints typically are logged by the date and nature of the complaint. Each complaint will be acknowledged by the board in writing and the complainant will be notified of the ultimate disposition of the complaint. Complaints may be dismissed on several grounds, including insufficient evidence or information, noncooperation of the complainant, or inability to prove or to refute charges due to lack of probable corroboration (e.g., hearsay evidence only).

Complainants to licensure boards may file complaints simultaneously against a suspected unethical practitioner with the professional associations to which the practitioner belongs (e.g., the ACA or APA). Counselors are obligated to disclose information about their professional qualifications and affiliations to interested parties. Withholding such information, especially to clients, may be considered a breach of ethics in and of itself, depending on state statute or professional ethical standards. The important issue is the availability of information so that complainants may make informed complaints to appropriate authorities; concerned individuals should not be impeded in their attempts to file complaints.

Counselors who are guilty of unethical conduct and who have the intention of practicing again have a responsibility to "rehabilitate" themselves and to seek guidance so they never repeat their actions (Chauvin & Remley, 1996). There is nothing more repulsive to the public or to professional colleagues than a repeat offender, especially in cases of serious ethical misconduct. In those instances, it becomes obvious that the unethical practitioner has become a predator, is incompetent, or is simply interested in personal gain. Such activity reflects badly on the profession of counseling, and all professionals have an obligation to prevent such activity.

The Development of the Ethical Professional Counselor

Professional associations such as the ACA and the APA have a special role in helping to develop ethical behavior in practitioners. In a recent survey of certified counselors who were asked to rate 16 sources of ethical information (Gibson & Pope, 1993), the ACA ethical code, the ACA ethics committee, and the ACA *Journal of Counseling and Development* were given the highest ratings. But good information may not be enough. The development of the ethically sensitive counselor is a complex process. It is not simply a matter of information, education, supervision, and training. As Pettifor (1996) stated:

> Psychologists who maintain high levels of professional conduct are encouraged by aspirational ethics to practice appropriately and . . . the measures they take to maintain competence are voluntary and targeted to specific professional needs. Aspirational ethics are based on moral principles that always place the well-being of the other, the consumer, above self-interest, as opposed to codes of conduct that define minimal levels of acceptable behavior. (pp. 91–92)

Professional training may not be enough. The works of Kohlberg (1964, 1971, 1981) have demonstrated that the application of moral thinking stems from a developmental process. It may be that training, no matter how targeted to moral development, may not inspire moral choice adequately in certain counselors. In the end, even the most trained counselor or psychologist may choose to act unethically. Therefore, it is as important to study what prevents unethical conduct as it is to study the correlates of unethical conduct. It may be that what prevents unethical conduct, as Pettifor implied, is a moral standard and moral directives that supersede even the most powerful motivations to breach an accepted ethical standard. Counselors must have the constitution to make moral choices when other needs enter into decisions.

This is not to imply that facilitating moral and ethical behavior is a fruitless or hopeless situation. Some might argue that no matter how sophisticated the profession becomes, there will always be practitioners who consciously will breach or challenge the limits of ethical behavior. Also, if a profession is struggling, that is, if trained professionals are having difficulty making a living, then temptations to sell clients short of ethical services may become more common. In this light, it is important for the leaders of the profession to help to ensure that ethical professionals are rewarded adequately in their professional practices; otherwise, the fringe ethical behaviors of desperate practitioners may erode the reputation of the profession as a whole.

Ideally, counselors should make the best of their education to take ethics to heart and develop a moral stance. A profession devoted to helping others should facilitate a personal as well as academic interest in defining what is right and wrong in the treatment of individuals in need. The clients of counselors deserve no less.

Summary

This text has been organized to provide the student of counseling and practicing counselors and psychologists with a clear and concise overview of ethical issues in counseling and psychology. The intent of the book is to provide a thorough and scholarly foundation, defining ethical concepts and practice, legal issues, philosophical frameworks, methods for clarifying values, a decision-making model, and contemporaneous and emerging issues. Additionally, we addressed issues related to some of the largest specialties of counseling. It is hoped that this text will inspire ethically sensitive counselors who will reflect before acting and who will consult with educated colleagues at those moments when ethical dilemmas arise. In the end, ethical counselors are those who have the best interests of their clients at heart, and who also respect the rights that derive from being professionals.

References

Bass, L. J., DeMers, S. T., Ogloff, J. R., Peterson, C., Pettifor, J. L., Reaves, R. P., Retfalvi, T., Simon, N. P., Sinclair, C., & Tipton, R. M. (1996). *Professional conduct and discipline in psychology.* Washington, DC: American Psychological Association.

Chauvin, J. C., & Remley, T. P. (1996). Responding to allegations of unethical conduct. *Journal of Counseling and Development, 74,* 563–568.

Garcia, J., Glosoff, H. L., & Smith, J. L. (1994). Report of the ACA Ethics Committee: 1993–1994. *Journal of Counseling and Development, 73,* 253–256.

Gibson, W. T., & Pope, K. S. (1993). The ethics of counseling: A national survey of certified counselors. *Journal of Counseling and Development, 71,* 330–336.

Kohlberg, L. (1964). Development of moral character and moral ecology. In M. L. Hoffman & L. W. Hoffman (Eds.), *Review of child development research*, Vol. 1. New York: Russell Sage Foundation.

Kohlberg, L. (1971). Moral development and the education of adolescents. In R. Purnell (Ed.), *Adolescents and the American high school.* New York: Holt, Rinehart & Winston.

Kohlberg, L. (1981). *Philosophy of moral development.* San Francisco: Harper & Row.

Pettifor, J. L. (1996). Maintaining professional conduct in daily practice. In Bass et al. (Eds.), *Professional conduct and discipline in psychology* (pp. 91–100). Washington, DC: American Psychological Association.

Reaves, R. P. (1996). Enforcement of codes of conduct by regulatory boards and professional associations. In Bass et al. (Eds.), *Professional conduct and discipline in psychology* (pp. 101–108). Washington, DC: American Psychological Association.

Schwab, R., & Neukrug, E. (1994). A survey of counselor educators' ethical concerns. *Counseling and Values, 39,* 42–54.

Glossary

This glossary defines italicized terms from parts one and two of the text with selected terms from other parts of the text.

Accreditation (general) the process whereby a college, university, or academic program voluntarily undergoes review by a recognized accrediting body. Accreditation allows for clear recognition of an institution's or a program's nature, intent, and quality.

Accreditation (professional) the process whereby an educational program meets high standards for preparation of professionals beyond standards required for offering a degree.

Active euthanasia the intentional termination of life, also referred to as mercy killing or assisted suicide.

Advance directives (type 1) living wills, which are specific substantive directives regarding medical procedures that should be provided or forgone in specific circumstances; and (type 2) durable power of attorney (DPA) for health care, or proxy directive.

Aspirational ethics a level of ethical guidance above mandatory ethics which involves consideration of the welfare of clients and the effects of actions on the profession as a whole.

Assessment the process that involves the collection and evaluation of information to address a client's counseling, rehabilitation concern, or problem. Typically, an individual is assessed against a normative standard, or a set of criteria, for diagnosis, cases planning, or treatment. Objective or projective testing may be involved.

Autonomy the principle which involves having a right to self-determination of choice and freedom from the control of others.

Autopoiesis Maturana and Varela's definition of living autonomous systems.

Balancing involves weighing which principles are more applicable or important in the ethical analysis.

Beneficence involves actively contributing to the well-being of others.

Benevolence the experience of sharing, helping, and acting generously toward others.

Biomedical ethics a way of understanding complexity and examining moral life as it pertains to the biological sciences, medicine, and health care.

Breach of contract a failure to provide agreed on services considered to be contracted services.

Burnout characterized by an emotional exhaustion in which the professional no longer has positive feelings, sympathy, or respect for clients.

Capacity ability to make a rational decision.

Career counseling counseling that focuses on a certain realm of the client's life—the world of work.

Case law legal precedents relevant to a law's interpretation in specific circumstances and jurisdictions.

Case management is focused on interviewing, counseling, planning programs, coordinating services, interacting with significant others, placing clients and following up with them, monitoring a client's progress, and solving problems.

Certification (specialty) a voluntary means of identifying oneself as a trained and qualified specialist in counseling, psychology, or other professions. Certification usually requires meeting standards of expertise beyond those required for general practice licensure.

Civil law involves the obligation of citizens to one another and the obligation must be asserted by the individual before the obligation is enforced by the government.

Competence (client) the capability of clients to make decisions—a precondition to be able to consent autonomously to services.

Competence (counselor) a counselor's capability to provide a minimum quality of service and within the counselor's (and his or her profession's) scope of practice.

Comprehension having sufficient information and being able to understand it.

Compulsory therapy therapy initiated and/or demanded by a third party, usually as a form of rehabilitation or ongoing assessment of a client.

Confidentiality is akin to an antigossip guarantee to clients; it is the obligation of professional counselors to respect the privacy of clients specifically related to the information communicated during counseling sessions. Legal confidentiality carries the penalty of law should there be a breach of confidentiality. Professional (non-legal) confidentiality does not carry the weight of law, but it carries the weight of sanctions by the professional associations or certifying organizations with which the counselor affiliates.

Conformity the following of rules and observation of societal regulations.

Consultation (professional) a paid formal arrangement where a consulting counselor obtains a second opinion, advice, or supervision on an issue or issues of concern from a knowledgeable, competent colleague.

Criminal law involves conduct required of all citizens or prohibited to all, and is enforced by the government's legal authorities.

Critical-evaluative level this level involves three hierarchically arranged stages or tiers of examination to resolve the dilemma.

Cybercounseling counseling on the Internet.

Differential diagnosis the process whereby one mental disorder is used to describe a client over another disorder with similar diagnostic signs, symptoms, or course.

Disability an identifiable condition that is medically stable and whose functional limitations, when manifested, are recognized and often overcome with appropriate accommodations.

Double effect involves the bioethical circumstance wherein unacceptable consequences such as death are deemed acceptable under certain circumstances, such as relief of pain.

Dual relationship a professional (treatment or supervisory) relationship and, additionally, a simultaneous or contiguous personal and non-professional relationship.

Duty to protect the counselor's responsibility to protect the intended victims of a client or others who may be harmed.

Duty to warn the counselor's responsibility to inform endangered party or parties when it is believed a client poses a serious and imminent danger to an identifiable potential victim.

Ethical climate one facet of an organizational climate that describes the shared perceptions that colleagues hold concerning ethical procedures and practices occurring within an organization.

Ethical dilemma conflicts that arise when competing standards of right and wrong apply to a specific situation in counseling practice.

Ethical principles higher order norms or fundamental assumptions that develop within society consistent with its moral principles and which constitute higher standards of moral behavior.

Ethics a branch of study in philosophy concerning how people ought to act toward each other, pronouncing judgments of value about those actions: a hierarchy of values that permits choices to be made based on distinguished levels of right or wrong. Ethics usually involves a judgment of human decisions or behaviors against an accepted standard primarily in a nonreligious context.

Euthanasia term originally derived from two Greek words meaning "good death".

Fidelity this principle is characterized by the keeping of commitments or promise keeping.

Four level model this model of ethical practice introduces an extended consideration of the contextual forces acting on ethical practice beyond the singular focus on the individual practitioner in relationship to the individual client.

Hospital privileges the right of a professional to admit and/or to treat patients in a hospital.

Impairment (professional)   a more covert, often insidious condition that suggests a level of diminished function (obtained by documentable evidence) that may be manifested on a continuum by varying degrees of loss of optimal function and may be caused by many reasons.

Independence   seeing oneself as being free to make one's own decisions and acting autonomously.

Informed consent   the client's right to agree to participate in counseling, assessment, or professional procedures or services after such services are fully described and explained in a manner that is comprehensible to the client.

Intuitive level   this level of decision making provides a forum to incorporate the richness and influence of the everyday personal and professional moral wisdom into the individual professional's process of ethical decision-making.

Justice   this concept involves the idea of fairness and equality in terms of access to resources and treatment by others.

Leadership   having the sense of responsibility, power, and authority over others.

Legal guardian   a person who is appointed by the court to make decisions regarding an individual's person and/or property.

Licensure   a type of professional regulation that restricts both the use of a professional title, such as "counselor," and/or the practice of the profession.

Limits of practice   the boundaries which demarcate the acceptable activities associated with a profession.

Malpractice   a violation of duty, requiring a determination of what constitutes "good professional practice" as applied to the actions of a professional.

Managed care   provision of health services through medical insurance managed or overseen by a contracted company that serves as a mediator between insurance carriers and health professionals.

Managed care contract   an agreement between a managed care company and the provider of counseling services; the contract usually defines the type of services that can be provided, the maximum fee, and other limitations of services.

Mandatory ethics   the most basic level of ethical guidance focusing on compliance with laws and dictates of professional codes of ethics.

Mental status examination   a structured interview designed to provide a controlled interpersonal setting for the emergence and observation of symptoms and signs of mental disorder.

Morals   conduct or behavior related to one's belief structure regarding the nature of right and wrong. Morals, as with morality, imply a religious standard.

Morality   judgments as to whether a human act conforms to the accepted rules of righteousness or virtue, which implies the application of religious standards.

Nonmaleficence   the requirement that we refrain from any action that might cause harm.

Normalization   a rehabilitation principle that dictates that persons with disabilities should be treated in a manner that allows them to participate both symbolically and actually in roles and lifestyles that are 'normal' for a person of their age and culture.

On-line forums (of counseling)   counseling on the Internet.

Organizational climate   the way people would characterize a system's practices, attitudes, and procedures.

Passive euthanasia   the practice of withdrawing or withholding life-sustaining treatments.

Personal counseling   counseling that involves professional helpers who assist clients to understand, accept, and resolve their problems by using basic counseling techniques so that their clients can lead more satisfying, well-adjusted lives.

Plagiarism   the act of stealing or passing off the ideas or words of another author or person as one's own original work.

Prima facie   Latin phrase meaning that the obligation in question must be considered in every case and only set aside if valid and compelling reasons are present to do so in a specific instance.

Principle ethics   objectively applying a system of ethical rules and principles to determine what is the right or moral decision when an ethical dilemma arises. It focuses on the objective, rational, and cognitive aspects of the decision-making process.

Privacy   the client's right to keep the counseling relationship a secret. Privacy is more inclusive than confidentiality, which addresses communications in the counseling context.

Privileged communication   a client's right that prevents the revelation of confidential information in a legal proceeding (e.g., a legal hearing or court room).

Pro bono publico   for the public good (usually meaning providing a service for no fee to those in need).

Recognition   the attraction of favorable notice and being considered important.

Responsibility (professional)   a counselor's obligation to clients and his or her profession to act in an appropriate and considerate manner.

Revocation (of a professional license)   refers to the loss of the right to practice in the licensing jurisdiction.

Scapegoating   a process whereby one member of a group is placed in an "odd person out" position or is treated by others as deviant, thereby receiving negative messages from other members of the group.

Scope of practice   the extent and limits of activities considered acceptable practice by an individual licensed or certified in a profession; a recognized area of proficiency or competence gained through appropriate education and experience.

Slippery slope argument   the progressive erosion of moral restraints.

Social constructivism   a philosophical framework that proposes that reality is a creation of individuals in interaction—a socially consensually agreed on definition of what is real.

Specifying   involves determining and naming the principles that are involved in the situation being considered.

Subpoena   a court ordered request to appear in a legal hearing with all requested information.

Support   the receiving of encouragement, understanding, and kindness from others.

Suspension (of a license to practice)   a temporary loss of the right to practice the profession within a jurisdiction.

Techno-anxious   fearful and avoiding computerization of the profession.

Techno-centered   comfortable with computer technology.

Techno-ethical   having ethical significance related to the development and use of technology.

Testing   the use of a test, or a specific tool used to gather information or measure some individual quality or characteristic.

Third party   an individual or organization that is somehow involved with a case (e.g., a referral source) but is not the counselor or the client.

Value system   a particular hierarchical rank-ordering of the degree of preference for the values expressed by a particular person or social entity.

Values   involve that which is intrinsically worthwhile, or worthy of esteem for its own sake, and reflects the value holder's world view, culture, or understanding of the world.

Valuing   the process of negotiating values with a client or other individual.

Virtue ethics   considers the characteristics of the counselors themselves as the critical element for responsible practice.

Voluntariness   giving consent by acting freely in the decision-making process.

World view   one's world view is constituted by the observable artifacts, values, and underlying assumptions the individual holds.

Name Index

Subject Index